CITYGUIDE
NEW YORK

FODOR'S TRAVEL PUBLICATIONS, INC.

NEW YORK • TORONTO • LONDON • SYDNEY • AUCKLAND

WWW.FODORS.COM/

1

A B C D

ELIZABETH BAYONNE St. George Station/ Ferry Terminal WESTCHESTER COUNTY

1

Newark Bay Kill Van Kull Richmond Ter. Prospect Ave. Bay St. Verrazano Narrows Bridge Broadway Van Cortlandt Park Woodlawn Cemetery E. 233rd St.

Castleton Ave. SILVER LAKE PARK Tompkins Ave.

Richmond Ter. Clove Rd. Victory Blvd. Van Duzer St. Bay St. Mosholu Pkwy. White Plains Rd. Gun Hill Rd.

CLOVE LAKES PARK Staten Island Expwy 278 Sand La. **5** Grand Concourse Jerome Ave. BRONX PARK Bronx Blvd.

Forest Ave. 440 Sea View Ave. Major Deegan Expwy. Fordham Rd.

2

South Ave. Victory Blvd. Bradley Ave. Todt Hill Rd. Manor Rd. Richmond Rd. Midland Ave. Inwood Hill Park 9A 9 THE BRONX

Latourette Park Railway Ave. New Dorp La. 9A Cross Bronx Expwy CROTONA PARK 895

Richmond Hill Rd. Richmond Ave. Hylan Guyon Ave. St. Nicholas Ave. Grand Concourse & Blvd Third Ave. Webster Ave. Bruckner

West Shore Expwy Emmet Ave. Geo. Wash. Br. **6** 95 Jerome Ave. 87

Arthur Kill Rd. Amboy Rd. GREAT KILLS PARK (GATEWAY NATIONAL RECREATION AREA) Hudson River Henry Hudson Pkwy. W. 155th St. 87 E. 138th St. Bruckner Blvd.

3

Huguenot Ave. Woodrow STATEN ISLAND Broadway W. 145th St. E. 125th St. Triborough Bridge

Arthur Kill Arthur Kill Rd. 440 Amboy Rd. Hylan Blvd. Riverside Dr. Amsterdam Ave. Columbus Ave. West End Ave. Central Park West Fifth Ave. E. 116th St. E. 110th St. **7** **8** 278

Outerbridge Crossing Page Ave. Amboy Rd. E. 96th St. E. 86th St. E. 79th St. F. D. R. Dr.

Hylan Blvd. ATLANTIC OCEAN 9A 72nd St. E. 72nd St. CENTRAL PARK 36th St. **9** MANHATTAN

W. 57th St. E. 59th St. Queensboro Bridge

5th Ave. 3rd Ave. 1st Ave.

W. 42nd St. Park Ave. Queens- Midtown Tunnel

SECAUCUS Lincoln Tunnel W. 34th St. E. 42nd St. E. 34th St.

NUTLEY LYNDHURST BERGEN 495 W. 23rd St. E. 23rd St. East River

5

21 17 9 11 W. 14th St. E. 14th St.

NEW JERSEY 95 Hudson River **10** **11** E. Houston St. Delancey St. Williamsburg Bridge

BELLEVILLE UNION CITY HOBOKEN Canal St. Manhattan Br.

KEARNY HUDSON Holland Tunnel Bklyn Bridge **12** 278

6

280 JERSEY CITY   y Park **4** Ellis Island Battery Park Hoyt St. Court St.

NEWARK 9 95 Statue of Liberty (Liberty Island) GOVERNORS ISLAND 278

ESSEX Upper New York Bay 4th Ave. Gowanus

7

78 Newark International Airport BAYONNE St. George Station/ Ferry Terminal

ELIZABETH Newark Bay Kill Van Kull Richmond Ter. Prospect Ave. Bay St. Verrazano Narrows Bridge

1 95 Bayonne Bridge Castleton Ave. Van Duzer St. Tompkins Ave.

8

UNION 440 Clove Rd. SILVER LAKE PARK 278

Richmond Ter. Forest Ave. CLOVE LAKES PARK Staten Island Expwy Sand La.

Goethals Bridge 278 440 Victory Blvd. Todt Hill Rd. Manor Rd.

STREETFINDER

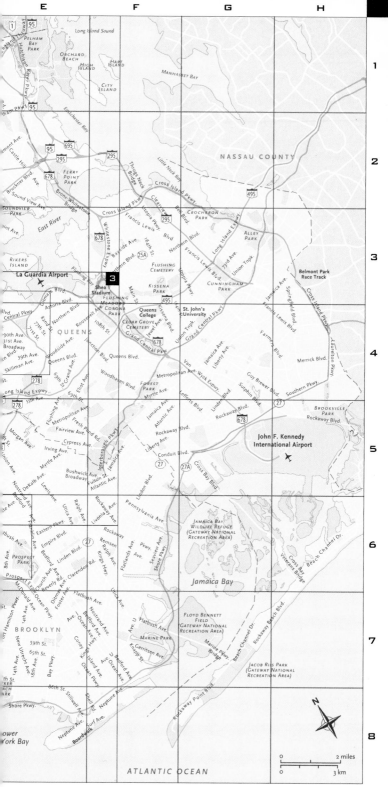

E   F   G   H

1

2

3

4

5

6

7

8

Long Island Sound

PELHAM
BAY
PARK

ORCHARD
BEACH

HIGH
ISLAND

HART
ISLAND

CITY
ISLAND

MANHASSET BAY

NASSAU COUNTY

Eastchester Bay

FERRY
POINT
PARK

Little Neck Bay

Cross Island Pkwy.

495

Bronx-Whitestone
Bridge

CROCHERON
PARK

ALLEY
PARK

BELMONT PARK
RACE TRACK

East River

RIKERS
ISLAND

Whitestone Expwy.

Cross Island Pkwy.

Francis Lewis Blvd.

FLUSHING
CEMETERY

CUNNINGHAM
PARK

Union Tnpk.

La Guardia Airport

3

Shea
Stadium

FLUSHING
MEADOWS
CORONA
PARK

KISSENA
PARK

Queens
College

CEDAR GROVE
CEMETERY

St. John's
University

Grand Central Pkwy.

Springfield Blvd.

Cross Island Pkwy.

Astoria Blvd.

Grand Central Pkwy.

QUEENS

Northern Blvd.

Roosevelt Ave.

Queens Blvd.

Union Tnpk.

Farmers Blvd.

Merrick Blvd.

BROOKVILLE
PARK

Long Island Expwy.

278

Woodhaven Blvd.

FOREST
PARK

Metropolitan Ave.

Van Wyck Expwy.

Liberty Ave.

Guy Brewer Blvd.

Sutphin Blvd.

Southern Pkwy.

27

678

JOHN F. KENNEDY
INTERNATIONAL AIRPORT

27

27A

Cross Bay Blvd.

Linden Blvd.

Conduit Blvd.

PROSPECT
PARK

27

Pennsylvania Ave.

Rockaway

JAMAICA BAY
WILDLIFE REFUGE
(GATEWAY NATIONAL
RECREATION AREA)

Cross Bay
Veterans Bridge

Beach Channel Dr.

BROOKLYN

Jamaica Bay

FLOYD BENNETT
FIELD
(GATEWAY NATIONAL
RECREATION AREA)

MARINE PARK

Marine Pkwy.
Bridge

Rockaway Beach Blvd.

JACOB RIIS PARK
(GATEWAY NATIONAL
RECREATION AREA)

N

Rockaway Point Blvd.

Lower
York Bay

Boardwalk   Surf Ave.

0   2 miles

0   3 km

ATLANTIC OCEAN

NEW YORK OVERVIEW

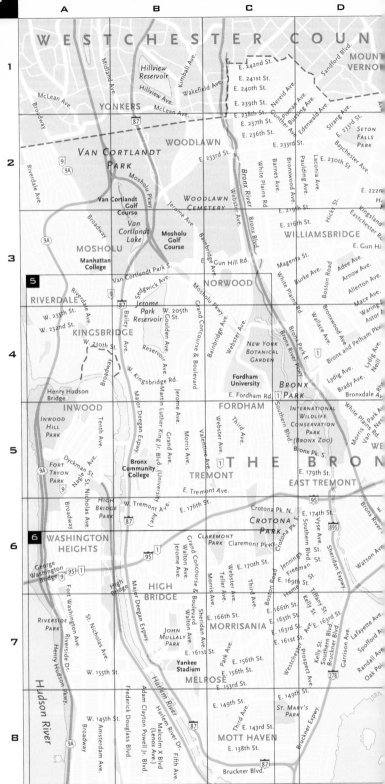

STREETFINDER

A B C D

7

W. 125th St.
Broadway
Riverside Dr.
RIVERSIDE PARK
Morningside Park
St. Nicholas Ave.
Manhattan Ave.
Marcus Garvey Park
Lexington Ave.
Park Ave.
Third Ave.
E. 125th St.
Second Ave.
First Ave.
RANDALLS ISLAND
278

8

ASTOR
20th Ave.
21st Ave.
Ditmars Blvd.

HARLEM
E. 116th St.
Central Park N.
E. 110th St.

1

UPPER WEST SIDE
Central Park W.
WARDS ISLAND
278
21st St.
31st St.

2

W. 96th St.
Amsterdam Ave.
Broadway
West End Ave.
Riverside Dr.
Columbus Ave.
Fifth Ave.
Madison Ave.
Lexington Ave.
Third Ave.
Second Ave.
First Ave.
E. 96th St.
E.D.R. Dr.
CARL SCHURZ PARK
26th Ave.
27th Ave.
Astoria Blvd.

W. 86th St.
W. 86th St. W.
UPPER EAST SIDE
E. 86th St.
York Ave.
East End Ave.
14th St.
23rd St.
29th St.
Crescent St.

W. 79th St.
E. 79th St.
ROOSEVELT ISLAND
Vernon Blvd.
12th St.
21st St.
34th St.
35th Ave.
36th Ave.
31st St.
33rd St.

3

9 A
W. 72nd St.
E. 72nd St.
37th Ave.
38th Ave.
39th Ave.
40th Ave.
41st Ave.

M A N H A T T A N
CENTRAL PARK
Broadway
Central Park S.
E. 59th St.
Queensboro Bridge
Queens Plaza N.
Queens Plaza S.

4

W. 57th St.
W. 50th St.
E. 57th St.
LONG ISLAND CITY
Thomson Ave.
47th
48th

Twelfth Ave.
Eleventh Ave.
Tenth Ave.
Ninth Ave.
Eighth Ave.
Seventh Ave.
Ave. of the Americas (Sixth Ave.)
Fifth Ave.
Madison Ave.
Park Ave.
Lexington Ave.
Third Ave.
Second Ave.
First Ave.
E. 50th St.
MIDTOWN

Lincoln Tunnel
W. 42nd St.
E. 42nd St.
Queens-Midtown Tunnel

5

W. 34th St.
MURRAY HILL
E. 34th St.
East River
GREENPO
McGuiness Blvd.
Manhattan Ave.
Franklin St.
Greenpoint Ave.
West St.
Messole Ave.
Norman Ave.
McCa

Broadway
MADISON SQUARE PARK
W. 23rd St.
E. 23rd St.

CHELSEA
GRAMERCY

6

10
W. 14th St.
UNION SQUARE PARK
E. 14th St.
4th Ave.
Ave. A
Ave. B
Ave. C
Ave. D
Kent Ave.
Wythe Ave.
Berry St.
Bedford Ave.
Driggs Ave.
N. 15th St.
N. 12th St.
PA

Hudson River
11
GREENWICH VILLAGE
4th St.
Greenwich St.
Hudson St.
WASHINGTON SQUARE PARK
Bleecker St.
Lafayette St.
Bowery
EAST VILLAGE
Grand St.
WILLIAMS

7

Holland Tunnel
W. Houston St.
Varick St.
W. Broadway
SOHO
E. Houston St.
Delancey St.
LOWER EAST SIDE
Williamsburg Bridge
EAST RIVER PARK
Broadway
S. 8th St.
Division Ave.
Wythe Ave.
Kent A
Bedf

Canal St.
LITTLE ITALY
Grand St.
E. Broadway

TRIBECA
Church St.
Broadway
Centre St.
CHINA-TOWN
Manhattan Bridge
Brooklyn Navy Yard

N

12
BATTERY PARK CITY
West St.
World Trade Center
Fulton St.
Wall St.
FINANCIAL DISTRICT
Brooklyn Bridge
SOUTH STREET SEAPORT
Adams St.
Flushing Ave.
278
LIU

8

1 mile
1 km
BATTERY PARK
BROOKLYN HEIGHTS
Joralemon St.
Fulton St.
Atlantic Ave.
Myrtle Ave.
Flatbush Ave.
DeKalb Ave.
Fo
Gr
Pa
Lafay

STREETFINDER

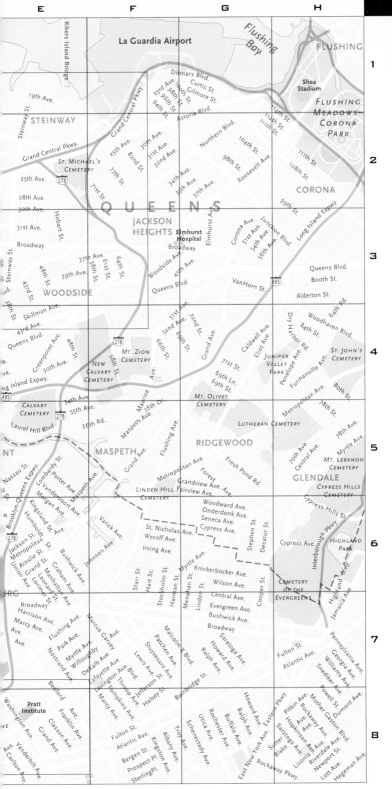

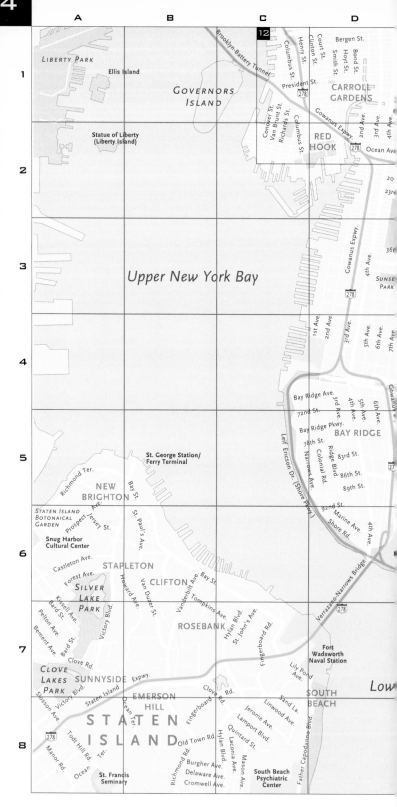

4

A B C D

LIBERTY PARK

Ellis Island

1

GOVERNORS ISLAND

Brooklyn-Battery Tunnel

Columbus St.
Henry St.
Court St.
Clinton St.
Bergen St.

President St.
Smith St.
Hoyt St.
Bond St.

278

CARROLL GARDENS

Statue of Liberty (Liberty Island)

Gowanus Expwy.

2nd Ave.
3rd Ave.
4th Ave.

Conover St.
Van Brunt St.
Richards St.
Columbus St.

RED HOOK

278 Ocean Ave.

2

20

23rd

Upper New York Bay

Gowanus Expwy.

4th Ave.

36t

SUNSE PARK

3

278

1st Ave.
2nd Ave.
3rd Ave.
5th Ave.
6th Ave.
7th Ave.

Gowanus

4

Bay Ridge Ave.
3rd Ave.
4th Ave.
5th Ave.
6th Ave.

72nd St.

Bay Ridge Pkwy.

BAY RIDGE

78th St.

Ridge Blvd.
Colonial Rd.
83rd St.
86th St.
89th St.

Richmond Ter.

St. George Station/ Ferry Terminal

Leif Ericson Dr. (Shore Pkwy.)

Narrows Ave.

27

5

92nd St.

Marine Ave.
Shore Rd.
4th Ave.

NEW BRIGHTON

Bay St.

Prospect Jersey St.

STATEN ISLAND BOTONAICAL GARDEN

St. Paul's Ave.

Snug Harbor Cultural Center

Castleton Ave.

STAPLETON

Forest Ave.

SILVER LAKE PARK

Howard Ave.

Van Duzer St.

CLIFTON

Bay St.

Vanderbilt Ave.
Tompkins Ave.

Verrazano-Narrows Bridge

278

6

Kissel Ave.
Bard St.
Pelton Ave.
Bement Ave.
Bard St.

Victory Blvd.

ROSEBANK

Hylan Blvd.
St. John's Ave.

Fingerboard Rd.

Fort Wadsworth Naval Station

Clove Rd.

Lily Pond Ave.

CLOVE LAKES PARK

SUNNYSIDE

Victory Blvd.

Staten Island Expwy.

Clove Rd.

Sand La.

SOUTH BEACH

Low

7

Sosson Ave.

Ocean Ter.

EMERSON HILL

Fingerboard Rd.

Clove Rd.

Linwood Ave.

Jerome Ave.

Lamport Blvd.

Father Capodanno Blvd.

278

STATEN ISLAND

Todt Hill Rd.
Manor Rd.
Ocean
Tet.

Old Town Rd.

Richmond Rd.

Hylan Blvd.

Quintard St.

Laconia Ave.

Mason Ave.

South Beach Psychiatric Center

8

St. Francis Seminary

Burgher Ave.

Delaware Ave.

Cromwell Ave.

STREETFINDER

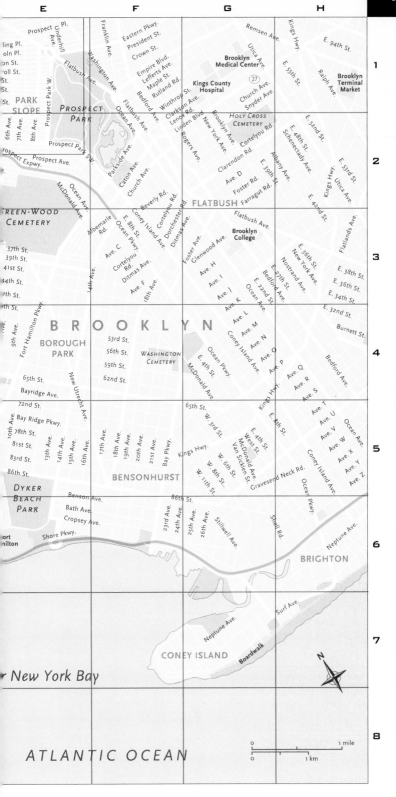

WESTERN BROOKLYN AND NORTHEASTERN STATEN ISLAND

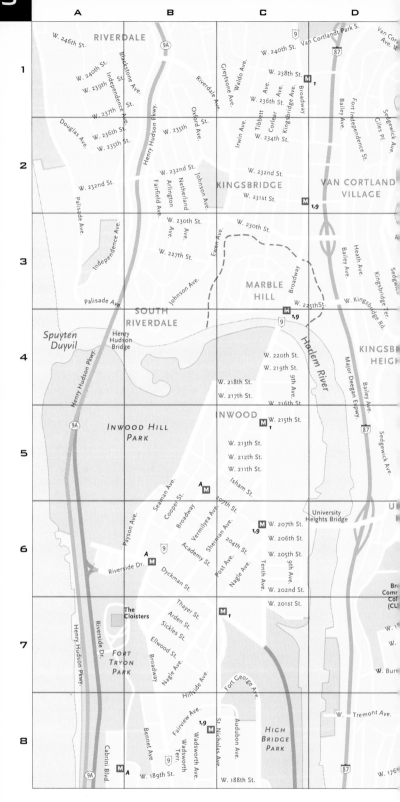

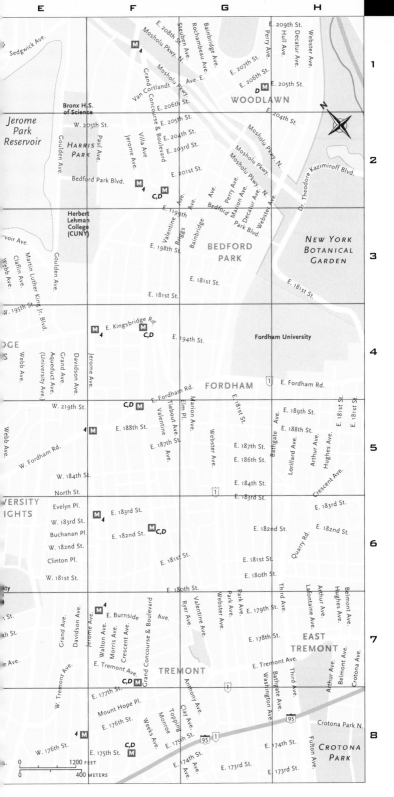

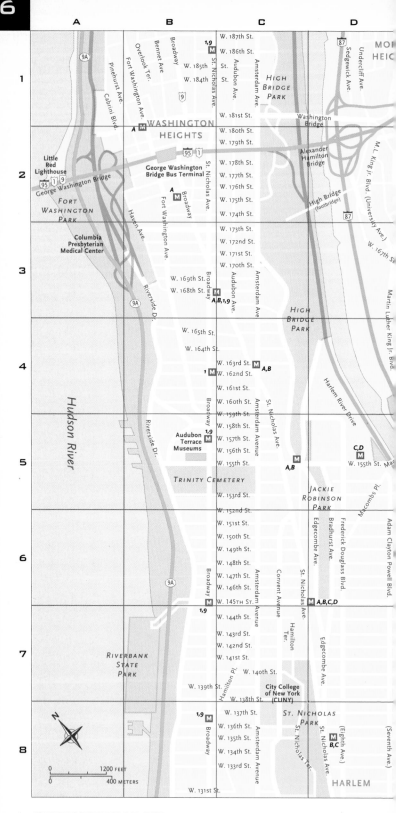

STREETFINDER

NORTHERN MANHATTAN AND THE SOUTH BRONX

A **B** **C** **D**

W. 130th

Lenox Ave.

W. 129th

W. 128th

W. 127th

W. 126th

Convent Ave.

St. Nicholas Ave.

St. Nicholas Ter.

Frederick Douglass Blvd. (Eighth Ave.)

Adam Clayton Powell Blvd. (Seventh Ave.)

1

¹,⁹ Ⓜ

W. 126th St.

Martin Luther King Jr. Blvd.

A,B,C,D
Ⓜ
(W. 125th St.)

La Salle St.

W. 124th St.

W. 124th St.

Ⓜ ²,³

General Grant National Memorial (Grant's Tomb)

W. 123rd St.

W. 122nd St.

2

Riverside Church

Broadway

Claremont Ave.

Amsterdam Ave.

W. 122nd St.

W. 120th St.

Morningside Ave.

W. 121st St.

W. 120th St.

W. 119th St.

St. Nicholas Ave.

W. 118th St.

W. 117th St.

9A

Barnard College

MORNINGSIDE HEIGHTS

HAR

Columbia University

Ⓜ
¹,⁹

MORNINGSIDE PARK

B,C Ⓜ

W. 116th St.

Ⓜ ²,³

Lenox Ave.

3

W. 114th St.

Morningside Dr.

W. 115th St.

W. 114th St.

RIVERSIDE PARK

W. 113th St.

W. 112th St.

W. 111th St.

W. 113th St.

W. 112th St.

W. 111th St.

¹,⁹ Ⓜ

Cathedral Parkway

Cathedral Church of St. John the Divine

Ⓜ
B,C

Central Park North

Ⓜ ²,³

Broadway

W. 109th St.

Amsterdam Ave.

W. 108th St.

Columbus Ave.

Manhattan Ave.

Frederick Douglass Circle

Harlem Mee

W. 107th St.

W. 106th St. (Duke Ellington Blvd.)

4

STRAUS PARK

W. 105th St.

The Loch

Muse the City

W. 104th St.

B,C

W. 103rd St.

Ⓜ ¹,⁹

Riverside Dr.

W. 102nd St.

Frederick Douglass Houses

The Pool

W. 101st St.

W. 100th St.

W. 99th St.

NORTH MEADOW

EAS MEAD

5

W. 98th St.

Park West Village

W. 97th St.

W. 96th St.

Ⓜ ¹,²,³,⁹

96th St. Transverse

Ⓜ
B,C

W. 95th St.

JOAN OF ARC PARK

W. 94th St.

W. 93rd St.

Columbus Ave.

Central Park West

Jacqueline Kennedy Onassis Reservoir

6

9A

West End Ave.

Broadway

Amsterdam Ave.

W. 92nd St.

W. 91st St.

W. 90th St.

W. 89th St.

UPPER WEST SIDE

RIVERSIDE PARK

W. 88th St.

W. 87th St.

B,C Ⓜ

7

Henry Hudson Pkwy.

Riverside Dr.

Ⓜ ¹,⁹

W. 86th St.

86th St. Transverse

E. A. Poe St.

W. 85th St.

CENTRAL PARK

W. 84th St.

W. 83rd St.

East Dr.

W. 82nd St.

GREAT LAWN

W. 81st St.

Hayden Planetarium

B,C Ⓜ

Belvedere Lake

8

W. 80th St.

¹,⁹ Ⓜ

W. 79th St.

79th St. Transverse

W. 78th St.

W. 77th St.

American Museum of Natural History

The Lake

0   1200 FEET

0   400 METERS

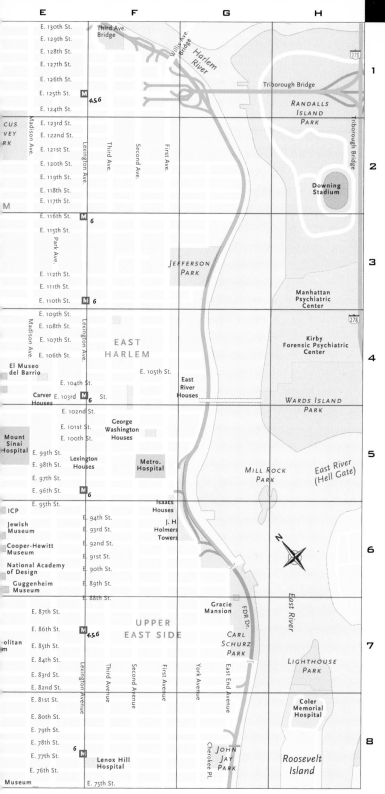

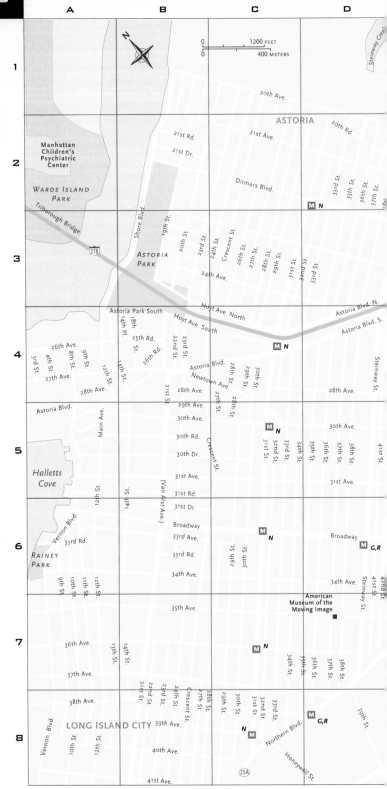

STREETFINDER

E   F   G   H

1

Steinway Pl.
Berrian
19th Ave.

Hazen St.

Bowery
Bay

La Guardia Airport

Ditmars Blvd.

STEINWAY

Marine
Air
Terminal

19th Rd.   19th Dr.

81st St.
80th St.
78th St.
Ditmars Blvd.
77th St.
76th St.

23rd Ave.

24th Ave.

Astoria Blvd.

2

45th St.
46th St.
21st Ave.
47th St.
48th St.
49th St.
21st Ave.
75th St.
77th St.
74th St.

41st St.
42nd St.
43rd St.
Ditmars Blvd.

72nd St.
71st St.

73rd St.

Grand Central Pkwy.

Astoria Blvd. S.

85th St.
84th St.
83rd St.
82nd St.
81st St.
80th St.
79th St.

3

278

ST. MICHAEL'S
CEMETERY

25th Ave.

Ave.

Brooklyn-Queens Expy.

30th Ave.

31st Ave.

79th St.

32nd Ave.
77th St.
78th St.
76th St.
75th St.
74th St.
73rd St.
Northern Blvd.

4

44th St.
45th St.
46th St.
47th St.
48th St.
49th St.
50th St.
Hobart St.
57th St.
31st Ave.

72nd St.
25A

JACKSON HEIGHTS

71st St.
70th St.
69th St.
34th Ave.

35th Ave.

37th Ave.

5

Newtown Rd.

32nd Ave.
56th St.
55th St.
54th St.
53rd St.
61st St.
60th St.
59th St.
58th St.
Northern Blvd.
62nd St.
34th Ave.

M G,R

M G,R

Broadway

M G,R
278

6

44th St.
45th St.
46th St.

25A

37th Ave.
57th St.
58th St.
59th St.
60th St.
61st St.

62nd St.
64th St.
65th St.

7
M

7

42nd Pl.

48th St.

Barnett St.

39th Ave.

Woodside Ave.

52nd St.
51st St.
50th St.
49th St.
48th St.
39th Rd.
39th Dr.

WOODSIDE

39th Ave.

M 7

Roosevelt Ave.
Woodside Ave.

67th St.
68th St.
69th St.
70th St.

43rd Ave.

39th Ave.

Woodside

61st St.

7

43rd St.
44th St.
45th St.
46th St.
47th St.

Skillman Ave.

49th St.
50th St.
51st St.

41st Ave.
54th St.
55th St.
56th St.
58th St.
44th Ave.
64th St.

Queens Blvd.

47th Ave.

Brooklyn-Queens Expressway

8

40th St.
41st St.
42nd St.
43rd St.

7 M

43rd Ave.

53rd St.

Greenpoint

NEW
CALVARY CEMETERY

278

A   **B**   **C**   **D**

The Lake

W. 73rd St.
W. 73rd St.
W. 72nd St.
W. 72nd St.

1

Broadway

W. 71st St.
W. 70th St.
W. 69th St.
W. 68th St.

West Dr.

Terrace Dr.

East Dr.

Freedom Place

Henry Hudson Pkwy.

W. 67th St.
W. 66th St.

Tavern on the Green

W. 66th St.
Lincoln Center

M 1,9

W. 65th St.

65th St. Transverse

2

W. 64th St.

Central Park W.

CENTRAL PARK

DAMROSCH PARK

Columbus Ave.

W. 63rd St.
W. 62nd St.

Wollman Rink

West End Ave.

Fordham University

W. 61st St.

W. 61st St.

The Pond

W. 60th St.

Columbus Circle

M A,B,C, D,1,9

Central Park South

Gra
Ar
Pla

W. 59th St.

W. 59th St.

W. 59th St.

Plaza Hotel

9A

W. 58th St.

W. 58th St.

Broadway

M N,R

M B,Q

3

W. 57th St.

Carnegie Hall

Eleventh Ave.

W. 56th St.
W. 55th St.

Tenth Ave.

W. 54th St.

M

E,

DeWitt Clinton Park

W. 53rd St.
W. 52nd St.

Seventh Ave.

West Side Highway

W. 51st St.

Hell's Kitchen

Radio City Music Hall

Rockefelle Center

4

W. 50th St.

M C,E

M 1,9

Rockefelle Plaza

W. 49th St.

M N,R

M B,D, F, Q

Hudson River

W. 48th St.
W. 47th St.

Eighth Ave.

Ninth Ave.

W. 46th St.

Actors Square

Ave. of the Americas

Intrepid Sea-Air-Space Museum

W. 45th St.
W. 44th St.

Times Square

W. 43rd St.

M A,C,E

M 1,2,3, N,R,S, 7,9

M B,D,F,Q

5

Twelfth Ave.

W. 42nd St.

Tenth Ave.

W. 41st St.

Port Authority Bus Terminal

BRYANT PARK

Lincoln Tunnel

W. 40th St.

(Sixth Ave.)

W. 39th St.

W. 38th St.

Dyer Ave.

W. 37th St.

Eighth Ave.

Seventh Ave.

Jacob K. Javits Convention Center

W. 36th St.

Herald Square

Empi Sta Buildin

6

Tenth Ave.

W. 35th St.

1,2, 3,9

W. 34th St.

M A,C,E

M

M B,D,F, N,Q,R

W. 33rd St.

U.S. Post Office (Main)

Penn Plaza Dr.

Penn Station/ Madison Square Garden

W. 32nd St.

Broadway

West Side Highway

W. 31st St.

Penn Plaza

W. 30th St.

W. 29th St.

7

Twelfth Ave.

W. 28th St.

M 1,9

M N

W. 27th St.

Eleventh Ave.

W. 26th St.

Ninth Ave.

W. 25th St.

Seventh Ave.

Wo Squ

W. 24th St.

W. 23rd St.

M C,E

M 1,9

M F,Q

N

W. 22nd St.

8

Hudson River

W. 21st St.
W. 20th St.

West Side Highway

W. 19th St.
W. 18th St.

Tenth Ave.

W. 17th St.

Eighth Ave.

Seventh Ave.

Ave. of the Americas

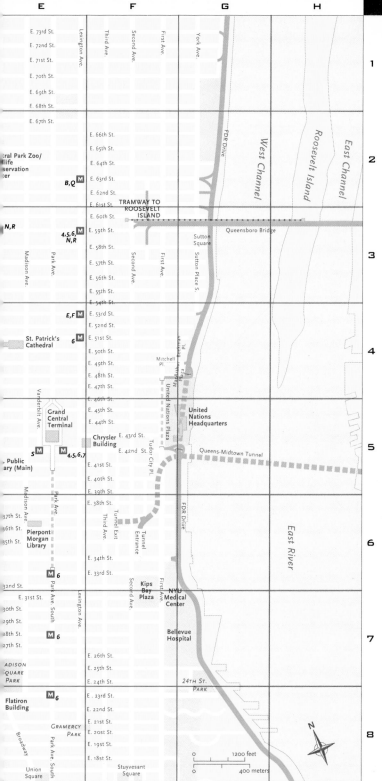

E   F   G   H

E. 73rd St.
E. 72nd St.
E. 71st St.
E. 70th St.
E. 69th St.
E. 68th St.
E. 67th St.

Lexington Ave.
Third Ave.
Second Ave.
First Ave.
York Ave.

1

E. 66th St.
E. 65th St.
E. 64th St.
E. 63rd St.
E. 62nd St.
E. 61st St.

ral Park Zoo/
llife
servation
er

B,Q M

West Channel
Roosevelt Island
East Channel

FDR Drive

2

TRAMWAY TO
ROOSEVELT
ISLAND

N,R

E. 60th St.
E. 59th St.
E. 58th St.
E. 57th St.
E. 56th St.
E. 55th St.
E. 54th St.

4,5,6,
N,R M

Madison Ave.
Park Ave.
Second Ave.
First Ave.

Queensboro Bridge
Sutton Square
Sutton Place S.

3

E,F M

St. Patrick's
Cathedral

6 M

E. 53rd St.
E. 52nd St.
E. 51st St.
E. 50th St.
E. 49th St.
E. 48th St.
E. 47th St.
E. 46th St.

Mitchell
Pl.

Beekman Pl.

United Nations Plaza

United
Nations
Headquarters

4

Vanderbilt Ave.

Grand
Central
Terminal

Chrysler
Building

E. 45th St.
E. 44th St.
E. 43rd St.
E. 42nd St.
E. 41st St.
E. 40th St.
E. 39th St.

Tudor City Pl.

Queens-Midtown Tunnel

5

S M
4,5,6,7 M

Public
ary (Main)

Madison Ave.
Park Ave.

37th St.
36th St.
35th St.

Pierpont
Morgan
Library

E. 38th St.
E. 34th St.
E. 33rd St.

Third Ave.

Tunnel Exit

Tunnel
Entrance

FDR Drive

6

East River

M 6

32nd St.
E. 31st St.
30th St.
29th St.
28th St.
27th St.

Park Ave. South
Lexington Ave.
Second Ave.
First Ave.

Kips
Bay
Plaza

NYU
Medical
Center

M 6

Bellevue
Hospital

7

ADISON
QUARE
PARK

E. 26th St.
E. 25th St.
E. 24th St.

24TH ST.
PARK

Flatiron
Building

M 6

GRAMERCY
PARK

Broadway
Park Ave. South

E. 23rd St.
E. 22nd St.
E. 21st St.
E. 20st St.
E. 19th St.
E. 18th St.

N

8

Union
Square

Stuyvesant
Square

0   1200 feet
0   400 meters

MIDTOWN MANHATTAN

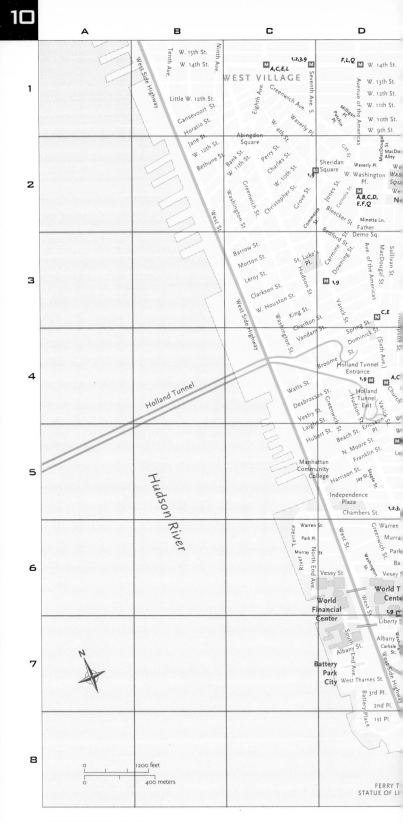

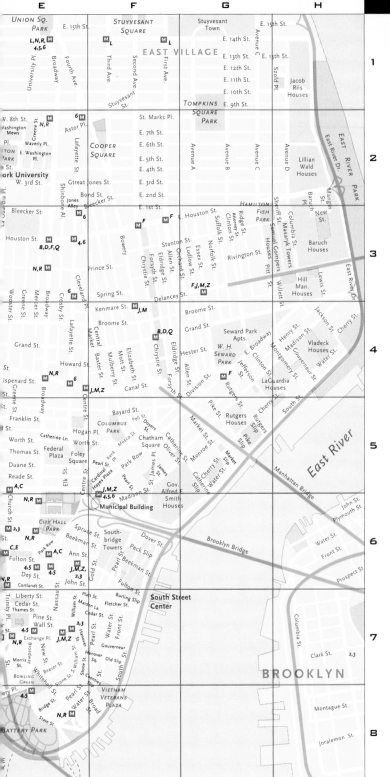

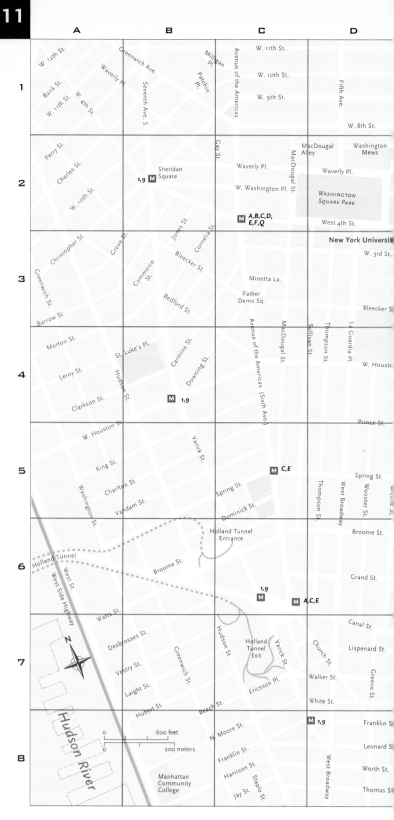

E   F   G   H

E. 11th St.

E. 10th St.

Stuyvesant St.

E. 9th St.

TOMPKINS SQUARE PARK

N,R Ⓜ   E. 8th St.

Ⓜ **6**

St. Marks Pl.

Astor Pl.

COOPER SQUARE

E. 7th St.

E. 6th St.

E. 5th St.

Avenue A

Greene St.
verly Pl.

Broadway

Lafayette St.

Fourth Ave.

Third Ave.

Second Ave.

First Ave.

Washington Pl.

E. 4th St.

Great Jones St.

E. 3rd St.

Shinbone Al.

Bond St.

E. 2nd St.

Jones Al.

Bleecker St.

E. 1st St.

Ⓜ **6**

Ⓜ **F**   E. Houston St.

Ⓜ **F**

Norfolk St.

Ⓜ **B,D,F,Q**

Ⓜ **4,6**

Stanton St.

Allen St.

Orchard St.

Ludlow St.

Essex St.

N,R Ⓜ

Prince St.

Bowery

Chrystie St.

Forsyth St.

Eldridge St.

Rivington St.

Cleveland Pl.

Mulberry St.

Mott St.

Elizabeth St.

F,J,M,Z Ⓜ

Delancey St.

6 Ⓜ

Spring St.

Mercer St.

Broadway

Crosby St.

Lafayette St.

Kenmare St.

Ⓜ **J,M**

Broome St.

Broome St.

B,D,Q Ⓜ

Grand St.

Central Market

Baxter St.

Mulberry St.

Mott St.

Elizabeth St.

Chrystie St.

Eldridge St.

Hester St.

Howard St.

Forsyth St.

Allen St.

N,R Ⓜ

6 Ⓜ

J,M,Z Ⓜ

Canal St.

Division St.

Pike St.

Broadway

Lafayette St.

Centre St.

Manhattan Bridge

Bayard St.

Pell St.

Doyers St.

Market St.

Catherine La.

COLUMBUS PARK

Hogan Pl.

Mosco St.

Chatham Square

St. James Pl.

Catherine St.

Madison St.

Worth St.

Park Row

Oliver St.

Monroe St.

Federal Plaza

Foley Square

Kent Pl.

GREENWICH VILLAGE AND SOHO

A · B · C · D

1

2

3

4

5

6

7

8

Manhattan Bridge

Marshall St.
John St.
Plymouth St.
Bridge St.
Water St.
Front St.
Hudson Ave.
York St.
Gold St.
Farragut

Wallabout Bay

CITY INDUSTRIAL PARK

New York Naval Shipyard

New Dock

Jay St.

Washington St.
Main St.
Front

Brooklyn Bridge
Fulton Ferry Landing
Fulton St.
Vine St.
Water St.

Brooklyn Queens Expwy.

Prospect St.
Pearl St.

Sands St.
Housing

Nassau St.
Navy St.

N. Elliott Pl.

J. BARRY PARK

Poplar St.
Middagh St.
Cranberry St.
Orange St.

A,C

Cadman Plaza W.
Cadman Plaza E.

Concord St.
Duffield St.
Cold St.

McLAUGHLIN PARK

Raymond Houses

278
Columbia Heights
The Promenade

Pineapple St.
Clark St.
Willow St.
Hicks St.
Love La.
Pierrepont St.
Montague St.

2,3
Henry St.
Monroe Pl.
Clinton St.

Tillary St.
Johnson St.
Tech Adams St.
Lawrence St.
Jay St.
Pearl St.

Flatbush Ave.
Willoughby St.

L I Brook Camp

M,N,R

2,3

A,C,F

M,N,R

D,M,N,Q,R

Fulton St.

2,3,

Furman St.

Remsen St.
Grace Ct.

A,5

Hunts La.
Joralemon St.
Sidney Pl.
Henry St.
Garden Pl.
State St.

Livingston St.
Court St.

Boerum Pl.

Smith St.

Livingston St.
Schermerhorn St.
State St.

Atlantic Ave.
Pacific St.
Dean St.
Bergen St.

A,C,G
Hoyt St.

East River

Willow Pl.
Columbia

Atlantic Ave.
Pacific St.

VAN VOORHEES PARK

Amity St.
Congress St.
Warren St.
Baltic St.

Baltic St.
Butler St.
Douglass St.
DeGraw St.

F,G

Wyckoff St.
Warren St.

Columbia Pl.

Kane St.
Irving St.
Sedgwick St.

Hicks St.
Tiffany Pl.

Henry St.
Cheever Pl.

Strong Pl.
Clinton St.
Tompkins Pl.

Bond St.
Hoyt St.

Brooklyn-Battery Tunnel

DeGraw St.
Van Brunt St.
Columbia St.

278

Sackett St.
Union St.
President St.

Court St.
Smith St.

CARROLL PARK

1st St.
F,G
2nd St.
3rd St.
4th St.

Buttermilk Channel

President St.
Carroll St.

Summit St.
Woodhull St.
Rapyle St.

1st Pl.
2nd Pl.
3rd Pl.

Summit

Hamilton Ave.
Bowne St.

4th Pl.
Luquer St.
Nelson St.

5th St.

Atlantic Basin

Conover St.
Imlay St.

Seabring St.
Commerce St.
Delavan St.
Verona St.
Visitation St.

Luquer St.
Nelson St.
Huntington St.
W. 9th St.

Gowanus Expwy.

Mill St.
Centre

Garnett St.

F,G
Second Ave.

Pioneer St.
King St.
Sullivan St.
Ferris St.
Wolcott St.
Dikeman St.
Coffey St.

Van Brunt St.

Richards St.

RED HOOK PARK

Dwight St.

Columbia St.
Hicks St.

Lorraine St.
Creamer St.
Bay St.
Sigourney

Otsego St.

Red Hook Housing

Henry St.
Clinton St.

Mill St.
Bush St.

RED HOOK PLAYGROUND

Halleck St.

Court St.
Smith St.
Hamilton Ave.

Vandyke St.
Beard St.

STREETFINDER

E F G H

1

Clinton Ave.
Flushing Ave.
Park Ave.
klyn-queens Expy.

U.S.
Naval Reserve

278

Emerson St.
Steuben St.
Grand Ave.
Ryerson St.
Hall St.

Myrtle Ave.
Taaffe St.
Kent Ave.
Franklin Ave.
Classon St.

Willoughby Ave.

Spencer St.
Bedford Ave.
Skillman St.
Walworth St.

De Kalb Ave.

Lafayette Ave.
Bedford Ave.

M G

2

Walt
Whitman
Houses

N. Portland
Auburn Pl.
Myrtle Ave.
Cumberland
Carlton Ave.
Adelphi Ave.
Clermont Ave.
Vanderbilt Ave.
Clinton Ave.
Waverly Ave.
Washington Ave.

Pratt
Institute

The
Quadrangles

Lafayette
Gardens

M G

Clifton Pl.
St. James Pl.
Greene Ave.
Grand Ave.
Classon St.
Franklin Ave.
Lexington Ave.
Quincy St.
Gates Ave.
Monroe St.
Madison St.
Downing Ave.

FT. GREENE
PARK

M G

3

Edwards St.
Rockwell Pl.
Ashland Pl.
Felix St.
Hudson Ave.
M

DeKalb Ave.
S. Oxford St.
S. Portland
Ft. Greene St.
S. Elliott St.
Lafayette Ave.
Greene Ave.
Fulton St.
Cumberland St.
Carlton Ave.
Adelphi Ave.
Clermont Ave.
Vanderbilt Ave.
Clinton Ave.
Waverly Ave.

M G
M
A,C

A,C
M

Putnam Ave.
Fulton St.
Atlantic Ave.

4

Brooklyn Academy
of Music

Flatbush Ave.
B,M,N,R M
D,Q,
2,3,4,5

Atlantic Ave.
Atlantic Ave.

Pacific St.
Dean St.
Bergen St.
St. Mark's Pl.
Carlton Ave.
Vanderbilt Ave.

Underhill Ave.
Washington Ave.
Grand Ave.

5

St. Mark's Pl.
Nevins St.
Baltic St.
Third Ave.
Butler St.
Douglass St.
DeGraw St.
Sackett St.

Fourth Ave.

Prospect Pl.
Park Pl.
Sterling Pl.
St. John's Pl.
Lincoln Pl.
Berkeley Pl.

Flatbush
D,Q
M
Park Pl.
Ave.

Montauk
Club
2,3,4
M

GRAND
ARMY
PLAZA

Butler Pl.
Stirling Pl.
St. Johns Pl.
Lincoln Pl.
2,3,4
M

Brooklyn
Public
Library

6

Union St.
N,R.
M
President St.

Fifth Ave.
Denton Pl.
Whitwell Pl.

Sixth Ave.

Carroll St.
Garfield Pl.
1st St.
2nd St.
3rd St.

Seventh Ave.
Fiske Pl.
Polhemus Pl.

Eighth Ave.
Montgomery Pl.

Flatbush Ave.
Eastern Pkwy.

3rd St.

PROSPECT
PARK

Prospect Park W.

7

4th St.
5th St.
6th St.
7th St.
8th St.
9th St.
10th St.

Methodist
Hospital

M F

Litchfield
Villa

F M M N,R.

M F

8

Third Ave.
Fourth Ave.
Fifth Ave.
Sixth Ave.
Seventh Ave.
Eighth Ave.

11th St.
12th St.
13th St.
14th St.
15th St.
16th St.

0   1200 FEET
0   400 METERS

Prospect Expwy.
N,R.
M

Bartel
Pritchard
Sq.
M F
Prospect Park S.W.

NORTHWESTERN BROOKLYN

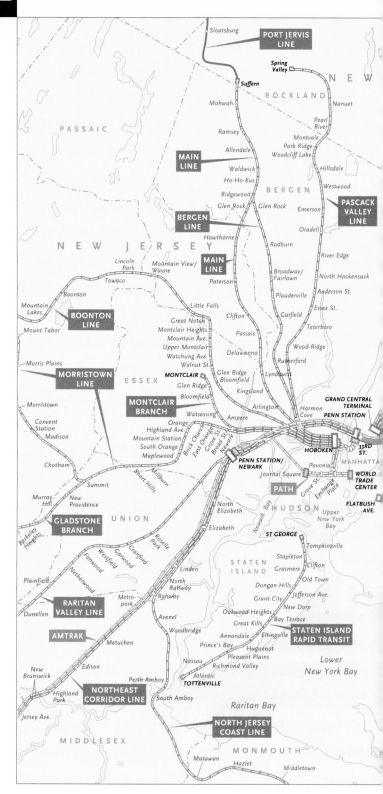

TRI-STATE COMMUTER RAIL

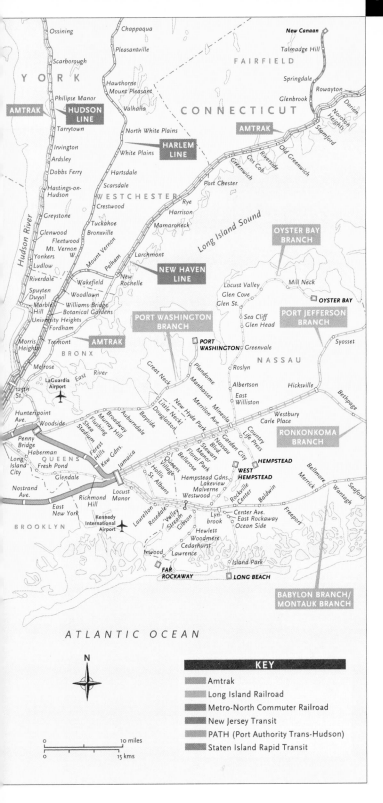

New Canaan
Talmadge Hill
FAIRFIELD
Springdale
Rowayton
Chappaqua
Ossining
Pleasantville
Scarborough
Hawthorne
Mount Pleasant
Glenbrook
Norton
Heights
Darien
Philipse Manor
Valhalla
AMTRAK
HUDSON
LINE
Stamford
CONNECTICUT
Old Greenwich
Riverside
Cos Cob
Greenwich
Tarrytown
North White Plains
AMTRAK
YORK
Irvington
Ardsley
White Plains
HARLEM
LINE
Dobbs Ferry
Hartsdale
Port Chester
Hastings-on-
Hudson
Scarsdale
WESTCHESTER
Rye
Greystone
Crestwood
Harrison
Long Island Sound
Tuckahoe
Mamaroneck
Glenwood
Bronxville
OYSTER BAY
BRANCH
Fleetwood
Mt. Vernon
Larchmont
Mill Neck
Yonkers
Mount Vernon
Pelham
New
Rochelle
Locust Valley
Glen Cove
Glen St.
OYSTER BAY
Ludlow
NEW HAVEN
LINE
Riverdale
Wakefield
Spuyten
Duyvil
Woodlawn
Sea Cliff
Glen Head
PORT JEFFERSON
BRANCH
Marble
Hill
Williams Bridge
Botanical Gardens
University Heights
Fordham
PORT WASHINGTON
BRANCH
Greenvale
Syosset
Morris
Heights
Tremont
AMTRAK
PORT
WASHINGTON
Roslyn
NASSAU
BRONX
Melrose
Plandome
Manhasset
Albertson
Hicksville
Bethpage
LaGuardia
Airport
East
River
Great Neck
East
Williston
Westbury
Carle Place
125th
St.
Little Neck
New Hyde Park
Merrilon Ave.
Mineola
Huntspoint
Ave.
Woodside
Broadway
Murray Hill
Flushing
Auburndale
Bayside
Douglaston
Garden City
Country
Life Press
RONKONKOMA
BRANCH
Penny
Bridge
Haberman
Shea
Stadium
Nassau
Blvd.
Stewart
Manor
Floral Park
Bellerose
Penny
Bridge
Forest
Hills
Kew Gdns.
Jamaica
Queens
Village
Hempstead
Bellmore
Merrick
Wantagh
Seaford
Long
Island
City
QUEENS
Fresh Pond
St. Albans
Hollis
WEST
HEMPSTEAD
Nostrand
Ave.
Glendale
Locust
Manor
Hempstead Gdns.
Lakeview
Malverne
Westwood
Rockville
Center
Baldwin
Freeport
East
New York
Richmond
Hill
Laurelton
Rosedale
Valley
Stream
Gibson
Lynbrook
Center Ave.
East Rockaway
Ocean Side
BROOKLYN
Kennedy
International
Airport
Hewlett
Woodmere
Cedarhurst
Lawrence
Inwood
Island Park
FAR
ROCKAWAY
LONG BEACH
BABYLON BRANCH/
MONTAUK BRANCH

Hudson River

ATLANTIC OCEAN

N

KEY

Amtrak
Long Island Railroad
Metro-North Commuter Railroad
New Jersey Transit
PATH (Port Authority Trans-Hudson)
Staten Island Rapid Transit

0   10 miles
0   15 kms

SUBWAYS

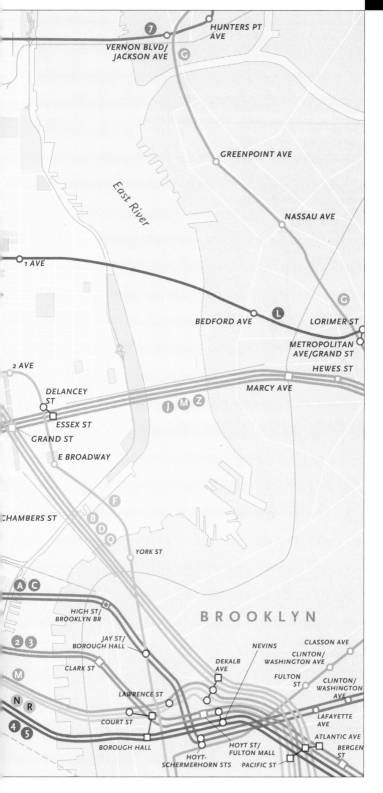

HUNTERS PT AVE

7

VERNON BLVD/
JACKSON AVE **G**

GREENPOINT AVE

East River

NASSAU AVE

1 AVE

BEDFORD AVE **L**

G

LORIMER ST

METROPOLITAN
AVE/GRAND ST

2 AVE

HEWES ST

MARCY AVE

DELANCEY
ST

J **M** **Z**

ESSEX ST

GRAND ST

E BROADWAY

CHAMBERS ST

F

B
D **Q**

YORK ST

A **C**

BROOKLYN

HIGH ST/
BROOKLYN BR

NEVINS

CLASSON AVE

CLINTON/
WASHINGTON AVE

2 **3**

JAY ST/
BOROUGH HALL

DEKALB
AVE

FULTON
ST

CLINTON/
WASHINGTON
AVE

CLARK ST

M

LAWRENCE ST

LAFAYETTE
AVE

N **R**

COURT ST

ATLANTIC AVE

4 **5**

BOROUGH HALL

HOYT-
SCHERMERHORN STS

HOYT ST/
FULTON MALL

PACIFIC ST

BERGEN
ST

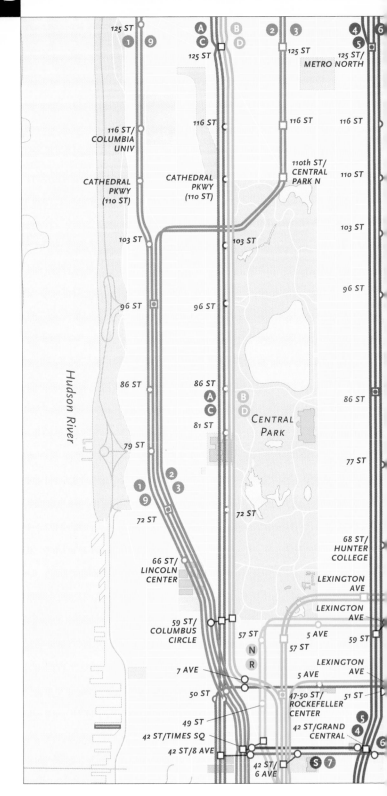

SUBWAYS

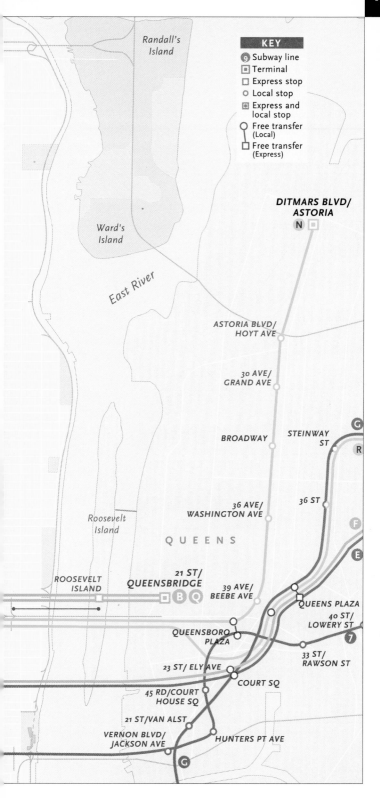

KEY
- ⑤ Subway line
- ▣ Terminal
- ☐ Express stop
- ○ Local stop
- ◉ Express and local stop
- Ⓞ Free transfer (Local)
- ▢ Free transfer (Express)

Randall's Island

Ward's Island

East River

Roosevelt Island

QUEENS

DITMARS BLVD/ ASTORIA
Ⓝ ▣

ASTORIA BLVD/ HOYT AVE

30 AVE/ GRAND AVE

BROADWAY   STEINWAY ST

Ⓖ

Ⓡ

36 AVE/ WASHINGTON AVE   36 ST

Ⓕ

Ⓔ

ROOSEVELT ISLAND

21 ST/ QUEENSBRIDGE
▣ Ⓑ Ⓠ

39 AVE/ BEEBE AVE

▢ QUEENS PLAZA

40 ST/ LOWERY ST

QUEENSBORO PLAZA

⑦

33 ST/ RAWSON ST

23 ST/ ELY AVE

COURT SQ

45 RD/COURT HOUSE SQ

21 ST/VAN ALST

VERNON BLVD/ JACKSON AVE   HUNTERS PT AVE

Ⓖ

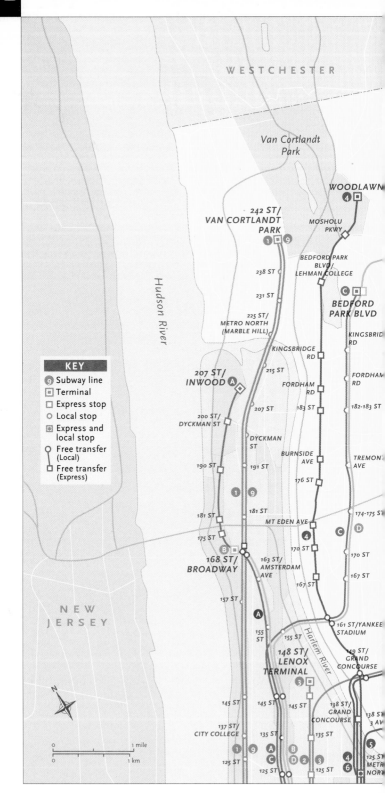

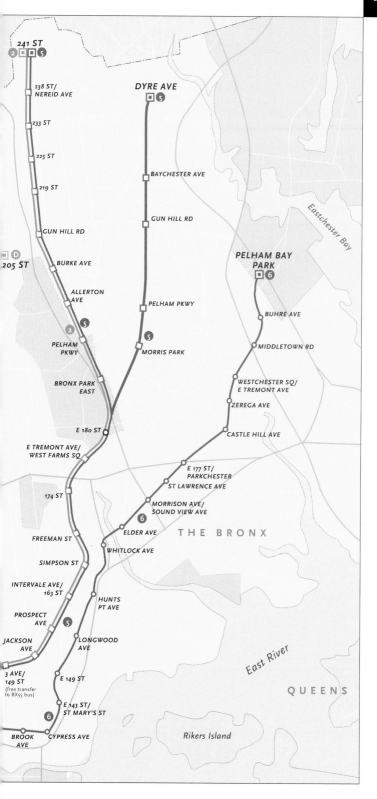

241 ST

238 ST/ NEREID AVE

233 ST

225 ST

219 ST

GUN HILL RD

205 ST

BURKE AVE

ALLERTON AVE

PELHAM PKWY

BRONX PARK EAST

E 180 ST

E TREMONT AVE/ WEST FARMS SQ

174 ST

FREEMAN ST

SIMPSON ST

INTERVALE AVE/ 163 ST

PROSPECT AVE

JACKSON AVE

3 AVE/ 149 ST
(free transfer to BX55 bus)

BROOK AVE

CYPRESS AVE

E 143 ST/ ST MARY'S ST

E 149 ST

LONGWOOD AVE

HUNTS PT AVE

WHITLOCK AVE

ELDER AVE

MORRISON AVE/ SOUND VIEW AVE

ST LAWRENCE AVE

E 177 ST/ PARKCHESTER

CASTLE HILL AVE

ZEREGA AVE

WESTCHESTER SQ/ E TREMONT AVE

MIDDLETOWN RD

BUHRE AVE

PELHAM BAY PARK

DYRE AVE

BAYCHESTER AVE

GUN HILL RD

PELHAM PKWY

MORRIS PARK

THE BRONX

Eastchester Bay

East River

QUEENS

Rikers Island

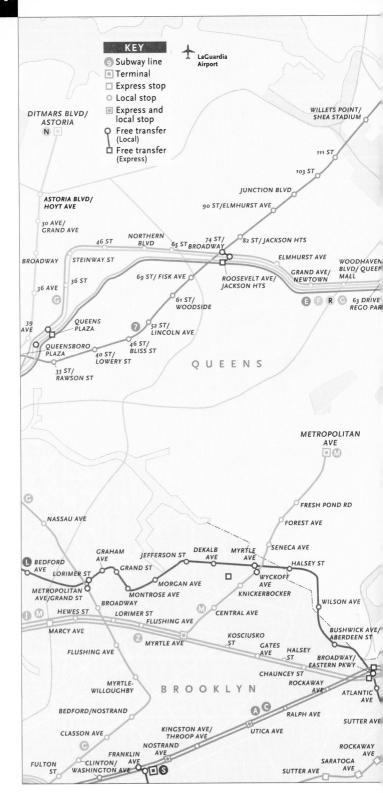

KEY

- **9** Subway line
- Terminal
- Express stop
- Local stop
- Express and local stop
- Free transfer (Local)
- Free transfer (Express)

LaGuardia Airport

DITMARS BLVD/ ASTORIA — **N**

WILLETS POINT/ SHEA STADIUM

111 ST

103 ST

JUNCTION BLVD

90 ST/ELMHURST AVE

ASTORIA BLVD/ HOYT AVE

30 AVE/ GRAND AVE

NORTHERN BLVD

74 ST/ BROADWAY

82 ST/ JACKSON HTS

46 ST

65 ST

ELMHURST AVE

BROADWAY

STEINWAY ST

WOODHAVEN BLVD/ QUEEN MALL

36 AVE

36 ST

69 ST/ FISK AVE

ROOSEVELT AVE/ JACKSON HTS

GRAND AVE/ NEWTOWN

61 ST/ WOODSIDE

E **F** **R** **G** 63 DRIVE REGO PAR

39 AVE

QUEENS PLAZA

7

52 ST/ LINCOLN AVE

QUEENSBORO PLAZA

46 ST/ BLISS ST

40 ST/ LOWERY ST

33 ST/ RAWSON ST

Q U E E N S

METROPOLITAN AVE — **M**

FRESH POND RD

FOREST AVE

NASSAU AVE

SENECA AVE

G

GRAHAM AVE

JEFFERSON ST

DEKALB AVE

MYRTLE AVE

HALSEY ST

L BEDFORD AVE

LORIMER ST

GRAND ST

WYCKOFF AVE

METROPOLITAN AVE/GRAND ST

MORGAN AVE

MONTROSE AVE

KNICKERBOCKER

WILSON AVE

BROADWAY

J **M**

HEWES ST

LORIMER ST

M CENTRAL AVE

FLUSHING AVE

MARCY AVE

BUSHWICK AVE/ ABERDEEN ST

KOSCIUSKO ST

FLUSHING AVE

Z MYRTLE AVE

GATES AVE

HALSEY ST

BROADWAY/ EASTERN PKWY

CHAUNCEY ST

MYRTLE- WILLOUGHBY

B R O O K L Y N

ROCKAWAY AVE

ATLANTIC AVE

BEDFORD/NOSTRAND

A **C**

RALPH AVE

SUTTER AVE

CLASSON AVE

UTICA AVE

KINGSTON AVE/ THROOP AVE

NOSTRAND AVE

ROCKAWAY AVE

G

FRANKLIN AVE

SARATOGA AVE

FULTON ST

CLINTON/ WASHINGTON AVE

S

SUTTER AVE

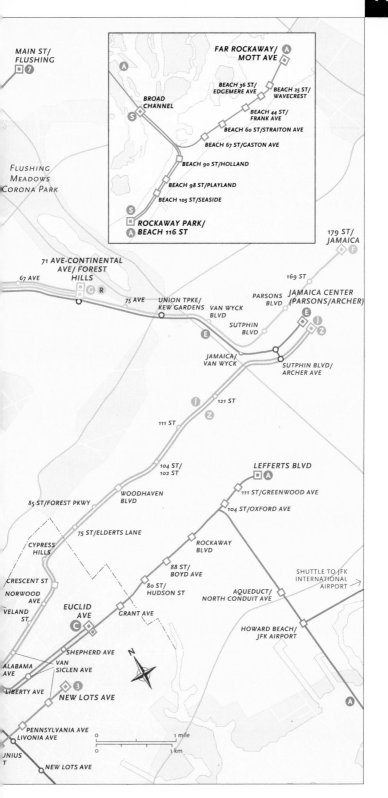

MAIN ST/
FLUSHING
7

FAR ROCKAWAY/
MOTT AVE   A

A

BEACH 36 ST/
EDGEMERE AVE

BEACH 25 ST/
WAVECREST

BROAD
CHANNEL

BEACH 44 ST/
FRANK AVE

S

BEACH 60 ST/STRAITON AVE

BEACH 67 ST/GASTON AVE

BEACH 90 ST/HOLLAND

FLUSHING
MEADOWS
CORONA PARK

BEACH 98 ST/PLAYLAND

BEACH 105 ST/SEASIDE

S

ROCKAWAY PARK/
BEACH 116 ST
A

179 ST/
JAMAICA
F

71 AVE-CONTINENTAL
AVE/ FOREST
HILLS

67 AVE

169 ST

G R

75 AVE

75 AVE

UNION TPKE/
KEW GARDENS

VAN WYCK
BLVD

PARSONS
BLVD

JAMAICA CENTER
(PARSONS/ARCHER)

E

E

J
2

SUTPHIN
BLVD

E

JAMAICA/
VAN WYCK

SUTPHIN BLVD/
ARCHER AVE

J

121 ST

Z

111 ST

104 ST/
102 ST

LEFFERTS BLVD
A

WOODHAVEN
BLVD

111 ST/GREENWOOD AVE

104 ST/OXFORD AVE

85 ST/FOREST PKWY

75 ST/ELDERTS LANE

ROCKAWAY
BLVD

SHUTTLE TO JFK
INTERNATIONAL
AIRPORT

CYPRESS
HILLS

88 ST/
BOYD AVE

CRESCENT ST

80 ST/
HUDSON ST

AQUEDUCT/
NORTH CONDUIT AVE

NORWOOD
AVE

VELAND
ST

EUCLID
AVE

GRANT AVE

HOWARD BEACH/
JFK AIRPORT

C

SHEPHERD AVE

N

ALABAMA
AVE

VAN
SICLEN AVE

LIBERTY AVE

3

NEW LOTS AVE

A

PENNSYLVANIA AVE
LIVONIA AVE

1 mile

JNIUS
T

1 km

NEW LOTS AVE

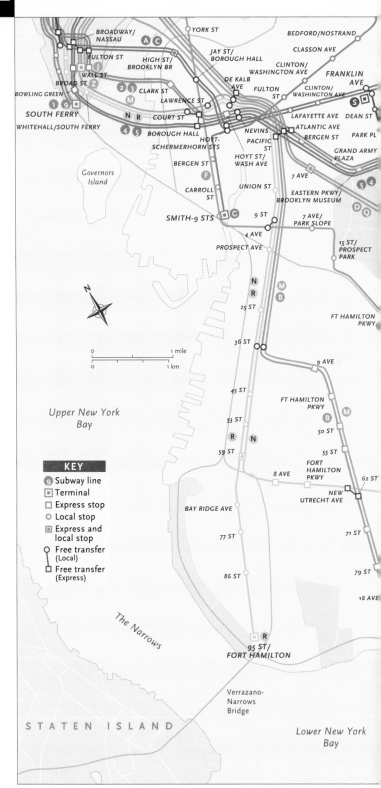

RALPH
AVE
UTICA AVE
KINGSTON AVE/
THROOP AVE
NOSTRAND
AVE
KINGSTON
AVE
NOSTRAND
AVE
SUTTER AVE/
RUTLAND RD
JUNIUS ST
SUTTER AVE
UTICA AVE
PRESIDENT ST
STERLING ST
FRANKLIN
AVE
BOTANIC
GARDEN
WINTHROP ST
PROSPECT
PARK
CHURCH AVE
PARKSIDE
AVE
BEVERLEY RD
CHURCH AVE
NEWKIRK AVE
BEVERLEY
RD
CORTELYOU
RD
CHURCH AVE
NEWKIRK AVE
DITMAS AVE
AVE H
18 AVE
AVE I
AVE J
BAY PKWY
AVE M
18 AVE
20 AVE
AVE N
BAY PKWY
AVE P
KINGS HWY
KINGS HWY
AVE U
BAY PKWY
AVE U
AVE U
NECK RD
20 AVE
25 AVE
AVE U
86 ST
AVE X
NEPTUNE AVE/
VAN SICKLEN
BAY 50 ST
STILLWELL AVE/
CONEY ISLAND
W 8 ST/
AQUARIUM
OCEAN PKWY

VAN SICLEN
AVE
PENNSYLVANIA
AVE
LIVONIA AVE
ROCKAWAY
AVE
NEW LOTS AVE
SARATOGA
AVE
E 105 ST
ROCKAWAY
PKWY
FLATBUSH AVE/
BROOKLYN
COLLEGE

B R O O K L Y N

KINGS HWY
SHEEPSHEAD
BAY
BRIGHTON BEACH

Rockaway Inlet

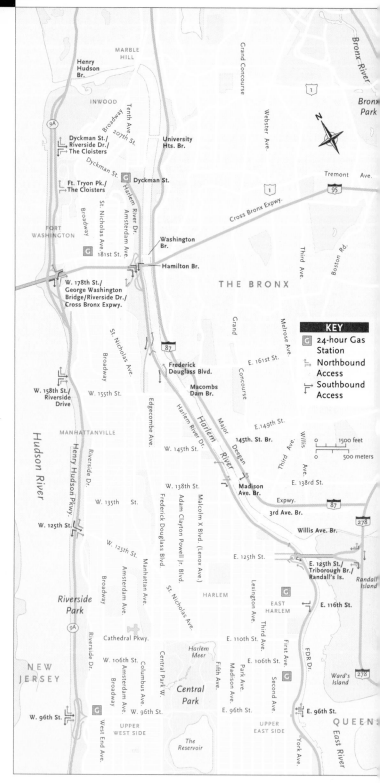

DRIVING UPTOWN: ENTRANCES & EXITS

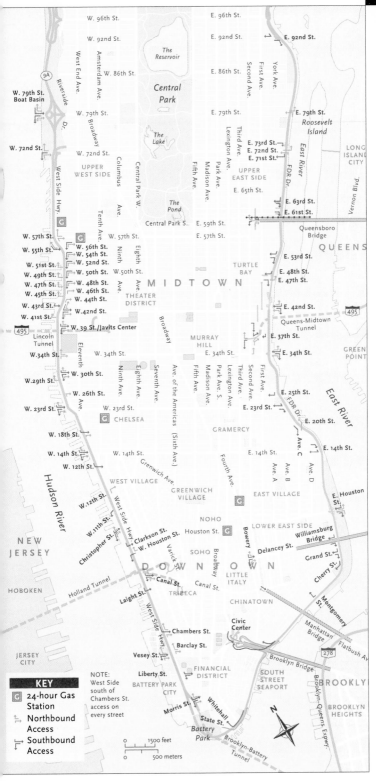

DRIVING DOWNTOWN: ENTRANCES & EXITS

KEY

- P Parking
- G Gasoline
- One-way street
- Two-way street
- Major thoroughfare

Lincoln Center

Fordham University

W. 65th St.
W. 64th St.
W. 63rd St.
W. 62nd St.
W. 61st St.
W. 60th St.
W. 59th St.
W. 58th St.
W. 57th St.
W. 56th St.
W. 55th St.
W. 54th St.
W. 53rd St.
W. 52nd St.
W. 51st St.
W. 50th St.
W. 49th St.
W. 48th St.
W. 47th St.
W. 46th St.
W. 45th St.
W. 44th St.
W. 43rd St.
W. 42nd St.
W. 41st St.
W. 40th St.
W. 39th St.
W. 38th St.
W. 37th St.
W. 36th St.
W. 35th St.
W. 34th St.
W. 33rd St.
W. 32nd St.
W. 31st St.
W. 30th St.
W. 29th St.
W. 28th St.
W. 27th St.
W. 26th St.
W. 25th St.
W. 24th St.
W. 23rd St.
W. 22nd St.

65th St. T

CENTRAL PARK

Columbus Circle
Central Park South
Carnegie Hall
TKTS Booth
Duffy Square
Times Square

Columbus Ave.
Central Park W.
Broadway
Seventh Ave.
Eighth Ave.
Ninth Ave.
Tenth Ave.
Eleventh Ave.
Twelfth Ave.
West Side Highway
Hudson River

DeWitt Clinton Park

9A

Lincoln Tunnel

Jacob K. Javits Convention Center

Port Authority Bus Terminal

Dyer Ave.

NY Post Office (Main)

Penn Plaza
Penn Plaza Dr.
Madison Square Garden/ Penn Station

600 feet
200 meters

DRIVING

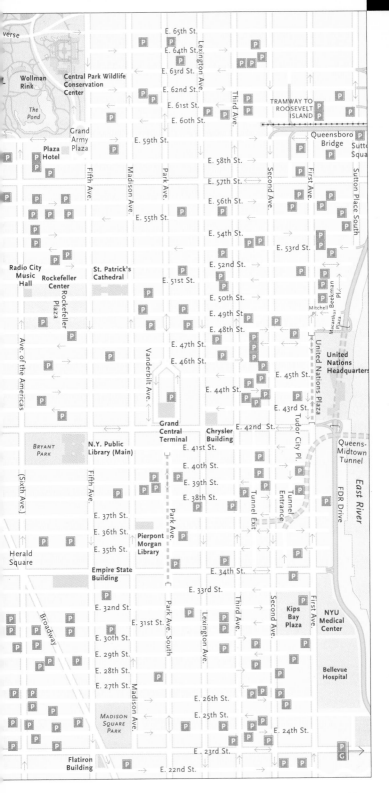

MIDTOWN MANHATTAN

W.16th St.
W.15th St.
W.14th St.
Eighth Ave.
Greenwich St.
West Side Hwy.
Seventh Ave. South
Ave. of the Americas (Sixth Ave.)
GREENWICH VILLAGE
W. 10th St.
Christopher St.
Varick St.
Hudson St.
W. Houston St.
West St.
Canal S
Holland Tunnel
TRIBECA
Hudson River
N. Moore St.
Harrison St.
Chambers St.
Vesey St.
X90
W. Thames
NEW JERSEY

KEY
Northbound
Southbound
Eastbound
Westbound
101 Route number
20 Terminal

BUSES

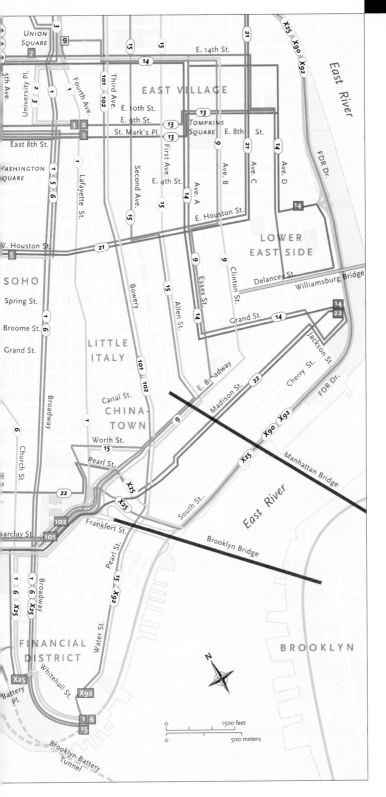

UNION
SQUARE
9
7

E. 14th St.

3
15
15
14
21

X25 X90 X92

East River

Fourth Ave.
101
102
2 3
1
1

Third Ave.

EAST VILLAGE

E. 10th St.
E. 9th St.
St. Mark's Pl.
13
13
13

TOMPKINS
SQUARE
E. 8th   St.

FDR Dr.

University Pl.

5th Ave.

East 8th St.
3 2
1

1

Ave. A
Ave. B
Ave. C
Ave. D

21
14

WASHINGTON
SQUARE

1 5 6

Lafayette St.

Second Ave.

First Ave.

E. 4th St.

1

15

15

14

E. Houston St.

LOWER
EAST SIDE

14

W. Houston St.
5
21

9
9

Essex St.
Clinton St.

Delancey St.

Williamsburg Bridge

SOHO

Spring St.

Broome St.
1
6

Grand St.

Bowery

LITTLE
ITALY

15

Allen St.

14

Grand St.
14

14
22

Jackson St.

101
102

Canal St.
CHINA-
TOWN

E. B'way

Madison St.
22

Cherry St.

FDR Dr.

Broadway

Worth St.
1
15

9

X90 X92

Pearl St.

X25

Manhattan Bridge

6

Church St.

22

102
101
Barclay St.

X25

Frankfort St.

South St.

X25

East River

Pearl St.

15
X92

Water St.

1 6
1 6
X25 X25

Broadway

Brooklyn Bridge

BROOKLYN

FINANCIAL
DISTRICT

X25

Whitehall St.

X92

Battery
Pl.

1 6
15

N

0   1500 feet
0   500 meters

Brooklyn-Battery
Tunnel

BUSES

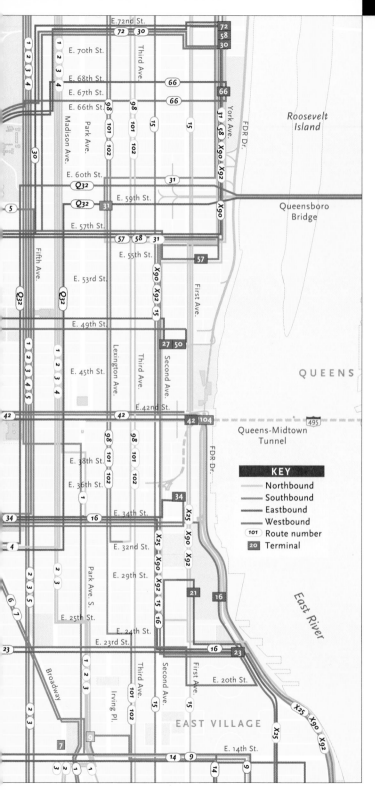

MIDTOWN

BUSES UPTOWN

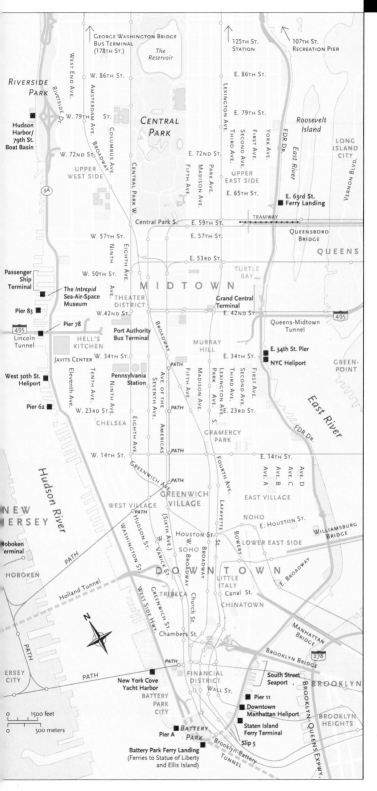

George Washington Bridge
Bus Terminal
(178TH ST.)

The
Reservoir

125TH ST.
STATION

107TH ST.
RECREATION PIER

RIVERSIDE
PARK

W. 86TH ST.

E. 86TH ST.

WEST END AVE.

RIVERSIDE DR.

AMSTERDAM AVE.

W. 79TH ST.

Hudson
Harbor/
79th St.
Boat Basin

ST.

BROADWAY

COLUMBUS AVE.

CENTRAL
PARK

E. 79TH ST.

Roosevelt
Island

LONG
ISLAND
CITY

W. 72ND ST.

LEXINGTON AVE.

THIRD AVE.

SECOND AVE.

FIRST AVE.

YORK AVE.

FDR DR.

East River

VERNON BLVD.

UPPER
WEST SIDE

E. 72ND ST.

E. 65TH ST.

UPPER
EAST SIDE

FIFTH AVE.

MADISON AVE.

PARK AVE.

E. 63rd St.
Ferry Landing

9A

CENTRAL PARK W.

Central Park S.

E. 59TH ST.

TRAMWAY

QUEENSBORO
BRIDGE

QUEENS

W. 57TH ST.

E. 57TH ST.

NINTH AVE.

EIGHTH AVE.

E. 53RD ST.

TURTLE
BAY

Passenger
Ship
Terminal

W. 50TH ST.

M I D T O W N

The Intrepid
Sea-Air-Space
Museum

Pier 83

THEATER
DISTRICT

Grand Central
Terminal

Pier 78

W. 42ND ST.

E. 42ND ST.

495

495

Lincoln
Tunnel

Port Authority
Bus Terminal

BROADWAY

MURRAY
HILL

Queens-Midtown
Tunnel

HELL'S
KITCHEN

Javits Center

W. 34TH ST.

PATH

FIFTH AVE.

MADISON AVE.

PARK AVE. S.

LEXINGTON AVE.

THIRD AVE.

SECOND AVE.

FIRST AVE.

E. 34TH ST.

E. 34th St. Pier
NYC Heliport

GREEN-
POINT

West 30th St.
Heliport

ELEVENTH AVE.

TENTH AVE.

NINTH AVE.

Pennsylvania
Station

SEVENTH AVE.

AVE. OF THE AMERICAS

PATH

W. 23RD ST.

E. 23RD ST.

East River

Pier 62

CHELSEA

EIGHTH AVE.

GRAMERCY
PARK

FDR DR.

W. 14TH ST.

PATH

E. 14TH ST.

FOURTH AVE.

AVE. A

AVE. B

AVE. C

AVE. D

N E W
J E R S E Y

Hudson River

GREENWICH AVE.

PATH

GREENWICH
VILLAGE

EAST VILLAGE

WEST VILLAGE

HUDSON ST.

(SIXTH AVE.)

W. VARICK ST.

BROADWAY

LAFAYETTE ST.

NOHO

E. HOUSTON ST.

WILLIAMSBURG
BRIDGE

Hoboken
Terminal

PATH

HOBOKEN

Holland Tunnel

WASHINGTON ST.

Houston St.

SOHO

BOWERY

LOWER EAST SIDE

E. BROADWAY

D O W N T O W N

WEST SIDE HWY

GREENWICH ST.

CHURCH ST.

TRIBECA

LITTLE
ITALY

Canal St.

CHINATOWN

N

MANHATTAN
BRIDGE

Chambers St.

BROOKLYN BRIDGE

278

ERSEY
CITY

PATH

PATH

FINANCIAL
DISTRICT

South Street
Seaport

BROOKLYN

ERSEY
CITY

New York Cove
Yacht Harbor

Wall St.

Pier 11

BROOKLYN-QUEENS EXPWY.

BROOKLYN
HEIGHTS

0   1500 feet

BATTERY
PARK
CITY

Downtown
Manhattan Heliport

0   500 meters

Battery
Pier A   Park

Staten Island
Ferry Terminal

Slip 5

Battery Park Ferry Landing
(Ferries to Statue of Liberty
and Ellis Island)

Brooklyn-Battery
TUNNEL

PIERS AND TERMINALS

Your Source
in the City

MANY MAPS • WHERE & HOW

FIND IT ALL • NIGHT & DAY

ANTIQUES TO ZIPPERS

BARGAINS • BAUBLES • KITES

ELEGANT EDIBLES • ETHNIC EATS

STEAK HOUSES • FISH HOUSES

BISTROS • TRATTORIAS

CLASSICAL • JAZZ • CABARET

COMEDY • THEATER • DANCE

BARS • CLUBS • BLUES

COOL TOURS

HOUSECLEANING • CATERING

LOST & FOUND • THE CABLE GUY

GET A LAWYER • GET A DENTIST

GET A NEW PET • GET A VET

MUSEUMS • GALLERIES

PARKS • GARDENS • RINKS

AQUARIUMS TO ZOOS

BASEBALL TO ROCK CLIMBING

FESTIVALS • EVENTS

DAY SPAS • DAY TRIPS

HOTELS • HOT LINES

PASSPORT PIX • TRAVEL INFO

HELICOPTER TOURS

DINERS • DELIS • PIZZERIAS

BRASSERIES • CAFÉS

BOOTS • BOOKS • BUTTONS

BICYCLES • SKATES

SUITS • SHOES • HATS

RENT A TUX • RENT A COSTUME

BAKERIES • SPICE SHOPS

SOUP TO NUTS

Fodor's

CITYGUIDE
NEW YORK

FODOR'S TRAVEL PUBLICATIONS, INC.

NEW YORK • TORONTO • LONDON • SYDNEY • AUCKLAND

WWW.FODORS.COM/

FODOR'S CITYGUIDE NEW YORK

EDITOR
Christine Cipriani

EDITORIAL CONTRIBUTORS
Rebecca Knapp Adams, Hannah Borgeson, Mitchell Davis, Matthew DeBord, Moira
Hodgson, Amy McConnell, Stasha Mills, Margaret Mittelbach, Jennifer Paull, Tom
Steele, Rima Suqi

EDITORIAL PRODUCTION
Linda K. Schmidt

MAPS
David Lindroth Inc., *cartographer*; Bob Blake, *map editor*

DESIGN
Fabrizio La Rocca, *creative director*; Allison Saltzman, *text design*; Tigist Getachew,
cover design; Jolie Novak, *photo editor*

PRODUCTION/MANUFACTURING
Robert B. Shields

COVER PHOTOGRAPH
James Lemass

Series created by Marilyn Appleberg

COPYRIGHT

SPECIAL SALES

CONTENTS

METROPOLITAN LIFE

O n a bad day in a big city, the little things that go with living shoulder-to-shoulder with a few million people wear us all down. But the special pleasures of urban life have a way of keeping us out of the suburbs—and thankful, even, for every second of stress. The field of daffodils in the park on a fine spring day. The perfect little black dress that you find for half price. The markets—so fabulously well stocked that you can cook any recipe without resorting to mail-order catalogs. The way you can sometimes turn a corner and discover a whole new world, so foreign you can hardly believe you're less than a mile from home. The never-ending wealth of possibilities and opportunities.

If you know where to find it all, the city cannot defeat you. With knowledge comes power. That's why Fodor's has prepared this book. It will put phone numbers at your fingertips. It'll take you to new places and remind you of those you've forgotten. It's the ultimate urban companion—and, we hope, your **new best friend in the city.**

It's the **citywise shopaholic,** who always knows where to find something, no matter how obscure. We've made a concerted effort to bring hundreds of great shops to your attention, so that you'll never be at a loss, whether you need a special birthday present for a great friend or some obscure craft items to make Halloween costumes for your kids.

It's the **restaurant know-it-all,** who's full of ideas for every occasion—you know, the one who would never send you to Café de la Snub, because he knows it's always overbooked, the food is boring, and the staff is rude. We'll steer you around the corner, to a perfect little place with five tables, a fireplace, and a chef on her way up.

It's a **hip barfly buddy,** who can give you advice when you need a charming nook, not too noisy, to take a friend after work. Among the dozens of bars and nightspots in this book, you're bound to find something that fits your mood.

It's the **sagest arts maven you know,** the one who always has the scoop on what's on that's worthwhile on any given night. In these pages, you'll find dozens of concert venues and arts organizations.

It's also the **city whiz,** who knows how to get you where you're going, wherever you are.

It's the **best map guide** on the shelves, and it puts **all the city in your brief-case** or on your bookshelf.

Stick with us. We'll lay out all the options for your leisure time—and gently nudge you away from the duds—so that you can truly enjoy metropolitan living.

YOUR GUIDES

No one person can know it all. To help get you on track around the city, we've hand-picked a stellar group of local experts to share their wisdom.

Rebecca Knapp Adams, who reported on Basics, Help!, and annual events, lives in Park Slope, Brooklyn, with her husband, Chris, and their two cats. When she's not out gallivanting in the "other" four boroughs, she's happy to revisit favorite spots in "the best borough of all," Brooklyn.

Bicycle activist **Hannah Borgeson** did most of the research for Parks, Gardens, & Sports on two wheels. She does most of her riding in Manhattan, commuting to her job as an editor and leading rides in Central Park for the group Time's Up. She has also written and updated portions of the annual *Fodor's New York City*.

Editor **Christine Cipriani** was born to Bronx and Queens parents, grew up in upstate New York, lives in Brooklyn, and works in Manhattan. To alleviate this confusion about where in New York she really belongs, she travels farther afield whenever possible. Here at home, she spends her free time dashing from Lincoln Center to Carnegie Hall, soaking up her favorite aspect of New York: the music.

Sometime between rating restaurants across the country, writing cookbooks, running a mail-order gift business, and hobnobbing with chefs at the James Beard Foundation, **Mitchell Davis** and his colleague **Yvette Fromer** have acquainted themselves personally with most New York City restaurants worth knowing, in all five boroughs.

Matthew DeBord, who advised us on art galleries and men's clothing, has written for several New York City guidebooks and is a frequent contributor to *Artforum,* as well as the *Boston Phoenix* and the on-line magazine *FEED.* He lives in Manhattan with his dog, Cooper.

Moira Hodgson is the restaurant critic for the *New York Observer.* She writes frequently on food and the arts and is the author of several cookbooks.

Amy McConnell can often be found in New York City's world-class hotels, roaming the lobbies and testing the depth of bathtubs and the softness of mattresses. As Fodor's regular lodging reviewer, she's developed a passion for Frette linens and Gilchrist & Soames bath amenities. She refuses to divulge the name of her favorite hotel.

Anastasia Mills, who crossed many a velvet rope and raised many a glass in her research for our nightlife section, has been going out in Manhattan for upward of 16 years.

Since moving to New York more than a decade ago, **Margaret Mittelbach** has written about all aspects of the city: animal, vegetable, and mineral.

On any given day you might find her examining the Art Deco interiors of midtown skyscrapers, ogling great blue herons at the Jamaica Bay Wildlife Refuge, or raising the ghost of Boss Tweed at Brooklyn's Green-Wood Cemetery. She is coauthor of *Wild New York*, an acclaimed guide to the city's wildlife, wild places, and natural history.

Shopping fanatic **Jennifer Paull**, our women's-clothing scout, has braved unkind dressing-room mirrors and slithered into embroidered silk, grubby denim, and talcum-dusted rubber in more stores than she cares to remember.

Arts writer **Tom Steele** was the founding editor of *TheaterWeek*, *Opera Monthly*, *Night and Day*, and *New York Native*, among other publications. He is currently the food editor of *Manhattan Spirit* and *Our Town* and is writing a cookbook intended to enrage the food police.

Shopping dynamos **Rima Suqi** and **Julie Fowler** specialize in home furnishings and style. Suqi, a former associate editor at *Metropolitan Home* and contributing editor for *Home*, produces style stories for the *New York Times*, *Marie-Claire*, and *House & Home* and is the author of *For Your Home: Kitchens*. Fowler, formerly an assistant decorating editor at *House Beautiful* and market editor for *American HomeStyle & Gardening*, is author of *British Country Style* and a contributing editor at *Redbook*.

Marilyn Appleberg, who conceived this series, is a city-lover through and through. She plots her urban forays from an archetypal Greenwich Village brownstone with two fireplaces.

It goes without saying that our contributors have chosen all establishments strictly on their own merits—no establishment has paid to be included in this book.

HOW TO USE THIS BOOK

The first thing you need to know is that everything in this book is **arranged by category and in alphabetical order within category.**

Now, before you go any farther, check out the **city maps** at the front of the book. Each map has a number, in a black box at the top of the page, and grid coordinates along the top and side margins. On the text pages, every listing in the book is keyed to one of these maps. Look for the map number in a small black box preceding each establishment name. The grid code follows in italics. For establishments with more than one location, additional map numbers and grid codes appear at the end of the listing. To locate a museum that's identified in the text as **7** *e-6*, turn to Map 7 and locate the address within the e-6 grid square. To locate restaurants nearby, simply skim the text in the restaurant chapter for listings identified as being on Map 7.

Where appropriate throughout the guide, we name the neighborhood in which each sight, restaurant, shop, or other destination is located. We also give you the nearest subway stop, plus complete opening hours and admission fees for sights; closing information for shops; credit-card, price, reservations, and closing information for restaurants; and credit-card information for nightspots.

At the end of the book, in addition to an **alphabetical index,** you'll find **directories of shops and restaurants by neighborhood.**

Chapter 1, Basics, lists essential information, such as entertainment hot lines (for those times you can't lay your hands on a newspaper). **Chapter 8, Help!,** covers resources for residents—everything from vet and lawyer-referral services to caterers worth calling.

We've worked hard to make sure that all of the information we give you is accurate at press time. Still, time brings changes, so always confirm information when it matters—especially if you're making a detour.

Feel free to drop us a line. Were the restaurants we recommended as described? Did you find a wonderful shop you'd like to share? If you have complaints, we'll look into them and revise our entries in the next edition when the facts warrant. So send us your feedback. Either e-mail us at editors@fodors.com (specifying *Fodor's CITYGUIDE New York* on the subject line), or write to the *Fodor's CITYGUIDE New York* editor at 201 East 50th Street, New York, New York 10022. We look forward to hearing from you.

Karen Cure
Editorial Director

chapter 1

BASICS
essential information

BANKS

Commercial banks are generally open weekdays from 9 AM to 3 PM and closed weekends and holidays. A few savings institutions are also open Friday evening and Saturday morning.

CURRENCY EXCHANGE

If you're going abroad, you may want to buy some foreign currency here at home before you leave, just in case there's a long line (or worse) in the airport you enter. You can buy and sell currency at the Manhattan branches of several national banks, or at old standby Thomas Cook. Chase sells foreign currency at most of its Manhattan branches, and buys currency at all branches if the buyer has 2 forms of I.D. (800/287–4054). You can pay for foreign currency in cash, debit your Chase account, or flash a Visa or MasterCard; if you charge it, the amount will be treated as a cash advance. Most exchanges are handled on the spot, but you may have to come back the next day for exotic currencies or very large amounts.

Most banks sell traveler's checks, which you can buy in U.S. dollars or in any of several foreign currencies. Traveler's checks are issued by American Express, MasterCard, or Visa and are accepted worldwide. Banks and nearly all stores in New York accept traveler's checks, though they may want to see a photo I.D. first.

american express travel services

American Express Travel Service Offices buy and sell foreign currency, buy and sell American Express traveler's checks (and buy other brands for a higher fee), issue refunds for lost checks, and provide all standard cardmember services. You can buy foreign currency with cash or, if you're a cardmember, with a personal check—just bring your AmEx card. If you *lose* your AmEx traveler's checks, call 800/221–7282.

65 Broadway (between Rector and Wall Sts.), 212/493–6500.

American Express Tower (200 Vesey St., World Financial Center), 212/640–5130.

Macy's (Broadway and 34th St., balcony level), 212/695–8075.

150 E. 42nd St., 212/687–3700.

New York Hilton and Towers (1335 6th Ave., at 53rd St.), 212/664–7798.

374 Park Avenue (at 53rd St.), 212/421–8240.

822 Lexington Avenue (at 63rd St.), 212/758–6510.

bank leumi

Bank Leumi has branches throughout the city, all with foreign-exchange departments and none with commissions or fees. The friendly staff is happy to quote exchange rates over the phone, and will even estimate the amount of currency you'll end up with. They'll then direct you to the branch nearest you. *212/343–5343.*

thomas cook currency services

Busy with other preparations? Thomas Cook can FedEx your foreign currency, traveler's checks, or foreign drafts right to your home. For general information and branch hours, call 800/287–7362 weekdays 8:30 AM–9 PM. The JFK office is open 7 days a week. If you *lose* your Thomas Cook traveler's checks, call 800/223–7373. *317 Madison Ave. (at 42nd St.); 511 Madison Ave. (at 53rd St.); 29 Broadway (at Morris St.); 1271 Broadway (at 32nd St.); 1590 Broadway (at 48th St.); JFK International Airport, International Arrivals building, terminals 4E and 4W.*

ENTERTAINMENT INFORMATION

Once you've decided what to do, give one of New York's entertainment hot lines a call for comprehensive listings and schedules.

Art (212/777–ARTS).

Film (212/777–FILM).

Jazz (212/866–3616).

Theater (212/768–1818). For details on this hot line—New York City Onstage—*see* Tickets *in* Chapter 5.

GAS STATIONS

In Manhattan, gas stations are most plentiful in SoHo and toward the island's outer rims, particularly in Hell's Kitchen and at various points on the West Side Highway. They're easy to stumble upon in the other four boroughs.

downtown

Amoco (Broadway at Houston St., 212/473–5924).

Gulf (FDR Dr. at 23rd St., 212/686–4546).

Mobil (E. Broadway at Pike St., 212/966–0571; 6th Avenue at Spring St., 212/925–6126).

uptown

Merit (7th Ave. at 145th St., 212/283–9354).

Mobil (11th Ave. at 51st St., 212/582–9269).

Shell (Amsterdam Ave at 181st St., 212/928–3100).

GEOGRAPHY

New York City's five boroughs—the Bronx, Brooklyn, Manhattan, Queens, and Staten Island—are linked by a series of bridges, tunnels, and ferries. Sightseers will most likely spend the bulk of their time in Manhattan, an island only 13.4 miles long and 2.3 miles wide (at its widest). The island's grid layout makes getting around easy. Avenues run north and south, with 5th Avenue dividing the east and west sides—the lower the house address on a street, whether it's east or west, the closer it is to 5th Avenue. Broadway, a former wagon trail, is the grand exception to the rule—it cuts diagonally through Manhattan from the Upper West Side to Lower Manhattan and the financial district. As it intersects other avenues on its way, Broadway creates Columbus Circle (at 59th St.), Times Square (at 42nd St.), Herald Square (at 34th St.), Madison Square (at 23rd St.), and Union Square (at 14th St.). Streets in Manhattan run east and west and ascend in numerical order going north. As a general rule, traffic is one-way going east on even-numbered streets, one-way going west on odd-numbered streets.

Most of Manhattan's downtown areas—those below 14th Street on the west and 1st Street on the east—were settled before the grid system and follow no particular pattern. These are among the city's oldest districts and

include Greenwich Village, SoHo, Tribeca, Chinatown, and the financial district. New Yorkers and visitors alike should remember that asking directions in an unfamiliar part of town will not get them killed; most New Yorkers are happy to give directions, and will then go quickly on their way. Try it.

HOLIDAYS

New York's banks, post offices, schools, offices, and most businesses close on these days. (*See* Events *in* Chapter 2 for holiday festivities.)

New Year's Day (January 1)

Martin Luther King Day (3rd Monday in January)

Presidents' Day (3rd Monday in Febuary)

Memorial Day (last Monday in May)

Independence Day (July 4th)

Labor Day (1st Monday in September)

Columbus Day (2nd Monday in October)

Election Day (1st Tuesday in November)

Veterans' Day (November 11th)

Thanksgiving (4th Thursday in November)

Christmas (December 25th)

LIQUOR LAWS

You must be 21 years old to purchase alcohol in New York State. Your proof of age is a government-issued photo ID, such as a driver's license or a passport. Most restaurants have a liquor license, but smaller places—many of the Indian restaurants in the East Village, for example—allow diners to bring their own beer. Some BYOB restaurants charge a corking fee when diners bring their own wine.

NO SMOKING

In 1988, New York City passed one of the toughest antismoking laws in the country: It is illegal to puff in hotel lobbies, banks, public rest rooms, and taxis and at playgrounds, sports stadiums, and race tracks. Smoking has also been restricted in restaurants seating more

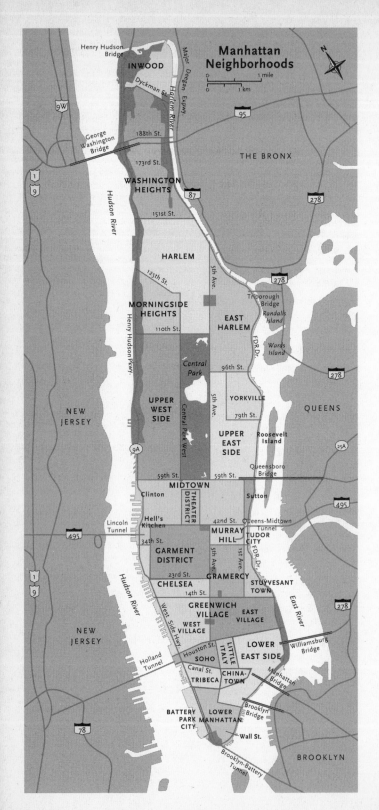

Manhattan Neighborhoods

1 mile

1 km

Henry Hudson Bridge

INWOOD

Dyckman St.

Harlem River

Major Deegan Expwy.

9W

George Washington Bridge

188th St.

THE BRONX

95

1 9

173rd St.

WASHINGTON HEIGHTS

87

Hudson River

151st St.

HARLEM

125th St.

5th Ave.

278

MORNINGSIDE HEIGHTS

110th St.

Triborough Bridge

Randalls Island

EAST HARLEM

FDR Dr.

Wards Island

Central Park

96th St.

278

Henry Hudson Pkwy.

NEW JERSEY

UPPER WEST SIDE

Central Park West

5th Ave.

YORKVILLE

79th St.

QUEENS

UPPER EAST SIDE

Roosevelt Island

25A

9A

59th St.

59th St.

Queensboro Bridge

MIDTOWN

Clinton

THEATER DISTRICT

Sutton

495

Hell's Kitchen

42nd St.

Queens-Midtown Tunnel

Lincoln Tunnel

495

34th St.

MURRAY HILL

TUDOR CITY

1 9

GARMENT DISTRICT

5th Ave.

1st Ave.

FDR Dr.

23rd St.

GRAMERCY

CHELSEA

STUYVESANT TOWN

Hudson River

14th St.

GREENWICH VILLAGE

EAST VILLAGE

East River

278

NEW JERSEY

West Side Hwy.

WEST VILLAGE

Holland Tunnel

Houston St.

LOWER EAST SIDE

Williamsburg Bridge

SOHO

LITTLE ITALY

Canal St.

CHINA-TOWN

Manhattan Bridge

78

TRIBECA

BATTERY PARK CITY

Brooklyn Bridge

LOWER MANHATTAN

Wall St.

Brooklyn-Battery Tunnel

BROOKLYN

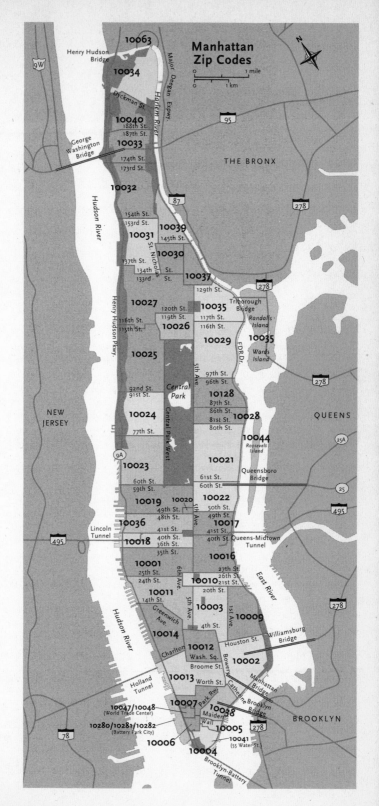

Manhattan Zip Codes

10063
Henry Hudson Bridge
10034
Dyckman St.
10040
188th St.
187th St.
George Washington Bridge
10033
174th St.
173rd St.
10032
154th St.
153rd St.
10031
145th St.
10039
10030
137th St.
134th St.
133rd St.
10037
129th St.
10027
120th St.
119th St.
10035
117th St.
116th St.
Triborough Bridge
Randalls Island
115th St.
10026
10029
10035
Wards Island
10025
97th St.
96th St.
Central Park
92nd St.
91st St.
10128
87th St.
86th St.
81st St.
10028
10024
80th St.
77th St.
10044
Roosevelt Island
10023
10021
Queensboro Bridge
60th St.
59th St.
10019
10020
61st St.
60th St.
10036
49th St.
48th St.
10022
50th St.
49th St.
10018
41st St.
40th St.
36th St.
35th St.
10017
41st St.
40th St.
Queens-Midtown Tunnel
Lincoln Tunnel
10001
25th St.
24th St.
10016
10011
14th St.
10010
27th St.
26th St.
21st St.
20th St.
10014
10003
4th St.
10009
10012
Wash. Sq.
Broome St.
Houston St.
10002
Williamsburg Bridge
Holland Tunnel
10013
Worth St.
Manhattan Bridge
10047/10048
(World Trade Center)
10007
10038
Maiden
Wall
Brooklyn Bridge
10280/10281/10282
(Battery Park City)
10005
10006
10041
(55 Water St.)
10004
Brooklyn-Battery Tunnel

THE BRONX
QUEENS
NEW JERSEY
BROOKLYN
Hudson River
Harlem River
East River
Henry Hudson Pkwy.
Major Deegan Expwy.
St. Nicholas St.
5th Ave.
Central Park West
6th Ave.
5th Ave.
1st Ave.
Greenwich Ave.
Charlton
Bowery
Catherine
Park Row
FDR Dr.

0   1 mile
0   1 km

9W
9
95
87
278
278
278
25A
25
495
495
78
278
9A

Avenue Address Finder

Streets	West End Ave.	Broadway	Amsterdam Ave.	Columbus Ave.	Central Park West
94–96	700–737	2520–2554	702–733	701–740	350–360
92–94	660–699	2476–2519	656–701	661–700	322–336
90–92	620–659	2440–2475	620–655	621–660	300–320
88–90	578–619	2401–2439	580–619	581–620	279–295
86–88	540–577	2361–2400	540–579	541–580	262–275
84–86	500–539	2321–2360	500–539	501–540	241–257
82–84	460–499	2281–2320	460–499	461–500	212–239
80–82	420–459	2241–2280	420–459	421–460	211
78–80	380–419	2201–2240	380–419	381–420	American Museum of Natural History
76–78	340–379	2161–2200	340–379	341–380	
74–76	300–339	2121–2160	300–339	301–340	145–160
72–74	262–299	2081–2114	261–299	261–300	121–135
70–72	221–261	2040–2079	221–260	221–260	101–115
68–70	176–220	1999–2030	181–220	181–220	80–99
66–68	122–175	1961–1998	140–180	141–180	65–79
64–66	74–121	1920–1960	100–139	101–140	50–55
62–64	44–73	Lincoln Center	60–99	61–100	25–33
60–62	20–43	1841–1880	20–59	21–60	15
58–60	2–19	Columbus Circle	1–19	2–20	Columbus Circle

	11th Ave.	Broadway	10th Ave.	9th Ave.	8th Ave.	7th Ave.	6th Ave.
56–58	823–854	1752–1791	852–889	864–907	946–992	888–921	1381–1419
54–56	775–822	1710–1751	812–851	824–863	908–945	842–887	1341–1377
52–54	741–774	1674–1709	772–811	782–823	870–907	798–841	1301–1330
50–52	701–740	1634–1673	737–770	742–781	830–869	761–797	1261–1297
48–50	665–700	1596–1633	686–735	702–741	791–829	720–760	1221–1260
46–48	625–664	1551–1595	654–685	662–701	735–790	701–719	1180–1217
44–46	589–624	1514–1550	614–653	622–661	701–734	Times Square	1141–1178
42–44	553–588	1472–1513	576–613	582–621	661–700		1100–1140
40–42	503–552	1440–1471	538–575	Port Authority	620–660	560–598	1061–1097
38–40	480–502	1400–1439	502–537		570–619	522–559	1020–1060
36–38	431–471	1352–1399	466–501	468–501	520–569	482–521	981–1019
34–36	405–430	Macy's	430–465	432–467	480–519	442–481	Herald Square
32–34	360–404	1260–1282	380–429	412–431	442–479	Penn Station	
30–32	319–359	1220–1279	341–379	Post Office	403–441	362–399	855–892
28–30	282–318	1178–1219	314–340	314–351	362–402	322–361	815–844
26–28	242–281	1135–1177	288–313	262–313	321–361	282–321	775–814
24–26	202–241	1100–1134	239–287	230–261	281–320	244–281	733–774
22–24	162–201	940–1099	210–238	198–229	236–280	210–243	696–732
20–22	120–161	902–939	162–209	167–197	198–235	170–209	656–695
18–20	82–119	873–901	130–161	128–166	162–197	134–169	613–655
16–18	54–81	860–872	92–129	92–127	126–161	100–133	574–612
14–16	26–53	Union Square	58–91	91–44	80–125	64–99	573–530

Crosstown Street Address Finder

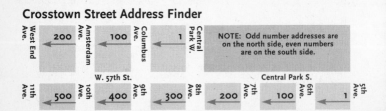

NOTE: Odd number addresses are on the north side, even numbers are on the south side.

5th Ave.	Madison Ave.	Park Ave.	Lexington Ave.	3rd Ave.	2nd Ave.	1st Ave.	Streets
1130–1148	1340–1379	1199–1236	1449–1486	1678–1709	1817–1868	1817–1855	94–96
1109–1125	1295–1335	1160–1192	1400–1444	1644–1677	1766–1808	1780–1811	92–94
1090–1107	1254–1294	1120–1155	1361–1396	1601–1643	1736–1763	1740–1779	90–92
1070–1089	1220–1250	1080–1114	1311–1355	1568–1602	1700–1739	1701–1735	88–90
1050–1069	1178–1221	1044–1076	1280–1301	1530–1566	1660–1698	1652–1689	86–88
1030–1048	1130–1171	1000–1035	1248–1278	1490–1529	1624–1659	1618–1651	84–86
1010–1028	1090–1128	960–993	1210–1248	1450–1489	1584–1623	1578–1617	82–84
990–1009	1058–1088	916–959	1164–1209	1410–1449	1538–1583	1540–1577	80–82
970–989	1012–1046	878–911	1120–1161	1374–1409	1498–1537	1495–1539	78–80
950–969	974–1006	840–877	1080–1116	1330–1373	1456–1497	1462–1494	76–78
930–947	940–970	799–830	1036–1071	1290–1329	1420–1454	1429–1460	74–76
910–929	896–939	760–791	1004–1032	1250–1289	1389–1417	1344–1384	72–74
895–907	856–872	720–755	962–993	1210–1249	1328–1363	1306–1343	70–72
870–885	813–850	680–715	926–961	1166–1208	1296–1327	1266–1300	68–70
850–860	772–811	640–679	900–922	1130–1165	1260–1295	1222–1260	66–68
830–849	733–771	600–639	841–886	1084–1129	1222–1259	1168–1221	64–66
810–828	690–727	560–599	803–842	1050–1083	1180–1221	1130–1167	62–64
790–807	654–680	520–559	770–802	1010–1049	1140–1197	1102–1129	60–62
755–789	621–649	476–519	722–759	972–1009	Queensborough Bridge		58–60
720–754	572–611	434–475	677–721	942–968	1066–1101	1026–1063	56–58
680–719	532–568	408–430	636–665	894–933	1028–1062	985–1021	54–56
656–679	500–531	360–399	596–629	856–893	984–1027	945–984	52–54
626–655	452–488	320–350	556–593	818–855	944–983	889–944	50–52
600–625	412–444	280–300	518–555	776–817	902–943	860–888	48–50
562–599	377–400	240–277	476–515	741–775	862–891	827	46–48
530–561	346–375	Met Life (200)	441–475	702–735	824–860	785	United Nations	44–46
500–529	316–345	Grand	395–435	660–701	793–823		42–44
460–499	284–315	Central	354–394	622–659	746–773	Tudor City	40–42
424–459	250–283	68–99	314–353	578–621	707–747	666–701	38–40
392–423	218–249	40–67	284–311	542–577	666–700	Midtown Tunnel	36–38
352–391	188–217	5–35	240–283	508–541	622–659	599–626	34–36
320–351	152–184	1–4	196–239	470–507	585–621	556–598	32–34
284–319	118–150	444–470	160–195	432–469	543–581	Kips Bay	30–32
250–283	79–117	404–431	120–159	394–431	500–541	NYU Hosp.	28–30
213–249	50–78	364–403	81–119	358–393	462–499	446–478	26–28
201–212	11–37	323–361	40–77	321–355	422–461	411–445	24–26
172–200	1–7	286–322	9–39	282–318	382–421	390–410	22–24
154–170		251–285	1–8	244–281	344–381	315–389	20–22
109–153		221–250	70–78	206–243	310–343	310–314	18–20
85–127		184–220	40–69	166–205	301–309	280–309	16–18
69–108		Union Square	2–30	126–165	230–240	240–279	14–16

(Park Ave. → Park Ave. S. → Lexington Ave. → Irving Pl. labels appear vertically between the Park Ave. and Lexington Ave. columns.)

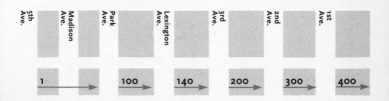

5th Ave. | Madison Ave. | Park Ave. | Lexington Ave. | 3rd Ave. | 2nd Ave. | 1st Ave.

1 →   100 →   140 →   200 →   300 →   400 →

than 36 people, in retail stores, and in schools.

PARKING

Street parking in Manhattan, if you can find it, is subject to a variety of restrictions. Metered street parking lasts from 20 minutes to an hour. Be sure to read the signs carefully, since understanding New York's parking rules requires a degree in quantum physics plus a few years' experience as a brain surgeon—and once you figure them out, you'll have to move your car periodically to allow for street-sweeping. To find out whether alternate-side-of-the-street rules are in effect on a given day, call 212/442–7080 or listen to a news-inclined radio station in the morning (*see* Radio Stations, *below*). Your car may be ticketed or towed away if illegally parked; both can be expensive and the latter a great hassle.

There are hundreds of private parking facilities in Manhattan, with costs varying by location, day, and time. Be sure to check the closing time, or you might lose your car for the night. Read the fine print on the price list, too; taxes and "special" conditions can make parking even more expensive than you expect. These short-term parking facilities have long hours and reasonable prices.

downtown
756 Parking Corp. (756 Washington St., near 12th St.).

midtown
Edison Park Fast (1120 Ave. of the Americas; entrances on 43rd and 44th Sts.).

Rapid 63 Street Corp. (411 W. 55th St.).

Real Pro Parking Corp. (330 E. 39th St.).

River Edge Sutton Garden Garage (425 E. 54th St.)

upper east side
Waterview (10 East End Ave., at 80th St.).

200 East 61st Street Garage Corp. (200 E. 61st St.).

upper west side
Hudson West Garage (101 W. 90th St.).

Edison Park Fast (214 W. 80th St.).

PARKS INFORMATION

For details on specific parks and for Parks Department headquarters in individual boroughs, *see* Parks *in* Chapter 6.

Department of Parks and Recreation (800/201–PARK). A staffed hot line for information and emergencies.

Citywide Special Events (212/360–3456; recorded). Listings of upcoming events on city properties.

Central Park Information (212/360–3444; recorded).

PERSONAL SECURITY

Common sense must dictate where you go and when you go there—anywhere in the world. New York has enjoyed a reduction in violent crime of late, but of course it's always better to travel with a companion late at night, and to know where you are and where you're going. It may be even more important to *look* like you know where you are and where you're going. Secure your wallet or purse—wallets are better off in a front pocket than a back pocket. Don't flaunt cash or jewelry. On a crowded subway or bus, keep your bag zipped or otherwise tightly shut.

PUBLICATIONS

New York is the publishing capital of the world, and its residents have a lot of commuting time to kill. Put the two together and you have an enormous reading public. All of these newspapers and magazines list goings-on, but each has a different angle. Pick them up at any newsstand and choose a favorite.

daily news
Subtitled "New York's Hometown Newspaper," the *Daily News* has a broader editorial range, with hearty metro and entertainment coverage, than its tabloid sibling, the *Post*—once you turn the grisly front page. Gossip columnists Rush & Molloy have a faithful following.

new york magazine
New York made its name being ultra-cool—is it now pursuing the main-

stream? Cover stories range from fashion to politics to food to social trends. Arts reviews are hefty. Weekly (Mon.).

new york observer

Easily spotted for its salmon-color paper, the *Observer* is New York's college newspaper for grown-ups. Gleefully trumpeting industry gossip on politics, publishing, and entertainment, it has many a closet addict. The focus shifts to the Hamptons in summer. Weekly (Wed.).

new york post

Owned by journalistic heavy hand Rupert Murdoch, the *Post* screams right-angle dish every day of the week, particularly on business and celebrity figures.

new york press

This downtown, Gen-X rag has aggressively targeted the *Village Voice*'s readership, but it's (even) more irreverent and gets some scary letters to the editor. Event listings are solid. Weekly (Tues.).

new york times

The *Times* still leads the national pack, though recent innovations aimed at widening its audience have stirred predictable debate. The Friday edition is the city's best source for that weekend's highbrow arts events. Daily; expanded edition Sunday.

new yorker

New York's most literate and literary source is for culture vultures. Longtime readers love to grouse that it's gone downhill in recent years, but they still can't live without it. The famous fact-checking department means that event listings are thorough and reliable, covering everything from classical recitals to nightly gigs at CBGB's. Weekly (Mon.).

timeout new york

Modeled on its London predecessor, this magazine calls itself "The Obsessive Guide to Impulsive Entertainment" and lives up to the claim. The tone is young and cheeky, but fans of all ages appreciate the virtually exhaustive event listings. Weekly (Wed.).

village voice

Culturally and politically lefty, the Voice is a great source for nightlife and music news and the last word on apartment listings. Pick it up Tuesday night in Manhattan if you're searching for digs. Weekly (Wed.).

RADIO STATIONS

fm stations

WALK 97.5 Adult contemporary

WAXQ 104.3 Rock

WBAB 102.3 Rock

WBAI 99.5 Varied

WBAU 90.3 Adelphi University

WBAZ 101.7 Light contemporary

WBGO 88.3 Jazz

WBLI 106.1 Adult contemporary

WBLS 107.5 Urban contemporary

WCBS 101.1 Oldies

WCWP 88.1 C. W. Post University

WDHA 105.5 Rock

WDRE 92.7 Progressive rock

WEBE 107.9 Adult contemporary

WEZN 99.9 Easy listening

WFAS 103.9 Adult contemporary

WFDU 89.1 Music/city-owned

WFMU 91.1 Varied

WFUV 90.7 Fordham University

WHCR 90.3 C.C.N.Y.

WHFM 95.3 Adult contemporary

WHPC 90.3 Nassau Community College

WHTZ 100.3 Top 40

WHUD 100.7 Light contemporary

WKCR 89.9 Columbia University

WKHL 96.7 Oldies

WKJY 98.3 Adult contemporary

WKTU 103.5 Dance/freestyle

WLNG 92.1 Oldies/adult contemporary

WLTW 106.7 Light contemporary

WMJC 94.3 Light contemporary

WMXV 105.1 Adult contemporary

WNEW 102.7 Rock

WNWK 105.9 Multi-ethnic

WNYC 93.9 Classical/NPR

WNYE 91.5 Community services

WPAT 93.1 Easy listening

WPLJ 95.5 Top 40

WPLR 99.1 Comedy/rock

WPSC 88.7 Top 40

WQCD 101.9 Contemporary jazz

WQHT 97.1 Top 40/urban

WQXR 96.3 Classical

WRCN 103.9 Rock

WRHU 88.7 Hofstra University

WRKS 98.7 Urban contemporary

WRTN 93.5 Big band/standards

WSOU 89.5 Seton Hall University

WUSB 90.1 SUNY/Stony Brook

WWHB 107.1 Adult contemporary

WXPS 107.1 Rock

WXRK 92.3 Alternative/progresive rock

am stations

WABC 77 Talk/news

WADO 128 Spanish

WALK 137 Adult contemporary

WBBR 113 News

WCBS 88 News

WEVD 105 News/sports/talk

WFAN 66 Sports

WFAS 123 Westchester news

WGBB 124 News/talk

WGSM 74 News/talk/nostalgia

WHLI 110 Oldies

WICC 60 Adult contemporary

WINS 101 News

WKDM 138 Spanish

WLIB 119 Talk/Caribbean/black

WLIM 158 Big band/talk

WMCA 57 Religion

WMTR 125 Pop standards

WNJR 143 Rhythm and blues

WNYC 82 News/talk

WNYG 144 Music

WOR 71 Talk/news

WPAT 93 Adult contemporary

WQEW 156 Pop standards

WRHD 157 Nostalgia

WVOX 146 Talk/nostalgia

WWDJ 97 Christian music

WWRL 160 Gospel/talk

WWRV 133 Ethnic

WZRC 148 Korean

SIGHTSEEING INFORMATION

new york convention & visitors bureau

The bureau's helpful, multilingual staff answers questions and provides printed guides and maps in six languages; tickets to TV shows; discount coupons for theater tickets; and a list of the city's current hotel rates, weekend packages, major attractions, and seasonal events. A new and larger facility is scheduled to open in spring 1998. *Embassy Theatre, 1564 Broadway (at 47th St.), Theater District, 212/484–1222 for general inquiries, 800/692/8474 for brochures. Subway: 49th St.; 42nd St./Times Sq.*

new york state department of economic development/ division of tourism

There is no office in New York City, but the state office has information on city tour packages and on vacations and recreation statewide. These folks are the geniuses behind the "I Love New York" campaign. *800/225–5697.*

tourist information carts

In late 1997, the Grand Central Partnership (a sort of civic Good Samaritans' group) installed a prototype of an unstaffed information kiosk near Grand Central Terminal and loaded it up with maps and helpful brochures on attractions throughout the city. Seasonal outdoor carts are now sprinkled throughout the area (near Vanderbilt Ave. and 42nd St.), staffed by friendly, knowledgeable, multilingual New Yorkers. A kiosk will return to the terminal's Main Concourse when renovations are complete, in 1998. The 34th Street Partnership runs a kiosk on the concourse level at Penn Station (33rd St. and 7th Ave.), and seasonal carts troll the streets surrounding the station. There's even a cart at the Empire State Building (5th Ave. at 34th St.).

SPORTS HOT LINES

Sportsphone, for scores and statistics (212/976–1313 or 212/976–2525; charge applies).

Ticketron, for schedules and ticket information (212/307–7171).

TAXES AND GRATUITIES

Expect a lot from New York—the city expects a lot from you in the form of sales tax and endless gratuities. Sales tax in the city is 8¼% and applies to all purchases not considered necessities. Guess what? That covers most store purchases and all restaurant meals. Gratuities are easy to figure, especially at restaurants: double the tax and round up a bit to bring the waiter's tip close to 20%. In elegant venues, give 5% to the captain and remember to give wine stewards about $5 per bottle of wine ordered. The coat-check clerk should receive $1 per coat. Cab drivers, hair stylists, your masseuse, and the like should be tipped at least 15%.

The total room tax at hotels is a hefty 13¼%, plus an occupancy charge of $2 per room, per night. Leave the hotel maid about $1 for each night of your stay; the bellhop should get about $2.

TELEVISION

major broadcasters

Channel 2—WCBS

Channel 4—WNBC

Channel 5—WNYW

Channel 7—WABC

Channel 8—ESPN

Channel 10—CNN

Channel 11—WPIX

Channel 13—WNET (PBS)

Channel 14—A&E

Channel 19—VH1

Channel 20—MTV

TRANSPORTATION

New York's mass-transit system is extensive and efficient. Subways offer speed and economy but minimal comfort and capricious schedules. Buses offer a view in exchange for a slower pace. Taxis can be expensive in rush-hour traffic jams and elusive during rainstorms, but a blessing when your feet hurt, or when you've simply had a long day. Many cabs are air-conditioned; you can bet that a cab with its windows rolled up in summer is cool. Flag one of these down—no sweat.

Information and directions to any destination by subway or bus are available daily between 6 AM and 9 PM from the Travel Information Bureau (718/330–1234), a courteous, knowledgeable bunch. The bureau staffs satellite booths at Penn Station, Grand Central Terminal, Port Authority Bus Terminal, and 370 Jay St. (lobby), Brooklyn Heights.

metrocard gold

With an eye toward dragging New York's subways and buses into the modern age, the Metropolitan Transit Authority (MTA) introduced the MetroCard in 1997, to quiet applause. The card was to supplement, or possibly supplant, the beloved token. To make the card more alluring, the MTA announced a long-awaited deal: use the MetroCard on the bus and your transfer to the subway (to complete your trip) is free. The same goes for subway-to-bus or bus-to-bus transfers, as long as riders don't try to use the transfer for the return fare of the same trip. The free transfers are good for two hours. The card is available at token booths in subway stations and at some convenience stores. Even those who don't need to transfer can make use of the card's portability: you can put as much as $80 on the card and stick it right into your wallet. Carting around the same value in tokens would make a silly picture.

At the dawn of 1998, the MTA announced the answer to New Yorkers' other transit prayer: a discount for frequent riders. You now get 11 rides for the price of 10 if you put $15 on your Metro-Card. Invest $30, and you'll get two free rides, and so on; the system will even prorate cents toward your next free ride if you put an odd amount on your card—as long as the amount is over $15.

bus

Bus fare is $1.50. Reduced fare for senior citizens and travelers with disabilities is 75¢, except during rush hour, when the full fare applies. You need exact change, a subway token, or a MetroCard to ride the bus—no bills, pennies, 50¢ pieces, or Susan B. Anthony dollars. Bus stops are marked with signs showing the numbers of the buses that stop there, approximate schedules, and route maps. North-south (uptown-downtown) buses usually stop every two to three blocks; east-west (crosstown) buses usually stop on every block. Many bus stops have glass-enclosed shelters. Route maps for the bus system are available at most subway stations.

Board and deposit your fare (or insert your card) in the machine at the front of the bus; exit in the rear. Smoking is not allowed, nor are animals, with the exceptions of pets in carrying cases and seeing-eye dogs. Most buses run 24 hours daily, though schedules are reduced during off-peak hours and days.

If you don't have a MetroCard (see above) but want to transfer from an uptown or downtown bus to a crosstown bus, or vice versa, ask the driver for a transfer slip upon boarding; they're still free.

COMMUTER & LONG-DISTANCE

George Washington Bridge Bus Terminal (Broadway at 178th St., 212/564–1114).

Port Authority Bus Terminal (42nd St. and 8th Ave., 212/564–8484).

ferry

There is, in fact, such a thing as a free ride. The Staten Island Ferry's 50¢ fare was abolished in July 1997. The ride from South Street Seaport to Staten Island has wonderful views of the Statue of Liberty and Ellis Island, not to mention the Manhattan skyline. Did we mention that it's free? Call 718/815–2628 for schedules.

subway

Subway fare is $1.50. Reduced fare for senior citizens and travelers with disabilities is 75¢, except during rush hour, when the full fare applies. You need a token or a MetroCard to access the subway platform. If you'll be riding the subway often, buy a supply of tokens or a MetroCard to save time. Free subway maps and information are available at every token booth. Break that $50 bill before your trip; subway staff can't change anything larger than a twenty.

Smoking is not allowed in either stations or trains; stubborn smokers will most likely be fined by the transit police. Animals are not allowed on trains, with the exceptions of pets in carrying cases or seeing-eye dogs.

The subways run 24 hours daily, though schedules are reduced during off-peak hours and days.

taxi

Taxicabs are readily available in New York City, except during peak rush hours and rain. Simply walk to the curb (ideally at a street corner) and extend your arm. Licensed taxis are always yellow (avoid gypsy cabs, which are not); when the rooftop cab number is lit, the cab is available; if it's not lit, the cab is occupied. If the cab is off duty, the rooftop banner is lit at both ends, reading "Off Duty"; these taxis will not stop. It takes a trained eye to spot an available cab from a distance.

Base fare for a cab ride is $2, then 30¢ for each additional ⅕ of a mile and 20¢

for each minute in stopped traffic. Pay only what's on the meter (there is a 50¢ surcharge from 8 PM to 6 AM) plus a 15%–20% gratuity. Make sure the driver remembers to start the meter. According to the rules, drivers must take you anywhere you want to go within the five boroughs, Nassau or Westchester counties, or Newark International Airport, though in practice you may find drivers who aren't interested in leaving Manhattan (or who need directions when doing so). For more information or to report a problem, call the New York City Taxi and Limousine Commission (212/221–8294).

rail

Trains leave the city from **Grand Central Station** (Lexington Ave. at 42nd St.) and **Pennsylvania (Penn) Station** (33rd St. and 7th Ave.).

COMMUTER

Metro-North, Grand Central Station, serves lower New York State and Connecticut (212/532–4900; outside New York City 800/638–7646).

Long Island Rail Road (LIRR), Penn Station (718/217–5477).

New Jersey Transit (NJTransit), Penn Station (973/762–5100).

PATH serves New Jersey from various points in the city (800/234–7284).

SEPTA picks up where NJTransit leaves off, in Trenton, to form the New Yorker's cheapest ride to Philadelphia (215/580–7800).

LONG-DISTANCE

All long-distance rail service leaves from Penn Station (33rd St. and 7th Ave.).

Amtrak (800/872–7245).

getting to the airport

For general information on transportation to New York's three major airports—John F. Kennedy (JFK), La Guardia, and Newark—call the Port Authority of New York and New Jersey (800/247–7433).

BY SUBWAY & BUS

The subway is the most economical way to reach the airports, but it's bound to be slow given the length of the journey. That said, during rush hour the subway can beat cabs and car services by passing traffic altogether, particularly to JFK and La Guardia. For all subway and bus schedules, call 718/330–1234.

To reach JFK from Midtown and Queens, take the E or F train to Kew Gardens/Union Turnpike, then the Green Lines Q10 bus to the airport. From the West Side, Lower Manhattan, and Brooklyn, take the A train to the Howard Beach–JFK Airport station, then the free, 24-hour airport shuttle bus (every 10 mins 5 AM–midnight, every 30 mins all other times).

To return from JFK, reverse the above directions or take the Q3 bus from JFK's Main Terminal to the 179th Street subway station, where you can pick up the F or R train to Manhattan and Brooklyn. Buses run every 15 minutes until midnight, then every 30 minutes until 1:30 AM.

To reach La Guardia from Manhattan or Brooklyn, take the E, F, G, R, or 7 train to the 74th Street/Roosevelt Avenue subway station in Jackson Heights, Queens, then the Triboro Coach Lines Q33 bus to La Guardia's Main Terminal. The bus shuttles between Roosevelt Avenue and the airport every every 12 minutes during the day and evening, every 40 minutes after midnight. Alternatively, the Triboro Coach Q47 bus leaves La Guardia's Marine Terminal every 20 minutes between 5:20 AM and 12:45 AM for the Roosevelt Avenue station.

BY EXPRESS BUS

Carey Airport Express (718/632–0509) serves JFK and La Guardia airports from six midtown Manhattan stops (Park Ave. between 41st and 42nd Sts., opposite Grand Central Terminal; outside the Port Authority Bus Terminal, 42nd St. between 8th and 9th Aves.; the New York Hilton and Towers, 6th Ave. at 53rd St.; Sheraton Manhattan, 7th Ave. at 51st St.; Marriott Marquis, Broadway between 45th and 46th Sts.; Holiday Crowne Plaza, Broadway at 48th St.). From Park Avenue, buses run nonstop to JFK every 30 minutes 5 AM–1 AM (every 20 mins in the afternoon); from JFK, 6 AM–midnight. Service runs nonstop to La Guardia every 20 minutes 6 AM–midnight (every 15 mins in the afternoon); from La Guardia, 6:45 AM–midnight. Fare is $10 to La Guardia, $13 to JFK.

Olympia Trails Airport Express (212/964–6233) serves Newark Airport from

Airport Access

New Jersey · Newark International Airport · Hudson · Manhattan · Brooklyn

Airlines	Terminals		
	JFK	LaGUARDIA	NEWARK
Aer Lingus ☎ 212/557–1110	4E		A, B
Aeroflot ☎ 212/332–1050	3		
Aerolineas Argentinas ☎ 800/333–0276	4E		
AeroMexico ☎ 800/237–6639	2		B
Air Afrique ☎ 800/237–2747	4W		
Air Aruba ☎ 800/882–7822			B
Air Canada ☎ 800/776–3000		CTB-A	C
Air China ☎ 212/371–9898	3		
Air France ☎ 800/237–2747	4W		B
Air India ☎ 212/751–6200	4W		
Air Jamaica ☎ 800/523–5585	4W		B
Air Nova ☎ 800/776–3000			C
Air Ontario ☎ 800/776–3000			C
Alitalia ☎ 800/223–5730	4W		B, C
ALIA-Royal Jordanian ☎ 212/949–0050	4E		
All Nippon Airways ☎ 800/235–9262	3		
American ☎ 800/433–7300	8, 9	CTB-D	A
American Eagle ☎ 800/433–7300	9		
American Trans Air ☎ 800/435–9282	2		
America West ☎ 800/235–9292	2	CTB-A	C
Asiana Airlines ☎ 800/227–4262	4E		
Austrian Airlines ☎ 800/843–0002	3		
Avianca ☎ 800/284–2622	3		B
Balkan Bulgarian ☎ 800/796–5706	4E		
Biman Bangladesh ☎ 888/702–4626	4W		
British Airways ☎ 800/247–9297	7		B
Business Express ☎ 800/345–3400			B
BWIA ☎ 800/538–2942	8		
Canadian Airlines ☎ 800/426–7000	9	CTB-D	
Carnival ☎ 800/437–2110	4E	CTB-C	B
Cathay Pacific ☎ 800/233–2742	3		
China Airlines ☎ 800/227–5118	3		
Colgan Air ☎ 800/272–5488		CTB-B	A

14

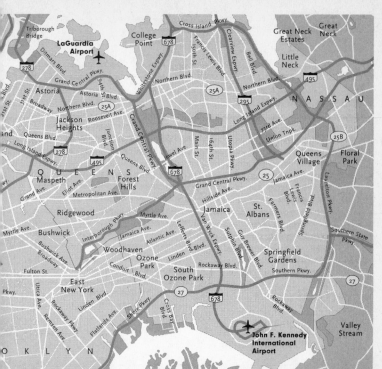

Airlines

Terminals (cont.)

Airlines	JFK	LaGUARDIA	NEWARK
Continental ☎ 800/525-0280		CTB-A	C
Continental Express ☎ 800/525-0280	2	CTB-A	C
Czech Airlines ☎ 212/765-6022			B
Delta International ☎ 800/241-1414	3	Delta	B
Delta Domestic ☎ 800/221-1212	3	Delta	B
Delta Shuttle ☎ 212/239-0700		MAT	
Ecuatoriana ☎ 800/328-2367	3		
Egypt Air ☎ 212/315-0900	4W		
El-Al ☎ 800/223-6700	4W		B
EVA Airways ☎ 800/695-1188	4E		B
Finnair ☎ 212/499-9026	2		
Ghana Airways ☎ 800/404-4262	4W		
Guyana ☎ 718/657-7474	4E		
Iberia ☎ 800/772-4642	4E		
Icelandair ☎ 800/223-5500	4E		
Japan ☎ 800/525-3663	4E		
KIWI ☎ 800/538-5494			A
KLM ☎ 212/759-3600; 800/374-7747	4E		B
Korean ☎ 800/438-5000	4W		B
Kuwait ☎ 212/308-5454	4E		
Lacsa Airlines ☎ 800/225-2272	7		
Lan Chile ☎ 800/488-0070	8		
LOT Polish ☎ 800/223-0593	8		B
LTU ☎ 800/888-0200	4E		
Lufthansa ☎ 800/645-3880	4E		
Malev Hungarian ☎ 212/757-6446	3		B
Mexicana ☎ 800/531-7921	4W		
Midway ☎ 800/446-4392		CTB-D	A
Midwest Express ☎ 800/452-2022		CTB-C	B
North American ☎ 718/656-3289	5		
Northwest International ☎ 800/447-4747	4E	Delta	B
Northwest Domestic ☎ 800/225-2525	4E	Delta	B
Northwest Airlink ☎ 800/225-2525	4E	Delta	B

JFK International Airport

D   C

Terminal 9

B   A

Terminal 8

CAR RENTAL RETURN AT FEDERAL CIRCLE

678

Van Wyck Expwy.

Tower Air Terminal

Lot 3

150 th St. JFK Expressway

N

Terminal 7

Lot 4

Terminal 6

Terminal 1 *

Lot 1

Parking Garage

Lot 2

Terminal 2

Terminal 5

Terminal 3

Rooftop Parking

Terminal 4W
Gates 23–35

Terminal 4E
Gates 9–22

International Arrivals Building (IAB)

600 feet
0
0
200 meters

* under construction

Airlines

Airlines	JFK	LaGUARDIA	NEWARK
Olympic ☎ 212/838–3600	4E	LaGUARDIA	NEWARK
Pakistan ☎ 212/370–9158	4W		
Pan Am ☎ 800/359–7262	4E		
Philippine Airlines ☎ 800/435–9725			
Precision Airlink ☎ 888/635–5293			B
Qantas ☎ 800/227–4500	4	Delta	
Royal Air Maroc ☎ 212/750–6071	4E		
SAS ☎ 800/221–2350	7		
Sabena ☎ 800/955–2000	3		C
SAETA ☎ 212/302–0004	7		
Singapore Airlines ☎ 800/742–3333	3		
South African Airways ☎ 212/826–0995	8		
Sun Country ☎ 800/359–5786	6		
Sun Jet ☎ 800/478–6538			
Swissair ☎ 800/221–4750	3		A
Tarom-Romanian ☎ 212/687–6013	3		B
TACA International ☎ 800/535–8780	2		
TAP Air Portugal ☎ 800/221–7370	3		
Tower Air ☎ 718/553–8500	Tower		B
TransBrasil ☎ 800/872–3153	4W		
TWA ☎ 212/290–2141; 201/643–3339	5, 6		
Turkish Airlines ☎ 212/339–9650		CTB-B	A
TW Express ☎ 212/290–2141;201/643–3339	5		B
	7		A
United ☎ 800/241–6522	7		A
United Express ☎ 800/241–6522	7	CTB-C	A
US Airways ☎ 800/428–4322	7	CTB-C	A
US Airways Express ☎ 800/428–4322		US Airways	A
US Airways Shuttle ☎ 800/428–4322	4W	US Airways	
Uzbekistan Airways ☎ 212/489–3954	2	US Airways Shuttle	
Varig ☎ 212/682–3100	4W		
VASP ☎ 718/955–0540	2		
Virgin Atlantic ☎ 800/862–8621			B

16

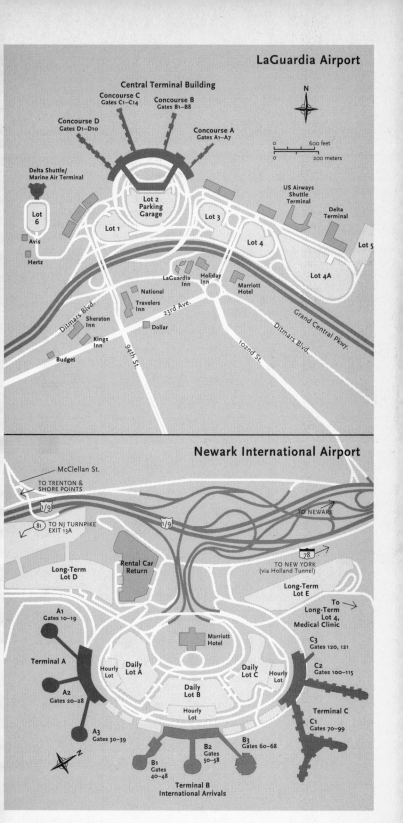

LaGuardia Airport

Central Terminal Building

Concourse C
Gates C1–C14

Concourse B
Gates B1–B8

Concourse D
Gates D1–D10

Concourse A
Gates A1–A7

N

0   600 feet
0   200 meters

Delta Shuttle/
Marine Air Terminal

US Airways
Shuttle
Terminal

Delta
Terminal

Lot
6

Avis

Hertz

Lot 2
Parking
Garage

Lot 1

Lot 3

Lot 4

Lot 5

Lot 4A

LaGuardia
Inn

Holiday
Inn

Marriott
Hotel

National

Travelers
Inn

23rd Ave.

Ditmars Blvd.

Sheraton
Inn

Dollar

Grand Central Pkwy.

Kings
Inn

Ditmars Blvd.

Budget

94th St.

102nd St.

Newark International Airport

McClellan St.

TO TRENTON &
SHORE POINTS

1/9

81 TO NJ TURNPIKE
EXIT 13A

1/9

TO NEWARK

78

TO NEW YORK
(via Holland Tunnel)

Rental Car
Return

Long-Term
Lot D

Long-Term
Lot E

To
Long-Term
Lot 4,
Medical Clinic

A1
Gates 10–19

Marriott
Hotel

C3
Gates 120, 121

Terminal A

Daily
Lot A

Hourly
Lot

Daily
Lot C

Hourly
Lot

C2
Gates 100–115

A2
Gates 20–28

Daily
Lot B

Terminal C

A3
Gates 30–39

Hourly
Lot

C1
Gates 70–99

N

B1
Gates
40–48

B2
Gates
50–58

B3
Gates 60–68

Terminal B
International Arrivals

Penn Station, Grand Central Terminal, and 1 World Trade Center (West St., Lower Manhattan). The bus leaves Newark for Penn Station and Grand Central Terminal every 20 minutes 6:15 AM–midnight; for the World Trade Center, every 30 minutes 6:45 AM–8:15 PM. Fare is $10.

Gray Line Air Shuttle (212/757–6840) operates door-to-door minibuses to all three airports from Manhattan hotels between 23rd and 63rd streets, 7 AM–11 PM. Fare to JFK is $16.50; to La Guardia, $13.50; to Newark, $18.50.

BY HELICOPTER

National Helicopter (516/756–9355) flies Twinstar and Bell 206L copters from three city heliports to all three airports daily 7 AM–9 PM. The fare is a flat $389 per helicopter; each helicopter carries up to five people.

WEATHER

New York has four distinct seasons, each lending the city its own character. Spring and fall bring moderate temperatures; the mercury in summer averages 75°F (23°C) with fairly high humidity; and winter temperatures often hover near 32°F (0°C). But remember that indoor temperatures are often the opposite of those outdside—chilly in summer due to air-conditioning and toasty in winter due to central heating. Things are further complicated if you ride the subway: subterranean stations are subtropical in summer. Dress for comfort, preferably in removable layers. In winter, snow and slush can turn sidewalks and corner crosswalks into treacherous courses and hazardous pools, so think seriously about boots, and tread with care. Remember to enjoy the view; the city is gorgeous under a blanket of snow, however fleeting.

chapter 2

PLACES TO EXPLORE

galleries, gargoyles, museums, and more

Think you've seen it all? Whether you're into art, architecture, scenery, history, people-watching, or something else altogether, each of New York's dozens of neighborhoods hides something appealing. You can search for ghosts in old mansions, explore changing ethnic neighborhoods, sail the East River in a historic tall ship, wander backstage at the Met, climb the Statue of Liberty (isn't it time?), or just take in Warhol at the MOMA. New York also offers subtler pleasures; sometimes just getting from place to place—riding an el train, passing through Grand Central Terminal, or taking a long bus ride—is an experience in itself. And walks through the city's many historic areas, such as SoHo and Brooklyn Heights, reveal wonderful old churches or architectural details on virtually every block. To borrow from an old cliché, stop and smell the roses. As New Yorkers know all too well, sightseeing in the Big Apple is mostly a matter of finding the time.

where to go

ARCHITECTURE

Each site is introduced with the name of its architect and the year the project was completed.

7 *b-8*
ANSONIA HOTEL
(Paul E.M. Duboy, 1904) An exuberant architectural masterpiece, complete with turrets, a mansard roof, and filigreed-iron balconies, the Upper West Side's Ansonia Hotel was inspired by turn-of-the-century Beaux Arts buildings in Paris. The luxury doesn't stop on the outside; the apartments inside are soundproof, and once attracted such musical stars as Enrico Caruso, Igor Stravinsky, Lily Pons, and Arturo Toscanini as longtime residents. *2109 Broadway (between 73rd and 74th Sts.), Upper West Side. Subway: 1, 2, 3, 9 to 72nd St.*

10 *d-6*
BATTERY PARK CITY
Not since Rockefeller Center has New York undertaken such an ambitious physical project. Battery Park City was a mere gleam in urban planners' eyes until the 1980s, and though it's largely complete, parts of it are still under construction. Built on a 92-acre stretch of landfill along the Hudson River at Manhattan's southern tip, this city within a city combines high-rise office towers with open space, outdoor sculpture, and a delightful, riverside public esplanade. Its stone, ceramic, glass, and bronze buildings—in shapes recalling the '30s—are a spectacular addition to the downtown skyline. The most impressive of these, the four-tower World Financial Center (Cesar Pelli, 1988) has 6 million square ft of office space and 220,000 square ft of shops and restaurants. Its centerpiece, the Winter Garden, a towering glass pavilion–cum–urban greenhouse, houses 16 palm trees (New York's first) under its 120-ft vaulted roof and overlooks a three-acre river plaza and yacht marina. Nearby, a little commuter ferry shuttles workers to and from New Jersey. *Hudson River from Battery Pl. to Vesey St., Lower Manhattan. Subway: South Ferry; Bowling Green; Cortlandt St./World Trade Center.*

9 *d-3*
CBS BUILDING
(Eero Saarinen & Associates, 1965) Framed in concrete and covered with dark granite, this 38-story midtown highrise is sometimes known as the Black Rock. Recently declared a landmark, it's still the TV network's home base. *1 W. 52nd St., Midtown. Subway: E, F to 5th Ave.*

9 *e-5*
CHANIN BUILDING
(Sloan & Robertson, 1929) Like the nearby Chrysler Building (*see below*), the Chanin Building is an Art Deco winner. Most notable are its stylized ornamentation and intricate detail, ranging from the terra-cotta bas-relief and bronze frieze on the lower facade to the bronze grills and "jeweled" clocks in the lobby. *122 E. 42nd St. Subway: 42nd St./Grand Central.*

10 *e-7*
CHASE MANHATTAN BANK TOWER & PLAZA
(Skidmore, Owings & Merrill, 1960) Lower Manhattan's first boxy, alu-

minum-and-glass high-rise, this 65-story tower is surrounded by interesting touches. The plaza contains a fountain designed by famed sculptor Isamu Noguchi (*see* Isamu Noguchi Garden Museum *in* Art Museums, *below*) and a whimsical, black-and-white sculpture by Jean Dubuffet, "Group of Four Trees," designed to resemble papier-mâché. *1 Chase Manhattan Plaza (between Nassau & William Sts.), Lower Manhattan. Subway: Wall St.*

9 *e-5*

CHRYSLER BUILDING

(William Van Alen, 1930) New York has more than its share of stunning skyscrapers, but many residents agree that if they had to pick a favorite, it would have to be the Chrysler Building—particularly at dusk, when the setting sun makes the building's gleaming Art Deco spire practically glow. The Chrysler was one of the first skyscrapers to be faced with stainless steel—including the gargoyles, which were modeled after car-hood ornaments. At 1,048 ft, it was the tallest building in the world until the Empire State Building was completed—alas, only a few months later. *405 Lexington Ave. (at 42nd St.), Midtown. Subway: 42nd St./Grand Central.*

9 *e-3*

CITICORP CENTER

(Hugh Stubbins & Associates, 1977) With its uniquely angled silhouette and greenish-silver satin veneer, the Citicorp Center is among the most eyecatching forms in the Midtown skyline. At street level it appears to stand on monster stilts, and its sunlit, three-level atrium—one of the city's most successful—is a modern agora of shops and pedestrian activity. Interestingly, the building's jauntily slanted top was meant to be practical: It was intended for a solar-energy collector that was never installed. (*See* St. Peter's Church at the Citicorp Center *in* Churches & Synagogues, *below*.) *Lexington Ave. between 53rd and 54th Sts., Midtown. Subway: 51st St./Lexington–3rd Aves.*

9 *f-5*

DAILY NEWS BUILDING

(Howells & Hood, 1930) Although the *News* moved out in 1995, this building's inspiring Art Deco ornamentation, commissioned by Joseph Patterson, the founder of the nation's first tabloid

newspaper, remains. After admiring the striped brickwork and the relief above the entrance depicting light dawning on the urban populace (an obvious reference to the enlightening power of the press), check out the lobby, which houses a huge, revolving globe (12 ft in diameter) and a floor that resembles a gigantic compass. *220 E. 42nd St., Midtown. Subway: 42nd St./Grand Central.*

10 *f-7*

88 PINE STREET

(I. M. Pei & Associates, 1974) This elegant aluminum-and-glass structure overlooks the South Street Seaport. *Wall Street Plaza (between Water and Front Sts.), Lower Manhattan. Subway: Wall St.*

9 *d-6*

EMPIRE STATE BUILDING

(Shreve, Lamb & Harmon, 1931) Although at 1,454 ft it's no longer the world's tallest building, the Empire State Building remains one of the most famous and most photographed structures in the world. Its enormity (the steel frame alone weighs 60,000 tons) is belied by the delicacy and balance of its design; the needlelike spire and careful setbacks create a sense of height and majesty. The building heightens its own romance by lighting its peak in colors for seasonal and special occasions: red, white, and blue for July 4; red and green at Christmastime; blue and white when the Yankees win big (blue and orange for the Mets). *350 5th Ave. (at 34th St.), Garment District. Subway: 34th st./Herald Sq. For admission to observatory, see Viewpoints, below.*

10 *e-7*

EQUITABLE BUILDING

(Ernest R. Graham, 1915) An unrelenting mass that blotted out the sun, the 40-story Equitable Building swallowed up so much airspace from such a small plot of land (less than one acre) that it inspired the nation's first zoning laws in 1916. *120 Broadway (at Cedar St.), Lower Manhattan. Subway: 4, 5 to Wall St.*

9 *d-7*

FLATIRON BUILDING

(D. H. Burnham & Co., 1902) Thanks to its alluring triangular shape (conceived to fit its triangular plot between 5th Ave., Broadway, and 23rd St.), this 286-ft-tall example of early "modern" architecture was once New York's most famous building and was really the city's first skyscraper. Covered with a limestone skin in the Italian Renaissance style, the shiplike structure was the most popular subject of picture postcards at the turn of the century, appearing to sail intrepidly up the avenue. The phrase "23 Skiddoo" originated at the building's prow, where policemen were assigned to chase away men who stopped to gaze at the upturned skirts of ladies at one of the windiest corners in the city. *175 5th Ave. (at 23rd St.). Subway: N, R to 23rd St.*

9 *f-5*

FORD FOUNDATION BUILDING

(Kevin Roche, John Dinkeloo & Associates, 1967) Home to one of the largest philanthropic organizations in the world, the Ford Foundation Building is best known for its glass-walled, 130-ft-high atrium. Filled with trees, shrubs, a still-water pool, and all manner of greenery, this enclosed garden is a real respite from the crush around Grand Central Terminal. *320 E. 43rd St., Midtown. Closed weekends. Subway: 42nd St./Grand Central.*

9 *d-3*

GENERAL MOTORS BUILDING

(Edward Durell Stone, Emery Roth & Sons, 1968) Generally considered a pretentious disaster by architecture critics, this 50-story, white marble tower was built on the site of the beautiful old Savoy Plaza Hotel, across from Central Park's Grand Army Plaza (which includes the distinguished Plaza Hotel). It's out of context, they say: an example of what not to do when combining the old with the new. Many people forgive the place, though, since it now houses both a public showroom for GM's finest cars and the beloved upscale toy store F.A.O. Schwartz. *767 5th Ave. (between 58th and 59th Sts.), Midtown. Subway: E, F, N, R to 5th Ave.*

9 *e-5*

GRAND CENTRAL TERMINAL

(Warren & Wetmore, Reed & Stem, 1913) This massive Beaux-Arts pile boasts the grandest interior space anywhere in New York. Crossed by more than 400,000 commmuters every weekday, its main concourse (470 ft long) resembles a cathedral, surmounted by a 150-ft-high vaulted ceiling with a teal-blue mural of the night sky. The exterior isn't bad, either; Grand Central's southern facade, with three 75-ft-high arched windows overlooking Park Avenue, is topped by a statue of Mercury, Hercules, and Minerva and a giant clock. Underground, more than 60 ingeniously integrated railroad tracks lead trains upstate and to Connecticut via MetroNorth Commuter Rail. In 1978, the U.S. Supreme Court upheld Grand Central's status as a landmark, affirming the city's tough landmark laws to prevent the station's owners from building an office tower on top of the terminal. *Vanderbilt Ave. and 42nd St., Midtown. Subway: 42nd St./Grand Central.*

9 *d-5*

GRACE BUILDING

(Skidmore, Owings & Merrill, 1974) Across from Bryant Park, this swooping glass behemoth—derided as "flashy" and "flamboyant" by architecture critics—has a curved facade that makes the bottom of the building look like a ski jump. *41 W. 42nd St., Midtown. Subway: B, D, F, Q to 42nd St.*

7 *e-6*

GUGGENHEIM MUSEUM

(Frank Lloyd Wright, 1959) The Guggenheim is one of only two buildings in Manhattan designed by Frank Lloyd Wright (the other is a Mercedes-Benz showroom at Park Avenue and 56th Street), and is often visited as much for its architecture as for the art inside. The white exterior resembles an inverted cone; the much-vaunted interior houses a six-story rotunda under a skylit glass dome. A spiraling ramp leads down past exhibitions of modern art (*see* Art Museums, *below*). *1071 5th Ave. (at 89th St.), Upper East Side. Subway: 4, 5, 6 to 86th St.*

11 *e-5*

HAUGHWOUT BUILDING

(J. P. Gaynor, 1857) With each window framed by Corinthian columns and rounded arches, this five-story, Palladio-inspired building is considered one of the best examples of cast-iron architecture in the world. It was equipped with the world's first elevator, designed by Elisha Graves Otis, who went on to found an elevator empire and make high-rises (and the modern skyscraper) practical possibilities. *See* SoHo Cast-Iron Historic District, *below. 488–492*

Broadway (at Broome St.), SoHo. Subway: N, R to Canal St.; 6 to Spring St.

9 *d-3*

IBM BUILDING

(Edward Larrabee Barnes, 1982) A sleek, green-granite-and-glass tower shaped like a prism, the entry to this building is set back under the 40 cantilevered floors. The huge, glass atrium, filled with bamboo trees, is a tranquil public plaza for sitting and sipping. *590 Madison Ave. (at 57th St.), Midtown. Subway: E, F, N, R to 5th Ave.*

9 *a-6*

JACOB K. JAVITS CONVENTION CENTER

(I. M. Pei & Partners, 1986) The Javits Center is New York's mecca for conventions and trade shows. With 1.8 million square ft of floor space on a 22-acre site, it is built almost entirely of glass. Sometimes called the Crystal Palace, the lobby alone is 150 ft high. The dark green, crystalline-glass exterior is made up of 16,100 panes. *11th and 12th Aves. from 34th to 39th Sts. Subway: 34th St./Penn Station.*

9 *f-6*

KIPS BAY PLAZA

(I. M. Pei & Associates & S. J. Kessler, 1960 & 1965) I. M. Pei strikes again. New York's first apartment buildings with exposed concrete, these two block-like structures squatting next to a barren, hardtop "park" were considered visionary in their day but are now considered mistakes. Rather than working with the surrounding streetscape, they ignore it, creating their own sterile world. *1st and 2nd Aves. from 30th to 33rd Sts., Murray Hill. Subway: 33rd St.*

9 *f-4*

LESCAZE HOUSE

(William Lescaze, 1934) Designed by pioneering architect William Lescaze as his own home and office, this town house—with its glass-block and rib-boned windows—is considered the first modernist building in the city. *211 E. 48th St., Midtown. Subway: 51st St./Lexington–3rd Aves.*

9 *e-3*

LEVER HOUSE

(Gordon Bunschaft of Skidmore, Owings & Merrill, 1952) One of the first metal-and-glass skyscrapers, this slim, blue-green tower stands on a one-story horizontal slab supported by chrome columns. Made for the soap-and-detergent empire Lever Brothers, it was designed to exude an aura of cleanliness. Its completion was considered an architectural watershed, leaving older skyscraper designs behind in favor of the increasingly sleek and commercial International Style. Interestingly, Lever House takes up so litte airspace on its enormous lot that the reflections of surrounding buildings can be seen clearly in its mirrorlike sides. *390 Park Ave. (between 53rd and 54th Sts.), Midtown. Subway: 51st St./Lexington–3rd Aves.*

9 *b-2*

LINCOLN CENTER FOR THE PERFORMING ARTS

(Various architects, 1962–68). Although Lincoln Center is unsurpassed for artistic variety and integrity, its architectural whole is greater than the sum of its parts. The center's buildings, all classical imitations decked out in the same cream-colored travertine, include Avery Fisher Hall, the New York State Theater, the Metropolitan Opera House, the Juilliard School of Music, and the Vivian Beaumont Theater. None of the buildings is terribly impressive on its own, yet there is something tremendously freeing about the open spaces and plazas here at the foot of the Upper West Side. The public art is also notable: murals by Marc Chagall inside the Met, a Henry Moore sculpture in the reflecting pool, and two white marble sculptures by Elie Nadelman in the foyer of the New York State Theater. *Columbus and Amsterdam Aves. from 62nd to 66th Sts., Upper West Side. Subway: 66th St./Lincoln Center.*

9 *f-3*

THE LIPSTICK BUILDING

(Philip Johnson for John Burgee Architects, 1986) Architecture buffs love this rose-color office tower, a truly unique design by Philip Johnson, the founder of American Modernism. Elliptical in shape, the smooth, 34-story exterior has no corners, making it a dramatic departure from the rectangular megaboxes that dominate the rest of Midtown. "Effect before everything" was Johnson's personal motto. The building gets its name from two setbacks in its midsection, which make it look like a tube of lipstick. *885 3rd Ave. (between 53rd and 54th Sts.), Midtown. Subway: 51st St/Lexington–3rd Aves.*

9 *d-5*

MCGRAW-HILL BUILDING

(Raymond Hood, Godley & Fouilhoux, 1931) Sometimes said to look like a jukebox, this Art Moderne–cum–International Style high-rise is considered a masterpiece of design. Covered in sea-green terra-cotta, it has Art Deco details at street level and Carrera glass in the lobby. *330 W. 42nd St., Midtown. Subway: 47th–50th Sts./Rockefeller Center.*

9 *e-1*

PAUL MELLON HOUSE

(Mazza & Seccia, 1965) Snug alongside Italianate brownstones and neo-Georgian mansions on one of the city's most beautiful residential blocks, this light-as-air postwar town house is characterized by the experts as "French provincial." *125 E. 70th St., Upper East Side. Subway: 68th St./Hunter College.*

9 *e-4*

METROPOLITAN LIFE BUILDING (FORMERLY PAN AM BUILDING)

(Emery Roth & Sons, Pietro Belluschi, and Walther Gropius, 1963) Plunked down in the middle of Park Avenue, hovering over Grand Central Station, the Pan Am Building was reviled as an outsize monstrosity when it was built in the 1960s. With 2.4 million square ft of office space, it was the largest office building in Manhattan, and it destroyed a cherished vista down Park Avenue. Since the 60s, however, it's become such an integral part of the city's skyline that people were upset when the name on the top of the building was changed from Pan Am to MetLife in the early '90s. *200 Park Ave. (at 46th St.), Midtown. Subway: 42nd St./Grand Central.*

9 *d-5*

NEW YORK PUBLIC LIBRARY

(Carrère & Hastings, 1911) Flanked by its two famous stone lions, the Public Library's Central Research Library is considered, along with Grand Central Terminal, New York's most magnificent Beaux-Arts building. The beauty of its broad, plaza-like stairway and columned exterior is matched by the interior, particularly the grand third-floor reading room, with row after row of long wooden tables illuminated by brass reading lamps and watched over by massive arched windows. The beloved reading room will reopen in 1999 after a complete renovation. (*See Libraries, below.*) *5th Ave. and 42nd St., Midtown. Subway: B, D, F, Q to 42nd St.*

9 *d-5*

NEW YORK YACHT CLUB

(Warren & Wetmore, 1899) Built on land donated by yacht-club member J. P. Morgan, this Beaux Arts structure is famous for its three decorative bay windows fashioned after the sterns of 18th-century sailing ships. The fanciful limestone facade is adorned with carvings of dolphins and waves. *37 W. 44th St., Midtown. Subway: B, D, F, Q to 42nd St.*

9 *f-3*

919 THIRD AVENUE

(Skidmore, Owings, & Merrill, 1970). What's most interesting about this brown-glass office structure is the little, redbrick 1890 building that seems to stand as its sentry box—P. J. Clarke's Tavern, famed watering hole and holdout against Tishman Realty. (*See American Casual in Chapter 3.*) *919 3rd Ave. (at 55th and 56th Sts.), Midtown. Subway: 59th St.*

9 *e-4*

OLYMPIC TOWER

(Skidmore, Owings & Merrill, 1976) With shops, offices, and apartments, the multipurpose Olympic Tower also has a nicely landscaped public arcade, complete with waterfall, and is conveniently located across from St. Patrick's Cathedral. *645 5th Ave. (at 51st St.), Midtown. Subway: E, F to 5th Ave.*

10 *e-7*

140 BROADWAY

(Skidmore, Owings & Merrill, 1967) A more successful version of Skidmore, Owings & Merrill's earlier Chase Manhattan Bank Tower & Plaza, this sleek, elegant glass skyscraper rises 52 orderly stories above an attractive travertine plaza—home to Isamu Noguchi's delicately balanced red sculpture "Cube." When the building was completed, architecture critic Ada Louise Huxtable wrote, "Sometimes we do it right." *140 Broadway (at Cedar St.), Lower Manhattan. Subway: 4, 5 to Wall St.*

9 *e-3*

135 E. 57TH STREET

(Kohn Pedersen Fox, 1988) This classically inspired pile has a 32-story concave curve that creates a corner plaza worthy of Delphi. *135 E. 57th St., Midtown. Subway: 59th St.*

10 *f-6*

127 JOHN STREET

(Emery Roth & Sons, 1969; lobby & plaza, Corchia deHarak Associates) This otherwise bland office tower is equipped with a whimsical—and now somewhat retro—lobby and plaza designed to delight pedestrians. You can climb on canvas-and-pipe structures without losing track of the time; just glance over at the 45-by-50-ft digital clock. *127 John St. (at Water St.), Lower Manhattan. Subway: 2, 3 to Fulton St.*

9 *f-5*

ONE & TWO UNITED NATIONS PLAZA

(Kevin Roche, John Dinkeloo & Associates One: 1976; Two: 1984) This elegant pair of aquamarine, glass-and-aluminum towers holds offices and the Regal U.N. Plaza Hotel (*see* Very Expensive Lodgings *in* Chapter 7). Cool, green-and-white marble makes this lobby one of the most attractive in the city. *1st Ave. and 44th St., Midtown. Subway: 42nd St./Grand Central.*

9 *e-5*

PHILIP MORRIS

(Ulrich Franzen & Associates, 1983) This 26-story, granite corporate facility was the first to use its building bonus (extra bulk in exchange for constructing a public amenity) as a cultural facility. The appealing pedestrian space is an enormous enclosed sculpture court, a branch of the Whitney Museum of Modern Art (*see* Art Museums, *below*). The building is also notable for such rare, energy-saving features as ceiling fans and windows that *open*. *120 Park Ave. (at 42nd St.), Midtown. Subway: 42nd St./Grand Central.*

10 *f-1*

RENWICK TRIANGLE

Attributed to James Renwick, Jr., the architect of both St. Patrick's Cathedral and Grace Church (downtown), these 1861 brick row houses form a handsome historic enclave in the bustling East Village. A postmodern NYU dormitory, bitterly contested by area residents, is an ungainly and unworthy addition at the triangle's 3rd Avenue base. *112–128 E.*

10th St. and 2335 Stuyvesant St. (between 2nd and 3rd Aves.), East Village. Subway: Astor Pl.

9 *g-3*

RIVER HOUSE

(Bottomly, Wagner & White, 1931) Then and now, a classic residential building for the very rich, the 26-story River House boasts a gated entrance for cars and a cobbled circular driveway. When the house was first built, residents had their own private yacht mooring, but alas, it was displaced by the construction of the FDR Drive in the 1940s. *435 E. 52nd St. (at Sutton Pl.), Midtown. Subway: 51st St./Lexington–3rd Aves.*

7 *a-4*

RIVERSIDE DRIVE– WEST 105TH STREET HISTORIC DISTRICT

Limestone Beaux-Arts houses built between 1899 and 1902 form a tiny enclave beside Riverside Park. *Riverside Dr. between 105th and 106th Sts., Upper West Side. Subway: 103rd St.; 110th St./Cathedral Pkwy.*

9 *d-4*

ROCKEFELLER CENTER

(Various architects, dir. by Raymond Hood, mostly 1931–40) A building complex with an unusual sense of harmony, grace, and wealth, Rockefeller Center combines the best of both worlds— functional verticality and street-level life. Despite its scale, Rockefeller Center remains a people's place. The Channel Gardens, with their rock pools, topiary, and colorful flower beds, lead past high-quality shops to the sunken Lower Plaza, which is turned into an ice rink in winter. Beyond the plaza is a gold-leaf statue of Prometheus, punctuating the G.E. Building (formerly the RCA Building, and now home to NBC Studios), with its black granite lobby and, at the top, the Art Deco Rainbow Room. And nothing evokes the power and scale of Manhattan more specifically than the enormous statue of Atlas supporting the world before the International Building (*see* Atlas *and* Prometheus *in* Statues & Monuments, *below*; Radio City Music Hall *in* Historic Buildings and Areas, *below*; *and* Rainbow Room *in* Dining and Dancing, Chapter 5.) *5th and 6th Aves. from 48th to 51st Sts., Midtown. Subway: 47th–50th Sts., Rockefeller Center.*

`9` *e-3*

SEAGRAM BUILDING

(Ludwig Mies van der Rohe and Philip Johnson, Kahn & Jacobs, 1958) An austere tribute to modernity by Mies van der Rohe, this sleek, bronze-color skyscraper and its plaza and fountains—all highly innovative at the time of construction—create a pleasing geometry. Although this International Style skyscraper inspired many less-successful imitations, *Times* architecture critic Paul Goldberger still calls this "one of the great buildings of the twentieth century." The interior, much of which was designed by Philip Johnson, also features exquisite, minimalist detail. Tours of the building start in the lobby every Tuesday at 3. *375 Park Ave. (between 52nd and 53rd Sts.), 212/572–7000 for tours (ask for office management). Midtown. Subway: 51st St./Lexington–3rd Aves.*

`10` *e-8*

17 STATE STREET

(Emery Roth & Sons, 1988) A sleek, wedge-shape, reflective-glass tower following the arc of State Street, this late-model International Style building has a twist: a high-tech glass-enclosed lobby 25 ft up. *Lower Manhattan. Subway: Bowling Green; South Ferry.*

`10` *f-7*

77 WATER STREET

(Emery Roth & Sons; street-level design, Corchia deHarak Associates, 1970) Like 127 John Street, which was financed by the same developer (Mel Kaufmann), this sleek skyscraper near South Street Seaport invites and involves pedestrians at street level, this time with pools and bridges. *Between Old Slip, Gouverneur La., and Front St., Lower Manhattan. Subway: 2, 3 to Wall St.*

`11` *e-4*

SINGER BUILDING

The SoHo Singer is sometimes known as the Little Singer Building to distinguish it from the beautiful Singer Tower, also designed by Ernest Flagg but demolished 30 years ago to make way for the hulking One Liberty Plaza in the financial district. The building is unique in its use of decorative terra-cotta paneling, recessed plate glass, and filigreed iron. Above 11 stories of recessed balconies, the facade culminates in a graceful iron arch. *561 Broadway (between Spring and Prince Sts.). Subway: Prince St.; 6 to Spring St.*

`9` *d-3*

666 5TH AVENUE

(Carson & Lundin, 1957) This embossed-aluminum skyscraper is most notable for the Isamu Noguchi waterfall in its arcade and the sculpted Noguchi ceiling in its lobby. *666 5th Ave. (between 52nd and 53rd Sts.), Midtown. Subway: E, F to 5th Ave.*

`10` *e-3*

SOHO CAST-IRON HISTORIC DISTRICT

One of the city's most vibrant areas, full of art galleries and upscale shops, SoHo is also home to the world's largest concentration of cast-iron architecture. In the mid-19th century, commercial builders successfully duplicated elaborate, carved masonry by buying prefabricated facades made from cast iron. Though made from molds, the results were anything but dull; SoHo is filled with five- and six-story commercial buildings that look like Italian palazzos, featuring Corinthian columns, multiple tiers of arched windows, and elaborate French Empire pediments. SoHo's Haughwout Building (*see above*) is generally considered the finest example of cast-iron architecture in the world. Tribeca and the Village have some cast-iron gems as well. For more information, call Friends of Cast-Iron Architecture at 212/886–3742. *Canal and Houston Sts. from W. Broadway to Crosby St. Subway: Prince St.; Spring St.; A, C, E, N, R to Canal St.*

`9` *e-3*

SONY BUILDING

(Johnson & Burgee, 1984) Formerly the headquarters of AT&T, this monumental corporate statement is considered the first postmodern skyscraper. Its 36 stories of rose-color granite climb 660 ft (normally the equivalent of 60 stories) and are topped by a much-ballyhooed "Chippendale" pediment. Archways worthy of Imperial Rome lead to a six-story arcade with public seating and an elevator that whisks you to the Sony Wonder Technology Lab. *550 Madison Ave. (at 56th St.), Midtown. Subway: E, F, N, R to 5th Ave.*

`9` g-8

STUYVESANT TOWN

(Irwin Clavan and Gilmore Clarke, 1947) A densely populated apartment complex built by the Metropolitan Life Insurance Company for returning World War II servicemen, Stuy Town is essentially a gargantuan housing project. Now home to over 8,000 families, it's one that works. Though the multiple redbrick towers are essentially identical, the decades-old trees, benches, and curving paths ease the sense of anonymity. *1st Ave. and FDR Dr. from 14th to 20th Sts., Gramercy. Subway: 1st Ave.*

`9` d-4

TIME-LIFE BUILDING

(Harrison & Abramovitz, 1960) The construction of the Time-Life Building, next to Rockefeller Center, led to a corporate Avenue of the Americas building boom, including such towers as the Exxon (at 1251), McGraw-Hill (1221), and Celanese (1211) buildings. Architect Harrison was married to a Rockefeller—go figure. *1271 6th Ave. (at 50th St), Midtown. Subway: 47th–50th Sts./Rockefeller Center.*

`9` e-3

TRUMP TOWER

(Swanke, Hayden, Connell & Partners, 1983) A 68-story, bronze-glass megastructure named for the headline-grabbing developer Donald Trump, Trump Tower is most famed for the prices of its condos (90% cost over $1 million) and for its huge, glitzy atrium of peach-color marble—chosen because it flatters certain complexions. Manhattan's first vertical shopping mall, the public atrium comes complete with a five-story waterwall which, depending on your mood, is either glorious or just plain silly. *725 5th Ave. (at 56th St.), Midtown. Subway: E, F, N, R to 5th Ave.*

`9` f-5

TUDOR CITY

(Fred F. French Co., 1925–28; head architect, H. Douglas Ives) Built in the 1920s to attract middle-income residents, this private "city" centers around 12 buildings containing 3,000 apartments. Situated on a bluff above 1st Avenue, Tudor City now affords great views of the United Nations and the East River. *1st and 2nd Aves. from 40th to 43rd Sts., Midtown. Subway: 42nd St./Grand Central.*

`9` f-4

UNITED NATIONS HEADQUARTERS

(International Committee of Architects, Wallace K. Harrison, chairman, 1947–53) These buildings became the U.N.'s permanent headquarters in 1952. The tall, slim, green-glass Secretariat Building; the much smaller, domed General Assembly Building; and the Dag Hammarskjold Library (Harrison, Abramovitz & Harris, 1963) form the complex, before which the flags of its member nations fly in alphabetical order when the General Assembly is in session. Built on 17 acres, the U.N. was profoundly influenced in design by Le Corbusier's "towers in open space" philosophy. Although the buildings may look a bit dated today, their windswept park and plaza remain visionary: There is a beautiful riverside promenade, a rose garden with 1,400 rosebushes, views of open sky (rare in Manhattan), and thought-provoking sculptures donated by member nations. *1st Ave. from 42nd to 48th Sts. (enter at 46th St.), Midtown. Subway: 42nd St./Grand Central.*

`9` g-7

WATERSIDE PLAZA

(Davis Brody & Associates, 1974) Constituting one of the city's first efforts to utilize the Manhattan waterfront for residential living, these odd-shaped towers arrange 1,600 apartments, shops, and restaurants around an isolated public plaza. Despite the plaza's coldness, it does provide access to a waterfront promenade with excellent views. *FDR Dr. from 25th to 30th Sts., Murray Hill. Subway: 6 to 28th St.*

`10` e-6

WOOLWORTH BUILDING

(Cass Gilbert, 1913) One of New York's most dramatic commercial buildings, this neo-Gothic tower rises 792 ft in the air and, clad in terra-cotta, is the jewel of the downtown skyline. Fittingly dubbed a "cathedral of commerce," it was the world's tallest building until 1930. Don't miss the ornate lobby: Carved figures on the ceiling represent the architect holding a model of the building and F. W. Woolworth himself, counting nickels and dimes. (He paid $13 million in cash to have the place built.) *233 Broadway (between Park Pl. and Barclay St.), Lower Manhattan. Subway: Park Pl.; Cortlandt St./World Trade Center.*

10 *d-6*
WORLD FINANCIAL CENTER
See Battery Park City, *above.*

10 *d-6*
WORLD TRADE CENTER
(Minoru Yamasaki & Associates and
Emery Roth & Sons, 1962–77) Dreamed
up by the Port Authority of New York
and New Jersey to replace an aging
neighborhood of electronics shops and
other low-rent businesses, the World
Trade Center consists of seven commercial buildings containing a staggering 12
million square ft of office space. With
more than 50,000 workers pouring into
the complex every day, the WTC not only
transformed the city's already famous
skyline; it redefined all of lower Manhattan. The stainless-steel "Twin Towers"
are the city's tallest buildings—1,350 ft
and 110 stories high, they loom over a
vast open plaza. The 1993 terrorist
bombing of one of the center's parking
garages killed six people, caused extensive damage, and made this New York
icon seem momentarily vulnerable; but
since then, repairs have been made,
security has been tightened, and the
wheels of commerce have kept turning.
(*See* Viewpoints, *below.*) *Bordered by
West, Vesey, Church, and Liberty Sts.,
Lower Manhattan. Subway: Cortlandt
St./World Trade Center.*

9 *c-4*
WORLDWIDE PLAZA
(Skidmore, Owings & Merrill, 1990) The
old Madison Square Garden was razed
from this site in 1968. In its place are a
mammoth office tower (48 stories), a
residential condominium complex (38
stories, with low-rise wings), eateries,
and a popular discount movie theater.
*8th and 9th Aves. from 48th to 49th Sts.,
Hell's Kitchen. Subway: C, E to 50th St.*

10 *e-1*
ZECKENDORF TOWERS
(Davis, Brody & Associates, 1987)
Looming above Union Square from a
massive commercial base, each of these
four apartment towers is topped by an
illuminated pyramid. The buildings have
radically transformed the Village skyline
and, unfortunately, blocked the far more
attractive Con Edison clock tower from
general view. *1 Irving Pl. (between 14th
and 15th Sts.), Flatiron. Subway: 14th
St./Union Sq.*

ART GALLERIES

The art world decamps for Europe from
June through August to scour assorted
international exhibitions for fresh talent
and fresh gossip. Galleries have limited
hours and shorter weeks during the
summer, and some spaces close down
altogether in August. Galleries that do
stay open tend to present smaller-scale
shows and group shows. In general, call
for summer hours before you make the
trek.

uptown galleries
These exclusive, white-glove spaces,
catering largely to serious collectors and
often emphasizing furniture and prints
over paintings, are located primarily on
and off Madison Avenue from 57th to
86th Street.

9 *e-3*
ACA GALLERIES
This standout Midtown gallery shows
both contemporary art and 19th-century
American works from its impressive col-
lection. *41 E. 57th St, Midtown, 212/644–
8300. Closed Sun. and Mon. Subway: E,
F, N, R to 5th Ave.*

7 *e-8*
**ACQUAVELLA
GALLERIES, INC.**
Acquavella's Impressionist and post-
Impressionist holdings include Monet,
Matisse, Picasso, Miró, and Pissarro.
Downstairs you'll find post–World War
II and contemporary paintings by such
artists as Guston, Gottlieb, Lichtenstein,
and Pollock. *18 E. 79th St., Upper East
Side, 212/734–6300. Closed Sun. Subway:
77th St.*

9 *d-3*
BABCOCK GALLERIES
Established in 1852, this old-line gallery
specializes in art of the 19th and 20th
centuries, but also has plenty of contemporary paintings, drawings, and sculpture. *724 5th Ave. (between 56th and 57th
Sts.), Midtown, 212/535–9355. Closed Sun.
and Mon. Subway: E, F, N, R to 5th Ave.*

7 *e-8*
CLAUDE BERNARD GALLERY
Claude Bernard showcases 19th- and
20th-century South American, American, and European artists including Fernando Botero, Balthus, Jim Dine, Jean

Dubuffet, Ferdinand Leger, Miró, Picasso, and Toledo. *33 E. 74th St., Upper East Side, 212/288–2050. Closed Sun. and Mon. Subway: 77th St.*

9 *e-1*

BERRY HILL GALLERIES, INC.

American painting and sculpture from the 19th and 20th centuries, plus 19th century China Trade paintings, are the order of the day. *11 E. 70th St., Upper East Side, 212/371–6777. Closed Sun. Subway: 68th St./Hunter College.*

9 *d-3*

BREWSTER GALLERY

Brewster specializes in 20th-century European and Latin American masters and is one of the world's largest dealers in Miró and Chagall. The gallery serves as exclusive representative for Branko Bahunek and Leonora Carrington, and publishes Francisco Zuñiga. *41 W. 57th St., Midtown, 212/980–1975. Closed Sun. Subway: B, Q to 57th St.*

9 *e-2*

BRUTON GALLERY

Just the place to go if you have a spare pedestal to cover: Bruton offers French and European sculpture of the 19th and 20th centuries by Joseph Bernard, Antoine Bourdekke, Stephen Buxin, Jean Carton, Paul Cornet, Aristide Maillol, Auguste Rodin, and others. *40 E. 61st St., Upper East Side, 212/980–1640. By appointment only. Subway: 59th St.*

7 *e-8*

CDS

CDS is one of Manhattan's more formidable galleries for the lions of midcentury abstraction. If Motherwell and de Kooning are your thing, put this space high on your list. *76 E. 79th St., Upper East Side, 212/772–9555. Closed Sun. and Mon. Subway: 77th St.*

9 *d-3*

GARTH CLARK

Clark's is a niche gallery specializing in high-quality sculpture and crafts from around the world. The pieces are exquisite, the usual crowd armored with wealth. *24 W. 57th St., Midtown, 212/246–2205. Closed Sun and Mon. Subway: B, Q to 57th St.*

9 *e-2*

DAVIS & LANGDALE CO.

Dignified 18th-, 19th-, and 20th-century American and English paintings, watercolors, and drawings—as well as contemporary American work by such artists as Lennart Anderson, Aaron Shikler, Albert York, and Harry Roseman—hang at this gallery, which caters to the Ralph Lauren/Prince of Wales look. *231 E. 60th St., Upper East Side, 212/838–0333. Closed Sun. and Mon. Subway: 59th St.*

9 *d-3*

TIBOR DE NAGY GALLERY

A recent show featuring the late painter Joe Brainard—along with shows highlighting other respected, poetic artists along the lines of Fairfield Porter—helped define this gallery as one of the city's prime purveyors of good taste with a forward eye. *41 W. 57th St., Midtown, 212/421–3780. Closed Sun. and Mon. Subway: B, Q to 57th St.*

7 *e-8*

THE ELKON GALLERY

Twentieth-century masters are the focus here: paintings, drawings, and sculpture from Balthus, Botero, Dubuffet, Ernst, Leger, Magritte, Matisse, Miró, and Picasso. *18 E. 81st St., Upper East Side, 212/535–3940. Closed Sun. and Mon. Subway: 77th St.*

9 *e-3*

ANDRE EMMERICH GALLERY

Painters represented include Al Held, Hans Hofmann, Morris Louis, David Hockney, and Helen Frankenthaler; sculptors include Anthony Caro, Beverly Pepper, and Anne Truitt. *41 E. 57th St., Midtown, 212/752–0124. Closed Sun. and Mon., also closed July and Aug. except by appointment. Subway: E, F, N, R to 5th Ave.*

9 *e-3*

WALLY FINDLAY

Findlay offers Impressionist, post-Impressionist, and contemporary art of the French school, all with mass appeal. *17 E. 57th St., Midtown, 212/421–5390. Closed Sun. Subway: E, F, N, R to 5th Ave.*

9 *d-3*

FISCHBACH GALLERY

Fischbach is a showcase for 20th-century American paintings and drawings—very eclectic, very New York. *24 W. 57th*

St., Midtown, 212/759–2345. Closed Sun. and Mon.; July and Aug., closed weekends. Subway: B, Q to 57th St.

9 e-3

FORUM GALLERY

Forum features contemporary American figurative paintings and sculpture. 745 5th Ave. (between 57th and 58th Sts.), Midtown, 212/355–4545. Closed Sun. and Mon. Subway: E, F, N, R to 5th Ave.

9 d-3

FRANCIS FROST

Stop in here if you fancy 20th-century prints and drawings by the likes of Grosz, Picasso, Munch, and Derain. 50 W. 57th St., Midtown, 212/459–1950. Closed Sun. and Mon. Subway: B, Q to 57th St.

9 d-3

GALERIE LELONG

Wander among contemporary American and European sculpture, drawings, and paintings. 20 W. 57th St., Midtown 212/315–0470. Closed Sun. and Mon. Subway: B, Q to 57th St.

9 d-3

GALERIE ST. ETIENNE

This private dealer specializes in 19th- and 20th-century Austrian and German expressionism, 19th- and 20th-century folk art, and Grandma Moses. 24 W. 57th St., Midtown, 212/245–6734. Closed Sun. and Mon. Subway: B, Q to 57th St.

9 e-3

JAMES GOODMAN GALLERY

A haven for 20th-century American and European paintings, drawings, watercolors, and sculpture, Goodman's roster includes Botero, Calder, de Kooning, Dubuffet, Giacometti, Leger, Lichtenstein, Matisse, Miró, Henry Moore, and Rauschenberg. 41 E. 57th St., Midtown, 212/593–3737. Closed Sun.; closed Mon. except by appointment. Subway: E, F, N, R to 5th Ave.

9 e-3

NOHRA HAIME GALLERY

Contemporary Latin American, American, and European art are the main courses at this standby. 41 E. 57th St., Midtown, 212/772–7760. Closed Sun. Subway: E, F, N, R to 5th Ave.

9 d-3

HAMMER GALLERIES

Got in in your head to check out sports painter LeRoy Neiman's fundamentally mediocre work? Head for Hammer. If it's prints you seek, try Hammer Graphics, on the 3rd of this emporium's many floors. 33 W. 57th St., Midtown, 212/644–4400. Closed Sun. Subway: B, Q to 57th St.

7 e-1

HIRSCHL & ADLER FOLK

If rustic chic turns you on, make tracks here for fine 19th-century American folk art, including paintings, coverlets and quilts, furniture, weathervanes, and glass. 851 Madison Ave. (at 70th St.), Upper East Side, 212/988–3655. Closed Sun. Subway: 68th St./Hunter College.

7 e-1

HIRSCHL & ADLER GALLERIES

Top-quality 18th-, 19th-, and 20th-century American painting, sculpture, and drawing rest here, and they're the kind of work that would send Robert Hughes scurrying for a thesaurus. Also on offer are European Impressionist and modern painting and drawing, as well as the patron saint of bird painting, John J. Audubon. Mary Cassatt, Frederick Church, John Singleton Copley, Childe Hassam, Homer, Hopper, Matisse, O'Keeffe, Picasso, and Renoir flesh out the reserves. 21 E. 70th St., Midtown, 212/535–8810. Closed Sun. and Mon. Subway: 68th St./Hunter College.

7 e-1

HIRSCHL & ADLER MODERN

Hirschl & Adler's 20th-century gallery shows both American and European art. 21 E. 70th St., Upper East Side, 212/535–8810. Closed Sun. and Mon. Subway: 68th St./Hunter College.

7 e-8

LEONARD HUTTON GALLERIES

German Expressionists and Russian avant-garde art reign supreme. 33 E. 74th St., Upper East Side, 212/249–9700. Closed Sun. and Mon; closed Aug. except by appointment. Subway: 77th St.

9 *d-3*

JANIS GALLERY

This important gallery shows four generations of modern art, from cubism to pop to minimalist painting to post-graffiti. *110 W. 57th St., Midtown, 212/586–0110. Closed Sun. Subway: B, Q to 57th St.*

9 *e-1*

JANE KAHAN

Kahan nearly always has a stunning roster of greats—everyone from Arp to Calder, from Delaunay to Picasso. *922 Madison Ave. (at 73rd St.), Upper East Side, 212/744–1490. Closed Sun. and Mon. Subway: 77th St.*

7 *e-3*

KENNEDY GALLERIES

American paintings, sculpture, and graphics of the 18th, 19th, and 20th centuries share space with European fine prints. *40 W. 57th St., Midtown, 212/541–9600. Closed Sun. and Mon. Subway: B, Q to 57th St.*

9 *e-1*

KNOEDLER & CO.

One of Manhattan's top-flight galleries, Knoedler is a must stop for contemporary European and American paintings and sculpture. *19 E. 70th St., Upper East Side, 212/794–0550. Closed Sun. Subway: 68th St./Hunter College.*

9 *e-3*

KRAUSHAAR GALLERIES

The vibe here is distinctly unflamboyant: paintings, drawings, and sculpture by 20th-century American artists such as Peggy Bacon, William Glackens, Leon Goldin, Elsie Manville, Ben Frank Moss, and John Sloan. (You may never have heard of these folks, but you'll be glad to know them.) *724 5th Ave. (at 57th St.), Midtown, 212/307–5730. Closed Sun. and Mon. Subway: E, F, N, R to 5th Ave.*

9 *d-3*

MARLBOROUGH GALLERY

Along with Knoedler, Robert Miller, and Gagosian, Marlborough is an important stop on any uptown gallery tour. The focus is on 20th-century and contemporary paintings, sculpture, photographs, and graphics; artists represented include Frank Auerbach, Francis Bacon, Fernando Botero, Red Grooms, Barbara Hepworth, Alex Katz, Antonio Lopez Garcia, Henry Moore, Larry Rivers, and

Rufino Tamayo. *40 W. 57th St., Midtown, 212/541–4900. Closed Sun. Subway: B, Q to 57th St.*

9 *e-3*

MCKEE GALLERY

McKee exhibits contemporary paintings, drawings, sculpture, and prints. *41 E. 57th St., Midtown, 212/688–5951. Closed Sun. and Mon. Subway: E, F, N, R to 5th Ave.*

9 *e-3*

PACE/WILDENSTEIN

PACE/WILDENSTEIN/ MACGILL

PACE MASTER PRINTS, PACE PRINTS, PACE PRIMITIVE

The mighty Pace, a corporate art empire ruled by superdealer Arne Glimcher, is so big, so vast, and so connected that nothing as trivial as the '87 stock crash could even dent its business. After the merger with Wildenstein, one of New York's older and most venerable dealer clans, Glimcher's reach extended even farther. Pace/Wildenstein, on the 2nd floor, exhibits paintings and sculpture; Pace/Wildenstein/MacGill, on the 9th floor, shows photography. Some of the heavyweights represented are Rothko, Nevelson, Mangold, and Steinberg. (For Pace Primitive, *see* Eastern Art, *below;* for Pace Master Prints and Pace Prints, *see* Prints, *below.*) *32 E. 57th St., Midtown, 212/421–3292. Closed Sun. Subway: 57th St.*

7 *e-8*

SALANDER O'REILLY GALLERIES

One of uptown's more significant galleries, Salander O'Reilly represents 19th to 20th century American modernist paintings, primarily from the Ashcan, precisionist, and New York schools, as well as contemporary and 19th-century European painters and antique European and American frames. *2 E. 79th St., Upper East Side, 212/879–6606. Closed Sun. Subway: 77th St.*

9 *d-3*

SCHMIDT BINGHAM GALLERY

The focus here is contemporary American realism. *41 W. 57th St., Midtown, 212/888–1122. Closed Sun. Subway: B, Q to 57th St.*

7 *e-8*

SOLOMON & CO. FINE ART

Solomon's roster of 20th-century American and European painters and sculptors includes Avery, Calder, de Kooning, Dubuffet, Hoffman, Pollock, and Stella. *959 Madison Ave. (at 75th St.), Upper East Side, 212/737–8200. Closed Sun. Subway: 77th St.*

7 *e-8*

SOUFER

Post-impressionist and European paintings of the 1920s–1940s are this gallery's forte, but there's also a cluster of German Expressionist works. *1015 Madison Ave. (between 78th and 79th Sts.), Upper East Side, 212/628–3225. Closed Sun. and Mon. Subway: 77th St.*

9 *d-3*

TATISTCHEFF & COMPANY

Tatistcheff showcases contemporary American painting and works on paper. *50 W. 57th St., Midtown, 212/664–0907. Closed Sun. and Mon. Subway: B, Q to 57th St.*

7 *e-8*

UBU GALLERY

This fresh new space engages art that deviates from the tried-and-true. Shows focus on unusual practices—photomontage, for instance—as well as the funkier products of surrealist and Eastern European art. *16 E. 78th St., Upper East Side, 212/794–4444. Closed Sun. and Mon. Subway: 77th St.*

7 *e-8*

VANDERWOUDE/ TANANBAUM

This mixed bag holds American modernist and post–World War II art, contemporary painting and sculpture, and works by emerging artists. *24 E. 81st St., Upper East Side, 212/879–8200. Closed Sun. and Mon. Subway: 77th St.*

9 *d-3*

VIRIDIAN GALLERY

Viridian specializes in contemporary art, painting, sculpture, and graphics. *52 W. 57th St., Midtown, 212/245–2882. Closed Sun. and Mon. Subway: B, Q to 57th St.*

9 *e-3*

WASHBURN GALLERY

American abstract art of the 1930s and '40s is mixed here with folk art and contemporary paintings, sculpture, and drawings. *41 E. 57th St., Midtown, 212/753–0546. Closed Sun. and Mon. Subway: E, F, N, R to 5th Ave.*

9 *d-3*

ZABRISKIE GALLERY

Early-20th-century American painting, sculpture, and drawing, along with contemporary, large-scale sculpture and photography, have built this gallery a loyal following. *724 5th Ave. (at 56th St.), Midtown, 212/307–7430. Closed Sun. and Mon. Subway: E, F, N, R to 5th Ave.*

soho galleries

In stark contrast to the uptown galleries—many of which might share the "white cube" aesthetic and little else—SoHo remains the neighborhood where art trends, as opposed to century-old art works, trace their roots. With few exceptions (Mary Boone, for one), almost every gallerist wants a space south of Houston, and every artist wants to show there—despite the advent of the chain retailers and West Chelsea.

This wasn't always the case, of course; SoHo has only been SoHo since the late '70s. Before that, it was a scary nether zone of abandoned factories and warehouses that artists colonized (along with nearby Tribeca), often illegally—they needed the light, needed the space. What was once free for the taking, however, now goes for millions, and this is due to the influx of dealers who established galleries that brought crowds that demanded restaurants, Dean & Deluca, and J. Crew. SoHo remains ground zero for contemporary art, but Los Angeles is coming up fast. Avoid galleries that put art in the windows; stick to the places that either look intimidating or inhabit upper floors. Another option is to head down toward Canal Street, where the more serious spaces have set up shop far from the madding crowds.

Crosby Street, which has only a few galleries, has remained largely and intriguingly untouched by the the mallification that has altered the rest of the area; it looks the way all of SoHo looked in the 1970s. A trot down the street's cobblestones is like boarding a time machine, particularly since it terminates to the north at the foot of the only building in New York designed by turn-of-the-century architect Louis Sullivan.

11 *b-4*

A.C.E. GALLERY

This major-league space recently hosted a section of the Guggenheim SoHo's massive Robert Rauschenberg retrospective. It's more serious, perhaps, than some of the other players, but not quite avant-garde—a superb example of the middle ground. *275 Hudson St. (at Spring St.), West Village, 212/255–5599. Closed Mon. and Tues. Subway: A, C to Spring St.; 1, 9 to Canal St.*

11 *b-5*

AC PROJECT ROOM

It's just what it sounds like: an experimental space devoted to newer forms of expression (i.e., not painting)—video, performance, and installation. *15 Renwick St. (west of Hudson St., between Canal and Spring Sts.), 212/219–8275. Closed Sun. and Mon. Subway: C, E to Spring St.; 1, 9 to Canal St.*

11 *d-5*

A.I.R. GALLERY

A.I.R. is a cooperative gallery for women artists. Special events include talks (say, women artists in history) and seminars on the biz of art. *40 Wooster St. (between Broome and Grand Sts.), 212/966–0799. Closed Sun. and Mon. Subway: A, C, E, N, R to Canal St.*

11 *d-5*

BROOKE ALEXANDER

Having weathered the art-market storms of the late '80s and early '90s, Alexander continues to show the cream, if not the cutting edge, of the contemporary scene, as well as prints. *59 Wooster St. (at Broome St.), 212/925–4338. Closed Sun. and Mon. Subway: A, C, E, N, R to Canal St.*

11 *d-5*

BASILICO FINE ARTS

Basilico is one of those terrific little galleries below Spring St. that remain must-sees for even a casual surveyor of the state of SoHo. On display are photography, group work, installations, and some painting. *26 Wooster St. (at Grand St.), 212/966–1831. Closed Sun. and Mon. Subway: A, C, E, N, R to Canal St.*

11 *c-5*

GAVIN BROWN'S ENTERPRISE

The buzz was on this extremely small, SoHo-frontier gallery (it's a good ten-minute walk from the neighborhood center, and has thus avoided the shopping-mall scene) almost from the beginning, when Brown was identified as the Generation X dealer. Of course, he's a bit older now, as is his roster of artists, which includes recent breakout painter Elizabeth Peyton. *558 Broome St. (at Varick St.), 212/966–1831. Closed Sun. and Mon. Subway: 1, 9 to Canal St.; C, E to Spring St.*

11 *e-4*

LEO CASTELLI GALLERY

This warehouse space, run by the éminence grise of the New York art world, shows the equally *grise* champions of pop art: Johns, Kelly, Lichtenstein, Rosenquist, Stella, and Naumann, among others. *420 W. Broadway (between Prince and Spring Sts.), 212/431–5160. Closed Sun. and Mon. Subway: C, E to Spring St.*

11 *d-4*

PETER BLUM

Blum's is an intelligent space with an ongoing passion for contemporary painting. *99 Wooster St. (between Prince and Spring Sts.), 212/343–0441. Closed Sun. and Mon. Subway: Prince St.*

11 *d-4*

TANYA BONAKDAR

Tanya Bonakdar is one of Manhattan's young art turks, along with Gavin Brown and West Chelsea's Matthew Marks. Bonakdar first established a space uptown and staged serious shows with a commercial edge, giving her a Castelli-meets-Gagosian reputation. Her early coup was to bring British enfant terrible Damien Hirst across the pond, but she soon lost him to Gagosian. The move downtown was followed by a retreat into less media-frenzied shows of painting, photography, sculpture, and installation. *130 Prince St. (at Wooster St.), 212/925–8035. Closed Sun. and Mon. Subway: Prince St.*

11 *d-5*

SPENCER BROWNSTONE

Another of those terribly contemporary spaces, Spencer Brownstone specializes in installation, which has lately displaced painting and sculpture as the young artist's métier of choice. 39 Wooster St. (between Broome and Grand Sts.), 212/334–3455. Closed Sun. and Mon. Subway: A, C, E, N, R to Canal St.

11 e-4

CHARLES COWLES

Cowles focuses on contemporary paintings, photography, and sculpture. 420 W. Broadway (between Prince and Spring Sts.), 212/925–3500. Closed Sun. and Mon. Subway: C, E to Spring St.

11 d-4

JAMES DANZIGER

Danziger features old school photography, such as Weegee, alongside more contemporary work. 130 Prince St. (between Wooster St. and W. Broadway), 212/226–0056. Closed Sun. and Mon. Subway: Prince St.

11 e-5

DEITCH PROJECTS

This avant-garde, sometimes downright weird gallery shows a variety of work, from contemporary painting to installation to long-term performance pieces. 76 Grand St. (between Wooster and Greene Sts.), 212/343–7300. Closed Sun. and Mon. Subway: N, R to Canal St.

11 d-5

THE DRAWING CENTER

This far-SoHo stalwart refuses to bow to caprice, preferring instead to mount idiosyncratic shows—a group of artists with similar styles, say—or simply focus on the Center's ostensible purpose, drawing. Perhaps the most celebrated show of the past few years was on the history of tattooing. Rising big-timers, such as Kara Walker, have exhibited large-scale works in the impressive quarters. Hey! Wasn't that Laurie Anderson? 35 Wooster St. (between Grand and Broome Sts.), 212/ 219—2166. Closed Sun. and Mon. Subway: A, C, E, N, R to Canal St.

11 e-6

RONALD FELDMAN FINE ARTS

Feldman has long been renowned as one of SoHo's prime tastemakers, not because he shows the big shots, but because he shows truly significant work by the likes of Ida Applebroog. As at Kent, Basilico, and Fredrich Petzel, scarcely a false note is struck here, so

dive in if the rest of the long march through Art Land has been getting you down. 31 Mercer St. (between Grand and Canal Sts.), 212/226–3232. Closed Sun.; closed Mon., July, and Aug. except by appointment. Subway: N, R to Canal St.

11 e-6

KIM FOSTER

How does the show title "Baby Doll Clown Killers" grab you? If it strikes a chord, duck into this way-south space (practically Canal St.), where the emphasis is on groundbreaking Gen-X artists. 62 Crosby St. (between Spring and Broome Sts.), 212/966–9024. Closed Sun. and Mon. Subway: 6 to Spring St.

11 d-3

GAGOSIAN

Well, what can you say? Twenty years ago the guy was selling posters on the beach in Venice, California. Now, with Arne Glimcher of Pace, he competes for the "Biggest Dealer" title on both coasts. Larry Gagosian's roster, featuring Schnabel, Salle, and Serra, might be starting to look a little too go-go art-star for the splintered market of the '90s, but he continues to add new talent, including Ivory Coast painter Ouattara. Unlike his uptown temple, Gagosian's downtown space is spare—more like a garage than a gallery—which suits it to Serra's enormous iron curves and blocks, Damien Hirst's bisected livestock, and Annette Messager's creepy, gallery-filling installations of yarn, photos, and stuffed varmints. While Pace is the scene for openings that require socialites and bankers, Gagosian is the place to spot David Geffen, rock stars, matinee idols, and the fashion tribe. 136 Wooster St. (between Prince and Houston Sts.), 212/228–2828. Closed Sun. and Mon. Subway: Prince St.; Broadway–Lafayette St.

11 e-4

JAY GORNEY MODERN ART

Another newish establishment with a taste for the young 'uns, Jay Gorney represents Jessica Stockholder, one of the stars of contemporary art. The rule here is the edgy, forward-looking show that garners attention and accolades. 100 Greene St. (between Spring and Prince Sts.), 212/966–8545. Closed Sun. and Mon. Subway: Prince St.; 6 to Spring St.

11 *e-5*

HELLER GALLERY

Contemporary glass sculpture gets its due. *71 Greene St. (between Broome and Spring Sts.), 212/966–5948. Closed Mon. Subway: 6 to Spring St.*

11 *d-4*

NANCY HOFFMAN

Hoffman shows good contemporary art, including works by Carolyn Brady, Don Eddy, Juan Gonzalez, Joseph Raffael, Rafael Ferrer, Howard Buchwald, John Okulick, and Alan Siegel. *429 W. Broadway (between Spring and Prince Sts.), 212/966–6676. Closed Sun. and Mon. Subway: C, E to Spring St.*

11 *d-5*

PAUL KASMIN

This lively, contemporary space keeps an eye on traditional media, mainly painting and drawing. *74 Grand St. (at Wooster St.), 212/219–3219. Closed Sun. and Mon. Subway: A, C, E, N, R to Canal St.*

11 *f-6*

BRONWYN KEENAN

One of Manhattan's newest gallerists, Keenan features edgy, younger artists on their way up, working in a variety of media. The space is trendy, but intimate—a nice way of saying that it's very small. *3 Crosby St. (at Howard St.), 212/431–5083. Closed Sun. and Mon. Subway: N, R, 6 to Canal St.*

11 *e-4*

JUNE KELLY

June Kelly's taste is solid, with a focus on a multicultural roster. *591 Broadway (between Prince and Houston Sts.), 212/226–1660. Closed Sun. and Mon. Subway: Prince St.; Broadway–Lafayette St.*

11 *e-5*

SEAN KELLY

Sean Kelly's stable includes such luminaries as Julie Roberts, Cathy de Monchaux, Lorna Simpson, and Ann Hamilton. Detect a theme? This is one of New York's most important spaces for women artists. *43 Mercer St. (between Grand and Broome Sts.), 212/343–2405. Closed Sun. and Mon. Subway: N, R to Canal St.*

11 *e-4*

KENT GALLERY

This tidy, two level space is squeezed between SoHo and Little Italy, in a sliver of neighborhood just shy of the mythical NoHo in flavor. Kent shows mainly "smart" work, from such artists as Vivienne Koorland and Richard Artschwager. It's not a rock-the-world gallery, but it can be relied on show after show to mount lively, intelligent work that steers clear of obvious trends. *67 Prince St. (between Broadway and Lafayette Sts.), 212/966–4500. Closed Sun. and Mon. Subway: Prince St.; Broadway–Lafayette St.*

11 *e-4*

PHYLLIS KIND GALLERY

Kind specializes in contemporary American, Soviet, and European art, as well as 20th-century American and European art brut. *136 Greene St. (between Prince and Houston Sts.), 212/925–1200. Closed Sun. and Mon.; closed Aug. except by appointment. Subway: Prince St.; Broadway–Lafayette St.*

11 *d-5*

CHUCK LEVITAN GALLERY

Levitan is a haven for contemporary American paintings and sculpture, featuring such artists as Will Barnet, Romare Bearden, and Marisol. *42 Grand St. (between W. Broadway and Thompson St.), 212/966–2782. Closed Sun. and Mon.; closed July and Aug. Subway: A, C, E to Canal St.*

11 *d-4*

LOUIS K. MEISEL

Photorealist art by Audrey Flack, Charles Bell, and Hilo Chen covers the walls at this reliable space. *141 Prince St. (between Wooster St. and W. Broadway), 212/677–1340. Closed Sun. and Mon. Subway: Prince St.*

11 *d-4*

LUHRING AUGUSTINE GALLERY

Luhring shows sculpture, drawings, prints, and paintings by modern and contemporary American and European artists. This is one of SoHo's standout galleries, an essential space on any tour of the neighborhood's highlights; the casual visitor is bound to find something suitably arty yet not unsuitably bizarre. *130 Prince St. (between Wooster St. and W. Broadway), 212/219–9600. Closed Sun. and Mon. Subway: Prince St.*

11 *e-5*

JOHN MCENROE

The former tennis champion is trying to make the shift to a more buttoned-up profession, with some success; he's put together some superb little shows since opening a few years ago. *41 Greene St. (between Grand and Broome Sts.), 212/ 219–0395. Closed Sept.–May, Sun. and Mon.; June–Aug., weekends. Subway: A, C, E, N, R to Canal St.*

11 *e-4*

PLEIADES GALLERY

Figurative, abstract, and experimental art have their way here. *591 Broadway (between Prince and Houston Sts.), 212/ 274–8825. Closed Sun. and Mon. Subway: Prince St.; Broadway–Lafayette St.*

11 *e-5*

P.P.O.W.

Contemporary international artists have the spotlight here. *476 Broome St. (between Greene and Wooster Sts.), 212/ 941–8642. Closed Sun. and Mon. Subway: A, C, E, N, R to Canal St.*

11 *d-4*

PRINCE ST. GALLERY

This gallery shows contemporary expressionist and representational paintings, sculpture, and drawings; nothing anyone is going to be talking about in café society. *121 Wooster St. (between Spring and Prince Sts.), 212/ 226–9402. Closed Sun. and Mon. Subway: Prince St.; Spring St.*

11 *d-4*

ANDREA ROSEN

With the likes of Sean Landers and John Cullen on her heavily Gen-X roster, Rosen has claimed territory in areas of the gallery business that tend to set the critics frothing. Her closest competition is Gavin Brown, who has more dignified ideas about what to show. If you dig surveillance videos, drop in and get spied on for Julia Sherr's. *130 Prince St. (between Wooster St. and W. Broadway), 212/941– 0203. Closed Sun. and Mon. Subway: Prince St.*

11 *d-4*

TONY SHAFRAZI GALLERY

This huge space is presided over by an '80s style megadealer who, after he defaced Picasso's *Guernica* by spray-painting an obscure slogan on the canvas, went on to show graffiti artists such as Kenny Scharf and Jean-Michel Basquiat. *119 Wooster St. (between Spring and Prince Sts.), 212/274–9300. Closed Sun. and Mon. Subway: Prince St.; Spring St.*

11 *d-4*

SONNABEND GALLERY

This respectable, thoughtful establishment specializes in contemporary photography, but also mounts shows by such seminal figures as conceptualist John Baldassari. *420 W. Broadway (between Prince and Spring Sts.), 212/ 966–6160. Closed Sun. and Mon. Subway: C, E to Spring St.*

11 *e-4*

SPERONE WESTWATER

Westwater's bent is European and American contemporary art. *142 Greene St. (between Prince and Houston Sts.), 212/431–3685. Closed Sun. and Mon. Subway: Prince St.; Broadway–Lafayette St.*

11 *e-4*

EDWARD THORP

Contemporary American painting and sculpture get top billing here. *103 Prince St. (between Greene and Mercer Sts.), 212/431–6880. Closed Sun. and Mon. Subway: N, R to Prince St.*

11 *f-5*

THREAD WAXING SPACE

So called because it used to be a thread factory, this exceptional space features installation and performance art. It's a slightly more austere alternative to Exit Art *(see Alternative Exhibition Spaces, below)*. *476 Broadway (between Grand and Broome Sts.), 212/966–9520. Closed Sun. and Mon. Subway: N, R to Canal St.; 6 to Spring St.*

11 *d-4*

VORPAL SOHO

Vorpal SoHo can claim the world's largest collection of M. C. Escher prints; other holdings include contemporary paintings, sculpture, and prints. *459 W. Broadway (between Prince and Houston Sts.), 212/777–3939. Closed Sun. and Mon. Subway: Prince St.; Spring St.*

11 *d-4*

WARD NASSE GALLERY

This cooperative gallery displays all media. *178 Prince St. (between Thompson and Sullivan Sts.), 212/925–6951. Closed Sun. and Mon. Subway: C, E to Spring St.*

11 *e-5*

DAVID ZWIRNER

Zwirner is another far-SoHo gallery that's snatching the bright young things up. In this case, the star is installationist Jason Rhoades, whose postmodern gatherings of brightly colored junk and everyday objects, arranged into Rube Goldbergesque clusters that fill entire spaces, have made him a favorite of the *Parkett*-magazine crowd. *43 Greene St. (between Grand and Broome Sts.), 212/966–9074. Closed Sun. and Mon. Subway: A, C, E, N, R to Canal St.*

west chelsea galleries

West Chelsea is Manhattan's newest playland for art types, a cluster of enormous galleries—many hewn from former taxi garages—west of 10th Avenue between 22nd and 26th Sts. The real action is here on Friday nights. No one could have known that West Chelsea would work out so well; even a quick glance at the fashion-plate mobs trekking across town reveals how hip the scene has become. The transformation was rapid, and some critics argue that the neighborhood's new galleries are more about architecture and ego than the art inside. Sour grapes? Maybe, but at least now we have a few refueling options beyond the Empire Diner.

To reach this new frontier, take the A, C, or E train to 23rd St. and 8th Avenue.

9 *b-8*

CLEMENTINE

This small, smartly managed space has mounted a dozen fine exhibits of painting and photography since opening in late 1996. A gallery specialty is the two-person show, with each artist getting one side of the space. *526 W. 21st St., 212/255–1105. Closed Sun. and Mon.*

9 *b-8*

PAULA COOPER

Gagosian's former neighbor in SoHo gave it all up for the desolate West Side, but photographer and bête noire Andres Serrano has followed her; so at the very least, those in search of an illicit burst of porno-religious imagery will flock to the openings. With any luck her pioneering spirit will be rewarded, and she'll trump the big boys in the end. *534 W. 21st St., 212/255–1105. Closed Sun. and Mon.*

9 *b-7*

BARBARA GLADSTONE GALLERY

Gladstone has on her commendable roster one of the most important artists currently working, Russian conceptualist Ilya Kabakov. *515 W. 24th St., 212/206–9300. Closed Sun. and Mon.*

9 *b-8*

PAT HEARN

Hearn emerged from the style wars of the '80s such a beloved figure that her current bout with liver cancer has galvanized the support of the entire art world, which established the Pat Hearn Fund so the gallerist can get a liver transplant (her insurance won't pay) and continue to show incisive contemporary work. *530 W. 22nd St., 212/727–7366. Closed Sun. and Mon.*

9 *b-7*

MATTHEW MARKS

Same telephone number, two vast and formidable spaces only two blocks apart. Marks was the first major gallerist to make the move west, and he can really be credited with setting the architectural tone for the area: big. His 24th Street space could shelter a blimp. He has cutting-edge taste, as well as the savvy to show older artists, such as arch-abstractionist Ellsworth Kelly, whose massive orange-and-blue curves and circles look right at home in Marks's white caverns. *523 W. 24th St., 212/243–0047. Closed Sun. and Mon.*

9 *b-8*
522 W. 22nd St.

9 *b-7*

GREENE NAFTALI

Of West Chelsea's smaller galleries, this one gets the most ink, for its zany contemporary-art installations. *526 W. 26th St., 212/463–7770. Closed Sun. and Mon.*

9 *b-7*

METRO PICTURES

Formerly on the northern edge of SoHo, Metro Pictures joined the exodus and opened a huge and spectacular space out west. Major artists represented include photographer Cindy Sherman and painter Carroll Dunham. *519 W. 24th St., 212/337–0070. Closed Sun. and Mon.*

9 *b-8*

ANNINA NOSEI

Life springs eternal for the gallerist who gave the late Jean-Michel Basquiat a basement in which to crank out paintings, and signed on as his first dealer. Now in West Chelsea, Nosei continues to champion new painting. *530 W. 22nd St., 212/741–8695. Closed Sun. and Mon.*

9 *b-8*

MAX PROTECH

Groovy name, huh? This brand new space sponsors the frisky, youthful work that has come to define this 'hood. *511 W. 22nd St., 212/633–6999. Closed Sun. and Mon.*

9 *b-8*

303

This medium-size, street-level space has defined itself with medium-size shows by up-and-coming photographers and installationists. *525 W. 22nd St., 212/255–1121. Closed Sun. and Mon.*

9 *b-8*

JOHN WEBER GALLERY

Weber shows European and contemporary artists, with an emphasis on minimalist and conceptual art. *529 W. 20th St., 212/691–5711. Closed Sun. and Mon.*

9 *b-7*

WESSEL & O'CONNOR

This interesting new space specializes in photography, sculpture, and installation. *242 W. 26th St., 212/242–8811. Closed Sun. and Mon.*

eastern art

7 *e-6*

ART OF THE PAST

The collection features art from Nepal, Tibet, and India. *1242 Madison Ave. (at 89th St.), Upper East Side, 212/860–7070. Closed Sun. Subway: 86th St.*

7 *e-8*

E & J FRANKEL LTD

E & J Frankel specializes in Oriental art from China (porcelain and jade from the Shang Dynasty through the 1840s) and Japan (screen paintings and furnishings from all periods). *1040 Madison Ave. (at 79th St.), Upper East Side, 212/879–5733. Closed Sun. Subway: 77th St.*

11 *e-4*

JACQUES CARCANAGUES

Carcanagues features ethnographic items from Afghanistan, Central America, Guatemala, India, Thailand, Indonesia, Japan, Korea, the Philippines, and more. *106 Spring St. (between Greene and Mercer Sts.), SoHo, 212/925–8110. Subway: Prince St.; 6 to Spring St.*

7 *e-7*

MERTON SIMPSON GALLERY

Most of this art is from Africa, but Oceanic and American Indian works are mixed in. *1063 Madison Ave. (at 81st St.), Upper East Side, 212/988–6290. Closed Sun. and Mon. Subway: 77th St.*

9 *e-3*

PACE PRIMITIVE

This branch of the Pace tree features antique African masks and sculpture, and Himalayan masks. *32 E. 57th St., Midtown, 212/421–3688. Closed Sun. and Mon. Subway: 57th St.*

9 *e-3*

RALPH M. CHAIT GALLERIES, INC.

Chait shows top-quality Chinese art, including export silver; porcelain; and pottery from the Neolithic period to 1800. *12 E. 56th St., Midtown, 212/758–0937. Closed Sun. Subway: E, F, N, R to 5th Ave.*

9 *e-3*

RONIN GALLERY

Ronin has a large selection of 17th- to 20th-century Japanese woodblock prints, as well as *netsuke*. *605 Madison Ave. (between 57th and 58th Sts.), Midtown, 212/688–0188. Closed Sun. Subway: 59th St.*

prints & original posters

9 *d-3*

ASSOCIATED AMERICAN ARTISTS (A.A.A.)

America's largest print dealer has prints from the 16th–20th centuries and original etchings, lithographs, woodcuts, and serigraphs from the 15th–20th centuries. *20 W. 57th St., Midtown, 212/399–5510. Closed Sun. and Mon.; also closed June–Aug., weekends. Subway: B, Q to 57th St.*

11 d-5
BROOKE ALEXANDER EDITIONS
These contemporary prints, multiples, and illustrated books come from such heavyweights as Richard Artschwager, Richard Bosman, Jasper Johns, Claes Oldenburg, and Andy Warhol. *59 Wooster St. (at Broome St.), SoHo, 212/925–2070. Closed Sun. and Mon. Subway: A, C, E, N, R to Canal St.*

7 e-8
DAVID TUNICK, INC.
Tunick carries fine old masters, modern prints, and drawings by such as Rembrandt, Dürer, Tiepolo, Bruegel, and Canaletto; 19th-century prints by Bonnard, Goya, Cezanne, Degas, Delacroix, Gericault, Manet, Toulouse-Lautrec, and Pissarro; and 20th-century works by Picasso, Matisse, Braque, Whistler, Bellows, and Villon. *21 E. 81st St., Upper East Side, 212/570–0090. Closed weekends; appointment advised. Subway: 77th St.*

9 e-3
FITCH-FEBVREL GALLERY
Fitch-Febvrel specializes in fine prints and drawings from the 19th and 20th centuries. *5 E. 57th St., Midtown, 212/688–8522. Closed Sun. and Mon.; closed Aug. except by appointment. Subway: E, F, N, R to 5th Ave.*

7 e-8
ISSELBACHER GALLERY
This uptowner features late-19th- and 20th-century prints, woodcuts, and etchings, including works by Beckmann, Bonnard, Chagall, Klee, Matisse, Miró, Picasso, Toulouse Lautrec, and Vuillard. *41 E. 78th St., Upper East Side, 212/472–1766. Closed Sun. and Mon. Subway: 77th St.*

9 e-3
JANE KAHAN GALLERY
Kahan has a large collection of Chagall prints, as well as works by Appel, Calder, Delaunay, Dubuffet, Francis, Lichtenstein, Matisse, Matta, Miró, Picasso, Pissarro, and Stella. *922 Madison Ave. (at 73rd St.), Upper East Side, 212/744–1490. Closed Sun. Subway: 77th St.*

7 e-7
JAPAN GALLERY
Here the focus is Japanese woodblock prints from the 18th century to the present. *1210 Lexington Ave. (at 82nd St.), Upper East Side, 212/288–2241. Closed Sun. and Mon. Subway: 86th St.*

9 d-2
MARGO FEIDEN GALLERIES
Feiden has a thorough collection of Al Hirschfield's drawings, watercolors, lithographs, and etchings. *699 Madison Ave. (between 62nd and 63rd Sts.), Upper East Side, 212/223–4230. Subway: 68th St./Hunter College.*

11 e-4
MULTIPLE IMPRESSIONS, LTD.
These contemporary American and European original graphics come from artists like Kozo, Andre Masson, Johnny Friedlaender, Harold Altman, Elizabeth Schippert, and Mikio Watanabe. The gallery mounts several solo shows annually. *128 Spring St. (at Greene St.), SoHo, 212/925–1313. Subway: Spring St.*

9 f-7
OLD PRINT SHOP
This is the place to retreat for original prints of Audubon, Currier & Ives, 18th-century maps, and nauticalia, as well as some American paintings. *150 Lexington Ave. (between 29th and 30th Sts.), Murray Hill, 212/683–3950. Closed Sun. and Mon.; June–Aug., closed weekends. Subway: 28th St.*

9 e-3
PACE MASTER PRINTS
This substantial collection includes 15th-century old-master prints and drawings, and 19th- and 20th-century master prints by Canaletto, Dürer, Goya, Kandinsky, Matisse, Miró, Picasso, Piranesi, Rembrandt, Tiepolo, Toulouse-Lautrec, and Whistler. It's probably the finest print annex (of a major gallery) in town. *32 E. 57th St., Midtown, 212/421–3688. Closed Sun. and Mon. Subway: 57th St.*

9 e-3
PACE PRINTS
Stop off on Pace's 3rd floor for contemporary prints and multiples. *32 E. 57th St., Midtown, 212/421–3237. Closed Sun. and Mon.; summer, closed weekends. Subway: 57th St.*

7 *e-8*

SINDIN GALLERIES

Sindin shows 20th-century master graphics, drawings, etchings, and sculpture from Botero, Miró, Motherwell, Picasso, Stella, and Zuñiga. *1035 Madison Ave. (at 79th St.), Upper East Side, 212/288–7902. Closed Sun. and Mon. Subway: 77th St.*

9 *e-3*

WILLIAM H. SCHAB GALLERY

Here hang modern and old master prints, lithographs, woodcuts, engravings, and etchings by Dürer, Rembrandt, and Goya, and old master drawings by Tiepolo and Tintoretto. *11 E. 57th St., Midtown, 212/758–0327. Closed Sun. and Mon. Subway: E, F, N, R to 5th Ave.*

9 *e-3*

ROBERT MILLER

Miller shows both contemporary American art and 19th- and 20th-century photography by such greats as Berenice Abbott, Diane Arbus, Jean-Michel Basquiat, Walker Evans, Man Ray, Robert Mapplethorpe, David McDermott and Peter McGough, Alice Neel, and Bruce Weber. *41 E. 57th St., Midtown, 212/980–5454. Closed Sun. and Mon.; closed Aug. except by appointment. Subway: E, F, N, R to 5th Ave.*

11 *e-4*

WITKIN GALLERY

Witkin concentrates on photographs and photographic books, including out of print photo literature. The vintage and contemporary prints include work by Andre Kertesz, Evelyn Hofer, Joel Meyerowitz, George Tice, and Jerry Uelsmann. *415 W. Broadway (between Spring and Prince Sts.), SoHo, 212/925–5510. Closed Sun. and Mon. Subway: C, E to Spring St.; Prince St.*

alternative exhibition spaces

Some in the hinterlands of Williamsburg, Brooklyn, some a little closer to art's traditional center, these spaces draw devoted art junkies with the very newest of the new, and sometimes the very strangest of the strange. In contrast to the scenes at SoHo or West Chelsea openings—and, frankly, about as far from Midtown and the Upper East Side as you can get—fashion and money are not the key concepts here. The sites can be difficult to find, the intrepid visitors a bit shaggy, but many art world veterans figure that these galleries and "complexes" are gestational holds for the future of American art.

3 *d-3*

P.S. 1 CONTEMPORARY ART CENTER

After years of renovation this seminal alternative space reopened amid much hoopla in late 1997. A former public school, this wonderful old Romanesque building is the world's largest space for showing art, providing curators with vast galleries plus an enormous outdoor space. The emphasis is on an ever-changing cast of innovative new artists, plus old hands at the experimental game. It's well worth the trip to Queens, a mere hop, skip, and jump across the East River. *22–25 Jackson Ave., Long Island City, Queens, 718/784–2084. Closed Mon. and Tues. Subway: E, F to 23rd St./Ely Ave.*

11 *e-4*

EXIT ART/ THE FIRST WORLD

This large SoHo space is atypical in that it encourages hanging out—in the gift shop or the café—rather than quick visits. The shows, mounted by freelance curators as well as staff, tend to focus on social concerns, so the place has a late '60s–early '90s feel that counters the cash chase currently raging elsewhere. Recent installations have included a clever show of artists invited to live and work in the space for a few weeks. *548 Broadway (between Spring and Prince Sts.), SoHo, 212/966–7745. Closed Mon. Subway: Prince St.*

ART MUSEUMS

Some landmark buildings and mansions have their own art collections and period furnishings; *see* Historic Buildings & Areas, *below*.

6 *d-5*

AMERICAN ACADEMY OF ARTS & LETTERS

Although the Academy is not usually open to the public, its doors are thrown open for three annual exhibitions, featuring the work of American sculptors, painters, architects, composers, and authors. For more on the Academy's attractive Italian Renaissance surroundings, *see* Audubon Terrace Historic District *in* Historic Buildings & Areas, *below. 633 W. 155th St. (Audubon Terrace Museum Complex), Washington Heights, 212/368–5900. Call for exhibit schedules and hours. Subway: 157th St.; 155th St.*

9 d-3
AMERICAN CRAFT MUSEUM
Right across the street from the Museum of Modern Art, the thoughtful exhibitions at the American Craft Museum raise crafts—often taken for granted—to the level of high art. The museum's changing exhibits feature quilts, handblown glass, pottery, basketry, woodwork, and hand-woven textiles. Classes, workshops, and lectures bring expert craftspeople to New York and give novices a chance to weave, mold, carve, and create. *40 W. 53rd St., Midtown, 212/956–6047. Admission: $5, free Thurs. evenings; $2.50 students and seniors, free children under 12. Open Tues., Wed., and Fri.–Sun. 10–6; Thurs. 10–8. Subway: E, F to 5th Ave.*

9 e-1
AMERICAS SOCIETY
In a mansion that once housed the Soviet Union's mission to the U.N., this small art gallery mounts exhibits from South and Central America, the Caribbean, and Canada, covering everything from pre-Columbian art to contemporary painting, sculpture, photography, and the decorative arts. *680 Park Ave. (at 68th St.), Upper East Side, 212/249–8950. Suggested contribution: $3. Open Tues.–Sun. noon–6. Subway: 68th St./Hunter College.*

9 e-1
ASIA SOCIETY
A nonprofit educational organization, the Asia Society regularly sponsors lectures, films, dance, and musical programs in addition to its art exhibits, which have included Japanese painting, Korean ceramics, South Asian stone and bronze sculpture, and artworks from China, Nepal, India, Pakistan, and Afghanistan. *725 Park Ave. (at 70th St.), Upper East Side, 212/288–6400. Admission: $3. Open Tues.–Sat. 11–6, Sun. noon–5. Subway: 68th St./Hunter College.*

6 f-4
BRONX MUSEUM OF THE ARTS
The permanent collection contains 20th-century works on paper by African, African-American, Latin, Latin American, South Asian, and Asian-American artists. Rotating exhibits feature contemporary works by international artists and often focus on the cultural and social history of the Bronx. *1040 Grand Concourse (at 165th St.), Bronx, 718/681–6000. Suggested donation: $3. Open Wed. 3–9, Thurs. and Fri. 10–5, weekends 1–6. Subway: 167th St.*

4 e-1
BROOKLYN MUSEUM OF ART
With approximately 1½ million pieces, the Brooklyn Museum ranks as the second-largest art museum in New York City. Its temporary exhibits are often among the city's best, and several of its permanent exhibits are world-renowned. Most notable are the Egyptian Art Collection, with its hieroglyphic-covered sarcophagi; the American Painting and Sculpture Galleries, with works by Georgia O'Keeffe, Mark Rothko, Winslow Homer, Gilbert Stuart, and John Singer Sargent; and the outdoor Sculpture Garden, with 19th-century architectural ornaments, including fragments of the original Pennsylvania Station. *200 Eastern Pkwy. (at Washington Ave.), Brooklyn, 718/638–5000. Suggested contribution: $4. Open Wed.–Fri. 10–5, Sat. 11–9, Sun. 11–6. Subway: Eastern Pkwy./Brooklyn Museum.*

9 e-2
CHINA HOUSE GALLERY
Housed in a redbrick mansion flanked by two stone lions, the China Institute's gallery features changing exhibits of traditional and contemporary Chinese art. *125 E. 65th St., Upper East Side, 212/744–8181. Suggested contribution: $5. Open Mon. and Wed.–Sat. 10–5, Tues. 10–8. Subway: 68th St./Hunter College.*

5 b-7
THE CLOISTERS
One of New York's artistic and spiritual treasures, the Cloisters is situated high on a hill in Upper Manhattan's wooded Ft. Tryon Park, overlooking the Hudson River. The castlelike structure incorporates parts of five different cloisters from medieval monasteries, including a Romanesque chapel and a 12th-century Spanish apse. A branch of the Metropolitan Museum of Art, the Cloisters' collection of medieval artwork includes the famed Unicorn Tapestries from the 15th

and 16th centuries, illuminated manuscripts, and the Chalice of Antioch. Outside, three enchanting gardens shelter more than 250 species of plants similar to those grown during the Middle Ages, including herbs and medicinals. *Ft. Tryon Park (Riverside Dr. and Broadway from 192nd to Dyckman Sts.), Inwood, 212/923–3700. Suggested contribution: $8. Open Mar.–Oct., Tues.–Sun. 9:30–5:15; Nov.–Feb., Tues.–Sun. 9:30–4:45. Subway: 190th St.*

7 *e-6*

COOPER-HEWITT NATIONAL DESIGN MUSEUM

Beautifully restored, this 64-room 5th Avenue mansion—once the home of industrialist Andrew Carnegie—now houses the Smithsonian Institution's design and decorative arts collections. With over 300,000 objects spanning 3,000 years of design history, the museum's collections include ceramics, textiles, drawings, prints, glass, furniture, metalwork, book papers, woodwork, wall coverings, embroidery, and lace. The collection of drawings and prints is America's largest. In summer 1998 the museum will expand into two neighboring town houses and gain a new home for much of its permanent collection. *2 E. 91st St., Upper East Side, 212/849–8300. Admission: $3, free Tues. 5–9. Open Tues. 10–9, Wed.–Sat. 10–5, Sun. noon–5. Subway: 4, 5, 6 to 86th St.*

9 *e-4*

DAHESH MUSEUM

While the Whitney, MOMA, and Guggenheim vie for the latest contemporary artworks, the Dahesh revels in tradition. Founded in 1995 by Lebanese art-collector Salim Moussa Achi, this free Midtown museum is devoted to 19th-century European "academic" art, most notably works by Bouguereau and Gérôme, who taught an entire generation of artists, including the Impressionists. Shows are clever and highly informative, often reintroducing works by artists once famed, now forgotten. *601 5th Ave. (between 48th and 49th Sts.), Midtown, 212/759–0606. Open Tues.–Sat. 11–6. Subway: E, F to 5th Ave.*

9 *d-4*

THE EQUITABLE GALLERY

This free, eclectic museum in the lobby of the Equitable Building in Midtown has changing exhibits on everything from folk to fine art. Recent offerings have included exhibits on Colonial American furniture, Haitian sculpture and painting, and the stateside photography of Henri Cartier-Bresson. *787 7th Ave. (at 51st St.), Midtown, 212/554–4818. Open weekdays 11–6, Sat. noon–5. Subway: 49th St.; 1, 9 to 50th St.*

9 *e-1*

FRICK COLLECTION

Don't miss this tranquil jewel. Coke-and-steel baron Henry Clay Frick's former mansion houses masterpieces of 14th- to 19th-century European painting, including pieces by Rembrandt, Vermeer, Gainsborough, Turner, Titian, Goya, and El Greco; exquisite 18th-century French and Italian Renaissance furniture; Oriental porcelain; and Limoges enamel. The intimate interior is wonderfully illuminated by overhead skylights, and there's a lovely outdoor garden court with a splashing fountain. *1 E. 70th St., Upper East Side, 212/288–0700. Admission: $5, no children under 10. Open Tues.–Sat. 10–6, Sun. 1–6. Subway: 68th St./Hunter College.*

7 *e-7*

GOETHE HOUSE NEW YORK

Smack in the middle of Museum Mile, in a 1907 Beaux Arts town house, Goethe House promotes German art, film, and culture. The gallery features changing exhibits of contemporary German art. *1014 5th Ave. (between 82nd and 83rd Sts.), Upper East Side, 212/439–8700. Open Tues. and Thurs. 10–7, Wed. and Fri. 10–5, Sat. noon–5. Subway: 4, 5, 6 to 86th St.*

7 *e-6*

GUGGENHEIM MUSEUM

Frank Lloyd Wright's building (*see* Architecture, *above*) provides a unique setting for modern art, from impressionism to the present day. Holdings include a renowned Kandinsky collection, Paul Klee, Picasso, early impressionism, minimalism, and an outdoor sculpture terrace. A major restoration and expansion, completed in 1992, added a 10-story tower annex, which reflects Wright's original conception for the museum and provides more space for copper magnate Solomon Guggenheim's collection. *1071 5th Ave. (at 89th St.), Upper East Side, 212/423–3500. Admission: $10 adults, $7 students and seniors, free children under 12; pay what you wish Fri. 6–8. Open*

Sun.–Wed. 10–6, Fri. and Sat. 10–8. Subway: 4, 5, 6 to 86th St.

11 e-4

GUGGENHEIM MUSEUM SOHO

Perhaps best known for its enormous museum shop, featuring giant, build-'em-yourself mobiles, the Guggenheim's downtown space focuses primarily on multimedia installations, such as video art by Nam June Paik and installations by Jenny Holzer. Such works are flattered by this landmark building, the interiors of which were redesigned by architect Arata Isokaki for the museum's 1992 opening. *575 Broadway (at Prince St.), SoHo, 212/423–3500. Admission: $8 adults, $5 students and seniors, free children under 12. Open Wed.–Fri., Sun. 11–6, Sat. 11–8. Subway: Prince St.; Broadway–Lafayette St.*

6 d-5

HISPANIC SOCIETY OF AMERICA

The Hispanic Society displays Spanish and Portuguese paintings, sculptures, and decorative artworks from prehistoric times to the present, including pieces by Goya, El Greco, and Velazquez. For more on the handsome surroundings, *see* Audubon Terrace Historic District *in* Historic Buildings and Areas, *below. Broadway and 155th St. (Audubon Terrace Museum Complex), Morningside Heights, 212/926–2234. Open Tues.–Sat. 10–4:30, Sun. 1–4. Subway: 157th St.; 155th St.*

7 e-6

INTERNATIONAL CENTER OF PHOTOGRAPHY (ICP)

Founded in 1974 in a lovely Georgian-revival building, ICP is devoted exclusively to photography as both an art and a medium of communication. The permanent collection contains works by important 20th-century photographers including Robert Capa, W. Eugene Smith, Henri Cartier-Bresson, Yousuf Karsh, Man Ray, Lee Miller, Gordon Parks, Roman Vishniac, and Ernst Haas. Temporary exhibitions focus on individual photographers and themes. *1130 5th Ave. (at 94th St.), Upper East Side, 212/860–1777. Admission: $4 adults, $2.50 students and seniors; pay what you wish Tues. 6–8. Open Tues. 11–8, Wed.–Sun. 11–6. Subway: 96th St.*

9 d-5

ICP MIDTOWN

A smaller branch of the original, ICP Midtown presents several photography shows annually, including selections from the extensive permanent collection. *1133 6th Ave. (at 43rd St.), Midtown, 212/860–1777. Admission: $4, $2.50 students and seniors; pay what you wish Tues. 6–8. Open Tues. 11–8, Wed.–Sun. 11–6. Subway: B, D, F, Q to 42nd St.*

8 a-8

ISAMU NOGUCHI GARDEN MUSEUM

A large, open-air garden and two floors of gallery space hold over 250 pieces by the renowned American-born sculptor Isamu Noguchi. Originally a photoengraving plant, the building was converted by Noguchi himself, and now houses his sculptures (in stone, bronze, wood, clay, and steel), models, drawings, and even stage sets for dances by Martha Graham. *32–37 Vernon Boulevard (at 33rd Rd.), Long Island City, Queens, 718/204–7088. Suggested contribution: $4. Open Apr.–Nov., Wed.–Fri. 10–5, weekends 11–6. Weekend shuttle bus service leaves from the Asia Society (see above) 11:30–3:30 every hour on the half-hour; $5. Subway: N to Broadway.*

1 b-2

JACQUES MARCHAIS MUSEUM OF TIBETAN ART

This replica of a Buddhist temple houses a major collection of Tibetan art, including bronzes, paintings, scrolls, and ritual objects. Surrounded by lovely gardens, it's the perfect spot for a day of contemplation. *338 Lighthouse Ave. (off Richmond Rd.), Staten Island, 718/987–3500. Admission: $3 adults, $1 children. Open Apr.–Nov., Wed.–Sun. 1–5; shorter hrs winter. Take S74 bus from Staten Island Ferry terminal to Lighthouse Ave. and walk a quarter of a mile up Lighthouse Hill.*

9 f-4

JAPAN SOCIETY GALLERY

This spare and serene space displays ancient as well as contemporary Japanese art and sponsors films, performances, and lectures. *333 E. 47th Street, Midtown, 212/832–1155. Suggested contribution: $3. Open Tues.–Sun. 11–5. Subway: 47th St.*

7 *e-6*

THE JEWISH MUSEUM

Housed in a French Gothic mansion facing Central Park, the Jewish Museum is one of the largest and most beautiful collections of Judaica in the country. Ceremonial objects, paintings, prints, drawings, sculpture, manuscripts, photographs, videos, and antiquities trace the development of Jewish culture over the past 4,000 years. *1109 5th Ave. (at 92nd St.), Upper East Side, 212/423–3230. Admission: $7 adults, $5 students and seniors, free children under 12; pay what you wish Tues. 5–8. Open Sun., Mon., Wed., and Thurs. 11–5:45, Tues. 11–8. Subway: 96th St.*

7 *e-7*

METROPOLITAN MUSEUM OF ART

One of the world's great museums, the Met is the largest museum in the Western Hemisphere, with 1.6 million square ft of gallery space and a permanent collection of over 2 million works of art. Covering 5,000 years of cultural history, the Met is so enormous that it's hard to know where to begin. The galleries for **classical art** contain Greek and Roman statuary, perfectly preserved Grecian urns, and rare Roman wall paintings excavated from the lava of Mt. Vesuvius. The renowned **Egyptian collection** centers around the Temple of Dendur, an entire Roman-period temple transported to the museum from Egypt and housed in its own, specially built atrium. A stunning collection of **European paintings** features 30 paintings by Monet, 17 by Cézanne, seven by Vermeer (more than any other museum in the world), and works by Gauguin, Van Gogh, Degas, El Greco, Rembrandt, and Rubens. Monumental Chinese Buddhas, Ming Dynasty furniture, and the re-creation of a Ming scholar's garden are highlights of the **Asian galleries.** Three floors of 20th-century art, centering on Picasso's portrait of Gertrude Stein, make up the **Lila Acheson Wallace Wing.** The **American Wing** contains 25 period rooms, and paintings by Thomas Cole and Winslow Homer. The **arms and armor** collection holds over 14,000 weapons and a cavernous hall of knights in helmets and chain mail, mounted on their steeds and ready for jousting. Moral of the story: don't try to pop in for a quick peek. *5th Ave. at 82nd St., Upper East Side, 212/535–7710. Suggested contribution: $8 adults, $4 students and seniors, free children under 12. Open Sun. and Tues.–Thurs. 9:30–5:15, Fri. and Sat. 9:30–8:45. For sculpture garden, see Viewpoints, below. Subway: 4, 5, 6 to 86th St.*

7 *e-4*

EL MUSEO DEL BARRIO

The art and culture of Latin America speak here through artifacts, photographs, and paintings. The permanent collection of 8,000 objects contains several pre-Columbian artifacts and is particularly strong on Puerto Rican art, featuring numerous Puerto Rican *santos*. *1230 5th Ave. (at 104th St.), East Harlem, 212/831–7272. Suggested contribution: $4 adults, $2 students and seniors, free children under 12. Open Wed. and Fri.–Sun. 11–5, Thurs. 11–8. Subway: 103rd St.*

9 *c-2*

MUSEUM OF AMERICAN FOLK ART

Like the American Craft Museum (*see above*), the Museum of American Folk Art brings crafts, pastimes, and commercial work by traditional American artisans to a new level. Changing exhibitions feature folk paintings, textiles (especially quilts), and sculpture (often in the form of weather vanes) from colonial times to the present. *2 Lincoln Sq. (Columbus Ave. between 65th and 66th Sts.), Upper West Side, 212/595–9533. Suggested contribution: $3. Open Tues.–Sun. 11:30–7:30. Subway: 66th St./Lincoln Center.*

9 *e-2*

MUSEUM OF AMERICAN ILLUSTRATION

This specialized museum was founded in 1901 to "promote and stimulate interest in the art of illustration, past, present, and future." The Society of Illustrators assembles highly eclectic monthly exhibitions, focusing on everything from *New Yorker* cartoons and Norman Rockwell paintings to pictures from *Mad* magazine and children's books. *128 E. 63rd St., Upper East Side, 212/838–2560. Open Tues. 10–8, Wed.–Fri. 10–5, Sat. noon–4. Subway: 59th St.*

11 *e-4*

MUSEUM FOR AFRICAN ART

Celebrating the art of an entire continent in one small space is a tall order, but the Museum of African Art manages to do it, and with panache. Exhibits range from ceremonial masks to contemporary painting. The unique interior, with galleries connected by a spiral staircase, was designed by Maya Lin, best known for her design of the Vietnam Veterans Memorial in Washington, D.C. *593 Broadway (between Houston and Prince Sts.), SoHo, 212/966-1313. Admission: $5 adults, $2.50 students, seniors, and children. Open Tues.–Fri. 10:30–5:30, weekends noon–6. Subway: Prince St.; Broadway–Lafayette St.*

9 *d-3*

MUSEUM OF MODERN ART (MOMA)

MOMA is the greatest repository of modern art in the world, its six stories brandishing such works as Van Gogh's *Starry Night*, Monet's *Water Lilies*, Matisse's *Dance*, Picasso's *Les Demoiselles d'Avignon*, and Warhol's *Marilyn Monroe*. Altogether, there are more than 100,000 works on display, including paintings and sculpture; architecture and design; drawings; prints and illustrated books; photography; and film and video. The first museum to recognize film as an art form, MOMA has documented the development of motion pictures for nearly 50 years, and still screens six films daily in its two theatres (call 212/708–9490 for listings). The museum's sculpture garden, around which the galleries are built, remains one of New York's most treasured spaces and contains works by Rodin, Matisse, and Moore; in the summer it hosts an outdoor classical concert series. The rest of the year, jazz concerts are held in MOMA's Garden Cafe on Friday nights. The museum shop has unusually fine art books, design objects, and gifts. *11 W. 53rd St., Midtown, 212/708–9400. Admission: $9.50 adults, $6.50 student, seniors, and children, free children under 16; pay what you wish Fri. 4:30–8:30. Open Sat.–Tues., Thurs. 10:30–6, Fri. 10:30–8:30. Subway: E, F to 5th Ave.*

7 *e-6*

NATIONAL ACADEMY OF DESIGN

Founded in 1825 as a drawing society and school, the academy is devoted to America's artistic heritage. The extensive collection of 19th- and 20th-century paintings, prints, drawings, photography, and sculpture includes works by Mary Cassatt, Winslow Homer, Frank Lloyd Wright, and Robert Rauschenberg—all of whom were members of the academy. *1083 5th Ave. (at 89th St.),*

Upper East Side, 212/369–4880. Admission: $5 adults, $2.50 students and seniors; free Friday 5–8. Open Tues.–Sun. noon–5, Fri. noon–8. Subway: 4, 5, 6 to 86th St.

11 *e-4*

NEW MUSEUM OF CONTEMPORARY ART

Founded in 1977, this avant-garde center for art and ideas focuses exclusively on art by living artists, most of them emerging or experimental. Currently undergoing extensive renovations and scheduled to re-open in December 1997, the new design will spotlight international artists and include a subterranean "project space"—free to the public— that will host performance art, film and video screenings, and visual art. *583 Broadway (between Prince and Houston Sts.), SoHo, 212/219–1222. Admission: $5 adults, $3 students and seniors, free under age 18; free Sat. 6–8. Open Wed.–Sat. noon–6, Sat. 12–8. Subway: Prince St.; Broadway–Lafayette St.*

7 *a-4*

NICHOLAS ROERICH MUSEUM

In a far–Upper West Side town house, this eccentric little museum's permanent collection focuses exclusively on the work of the Russian artist Nicholas Roerich, who came to New York in the 1920s and quickly developed an ardent following. The museum centers on Roerich's vast paintings of the Himalayas. The museum also hosts a chamber-music series and occasional poetry readings. *319 W. 107th St., Upper West Side, 212/864–7752. Open Tues.–Sun. 2–5. Subway: 110th St./Cathedral Pkwy.*

9 *e-6*

PIERPONT MORGAN LIBRARY

See Libraries, *below.*

3 *h-2*

QUEENS MUSEUM OF ART

On the site of two famous World Fairs, the Queens Museum features changing painting and sculpture exhibitions from the classical to the avant-garde, often with an emphasis on New York City's own art history. On permanent view is Panorama, a detailed (9,000-square-ft) scale model of New York City's five boroughs that includes nearly every building—fascinating, and updated constantly. *New York City Building (111th*

St. at 49th Ave., next to the Unisphere),
Flushing Meadows–Corona Park, Flushing, Queens, 718/592–5555. Admission: $4
adults, $2 students and seniors, free chil-
dren under 5. Open Wed.–Fri. 10–5, weekends noon–5. Subway: 111th St.

7 d-1

STUDIO MUSEUM
IN HARLEM

This distingushed museum is devoted
to the study, documentation, collection,
promotion, and exhibition of the arts
and artifacts of African-Americans. Temporary exhibits feature both established
and emerging black artists. 144 W. 125th
St. (between Lenox and 7th Aves.),
Harlem, 212/864–4500. Admission: $5
adults, $3 students and seniors, $1 children
under 12; free first Sat. of each month.
Open Wed.–Fri. 10–5, weekends 1–6. Subway: 2, 3 to 125th St.

10 f-1

UKRAINIAN MUSEUM

This small East Village gallery celebrates
the cultural history of the Ukraine.
Ceramics, jewelry, folk costumes, and
the hundreds of brilliantly colored
Easter eggs—the museum's pride and
joy—are on permanent display. 203 2nd
Ave. (between 12th and 13th Sts.), East
Village, 212/228–0110. Admission: $1.
Open Wed.–Sun. 1–5. Subway: Astor Pl.;
3rd Ave.; 1st Ave.

7 e-8

WHITNEY MUSEUM
OF AMERICAN ART

Founded in 1930 in the studio of artist
Gertrude Vanderbilt Whitney, who
wanted to highlight the work of living
American artists, the Whitney now occupies a striking modern building (it's an
upside-down ziggurat) designed by the
Bauhaus architect Marcel Breuer. Inside
the cubist structure are three floors of
modern works, including Georgia
O'Keeffe's White Calico Flower, sculptor
Alexander Calder's playful Circus, and
Edward Hopper's haunting Early Sunday
Morning. Special exhibits focus on major
20th-century artists, including photographers, filmmakers, and video artists;
and every odd year, the Whitney hosts
its controversial Biennial, featuring the
best (or the worst, depending on your
point of view) new works of living American artists. 945 Madison Ave. (at 75th
St.), Upper East Side., 212/570–3676.
Admission: $8, free Thurs. 6–8. Open

Wed. and Fri.–Sun. 11–6, Thurs. 1–8. Subway: 77th St.

9 e-5

WHITNEY MUSEUM
OF AMERICAN ART
AT PHILIP MORRIS

A wonderful retreat from Grand Central
Terminal's maddening crowds, the Whitney's free Midtown branch in the Philip
Morris building (see Architecture, above)
features a 42-ft-high sculpture court
with outstanding examples of 20th-cen-
tury sculpture, many of which are simply
too big for the Whitney's uptown base.
Such Whitney icons as Claes Oldenberg
and Alexander Calder have works here.
In the adjacent gallery, five shows annually cover all aspects of American art.
120 Park Ave. (at 42nd St.), Midtown, 212/
878–2550. Sculpture court Mon.–Sat.
7:30–9:30, Sun. 11–7; gallery Mon.–Wed.
and Fri. 11–6, Thurs. 11–7:30. Subway:
42nd St./Grand Central.

BRIDGES

New York has 65 bridges, connecting its
boroughs and islands to each other and
to the world beyond. Here are some of
the most impressive.

10 g-6

BROOKLYN BRIDGE

(John A., Washington, and Emily Roebling, 1867–83.) A triumph of Victorian
engineering, this graceful 1,595-ft-long
suspension bridge was the world's
longest when it opened in 1883. Spanning the East River, it connected Manhattan island to the then-independent city of
Brooklyn, and instantly became one of
the city's most enduring symbols. Alas,
the bridge's construction was fraught
with peril. Designer John A. Roebling was
killed in a construction accident while the
bridge was being built; his son, Washington, took over the project and was himself permanently crippled in another
accident. With the help of his wife, Emily,
Washington nonetheless saw the bridge's
construction through to completion.
Today, a walkway across the bridge
affords unparalleled views of the East
River and the downtown skyline (see
Viewpoints, below), as well as a unique
look at the bridge's Gothic stone towers
and arching steel cables. City Hall Park,
Manhattan, to Cadman Plaza, Brooklyn.
Subway: Brooklyn Bridge/City Hall; High
St./Brooklyn Bridge.

6 a-2

GEORGE WASHINGTON BRIDGE

(O. H. Ammann, engineer, and Cass Gilbert, architect, 1931) New York City's only bridge to New Jersey, the GWB is one pure, 3,500-ft line across the Hudson River. A suspension bridge made entirely of exposed steel, the GWB was originally going to have its towers sheathed in concrete, but that plan was scrapped to save money. Most of the bridge's fans don't seem to mind its raw structure; according to architecture critic Paul Goldberger, the bridge "leaps over space in a way that still causes the heart to skip a beat." A walkway and bikeway on the upper deck provide stunning views of the Hudson and the New Jersey Palisades. *Hudson River and 178th St. to Fort Lee, N.J. Subway: 175th St.; 181st St.*

10 g-5

MANHATTAN BRIDGE

(O.F. Nichols and Gustav Lindenthal, 1909.) A 1,470-ft-long suspension bridge of exposed steel, the Manhattan Bridge spans the East River just north of the Brooklyn Bridge and carries cars, trucks, *and* several subway lines between Manhattan and Brooklyn. Inspired by the Porte St. Denis in Paris and the Bernini Colonnade in Rome, its Manhattan entrance is adorned by a regal arch and colonnade by Carrère and Hastings (1915). *Canal St. and Bowery (Manhattan) to Flatbush Ave. Extension (Brooklyn). Subway: Grand St.; E. Broadway.*

9 g-3

QUEENSBORO BRIDGE

(Gustav Lindenthal, engineer; Palmer & Hornbostel, architects, 1909) An ornate, cantilevered mass of exposed steel, the 1,182-ft-long Queensborough Bridge spans the East River, connecting Queens to Manhattan and offering fantastic views of the Midtown skyline. In *The Great Gatsby*, F. Scott Fitzgerald writes, on driving into Manhattan: "The city seen from the Queensboro Bridge is always the city seen for the first time, in its wild promise of all the mystery and the beauty in the world." *E. 59th St. (Manhattan) to Queens Plaza. Subway: 4, 5, 6 to 59th St.*

7 g-1

TRIBOROUGH BRIDGE

(O. H. Ammann, engineer; Aymar Embury II, architect; 1936) Spanning three bodies of water and connecting three boroughs via islands in the East River, the Triborough was considered the ultimate congestion-buster when it opened to auto traffic in 1936. A series of four interconnecting bridges, it crosses the East River, Harlem River, and Bronx Kills, joining Manhattan, the Bronx, and Queens—with one million cars passing through every day. Lewis Mumford called the view from the Triborough's walkway "one of the most dazzling urban views in the world." *Subway: 4, 5, 6 to 125th St.*

4 c-7

VERRAZANO-NARROWS BRIDGE

(O. H. Ammann, 1964.) At 4,260 ft long, the beautiful Verrazano is the world's second-longest suspension bridge, surpassed only by the Humber Bridge in England. Named for Giovanni da Verrazano, the first European to sight New York Harbor (in 1524), it spans the mouth of New York Harbor to link Brooklyn and Staten Island. The bridge inspired a development boom on Staten Island; before its construction, Staten Island was accessible from the other boroughs only by ferry. *Ft. Hamilton at 92nd St., Bay Ridge (Brooklyn) to Lily Pond Road, Fort Wadsworth (Staten Island). Subway: 95th St./Ft. Hamilton.*

3 c-7

WILLIAMSBURG BRIDGE

(Leffert L. Buck, 1903) When it was first completed, this 1,600-ft steel suspension bridge snatched the title of "World's Longest" from the Brooklyn Bridge and had a profound effect on the city's makeup, offering Lower East Side immigrants easy access to a new promised land: Brooklyn. But time and tides have not been kind to this structure; in 1988, the bridge was found to be deteriorating so seriously that it was temporarily closed. An ongoing repair project is bringing the bridge back up to speed, and the plans include a new walkway and bikeway. *Delancey and Clinton Sts. (Manhattan) to Washington Plaza (Brooklyn). Subway: Delancey St.; Marcy Ave.*

CHILDREN'S MUSEUMS

3 f-8
BROOKLYN CHILDREN'S MUSEUM

The world's oldest museum designed specifically for children (founded in 1899), the Brooklyn Children's Museum is the place to go for hands-on involvement. Recently renovated, the new interactive exhibits are full of tunnels to crawl through, animals to pet, stories to read, and plants to water. *145 Brooklyn Ave. (at St. Mark's Ave.), Crown Heights, Brooklyn, 718/735–4432. Suggested contribution: $3. Open June–Aug., Mon. and Wed.–Sun. noon–5; Sept.–May, Wed.–Fri. 2–5, weekends noon–5. Subway: A to Kingston–Throop Aves.; 3 to Kingston Ave.; 2 to President St.*

7 b-7
CHILDREN'S MUSEUM OF MANHATTAN

In a wonderful five-story building, kids ages 1–10 can climb, crawl, paint, make collages, try on costumes, and even film their own newscasts. Every half-hour there's an art workshop, storytelling session, science program, or drama workshop. *212 W. 83rd St., Upper West Side, 212/721–1234. Admission: $5. Open Wed.– Sun. 10–5. Subway: 1, 9 to 86th St.*

4 a-6
STATEN ISLAND CHILDREN'S MUSEUM

This award-winning museum assembles changing exhibitions with the help of consulting artists and educators. Hands-on exhibits have focused on the mysteries of water, costuming for film and theater, and the five senses. There are special events every weekend. *Snug Harbor Cultural Center, 1000 Richmond Terr., Staten Island, 718/273–2060. Admission: $4. Open Tues.–Sun. noon–5.*

CHURCHES & SYNAGOGUES

New York City has over 2,250 churches and 600 synagogues. Here are some of the most historic and architecturally interesting. We list phone numbers for those that welcome sightseers when services are not in session.

10 g-3
ANSHE CHESED (OLD CONGREGATION)

(Alexander Saeltzer, 1849) Despite its designation as a city landmark, New York's oldest surviving synagogue, and at one time its largest, is in a state of woeful disrepair. The Lower East Side's well-remembered Jewish community has largely dispersed, and the Anshe Chesed congregation has long since moved uptown. Brooding, Gothic-revival architecture gives this abandoned building a ghostly air. *172–176 Norfolk St. (between Stanton and E. Houston Sts.), Lower East Side. Subway: 2nd Ave.*

10 h-4
BIALYSTOKER SYNAGOGUE

A Federal-style stone building erected in 1826, this synagogue, like many others in the city, was originally a Protestant church. In 1908, reflecting the massive influx of Eastern European Jews into New York City and the Lower East Side in particular, it was turned into a synagogue and became the home of a congregation originally founded in Bialystok, Poland. *713 Bialystoker Pl. (at Grand St.), Lower East Side. Subway: Delancey St.*

1 b-1
BRIGHTON HEIGHTS REFORMED CHURCH

A lovely, white wood-framed building dating from 1864, this Dutch Reformed Protestant church is crowned with a tall spire that's visible from incoming Staten Island ferries. *320 St. Mark's Pl. (at Fort Pl.), Staten Island.*

9 e-8
BROTHERHOOD SYNAGOGUE

Built in 1859 alongside Gramercy Park, this landmark house of worship was long the Friends' Meeting House, one of two original Quaker meeting houses in Manhattan. Simple in design, built from yellow sandstone, it was lovingly renovated and turned into a synagogue in 1975. *28 Gramercy Park S (between Irving Pl. and 3rd Ave.), Gramercy. Subway: N, R, 6 to 23rd St.*

7 b-3
CATHEDRAL CHURCH OF ST. JOHN THE DIVINE (EPISCOPAL)

Construction of the cathedral in Morningside Heights began on St. John's

Day, December 27, 1892, and continued until 1941, when it was halted—still unfinished—by World War II. Work resumed in 1979 and is still going on in the medieval manner, each stone hand-cut. Two football fields (601 ft) long and 14 stories high, this massive, architec-turally eclectic structure will be the world's largest Gothic cathedral when complete. The church hosts several spe-cial events each year, including concerts and an enormous Halloween bash; the high point is the blessing of the ani-mals, in honor of St. Francis (October), when the cathedral's bronze doors are opened to circus elephants and pet tarantulas. (*See* Events, *below.*) *Amster-dam Ave. at 112th St. 212/316–7540. Open Mon.–Sat. 7–6, Sun. 7 AM–7:30 PM. Sub-way: 110th St./Cathedral Pkwy.*

9 *e-3*

CENTRAL SYNAGOGUE (REFORM)

(Henry Fernbach) Founded in 1872, this Moorish Revival edifice—crowned by two fanciful onion-shaped domes and now surrounded by high-rises—is the oldest synagogue in the city in continu-ous use. Its Eternal Light, kindled in 1872 and replaced by an electric bulb in 1946, continues to burn. *652 Lexington Ave. (at 55th St.), Midtown. Subway: 51st St./Lexington–3rd Aves.*

5 *c-2*

CHRIST CHURCH (EPISCOPAL)

(R.M. Upjohn, 1866) This small, pic-turesque stone church in hilly Riverdale was designed to look like a medieval English parish church. *5030 Riverdale Ave., Riverdale, Bronx. Subway: 1, 9 to 231st St.*

10 *d-1*

CHURCH OF THE ASCENSION (EPISCOPAL)

(Richard Upjohn, 1841; interior remod-eled by McKim, Mead & White, 1889) In the heart of Greenwich Village, New York's first Gothic Revival church fea-tures a beautiful altar mural, *The Ascen-sion,* and illuminated stained-glass windows, both by John La Farge. *36–38 5th Ave. (at 10th St.). Subway: 8th St.*

6 *d-5*

CHURCH OF THE INTERCESSION COMPLEX (EPISCOPAL)

(Bertram Goodhue for Cram, Goodhue & Ferguson, 1914) Beautifully situated in rural Trinity Cemetery (*see* Graveyards, *below*), this large, English Gothic–style country church was founded in 1846. Once the farm of famed artist and ornithologist John J. Audubon, the com-plex is also home to an impressive parish house, cloister, and vicarage. *Broadway at 155th St., Harlem. 212/283–6200. Subway: 157th St.; 155th St.*

1 *b-2*

CHURCH OF ST. ANDREW (EPISCOPAL)

(William H. Mersereau, 1872.) As if transplanted from New England, or even old England, this fieldstone parish church and its ramshackle graveyard sit on a picturesque green hillock near Staten Island's Historic Richmondtown. *4 Arthur Kill Rd. (at Old Mill Rd.), Rich-mondtown, Staten Island.*

7 *e-7*

CHURCH OF ST. IGNATIUS LOYOLA (ROMAN CATHOLIC)

(Ditmas & Schickel, 1898) This land-mark limestone Beaux-Arts pile on Park Avenue was modeled on Jesuit churches in Rome. The main altar is dedicated to St. Ignatius Loyola, founder of the Jesuits, and the church is built upon an earlier house of worship (never com-pleted) dedicated to St. Laurence O'Toole, a popular saint with the city's 19th-century Irish immigrants. *980 Park Ave. (at 84th St.), Upper East Side. Sub-way: 4, 5, 6 to 86th St.*

9 *d-4*

CHURCH OF ST. MARY THE VIRGIN (EPISCOPAL) COMPLEX

Now surrounded by the theater district (TKTS is just around the corner), this 1895 French Gothic–style church is accompanied by a brick clergy house, a chapel, a rectory, and a mission house. The church is believed to be the first built on a steel frame à la the modern-day skyscraper. *133–145 W. 46th St. (between 6th Ave. and Broadway). Sub-way: 42nd St./Times Sq.*

`9` e-2

CHURCH OF ST. VINCENT FERRER (ROMAN CATHOLIC, DOMINICAN ORDER)

(Bertram Goodhue, 1918) Set inside a large Midtown church complex, Goodhue's Gothic-inspired church of granite with limestone carvings features a magnificent rose window. Nearby is the Victorian Gothic Old Priory of the Dominican Fathers (William Schickel, 1881), the Holy Name Society Building, and the St. Vincent Ferrer School. *869 Lexington Ave. (at 66th St.), Upper East Side. Subway: 68th St./Hunter College.*

`10` e-4

CIVIC CENTER SYNAGOGUE (SHAARE ZEDEK)

(William N. Breger Associates, 1967) An incongruous marble swirl tucked between two blackened tenement buildings, this synagogue is shaped like a breaking wave. *49 White St. (between Church St. and Broadway), Lower Manhattan. Subway: Franklin St.*

`7` b-6

CONGREGATION B'NAI JESHURUN

(Henry B. Herts & Walter Schneider, 1918) An exotic Byzantine edifice with a high, Romanesque entryway, this conservative Upper West Side synagogue has an extremely active congregation. *257 W. 88th St., Upper West Side. Subway: 1, 9 to 86th St.*

`10` g-3

CONGREGATION CHASAM SOFER

Built in 1853 and now one of the many abandoned relics of the Lower East Side, Chasam Sofer is the city's second-oldest standing synagogue, after Anshe Chesed, two blocks west. *810 Clinton St. (between Stanton and Houston Sts.), Lower East Side. Subway: 2nd Ave.*

`10` f-4

ELDRIDGE STREET SYNAGOGUE

(Herter Brothers, 1887) The most luxurious of the hundreds of synagogues that once thrived on the Lower East Side, this Orthodox temple is lined with keyhole-shape arches and has an enormous Gothic-wheel window in its center. Although the main sanctuary was abandoned in the 1950s, it is currently being restored by the Eldridge Street Project,

which also offer tours of the synagogue focusing on Jewish-American history and the history of the Lower East Side. Services, weddings, and bar mitzvahs are still held downstairs. *12 Eldridge St. (between Canal and Division Sts.), Lower East Side, 212/219–0888. Open only for drop-in tours, Tues. and Thurs. at 11:30 and 2:30, Sun. hourly starting at 11; admission $4, $2.50 children, students, and seniors. Subway: Grand St.; E. Broadway.*

`9` c-1

CONGREGATION SHEARITH ISRAEL (JEWISH)

(Brunner & Tryon, 1897) Founded by North America's oldest Jewish congregation, this Sephardic (of Spanish and Portuguese origin) synagogue on the Upper West Side contains religious articles from three centuries. For the synagogue's annual fair, *see* Events, below; for its three associated burial grounds, *see* Graveyards & Cemeteries, *below. 99 Central Park West (at 70th St.), Upper West Side. Subway: B, C to 72nd St.*

`9` e-2

5TH AVENUE SYNAGOGUE

(Percival Goodman, 1959) This modern limestone temple is adorned with stained-glass windows that are best appreciated after dark, when the interior lights come on. *5 E. 62nd St., Upper East Side. Subway: N, R to 5th Ave.*

`9` e-7

FIRST MORAVIAN CHURCH

This lovely, circa-1845 brick church has a gabled roof. *154 Lexington Ave. (at 30th St.), Murray Hill. Subway: 6 to 28th St.; 33rd St.*

`10` d-1

FIRST PRESBYTERIAN CHURCH

(Joseph C. Wells, 1846) Near the Church of the Ascension (*see above*) and just a few years younger, this Gothic Revival church is considered the finer of the two, and its grounds are surrounded by a lovely fence of wood and cast iron. *48 5th Ave. (between 11th and 12th Sts.), Greenwich Village. Subway: 8th St.; F to 14th St.*

`2` g-8

FIRST REFORMED CHURCH OF COLLEGE POINT

This 1872 country church is a New York City rarity, built of wood and dressed with ornate details in the style of the well-known 19th-century architect Charles Eastlake. *14th Ave. at 119th St., College Point, Queens.*

10 *f-3*

FIRST WARSAW CONGREGATION

Built in 1903, this synagogue originally housed the Congregation Adath Jeshurun of Jassy, Romania, and then the First Warsaw Congregation. Vacant and vandalized, it's now another Lower East Side ghost, but its ornate facade survives as a reminder of another era. *5860 Rivington St. (between Eldridge and Allen Sts.), Lower East Side. Subway: 2nd Ave.*

4 *f-2*

FLATBUSH DUTCH REFORMED CHURCH

Built 1793–98 with an elegant clock tower and steeple, this Federal-style church still has its original bell, imported from Holland; it tolled the death of President Washington in 1799 and still rings each year on the anniversary of his demise. Behind the church is an old cemetery, with graves going back to the 1600s. *890 Flatbush Ave. (at Church Ave.), Brooklyn. Subway: Church Ave.*

4 *h-3*

FLATLANDS DUTCH REFORMED CHURCH

This Georgian Federal church, with white-clapboard siding and a tall steeple, dates from 1848, when this part of Brooklyn was still farmland and many of its residents still spoke Dutch. *3931 Kings Highway (between Flatbush Ave. and E. 40th St.), Brooklyn. Subway: 2, 5 to Flatbush Ave./Brooklyn College (from station, walk 1 mile down Flatbush Ave.).*

1 *f-3*

FRIENDS' MEETING HOUSE

This plain, wood-shingle building with cast-iron door hinges and latches is the oldest house of worship in New York City, and one of the oldest in the United States. It has been in continuous use since 1694, except for a period during the American Revolution when the occupying British used it successively as a prison, storehouse, and hospital. The two wooden doors in the rear were originally separate entrances for men and women. The Friends (popularly known as the Quakers) were pioneers in asserting the right of religious freedom; the meeting house was built following the trial and acquittal of John Bowne after he was arrested for "illegal worship and assembly." *(See Bowne House in Historic Buildings & Areas, below.) 137-16 Northern Blvd. (between Main and Union Sts.), Flushing, Queens, 718/358–9636. Subway: 7 to Main St./Flushing.*

10 *f-1*

FRIENDS' MEETING HOUSE & SEMINARY

(Charles T. Bunting, 1860) These simple but elegant buildings of redbrick and brownstone embody the no-frills Quaker style. *221 E. 15th St.and Rutherford Pl., Gramercy. Subway: 14th St./Union Sq.*

10 *e-1*

GRACE CHURCH & RECTORY (EPISCOPAL)

(James Renwick, Jr., 1846) One of the most magnificent examples of Gothic Revival architecture in the nation, Grace Church was designed by James Renwick—later celebrated for his masterpiece, St. Patrick's Cathedral. The church's ornate marble tower, surmounted by a tall spire, is among Lower Manhattan's most picturesque sights. Countless society couples have wed here over the years, but one particular union—that of P. T. Barnum's little trouper, Tom Thumb, in 1863—particularly scandalized the congregation. *800 Broadway (at 10th St.), Greenwich Village. Subway: 8th St.*

1 *g-4*

GRACE EPISCOPAL CHURCH

The third church to be built on this site, this rugged Gothic Revival building serves a congregation that first assembled in 1702. Statesman and four-time U.S. senator Rufus King is buried in the charming churchyard, which dates from 1734. *(See King Manor Museum in Historic Buildings & Areas, below.) 155-03 Jamaica Ave. (between 155th St. and Parsons Blvd.), Jamaica, Queens. Subway: Jamaica Center.*

12 *b-3*

GRACE CHURCH, BROOKLYN HEIGHTS (EPISCOPAL)

(Richard Upjohn, 1848) This neo-Gothic brownstone church in the heart of historic Brooklyn Heights features three stained-glass Tiffany windows. The church is particularly popular for its outdoor entrance court, where benches are shaded by an old elm. (See Grace Court Alley in Historic Buildings & Areas, below.) *254 Hicks St. (at Grace Ct.), Brooklyn Heights. Subway: Borough Hall; Court St.*

10 e-6
JOHN STREET UNITED METHODIST CHURCH

Now dwarfed by Wall Street high-rises, this Georgian-style brownstone is the home of America's oldest Methodist congregation. Built in 1841, it was already the third church on this site; the first was built in 1768. *44 John St. (between Nassau and William Sts.), Lower Manhattan. Subway: Fulton St.*

10 d-2
JUDSON MEMORIAL BAPTIST CHURCH

(McKim, Mead & White, 1892) Best known for its 10-story campanile (now an NYU dormitory), this church is considered one of architect Stanford White's most significant buildings. Designed in the Italian Renaissance style, it's adorned with 12 stained-glass windows by the artist John LaFarge. *55 Washington Sq. S (between Thompson and Sullivan Sts.), Greenwich Village. Subway: W. 4th St./Washington Sq.*

9 e-7
THE LITTLE CHURCH AROUND THE CORNER (CHURCH OF THE TRANSFIGURATION) (EPISCOPAL)

Founded in 1849, this Gothic Revival complex is set back from the street in a well-landscaped garden. Here's how it got its nickname: In 1870, the minister at another local church refused to perform funeral services for the actor George Holland, and suggested that Holland's friends try "the little church around the corner." The name stuck, and the church's popularity with theater folks is now a tradition. The stained-glass windows—once again by John LaFarge—are dedicated to actors; one depicts the 19th-century superstar Edwin Booth in his most celebrated role, Hamlet. *1 E. 29th St., Murray Hill. Subway: N, R, 6 to 28th St.*

9 d-7
MARBLE COLLEGIATE CHURCH (DUTCH REFORMED)

(S. A. Warner, 1854) This Gothic Revival church in Murray Hill gets its name from the Tuckahoe marble in which it is clad. Its congregation traces its roots back to the city's very first church, which was founded by the Reformed Protestant Dutch Congregation organized by the Dutch governor, Peter Minuit, in 1628. Dr. Norman Vincent Peale (*The Power of Positive Thinking*) was the pastor here from 1932 to 1984. *272 5th Ave. (at 29th St.). Subway: N, R, 6 to 28th St.*

10 f-5
MARINERS' TEMPLE (BAPTIST)

(Isaac Lucas, 1842) The *AIA* [American Institute of Architects] *Guide to New York City* refers to this building as a "temple to Athena"; indeed, the two Ionic columns at the church's entrance make this Greek Revival structure look like a shrine. Now in what has become part of Chinatown, the church was originally built to lift the spirits—and morals—of the many lonely sailors who passed through the city during the 19th century. *12 Oliver St. (at Henry St.), Chinatown. Subway: Brooklyn Bridge/City Hall.*

7 e-5
MOSQUE OF NEW YORK

(Main Building: Skidmore, Owings, & Merrill; Minaret: Swanke, Hayden, Connell, Ltd, 1991) A new focal point for New York's Muslims and a new landmark on the uptown skyline, this granite-and-glass pile, topped with a copper dome and a thin gold crescent, is the first building in New York City to be built as a mosque. The cornerstone of the 130-ft minaret was laid by the Emir of Kuwait in 1988. *Islamic Cultural Center of New York, 1711 3rd Ave. (at 96th St.), Upper East Side, 212/722–5234. Subway: 96th St.*

1 f-6
NEW LOTS REFORMED DUTCH CHURCH

Built in 1824, this one-story, white, wooden church with simple, Gothic-style windows and a short tower, stands virtually unaltered. Records show that the Dutch farmers of New Lots built it for $35. *630 New Lots Ave. (at Schenck*

Ave.), East New York, Brooklyn. Subway: 3 to Van Siclen Ave.

4 *f-5*

NEW UTRECHT REFORMED CHURCH

The fieldstone for this 1828 Georgian Gothic edifice came from the original 1699 church that stood on the same site. The windows are made of Victorian milk glass. *18th Ave. between 83rd and 84th Sts., Bensonhurst, Brooklyn. Subway: 18th Ave.*

11 *f-4*

OLD ST. PATRICK'S CATHEDRAL (ROMAN CATHOLIC)

(Joseph Mangin, 1815) New York's original Roman Catholic cathedral, Old St. Patrick's was replaced by the uptown St. Patrick's in 1879, after a disastrous fire in 1866. Although the building was restored in 1868, the cathedral was "demoted" to a parish church. Note the high walls surrounding the churchyard, designed to protect the cathedral from the anti-Catholic mobs who once threatened to burn the place down. (*See Graveyards, below.*) *260–264 Mulberry St. (between Prince and Houston Sts.), SoHo. Subway: Broadway–Lafayette St.; Prince St.*

12 *b-3*

OUR LADY OF LEBANON ROMAN CATHOLIC CHURCH

(Richard Upjohn, 1846) A Romanesque Revival by the architect of Manhattan's famous Trinity Church, this was the Congregational Church of the Pilgrims until 1934; it is said that a fragment of Plymouth Rock projects from one of its walls. Sadly, the church's original steeple has been removed, but two interesting post-Upjohn touches are the west and south doors, which were salvaged from the ocean liner *Normandie* after it was scuttled in the Hudson River in 1942. Look for the panel picturing an ocean liner. *113 Remsen St. (at Henry St.), Brooklyn Heights. Subway: Borough Hall; Court St.*

12 *b-2*

PLYMOUTH CHURCH OF THE PILGRIMS

(Joseph C. Wells, 1849) The abolitionist minister Henry Ward Beecher delivered fiery sermons in this simple church from 1847 to 1887, preaching against slavery and for women's rights. Along with a fine statue of Beecher in the garden, the church has a preserved piece of Plymouth Rock on display. Inside, a plaque on Pew 89 points out that Abraham Lincoln once worshipped here. *75 Hicks St. (at Orange St.), Brooklyn Heights. Subway: Clark St.*

3 *g-3*

REFORMED DUTCH CHURCH OF NEWTOWN

Topped with an elegant cupola, this white-clapboard church from 1831 is one of the oldest wooden churches in the city. *85-15 Broadway (at Corona Ave.), Elmhurst, Queens. Subway: R to Grand Ave.*

1 *c-2*

RIVERDALE PRESBYTERIAN CHURCH AND MANSE

(James Renwick, Jr., 1863) A Gothic Revival by master church-builder James Renwick, this charming stone church in Riverdale is very much in the style of the English parish church, surrounded by trees. *4765 Henry Hudson Pkwy. West (at 249th St.), Bronx. Subway: 242nd St./Van Cortlandt Park.*

7 *a-2*

RIVERSIDE CHURCH (INTERDENOMINATIONAL)

(Allen & Collens and Henry C. Pelton, 1930) Modeled after Chartres Cathedral, this impressive Gothic-style church is prominently sited above the Hudson River, right next to Riverside Park. Rising 21 stories (392 ft), the tower offers an astonishing view of the river (*see Viewpoints, below*) and houses a 74-bell carillon, the largest in the world. The church's interracial, interdenominational congregation sponsors numerous community, cultural, and political projects. *490 Riverside Dr. (at 122th St.), Morningside Heights, 212/870–6700. Open Mon.–Sat. 9–5, Sun. noon–4. Subway: 116 St./Columbia University; 1, 9 to 125th St.*

11 *g-7*

ROMAN CATHOLIC CHURCH OF THE TRANSFIGURATION

This unpretentious Gothic-Georgian blend, built from locally quarried Manhattan schist, was built in 1801 by English Lutherans. It's now in Chinatown. *25 Mott St. (at Pell St.), Chinatown. Subway: J, M, Z to Canal St.*

12 b-3

ST. ANN & THE HOLY TRINITY

(Minard Lafever, 1847) The stained-glass windows at this neo-Gothic brownstone church are the first ever made in the United States. The church has its own performing arts center, "Arts at St. Ann's." *157 Montague St. (at Clinton St.), Brooklyn Heights, 718/858–2424. Subway: Borough Hall; Court St.*

12 b-3

ST. ANN'S CHURCH (EPISCOPAL)

(James Renwick, Jr., 1869) Here, Renwick—of St. Patrick's Cathedral and Manhattan's Grace Church—gave Brooklyn its only example of the Venetian Gothic, characterized primarily by a facade of varying colors and textures of stone. *Clinton St. (at Livingston St.), Brooklyn Heights. Subway: Borough Hall; Court St.*

2 c-8

ST. ANN'S CHURCH (EPISCOPAL)

Gouverneur Morris, Jr., built this fieldstone church on his estate for family worship. Consecrated in 1841, it's the earliest surviving church in the Bronx. The cemetery and crypts contain many members of the Morris family—after which the Bronx neighborhood Morrisania was named. Among the family's most prominent members was Gouverneur Morris, Sr., who helped draft the U.S. Constitution. *295 St. Ann's Ave. (between 139th and 141st Sts.), Bronx. Subway: 6 to Brook Ave.*

10 h-4

ST. AUGUSTINE'S CHAPEL (EPISCOPAL)

A landmark Georgian-Gothic building dating from 1828, this Lower East Side fieldstone church was originally All Saints' Free Church—"free" meaning that you didn't have to pay to worship. *290 Henry St. (between Montgomery and Jackson Sts.), Lower East Side. Subway: E. Broadway.*

12 f-4

ST. AUGUSTINE'S ROMAN CATHOLIC CHURCH

(Parfitt Brothers, 1897) Among the elegantly preserved brownstones on Park Slope's 6th Avenue is this monumental church, with its tall bell-tower, intricate sculptural detail (including carved owls on the exterior), and splendid stained-glass windows. Architects consider it one of Brooklyn's finest churches. *116 6th Ave. (between Park and Sterling Pls.), Park Slope, Brooklyn. Subway: Bergen St.; 7th Ave.*

9 e-4

ST. BARTHOLOMEW'S CHURCH (EPISCOPAL)

(Bertram Grosvenor Goodhue, 1919) Time and again, historic preservationists have saved this Byzantine-domed Park Avenue landmark from becoming one of the skyscrapers around it. The church's impressive triple-arch entry (McKim, Mead & White, 1902) was actually moved here from the congregation's former building on Madison Avenue. *Park Ave. at 50th St., Midtown. Subway: 51st St./Lexington–3rd Aves.*

9 c-3

ST. BENEDICT'S CHURCH (ROMAN CATHOLIC)

Formerly known as the Church of St. Benedict, the Moor, this congregation was founded in 1883 by a group of black Catholics. The group moved into its present neo-Italianate home (formerly a Protestant church) in the 1890s. *342 W. 53rd St., Hell's Kitchen. Subway: C, E to 50th St.*

9 b-4

ST. CLEMENT'S CHURCH (EPISCOPAL)

This picturesque parish church was built around 1870. Perhaps reflecting its proximity to the theater district, the church regularly hosts dance and drama performances. *423 W. 46th St., Hell's Kitchen. Subway: A, C, E to 42nd St.*

9 f-8

ST. GEORGE'S EPISCOPAL CHURCH

(Blesch & Eidlitz, 1856) A Romanesque brownstone known as "Morgan's church" after founding member and financier J. P. Morgan, this beautiful complex features rounded exterior arches and, inside, lovely stained-glass windows. *Rutherford Pl. and 16th St. (off Stuyvesant Sq.), Gramercy. Subway: 14th St./Union Sq.*

11 *d-1*

ST. GEORGE'S UKRAINIAN CATHOLIC CHURCH

Topped by an impressive dome, this is the new (1977) religious centerpiece of an old Ukrainian neighborhood. It's also the focal point of the annual Ukrainian Festival (*see* Events, *below*). *30 E. 7th St., East Village. Subway: Astor Pl.; 2nd Ave.*

10 *f-5*

ST. JAMES CHURCH (ROMAN CATHOLIC)

Founded by Irish immigrants in 1837, the city's second-oldest Roman Catholic Church is a stately building with a brownstone facade and two Doric columns. Al Smith, former governor of New York and renowned political reformer, was an altar boy here when this was still a predominantly Irish neighborhood. *32 James St. (between St. James Pl. and Madison St.), Chinatown. Subway: Brooklyn Bridge/City Hall.*

7 *e-8*

ST. JEAN BAPTISTE CHURCH (ROMAN CATHOLIC)

(Nicholas Serracino, 1913) A single patron, Thomas Fortune Ryan, paid for the construction of this two-tower, dome building after he could not find a seat one Sunday in the crowded little church that stood here earlier. The original congregation was French-Canadian. *Lexington Ave. and 76th St., Upper East Side. Subway: 77th St.*

9 *c-7*

ST. JOHN THE BAPTIST CHURCH (ROMAN CATHOLIC)

(Napoleon Le Brun, 1872) A brownstone church with one spire, this exquisite building near Penn Station has a lovely, white-marble interior. *211 W. 30th St., Garment District. Subway: 34th St./Penn Station.*

1 *c-1*

ST. JOHN'S EPISCOPAL CHURCH

(Arthur D. Gilman, 1871) Ferry magnate Cornelius Vanderbilt was baptized in this Gothic Revival church of rose-color granite. *1331 Bay St. (at New Lane), Rosebank, Staten Island.*

12 *f-4*

ST. JOHN'S PROTESTANT EPISCOPAL CHURCH

(Edward T. Potter, 1869) This Park Slope intersection boasts a wonderful trio of Gothic Revival churches. The oldest is St. John's, which resembles an English country church. Memorial Presbyterian (Pugin & Walter, 1883) is a brownstone church with a tall octagonal spire and stained-glass Tiffany windows. Grace United Methodist Church (Parfitt Brothers, 1882) completes the trio with variegated brownstone facade. Standing on this corner, you begin to understand why Brooklyn once was nicknamed "the city of churches." *St. John's Place and 7th Ave., Park Slope, Brooklyn. Subway: D, Q to 7th Ave.*

11 *c-1*

ST. JOSEPH'S ROMAN CATHOLIC CHURCH

(John Doran, 1834) Just west of Washington Square Park is Manhattan's oldest surviving Roman Catholic church. Like fellow St. James Church and the Mariner's Temple—also in the Greek Revival style—it is topped with a simple triangular pediment, and its entryway is supported by two columns. *365 6th Ave. (at Washington Pl.), Greenwich Village. Subway: W. 4th St./Washington Sq.*

11 *a-2*

ST. LUKE-IN-THE-FIELDS CHURCH (EPISCOPAL)

(James N. Wells, 1822) To this church's early parishioners, today's West Village was the sticks; hence their name for what was then a charming country parish, an annex of Trinity Church, downtown. A tragic fire devastated the building in 1981, but it was successfully restored in 1986. A peaceful little garden (open to the public) preserves some of the church's original country spirit. *485 Hudson St. (between Barrow and Christopher Sts.), West Village. Subway: Christopher St./Sheridan Sq.*

10 *f-1*

ST. MARK'S CHURCH IN-THE-BOWERY (EPISCOPAL)

Originally a stark Georgian structure (1799), St. Mark's served as the first parish in Manhattan that was independent of Trinity Church, further downtown. The Greek Revival steeple, an East Village landmark, was completed in

1828; the cast-iron Italianate portico was added in 1854. Beautifully restored following a devastating fire in 1978, St. Mark's stands on the site of Dutch governor Peter Stuyvesant's family chapel. Stuyvesant is buried in the churchyard (*see* Haunted Places, *below*).

Even in its early days, St. Mark's was considered progressive, and historically it has been a haven for the arts as well as the spirit. Ballerina Isadora Duncan once danced here, and poets Edna St. Vincent Millay and Robert Frost read their works; today, Danspace and the Poetry Project stage performances and readings. (*See* St. Mark's Historic District *in* Historic Buildings & Areas, *below*.) *2nd Ave. and 10th St., East Village, 212/674–6377. Subway: Astor Pl.; 3rd Ave.*

9 *e-4*

ST. PATRICK'S CATHEDRAL (ROMAN CATHOLIC)

(James Renwick, Jr., 1858–79) The most famous church in New York City, St. Patrick's Cathedral is also one of the most architecturally significant churches in the nation. Designed by the famed 19th-century church architect James Renwick (and considered his masterpiece), the marble Gothic Revival edifice is based on Germany's Cologne Cathedral and took 21 years to build. The tallest structures in the area when first erected, the cathedral's two 330-ft-high towers are now dwarfed by Midtown's skyscrapers. St. Patrick's is the seat of the Archdiocese of New York. *5th Ave. and 50th St., Midtown, 212/753–2261. Open daily 7 AM–9 PM. Subway: E, F to 5th Ave.*

7 *b-2*

ST. PAUL'S CHAPEL (EPISCOPAL)

(Howells & Stokes, 1907) Considered one of Columbia's finest buildings, this wonderful brick, terra-cotta, and limestone chapel has 24 windows in its dome, decorated with the coats-of-arms of old New York families associated with city and university history. *Columbia University, Amsterdam Ave. (between 116th and 117th Sts.), Morningside Heights. Subway: 116th St./Columbia University.*

10 *e-6*

ST. PAUL'S CHAPEL (EPISCOPAL)

(Archibald Thomas McBean, 1764–66; tower, steeple, porch by James Cromelin Lawrence, 1794) This Georgian-style church, with its distinctive brownstone spire, is Manhattan's oldest surviving building. Early worshippers included George Washington; New York's first governor, George Clinton; the Marquis de Lafayette; and General Cornwallis. The oak interior was designed primarily by architect Pierre L'Enfant, who later laid out the city plan for Washington, D.C. The chapel is fronted by a peaceful 18th-century cemetery, a unique bit of open space in the pit of Manhattan's bustling financial district (*see* Graveyards & Cemeteries, *below*). *Broadway and Fulton St., Lower Manhattan, 212/602–0874. Subway: Fulton St.*

9 *c-8*

ST. PETER'S CHURCH (EPISCOPAL)

(James W. Smith, 1836–38) Based on designs by Clement Clarke Moore, this fieldstone church in Chelsea was one of the first of the English-style Gothic Revival churches that became so popular here in the years to follow. *344 W. 20th St., Chelsea. Subway: C, E to 23rd St.*

2 *f-4*

ST. PETER'S CHURCH (EPISCOPAL)

(Leopold Eidlitz, 1855) This picturesque Gothic Revival church serves the community of Westchester Square. The gravestones in the adjacent cemetery go back to the 1700s. *2500 Westchester Ave. (near St. Peter's Ave.), Bronx. Subway: 6 to Westchester Sq./E. Tremont Ave.*

9 *e-3*

ST. PETER'S CHURCH (LUTHERAN)

(Hugh Stubbins & Associates, 1977) When the original St. Peter's Church was torn down to make way for Citicorp Center (*see* Architecture, *above*), this ultramodern church—complete with a chapel by artist Louise Nevelson—went up on the same site, nesting in the skyscraper's shadow. *Lexington Ave. at 54th St., Midtown, 212/935–2200. Subway: 51st St./Lexington–3rd Aves.*

10 *e-6*

ST. PETER'S CHURCH (ROMAN CATHOLIC)

(John R. Haggerty and Thomas Thomas, 1838) An impressive Greek Revival building made of smooth blocks of granite,

St. Peter's, like Trinity and St. Paul's, is a piece of early New York history that survives amid the glass-and-steel pillars of Wall Street. Its first incarnation, built on this site in 1786, was the city's second Catholic church. *22 Barclay St. (at Church St.), Lower Manhattan. Subway: Park Pl.*

`9` *e-7*

ST. STEPHEN'S CHURCH (ROMAN CATHOLIC)

(James Renwick, Jr., 1854) A brownstone Romanesque Revival in Murray Hill, this church has a large cast-iron interior that features a mural by Constantino Brumidi. *149 E. 28th St., Murray Hill. Subway: 28th St.*

`10` *g-4*

ST. TERESA'S ROMAN CATHOLIC CHURCH

Built in 1841 in the then-popular Gothic Revival style, this was originally the First Presbyterian Church of New York. Converted into a Catholic church in 1863 to serve the Lower East Side's growing Irish population, it conducts services today in English, Spanish, and Chinese, reflecting the area's current ethnic makeup. *1618 Rutgers St. (at Henry St.), Lower East Side. Subway: E. Broadway.*

`9` *d-3*

ST. THOMAS CHURCH 5TH AVENUE (EPISCOPAL)

(Cram, Goodhue & Ferguson, 1914) Just two blocks north of St. Patrick's Cathedral, this richly detailed Gothic church gives its more-famous 5th Avenue counterpart a run for its aesthetic money. Architects consider St. Thomas the more beautiful of the two; "St. Patrick's seems to want to be off in a tiny village somewhere," says New York Times architecture critic Paul Goldberger, while "St. Thomas was made to be on a Manhattan street and nowhere else." The elaborate interior is gloriously detailed, and the carvings on the "Bride's Door" include both a love knot and a dollar sign—the stonemason's comment on the institution of matrimony. *1 W. 53rd St., Midtown. Subway: E, F to 5th Ave.*

`10` *f-5*

SEA AND LAND CHURCH

A Georgian Federal church with Gothic windows—and one of four downtown churches of this period made from locally quarried Manhattan schist—this Lower East Side landmark was originally built in 1817 as the Northern Reformed Church. In 1865 it became the Sea and Land Church, dedicated to serving the city's seafaring population. It's now the First Chinese Presbyterian Church. *61 Henry St. (at Market St.), Lower East Side. Subway: E. Broadway.*

`9` *d-7*

SERBIAN ORTHODOX CATHEDRAL OF ST. SAVA

(Richard Upjohn, 1855) Originally Trinity Chapel, part of downtown's Trinity Parish, this brownstone church was transferred to the Serbian Orthodox Church in 1943. The neighboring parish house, designed by J. Wrey Mould in the Victorian Gothic style in 1860, stands in contrast to the church's Gothic heaviness. *15 W. 25th St., Chelsea. Subway: F to 23rd St.*

`9` *e-2*

TEMPLE EMANUEL (REFORM)

(Robert D. Kohn, Charles Butler, and Clarence Stein, 1929) Built in the Byzantine-Romanesque style and covered with mosaics, this fashionable Upper East Side synagogue seats 2,500, making it the largest Reform temple in the nation. *1 E. 65th St., Upper East Side, 212/744-1400. Subway: N, R to 5th Ave.*

`10` *e-7*

TRINITY CHURCH (EPISCOPAL)

(Richard Upjohn, 1846) Founded by royal charter during the reign of England's King William III in 1697, Trinity Church was the city's first Episcopal congregation. The first church built on this site was destroyed by fire during the Revolution; Upjohn's Gothic Revival edifice is the third, and remains one of New York's best-known landmarks. Its 280-ft spire made it New York's tallest building for the second half of the 19th century, and it is still sometimes credited as the city's first skyscraper—author Judith Dupré calls Trinity an "ecclesiastical exclamation point in Wall Street's sea of corporate towers." The adjacent 2½-acre cemetery is also a landmark, and a quiet green oasis in summertime (*see* Graveyards & Cemeteries, *below*). The church hosts a popular noontime concert series. *Broadway and Wall St., Lower Manhattan, 212/602-0872. Subway: Wall St.*

`10` d-1

VILLAGE COMMUNITY CHURCH

(Samuel Thompson, 1846) With six Doric columns, this former Village church was once considered one of the finest Greek Revival houses of worship in New York, and a synagogue and a church shared its quarters. It's now a residential coop complex. *143 W. 13th St., Greenwich Village. Subway: F, 1, 2, 3, 9 to 14th St.*

`1` a-3

WOODROW UNITED METHODIST CHURCH

Built in 1842, this simple church is pure Greek Revival—except for the tower and belfry added in 1876. *1109 Woodrow Rd. (near Rossville Ave.), Woodrow, Staten Island.*

graveyards & cemeteries

In the 18th and early 19th centuries, New Yorkers buried their dead in churchyards or in nearby cemeteries. Of some 90 known burial grounds from that time, only a few remain, especially within the confines of "the City." After 1830 one needed a special permit for burial south of Canal Street, and after 1852, burial in Manhattan was prohibited altogether. Trinity Cemetery is still active, but interment is above ground in crypts.

`10` f-5

FIRST SHEARITH ISRAEL GRAVEYARD

Dating from its members' arrival from Brazil in 1654, the Congregation Beth Shearith is the oldest Jewish congregation in America. Tucked into present-day Chinatown, this small graveyard is the earliest surviving burial ground of these Sephardic Jews. The graveyard was consecrated in 1656, and the oldest remaining gravestone is dated 1683; the newest dates from 1828. An English translation on one of the tombstones reads:

Here lies buried
The unmarried man Walter J. Judah
Old in wisdom, tender in years

55 St. James Pl. (between Oliver and James Sts.) Lower Manhattan. Subway: E. Broadway; Brooklyn Bridge/City Hall.

`4` d-2

GREEN-WOOD CEMETERY

(Grounds: Henry Pierrepont, 1840; Gates: Richard Upjohn, 1861–65.) Breaking with the traditional forms of interment—churchyards, family plots, and compact enclosures—ingenious Brooklyn planner Henry Pierrepont laid out Green-Wood's 478 rolling acres to create a cemetery full of hills, ponds, lakes, and meandering drives. Encompassing Brooklyn's highest point, 216 ft above sea level, the cemetery's natural setting is unsurpassed, and when it first opened in 1840 it was as much a public park as a burial ground. Magnificent Gothic Revival mausoleums and monuments decorate many of the 500,000 graves, and the list of those interred reads like a *Who's Who* of the 19th century, including artists Nathaniel Currier, James Merrit Ives, and Louis Comfort Tiffany; Governor De Witt Clinton; William Marcy "Boss" Tweed; piano manufacturer Henry Engelhard Steinway; newspaper king Horace Greeley; abolitionist minister Henry Ward Beecher; and inventors Samuel F. B. Morse (telegraph), Peter Cooper (steam locomotive), and Elias Howe (sewing machine). Green-Wood still operates as a full-service, nonsectarian, nonprofit cemetery; composer/conductor Leonard Bernstein was laid to rest here in 1990. For information on 2-hour walking tours on Sundays in spring and fall, call 718/469–5277. *Main Gate: 5th Ave. and 25th St., Sunset Park, Brooklyn, 718/768–7300. Subway: 25th St.*

`8` d-4

LAWRENCE FAMILY GRAVEYARD

Relatives of George Washington, the distinguished Lawrence family first settled in Queens in 1664. Their private burial ground spans an incredible 272 years of family history, with the earliest of 89 graves dated 1703 and the last dated 1975. *20th Rd. and 35th St., Steinway, Queens. Subway: N to Ditmars Blvd.*

`1` g-3

LAWRENCE MEMORIAL PARK

A second Lawrence-family graveyard, first used in 1832, contains the remains of a New York City mayor, Cornelius W. Lawrence, and an Indian named Moccasin, who was given the first name Lawrence and buried with the family. *216th St. and 42nd Ave., Bayside, Queens.*

1 *b-2*

MORAVIAN CEMETERY
(Frederick Law Olmsted, 1866) Best known as the site of a million-dollar mausoleum designed by Richard Morris Hunt for Cornelius Vanderbilt and his family, the Moravian Cemetery covers 80 terraced acres, with the earliest grave dating back to 1740. *Richmond Rd. at Otis Ave. (between Todt Hill Rd. and Altamont), New Dorp, Staten Island, 718/351–0136.*

11 *g-2*

NEW YORK CITY MARBLE CEMETERY
The markers and headstones in this private East Village cemetery (opened in 1832) can be viewed from the sidewalk through a handsome iron fence. Shipping merchant Preserved Fish (his real name) and James Henry Roosevelt (the founder of Roosevelt Hospital) are among those buried here. *52–74 E. 2nd St., East Village. Subway: Bleecker St.*

11 *g-2*

NEW YORK MARBLE CEMETERY
Opened in the East Village in 1830, this was Manhattan's first nonsecterian graveyard and offered prominent New Yorkers an opportunity for burial in what was then a fashionable area. Among the 156 New Yorkers buried below ground in Tuckahoe marble vaults are members of the Scribner, Hoyt, Varick, and Beekman families. Instead of headstones, tablets on the brick wall serve as the only markers. The cemetery is closed to the public, but is just visible from its gates. *Entrance on 2nd Ave. between 2nd and 3rd Sts., East Village. Subway: 2nd Ave.*

11 *f-4*

OLD ST. PATRICK'S CEMETERY
On a quiet street in Little Italy next to Old St. Patrick's Cathedral, a 9-ft brick wall hides most of this churchyard from view. The crypt beneath the church holds the remains of two of New York's early bishops, as well as some of the country's first Irish-Catholic settlers. (The high wall and underground burials were a prudent response to anti-Catholic vandalism and, occasionally, violence.) The earliest graves date from 1804. The remains of Pierre Toussaint (1766–1863) were recently exhumed and sent to the Vatican, a step toward possible canonization of the former slave famous for his acts of charity. (*See* Old St. Patrick's Cathedral *in* Churches & Synagogues, *above.*) *Mulberry St. (between Prince and Houston Sts.), SoHo. Subway: Broadway–Lafayette St.; Prince St.*

2 *d-5*

OLD WEST FARMS SOLDIER CEMETERY
Forty veterans of the War of 1812, the Civil War, the Spanish-American War, and World War I are buried in this small public cemetery. *Bryant Ave. and 180th St., Bronx. Subway: 2, 5 to E. 180th St.*

10 *f-1*

ST. MARK'S IN-THE-BOWERY EAST & WEST YARDS
The former site of Peter Stuyvesant's country chapel, this peaceful graveyard has been covered over by cobblestones, but some memorial tablets and markers are still visible. Stuyvesant himself is buried in a crypt beneath the church. The East Yard is now a children's play area. (*See* St. Mark's Church in-the-Bowery *in* Churches & Synagogues, *above.*) *2nd Ave. and 10th St., East Village. Subway: Astor Pl.; 3rd Ave.*

10 *e-6*

ST. PAUL'S CHURCHYARD
Though not as old as Trinity's graveyard, St. Paul's churchyard, with its tumble of blackened headstones, offers a pleasant, albeit somber, spot to reflect upon the city's past in the shadow of modern life: the World Trade Center towers above. (*See* St. Paul's Chapel *in* Churches & Synagogues, *above.*) *Broadway and Fulton St., Lower Manhattan. Subway: Fulton St.*

10 *d-1*

SECOND SHEARITH ISRAEL GRAVEYARD
Active from 1805 until 1829, the original burial ground was reduced and made triangular by the laying out of West 11th Street, making this the smallest surviving graveyard in Manhattan. The displaced graves were moved to the congregation's third cemetery, on West 21st Street. *72–76 W. 11th St., Greenwich Village. Subway: 8th St.; F to 14th St.*

1 *a-3*

SLEIGHT FAMILY GRAVEYARD

Also known as the Rossville or Blazing Star Burial Ground, this was originally a family plot and later served the entire village of Rossville. The graveyard was in use from 1750 to 1850; many of Staten Island's early settlers are buried here. *Arthur Kill Rd. at Rossville Ave., Rossville, Staten Island.*

9 *d-8*

THIRD SHEARITH ISRAEL GRAVEYARD

The northernmost burial ground of the Congregation Shearith Israel, this picturesque little graveyard, used 1829–51, is now surrounded by buildings. *W. 21st St. between 6th and 7th Aves., Chelsea. Subway: F, 1, 9 to 23rd St.*

6 *c-5*

TRINITY CEMETERY

Once part of the farm belonging to artist and naturalist John James Audubon, who is buried here, Trinity Cemetery became the rural burial place for Wall Street's Trinity Church in 1842. In an uncrowded area of Upper Manhattan next to the Church of the Intercession, rural peace still prevails on these grounds, which climb from the Hudson River up to Amsterdam Avenue. Among those buried here are John Jacob Astor; Eliza Brown Jumel, owner of the Morris Jumel Mansion; and Clement Clarke Moore, author of "A Visit from St. Nicholas." (*See* Church of the Intercession *in* Churches & Synagogues, *above*.) *153rd–155th Sts. (between Riverside Dr. and Amsterdam Ave.), Washington Heights., 212/368–1600. Open daily 8–4:30. Subway: 157th St.; 155th St.*

10 *e-7*

TRINITY CHURCH GRAVEYARD

The oldest stone in this 2½-acre graveyard is dated 1681, predating the church and making it Manhattan's earliest burial ground. Here beneath the trees are Alexander Hamilton; Robert Fulton, the inventor of the steamboat; William Bradford, the editor of New York City's first newspaper; and Captain James Lawrence, the War of 1812 hero who exhorted, "Don't give up the ship!" Also of note is the Martyr's Monument, honoring the rebel soldiers who died imprisoned at the old sugar house on

nearby Liberty Street during the American Revolution. At the north end of the cemetery, a faded stone reads "Hark from tombs a doleful sound / Mine ears attend the cry / Ye living men come view the ground / Where you must shortly lie."

Broadway and Wall St., Lower Manhattan, 212/607–0747. Open spring–fall, weekdays 7–5, Sat. 8–3, Sun. 7–3; winter, weekdays 7–4, Sat. 8–3, Sun. 7–3. Subway: Wall St.

1 *b-2*

VAN PELT–REZEAU CEMETERY

A homestead burial plot containing five generations of the Van Pelt–Rezeau families, this private cemetery (begun circa 1780) is on the grounds of Historic Richmondtown. (*See* Historic Richmondtown *in* Historic Buildings & Areas, *below*.) *Tysen Court, Historic Richmondtown, Staten Island.*

2 *c-3*

WOODLAWN CEMETERY

Along with Green-Wood Cemetery in Brooklyn, Woodlawn Cemetery is one of the most ornate and star-studded burial grounds in the world. First opened in 1863, it is filled with elaborate tombs, some of them replicas of European chapels and Egyptian burial sites. Among the resting luminaries are Mayor Fiorello LaGuardia, Bat Masterson, F. W. Woolworth, R. H. Macy, J. C. Penney, Jay Gould, Henry H. Westinghouse, Joseph Pulitzer, Elizabeth Cady Stanton, Herman Melville, Damon Runyon, Duke Ellington, and Miles Davis. Maps are available at the cemetery office, and guided tours are offered in spring and fall. *Entrances on Jerome Ave. north of Bainbridge Ave., 233rd St., and Webster Ave., Woodlawn, Bronx, 718/920–0500. Open daily 9–4:30. Subway: 4 to Woodlawn.*

HAUNTED PLACES

In which we lead you where lively spirits dwell.

9 *c-1*

THE DAKOTA

Let's face it: the Dakota is creepy. It has the severe miasma of a mad French marquis's torture castle, and the wrought-iron fence surrounding the building features "decorative" masks that seem to shriek, "STAY AWAY!" The creep value is so high here that film director Roman Polanski chose the building as the setting for *Rosemary's Baby*, in which Mia Farrow's character gives birth to the son of Satan. If that's not enough to give you pause, remember that John Lennon was murdered just outside the building by a deranged fan in 1980. The Dakota's supernatural history is said to go back even further; when John and Yoko first moved in, they supposedly conducted a séance to raise the ghost of a former tenant. *1 W. 72nd St., Upper West Side. Subway: B, C to 72nd St.*

10 *c-1*

JANE STREET, BETWEEN WASHINGTON AND HUDSON STREETS

Here the ghost of founding father Alexander Hamilton wanders from walk-up to walk-up, no doubt restless after his nearby death from a pistol wound sustained in a duel with Vice President Aaron Burr. According to legend, Hamilton shot into the air while Burr went straight for Hamilton's heart. Hamilton most commonly makes his presence known by flicking lights on and off, flushing toilets, and turning on blenders; according to Jane Street's residents, he's fascinated by modern technology.

6 *d-4*

MORRIS-JUMEL MANSION

George Washington's headquarters during the victorious Battle of Harlem Heights in 1776, this mansion was later purchased by the French merchant Stephen Jumel for his wife, Elizabeth, who later lived here with her second husband, former Vice President (and duelist) Aaron Burr, after Jumel's death. Elizabeth's insubstantial form is said to wander the house now, along with the ghosts of a smiling soldier and a sad-faced servant girl believed to have committed suicide here. (*See* Historic Buildings & Areas, *below.*) *Edgecombe Ave. and W. 160th St., Washington Heights. Subway: 163rd St.*

11 *f-2*

OLD MERCHANT'S HOUSE

Once owned by the wealthy merchant Seabury Tredwell, this house is reputed to be haunted by a lovely young woman in 19th-century dress. She is assumed to be Tredwell's daughter, Gertrude, who became a solitary recluse following a romance thwarted by her father. (*See*

Historic Buildings & Areas, *below.*) *29 E. 4th St., East Village. Subway: W. 4th St./Washington Sq.*

10 *f-1*

ST. MARK'S CHURCH IN-THE-BOWERY

Our 17th-century Dutch governor, Peter Stuyvesant, once owned this land, and he's buried in a vault right under the church's garden. Worshippers have occasionally been disturbed by a strange tapping, which the psychically attuned have identified as the sound of the old governor angrily approaching on his peg leg, craving revenge for the crowds now scampering willy-nilly over his resting place. (*See* Churches & Synagogues, *above.*) *2nd Ave. and 10th St., East Village. Subway: Astor Pl.; 3rd Ave.*

11 *d-2*

WASHINGTON SQUARE

This popular Greenwich Village oasis was once a potter's field, estimated to have housed the graves of some 20,000 impoverished souls and executed convicts. Moreover, an old elm tree that still stands in the park's northwest corner was once known as the "Hanging Elm"; according to local historians, public hangings took place here until 1819, and the executioner lived just around the corner. *Subway: W. 4th St./Washington Sq.*

10 *c-1*

THE WHITE HORSE TAVERN

"Do not go gentle into that good night," wrote the poet Dylan Thomas—and he didn't. Thomas died at this Greenwich Village hangout in 1958 after downing close to 20 shots of scotch. Regulars say that his ghost still drops in late at night, sitting at an unobtrusive corner table and scribbling. *567 Hudson St. (at 11th St.), West Village, 212/243–9260. Subway: Christopher St./Sheridan Sq.*

HISTORIC BUILDINGS & AREAS

New York City's architecture and layout are deeply layered in history, ranging from the days of Dutch rule over Nieuw Amsterdam to the colonial days of the American Revolution, and from the horse-drawn carriages of the gaslit Victorian era to the waves of European immigrants who transformed the city's neighborhoods.

The Metropolitan Historic Structures Association is a coalition of 70 small history museums, including historic houses, religious sites, military sites, and historical societies. Write or call the association for information on historic sites throughout the five boroughs or for workshops on preserving historic buildings and their interiors. *15 Gramercy Park S, New York, NY 10003, 212/473–6045.*

bronx

1 *e-1*

BARTOW-PELL MANSION

A Greek Revival country house built circa 1836, this old mansion is filled with period furnishings and surrounded by beautiful sunken gardens. *Shore Rd., Pelham Bay Park, 718/885–1461. Open Sept.–July, Wed. and weekends noon–4.*

1 *f-1*

CITY ISLAND

A narrow, 230-acre island with a salty, New England flavor, City Island is just off the Bronx shore, attached to the mainland by a single narrow bridge. Discover it: You'll find weathered bungalows, Victorian houses, boatyards, seafood restaurants, and sea breezes. *6 to Pelham Bay Park, then BX29 bus to City Island Ave.*

1 *d-2*

LORILLARD SNUFF MILL

Built on the Bronx River in 1840 by the Lorillard tobacco family, this fieldstone building was orginally a mill used to grind snuff. It's currently a public café, with a lovely outdoor terrace, at the New York Botanical Garden. *New York Botanical Garden (see Gardens in Chapter 6), Bronx Park. Subway: Bedford Park Blvd.*

5 *f-4*

POE COTTAGE

Built in 1812, this little cottage was the home of Edgar Allan Poe and his consumptive young wife, Virginia, from 1846 to 1849. Here, Poe wrote such haunting works as "Annabelle Lee" and "The Bells." Administered by the Bronx Historical Society. *2640 Grand Concourse (at E. Kingsbridge Rd.), Fordham, 718/881–8900. Admission: $2. Open Sat. 10–4, Sun. 1–5. Subway: C, D to Kingsbridge Rd.*

5 *g-1*

VALENTINE-VARIAN HOUSE (BRONX COUNTY HISTORICAL SOCIETY MUSEUM)

Dating from 1758, this pre-Revolution fieldstone farmhouse now serves as a museum of local history. *3266 Bainbridge Ave. (between Van Cortlandt Ave. and 208th St.), Norwood, 718/881–8900. Admission: $2, free children under 12. Open Sat. 10–4, Sun. 1–5. Subway: D to 205th St.*

1 *d-1*

VAN CORTLANDT MANSION

Built in 1748, this Georgian-style, fieldstone manor house was Washington's headquarters at various times during the American Revolution. The interior is a wealth of Colonial artifacts and furnishings. *Van Cortlandt Park (Broadway north of 242nd St.), Riverdale, 718/543–3344. Admission: $2, $1.50 seniors, free children under 12. Open Tues.–Fri. 10–3, weekends 11–4. Subway: 242nd St./Van Cortlandt Park.*

brooklyn

4 *f-2*

ALBEMARLE-KENMORE TERRACES HISTORIC DISTRICT

In the heart of Flatbush, behind the Flatbush Dutch Reformed Church (*see* Churches & Synagogues, *above*), these two attractive dead-end streets are lined with landmark Georgian Revival row houses built 1916–20. *South of Church Ave. and east of 21st St. between Flatbush and Ocean Aves. Subway: Church Ave.*

1 *d-6*

BROOKLYN HEIGHTS

Called *Ihpetonga* (high, sandy bank) by the Canarsie Indians, Brooklyn Heights sits high on a bluff above the East River. Its airy location attracted 19th-century financiers to build their mansions here—they could take the Fulton Ferry to their jobs on Wall Street—and today, its fifty blocks of incredibly rich 19th-century architecture are among the best-preserved in the city. Almost every block has some kind of architectural gem; try wandering down Columbia Heights, Pierrepont Street, Joralemon Street, and Willow Place in particular. Save time at the end of your stroll for the Brooklyn Heights Promenade, with its breathtaking vista of the downtown-Manhattan skyline (*see* Viewpoints, *below*). *Bordered roughly by the East River (the Promenade), Atlantic Ave., Cadman Plaza W, and Brooklyn Bridge. Subway: Borough Hall; Court St.; Clark St.; High St./Brooklyn Bridge.*

12 *b-3*

GRACE COURT ALLEY

A charming mews, this was once the stable alley for mansions on neighboring Remsen and Joralemon Streets. Today, those stables and brownstone carriage houses are luxury homes. *East of Hicks St. (between Joralemon and Remson Sts.), Brooklyn Heights. Subway: Borough Hall; Court St.*

12 *g-5*

GRAND ARMY PLAZA

(Frederick Law Olmsted and Calvert Vaux, 1870) *Grand* is indeed the word for this Park Slope plaza, designed in the spirit of L'Etoile (a.k.a., Place Charles-de-Gaulle) in Paris. At its center is the 80-ft-square Soldiers and Sailors Memorial Arch (1892), reminiscent of the Arc d'Triomphe, with enormous bronze sculptures honoring the Union Army's efforts in the Civil War. The Plaza is a fitting entry to Brooklyn's beloved Prospect Park (*see* Parks *in* Chapter 6.) *Intersection of Flatbush Ave., Prospect Park W, Eastern Pkwy., and Vanderbilt Ave. Arch open to climbers mid-May–early July weekends and holidays 1–5. Subway: Grand Army Plaza; D, Q to 7th Ave.*

12 *c-4*

JENNIE JEROME HOUSE

Tucked away in Cobble Hill, this old Greek Revival was the birthplace of Jennie Jerome on January 9, 1854. While Jerome Avenue in the Bronx is named after her father, financier Leonard Jerome, Jennie herself became better known for marrying a British lord and becoming the mother of Winston Churchill. *197 Amity St. (between Clinton and Court Sts.). Subway: F to Bergen St.*

4 *f-1*

LEFFERTS HOMESTEAD

A Dutch Colonial farmhouse built in 1783 on Flatbush Avenue, the Lefferts Homestead was moved to its current Prospect Park location in 1918. Today, it's a historic museum geared toward children, with reproductions of period furnishings. Next door is a painstakingly restored 1912 carousel that operates on weekends. *Prospect Park, Flatbush Ave. at Empire Blvd., 718/ 965–6505. Subway: Prospect Park.*

12 *g-6*

LITCHFIELD VILLA

(Alexander Jackson Davis, 1857) A romantic Italianate pile built for railroad baron Edwin C. Litchfield, the villa was once the heart of a vast estate that took in virtually all of present-day Park Slope. It now serves as the Department of Parks and Recreation's Brooklyn headquarters. *Prospect Park, Prospect Park W between 4th and 5th Sts., Park Slope. Subway: Grand Army Plaza; F to 7th Ave.*

12 *b-2*

MIDDAGH STREET

One of the first streets laid out in Brooklyn Heights (circa 1817), Middagh Street retains some of its oldest houses, many made from wood. Take particular note of No. 24 (1824), a gambrel-roof Federal house—one of the finest in the city. *Between northern ends of Willow and Hicks Sts., Brooklyn Heights. Subway: Clark St.; High St./Brooklyn Bridge.*

12 *b-3*

MONTAGUE TERRACE

This delightful stretch of English-style row houses was built in 1886 and has been wonderfully preserved. In the 1930s, novelist Thomas Wolfe lived at No. 5, where he wrote *You Can't Go Home Again. 113 Montague Terr. (between Remsen and Montague Sts.), Brooklyn Heights. Subway: Borough Hall; Court St.*

12 *g-5*

PARK SLOPE
HISTORIC DISTRICT

Covering more than 30 blocks, this beautiful, tree-lined residential area contains 1,900 structures of architectural interest, including some of the finest Queen Anne and Romanesque Revival homes in the nation. Don't miss the dazzling 1880s and -'90s gems on Montgomery Place and Carroll Street just below Prospect Park, or the palazzo-like Montauk Club, at Lincoln Place and 8th Avenue, with its friezes depicting the history of the Montauk Indians. Prospect Park itself, designed by Frederick Law Olmsted and Calvert Vaux (the same pair who designed Central Park) is a triumph of landscape design; Olmsted and Vaux openly preferred it to Central Park. (See Parks *in* Chapter 6.) *Grand Army Plaza to Bartel Pritchard Sq. (15th St.) bordering Prospect Park W. Subway: Grand Army Plaza; D, Q to 7th Ave.; F to 7th Ave.*

1 *f-7*

SHEEPSHEAD BAY

A small but active fishing port, Sheepshead Bay is best known for its fleet of "party boats," which whisk anglers to secret fishing holes out on the ocean. This salty old neighborhood is also known for its seafood restaurants, the preeminent of which— Lundy's—recently reopened with much fanfare. *Emmons Ave. from Knapp St. to Shore Ave. Subway: Sheepshead Bay.*

4 *g-3*

VAN NUYSE HOUSE (COE HOUSE)

When the Dutch first settled New York, the southern part of Brooklyn was prime farmland. Parts of this landmark Dutch house date back to 1744, when it was part of Joost and Elizabeth Van Nuyse's 85-acre farm. *1128 E. 34th St. (between Flatbush Ave. and Ave. J). Subway: 2, 5 to Flatbush Ave.*

4 *g-3*

VAN NUYSE–MAGAW HOUSE

A Dutch Colonial house from around 1800, this gambrel-roof structure was transported to its present site in 1916 to ensure permanent preservation. *1041 E. 22nd St. (between Aves. I and J), Midwood. Subway: D to Ave. J.*

4 *h-4*

WYCKOFF-BENNETT HOUSE

Built around 1766, complete with little dormers and a six-column porch, this house is considered Brooklyn's finest example of Dutch Colonial architecture. Two glass windowpanes are etched with the name and rank of two Hessian soldiers quartered here during the Revolution. *1669 E. 22nd St. (at Kings Hwy.). Subway: D to Kings Highway.*

manhattan

9 *f-2*

ABIGAIL ADAMS SMITH MUSEUM

Built in 1799, this elegant, Federal-style stone carriage house was converted into a country resort (the Mt. Vernon Hotel)

in 1826 and a residence in 1833. Restored by the Colonial Dames of America, it is one of the few 18th-century historic structures left on Manhattan. Open to the public, its nine period rooms are decorated in the style of the old hotel, with Federal and Empire-style furniture. A charming Colonial-style garden adjoins the house. *421 E. 61st St., Upper East Side, 212/838–6878. Open Sept.–May, Tues.–Sun. 11–4; June and July, Tues. 11–9, Wed.–Sun. 11–4. Admission: $3. Subway: 4, 5, 6 to 59th St.*

9 *e-2*

THE ARSENAL

(Martin E. Thompson, 1848) Predating the completion of the park itself by 10 years, this brick fortress was originally built to house the state's cache of artillery and ammunition. Troops were then quartered here during the Civil War. Over the years, the Arsenal has served variously as a police station and the original home of the American Museum of Natural History; today, it houses the main offices of the city's Department of Parks and Recreation. *Central Park, 5th Ave. and 64th St., Upper East Side. Subway: 68th St./Hunter College.*

6 *d-5*

AUDUBON TERRACE HISTORIC DISTRICT

Originally part of the estate belonging to artist and naturalist John James Audubon, Audubon Terrace was turned into a cultural center in 1908 by philanthropist Archer M. Huntington and his cousin, architect Charles Pratt Huntington. Several cultural institutions, all designed in the Italian Renaissance style, surround a small plaza; they include the American Numismatic Society, with a collection of coins dating from ancient times to the present; the Hispanic Society of America; and the American Academy of Arts & Letters. (*See Art Museums, above.*) *Broadway between 155th and 156th Sts., Washington Heights. Subway: 157th St.; 155th St.*

9 *f-4*

BEEKMAN PLACE

A retreat from Manhattan's chaos, this charming and exclusive two-block street on a bluff overlooking the East River is one of New York's almost-hidden treasures. Town-house residents have included Irving Berlin, Ethel Barrymore, and the Rockefellers. *East of (and parallel* to) *1st Ave., from 49th to 51st Sts. Subway: 51st St./Lexington–3rd Aves.*

11 *f-2*

BOUWERIE LANE THEATRE

(Henry Englebert, 1874) Originally the Bond Street Savings Bank, and later the German Exchange Bank (catering to the neighborhood's many German immigrants), this unusual cast-iron building is in the French Second Empire style, with paired Corinthian and Ionic columns running up the facade. *330 Bowery (at 2nd St.), East Village. Subway: Astor Pl.; 2nd Ave.*

9 *d-3*

CARNEGIE HALL

(William B. Tuthill, 1891) Built by steel magnate–cum–philanthropist Andrew Carnegie, this world-famous music hall opened in 1891 with a concert conducted by Tchaikovsky. Since then it has seen the likes of Arturo Toscanini, Leonard Bernstein, Isaac Stern, Yo-Yo Ma, the Beatles, and countless other stars. It reopened in 1987 following a loving restoration, and triumphantly celebrated its centennial in 1991. Bravo! (*See* Concert Halls *in* Chapter 5.) *154 W. 57th St., Midtown. Subway: 57th St.; 7th Ave.*

10 *e-8*

CASTLE CLINTON NATIONAL MONUMENT

(John McComb, Jr., 1807–11) This circular brownstone fortress in Battery Park was first built as a defense for New York Harbor, in preparation for the War of 1812. Originally sited on an island 200 ft from shore, it was eventually connected to Lower Manhattan by landfill. Given to the city in 1823 by the U.S. government, the old fort successively became Castle Garden, an enormously popular concert hall where impresario P. T. Barnum presented "Swedish nightingale" Jenny Lind in 1850; the Emigrant Landing Depot, 1855–90, where 8 million of New York's immigrants were processed before the opening of Ellis Island; and then, until 1941, the city's first aquarium. Today, Castle Clinton houses a small museum, as well as the ticket office for ferries to the Statue of Liberty and Ellis Island. (*See* Parks *in* Chapter 6.) *Battery Park (State St. and Battery Pl.), Lower Manhattan, 212/269–5755. Daily 8:30–5. Free. Subway: Bowling Green.*

10 *d-6*

CHAMBER OF COMMERCE OF THE STATE OF NEW YORK

(James B. Baker, 1901) Deep in the heart of the financial district, this homage to trade is now the home of the International Bank of China. An ornate Beaux-Arts landmark, it features white-marble Ionic columns and a mansard roof. *65 Liberty St. (at Liberty Pl.), Lower Manhattan. Subway: Cortlandt St./World Trade Center.*

11 *b-4*

CHARLTON-KING-VANDAM HISTORIC DISTRICT

Below Houston Street on the far west side is the city's largest concentration of Federal-style row houses (characterized by redbrick, high stoops, narrow dormers, and leaded-glass windows). Now surrounded by large commercial buildings, this area belonged originally to Aaron Burr and later to John Jacob Astor. Walking down these streets is like stumbling upon the turn of the 19th century. *9–43 and 20–42 Charlton St.; 1–49 and 16–54 King St.; 9–29 Vandam St.; 43–51 MacDougal St. West Village. Subway: Houston St.*

9 *b-8*

CHELSEA HISTORIC DISTRICT

Composed mainly of land from the estate of Clement Clark Moore, an influential 19th-century clergyman and the author of "A Visit from St. Nicholas" (better known as "T'was the Night Before Christmas"), Chelsea was developed on Moore's plan between 1825 and 1860. Among the lovely buildings here are Greek Revival row houses (the best of which are on West 20th Street's "Cushman Row," named for Moore's friend Don Alonzo Cushman, dry-goods merchant); 1890s apartment buildings; St. Peter's Episcopal Church (*see* Churches & Synagogues, *above*); and the block-long, high-fenced General Theological Seminary, which has a redbrick-and-brownstone campus accessible to the public from 175 9th Ave. *8th–10th Aves. from 20th to 22th Sts. Subway: A, C, E to 23rd St.*

9 *c-7*

CHELSEA HOTEL

(Hubert, Pirsson & Co., 1884) Constructed of redbrick with intricate wrought-iron balconies, this 12-story literary landmark began life as a cooperative apartment house in the late 19th century. In 1905 it became a hotel catering to long-term tenants and attracted many famous authors, artists, and musicians, including Thomas Wolfe, Dylan Thomas, O. Henry, Mark Twain, Vladimir Nabokov, Tennesee Williams, Arthur Miller, and William S. Burroughs. Although this is probably *not* why the hotel gained official landmark status, it's also where punk-rock star Sid Vicious stabbed his girlfriend Nancy Spungen to death. (*See* Moderately Priced Lodgings *in* Chapter 7.) *222 W. 23rd St. Subway: A, C, E, 1, 9 to 23rd St.*

10 f-4
CHINATOWN
Traditionally contained within Canal, Worth, and Mulberry Streets, the Bowery, and Chatham Square, Chinatown has recently expanded on all sides due to an influx of new immigrants and capital, primarily from Hong Kong. A feast for the senses—full of tea and rice shops, Asian vegetable stands, and Chinese apothecaries—this bustling enclave has been the heart of New York's Chinese immigrant community since the mid-1800s. Originally hailing mainly from the province of Canton, Chinatown's residents today are highly diverse, a fact reflected in the multiple dialects spoken, the seven different Chinese newspapers, and cuisine ranging from Hunan and Szechuan to Mandarin, Shanghai, and Southeast Asian. For restaurant selections, *see* Chinese *in* Chapter 3. *Subway: Grand St.; N, R, 6, J, M, Z to Canal St.*

10 e-6
CITY HALL
(Mangin and McComb, 1802–1811) A surprisingly diminutive building, City Hall has been the seat of city government since 1811. Its architecture is Federal, enriched by French Renaissance detailing. The interior is striking: The main entrance opens into a domed rotunda with a graceful twin stairway that curves upward to second-floor rooms containing original 19th-century furnishings and portraits. *City Hall Park, Broadway and Park Row. Open weekdays 9–5. Subway: Brooklyn Bridge/City Hall.*

10 f-5
WILLIAM CLARK HOUSE
A superb, four-story Federal structure built in 1824, this house was built for grocer William Clark and his wife, Rosamond, and still has its original fanlit entrance and window lintels. *51 Market St. (between Monroe and Madison Sts.), Lower East Side. Subway: E. Broadway.*

11 f-2
COLONNADE ROW
(LA GRANGE TERRACE)
(Attributed to Alexander Jackson Davis, 1833) Across from Joseph Papp's Public Theater are four survivors of nine original Greek Revival town houses that were the most coveted addresses in New York in their day. For a few years in the 1830s and '40s, these now-dilapidated marble buildings, lined by a patrician row of Corinthian columns, housed New York's elite—John Jacob Astor, Cornelius Vanderbilt, and Warren Delano (FDR's grandpa)—before the millionaires moved en masse to spanking-new 5th Avenue mansions. *428–434 Lafayette St. (between Astor Pl. and 4th St.), East Village. Subway: Astor Pl.*

10 e-2
COOPER UNION
(Frederick A. Peterson, 1859) An enormous, Italianate brownstone with high-arched windows, this is the oldest building in America framed with steel beams. The beams—actually railroad rails—were provided by the college's benefactor, the 19th-century inventor and steel magnate Peter Cooper (whose statue dominates neighboring Cooper Square), who founded the school to provide free technical education to the working class. Cooper Union remains a tuition-free private college to this day—one of the city's best for architecture, design, and engineering. In 1860, Abraham Lincoln delivered his famous "Right Makes Right" speech here, which catapulted him into the White House. *7th St. between 4th Ave. and Bowery, East Village. Subway: Astor Pl.*

9 c-1
THE DAKOTA
(Henry J. Hardenbergh, 1884) Built by Singer Sewing Machine heir Edward Clark amid rundown farms and shanties, New York's first luxury apartment house was initially criticized for being as remote as the "Dakotas in Indian territory." Though it's difficult to imagine now, the Dakota's severe triangular turrets loomed alone, like a provincial castle, when it first went up on the edge of Cen-

tral Park. In the end, of course, the Dakota became a prestigious address and served as a sort of grand corner-stone for the Upper West Side. Lauren Bacall, Boris Karloff, Rudolf Nureyev, Leonard Bernstein, Rosemary Clooney, and Gilda Radner all called this house home at some point, as did John Lennon, who was murdered outside by a "fan" on December 8, 1980. (*See* Haunted Places, *above.*) *1 W. 72 St., Upper West Side. Subway: B, C, to 72nd St.*

9 d-4

DIAMOND & JEWELRY WAY

This is really the only street in America that comes close to being paved with gold. Eighty percent of all the diamonds in the country are bought and sold here, mainly by Hasidic Jews, who can some-times be seen walking around with gem-packed briefcases handcuffed to their arms. Before World War II, the diamond district was on the Lower East Side, but, following the money, it eventually moved uptown. Lined with slightly retro jewelry stores, West 47th Street crackles with activity on weekdays. *W. 47th St. between 5th and 6th Aves., Midtown. Sub-way 47th–50th Sts./Rockefeller Center; E, F to 5th Ave.*

5 c-6

DYCKMAN HOUSE

This gambrel-roof fieldstone building is the only 18th-century Dutch farmhouse still standing in Manhattan. Built in 1785, it was restored and furnished with Dutch and English Colonial antiques and now serves as a museum of Dutch New York. *4881 Broadway (at W. 204th St.), Inwood, 212/304–9422. Open Tues.– Sun. 11–4. Subway: 207th St./Inwood.*

3 b-6

EAST VILLAGE

For a short time in the 1820 and 1830s, the East Village was aristocratic; later in the century, it housed a large German community; at the turn of the century, it was an extension of the Lower East Side, packed with Eastern Europeans; and in the 1960s, hippies and flower children put the area on the wider cultural map. Pieces of all of these eras, and particu-larly of the last, remain; the area is now favored by twentysomethings with an anti-establishment bent. East of Avenue A, the predominantly Puerto Rican pop-ulation has renamed their turf Loisaida. *Houston–14th Sts., from 4th Ave./Bowery*

to East River. Subway: Astor Pl.; Bleecker St.; 1st Ave.; 2nd Ave.; 3rd Ave.

1 c-6

ELLIS ISLAND
NATIONAL MONUMENT

(Boring & Tilton, 1898; restored 1990) Ellis Island was the first glimpse of America for more than 17 million Euro-pean immigrants, from 1892 to 1954. Long abandoned, its buildings under-went an extraordinary restoration in the 1980s, and reopened in 1990 as the Ellis Island Immigration Museum—now one of the city's busiest tourist attractions. Through the magnificent, Victorian Great Hall; the enormous Registry Hall; the Baggage Room; and the Ticket Office, visitors can retrace the steps of their immigrant forebears. The major exhibits—including excellent pho-tographs, demographic explanations, and tapes of immigrants' reminis-cences—are poignant reminders of many Americans' roots. It's estimated that more than 40% of U.S. citizens have ancestors who passed through here. *Ferries to Ellis Island depart from Battery Park, Lower Manhattan. Ferry information: 212/269–5755. Admission: $7. Departures: Weekdays every 30–45 mins 9:30–3:15, weekends every 30 mins 9:30– 3:15. Subway: South Ferry.*

10 d-1

ENGLISH TERRACE ROW

(James Renwick, Jr., 1856–58) When the Dutch settled New Amsterdam, they brought their architectural styles with them, and one of the most enduring was the "stoop," a high stairway leading up to the front door. The stoop has become a fixture on New York brown-stones and row houses, serving as a playground for children and a front porch for adults. These elegant homes on West 10th Street, however, were modeled on the English style—they were the first houses in the city *without* stoops. *20–38 W. 10th St., Greenwich Vil-lage. Subway: 8th St.; W. 4th St./Wash-ington Sq.*

10 e-7

FEDERAL HALL
NATIONAL MEMORIAL

(Town & Davis, 1842) Just up the street from the New York Stock Exchange, this imposing Greek Revival building occu-pies one of the most historic sites in the city. Originally the site of New York's second city hall, Federal Hall later served as the nation's capital, in which the Bill of Rights was adopted and George Washington took his presidential oath in 1789. The present building served as a customs house from 1842 to 1862, and then as the U.S. subtreasury until 1920. Now a National Historic Site, with a statue of George Washington on the very spot where he took the oath of office, Federal Hall houses artifacts from Colonial and early Federal New York, including Washington's inaugural suit. Free brochures outline self-guided walking tours through Lower Manhattan. *26 Wall St. (at Nassau St.), Lower Manhattan, 212/264–8711. Admission: Free. Open weekdays 9–5. Subway: Wall St.*

7 *e-2*

FIRE WATCHTOWER

Built in 1856 on the rocky high ground of what was once called Mt. Morris Park, this is the last remaining fire tower in the city. A landmark cast-iron structure with a spiral iron staircase and octagonal lookout, it became obsolete when fire-alarm boxes were invented in 1883. *Marcus Garvey Park, Madison Ave. and 121st St., East Harlem. Subway: 4, 5, 6 to 125th St.*

9 *c-6*

GENERAL POST OFFICE

(McKim, Mead & White, 1913) Topping off an imposing row of enormous Corinthian columns and a two-block-long staircase, the letter carrier's famous motto is carved in stone, looking terribly inspiring: "Neither snow, nor rain, nor heat, nor gloom of night stays these couriers from the swift completion of their appointed rounds." This monumental post office is open 24 hours, 365 days a year, making it the site of an annual midnight frenzy on April 15th. Despite the sonorous credo, the building is slated to retire as a U.S. post office and become the new home of Amtrak's passenger trains, now harbored just across 8th Avenue in Penn Station. *8th Ave. from 31st to 33rd Sts., Garment District. Subway: 34th St./Penn Station.*

1 *d-6*

GOVERNOR'S ISLAND

Sitting squarely at the mouth of the East River, this island was reputedly purchased by the Dutch governor of New Netherland from the Native Americans in 1637 for a bunch of trinkets. When the British arrived, they co-opted the island for the use of colonial governors; their circa-1708 Governor's House is one of the city's only surviving Georgian buildings. From the 1790s on, the island was used mainly as a military fortification; the 1811 Castle William—a 40-ft-high circular fort with walls 8 ft thick—housed Rebel P.O.W.s during the Civil War. In 1966 the U.S. Coast Guard moved in, but they are now planning to leave, and the next chapter in the island's story has yet to be determined. *New York Harbor. Subway: Whitehall St./South Ferry.*

7 *g-6*

GRACIE MANSION

A Federal country villa built in 1799 by wealthy merchant Archibald Gracie, Gracie Mansion has served as the residence for New York's mayors since 1942. *East End Ave. and 88th St., Upper East Side. Tour reservations: 212/570–4751. Admission: $4. Tours of the public rooms, the garden, and the private quarters (except the mayor's bedroom) are arranged by appointment. only, mid-Mar.–mid-Nov., Wed. Subway: 4, 5, 6 to 86th St.*

7 *a-2*

GENERAL GRANT NATIONAL MEMORIAL (GRANT'S TOMB)

(John H. Duncan, 1897) Civil War general and U.S. President Ulysses S. Grant and his wife, Julia Dent Grant, are entombed in this colossal white-granite mausoleum—made from 8,000 tons of stone. *Riverside Dr. and 122nd St., Morningside Heights, tel.212/666–1640. Open daily 9–5. Subway: 116th St./Columbia University; 1, 9 to 125th St.*

1 *c-6*

GREENWICH VILLAGE

The largest designated historic district in New York City, Greenwich Village was a semirural retreat for the well-to-do in the early 19th century. It has since become a haven for students, artists, immigrants, and bohemians. Its winding streets (laid out before Manhattan adopted its orderly street grid pattern) offer a wealth of architectural treasures, charming bistros, coffeehouses, and trendy boutiques. The best way to experience the Village is simply to meander. *Houston–14th Sts., from roughly University Pl. to Hudson River (including West Village).*

11 *a-2*

GROVE COURT

Built in 1854 as laborers' quarters, this charming secluded mews in Greenwich Village was then known as Mixed Ale Alley for its residents' affinity for pooling beverages. The surrounding row houses on Grove Street—brick-and-clapboard Federal and Greek Revival—date from the early 1800s. *10–12 Grove St. (between Bedford and Hudson Sts.), West Village. Subway: Christopher St./Sheridan Sq.*

6 *d-7*

HAMILTON GRANGE NATIONAL MONUMENT

Just north of City College, in Hamilton Heights, is founding father Alexander Hamilton's country retreat, designed by John McComb, Jr., and built in 1801. It's one of the few Federal frame houses still standing in Manhattan, and is now a National Historic Site administered by the National Park Service. *287 Convent Ave. (near W. 141st St.), 212/283–5154. Admission: Free. Open Fri.–Sun. 9–5. Subway: 137th St./City College.*

1 *c-3*

HARLEM

A thriving 17th- and 18th-century farming community, Harlem took off as a fashionable address in the 1880s, with brownstones, high-class apartments, and polo on horseback at the original Polo Grounds. In the decades that followed, Harlem housed succeeding waves of immigrants, first German and Irish, then Jewish and Italian; but by 1910, it was well on its way to becoming the largest black community in America. In the Roaring '20s, nightclubs and dance halls like the Cotton Club and the Savoy Ballroom showcased Duke Ellington, Louis Armstrong, and Cab Calloway, and artists and writers helped round out the fabulous Harlem Renaissance. Vestiges of Harlem's proud past—elegant row houses, fine commercial structures, historic churches—stand within a blighted present. *Broadway–5th Ave. from 125th to 155 Sts.*

7 *e-2*

HARLEM COURTHOUSE

(Thom & Wilson, 1893) A richly decorated brick-and-stone courthouse with gables and a four-faced clock, the Harlem Courthouse is now a landmark. *170 E. 121st St. (at Sylvan Pl.), East Harlem. Subway: 4, 5, 6 to 125th St.*

11 *b-2*

ISAACS-HENDRICKS HOUSE

Built in 1799, Isaacs-Hendricks House is the oldest surviving house in Greenwich Village. Though some alterations have been made, the side and rear retain restored versions of the original Federal clapboard structure. The "Narrowest House" (*see below*) is next door. *77 Bedford St. (at Commerce St.), West Village. Subway: Christopher St./Sheridan Sq.*

10 *d-1*

JEFFERSON MARKET LIBRARY

(Vaux & Withers, 1877; renovated interiors: Giorgio Cavaglieri, 1967) Originally a courthouse built on the site of an old market, this extraordinary building and its fanciful clock tower are a veritable celebration of the Victorian Gothic. Threatened with destruction in the 1960s, the building was saved by a determined band of Greenwich Village residents and is now a branch of the New York Public Library. *425 6th Ave. (at 10th St.), West Village, 212/243–4334. Subway: W. 4th St./Washington Sq.*

9 *d-8*

LADIES' MILE HISTORIC DISTRICT

At the heart of the Gilded Age, the Ladies' Mile was the 5th Avenue of its day—a shopping district traversed by mostly female, mostly elegant, turn-of-the-century shoppers. Once populated by well-known department stores, such as the original Macy's and Lord & Taylor, the Ladies' Mile was lined with imposing, block-long buildings—grandiose emporiums designed to impress shoppers both inside and out. A surprising number of these wonderful old buildings still have their original cast-iron and otherwise decorative facades; others have been restored as "superstores" like Bed, Bath, & Beyond. Today's Man, Barnes & Noble, and Old Navy have moved in and re-established this area as one of the city's most popular shopping districts. *6th Ave. from 14th to 23rd Sts., Chelsea. Subway: N, R to 8th St., 14th St., 23rd St.*

11 *f-5*

LITTLE ITALY

First settled between 1880 and 1924, New York's old Italian community is shrinking as Chinatown expands, but visitors still clog the narrow streets in search of hearty Neapolitan fare, cappuccino, and cannoli at the area's many cafés. Mulberry Street remains the main drag, and becomes a proud, pedestrian-only fairground during the 10-day Feast of San Gennaro (see September in Events, below). *Canal–Houston Sts. from Lafayette St. to Bowery. Subway: 6 to Spring St.; Bowery.*

6 *a-2*

LITTLE RED LIGHTHOUSE (JEFFREY'S HOOK LIGHT)

Tucked under the George Washington Bridge is this 40-ft-tall namesake from the beloved children's story "The Little Red Lighthouse and the Great Gray Bridge." Originally constructed in 1880, and once a critical warning signal that kept Hudson River barges from dashing themselves against the rocky shore, the lighthouse is now a landmark, occasionally brought to life in tours given by the New York City Parks Department. *Ft. Washington Park off 178th St., Washington Heights., 800/201–7275. Subway: 175th St.*

3 *c-7*

LOWER EAST SIDE

Historically the absorption center for New York's floods of Jewish immigrants in the 1880s and 1890s, the Lower East Side was at one time the world's largest Jewish community. Today the pushcarts are gone, and many of the synagogues stand abandoned. Lately, however, the neighborhood is being revitalized, and it's probably just around the corner from becoming a "hot" community. For a closer look, take one of the fascinating tours presented by the Lower East Side Tenement Museum. *Roughly Houston–Canal Sts. from Bowery to East River.*

11 *d-1*

MACDOUGAL ALLEY

A charming little dead-end street in Greenwich Village, McDougal Alley is lined with tiny houses, originally built as stables in the 19th century. *Off MacDougal St. between Washington Sq. N and 8th St., Greenwich Village. Subway: W. 4th St./Washington Sq.; 8th St.*

10 *e-7*

MERCHANTS' EXCHANGE (CITIBANK)

(Isaiah Rogers, 1836–42; remodeled by McKim, Mead & White, 1907) This massive building with two colonnades originally had only one floor, serving first as a merchants' exchange and later as the U.S Customs House (1863–99). The second set of columns and the second story were added in 1907, when the building was turned into a bank. *55 Wall St. (between William and Hanover Sts.), Lower Manhattan. Subway: Wall St.*

10 *d-1*

MILLIGAN PLACE/ PATCHIN PLACE

The houses on these two secluded Greenwich Village cul-de-sacs were originally built in 1848–49 as boardinghouses for the Basque employees of a nearby hotel. Later many famous writers lived on Patchin Place, including Theodore Dreiser and e. e. cummings. *Off 6th Ave. (west side) between 10th and 11th Sts.; off W. 10th St. (north side) between Greenwich and 6th Aves. Subway: W. 4th St./Washington Sq.; F to 14th St.*

11 *g-7*

EDWARD MOONEY HOUSE

Chinatown's Georgian Mooney House is thought to be Manhattan's oldest surviving row house. Restored in 1971, it was built between the British evacuation (1785) and Washington's inauguration (1789) by merchant Edward Mooney, known in his day as a breeder of championship racehorses. *18 Bowery (at Pell St.), Chinatown. Subway: J, M, Z to Canal St.*

6 *d-4*

MORRIS-JUMEL MANSION

This pre-Revolution Georgian mansion, built in 1765 in the Palladian style (remodeled 1810), is the oldest surviving private dwelling on Manhattan. Originally the "summer villa" of British officer Roger Morris's family, it later served famously as General George Washington's headquarters in 1776. Bought in 1810 by the wealthy French merchant Stephen Jumel, it was occupied by his widow, Eliza Bowen (who married Aaron Burr in 1833) until 1865. (See Haunted Places, above.) The mansion contains nine rooms with magnificent Georgian, Federal, and French Empire furnishings, silver, and china, a Colonial kitchen, and a lovely herb and rose garden. While you're here: nearby Sylvan Terrace, a completely restored cobblestone street between Jumel Terrace and St. Nicholas Ave., is lined with rare wooden row houses dating from 1882. *Edgecombe Ave. at 160th St., Washington Heights,*

212/923–8008. Admission: $3. Open Wed.–Sun. 10–4. Subway: 157th St.

10 *e-5*

MUNICIPAL BUILDING

(McKim, Mead & White, 1914) Straddling Chambers Street, the Beaux-Arts Municipal Building is an almost imperial civic skyscraper. Like a wedding cake, the building is topped with a 10-story turreted central tower at whose pinnacle stands "Civic Fame," a 25-ft-high gilt statue. Inside the building is jumble of city offices; each year thousands of couples get married in a civil chapel on the second floor. *Centre St. at Chambers St. Subway: Chambers St.*

11 *b-2*

"NARROWEST HOUSE"

Only 9½ ft wide, the "narrowest house" occupies what was once a carriageway. Built in 1873, it has the honor of snuggling up to the oldest residence in Greenwich Village, the Isaacs-Hendricks House next door. Poet Edna St. Vincent Millay lived here in 1923. *75½ Bedford St. (between Morton and Commerce Sts.), West Village. Subway: Christopher St./Sheridan Sq.*

11 *f-2*

OLD MERCHANT'S HOUSE

(Attributed to Minard Lafever, 1832) A hidden treasure in the East Village, this completely intact, four-story Greek Revival house became the property of Seabury Tredwell, a wealthy merchant and hardware importer, in 1835. It retains most of its original fittings and furniture, as well as clothing belonging to Tredwell's daughter Gertrude, who lived here until her death in 1933 at the age of 93. Restored and open to the public, the house is particularly appealing during the Christmas season, when it's decorated in the style of a 19th-century holiday party. *29 E. 4th St. (between Lafayette St. and Bowery), East Village, 212/777–1089. Admission: $3, $2 students and seniors. Open Sun.–Thurs. 1–4. Subway: Astor Pl.; Bleecker St.*

10 *e-5*

OLD NEW YORK COUNTY COURTHOUSE

(John Kellum, 1872) This stately Italianate edifice is better known as the Tweed Courthouse. Built during political boss William Tweed's iron reign over city government, its construction

dragged on for nine years at a then-unheard-of cost of $8–$12 million, most of which lined the pockets of Boss Tweed and his cronies. *52 Chambers St. (between Broadway and Centre St., behind City Hall), Lower Manhattan. Subway: Chambers St.*

10 *d-1*

PATCHIN PLACE

See Milligan Place/Patchin Place, above.

10 *f-6*

PEARL STREET

Now in the financial district, this street formed the shoreline of the East River in Dutch colonial times, and was named for the mother-of-pearl oyster shells scattered along the beach. *Lower Manhattan. Subway: Whitehall/South Ferry.*

9 *e-8*

PLAYERS CLUB

Built in 1845, the Players Club was remodeled by Stanford White in 1888, when actor Edwin Booth turned it into a private club for members of the "theatrical profession." Peek through the bars of adjacent Gramercy Park to see a statue depicting Booth playing Hamlet (*see Statues & Monuments, below*). *16 Gramercy Park S (between Irving Pl. and Park Ave. S). Subway: 6 to 23rd St.*

9 *d-2*

THE PLAZA HOTEL

(Henry J. Hardenbergh, 1907) This 18-story French Renaissance building by the same architect who designed the Dakota is more than an architectural landmark. Its exuberant style; its fortuitous location on spacious Grand Army Plaza, across from Central Park; and its legendary past make it a sentimental favorite. Ernest Hemingway supposedly recommended to F. Scott Fitzgerald that when he died, he should leave his liver to Princeton but his heart to the Plaza. (*See Expensive Lodgings in Chapter 7.*) *5th Ave. and 59th St., Midtown, 212/759–3000. Subway: N, R to 5th Ave.*

11 *f-5*

POLICE HEADQUARTERS

(Hoppin & Koen, 1909) A baroque beauty with an impressive dome, this was the city's main police station when future President Teddy Roosevelt was the New York City's police chief. The police moved out in 1973, and this lovely old building became a luxury coop residence in the booming '80s. *240 Centre St. (between Broome and Grand Sts.), Little Italy. Subway: 6 to Spring St.; J, M, Z to Canal St.*

9 *g-7*

PUBLIC BATHS, CITY OF NEW YORK

(Arnold W. Brunner and William Martin Aiken, 1906) Public baths worthy of ancient Rome, these relics are now incorporated into the municipal swimming pool at the Asser Levy Recreation Center. *E. 23rd St. near FDR Dr., Gramercy. Subway: 6 to 23rd St.*

11 *f-1*

PUBLIC THEATER

(Alexander Saeltzer, 1849; additions by Griffith Thomas, 1859, and Thomas Sent, 1881; renovation by Giorgio Cavaglieri, 1967) Designed in the style of an Italian palazzo, the Public Theatre was originally the Astor Library, New York's first free public library. Today, after a 1967 interior renovation, it houses the creative legacy of theater impresario Joseph Papp: the old reading rooms became auditoriums, which function as five different theaters. *Hair* and *A Chorus Line* both premiered here. *425 Lafayette St. (near Astor Pl.), East Village, 212/598-7150. Subway: Astor Pl.; 8th St.*

11 *f-3*

PUCK BUILDING

(Albert Wagner, 1886-1993) This giant, redbrick Romanesque Revival was home to the satirical weekly *Puck* from 1887 to 1916, and eventually housed the world's largest concentration of lithographers and printers. Today, it holds gallery and studio space and the Manhattan campus of Pratt Institute. Two gold-leaf statues of Puck continue to gaze whimsically at passersby. *295-307 Lafayette St. (at Houston St.), SoHo. Subway: Bleecker St.; Broadway-Lafayette St.*

9 *d-4*

RADIO CITY MUSIC HALL

(Edward Durrell Stone and Donald Deskey) This 1932 Art Deco theater can seat 6,200. Its interior is magnificence on a grand scale, with the world's largest chandeliers hanging from a 50-ft ceiling in the foyer, to 32-ft organ pipes. (*See* Concert Halls *in* Chapter 5.) *1260 6th Ave. (at 50th St.), Midtown. Subway: 47th-50th Sts./Rockefeller Center.*

9 *h-2*

ROOSEVELT ISLAND

Known earlier as Welfare Island, in which incarnation it housed the city's poor and chronically ill, this 2-mile long strip of land in the middle of the East River became a "self-sufficient" residential complex in the 1970s. Burnt-out traces of the old institutions peek out from the edges of this otherwise clean-lined environment, and north-south promenades offer impressive river views. Getting to Roosevelt Island is a delight: opened in 1976, the Roosevelt Island tramway is the only aerial commuter tram in the United States. From the tram plaza at 2nd Avenue and 60th Street, the 25-person cabin rises 250 ft in the air above the East River and glides to a stop on the island in four minutes. *East River, roughly parallel to 50th-86th Sts. Subway: Roosevelt Island.*

9 *e-2*

SARA DELANO ROOSEVELT MEMORIAL HOUSE

(Charles A. Platt, 1907-1908) Mrs. Roosevelt commissioned Platt to build twin town houses, one for her son Franklin and his future wife, Eleanor, and one for herself. FDR lived here until he became governor of New York, in 1928; his mother lived at No. 47 until her death in 1941. *47-49 E. 65th St., Upper East Side. Subway: 68th St./Hunter College; N, R to 5th Ave.*

9 *e-8*

THEODORE ROOSEVELT BIRTHPLACE NATIONAL HISTORIC SITE

Theodore Roosevelt, the 26th President and the only U.S. president from New York City, was born on this site in 1858. The original 1848 brownstone was demolished in 1916, but this Gothic Revival replica was constructed in 1923. Now administered by the National Park Service, Roosevelt's restored boyhood home has a fascinating collection of Teddyana in five Victorian period rooms. *28 E. 20th St., Gramercy, 212/260-1616. Admission: $2. Open Wed.-Sun. 9-5. House tours on the hour; chamber-music concerts Sat. at 2. Subway: N, R, 6 to 23rd St.*

11 *b-3*

ST. LUKE'S PLACE

In Greenwich Village, this handsome block of 1850s brick and brownstone row houses has billeted many famous residents. New York mayor Jimmy Walker (elected in 1926) lived in No. 6, poet Marianne Moore lived in No. 14, and novelist Theodore Dreiser wrote *An American Tragedy* in No. 16. *Between Hudson St. and 7th Ave. S. Subway: 1, 9 to Houston St.*

6 *e-7*
ST. NICHOLAS HISTORIC DISTRICT ("STRIVERS ROW")
In 1891, builder David H. King commissioned several leading architects of the day—James Brown Lord, Bruce Price and Clarence S. Luce, and McKim, Mead & White—and the results were the King Model Houses, a harmonious grouping of row houses and apartments. Originally built for well-to-do white residents, they were purchased by aspiring African-American professionals in the '20s and '30s and acquired the collective nickname "Strivers Row" as Harlem evolved into a black community. *Adam Clayton Powell–Frederick Douglass Blvds. from 138th to 139th Sts., Harlem. Subway: 135th St.*

10 *f-1*
ST. MARK'S HISTORIC DISTRICT
This historic East Village oasis contains three of Manhattan's earliest Federal buildings: St. Mark's Church in-the-Bowery (1799), the Stuyvesant-Fish House (1804), and 44 Stuyvesant Street (1795), all traceable back to Dutch governor Peter Stuyvesant, on whose farmland the district rests. Stuyvesant Street, the only true east-west street in Manhattan, was the driveway to the governor's mansion. *E. 10th and Stuyvesant Sts. between 2nd and 3rd Aves. Subway: Astor Pl.*

10 *f-2*
ST. MARK'S PLACE
In the 1960s, the 1830s Greek Revival row houses lining these blocks went psychedelic and formed the main street of the hippie phenomenon. Later, St. Mark's became a haven for punk rockers, and though a few punks remain, the counterculture has largely given way to tourism. Jewelry stands, T-shirt stalls, ethnic restaurants, and body piercers now line the East Village's gritty main drag. *Between 3rd Ave. and Tompkins Sq. Park, East Village. Subway: Astor Pl.*

10 *f-6*
SCHERMERHORN ROW
Dating from the early 19th century, these 12 peak-roof Georgian Federal and Greek Revival buildings were originally warehouses and countinghouses serving New York's then-bustling seaport. Now landmarks, they have been carefully restored as part of the South Street Seaport Museum's efforts to evoke the area's rich history (*see* History Museums, *below*). *218 Fulton, 91–92 South, 159–171 John, and 189–195 Front Sts., Lower Manhattan. Subway: Fulton St.*

9 *e-1*
SEVENTH REGIMENT ARMORY
(Charles W. Clinton, 1879) A Victorian incarnation of a medieval fortress, the vast armory houses a great drill hall (187 ft by 290 ft) and a Veterans' Room and library decorated under the direction of Louis Comfort Tiffany. Every January, this behemoth fills with the renowned Winter Antiques Show (*see* Events, *below*). *643 Park Ave. (between 66th and 67th Sts.), Upper East Side, 212/744–2968. Tours avail. by appointment. Subway: 68th St./Hunter College.*

9 *c-4*
SHUBERT ALLEY
Now just a glitzy shortcut in the theatre district, this private alley was the commercial domain of brothers J. J., Lee, and Sam Shubert, theater impresarios, in the early 1900s. Actors and chorus girls thronged to Shubert Alley whenever new shows were being cast. *Between 44th–45th Sts., west of 7th Ave. Subway: 42nd St./Times Sq.*

9 *e-6*
SNIFFEN COURT HISTORIC DISTRICT
In Murray Hill, New York's smallest designated historic district is a charming 19th-century mews of 10 Romanesque Revival brick carriage houses. Built as stables in the 1860s, they were converted to residences in the 1920s. *150–158 E. 36th St., Murray Hill. Subway: 33rd St.*

10 *e-3*
SOHO
An acronym meaning south of Houston Street, SoHo is bounded by West Broadway, Canal, and Lafayette streets. Filled with galleries, trendy boutiques, shops,

restaurants, and artists' lofts, this wonderfully with-it neighborhood is also a splendid treasure trove of 19th-century cast-iron architecture (see Cast-Iron Historic District in Architecture, above). *Subway: Prince St.; Spring St.*

11 *g-1*

STUYVESANT-FISH HOUSE

Dating from 1804, this brick Federal house in the East Village was built by the Dutch governor Peter Stuyvesant's great-grandson as a wedding gift for his daughter Elizabeth and her husband, Nicholas Fish. *21 Stuyvesant St. (at 9th St., between 2nd and 3rd Aves.), East Village. Subway: Astor Pl.*

10 *e-5*

SURROGATE'S COURT/ HALL OF RECORDS

(John R. Thomas, Horgan & Slattery, 1899–1907) The Surrogate's Court forms a delightful and impressive civic monument opposite City Hall Park. With marble walls, a vaulted ceiling, and encircling corridors, its central hall is one of the finest Beaux-Arts rooms this side of the Paris Opera House. *31 Chambers St. (at Centre St.), Lower Manhattan. Subway: Chambers St.*

9 *g-3*

SUTTON PLACE

Overlooking the East River, Sutton Place is a quiet and prestigious enclave of luxury apartments and lavish town houses with private gardens. The address is synonymous with status, affluence, and, in the case of former resident Greta Garbo, mystery. *1 block east of 1st Ave., from 53rd to 59th Sts., Upper East Side. Subway: 4, 5, 6 to 59th St.*

9 *c-4*

TIMES SQUARE

Named for the Times Tower—which no longer houses the *New York Times,* but still "drops the ball" on hundreds of thousands of revelers every New Year's Eve—Times Square has long been synonymous with Broadway shows, bright lights, and seedy doings. In a somewhat surprising recent turn, however, a controversial redevelopment scheme has almost completely sanitized Times Square. The neon lights remain, but the porn businesses, which long occupied abandoned theaters on 42nd Street, have been booted out, and 42nd Street is filling with gleaming megastores,

each visually louder than the last. Although tourists seem to like it, many New Yorkers smell Disneyland in this unlikely metamorphosis. Once just crass, Times Square is now crassly commercial. *42nd–47th Sts. at Broadway and 7th Ave.*

11 *e-1*

TRIANGLE FIRE PLAQUE

Just east of Washington Square is a plaque commemorating a tragic fire in the building that once housed the Triangle Shirtwaist Company. On March 25, 1911, fire broke out on the upper floors of this sweatshop, and within a single hour 146 young women were killed, many of them leaping in flames to their deaths on the streets below. The building was equipped with fire escapes, and was supposed to be fireproof, but supervisors had locked the workers into their workrooms. A state investigation following the fire led to new labor laws and improved safety conditions for factory workers. *Washington Pl. and Greene St., Greenwich Village. Subway: 8th St.; Astor Pl.*

10 *d-5*

TRIBECA

Tribeca translates as the *Triangle Below Canal.* Once a 19th-century wholesaling district (there are still some aging signs advertising fresh dairy products), Tribeca is the city's newest fashionably transformed neighborhood and is still very much in flux. The surprisingly attractive old warehouses—many clad in cast iron and patterned brick—are rapidly turning into artists' lofts, luxury condos, and offices. Reflecting this hip influx, Tribeca now boasts several of the city's trendiest and priciest restaurants. *Broadway–West St. from Chambers St. to Canal St. Subway: Franklin St.; Chambers St.; 1, 9 to Canal St.*

9 *e-1*

UNION CLUB

(Delano & Aldrich, 1932) This limestone-and-granite behemoth houses the oldest private club in New York. *101 E. 69th St., Upper East Side. Subway: 68th St./Hunter College.*

10 *e-7*

U.S. CUSTOMS HOUSE

(Cass Gilbert, 1907) A monumental Beaux-Arts building with 44 Corinthian columns, the Customs House is now home to the National Museum of the American Indian (*see* History Museums, *below*). Since the building was originally used to collect import taxes on foreign goods shipped into the Port of New York, its architectural theme is "world trade": Four massive limestone sculptures embedded in the facade represent Asia, the Americas, Europe, and Africa, while 12 smaller ones arrayed above represent the world's "greatest trading nations." The huge oval rotunda has 1937 WPA murals by Reginald Marsh. *1 Bowling Green, Lower Manhattan. Subway: Bowling Green.*

9 *e-4*
VILLARD HOUSES
(McKim, Mead & White, 1882–85) Surrounding a peaceful courtyard, this cluster of Italian Renaissance–style brownstones was modeled on Rome's Palazzo della Cancelleria. Built by newspaper owner and railroad entrepreneur Henry Villard, they have served variously as the home of the Catholic Archdiocese of New York and Random House Publishing Co. Today they comprise the landmark section of the New York Palace Hotel (*see* Very Expensive Lodgings *in* Chapter 7), containing its opulent public rooms and the hot, new Le Cirque 2000 (*see* French *in* Chapter 3). *451–457 Madison Ave.; 24 E. 51st St., Midtown. Subway: 51st St./Lexington–3rd Aves.*

10 *e-7*
WALL STREET
In 1653 this was the northern frontier of the city, fortified against attack by a Dutch wall of thick wooden planks. The wall was completely dismantled by the English in 1699, but the name stuck, and The Street is now synonymous with the downtown financial district and the world of high finance in general. *Subway: Wall St.*

11 *d-1*
WASHINGTON MEWS
Lined with converted stables, this 19th-century Greenwich Village mews once housed the carriage horses of fashionable Washington Square area residents. *University Pl. to 5th Ave., between 8th St. and Washington Sq. N. Subway: 8th St.*

11 *d-1*
WASHINGTON SQUARE NORTH
(Town & Davis, ca. 1831) Immortalized in Henry James's *Washington Square*, "the Row" housed New York's most prominent citizens when it was first built. No. 8 was the mayor's official residence. Lovingly preserved, these stylish Greek Revival row houses are an affecting reminder of Old New York. *1–13 and 21–26 Washington Sq. N (between 5th Ave. and University Pl.), Greenwich Village. Subway: W. 4th St./Washington Sq.*

7 *f-7*
YORKVILLE
A remote hamlet known as *klein Deutschland* (little Germany) in the 19th century, Yorkville has also been a haven for immigrants from Austria, Hungary, and Czechoslovakia. *Lexington–York Aves. from 75th to 88th Sts., Upper East Side. Subway: 77th St.; 4, 5, 6 to 86th St.*

queens

1 *f-3*
BOWNE HOUSE
The oldest building in Queens and the former home of Quaker John Bowne, this 1661 Colonial residence was a clandestine meeting place for the then-forbidden Society of Friends (Quakers). Bowne's arrest and subsequent acquittal by Dutch authorities set a precedent for freedom of worship in the New World. (*See* Friends Meeting House *in* Churches & Synagogues, *above*.) *3701 Bowne St. (between 37th and 38th Aves.), Flushing, 718/359–0528. Guided tours Tues., Sat., Sun. between 2:30 and 4:30; tours for larger groups other days by appointment. Subway: 7 to Main St./Flushing.*

1 *g-2*
CORNELIUS VAN WYCK HOUSE
Built in 1735, this Dutch Colonial farmhouse on the edge of Little Neck Bay was built by Revolutionary War patriot Cornelius Van Wyck. *3704 Douglaston Pkwy. at Alston Pl., Douglaston.*

3 *c-4*
HUNTER'S POINT HISTORIC DISTRICT
Dating from the 1870s, this block of middle-income row houses is excellently

preserved. *45th Ave. (between 21st and 23rd Sts.), Long Island City. Subway: 7 to 45th Rd.*

1 g-4

KING MANOR MUSEUM

The home of Rufus King—member of the Continental Congress, U.S. senator, and unsuccessful candidate for president—this gambrel-roof farmhouse dates back to 1750. It's now a history museum with a nine-room interior restored and decorated in period furniture. *King Park, Jamaica Ave. between 150th and 153rd Sts., Jamaica, 718/206–0545. Admission: $2, $1 children. Open weekends noon–4. Subway: Jamaica Center.*

3 h-1

KINGSLAND HOMESTEAD

Home to the Queens Historical Society, this farmhouse, built in 1774 by a wealthy Quaker farmer, is an interesting mix of Dutch and English architectural traditions. Moved from its original location on 155th Street, it now houses period rooms and changing exhibits. *Weeping Beech Park, 143-35 37th Ave. (at Parsons Blvd.), Flushing, 718/939–0647. Admission: $2, $1 seniors and children. Open Tues., Sat., and Sun. 2:30–4:30. Subway: 7 to Main St./Flushing.*

8 f-4

LENT HOMESTEAD

Well preserved since its construction in 1729, this simple, Dutch Colonial farmhouse retains its original stonework and overhanging, wood-shingled roof. *7803 19th Rd. (at 78th St.), Astoria.*

3 h-1

WEEPING BEECH TREE

Samuel Parsons, a Flushing nurseryman, purchased a shoot from a rare Belgian tree in 1847; 150 years later, it became the first tree ever designated a New York City landmark. It's over 60 ft high, with an 85-ft spread and a trunk circumference of 14 ft. *37th Ave. between Parsons Blvd. and Bowne St., Flushing. Subway: 7 to Main St./Flushing.*

staten island

4 c-7

ALICE AUSTEN HOUSE (CLEAR COMFORT)

Probably built between 1700 and 1750, this Dutch-style cottage was the home of Alice Austen, a pioneering photographer, from 1866 to 1952. Austen's legacy: 3,000 glass-plate negatives of photos taken 1880–1930. View prints from those plates among Victorian furnishings at the house-cum-museum. *2 Hylan Blvd., Rosebank, 718/816–4506. Suggested contribution: $3. Open Thurs.–Sun. noon–5.*

1 a-4

CONFERENCE HOUSE (BILLOPP HOUSE)

Built by British naval captain Christopher Billopp circa 1675, this manor house is renowned as the site of the only attempted peace conference during the American Revolution. On September 11, 1776, rebels Ben Franklin, John Adams, and Edward Rutledge met with British Admiral Lord Howe and refused to negotiate a cease-fire unless the Colonies were granted complete independence. *7455 Hylan Blvd., Tottenville, 718/984–2086. Closed Dec. 15–Mar. 15; closed Mon. and Tues.*

1 b-1

GARDINER TYLER RESIDENCE

A grand mansion across from St. Peter's Cemetery, this 1835 house was the home of President John Tyler's widow, Julia Gardiner Tyler, from 1868 to 1874. *27 Tyler St. (between Clove Rd and Broadway), West Brighton.*

1 b-3

POILLON HOUSE

Frederick Law Olmsted lived in this 1720 house in his youth, and made extensive changes to the place in 1848. *4515 Hylan Blvd. (between Hales Ave. and Woods of Arden Rd.), Annadale.*

1 b-2

HISTORIC RICHMONDTOWN

Known as Cocclestown when it was founded in 1685 by Dutch, French Walloon, and English settlers, present-day Richmondtown is the site of approximately 26 buildings of major historical interest, 1690–1890. Highlights include the Voorlezer's House (1695), the oldest known elementary-school building in the United States, and the Stephens General Store & House, a reconstructed 19th-century store. In summer, costumed interpreters and craftspeople, such as a tinsmith, basketmaker, and shoemaker, recreate a 19th-century village; on Labor

Day weekend the County Fair takes over; and at the end of December, folks convene for candlelight tours and holiday revels. From January to April, there are tavern concerts in a period tavern lit by candles and heated by a woodburning stove. *Arthur Kill and Richmond Rds., Richmondtown, 718/351–1611. Open Apr.–June and Sept.–Dec., Wed.–Fri. and Sun. 1–5; July and Aug., Wed.–Fri. 10–5, weekends 1–5; Jan.–Mar., call for hrs. From Staten Island Ferry, take Bus 74.*

4 *a-6*

SNUG HARBOR CULTURAL CENTER
Sailor's Snug Harbor originally consisted of five magnificent Greek Revival buildings built in the 1830s and '40s as a home for "aged, decrepit and worn-out sailors." In all, there are now 28 buildings on 83 acres of park, and they serve as a performing- and visual-arts facility offering art exhibits, theater, recitals, concerts, and outdoor sculpture in a landmark maritime setting. Components include the Staten Island Botanical Garden (*see* Botanical Gardens *in* Chapter 6) and the Staten Island Children's Museum (*see* Children's Museums, *above*). *1000 Richmond Terr. (from Tysen St.to Kissel Avenue), Livingston, 718/448–2500. Open daily 8 AM–dusk. In summer, tours depart from the main gate Sun. at 2; shuttle bus from Staten Island Ferry Terminal.*

4 *a-5*

STATEN ISLAND BOROUGH HALL
(Carrère & Hastings, 1906) Just above the ferry landing in St. George, Staten Island's seat of government, with its slender clock tower, was designed in the style of a French château. *Richmond Terr. at Borough Pl.*

HISTORY MUSEUMS

Some landmark buildings and mansions have their own collections and period furnishings; *see* Historic Buildings & Areas, *above*.

8 *c-8*

AMERICAN MUSEUM OF THE MOVING IMAGE
Adjacent to the Kaufman-Astoria Studios, this unique museum is devoted to the art, technology, and history of the film and television industries. It contains a state-of-the-art, 190-seat theater, a 60-seat screening room, and 25,000 square ft of exhibit space. In addition to the Zoetrope—a giant spinning disk on which the first primitive movies were shown—and costumes worn by Marilyn Monroe, Marlene Dietrich, and Robin Williams, hundreds of classic films are "displayed" annually. *35th Ave. and 36th St., Astoria, Queens, 718/784–4520; Admission: $8 adults, $5 students and seniors, $4 children 4–17, free children under 4 (all screenings included). Open Tues.–Fri. noon–5, weekends 1–6. Subway: Steinway St.*

6 *d-5*

AMERICAN NUMISMATIC SOCIETY
Devoted to the study of coins and currency, the Numismatic Society has two public galleries, filled with coins that come from around the world and as far back as ancient Rome. *Audubon Terr. Museum Complex, Broadway and 155th St., Washington Heights, 212/234–3130. Open Tues.–Sat. 9–4:30, Sun. 1–4. Subway: 155th St.*

9 *c-2*

AMERICAN BIBLE SOCIETY GALLERY AND ARCHIVES
Outside the Vatican, this is the largest Bible collection in the world, with nearly 50,000 scriptural items in nearly 2,000 languages and dialects. Planning to reopen in April 1998 after renovation, the gallery normally offers exhibits of rare and historic Bibles; leaves of the original Gutenberg Bible; Helen Keller's braille Bible; and a Kai Feng Fu Torah scroll. *1865 Broadway (at 61st St.), Upper West Side, 212/408–1236. Open weekdays 9–4:30. Subway: 59th st./Columbus Circle.*

12 *b-3*

BROOKLYN HISTORICAL SOCIETY
The gallery here is eclectic, with Brooklyn Dodgers baseball bats and trick mirrors from Coney Island alongside changing exhibits on the history of the borough's neighborhoods, culture, and institutions. *128 Pierrepont St., Brooklyn Heights, 718/624–0890. Admission: $2.50. Open Mon. and Thurs.–Sun. noon–5. Subway: Clark St.; Borough Hall; Court St.*

9 *d-3*

CARNEGIE HALL MUSEUM

Built when Carnegie Hall was renovated for its centennial in 1991, this little museum holds memorabilia from the music hall's illustrious history, including photos of Maria Callas, Benny Goodman's clarinet, and a baton used by Arturo Toscanini. *881 7th Ave. (at 57th St.), Midtown, 212/903–9629. Open Mon., Tues., and Thurs.–Sun. 11–4:30. Subway: 57th St.; 7th Ave.*

4 *h-7*

CONEY ISLAND MUSEUM

In the same building as the Coney Island Sideshow, just a block away from the boardwalk, this museum documents the history of this beachside amusement park from the late 19th century to the present. On display are original horses from the old steeplechase, a wicker rolling chair in which older folks were pushed down the boardwalk for 75¢ an hour, and banners and photos from old sideshow acts. Musical performances are staged on weekend nights. *1208 Surf Ave. (at 12th St.), Brooklyn, 718/372–5159. Admission: 99¢. Open Fri.–Sun. noon–sunset; winter, weekends noon–sunset. Subway: W. 8th St./N.Y. Aquarium.*

1 *c-6*

ELLIS ISLAND IMMIGRATION MUSEUM

See Historic Buildings & Areas, *above.*

10 *d-1*

FORBES MAGAZINE GALLERIES

This minimuseum in the Village displays the Forbes family's idiosyncratic collections, including 12,000 toy soldiers, over 500 toy boats, 12 jeweled Fabergé eggs made for the last two Russian czars, and a wealth of historic American manuscripts and presidential papers, including letters from Abraham Lincoln. Kids tend to like the toy soldiers, while their parents may appreciate the adjacent picture gallery, with changing exhibitions. *62 5th Ave. (at 12th St.), 212/206–5548. Open Tues., Wed., Fri., and Sat. 10–4. Subway: 8th St.; F to 14th St.*

10 *e-7*

FRAUNCES TAVERN MUSEUM

This museum commemorates the site of the original tavern of Samuel Fraunces, where George Washington bade farewell to his officers in 1783 after having forced the redcoats from New York. Founded in 1907 in five reconstructed Federal buildings, the museum interprets the history and culture of colonial America through Revolutionary War artifacts and colonial-period rooms, decorative arts, prints, and paintings. Call for a current schedule of exhibits, lectures, performances, and walking tours. *54 Pearl St. (at Broad St.), Lower Manhattan, 212/425–1778. Admission: $2,50, $1 students and seniors, free children under 6. Open weekdays 10–4:45, weekends noon–4. Subway: Whitehall St./South Ferry.*

4 *c-2*

HUDSON WATERFRONT MUSEUM

In a historic wooden barge on the Brooklyn waterfront, this makeshift museum presents changing art exhibits and maritime artifacts (1860–1960) from New York Harbor. The adjacent pier and community garden offer stunning harbor views stretching from the Verrazano Bridge to the Statue of Liberty. *290 Conover St., Red Hook Garden Pier, Brooklyn, 718/624–4719. Donation suggested. Museum open by appointment only. Subway: Borough Hall, then Bus B61 (to Beard) or 77 (to Conover) toward Red Hook.*

1 *f-3*

LOUIS ARMSTRONG ARCHIVES

While Satchmo's former home at 34–56 107th Street in Corona, Queens, is being transformed into a museum, his personal effects—including 5,000 photographs, 650 homemade audiotapes, and five gold-plated trumpets—are on display at the Louis Armstrong Archives at Queens College. *Rosenthal Library, Queens College, 65-30 Kissena Blvd., Flushing, Queens, 718/997–3670. Open by appointment only, weekdays 10–5.*

11 *h-5*

LOWER EAST SIDE TENEMENT MUSEUM

This restored 1863 tenement building is a poignant tribute to the immigrants—aptly called urban pioneers—who lived on New York's Lower East Side in the 19th and early 20th centuries. You'll be guided through apartments furnished as they most likely appeared to those who lived here: the Gumpertz family, a German Jewish family from the 1870s, and the Baldizzis, a Sicilian Catholic family from the 1930s. Less than 10 years old, the museum is a work in progress; more apartments will be opened as the museum expands. *90 Orchard St. (at Broome St.), 212/431–0233. Admission: $8, $6 students and seniors. Open Tues.– Fri. noon–5, weekends 11–5. Subway: Delancey St.; Essex St.; Grand St.*

9 *c-7*

MUSEUM AT THE FASHION INSTITUTE OF TECHNOLOGY

Deep in the garment district, F.I.T. is home to a substantial museum space documenting the history of fashion both high and low. The textile collection holds more than 3 million indexed swatches, alongside ½ million costumes and accessories from the 18th century to the present. Recent shows have addressed topics ranging from the history of automobile upholstery to haute couture of the past five decades. *7th Ave. and 27th St., 212/217–5970. Open Tues.–Fri. noon–8, weekends 11–5. Subway: 1, 9 to 28th St.*

10 *e-7*

MUSEUM OF AMERICAN FINANCIAL HISTORY

This one-room museum displays artifacts from Wall Street and the financial markets, including a vintage ticker-tape machine. *28 Broadway (between Beaver St. and Exchange Pl.), Lower Manhattan, 212/908–4519. Open weekdays 11–2:30 or by appointment. Subway: Rector St.;4, 5 to Wall St.*

11 *f-7*

MUSEUM OF CHINESE IN THE AMERICAS

The permanent exhibit, "Where is Home," documents the vibrant history and culture of Chinese immigrants in New York, San Francisco, Canada, and Latin America. *70 Mulberry St. (at Bayard St.), 2nd floor, Chinatown, 212/ 619–4785. Admission: $3, $1 students and seniors, free children under 12. Open Tues.–Thurs. and Sat. noon–5. Subway: 6, J, M, Z to Canal St.*

10 *d-6*

MUSEUM OF JEWISH HERITAGE— A LIVING MEMORIAL TO THE HOLOCAUST

Opened in 1997 after years of planning, this museum is devoted to preserving the memory of the Holocaust through photographs, artifacts, and videotaped oral histories. *18 1st Pl., Battery Park City, Lower Manhattan, 212/968–1800; Admission: $7 adults, $5 students and seniors, free children under 5. Open Sun.–Wed. 9– 5, Thurs. 9–8, Fri. 9–2. Subway: South Ferry; Bowling Green.*

9 *d-3*

MUSEUM OF TELEVISION AND RADIO

If you harbor secret addictions to *Nick at Night* and *TVLand*, this is the place for you. With 75,000 radio and TV programs preserved forever in its permanent collection, the museum encourages visitors to select their favorite shows and watch away at over 100 personal consoles. Try the Beatles on the *Ed Sullivan Show*, the pilot episode of *Charlie's Angels*, or the original radio broadcast of Orson Welles' *War of the Worlds*. There are 96 television consoles, a 200-seat theater, a 96-seat theater, two 45-seat screening rooms, and a listening room for radio programs. Frequent special screenings bring rare programs back to light. *25 W. 52nd St, Midtown, 212/621–6800. Admission: $6, $4 seniors and students, $3 children under 13. Open Tues., Wed., and Fri.– Sun. noon–6, Thurs. noon–8. Subway: E, F to 5th Ave.; 47th–50th Sts./Rockefeller Center.*

7 *e-4*

MUSEUM OF THE CITY OF NEW YORK

The amazing life and history of New York City—from the Native Americans and early Dutch settlers through the present day—is chronicled in this massive Georgian mansion via costumes, furniture, paintings, artifacts, oral histories, dollhouses, and toys. Special exhibits usually run simultaneously, featuring such topics as Harlem, the Irish in New York, Tin Pan Alley, and *New Yorker* cover art. The museum also sponsors a wonderful series of urban walking tours. *1220 5th Ave. (at 103rd St.), Upper East Side, 212/ 534–1672; Admission: $5 adults; $4 students, seniors, and children. Open Wed.– Sat. 10–5, Sun. 1–5. Subway: 103rd St.*

10 *e-7*

NATIONAL MUSEUM OF THE AMERICAN INDIAN

With over 1 million artifacts, this is the world's largest and best collection of ethnology and archaeology on the Indians of North, South, and Central America and the West Indies. Run by the Smithsonian Institution, the museum is rich in sound and video recordings of Native Americans explaining the significance of specific exhibits. Live dance performances and craft demonstrations by masters, such as totem-pole carvers, bring the exhibits to life. For the history of the building, see U.S. Customs House in Historic Buildings & Areas, above. 1 Bowling Green (Broadway and Whitehall St.), Lower Manhattan, 212/668–6624. Open daily 10–5. Subway: Bowling Green.

9 e-3
NEWSEUM/NY
Opened in 1997, Newseum/NY, a branch of Newseum in Washington, D.C., presents changing exhibits on news and photojournalism, focusing on First Amendment issues and how news is made. Displays are accompanied by documentary films, lectures, and round-table discussions with newsmakers and newsbreakers. 580 Madison Ave. (between 56th and 57th Sts.), Midtown, 212/317–7596. Open Mon.–Sat. 10–5:30. Subway: 59th St.; N, R to 5th Ave.

11 c-4
NEW YORK CITY FIRE MUSEUM
Examine hand-pulled and horse-drawn firefighting apparatus, uniforms, and sliding poles at this restored 1904 firehouse in SoHo, which chronicles the efforts of New York's Bravest from the 18th century to the present. 278 Spring St. (between Hudson and Varick Sts.), West Village, 212/691–1303. Admission: $4, $2 seniors, $1 children under 12. Open Tues.–Sun. 10–4. Subway: C, E to Spring St.

7 c-8
NEW-YORK HISTORICAL SOCIETY
Founded in 1804, this is the oldest museum in the city. Changing exhibits are culled from the society's elegant collection of paintings, prints, folk art, and vintage toys, and cover everything from the history of Central Park to the lights of Times Square. The society houses a major research library of 600,000 volumes; an impressive collection of 18th-century New York newspapers; and over a million maps, prints, photos, lithographs, and architectural drawings—including the original watercolors for John James Audubon's Birds of America. 2 W. 77th St., Upper West Side, 212/873–

3400. Admission: $5, $3 students, seniors, and children. Open Tues.–Sun. 11–5. Subway: B, C to 72nd St.

12 c-3
NEW YORK TRANSIT MUSEUM
Appropriately located underground, in an authentic 1938 subway station, the Transit Museum contains full-size classic subway cars dating back to 1903, including wooden cars with rattan seating. It's great for kids, who for once can climb all over the seats and pretend they're driving without anyone looking askance. Volunteers dressed as subway conductors give impromptu tours. There are also vintage turnstiles, station signs, trolley models, and well-researched temporary exhibits on the history of the good old subway system. Boerum Pl. and Schermerhorn St., Downtown Brooklyn, 718/243–3060; Admission: $3, $1.50 students and seniors, free children under 5. Open Tues.–Fri. 10–4, weekends noon–5. Subway: Borough Hall.

9 e-8
POLICE MUSEUM
Right in the Police Academy, this large collection features cop paraphernalia from the Dutch era to the present, including guns, ammo, handcuffs, billy clubs, and uniforms. 235 E. 20th Street, 2nd floor, Gramercy, 212/477–9753. Open by appointment only, weekdays 9–3. Subway: 6 to 23rd St.

10 f-6
SOUTH STREET SEAPORT MUSEUM
Filling 11 square seaport blocks on the East River, this "museum without walls" features cobblestone streets, historic sailing ships, 18th- and 19th-century architecture, an old print shop, a boat-building center, and a children's crafts center with hands-on displays illuminating the history of seafaring. If you're feeling salty, book passage on the Pioneer, a 102-ft schooner built in 1885, and be sure to visit the other ships docked at Pier 16 as well, including the Peking, the second-largest sailing ship in the world; the lightship Ambrose; and the full-rigged Wavertree. Call for details on classes, programs, lectures, and events. Visitors' center: 12 Fulton St. (at South St.), Lower Manhattan, 212/748–8600. Admission: $6, $4 students, $3 children under 12. Open summer, Fri.–Wed. 10–6,

Thurs. 10–8; winter, Wed.–Mon. 10–5.
Subway: Fulton St.; Broadway–Nassau St.

9 c-1

YESHIVA UNIVERSITY MUSEUM

Changing exhibits of paintings, photographs, ceremonial objects, and architectural models of synagogues around the world reflect the Jewish historical and cultural experience. *2520 Amsterdam Ave. (at 185th St.), Washington Heights, 212/960–5390. Open Tues.–Thurs. 10:30–5, Sun. noon–6. Subway: 181st St.*

LIBRARIES

If nothing else, New Yorkers are certified readers. We love books, authors, stories . . . the whole literary idea. The five boroughs have close to 200 public libraries between them, which, in addition to loaning books, sponsor more than 500 free programs monthly, including film screenings, discussions with well-known and emerging authors, and storytelling hours for children. These are the city's most significant public and private collections; if you're conducting research in art, design, or history, tap the city's museums as well—many open their specialized collections to the public.

12 g-5

BROOKLYN PUBLIC LIBRARY (CENTRAL LIBRARY)

An art moderne pile erected in 1941, Brooklyn's central library is a grand affair—a fact that's understandably easy to forget when you're trying desperately to find a book or waiting in line for one of the library's Web-linked computers. A recent renovation opened up the library's long interior spaces, and the exterior, with its golden doorways, gilt bas-reliefs, and uplifting carved maxims, is as glorious as ever. A holdover from the days when Brooklyn was a separate city, Brooklyn's independent, 58-branch library system is headquartered here. *Grand Army Plaza (see Historic Buildings & Areas, above), Park Slope, 718/780–7700. Open Mon., Fri., and Sat. 10–6; Tues.–Thurs. 9–8, Sun. 1–5. Subway: Grand Army Plaza.*

9 e-6

PIERPONT MORGAN LIBRARY

(McKim, Mead & White, 1906) Housed in an austere, Italian Renaissance–style palazzo, the Pierpont Morgan was originally built for the collections of Wall Street baron J. Pierpont (J. P.) Morgan (1837–1913). The opulent interior is rich not only in furnishings and paintings, but in medieval and Renaissance illuminated manuscripts, old-master drawings and prints, rare books, and autographed literary and musical manuscripts. Augmented in recent years by the acquisition of the adjacent 45-room brownstone mansion—once the residence of J. P. Morgan, Jr.—the library now includes a graceful, glass-enclosed garden court, in which lunch and tea are served. Changing exhibits, drawn from the permanent collection, are almost always a delight. *Madison Ave. and 36th St., Murray Hill, 212/685–0008. Suggested donation: $5, $3 seniors and students, free children under 12. Open Tues.–Fri. 10:30–5, Sat. 10:30–6, Sun. noon–6. Tours of historic rooms Tues.–Fri. 2:30. Subway: 33rd St.*

9 d-5

NEW YORK PUBLIC LIBRARY

A national historic landmark covering two city blocks, the New York Public Library first opened its doors—guarded always by the famous stone lions—on May 24, 1911 (*see Architecture, above*). Today the library is one of the greatest research institutions in the world, with 6 million books, 12 million manuscripts, and 2.8 million pictures. Among the more unusual items in the research collection are magician Harry Houdini's personal library; a selection of 19th- and 20th-century restaurant menus; and the original stuffed animals on which A.A. Milne based his *Winnie-the-Pooh* stories. The library's famous Main Reading Room (closed for renovations until 1999) is 297 ft long and 78 ft deep, and still has its original long tables, wooden chairs, and bronze reading lamps. The library regularly mounts full-scale exhibits on such lettered topics as American novelists, early English Bibles, New York City history, and typography. *5th Ave. and 42nd St., Midtown, 212/930–0800. Current gallery exhibits: 212/869–8089. Open Mon. and Thurs.–Sat. 10–6, Tues.–Wed. 11–7:30; call for hrs for special collections. Tours Mon.–Sat. 11 and 2. Information on other branches: 212/661–7220. Subway: B, D, F, Q to 42nd St.*

9 *b-2*

NEW YORK PUBLIC LIBRARY FOR THE PERFORMING ARTS

While couch potatoes are gazing their way through the Museum of Television and Radio, the ear-trained should scrutinize this wonderful library's manuscript musical scores, videotapes of great ballets, and recordings of famous opera performances. Researchers will find staggering archival resources and a friendly staff. Temporary exhibits focus on specific topics relating to music, dance, and theater. *40 Lincoln Center Plaza (Broadway and 64th St., just north of Metropolitan Opera), Upper West Side, 212/870–1600. Open Mon. and Thurs. noon–8; Tues., Wed., Fri., and Sat. noon–6. Tours Tues. at 2. Subway: 65th St.*

6 *e-8*

SCHOMBURG CENTER FOR RESEARCH IN BLACK CULTURE

A branch of the New York Public Library, this internationally renowned cultural facility in the heart of Harlem began with Arthur Schomburg's personal collection of black literature and history. Now the largest collection of its kind in the world, the library has 20,000 microfilm reels of news clippings, over 1,000 rare books, 30,000 photographs, 15,000 hours of taped oral history, 10,000 records, and 3,000 videotapes and films. In addition to its research facilities, the library maintains a permanent exhibit of African and African-American art and artifacts from its collection. *515 Malcolm X Blvd. (at 135th St.), Harlem, 212/491–2200. Open Mon.–Wed. noon–8, Thurs.–Sat. 10–6; exhibit also open Sun. noon–5. Subway: 2, 3 to 135th St.*

9 *b-3*

YIVO INSTITUTE FOR JEWISH RESEARCH

Established in 1925 in Vilna, Lithuania, this academic-research center for Eastern European Jewry and Jewish culture contains more than 22 million archival documents, 100,000 photographs, and 300,000 books. *555 W. 57th, Midtown, 212/246–6080. Open Mon.–Thurs. 9:30–5:30. Subway: 59th St./Columbus Circle.*

SCIENCE MUSEUMS

7 *c-8*

AMERICAN MUSEUM OF NATURAL HISTORY

The largest museum of natural history in the world, this wonder-filled place is most famous for its towering dinosaur skeletons. Indeed, the first thing you encounter when you walk in the door is a 50-ft-tall Barosaurus, rearing up to fend off an enormous reptilian marauder. Next to 30 million artifacts and specimens, 800 staff members, and 42 exhibition halls, however, dinosaurs are just the beginning. Don't miss the Hall of Mammals and Their Extinct Relatives, with interactive video monitors on virtually every exhibit; the Hall of Meteorites, featuring the 4-billion-year-old *Ahnighito*, the largest meteorite ever retrieved from the Earth's surface; or the Hall of Human Biology and Evolution, with dioramas tracing human origins back to Lucy. IMAX films exploring the natural world are shown daily on the museums's colossal screen. The museum keeps late hours Friday and Saturday, and serves cocktails in the Hall of Ocean Life, beneath the memorable replica of a 94-ft blue whale. *Central Park West and 79th St., Upper West Side, 212/769–5100. Admission: $8 adults, $6 seniors and students, $4.50 children. Open Sun.–Thurs. 10–5:45, Fri. and Sat. 10–8:45. Subway: B, C to 81st St.*

7 *c-7*

HAYDEN PLANETARIUM

Closed for major renovations, the plantetarium has suspended its sky shows, but lectures on the science of space and exhibits on astronomy will continue at the neighboring American Museum of Natural History. Renovations, and the opening of a brand-new center for earth and space, are scheduled for completion in the year 2000. *Central Park West and 81st St., Upper West Side, 212/769–5100. Subway: B, C to 81st St.*

9 *a-4*

INTREPID SEA-AIR-SPACE MUSEUM

Formerly the U.S.S. *Intrepid*, this 900-ft aircraft carrier is serving out its retirement as the centerpiece of one of the city's grandest museums. On deck is a startling array of aircraft (such as the A-

12 Blackbird spy plane) as well as lunar landing modules, helicopters, seaplanes, and crew areas. Docked alongside, and also part of the museum, are the *Growler*, a strategic-missile submarine; the lightship *Nantucket*; and several other battle-scarred naval veterans. Kids will enjoy exploring the ships' skinny hallways and winding staircases, as well as manipulating countless knobs, buttons, and wheels. *Hudson River, Pier 86 (12th Ave. and 46th St.), Hell's Kitchen, 212/245–0072. Admission: $10 adults; $7.50 seniors, veterans, and students 12–17; $5 children 6–11; free children under 6 and U.S. military personnel. Open May–Sept., weekdays 10–5, weekends 10–6; Oct.–Apr., Wed.–Sun. 10–5. Subway: A, C, E to 42nd St.*

1 *c-6*

LIBERTY SCIENCE CENTER

Just across the Hudson River in Liberty State Park, New Jersey, the high-tech Liberty Science Center has three floors: Environment, Health, and Invention. Highlights include the insect zoo, the 100-ft touch tunnel, the 700-pound geodesic globe, IMAX movies, and 3-D laser shows. *Liberty State Park, 251 Philip St., Jersey City, NJ, 201/200–1000. Admission: $9.50, $8.50 students and seniors, $6.50 children 2–12; pay what you wish 1st Wed. of every month after 1. Open Apr.–Aug., daily 9:30–5:30; Sept.–Mar., Tues.–Sun. 9:30–5:30.*

3 *g-2*

NEW YORK HALL OF SCIENCE

A hop, skip, and a jump away on the No. 7 train, the New York Hall of Science is one of the nation's top 10 science museums. Children and other budding researchers are invited to explore, investigate, and experiment with 160 hands-on exhibits treating subjects from lasers to microbes. Preschoolers can make crafts at the Discovery Center; older kids will enjoy the museum's new, outdoor science playground. *111th St. and 46th Ave., Flushing Meadows–Corona Park, Queens; 718/699–0005. Admission: $6; $4 children and seniors; free children under 3; free Thurs. and Fri. 2–5. Open Tues. and Wed. 9:30–2, Thurs. and Fri. 9:30–5, weekends 11–5. Subway: 7 to 111th St.*

9 *e-3*

SONY WONDER TECHNOLOGY LAB

Right in the right-now Sony Building, a free, four-floor science and technology exhibit lets kids to log onto computers, play sound engineer, and be on TV. *550 Madison Ave. (at 56th St.), Midtown, 212/833–8100. Open Tues., Wed., Fri., and Sat. 10–6; Thurs. 10–8, Sun. noon–6. Subway: 4, 5, 6 to 59th St.; N, R to 5th Ave.*

1 *b-1*

STATEN ISLAND INSTITUTE OF ART & SCIENCE

Founded in 1881 and now just two blocks from the Staten Island Ferry terminal, the Staten Island Institute celebrates art, science, and history. The high point is the remarkable natural-history collection, with specimens covering anthropology to zoology. *75 Stuyvesant Pl., St. George, Staten Island, 718/727–1135. Suggested contribution: $2.50 adults, $1.50 children.*

STATUES & MONUMENTS

10 *c-1*

ABINGDON SQUARE MEMORIAL

(Philip Martiny, 1921) A memorial to those who perished in World War I, this statue depicts a doughboy planting the American flag. *Abingdon Sq., 8th Ave. and 12th St., Greenwich Village. Subway: A, C, E to 14th St.*

7 *d-8*

ALICE IN WONDERLAND

(Jose de Creeft, 1959) One of Central Park's most beloved statues, bronze Alice is climbed and crawled upon by local youngsters. *Central Park, Sailboat Lake (near E. 74th St.). Subway: 77th St.*

7 *b-2*

ALMA MATER

(Daniel Chester French, 1903) This 8-ft-tall seated lady in bronze has presided over hundreds of graduation ceremonies—and, in the 1960s, riots. *Low Library, Columbia University, east of Broadway and 116th St., Morningside Heights. Subway: 116th St./Columbia University.*

7 *d-8*

HANS CHRISTIAN ANDERSEN

(Georg John Lober, 1956) A gift to the city from Danish and American schoolchildren, bronze Hans provides the perfect setting for reading his fairy tales. (The Central Park Conservancy sponsors readings on weekends.) Sculptural sidekick the Ugly Duckling was stolen in 1974, but it was soon recovered and returned to its creator's side. *Central Park, Sailboat Lake (near E. 74th St.). Subway: 77th St.*

9 *c-1*

ANGEL OF THE WATERS (BETHESDA FOUNTAIN)

(Emma Stebbins, 1868) Central Park's centerpiece and the focal point of one of the many prettiest spots in the city, the bronze fountain lady is surrounded by cherubs representing Temperance, Purity, Health, and Peace. Behind her, rowboats and the occasional gondola drift by on the Lake. *Central Park, Bethesda Terr. (near 72nd St. Transverse). Subway: B, C to 72nd St.*

3 *h-2*

ARMILLARY SPHERE

(Paul Manship, 1964) A bronze group on a granite base, the famous sphere was commissioned for the 1964 World's Fair. *Flushing Meadows–Corona Park, Queens. Subway: Willets Pt./Shea Stadium.*

9 *d-4*

ATLAS

(Lee Lawrie, 1937) A 15-ft-tall bronze statue on a 9-ft-high granite pedestal, *Atlas*—terminally persistent in bearing the world on his shoulders—is the defining figure of Midtown's Rockefeller Center. Interestingly, the statue was picketed when originally installed because Atlas reputedly bore a resemblance to Benito Mussolini. *International Bldg., Rockefeller Center, 5th Ave. between 50th and 51st Sts. Subway: E, F to 5th Ave.; 47th–50th Sts./Rockefeller Center.*

9 *d-2*

BALTO

(Frederick George Richard Roth, 1925) Adoring schoolchildren supposedly helped finance this bronze statue commemorating Balto, a real-life sled dog who led a team of huskies carrying medicine through a blizzard to Nome, Alaska, during a 1925 diphtheria epidemic. Note the shiny patches where children have "petted" his snout and sat on his back. *Central Park near E. 66th St. Subway: N, R to 5th Ave.; 68th St./Hunter College.*

12 *c-3*

HENRY WARD BEECHER

(John Quincy Adams Ward, 1891) This fine bronze of the abolitionist minister was cast by an abolitionist sculptor, one of the most prolific creators of public art in his day. *Fulton St. at Court St., Brooklyn Heights. Subway: Borough Hall.*

9 *d-6*

JAMES GORDON BENNETT MEMORIAL

(Antonin Jean Carles, 1895) This bronze figure and clock (Bell Ringers' Monument) graced the top of newspaperman James Gordon Bennett's *New York Herald* building before it was razed. *Herald Sq., 6th Ave. and Broadway between 34th and 35th Sts., Garment District. Subway: 34th St./Herald Sq.*

9 *d-2*

SIMON BOLIVAR

(Sally James Farnham, 1921) One of the many enormous bronze statues fronting Central Park to the south, this one has the South American liberator on horseback atop a polished-granite pedestal. *6th Ave. and Central Park South. Subway: B, Q, N, R to 57th St.*

9 *e-8*

EDWIN BOOTH AS HAMLET

(Edmond T. Quinn, 1918) Booth was America's leading Shakespearean actor in his day. He lived at 16 Gramercy Park South from 1888 until his death in 1906. *Gramercy Park. Subway: 6 to 23rd St.*

9 *d-5*

WILLIAM CULLEN BRYANT

(Herbert Adams, 1911) A bronze statue of the famed 19th-century poet and journalist sits fittingly in the now-hip Midtown park that bears his name. *Bryant Park, 6th Ave. and 42nd St., Midtown. Subway: B, D, F, Q to 42nd St.*

9 *c-1*

CENTRAL PARK MALL

Several bronze statues of literary figures line the south end of Central Park's elm-shaded pedestrian mall, at 72nd Street. *Subway: B, C to 72nd St.*

Robert Burns Sir John Steell, 1880.

Fitz-Greene Halleck James Wilson Alexander MacDonald, 1877.

Victor Herbert Edmond T. Quinn, 1927.

Samuel F. B. Morse Byron M. Pickett, 1871.

Sir Walter Scott Sir John Steell, 1871.

William Shakespeare John Quincy Adams Ward, 1870. The sculptor was paid $20,000 for this work.

1 *f-4*
CIVIC VIRTUE
(Frederick William MacMonnies, 1922) This male (as opposed to the usual female) embodiment of virtue was banished from City Hall Park in 1941 by women protesters. *Queens Blvd. and Union Tpke., Forest Hills, Queens. Subway: E, F to Union Tpke./Kew Gardens.*

7 *d-8*
CLEOPATRA'S NEEDLE
Located behind the Metropolitan Museum of Art, this hieroglyphic-covered obelisk was a gift from Egypt in 1880. It is believed to date from the year 1600 BC. *Central Park near E. 80th St. Subway: 77th St.*

9 *c-4*
GEORGE M. COHAN
(Georg John Lober, 1959) Cast in bronze, the famed song-and-dance man now gives his regards to Broadway come rain or shine. Pay him a visit next time you're stuck in a queue at the TKTS booth. *Broadway and 46th St., Theater District. Subway: 42nd St./Times Sq.; 49th St.*

9 *c-2*
COLUMBUS MONUMENT
(Gaetano Russo, 1892) One of four Christopher Columbus statues in the city, this white marble statue perched on a 26-ft granite column was erected on the 400th anniversary of Columbus's first voyage to the New World. *Columbus Circle (Broadway and 59th St.), Upper West Side. Subway: 59th St./Columbus Circle.*

11 *f-1*
PETER COOPER
(Augustus Saint-Gaudens, 1897) Philanthropist Peter Cooper sits proudly in bronze (within a sort of temple designed by architect Stanford White) in front of Cooper Union, the free institution he founded to teach practical arts and sciences. *Cooper Sq. (3rd Ave. at 7th St.), East Village. Subway: Astor Pl.*

9 *d-2*
DELACORTE MUSICAL CLOCK
(Andrea Spadini, 1965) Almost as popular as the zoo's live residents, these bronze denizens do an hourly dance to the tune of one of 32 nursery songs. *Central Park Zoo, near 5th Ave. and 64th St. Subway: N, R to 5th Ave.; 68th St./Hunter College.*

10 *e-7*
ABRAHAM DE PEYSTER
(George Edwin Bissell, 1896) This bronze statue of prosperous colonial merchant Abraham de Peyster replaced an ill-fated model of King George III. George was pulled down by an angry colonial mob following the signing of the Declaration of Independence, and was then melted down to make bullets. *Bowling Green (Broadway at Whitehall St.), Lower Manhattan. Subway: Bowling Green.*

9 *c-4*
FATHER DUFFY MEMORIAL
(Charles Keck, 1937) Cast in bronze atop a polished granite base and cross, Father Duffy was a figure straight out of Damon Runyon. Duffy, whose parish was honky-tonk Times Square in the 1920s, was chaplain to the Fighting 69th in World War I. *Duffy Sq. (Broadway between 46th and 47th Sts.), Theater District. Subway: 49th St.; 42nd St./Times Sq.*

9 *c-1*
EAGLES AND PREY
(Kristin Fratin, 1850) This is one of Central Park's earliest sculptures. *Central Park northwest of the Mall. Subway: B, C to 72nd St.*

9 *c-1*
THE FALCONER
(George B. Simonds, 1871) This bronze statue rises a graceful 10 ft. *Central Park, 72nd St. Transverse. Subway: B, C to 72nd St.*

7 *a-5*
FIREMEN'S MEMORIAL
(Attilio Piccirilli, 1912) The representations of Duty and Courage pay tribute to New York's Bravest, and the bronze

plaque is a tribute to their horses, which once pulled the apparatus for the city's Fire Department. *Riverside Dr. and 100th St., Upper West Side. Subway: 1, 9 to 103rd St.*

`10` *e-6*

BENJAMIN FRANKLIN

(Ernst Plassmann, 1872) Here the founding father holds a copy of the newspaper he edited, the *Pennsylvania Gazette. Park Row at Nassau and Spruce Sts., Lower Manhattan. Subway: Brooklyn Bridge/City Hall.*

`10` *e-1*

MOHANDAS GANDHI

(Kantilal B. Patel, 1986) The famous Indian nationalist is memorialized in Union Square. *Union Sq. (Broadway and 14th St.), Flatiron. Subway: 14th St./Union Sq.*

`11` *d-1*

GIUSEPPE GARIBALDI

(Giovanni Turini, 1888) This tribute to Garibaldi's victorious efforts to unite Italy was erected by New York's Italian-Americans in the late 19th century. *Washington Sq. Park (at foot of 5th Ave.), Greenwich Village. Subway: 8th St.; W. 4th St./Washington Sq.*

`9` *f-4*

GOOD DEFEATS EVIL

(Zurab Tsereteli, 1990) The dragon that St. George is spearing was made of slices of what were once Soviet SS-20 and American Pershing ballistic missiles, chopped up in accordance with the 1988 treaty eliminating intermediate-range missiles. The statue was a gift from the Soviet government. Who knew? *United Nations (1st Ave. between 42nd and 48th Sts.), Midtown. Subway: 42nd St./Grand Central.*

`10` *e-6*

HORACE GREELEY

(John Quincy Adams Ward, 1916) Seated in an armchair, this bronze figure of Greeley holds a copy of the *New York Tribune*—fair enough, since he owned it. *City Hall Park (Broadway and Park Row), Lower Manhattan. Subway: Brooklyn Bridge/City Hall*

`10` *e-6*

NATHAN HALE

(Frederick MacMonnies, 1890) This imagined bronze portrait of Hale depicts a very real hero, who was executed by the British as a spy in 1776. *City Hall Park (see above).*

`7` *d-7*

ALEXANDER HAMILTON

(Carl Conrads, 1880) This granite statue of the famed Federalist was presented to the city by Hamilton's son John C. Hamilton. *Central Park, East Dr. near 83rd St. Subway: 4, 5, 6 to 86th St.*

`11` *d-1*

ALEXANDER LYMAN HOLLEY

(John Quincy Adams Ward, 1889) Holley was an American inventor; his bronze likeness is considered one of this prolific sculptor's best public works. *Washington Sq. Park (see Giuseppe Garibaldi, above).*

`5` *b-3*

HUDSON MEMORIAL COLUMN

(Karl Bitter, 1909–1939) This column was commissioned to commemorate the 300th anniversary of Hudson's discovery of the river down below. *Henry Hudson Pkwy. and 227th St., Bronx. Subway: 1, 9 to 225th St.*

`9` *c-1*

INDIAN HUNTER

(John Quincy Adams Ward, 1866) Initially cast in plaster, this bronze group grew out of sketches made during a visit to the American West. It was Central Park's first statue by an American sculptor. *Central Park northwest of the Mall. Subway: B, C to 72nd St.*

`4` *e-1*

WASHINGTON IRVING

(James Wilson Alexander MacDonald, 1871) This bronze bust depicts the author some consider the "father of American literature." *Concert Grove, Prospect Park, Brooklyn. Subway: D, Q to Prospect Park.*

`7` *a-6*

JOAN OF ARC

(Anna Vaughn Hyatt Huntington, 1915) This bronze statue on a granite pedestal contains stone fragments from the tower where Joan was imprisoned in Rouen, and from Rheims Cathedral. *Riverside Dr. and 93rd St., Upper West Side. Subway: 1, 2, 3, 9 to 96th St.*

12 *g-5*
JOHN F. KENNEDY MEMORIAL
(Neil Estern, 1965) This bronze bust is New York's only official memorial statue of the late president. *Grand Army Plaza, Park Slope, Brooklyn. Subway: Grand Army Plaza.*

10 *e-1*
LAFAYETTE
(Frederic-Auguste Bartholdi, 1876) Quoting the Marquis de Lafayette, the inscription reads: "As soon as I heard of American independence my heart was enlisted." *Union Sq. (Broadway and 14th St.), Flatiron. Subway: 14th St./Union Sq.*

7 *b-2*
LAFAYETTE AND WASHINGTON
(Frederic-Auguste Bartholdi, 1890) These two revolutionary allies were cast by the same French sculptor who gave New York the Statue of Liberty. *Morningside Park (110th–123rd Sts. from Morningside Dr. to Manhattan and Morningside Aves.), Upper West Side. Subway: B, C to 110th St., 116th St., or 125th St.*

4 *e-1*
ABRAHAM LINCOLN
(Henry Kirke Brown, 1869) Abe's right hand points to a manuscript that is now, alas, missing. History has not been kind to this statue; the nearby Kate Wollman Memorial Rink has directed pedestrian and skating traffic toward Lincoln's back. *Concert Grove, Prospect Park, Brooklyn. Subway: D, Q to Prospect Park.*

9 *d-5*
LIONS
(Edward Clark Potter, 1911) The closest thing New York has to a mascot, these stone lions are a matched pair. Dubbed Patience and Fortitude by Mayor Fiorello LaGuardia, they are dear to the hearts of New Yorkers and look especially smart at Christmastime, when they are bedecked with red-trimmed wreaths. *New York Public Library, 5th Ave. and 41st St., Midtown. Subway: B, D, F, Q to 42nd St.*

9 *c-2*
MAINE MONUMENT
(Attilio Piccirilli, 1913) A dramatic Beaux-Arts memorial in bronze and marble, it commemorates those who perished on the battleship *Maine* in 1898. *Columbus Circle (Broadway and 59th St.), Midtown. Subway: 59th St./Columbus Circle.*

4 *e-1*
MANHATTAN & BROOKLYN
(Daniel Chester French, 1916) This symbolic representation of the two boroughs originally stood at the Brooklyn end of the Manhattan Bridge. *Brooklyn Museum of Art, 200 Eastern Pkwy. (at Washington Ave.), Park Slope, Brooklyn. Subway: Eastern Pkwy./Brooklyn Museum.*

4 *e-1*
THOMAS MOORE
(John G. Draddy, 1879) Ireland's beloved poet is memorialized here in bronze. *Concert Grove, Prospect Park, Brooklyn. Subway: D, Q to Prospect Park.*

9 *d-1*
MOTHER GOOSE
(Frederick G. R. Roth, 1938) This 8-ft granite embodiment of the feathered matriarch stands on the site of the old Central Park Casino. *Central Park, East Dr. near 72nd St. Subway: 68th St./Hunter College.*

10 *e-7*
NEW YORK VIETNAM VETERANS MEMORIAL
(Pete Wormser, William Fellows) Unveiled on May 6, 1985, 10 years after the war ended, New York's Vietnam Veterans Memorial is a translucent wall of glass blocks, 14 ft high and 70 ft long, inscribed with excerpts of letters to and from those who served. Only some of those commemorated here came home. Visitors leave candles, notes, and flowers on the granite shelves. It's a poignant tribute. *Vietnam Veterans Plaza, 55 Water St. (near Broad St.), Lower Manhattan. Subway: Whitehall St./South Ferry.*

9 *e-1*
107TH INFANTRY
(Karl M. Illava, 1927) An alumnus of the 107th in World War I, the sculptor includes himself in this bronze depiction. *5th Ave. and 67th St., Upper East Side. Subway: 68th St./Hunter College.*

9 *f-4*

PEACE

(Antun Augustincic, 1954) This heroic bronze statue was presented to the U.N. by the government of Yugoslavia. *United Nations Gardens, near 1st Ave. and 46th St., Midtown. Subway: 42nd St./Grand Central.*

12 *e-2*

PRISON SHIP MARTYRS' MONUMENT

(McKim, Mead & White, 1908) The world's tallest Doric column—148 ft, 8 inches—is a memorial to the American patriots who died on British prison ships anchored in New York Harbor during the Revolution. *Ft. Greene Park, Brooklyn. Subway: Atlantic Ave.*

9 *d-4*

PROMETHEUS

(Paul Manship, 1934) Cast in bronze and finished in gold leaf, the fire thief is set in a flashing fountain-pool overseeing ice-skaters in winter and alfresco diners in summer. *Lower Plaza, Rockefeller Center, 5th–6th Aves. between 50th and 51st Sts., Midtown. Subway: 47th–50th Sts., Rockefeller Center.*

9 *d-3*

PULITZER FOUNTAIN

(Carrère & Hastings; sculptor: Karl Bitter, 1916) This fountain became a legendary icon of the Roaring '20s once F. Scott and Zelda Fitzgerald went wading in it. Originally built of limestone, it eventually deteriorated to the point of crumbling, and was virtually rebuilt in more-durable granite. The goddess Pomona was given a new patina. *Grand Army Plaza (5th Ave. between 58th and 59th Sts.), Midtown. Subway: N, R to 5th Ave.*

3 *h-2*

ROCKET THROWER

(Donald DeLue, 1964) This bronze work was commissioned for the 1964 World's Fair as a permanent fixture for the park. *Flushing Meadows–Corona Park, Flushing, Queens. Subway: Willetts Pt./Shea Stadium*

7 *c-8*

ROOSEVELT MEMORIAL

(James Earle Fraser, 1940) At 16 ft tall, this bronze group is one of the largest and best equestrian statues in the world. *American Museum of Natural History, Central Park West and 79th St., Upper West Side. Subway: B, C to 81st St.*

4 *e-1*

SCULPTURE GARDEN

The Brooklyn Museum's outdoor garden displays architectural sculpture and ornamentation salvaged from demolition sites around the city—most notably the original Penn Station. *Brooklyn Museum of Art, 200 Eastern Pkwy. (at Washington Ave.), Park Slope, Brooklyn. Subway: Eastern Pkwy./Brooklyn Museum.*

9 *c-1*

SEVENTH REGIMENT MEMORIAL

(John Quincy Adams Ward, 1873) The 58 members of this New York State regiment who died in the Civil War are memorialized here. *Central Park, West Dr. near 67th St. Subway: B, C to 72nd St.*

9 *e-7*

WILLIAM H. SEWARD

(Randolph Rogers, 1876) Truth or fiction? Word on the street is that the sculptor set Secretary of State Seward's head on President Lincoln's body—for which he already had molds from another project in Philadelphia. *Madison Sq. Park (5th–Madison Aves., 23rd–26th Sts.), Murray Hill. Subway: 6, N, R to 23rd St.*

9 *d-3*

SHERMAN MONUMENT

(Augustus Saint-Gaudens, 1903) A graceful equestrian group, this bronze tribute to the Civil War general is one of several monuments towering over the southern edge of Central Park. *Grand Army Plaza, 5th Ave. and 59th St., Midtown. Subway: N, R to 5th Ave.*

7 *a-6*

SOLDIERS' AND SAILORS' MEMORIAL

(Paul E.M. Duboy) Built in 1902 to commemorate the Civil War dead, this 96-ft white marble column along Riverside Park was fashioned after Athens' monument to Lysicrates. *Riverside Dr. and 89th St., Upper West Side. Subway: 1, 9 to 86th St.*

1 c-6

STATUE OF LIBERTY NATIONAL MONUMENT

Probably the most famous statue in the world, "Liberty Enlightening the World" was sculpted by Frederic-Auguste Bartholdi and presented to the United States as a gift from France in 1886. Since then she has since become a near-universal symbol of freedom, standing a proud 152 ft high on *top* of an 89-ft pedestal (executed by Richard Morris Hunt) on an island in New York Harbor. Gustav Eiffel designed the statue's iron skeleton, through which visitors can climb spiral stairs to reach the statue's crown (*see* Viewpoints, *below*). In anticipation of her centennial, Liberty underwent a long-overdue restoration in the mid-'80s and emerged with great fanfare on July 4, 1986, more beautiful and awe-inspiring than ever. *Liberty Island, New York Harbor, off Lower Manhattan. Subway: South Ferry. Ferry tickets: Castle Clinton, Battery Park, 212/269–5755. Admission: $7 adults, $5 seniors, $3 children under 17. Boats leave for the island daily 9:30–3:30, on the half-hour. For statue information, call the National Parks Service, 212/363–3200.*

7 d-8

STILL HUNT

(Edward Kemeys, 1883) Perched on one of the park's natural outcroppings, this crouched bronze panther is so realistic that you may feel the cat has snuck up on you. *Central Park, East Dr. near 76th St. Subway: 77th St.*

7 b-4

STRAUS MEMORIAL

(Henry Augustus Lukeman, 1915) Although women were offered space in the *Titanic*'s lifeboats, Ida Straus chose to stay with her husband, Isador, and both perished on the doomed ocean liner's maiden voyage. The philanthropist Strauses had lived near this memorial. *Broadway and 106th St., Upper West Side. Subway: 110th St./Cathedral Pkwy.*

11 f-1

PETER STUYVESANT

(Gertrude Vanderbilt Whitney, 1941) This life-size bronze was cast by the founder of the Whitney Museum. Standing on what was once part of his farm, it depicts New York's last Dutch governor, the peg-legged Peter Stuyvesant, buried at nearby St. Mark's Church in-the-Bowery (*see* Churches & Synagogues, *above*). *Stuyvesant Sq. (1st to 3rd Aves., between 15th and 17th Sts.), East Village. Subway: 3rd Ave.; 14th St./Union Sq.*

9 g-4

SWORDS INTO PLOWSHARES

(Evgeniy Vuchetich, 1958) This dramatic, 9-ft-tall bronze was a gift from the U.S.S.R. *United Nations Gardens, near 1st Ave. and 46th St., Midtown. Subway: 42nd St./Grand Central.*

7 c-7

TEMPEST

(Milton Hebald, 1966) Depicting Shakespeare's Prospero, the *Tempest* monument is dedicated to Joseph Papp, the theatrical guru who brought free Shakespeare to the park. This statue violated an 1876 law prohibiting commemorative statues until five years after the subject's death, but no one complained. Papp was around until 1991. *Central Park, near Delacorte Theater (enter at W. 81st St.). Subway: B, C to 72nd St. or 81st St.*

7 e-5

ALBERT BERTIL THORVALSDEN, SELF-PORTRAIT

(Donated by Denmark, 1894) Cast from the marble original, this self-portrait by the great neoclassical sculptor was donated by the Danish in recognition of Thorvalsden's influence on early American sculpture. *Central Park near E. 96th St. Subway: 6 to 96th St.*

7 e-4

UNTERMEYER FOUNTAIN (DANCING GIRLS)

(Walter Schott, 1947) These beautifully sculpted, spirited maidens from Untermeyer's Yonkers estate are among the showpieces of Central Park's only European-style garden. *Central Park, Conservatory Gardens, 5th Ave. and 104th St., Upper East Side. Subway: 103rd St.*

9 b-1

GIUSEPPI VERDI

(Pasquale Civiletti, 1906) Made of Carrara marble, this statue commemorates the great 19th-century composer. *Verdi Sq., Broadway and 73rd St., Upper West Side. Subway: 1, 2, 3, 9 to 72nd St.*

`10` *e-8*

GIOVANNI DA VERRAZANO

(Ettore Ximenes, 1909) Italian-Americans erected this monument to honor the captain of the ship that first sighted New York Harbor in 1524. *Battery Park, Battery Pl. and State St., Lower Manhattan. Subway: Bowling Green; South Ferry.*

`10` *e-1*

GEORGE WASHINGTON

(Henry Kirke Brown, with John Quincy Adams Ward, 1856) Washington and his horse head beautifully into battle, in bronze. *Union Sq. (Broadway and 14th St.) Flatiron. Subway: 14th St./Union Sq.*

`10` *e-7*

GEORGE WASHINGTON

(John Quincy Adams Ward, 1833) Occupying the site where Washington was inaugurated as the first president of the United States, the statue is said to contain a stone (in its pedestal) from the spot where Washington stood. *Steps of Federal Hall, Wall and Broad Sts., Lower Manhattan. Subway: Wall St.*

`11` *d-1*

WASHINGTON ARCH

(McKim, Mead & White, 1892) First erected in wood in 1889 for the centennial of Washington's inauguration, this marble arch was designed by famed New York architect Stanford White. The statues, *Washington at War* (1916) and *Washington at Peace* (1917), were added later; bodybuilder Charles Atlas is said to have modeled for the civilian version of Washington. *Washington Sq. Park (at foot of 5th Ave.), Greenwich Village. Subway: 8th St.; W. 4th St./Washington Sq.*

`9` *c-1*

DANIEL WEBSTER

(Thomas Ball, 1876) The famed American statesman and orator is here adorned with his own memorable maxim "Liberty and union, now and forever, one and inseparable." *Central Park, West Dr. near 72nd St., Upper West Side. Subway: B, C to 72nd St.*

VIEWPOINTS

One of the best ways to acquaint yourself with New York City's famous skyline is to join it in the clouds.

`10` *g-6*

BROOKLYN BRIDGE

No bridge in the world had an elevated promenade when John Roebling conceived one for his bridge in 1869 (*see* Bridges, *above*). Dedicated exclusively to pedestrians (and now bicycles), the boardwalk was designed to allow uninterrupted views in every direction. When the Great East River Bridge (as it was then called) was opened, in 1883, 150,300 pedestrians paid a penny each to walk the mile across it. The walk is free now, and the view considerably different, but the experience is no less magnificent. Don't miss this trek, even if you only go to the first tower; if you do cross to Brooklyn, wander over to the Brooklyn Heights Promenade (*see below*) for another famous view. *City Hall Park, Manhattan, to Cadman Plaza West, Brooklyn. Subway: Brooklyn Bridge/City Hall; High St./Brooklyn Bridge.*

`12` *a-3*

BROOKLYN HEIGHTS PROMENADE

Strolling, sitting on a classic park bench, and watching the sunset on this riverbank esplanade are divine here, backed by an incomparable, bird's-eye view of the Manhattan skyline. *1 block west of Columbia Heights from Remsen to Orange Sts.*

`9` *d-6*

EMPIRE STATE BUILDING

At 102 stories (1,250 ft), it's now only the fifth-tallest building in the world, but it's still the most elegant. The two observation decks—one outdoors on the 86th floor, one enclosed in glass on the 102nd—have 360-degree views, with 80-mi visibility on clear days. For a different kind of view, stop off on the second floor and take the *New York Skyride*, a big-screen "thrill ride" that simulates a flight over New York City. *See* Architecture, *above. 350 5th Ave. (at 34th St), 212/736–3100. Observatory admission: $6 adults; $3 seniors (over 62), military personnel, and children under 12; free children under 5. Open daily 9:30 AM–midnight; last elevator leaves at 11:30 PM. New York Skyride, 212/279–9777. Admission $11.50 adults and teens, $9.50 seniors and children under 12. Subway: 34th St./Herald Sq.*

7 *e-7*

METROPOLITAN MUSEUM OF ART ROOFTOP SCULPTURE GARDEN (THE IRIS AND B. GERALD CANTOR ROOF GARDEN)

Topping off the Lila Acheson Wallace wing, the Met's rooftop sculpture garden overlooks Central Park, with Midtown and the Upper West Side as beautiful backdrops. Come at twilight and watch the city's lights slowly and glamorously emerge as the sky darkens. *5th Ave. and 82nd St., Upper East Side. Sculpture Garden open May–Oct., weather permitting. Subway: 4, 5, 6 to 86th St.*

10 *f-6*

SOUTH STREET SEAPORT, PIER 17

This shopping and dining pier juts 500 yards into the East River, offering superb views of the Brooklyn Bridge and the harbor. Sunset is the best time to visit; head to the far end of the pier, where you can sit right on the river on the upper or lower promenade. (*See* History Museums, *above,* and Department Stores *in Chapter 4.) Fulton St. and East River, Lower Manhattan. Subway: 2, 3 to Fulton St.; Broadway–Nassau St.*

9 *d-4*

RAINBOW ROOM

See Dining & Dancing *in Chapter 5.*

7 *a-2*

RIVERSIDE CHURCH

The church's observation platform affords a lovely, unobstructed view of the Hudson River, New Jersey Palisades, and George Washington Bridge from 392 ft. (*See* Churches & Synagogues, *above.) Riverside Dr. at 120th St., Upper West Side, 212/870–6700. Admission: $2. Open Tues.–Sat. 11–4, Sun. noon–4:30. Subway: 116th St./Columbia Univ.*

1 *c-6*

STATUE OF LIBERTY NATIONAL MONUMENT

The 20-minute boat ride to resplendent Lady Liberty provides lovely vistas of New York Harbor. Once you're there, the view from Liberty's crown is unforgettable—just be prepared for a 1- to 1½-hour wait to ascend. *New York Harbor, off Lower Manhattan. Subway: South Ferry. Ferry tickets: Castle Clinton, Battery Park, 212/269–5755. Admission: $7 adults,*

$5 seniors, $3 children under 17. Boats leave for the island daily 9:30–3:30, on the half-hour.

10 *d-6*

WORLD TRADE CENTER, OBSERVATION DECK

At 1,377 ft tall, the World Trade Center's Twin Towers are New York's tallest buildings; the observation deck on the 107th floor of the south tower is a quarter of a mile high, making it the world's highest open-air viewing platform (*see* Architecture, *above*). Day or night the view is literally breathtaking. Also on the 107th floor, the newly reopened Windows on the World restaurant affords the most luscious excuse for lingering over the twinkling lights (*see* Continental *in Chapter 3). South Tower (No. 2), Lower Manhattan, 212/323–2340. Admission: $10 adults, $8 seniors, $5 children 6–12, free children under 5. Open Sept.–June, daily 9:30–9:30; July and Aug., daily 9:30 AM–11:30 PM. Subway: Cortlandt St./World Trade Center.*

guided tours

BUS TOURS

Rise just a bit above it all—physically, anyway—in a comfortable, air-conditioned bus. Commentaries are given en route.

9 *c-5*

GRAY LINE NEW YORK

Gray Line offers more than 20 bus tours of New York City, ranging from quick, two-hour trips to all-day excursions. A popular option is the double-decker "Hop on, hop off" bus, which shuttles tourists to major sights around town and lingers at each one as long as they like. *Port Authority Bus Terminal, north wing, 8th Ave. and 42nd St., Hell's Kitchen, 212/397–2600. Subway: A, C, E to 42nd St.*

9 *c-5*

HARLEM SPIRITUALS

This outfit offers four-hour Sunday gospel trips to Harlem, as well as bus tours of Brooklyn and the Bronx. *690 8th Ave. (at 43rd St.), Theater District, 212/757–0425. Subway: A, C, E to 42nd St.*

`9` *d-6*

NEW YORK DOUBLEDECKER TOURS

These authentic London double-decker buses make a loop, stopping every half-hour at the Empire State Building, Greenwich Village, Chinatown, the World Trade Center, the South Street Seaport, and the Statue of Liberty. Passengers board and re-board at their leisure. *Empire State Building (350 5th Ave., at 34th St.), Garment District, 212/967–6008. Subway: 34th St./Herald Sq.*

BOAT TOURS

`9` *a-5*

CIRCLE LINE CRUISES

Manhattan *is* an island, after all, and this 35-mile, three-hour cruise circumnavigates it, offering odd views and a funny and informative commentary. *Pier 83 (12th Ave. and 42nd St.), Hell's Kitchen, 212/563–3200. Subway: A, C, E to 42nd St.*

`1` *c-6*

ELLIS ISLAND NATIONAL MONUMENT

See Historic Buildings & Areas, *above.*

`10` *e-8*

PETREL

Sail New York Harbor on the same spectacular 70-foot yawl that JFK sailed as President; just take care to reserve two days in advance. Cruises last between 45 minutes and two hours. *Battery Park (State St. and Battery Pl.), Lower Manhattan, 212/825–1976. Subway: Bowling Green.*

`10` *f-6*

PIONEER

Take a 2- to 3-hour sail on a 102-foot twin-masted schooner built in 1885. *Pier 16, South Street Seaport (Fulton and South Sts.), Lower Manhattan, 212/748–8600 or 212/748–8786. Closed mid-Sept.–mid-May. Subway: Fulton St.*

`10` *f-6*

SEAPORT LIBERTY CRUISES

No time to waste? Hour-long sails around New York Harbor depart from the Seaport daily. *Pier 16, South Street Seaport (Fulton and South Sts.), Lower Manhattan, 212/639–8888. Closed mid-Dec.–Feb. Subway: Fulton St.*

`10` *e-8*

STATEN ISLAND FERRY

This 25-minute boat ride crosses Upper New York Bay and offers wonderfully panoramic views—and as of 1997, it's absolutely free. Who ever heard of a fare *dissolution? Whitehall St. at State St., Lower Manhattan. Departures: weekdays every 20 min, weekends every 15 min; every hour during very early morning. Subway: South Ferry. Foot of Bay Street, St. George, Staten Island, 718/727–2508.*

`1` *c-6*

STATUE OF LIBERTY NATIONAL MONUMENT

See Viewpoints, *above.*

`7` *d-8*

VENETIAN GONDOLA

What to do with that breathless summer evening? Try gliding the waters of Central Park Lake in an authentic Venetian gondola—the 37½ foot Daughter of Venice—expertly navigated by a traditionally trained and attired gondolier. It's expensive, but it's pure magic. The gondola can hold up to six people. *Loeb Boathouse, Central Park, near E. 74th St., 212/517–3623. Available May–Sept., nightly 5–10; not available Oct.–Mar. Subway: 77th St.*

`9` *a-5*

WORLD YACHT CRUISES

These luxury restaurant yachts offer 3-hour, four-course dinner and dancing cruises around the tip of Manhattan. You'll need to reserve in advance. *Pier 81 (12th Ave. and 41st St.), Hell's Kitchen, 212/630–8100. Subway: A, C, E to 42nd St.*

HELICOPTER TOURS

`9` *g-6*

ISLAND HELICOPTER

Fasten your seatbelt and choose from four different flights overlooking sights from the United Nations and Statue of Liberty to midtown's skyscrapers. The "Ultimate Delight" whisks you all the way from Yankee Stadium to Battery Park. *Heliport: E. 34th St. at FDR Dr., 212/683–4575. Purchase tickets at Gray Line New York (see above). Open daily 9–6. Subway: 6 to 33rd St.*

9 *a-6*

LIBERTY HELICOPTER

These four pilot-narrated tours range from the four-minute "Liberty Sampler" to the 18-minute "Big Picture." Get a whole new angle on life. *Heliport: 12th Ave. and 30th St., Garment District, 212/465–8905. Open daily 9–9. Subway: 34th St./Penn Station.*

SPECIALIZED TOURS

ARTTOURS OF MANHATTAN

Private guides take you through the city's museums, studios, and galleries and help you understand what you're staring at. *28 Scott Ln., Princeton, NJ 08540, 609/921–2647.*

9 *d-3*

CARNEGIE HALL

The hour-long tour of this performers' Mecca is full of history and backstage anecdotes. *154 W. 57th St., Midtown, 212/247–7800. Tours depart Mon., Tues., Thurs., and Fri. 11:30, 2, and 3. Subway: N, R to 57th St.*

7 *b-3*

CATHEDRAL OF ST. JOHN THE DIVINE

Tours focus on the cathedral's history; special "vertical" tours take you into the cathedral's neo-Gothic towers. Reserve in advance. *Amsterdam Ave. and 112th St., Upper West Side, 212/932–7347. Cathedral tours depart Tues.–Sat. 11 AM, Sun. 1 PM; vertical tours 1st and 3rd Sat. of month, noon and 2 PM. Subway: 110th St./Cathedral Parkway.*

DOORWAY TO DESIGN

These intriguing behind-the-scenes tours illuminate design, art, and architecture through entrée into private homes, sample sales, fashion designers' ateliers, and artists' studios. Itineraries are custom-designed for groups or individuals, and include shopping tours—everything from wholesale to haute couture. *1441 Broadway, Suite 338, New York, NY 10018, 212/221–1111 or 718/339–1542.*

10 *e-7*

FEDERAL RESERVE BANK

A block-long, 14-story stone behemoth, the Federal Reserve Bank in Lower Manhattan houses the largest stockpile of gold in the world—about $110 billion worth. Free tours of the Fed provide an overview of the bank's operations, an explanation of its role in the economy, a look at currency processing, and a visit to the gold vault, where you can salivate over bars of solid gold. Reserve a week in advance. *33 Liberty St. (near William St.), Lower Manhattan, 212/720–6130. Tours depart weekdays 10:30, 11:30, 1:30, and 2:30. Subway: Fulton St.; Wall St.*

10 *f-6*

FULTON FISH MARKET

Early birds who want to see the catch can take a 1¾-hour walking tour through the stalls of the Fulton Fish Market, opened in 1823 and still going strong. Reserve in advance. *South Street Seaport Museum, Fulton and South Sts., Lower Manhattan, 212/748–8590. Tours depart Apr.–Oct., 1st and 3rd Thurs. of month, 6 AM. Subway: Fulton St.*

9 *e-5*

GRAND CENTRAL TERMINAL TOUR

Try to forget the commute: the Municipal Art Society offers a free guided tour of New York's Beaux Arts beauty. *Meet at information booth on Grand Concourse, 212/935–3960 or 212/439–1049, Wed. 12:30 PM. Subway: 42nd St./Grand Central.*

HARLEM YOUR WAY! TOURS UNLIMITED

These tours cover Harlem's famous music, food, cultural institutions, brownstones, and nightlife. Customized walk, bike, bus, or limo tours are conducted by knowledgeable locals. Reserve in advance. *212/690–1687.*

9 *b-5*

KRAMER'S REALITY TOUR

Seinfeld's irascible Kramer is based on real-life New Yorker, Kenny Kramer, who, lacking no commercial spirit, has started his own tour company to take visitors past the show's New York sites. You'll visit the real-life Soup Nazi, and, of course Tom's Restaurant, where Jerry, Elaine, and George vent their respective spleens. Reserve in advance. *Pulse Theater, 432 W. 42nd St., Hell's Kitchen, 212/268–5525. Subway: A, C, E to 42nd St.*

9 *b-2*

METROPOLITAN OPERA BACKSTAGE

Opera singers love this six-tiered, 3,800-seat auditorium—and so does the Metropolitan Opera Guild. Their tours offer a fascinating backstage look at the often bustling scenery and costume shops, auditorium, stage area, and rehearsal facilities. They don't promise Pavarotti, but you never know. Reserve in advance. *Lincoln Center Plaza (Broadway at 64th St.), Upper West Side, 212/769–7020. Tours depart Oct.–June, weekdays 3:45, Sat. 10 AM. Subway: 66th St./Lincoln Center.*

9 *d-4*

NBC STUDIO TOUR

NBC has hung its hat in the GE Building for over 50 years. Daily hour-long tours let visitors onto the sets of "Saturday Night Live," "The Today Show," "Late Night with Conan O'Brien," and "The Rosie O'Donnell Show." *30 Rockefeller Plaza (50th St. between 5th and 6th Aves.), Midtown, 212/664–7174. Tours 9:30–4:30. Subway: 47th–50th Sts./Rockefeller Center.*

10 *e-7*

NEW YORK STOCK EXCHANGE

In front of what is now 60 Wall Street, 24 brokers met under a buttonwood tree in 1792 and agreed on some rules of business, thereby creating the New York Stock Exchange. The Exchange's neoclassical building dates from 1901. If you arrive before 1, you can take a self-guided look at the enormous trading floor, where brokers go about their frenetic business. *20 Broad St. (near Wall St.), 212/656–3000. Tours weekdays 9–4:30. Subway: Wall St.*

RADICAL WALKING TOURS

If you're into movements and causes, revolutionary thinking, or the anarchic ideal, Radical Walking Tours are for you. They cast a different light on the history of New York and the figures who have tried to rouse its rabble, from Thomas Paine to Ethel and Julius Rosenberg. *718/492–0069.*

ROCK AND ROLL TOURS OF NEW YORK

This tour of New York's rock-and-roll landmarks includes places where stars wrote and recorded their songs, where they bought their drugs, where their songs were inspired, and where their album covers were shot. Stops on the two-hour bus tour include Madonna's apartment building, the bar where the Rolling Stones shot the "Waiting on a Friend" video, and—amazingly—the RCA record studio (now Baruch College), where Elvis Presley recorded "Hound Dog." Custom tours can be arranged for fan clubs. The tours are designed for groups, but individuals can occasionally squeeze onto the bus. *212/941–9464.*

10 *g-3*

SCHAPIRO'S WINERY

Napa Valley it's not, but Schapiro's, founded in 1899, is Manhattan's only working winery. Its motto (no joke): "The wine you can cut with a knife." Tour the wine cellars, see the presses, and taste the wine. *126 Rivington St. (at Essex St.), Lower East Side, 212/674–4404. Tours depart hourly Sun. 11–4. Subway: Delancey St.*

WALKING TOURS

ADVENTURE ON A SHOESTRING

This group's motto is "Exploring the world within our reach, within our means." Jaunts include historic walking tours of Chinatown, Hell's Kitchen, and "haunted" Greenwich Village. *212/265–2663.*

BIG ONION WALKING TOURS

Focusing on urban history and the city's multiethnic neighborhoods, Big Onion leads two-hour walking tours in Manhattan each weekend. One of the most popular is "From Naples to Bialystock to Beijing: The Multiethnic Eating Tour," on which you can sample the Lower East Side's mozzarella, pickles, and dim sum. *212/439–1090.*

BROOKLYN CENTER FOR THE URBAN ENVIRONMENT

These unique walking tours traverse Brooklyn's lesser-known neighborhoods and occasionally include boat rides on such unlikely waterways as the Gowanus Canal, focusing always on the borough's unique history, culture, and ecology. *718/788–8500.*

CITYWALKS

Walking tours of Greenwich Village, the Lower East Side, Fifth Avenue, and Chelsea are led most weekends by the knowledgeable John Wilson. *212/989–2456.*

`9` *e-5*

GRAND TOUR

This Grand Central neighborhood tour, sponsored by the Grand Central Partnership is led by "urban detective" and historian Justin Ferate. Focusing on the area's architecture and history, the walk includes the station and its environs: the Art Deco interiors of the Chanin and Chrysler buildings, the Helmsley Building, and more. *Meet in front of Philip Morris Building (Park Ave. and 42nd St.), Midtown, 212/818–1777.*

`10` *e-7*

HERITAGE TRAILS

Choose from four self-guided tours of historic Lower Manhattan. Explore buildings, monuments, and open spaces representing key elements in the city's economic, social, and political evolution. *Pick up brochure at Heritage Trails Visitor Center, 120 Broadway (at Cedar St.), Lower Manhattan, 212/269–1500. Subway: Wall Street.*

JOYCE GOLD HISTORY TOURS OF NEW YORK

Historian and author Joyce Gold's enthusiastic and highly informative tours cover over 20 different New York City neighborhoods, from the financial district to Harlem. *212/242–5762.*

`9` *d-6*

MIRACLE TOUR OF 34TH STREET

The 34th Street Partnership offers free weekly walking tours of the architecture and history of this endlessly colorful street and its surroundings. *Meet at Empire State Building (350 5th Ave., between 33rd and 34th Sts.), Garment District, 212/868–0521, Thurs. 12:30 PM. Subway: 34th St./Herald Sq.*

MUNICIPAL ART SOCIETY

New York's premier preservationist group leads several walking tours each week, examining current happenings in city architecture and neighborhoods in light of their social history. *212/935–3960 or 212/439–1049.*

`11` *f-7*

THE MUSEUM OF THE CHINESE IN THE AMERICAS

Take a closer look at the largest, most vibrant Chinatown in the Western Hemisphere. *70 Mulberry St., 2nd floor, Chinatown, 212/619–4785. Subway: J, M, Z to Canal St.*

MUSEUM OF THE CITY OF NEW YORK

For over 30 years the museum has sponsored leisurely explorations of New York neighborhoods, highlighting architectural and social history. *212/534–1672.*

NEW YORK CITY CULTURAL WALKING TOURS

Longtime guide Alfred Pommer escorts folks around every Sunday at 2 to such theme 'hoods as Millionaire's Mile and Little Italy. He also organizes private tours for groups and individuals from a menu of over 25 different walks, ranging from "Gargoyles in Manhattan" to an Irish-heritage tour. *212/979–2388.*

92ND STREET Y

The Y organizes fascinating treks through neighborhoods of historic, social, and architectural importance throughout the five boroughs. *212/996–1100.*

RIVER-TO-RIVER DOWNTOWN WALKING TOURS

Ruth Alcher-Green's excursions through lower Manhattan are personal, chatty, and informed glimpses of the southern tip of Manhattan island. The two-hour walks cover history as well as the latest urban art, new architecture, and afford magnificent views of the harbor. Reserve in advance. *212/321–2823.*

SOHO ART EXPERIENCE

Customized tours led by SoHo native Joy Jacobs lead visitors to the hottest shows and galleries, artists' lofts, and the finest of SoHo's world-famous cast-iron architecture. *212/219–0810.*

STREET SMARTS NEW YORK

Street Smarts sponsors several excursions through downtown Manhattan each weekend, ranging from daytime tours of the Ladies' Mile Historic District to evening rambles through "Ghostly Greenwich Village." *212/969–8262.*

URBAN PARK RANGERS, NEW YORK CITY DEPARTMENT OF PARKS

Park rangers conduct several free walking tours in parks throughout the city each weekend. Topics include bird-watching, tree identification, general ecology, history, and geology. *800/201–PARK.*

events

New Yorkers may be cynical, but they turn out for parties in droves. It's hard to imagine this town without, say, the Feast of San Gennaro, the New York City Marathon, or the Halloween Parade. The New York Convention and Visitors' Bureau (212/484–1222, weekdays 9–5) has exact dates and times for many of the annual events listed below, and the bureau's Web site (www.nycvisit.com) has yet more information on free activities, vacation ideas, transportation, restaurants, hotels, and airports. Browsing the Web is much better than lingering on the phone, and the site has an invaluable directory of URLs for organizations across the city. All of these events are free unless otherwise indicated.

JANUARY

LEGAL HOLIDAYS
New Year's Day Jan. 1.

Martin Luther King Day 3rd Mon.

10 *f-5*
CHINESE NEW YEAR
This two-week celebration is launched with a barrage of fireworks and a colorful paper-dragon dance through the narrow streets of Chinatown. Local restaurants have extravagant banquets, making this a feast in more ways than one, and the price of flowering quince branches goes up all over the city. *212/ 484–1222. Mid-Jan.–late Feb.*

9 *b-6*
NATIONAL BOAT SHOW
New York's 10-day boat show is just the thing to float your spirits during a gray spell in early January. Check out the latest in pleasure craft (power- and sailboats) and equipment, and dream of the Caribbean. *Jacob K. Javits Convention Center, 11th Ave. at 35th St., Hell's Kitchen, 212/216–2000. Admission. Early Jan.*

11 *f-3*
OUTSIDER ART FAIR
This long weekend is a wild ride through the major artworks and practitioners of what's become known as outsider art, sometimes called naive art or art of the self-taught. If you like folk art, stop in

and be amazed at this oft-misunderstood genre. Just vow beforehand not to blurt, "My three-year-old could do that!" It's not true. *Puck Bldg., 295 Lafayette St. (at Houston St.), SoHo, 212/777–5218. Late Jan.*

10 *f-1*
POETRY PROJECT
Performances at the annual New Year's Benefit for the resident Poetry Project at this landmark church range from the traditionally modern to the East Village avant-garde. More than 100 poets, dancers, and musicians pop into the spotlight. *St. Mark's Church, 2nd Ave. at 10th St., East Village, 212/674–0910. Admission. Advance tickets available. Jan. 1, 2 PM–2 AM.*

9 *e-1*
WINTER ANTIQUES SHOW
The grande dame of New York antiques shows has been around for over 40 years. Dealers large and small converge from all over the country to show off their furniture, collectibles, clothing, and memorabilia at this 10-day extravaganza. *7th Regiment Armory, Park Ave. at 67th St., Upper East Side. Admission. Mid-Jan.–early Feb.*

7 *e-6*
WINTER ISRAELI FOLK DANCE MARATHON
Somewhere in the middle of the 92nd Street Y's immense calendar of events is the Winter Israeli Folk Dance Marathon, and it *is* a marathon: the dancing can continue for days. Hoofers are led by Ruth Goodman and Danny Uziel, touted as New York's favorite Israeli-dance teachers. *92nd St. Y, 1395 Lexington Ave. (at 92nd St.), Upper East Side, 212/996– 1100. Late Jan.*

FEBRUARY

In honor of Abraham Lincoln's and George Washington's birthdays, New York's major departments stores traditionally hold big sales in mid- to late February. Keep your eyes peeled for dates and details in the daily newspapers.

LEGAL HOLIDAYS
Lincoln's Birthday Feb. 12 (New York State holiday).

Presidents' Day 3rd Mon.

BLACK HISTORY MONTH

February is devoted to a celebration of black American history and culture. Check newspapers and magazines for events.

`10` *f-5*

CHINESE LANTERN DAY PARADE

In the middle of the month (depending on the lunar phase), schoolchildren in Chinatown parade to City Hall to present the mayor with handmade paper lanterns. There's singing, dancing, and Kung Fu, all free. *Chinatown; Lower Manhattan.*

`9` *e-6*

EMPIRE STATE BUILDING RUN-UP

Forget cinder tracks: This course starts in the Art Deco lobby and ends on the 86th-floor observation deck. Between the two is an elevator, right? The Run-Up is a New York Road Runners Club invitational, so contact them in advance if you've decided that gravity is no object. *Empire State Bldg., 350 5th Ave. (at 34th St.), Garment District. New York Road Runners Club, 212/860–4455. Late Feb.*

`9` *c-6*

WESTMINSTER KENNEL CLUB DOG SHOW

For two days in early February, it's a dog's life at Madison Square Garden. This show of shows draws nearly 3,000 dogs and their humans from every state of the union to join paws and hands in competition. *Madison Sq. Garden, 4 Penn Plaza (7th Ave. between 31st and 33rd Sts.), Garment District, 800/455–3647. Admission. Subway: 34th St./Penn Station.*

MARCH

`3` *b-3*

MODEL YACHT RACES

Every Saturday in the milder months, beautifully crafted radio-controlled boats buzz around Central Park's Conservatory Water, also known as the Sailboat Lake. *Central Park, entrance at 5th Ave. at 74th St., Upper East Side, 212/673–1102. Mid-Mar.–mid-Nov., Sat. 10–2 (rain date Sun.).*

`9` *c-6*

RINGLING BROS. AND BARNUM & BAILEY CIRCUS

Forget Groundhog Day: You know winter has ended when this world-famous, three-ring circus arrives, filling the subways and sidewalks with giddy children and their (giddy?) adults, clutching cotton candy and spewing popcorn. Just before opening night the Animal Walk takes the show's four-legged stars from their train at Penn Station to the Garden, along 34th Street; it happens around midnight but is well worth the effort. *Madison Sq. Garden, 4 Penn Plaza (7th Ave. between 31st and 33rd Sts.), Garment District, 212/465–6741 for tickets, 212/302–1700 for information. Late Mar.–early Apr.*

`9` *d-5*

ST. PATRICK'S DAY PARADE

New York's first parade in honor of St. Patrick took place in 1762, and the tradition has yet to gather a speck of dust. It's a boisterous affair, with traditional music that sticks in your brain for days and a sea of "Kiss Me—I'm Irish" buttons. Don't stop at a measly button, though; 'tis a fine day for wearin' the green. Views are excellent all along the route. *5th Ave., from 44th St. to 86th St, 212/484–1222. Mar. 17 at 11:30.*

`10` *d-6*

VERNAL EQUINOX

What are *you* doing for Vernal Equinox? Celebrate the very moment of spring's arrival by attempting to balance an egg on one end. The ritual is an ancient Chinese folk (yolk?) tradition, supposed to bring good luck for the coming year. Eggs are free. For details call performance artist Donna Henes, who initiated this annual event in 1976 at Mama Donna's Tea Garden and Healing Haven in Brooklyn. *World Trade Center Plaza (Church, Liberty, and Vesey Sts.), Lower Manhattan, 718/857–2247. Mar. 20 or 21.*

EASTER WEEKEND

`3` *b-3*

EASTER EGG ROLL

Children ages 4–11 scramble to this traditional Central Park event. Don't worry; the eggs are wooden. Refreshments, prizes, and entertainment add activity to the charming sight of a sea of Easter bonnets. *212/360–3456. Day before Easter 9–2.*

9 *d-4*

EASTER LILIES DISPLAY

Rockefeller Center's Easter feast of blooms is always dazzling. *Channel Gardens, Rockefeller Center, 5th Ave. between 49th and 50th Sts.*

9 *d-5*

EASTER PARADE

New York's traditional Easter procession is more a showcase of springtime finery—especially millinery—than a real parade. The excitement centers around St. Patrick's Cathedral, at 51st Street. *5th Ave. from 44th to 57th Sts., 11–2:30. Easter Sun.*

9 *e-6*

EASTER SUNRISE SERVICE

Reverend Frank Rafter, who began this tradition in 1973, leads a special, high-rise, sunrise Easter service at 6. Most churches don't have these views—you're in the Empire State Building observatory, on the 86th floor. Reserve in advance; space is limited. *Empire State Bldg., 350 5th Ave. (at 34th St.), Garment District, 718/849–3580. Easter Sun.*

9 *d-6*

MACY'S SPRING FLOWER SHOW

The week before Easter, Macy's sets its Broadway windows abloom, and arranges lush displays throughout the main floor. Step inside the emporium for a better whiff, and to hear talks by floral and interior designers. *Macy's Herald Sq., 151 W. 34th St., Garment District. Palm Sun.–Easter Sun.*

10 *f-1*

UKRAINIAN EASTER EGG EXHIBIT

The Ukrainian Museum rolls out the heavy cultural artillery in mid-February and keeps it out until summer, with a display of more than 400 *pysanky*—colorful Ukrainian Easter eggs. Egg-decorating workshops run through Easter; call for details. *Ukrainian Museum, 203 2nd Ave. (between 12th and 13th Sts.), 212/228–0110. Admission: children free. Wed.–Sun., 1–5.*

APRIL

It's time for the Mets and the Yankees to play ball (the Dodgers haven't returned from L.A. yet, but no true Brooklynite has given up hope), and for Coney Island Amusement Park to dust itself off. (*See* Sports & Outdoor Activities *in* Chapter 6.)

BIKE NEW YORK/ FIVE BORO BIKE TOUR

See Sporting Events *in* Chapter 6.

9 *d-2*

BROADWAY SHOW SOFTBALL LEAGUE

Is that Norma Desmond on the diamond? Two great American institutions merge when New York's theater people form a 20-team softball league. Generally, one Broadway show plays another—cast, crew, and all. *Heckscher Field, Central Park, near E. 62nd St. Mid-April–July, Thurs. noon–5:30 (weather permitting).*

4 *e-1*

CHERRY BLOSSOM FESTIVAL

See Sporting Events *in* Chapter 6.

9 *e-1*

NEW YORK ANTIQUARIAN BOOK FAIR

First editions, manuscripts, autographs, atlases, drawings, prints, maps—it's book-lovers' heaven at the Armory. Wear your tweed blazer and carry your leather checkbook: Prices range from $25 to more than $25,000. *7th Regiment Armory, Park Ave. at 67th St., Upper East Side, 212/944–8291. Admission. Mid-Apr.*

STREET ENTERTAINERS

Out of hibernation at last, New York's street performers—accordionists, mimes, jugglers, magicians,—reappear with the daffodils in May. (Wait—what daffodils?) Street theater tends to spring up where the crowds are. Here are some of the best "stages."

Battery Park & Wall Street Weekdays at noon.

Central Park The Mall (near E. 72nd St.). Mon.–Sun.

5th Avenue Artists and performers gather from Rockefeller Center (49th–50th Sts.) to Central Park (59th St.), especially around Grand Army Plaza

(59th St.), in front of the Plaza Hotel.
Mon.–Sun. noon–5.

Greenwich Village Washington Sq. Park.
Mon.–Sun.

New York Public Library 5th Ave. at 42nd
St. Weekdays at noon.

Theater District Intermission (matinee
and evening performances).

MAY

Check the April listings for ongoing
events.

LEGAL HOLIDAY
Memorial Day Last Mon.

PARADES
Armed Forces Day Parade

Bronx Day Parade

Salute to Israel Parade

Norwegian Constitution Day Parade

For exact dates and routes, call 212/
484–1222 or visit the New York Convention and Visitors' Bureau Web site at
www.nycvisit.com.

9 *c-1*

ADVIL MINI MARATHON
See Sporting Events *in* Chapter 6.

12 *a-3*

BROOKLYN HEIGHTS
PROMENADE ART SHOW
Over 100 artists, photographers, and
artisans display their work against the
backdrop of the Manhattan skyline.
*Brooklyn Heights Promenade, East River
from Remsen to Clark Sts., 718/625–0080.*

GREENMARKETS
Starved for pastoral touches, New Yorkers suppport at least one greenmarket
in each borough. Farm-fresh produce
and baked goods arrive in neighborhood
parks and plazas courtesy of farmers,
dairymen, butchers, and bakers from
upstate, New Jersey, and Pennsylvania.
Union Square Park's year-round greenmarket is the biggest and busiest (open
year-round, Mon., Wed., Fri., Sat. 8–6;
212/477–3220); most greenmarkets are
open May–December.

HISTORIC HOUSE TOURS
Private houses in several historic neighborhoods open their doors to the public
in May. The Park Slope Civic Council
sponsors an annual tour of 10 historic
Brooklyn homes on the third Sunday
(daytime 718/832–8227); the Brooklyn
Heights Association offers a self-guided
afternoon tour of five historic homes
and private gardens, often including the
sanctuary of the landmark Plymouth
Church of the Pilgrims, usually on the
second Saturday (718/858–9193). The
Village Community School sponsors a
tour of six Manhattan homes to benefit
its school fund (212/691–5146).

9 *c-5*

9TH AVENUE
INTERNATIONAL
FOOD FESTIVAL
A mile-long annual gustatory celebration
of New York's ethnic diversity greets
wanderers in Hell's Kitchen on the third
weekend in May. Try kebabs and kimchi,
chow mein and gazpacho, tempura and
falafel, ravioli and bratwurst . . . it's all
topped off with crafts and entertainment. *9th Ave., 37th–57th Sts., 11–7, 212/
581–7217.*

9 *c-1*

SEPHARDIC FAIR
Congregation Shearith Israel (The Spanish and Portuguese Synagogue) is the
landmark home of America's oldest
Orthodox Jewish congregation. Watch
artists making prayer shawls and craft-
ing jewelry, potters vending wine cups,
and scribes penning marriage contracts,
and nibble Sephardic delicacies. *Congregation Shearith Israel, Central Park West
at 67th St., Upper West Side, 212/873–
0300. One Sunday in mid-May, 10–5.*

3 *b-3*

STORYTELLING HOUR
If this town could talk, the stories it
would tell—well, maybe not *these* stories. Come hear wonderful children's
tales read aloud at the Hans Christian
Andersen statue, near Central Park's
Sailboat Lake—an appropriate and
charming site for storytelling. Selections are geared toward ages 3–7. *Central Park, entrance at 5th Ave. and 74th
St., 212/360–3456. Late May–Sept., Sat.
11–noon.*

STREET FAIRS

Street fairs and block parties have become traditional summer fare in New York, featuring music, games, food, and wares—often for the benefit of neighborhood and block beautification projects. Some street fairs have become epic events, but even the tiniest block parties make for fine people-watching and usually draw friendly folks. For each weekend's fairs and festivals, check the "Weekend" section of Friday's *New York Times* and watch for notices on billboards and lampposts.

1 *f-1*

UKRAINIAN FESTIVAL

Old-country music accompanies pierogi, polkas, *pysanky* (colored eggs), and dancing in the heart of the East Village Ukrainian community. *E. 7th St. between 2nd Ave. and Bowery, 212/674–1516. 3rd weekend in May.*

11 *d-2*

WASHINGTON SQUARE OUTDOOR ART EXHIBIT

For over half a century, Memorial Day has turned the Washington Square area into an open-air arts-and-crafts gallery, bringing some 600 exhibitors to lower 5th Avenue, Washington Square Park, and the surrounding streets. The action continues for three weekends, from noon to sundown. *Greenwich Village, 212/982–6255.*

1 *d-4*

YOU GOTTA HAVE PARK!

A variety of park-related festivities— races, concerts, games—celebrate our greenest patches and remind us why we've managed to live here for so many years. *212/315–0385.*

JUNE

Check the April and May listings for ongoing summer events.

PARADES

Puerto Rican Day Parade Possibly New York's loudest parade. *212/484–1222.*

9 *b-2*

AMERICAN CRAFTS FESTIVAL

Some 400 skilled artisans display their crafts at Lincoln Center on June weekends. Support the arts *and* carry something home: leather, jewelry, blown and stained glass, quilts, baskets, furniture, and toys are all for sale. *Lincoln Center Plaza, Broadway at 64th St., 212/677–4627. Mid- to late June, noon–9.*

1 *h-3*

BELMONT STAKES

This is New York's thoroughbred of horse races, and a jewel in the Triple Crown. *Belmont Park Racetrack, Hempstead Tpke. and Plainfield Ave., Belmont, Long Island, 718/641–4700. Admission. Early June.*

9 *d-5*

BRYANT PARK SUMMER FILM FESTIVAL

Monday nights in summer are classic-movie nights in the nearly bucolic Bryant Park, behind the New York Public Library. This hugely popular (read: get there early) outdoor series runs throughout the summer and becomes more of a scene each year. Dash from work around 5 to claim a spot on the lawn, spread out your blanket and snacks, and get comfortable—films start at sundown. *Bryant Park, 6th Ave. between 40th and 42nd Sts., 212/512–5700.*

12 *g-7*

CELEBRATE BROOKLYN PERFORMING ARTS FESTIVAL

From mid-June to late August, a delectable potpourri of music—pop, jazz, rock, classical, klezmer, African, Latin, Caribbean—comes to Prospect Park, along with dance, film, and more. Take advantage! *Prospect Park Band Shell, Prospect Park West at 9th St., Park Slope, Brooklyn, 718/855–7882, ext. 52.*

11 *d-4*

FEAST OF ST. ANTHONY OF PADUA

The music, games of chance, and kids' rides at this classic street festival beg you to inhale and ingest the glorious Italian food. *Sullivan St. between W. Houston and Spring Sts., 212/777–2755. Early June.*

JVC JAZZ FESTIVAL NEW YORK

This much-loved summer festival (which recently turned 25) brings giants of jazz and new faces alike to Carnegie Hall, Lincoln Center, the Beacon Theater, Bryant Park, and other theaters and clubs about town. Check newspapers for performers and schedules. Tickets are available through Ticketmaster. *212/501–1390. Admission. Late June.*

10 e-5
LOWER EAST SIDE JEWISH FESTIVAL
Yiddish is now mixed with Spanish and Chinese in these parts, but once a year the neighborhood's Old World kicks up its heels. Baked goods, kosher food, books, and entertainment fill East Broadway from Rutgers to Montgomery Streets. So go—would it kill you to have a good time? *212/475–6200. One Sun. in late May or early June.*

4 g-7
MERMAID PARADE
The Mermaid Parade is a pagan tribute to Coney Island, once the parade capital of the world. This weird and wild affair begins at Brooklyn's Surf Avenue and West 10th Street, right in front of that proto–roller coaster, the Cyclone. Break out your sequins and blond wig, and become a mermaid for the day (you'll fit right in)—or dress as King Neptune. If you're weak on maritime history, build a float, don flippers and goggles, and be Liza Minnelli. Whatever. *718/372–5159. 1st Sat. after summer solstice at 2.*

THE MET IN THE PARKS
This summer, have some Puccini with your tortillas and brie. Free outdoor performances by the Metropolitan Opera Company start at 8 PM in rotating city parks (*see below*). The acoustics are better elsewhere, and you might want to bring some bug spray, but the atmosphere and the price are unbeatable. *212/362–6000.*

Bronx Van Cortlandt Park

Brooklyn Prospect Park; Marine Park.

Manhattan Central Park.

Queens Cunningham Park.

Staten Island Snug Harbor; Miller Field; Great Kills Park.

9 b-2
MIDSUMMER NIGHT SWING
It's amazing to see: on balmy summer evenings, New York's highest-brow plaza becomes an enormous, old-fashioned dance hall. Top big bands provide jazz, Dixieland, R&B, calypso, and Latin rhythms, and zillions of people of all ages fill both the checkerboard dance floor (for a fee) and the periphery (no charge). Tuesday night is Tango Night, and Wednesday night you can take dance lessons 6:30–7:30. *Lincoln Center Plaza, Broadway at 64th St., Upper West Side, 212/875–5766. Late June–late July, Tues.–Sat. at 8:15.*

3 b-3
MUSEUM MILE FESTIVAL
One evening in mid-June, 10 of New York's cultural treasure chests open their doors free of charge. Upper 5th Avenue is closed to traffic, and musicians, clowns, and jugglers entertain strollers. *5th Ave. from 82nd to 104th Sts. 2nd or 3rd Tues. in June, 6–9.*

10 f-1
MUSIC IN ABE LEBEWOHL PARK
Burst from your cubicle at the stroke of noon and high-tail it to the East Village, where jazz, pop, and classical interludes relax the crowd every Thursday at 12:30 in June and July. Need another reason? The Second Avenue Deli provides post-performance snacks. *Abe Lebewohl Park, 2nd Ave. at 10th St., 212/777–3240. June–July.*

7 d-7
SHAKESPEARE IN THE PARK
Central Park's outdoor Delacorte Theater now hosts one of New York's most blazingly popular summer traditions. Joseph Papp's Public Theater stages two major productions here each year, most featuring one star performer from the big or small screen. The program does depart from Shakespeare, but only to celebrate another masterpiece, such as Leonard Bernstein's *On the Town*. The whole affair is free, so while the play might later come indoors if it's a smash (as *The Tempest* did, with Patrick Stewart), you won't get the same bang for your buck. Tickets are distributed the day of the performance, two per person, at the Public Theater (425 Lafayette St., East Village, 1–3) and the Delacorte (beginning at 1)—line up early and bring some *Mad Libs. Central Park, Delacorte Theater (enter at E. or W. 81st St.), 212/861–PAPP. Mid-June–late Aug., Tues.–Sun. at 8.*

`9` *d-1*

SUMMERSTAGE IN CENTRAL PARK

Talk about a crowd-pleaser: Summer-Stage offers free weekday-evening and weekend-afternoon blues, Latin, pop, African, and country music; dance; opera; and readings. You can often enjoy the sounds without stopping by in earnest. Recent performers have included Morrissey and the one and only James Brown. *Central Park (enter at 72nd St.), 212/360–2777. June–Aug.*

TEXACO NEW YORK JAZZ FESTIVAL

In 1997, Texaco climbed on board as primary sponsor of this decade-old festival, which began life as "What Is Jazz?", an alternative to the JVC Jazz Festival. If you need an excuse to give up your day job, the festival already sponsors 350 performances at clubs and public spaces around town. Exhaustion will most likely be the end of you, but it's not a bad closing riff. The Knitting Factory (74 Leonard St., Tribeca) is a main venue. *212/219–3006. Admission. 2 wks in mid-June.*

`12` *g-5*

WELCOME BACK TO BROOKLYN FESTIVAL

You can go home again, at least on the second Sunday in May. Street games, local-history exhibits, Junior's cheesecake, and Nathan's hot dogs educate tourists from Peoria, Pakistan, and Manhattan and confirm the locals' suspicions that they really do live in the coolest borough. *Eastern Pkwy, Grand Army Plaza (north end of Prospect Park) to Brooklyn Museum, Park Slope, 718/855–7882. Noon–5.*

INDEPENDENCE DAY WEEKEND

`10` *e-8*

GREAT 4TH OF JULY FESTIVAL

Manhattan's oldest quarter celebrates the nation's birthday with arts, crafts, ethnic food, live entertainment, and a parade from Bowling Green to City Hall. *Water St. from Battery Park–John St., 212/484–1222. July 4, 11–7.*

`9` *f-6*

MACY'S FIREWORKS DISPLAY

The nation's largest display of pyrotechnical wizardry—yes, we've got that, too—is launched from barges in the East River. The best viewing points are FDR Drive from 14th to 41st Sts. (access via 23rd, 34th, and 48th Sts.) and the Brooklyn Heights Promenade. The FDR Drive is closed to traffic, but you'll want to get there early, as police sometimes restrict even pedestrian traffic. *212/560–4060. July 4, 9:15.*

`10` *f-7*

SOUTH STREET SEAPORT INDEPENDENCE WEEKEND

The Seaport is awash in celebrations and jammed with visitors and residents alike for the entire weekend. Concerts, street performers, and other special events make for excellent people-watching. *South Street Seaport, Lower Manhattan.*

JULY

Check the April, May, and June listings for ongoing summer events.

LEGAL HOLIDAY

Independence Day July 4 (*see above* for listings).

NEW YORK PHILHARMONIC PARK CONCERTS

Bronx Van Cortlandt Park

Brooklyn Prospect Park

Manhattan Central Park

Queens Cunningham Park

Staten Island Miller Field

Each summer the New York Philharmonic Orchestra performs a light program under the stars, and caps each concert with fireworks. Bring a picnic. *212/875–5709. Mid-July–early Aug.*

`9` *d-3*

SUMMERGARDEN

Enjoy 20th-century classical music in the Museum of Modern Art's popular sculpture garden. Performers are graduate students and alumni of the Juilliard School. *Museum of Modern Art, 14 W. 54th St., Midtown, 212/708–9400. Early July–mid-Aug., Fri. at 6, Sat. at 8:30.*

11 *d-2*

WASHINGTON SQUARE MUSIC FESTIVAL

Washington Square Park gets even louder in midsummer, when one of the city's oldest open-air concert series kicks in. The first four concerts are chamber music; the ultimate one features big-band swing. *Washington Sq. Park (5th Ave. at University Pl.), Greenwich Village, 212/431–1088. Mid-July–mid-Aug., Tues. at 8.*

AUGUST

Check the April, May, June, and July listings for ongoing summer events.

1 *d-3*

HARLEM WEEK

Fortunately for all, the largest black and Hispanic festival in the world actually runs for about two weeks. Indoor and outdoor activities for every age celebrate the community's past, present, and future. Try to catch a feature at the Black Film Festival, and don't rush through the Taste of Harlem Food Festival. *212/283–3315. 1st Mon.–3rd Sun. in Aug.*

9 *b-2*

LINCOLN CENTER OUT-OF-DOORS

Lincoln Plaza devotes itself to a four-week open-air bonanza of music, dance, and theater. *Lincoln Center Plaza, Broadway at 64th St., Upper West Side, 212/875–5108.*

9 *b-2*

MOSTLY MOZART FESTIVAL

This world-renowned August concert series is just what it sounds like: a generous helping of Mozart, with dashes of other masters for good measure. The Mostly Mozart Festival Orchestra holds forth under the inspired baton of Gerard Schwarz, and various solo performers illuminate chamber works in recitals. Free outdoor afternoon concerts are followed by casual evening concerts at reasonable prices. *Avery Fisher Hall, 10 Lincoln Center Plaza (Broadway at 64th St.), Upper West Side, 212/875–5103. Aug.*

3 *b-6*

NEW YORK INTERNATIONAL FRINGE FESTIVAL

Modeled on the Edinburgh Festival, emerging theater companies and per-forming artists take over two dozen performance spaces on the Lower East Side for the last two weeks of August. Make the trip—summer's winding down, and this is what the Lower East Side does best. *212/307–1022. Admission. Daily 3:30 PM–2 AM.*

9 *d-6*

TAP-O-MANIA

Be a part of Broadway's—okay, 34th Street's—longest tapping chorus line, and try to outdo yourselves: The *Guinness Book of World Records* puts the last one at 6,600 dancers. *Macy's Herald Sq., Broadway at 34th St., Garment District, 212/494–5432. 3rd Sun. in Aug. Registration at 8.*

3 *g-1*

U.S. OPEN

See Sporting Events *in* Chapter 6.

SEPTEMBER

The New York Philharmonic, the New York City and Metropolitan Operas, and Broadway launch their new seasons, and the pace of the city quickens—especially on the first day of crisp fall weather.

LEGAL HOLIDAY
Labor Day 1st Mon.

PARADES
Labor Day Parade 1st Mon.

Steuben Day (German) Parade.

LABOR DAY WEEKEND

For many New Yorkers, the nation's unofficial end of summer marks the last chance for a beach-escape weekend. As a result, you'll hardly suffer for hanging around the city; a pleasant lull descends. The city is peaceful and almost quiet, providing great opportunities to visit otherwise jam-packed venues. Just the *thought* of going out for bagels and not standing in line should make your bowl of corn flakes that much more savory.

9 *b-2*

AUTUMN CRAFTS FESTIVAL

Over 400 craftspeople show up and sell their unique and comforting wares to world-weary New Yorkers. Think you've seen it all? Drop by for the sheep-shearing demonstration. *Lincoln Center Plaza,*

Broadway at 64th St., Upper West Side, 212/677–4627. Two weeks, early to mid-Sept.

3 c-8
ATLANTIC ANTIC

This 12-block-long festival celebrates downtown Brooklyn, and there is much to celebrate. Food, entertainment, antiques, and a parade (at 11:30) beckon all toward the Williamsburg Clock Tower. *Atlantic Ave. from Flatbush to Furman St. Downtown Brooklyn, 212/484–1222. 1st Sun. in late Sept., 10–6.*

10 f-4
FEAST OF SAN GENNARO

The oldest, grandest, largest, and most crowded *festa* of them all, in honor of the patron saint of Naples, begins with the "Triumphant March" from Verdi's *Aida* and continues for 11 days of eating and shenanigans. The city has recently imposed greater restrictions on San Gennaro, and vendors and visitors have complained that the festival's flavor has changed. Pay no attention; you're all but obliged to go. *Mulberry St. from Canal to Houston Sts., Little Italy, 212/764–6330. Mid- to late Sept., noon–midnight.*

7 e-7
5TH AVENUE MILE

The world's fastest runners crash New York's most exclusive strip, and thousands cheer them on—brief, but exhilarating. *5th Ave. from 62nd to 82nd Sts., Upper East Side, 212/860–4455. One Sat. in late Sept.*

9 b-2
NEW YORK FILM FESTIVAL

Founded in 1963, New York's exceptional international film festival is an autumn tradition for cinephiles. Afternoon and evening screenings provide plenty of temptations, and advance tickets make them real events. *Alice Tully Hall, Broadway at 65th St., Upper West Side, 212/875–5050. 2 wks, late Sept.–early Oct.*

9 d-4
NEW YORK IS BOOK COUNTRY

This midtown stretch of 5th Avenue contains—oops, used to contain—the country's largest concentration of bookstores, so on this Indian Summer day the street is filled with kiosks representing publishers of all stripes. Preview forthcoming books, meet authors, admire beautiful book jackets, chat with George Plimpton at the *Paris Review* booth, and enjoy live entertainment and bookbinding demonstrations. Bring the kids. *5th Ave. from 48th to 57th Sts., 212/207–7242. 3rd Sun. in Sept., 11–5.*

11 d-2
WASHINGTON SQUARE OUTDOOR ART EXHIBIT

Like its Memorial Day cousin (*see above*), this fair turns Washington Square Park and its environs into an alfresco art gallery. *Greenwich Village, 212/982–6255. 1st weekend in early Sept., noon–6.*

4 e-1
WEST INDIAN AMERICAN DAY PARADE

Labor Day weekend brings out the largest parade in New York City—no mean distinction. Modeled after the harvest carnival of Trinidad and Tobago, this Caribbean revel has been observed in New York since the 1940s, when it sprang up in Harlem. The festivities begin with a Friday-evening salsa, reggae, and calypso extravaganza at the Brooklyn Museum (admission), and end on Monday afternoon with a gigantic, Mardi Gras–style parade of floats, elaborately costumed dancers, stilt-walkers, and West Indian food and music. *Eastern Pkwy. from Utica Ave. to Brooklyn Museum, 212/484–1222.*

OCTOBER

The New York Rangers and New York Knicks snap into public action at Madison Square Garden. (*See* Sporting Events *in* Chapter 6 for details.)

LEGAL HOLIDAY
Columbus Day 2nd Mon.

PARADES
Columbus Day Parade

Hispanic Day Parade

Pulaski Day Parade

9 b-2
BIG APPLE CIRCUS

No one is more than 50 ft from the action at this heated little big top in Lincoln Center's Damrosch Park. From late

October through early January, this new New York tradition tips its hat to the classical American circus with simplicity, charm, and magic in one ring. Advance tickets are available. *Damrosch Park, Lincoln Center, Columbus Ave. at 63rd St., Upper West Side, 212/268–2500. Late Oct.–early Jan., generally Tues.–Sun., matinee and evening shows.*

12 *a-3*

BROOKLYN HEIGHTS PROMENADE ART SHOW

Like its predecessor in May, this show draws over 100 art lovers to the water's edge. Need a push? Last we checked, there was a quietly flourishing Baskin-Robbins on Montague Street. *Brooklyn Heights Promenade, East River from Remsen to Clark Sts., 718/625–0080.*

9 *e-1*

FALL ANTIQUES SHOW

Over 75 dealers converge from all over the U.S. for this relaxed yet refined affair, the foremost American-antiques show in the country and a bonanza for collectors of Americana. The Museum of American Folk Art benefits. *7th Regiment Armory, Park Ave. at 67th St., Upper East Side, 212/777–5218 or 212/581–2676. Admission. 4 days in late Sept.*

7 *b-3*

FEAST OF ST. FRANCIS DAY

Obedience school too pricey? Ask for divine intervention at this wonderful service, otherwise known as the Blessing of the Animals. Most of the blessed are garden-variety cats and dogs, but you never know; often an elephant shows up. *Cathedral Church of St. John the Divine, 1047 Amsterdam Ave. (at 112th St.), Upper West Side, 212/662–2133. 1st Sun. in Oct., mass at 11, blessings 1–5.*

7 *b-3*

HALLOWEEN EXTRAVAGANZA AND PROCESSION OF GHOULS

The massive Cathedral Church of St. John the Divine lends gothic cachet to these creepy goings-on: a silent movie is accompanied by organ music, and a procession of giant puppets brings on spiders, skeletons, ghouls, and spooks courtesy of Ralph Lee and the Mettawee River Theater Company. And who better to scare you? Ralph Lee basically founded the Village Halloween Parade

(see below). Cathedral Church of St. John the Divine, 1047 Amsterdam Ave. (at 112th St.), Upper West Side, 212/662–2133. Oct. 31 at 7 and 10.

NEW YORK CITY MARATHON
See Sporting Events in Chapter 6.

3 *b-6*

VILLAGE HALLOWEEN PARADE

What started as a handful of weirdos in the streets now draws 50,000 yahoos of all ages and persuasions. This anything-goes annual procession features some bizarre but brilliant costumes and exuberant live music. Join the march or just watch the massive spectacle from the sidelines. *6th Ave. from Spring to 23rd Sts., SoHo/W. Village/Chelsea. Oct. 31st, sundown (about 7)–about 10.*

NOVEMBER

LEGAL HOLIDAYS
Veteran's Day Nov. 11.

Thanksgiving Day 4th Thurs.

9 *d-5*

LORD & TAYLOR'S CHRISTMAS WINDOWS

Early in the season the mannequins disappear, and lavish, animated holiday scenes fill this classic store's 5th Avenue windows. The line moves quickly, but the best viewing is after 9 PM, when the shoppers have cleared out. *Lord & Taylor, 424 5th Ave. (at 39th St.), 212/391–3344. Tues. before Thanksgiving–Jan. 1.*

9 *d-6*

MACY'S SANTA CLAUS ADVENTURE AT MACYLAND

St. Nick is in residence— and in demand—at Macy's from the day after Thanksgiving until Christmas Eve, greeting and posing with children of all ages. So who's stuck managing the elves? The Mrs.? There is a 20-minute holiday marionette show every hour 10:30–4:30. *Macy's Herald Sq., Broadway at 34th St., Garment District, 212/494–5432.*

9 *d-6*

MACY'S THANKSGIVING DAY PARADE

You watched it on TV growing up; now break away from the set and watch the real thing. Macy's Thanksgiving Day parade moves south from Central Park West and 77th Street to Columbus Circle, then down Broadway to the float-reviewing stand at Macy's Herald Square (Broadway and 34th St.). The biggest stars are the gigantic balloons, which are inflated the night before the parade to antic effect (77th and 81st Sts. between Central Park West and Columbus Ave., 6–wee hours). Santa's arrival provides the grand finale, though the occasional unscripted event can upstage even Santa, as when a Sonic the Hedgehog balloon broke free and ran amok. Dress warmly, and take your postion by 8. *212/494–5432. Thanksgiving Day, 9–noon.*

9 *d-4*

RADIO CITY CHRISTMAS SPECTACULAR

The famed Christmas Spectacular at the famed music hall features the famed Rockettes. A quieter tradition within the show is the Nativity Pageant, with live donkeys, camels, and sheep. Buy tickets in advance. *Radio City Music Hall, 1260 6th Ave. (at 50th St.), Midtown, 212/247–4777. Mid-Nov.–early Jan.*

9 *a-4*

TRIPLE PIER EXPO

This annual collectibles and antiques extravaganza is not for the faint of heart, even if the faint of heart love antiques. Wear comfortable shoes and be prepared for a feast of Art Deco furniture, 19th-century decorative arts, American quilts, memorabilia, silver, prints, jewelry, dolls, and much more. The price range is pleasingly broad. *Passenger Ship Terminals, Piers 88, 90, 92, 12th Ave. from 48th to 55th Sts., Hell's Kitchen, 212/255–0020. Admission. 1st weekend in early Nov.*

DECEMBER

New York's holiday pleasures are sweet but not cloying. It's bloody difficult to remain unmoved by the strings of lights, classic store windows, concerts, and general hullabaloo. Feel like Handel's *Messiah*? You'll have to choose from a dozen different performances—each week. (*See* November, *above,* for ongoing holiday festivities.)

LEGAL HOLIDAY
Christmas Day Dec. 25.

9 *e-3*

CAROUSEL AND HOLIDAY DISPLAY

An animated carousel and colorful decorations will delight kids of all ages. Tantrum-prevention tip: Kids may look at, but may not ride, the carousel, so you may want to call a conference before taking Junior to see this gorgeous machine. *Lever House, 390 Park Ave. (at 53rd St.), lobby, Midtown, 212/688–6000. Early Dec.–Jan. 2.*

9 *e-3*

CHANUKAH CELEBRATIONS

A 32-ft-tall menorah at Grand Army Plaza (5th Ave. and 59th St.) makes for a grand candle-lighting ceremony each night at sundown during the 8-day Festival of Lights (212/427–6000). The 92nd St. Y (395 Lexington Ave., at 92nd St., 212/996–1100) holds a family celebration, geared toward ages 4–12, at which the gang can make holiday crafts, sing along to holiday music, hear an expert storyteller, and nibble refreshments (usually the Sun. before Chanukah, 10:45–1:15).

1 *b-2*

CHRISTMAS IN RICHMONDTOWN

Restored buildings are decorated for Christmas in period (18th- and 19th-century) fashion and open to the public. Costumed guides explain local history, parlor games and popcorn stringing keep the kids occupied, and homemade food and gifts make a dent in your shopping list. *Historic Richmondtown, 441 Clarke Ave. (near Arthur Kill Rd.), Staten Island, 718/351–1611. Admission to Historic Richmondtown. 1st or 2nd Sun. in Dec., 10–4.*

KWANZAA

Kwanzaa is a seven-day African-American cultural festival (Dec. 26–Jan. 1) celebrating the traditional first fruit of the harvest. Events are citywide; check newspapers for details.

7 *B-8*

KWANZAA AT THE AMERICAN MUSEUM OF NATURAL HISTORY

Music and dance help augment the re-creation of an African marketplace, complete with African-style gifts for sale.

American Museum of Natural History, Central Park West at 79th St., Upper West Side, 212/769–5000. Admission to museum. One afternoon, late Dec.

9 *e-2*

MIRACLE ON MADISON AVENUE

Madison Avenue's slickest shopping stretch is closed to traffic on the first Sunday in December for an afternoon of (civilized?) holiday shopping, with participating stores donating 20 percent of every sale to children's charities. Festive heated tents keep the wee ones warm as they enjoy the strolling musicians and the hot cider and cookies. *Madison Ave. from 55th to 79th Sts., 212/988–4001. Noon–5.*

9 *b-2*

MESSIAH SING-IN

Led by 21 different conductors and punctuated by four soloists, the chorus for this *Messiah* consists of everyone else who shows up—a good three thousand. Handel never sounded so good. Make your big break from the shower to Lincoln Center; bring the score or buy one in the lobby from the National Choral Council. *Avery Fisher Hall, Lincoln Center, Broadway at 64th St., Upper West Side, 212/333–5333. Admission. 1 evening several days before Christmas at 8.*

7 *e-7*

METROPOLITAN MUSEUM OF ART CHRISTMAS TREE

Folks come from far and wide to see the Met's stunning tree in the solemn Medieval Sculpture Hall. The 30-ft Baroque wonder is decorated with 18th-century cherubs and angels and accompanied by an elaborate Neapolitan nativity scene. *Metropolitan Museum of Art, 5th Ave. at 82nd St., Upper East Side, 212/879–5500. Dec.–early Jan.*

9 *b-2*

THE NUTCRACKER

The Nutcracker is the most popular ballet in the world, and who better than the New York City Ballet to perform it? The company is ably assisted by children from the School of American Ballet. This magical show is as much a holiday tradition in New York as anywhere, so buy tickets well in advance. *New York State Theater, Lincoln Center, Broadway and 64th St., Upper West Side, 212/870–5590. Late Nov.–early Jan.*

9 *d-5*

TREE-LIGHTING CEREMONY

Perhaps New York's most famous holiday tradition, the Rockefeller Center tree-lighting began in 1933 and has only picked up steam since. All at once, on the first Tuesday in December, the 20,000 lights on Rockefeller Center's mammoth Christmas tree come into view, accompanied by cheers, carols, and, of course, figure skating down below. It's a magical sight—if you can see it, which is unlikely, as thundering hordes of people pack several of the plaza's surrounding blocks. *Rockefeller Plaza, 5th Ave. between 49th and 50th Sts., 212/632–3975. Early evening.*

6 *c-5*

"'TWAS THE NIGHT BEFORE CHRISTMAS"

In a charmingly esoteric tradition that dates from 1911, a procession of carolers lays a wreath on Clement Clarke Moore's grave in Trinity Cemetery and reads his beloved poem, "A Visit from St. Nicholas." *Church of the Intercession, Broadway at 155th St., Harlem, 212/283–6200. Sun. before Christmas at 4.*

NEW YEAR'S EVE

FIREWORKS

Fireworks greet the New Year at midnight in Central Park. Catch the best views at Bethesda Fountain, 72nd St.; Tavern-on-the-Green, Central Park West and 67th St.; Central Park West and 96th St.; and 5th Ave. at 90th St. Fireworks also light up Brooklyn's Prospect Park; in Park Slope's Grand Army Plaza, the show is tastefully accompanied by music, hot cider, and cookies; festivities begin at 11:30 PM. If it's just too cold to stand around until midnight, watch the 'works at South Street Seaport at 11:30 PM. *212/397–3111.*

9 *e-6*

EMPIRE STATE BUILDING

It's a grand place to be at midnight—even if you're not sleepless in Seattle. The last ticket is sold at 11:25 PM. *Empire State Bldg., 350 5th Ave. (at 34th St.), Garment District. Admission.*

9 *e-5*

FIRST NIGHT

Sponsored by the Grand Central Partnership, New York's First Night is a wonderful new tradition, begun in 1991. It's a family-oriented alternative to high-priced, high-octane celebrations, though most revelers are in fact adults. Choose from over 40 events—ice-skating, concerts, storytelling, circus arts, dance, and more—in places like the MetLife Building, the Winter Garden at the World Financial Center, and Grand Central Terminal. When did you last waltz in the Grand Concourse? A First Night button buys you admission to all events; children 3 and under get in free. *Grand Central Terminal, and environs. Park Ave. and 42nd St., 212/922–9393. Dec. 31 noon–1 AM.*

9 c-1
MIDNIGHT RUN
Beginning and ending at Tavern-on-the-Green, some 3,000 men and women take a chilly but relatively short run around Central Park. Lose the sweats: many run in evening dress, others in costume. Prizes go to the fastest and best-dressed, and every runner gets champagne and a T-shirt. *Tavern-on-the-Green, Central Park West and 67th St., 212/860–4455. Registration fee. Jan. 1, midnight.*

7 b-3
NEW YEAR'S EVE CONCERT FOR PEACE
Leonard Bernstein used to conduct this stirring, 2-hour program at St. John the Divine. Like the cathedral itself, the music still soars. Doors open at 6 PM, a fact you should heed if you want a seat. *Cathedral Church of St. John the Divine, 1047 Amsterdam Ave. (at 112th St.), Upper West Side, 212/662–2133. Dec. 31 at 7:30; doors open at 6.*

9 d-5
TIMES SQUARE
There are people who spend every New Year's Eve in Times Square; this is not necessary. But there's nothing quite like Times Square on December 31. Ever since 1907 (well—minus a few electric-apple years in the '80s), a 6-ft, illuminated, wrought-iron ball has welcomed the new year by moving slowly down a flagpole atop the Times Tower, now 1 Times Square Building. The descent takes the last 59 seconds of the old year, and at midnight the ball is illuminated at the pole's base. Hardy revelers start to gather in the square at 10 PM; the rest of the country watches Dick Clark nar-

rate the event on TV. *Times Sq., Broadway and 42nd St., Theater District, 212/484–1222.*

day trips out of town

Escape! In case hauling yourself efficiently out of the city seems as nerve-wracking as staying in it, Metro-North and the Long Island Rail Road (*see* Transportation *in* Chapter 1) offer package day trips to a variety of intriguing destinations, such as Long Island wineries and various historic homes. The tours are escorted and include all admission fees.

ATLANTIC CITY, NJ

If you're itchy for a little action, catch a bus down to Atlantic City, where casinos line the seaside boardwalk. Try your hand at craps, the slots, roulette, and table after table of blackjack. If your luck turns sour, you've still got the saltwater taffy and the ocean breezes. Gray Line's one-day bus trips (212/397–2600) make transport a snap.

BAYARD CUTTING ARBORETUM

An easy jaunt from the city, this 690-acre arboretum is just a ten-minute walk from the train station. Spread out along the lazy Connetquot River, the arboretum is best known for its stands of pines, native woods and bogs, meandering paths, and carefully laid rows of rhododendrons and azaleas. *Oakdale, NY, 516/581-1002. Open Tues.–Sun. 10 AM–sunset. Long Island Rail Road: Montauk Line to Great River.*

BOSCOBEL RESTORATION

A grand Federal-style mansion surrounded by formal gardens and lawns and overlooking the Hudson River, Boscobel (from *bosco bello,* "beautiful woods") was built in 1808 by Morris Dyckman. You can tour both the grounds and the interior, with its canopy beds, elaborate woodwork, and wonderful collection of 19th-century furniture, including some pieces by the famous New York cabinetmaker Duncan Phyfe. Special events include nature walks, lectures on horticulture, concerts, and storytelling hours. *Rte. 9D (8 mi north of Bear Mtn. Bridge), Garrison-on-Hudson, NY, 914/265–3638. Open Apr.–Oct., Mon. and Wed.–Sun. 10–5; Nov., Dec., and Mar., Mon. and Wed.–Sun. 10–3:15. Metro-North: Hudson Line to Cold Spring.*

LYNDHURST

An 1838 Gothic Revival mansion designed by Alexander Jackson Davis for Gen. William Paulding, an early New York City mayor, Lyndhurst was later purchased by railroad tycoon Jay Gould in 1870. Perched above the Hudson River and surrounded by 67 acres of lush grounds, the house itself—often referred to as "the castle"—is characterized by grandiose rooms and holds period furnishings and paintings. *635 S. Broadway, Tarrytown, NY, 914/631–4481. Open May–Oct., Tues.–Sun. 10–5; Nov.–Apr., weekends, 10–5. Metro-North: Hudson Line to Tarrytown.*

OLD BETHPAGE VILLAGE RESTORATION

This animated history museum re-creates a rural Long Island village circa 1850. Costumed craftspeople, farmers, and villagers populate the grounds and the 15 historic buildings. *Round Swamp Road, Old Bethpage, NY, 516/572–8401. Open Wed.–Sun. 10–5, shorter hrs winter. Long Island Rail Road: Port Jefferson Line to Hicksville; Ronkonkoma Line to Bethpage or Farmingdale.*

OLD WESTBURY GARDENS

Several hundred acres of formal English gardens surround a beautifully furnished, Georgian-style country house, once the property of millionaire John S. Phipps. Each weekend brings concerts, hay rides, walking tours, art exhibits, and other activities. *71 Old Westbury Rd., Old Westbury, NY, 516/333–0048. Open Apr.–Oct., Wed.–Mon. 10–5; longer hrs summer. Long Island Rail Road: Port Jefferson Line to Westbury.*

PLANTING FIELDS ARBORETUM STATE HISTORIC PARK

This 409-acre country estate comprises extensive European-style gardens, greenhouses, woodlands, and Coe Hall, a 65-room Tudor-style mansion. *Planting Fields Rd., Oyster Bay, Long Island, 516/922–9201. Gardens open daily 9–5; mansion open daily 12:30–3:30. Long Island Rail Road: Oyster Bay Line to Locust Valley or Oyster Bay.*

SAG HARBOR, LONG ISLAND

For a charming getaway, try this 19th-century whaling center on Long Island's South Fork. Along with historic houses and chic boutiques and cafés, there's an old cemetery, a Customs House dating from 1793, and a Whaling Museum (516/725–0770).

HISTORIC HUDSON VALLEY

These three Hudson River Valley mansions, ranging in age from pre-Revolutionary to Federal, can be toured with guides dressed in period costumes. All three estates are designated as National Historic Landmarks; visits are free, and you're welcome to bring a picnic.

PHILIPSBURG MANOR

Once owned by Frederick Philips, a Dutch carpenter who rose to become the richest man in the colony, this working farm dates from the early 1700s, when it was run by African slaves. Now restored, Philipsburg features a stone manor house, a water-powered grist mill and mill pond, and a barn filled with farm animals. Guides in Colonial dress demonstrate spinning and weaving. *Rte. 9, Sleepy Hollow, NY (2 mi north of Tappan Zee Bridge). 914/631–3992. Closed Tues.; closed Jan.–Feb. Metro-North: Hudson Line to Tarrytown.*

SUNNYSIDE

Covering 20 acres is the picturesque home of Washington Irving, author of the classic American stories "The Legend of Sleepy Hollow" and "Rip Van Winkle." Purchased in 1835, Irving's charming cottage, topped by a Spanish-style tower, is filled with his personal furnishings and memorabilia, including over 3,000 books. On the surrounding grounds, garden plantings and walkways follow a plan devised by Irving himself. *W. Sunnyside Ln. (off Rte 9; 1 mi south of Tappan Zee Bridge), Tarrytown, NY, 914/591–8763. Closed Tues.; closed Jan.–Feb. Metro-North: Hudson Line to Tarrytown.*

VAN CORTLANDT MANOR

The centerpiece of this Revolutionary War estate is an 18th-century brick manor house filled with Georgian and Federal period furniture and paintings; also on the grounds is a restored 18th-century tavern. Frequent demonstrations of open-hearth cooking, brickmaking, and blacksmithing appeal to all five senses; and in summer, the staff cooks colonial-style dinners according to 18th-century recipe books. *S. Riverside Ave. (off Rte. 9, Croton Pt. Ave. exit), Croton-on-Hudson, NY, 914/271–8981. Closed weekdays Nov.–Dec. Metro-North: Hudson Line to Croton-Harmon.*

VANDERBILT MANSION

Designed by McKim, Mead & White, this sumptuous 1898 Italian Renaissance pile was the home of Frederick Vanderbilt, the commodore's son. Inside you'll find opulent furnishings and paintings from the 16th to 18th centuries. *Rte. 9, Hyde Park, NY, 914/229–9115. Open daily 9–5. Metro-North: Hudson Line to Poughkeepsie.*

chapter 3

RESTAURANTS

New York has become the restaurant capital of the planet. No other city has New York's variety of cuisine, from ethnic and haute French to pan-Asian and New American. Downtown in particular has seen a veritable avalanche of restaurant openings in the 1990s, as old areas are renovated, lofts are fancifully redesigned, and discriminating diners move in. Loft locus Tribeca now packs some of the city's finest restaurants. Chelsea, with its rash of new galleries, and Flatiron have also become hot dining districts. SoHo continues to add venues to its stylish roster; you can find somewhere to dine in this area virtually around the clock. Watch for new eateries even further downtown, in the Wall Street area, as the loft-conversion frenzy presses south.

general information

NO SMOKING

All New York City restaurants with seats for 36 or more diners must set aside at least half of those seats for nonsmokers. You may state your preference for non-smoking or smoking when you make a reservation. Restaurant owners or patrons who break this law are subject to a fine.

RESERVATIONS

If you have the slightest whiff of a restaurant's popularity, phone ahead to make a reservation. If the restaurant doesn't take reservations, try to get an estimate on the waiting time for a table.

TIPPING

The rule of thumb for wait-service tips is *at least* 15% of the total (exclusive of tax), a figure easily calculated by doubling the amount of the 8¼% city sales tax. It's safe to say that New Yorkers tend to leave closer to 20%. Most restaurants add a service charge for large parties, so if you are dining with a group of six or more, be sure to check the bill carefully before leaving a tip.

Very Expensive ($$$$)	over $60
Expensive ($$$)	$40–$59
Moderate ($$)	$20–$39
Inexpensive ($)	under $20

Price for dinner per person, minus drinks, service, and tax.

restaurants by cuisine

AFGHAN

9 *f-3*
PAMIR
A popular place for a quick, light dinner, Pamir serves dependable, budget-priced, Afghan fare in an exotic setting. Locals like the large portions of shish kebabs and other grilled meats and stews. *1065 1st Ave. (at 58th St.), Upper East Side, 212/644-9258. AE, D, DC, MC, V. Closed Mon. Subway: 59th St. $*

7 *f-8*
1437 2nd Ave. (at 75th St.), Upper East Side, 212/734–3791. Subway: 77th St. $

AMERICAN

7 *f-6*
ACROSS THE STREET
This newcomer is named for its location—across the street from Eli Zabar's East Side gourmet market, The Vinegar Factory. Because Zabar's warm and casual restaurant features the freshest goodies from the shop, the menu changes nightly. There's probably no need to mention that the bread is addictive; Zabar created the city's bread craze. Locals flock here for the simple but robust fare. Try the sea scallops with bacon and beets, and don't miss the chocolate bread pudding, if you catch it on the menu. *444 E. 91st St., Upper East Side, 212/722–4000. AE, D, DC, MC, V. No lunch. Subway: 86th St. $$$*

9 *e-8*
ALVA
Alva is the ultimate neighborhood restaurant, its cozy bar draped with reg-

ulars enjoying the perfect combination of intimacy and excitement. Don't be fooled: past the bar lies a sophisticated dining room that pays homage to its namesake, Thomas Alva Edison, with dim, exposed bulbs and black-and-white photographs. The American bistro fare is above average, and it's a bargain considering the location. Look for the fabulous Cuban sandwich. *36 E. 22nd St., Flatiron, 212/228–4399. AE, DC, MC, V. No lunch weekends. Subway: 6 to 23rd St. $$*

9 *e-6*

AN AMERICAN PLACE

On an unassuming Murray Hill side street, celebrated chef Larry Forgione wins raves for his artfully presented, American-grown foodstuffs. The setting is handsome and spacious, and the wine selection (American only) is excellent. Enjoy barbecued mallard, Key West shrimp with mustard sauce, chicken breast sautéed with apple-cider vinegar, three-smoked-fish terrine, or sweet-potato ravioli. *2 Park Ave. (at 32nd St.), 212/684–2122. Reservations essential. Jacket and tie. AE, DC, MC, V. Closed Sun. No lunch Sat. Subway: 33rd St.; 34th St. Herald Sq. $$$$*

11 *d-4*

BLUE RIBBON

The line spills onto the street outside this cheerful storefront, which serves until 4 AM. (Tip: it's a popular late-night haunt for chefs.) There's a raw bar, a pupu platter, a shrimp Provençal, and a heavenly, dark mousselike chocolate cake. The place is noisy, and waits can be long, but the food is worth it. *97 Sullivan St. (between Spring and Prince Sts.), SoHo, 212/274–0404. AE, D, DC, MC, V. Closed Mon. No lunch. Subway: Spring St.; Prince St. $$*

10 *f-6*

BRIDGE CAFE

Nestled beneath the Brooklyn Bridge in a wood-frame building from around 1800, this cozy and friendly former longshoremen's café is now a favorite with Wall Street suits. Try soft-shell crabs in season, grilled trout, red snapper with vegetable risotto, and the excellent pecan pie. *279 Water St. (at Dover St.), Lower Manhattan, 212/227–3344. AE, DC, MC, V. No lunch Sat. Brunch Sun. Subway: Fulton St. $$*

11 *d-7*

BUBBLE LOUNGE

And what a lounge it is! Quaff some bubbly from the impressive champagne list and find yourself flattered by the red velvet, brick walls, high ceilings, comfortable couches, and other beautiful people. The food is secondary; have some caviar or pâté, then go somewhere else for dinner. Reserve ahead with a party of six or more. *228 W. Broadway (between Franklin and White Sts.), Tribeca, 212/421–3433. AE, DC, MC, V. No lunch. Subway: Franklin St. $$*

9 *e-8*

CANDELA

This former brick warehouse near Union Square has been transformed into something of a baronial hall, with wrought-iron railings, huge, dark mirrors, lighted tapers, and wooden booths. The menu is broad-ranging—spicy focaccia, hummus, fried calamari, chicken wontons, short ribs—and the crowd is young. *116 E. 16th St., Gramercy, 212/254–1600. AE, MC, V. Brunch Sun. $$*

11 *f-5*

CASCABEL

Despite some chef switcheroos, the food has remained consistently good at this trendy SoHo spot. The smart, chic dining room has red lacquered walls and shines spotlights on the tables. The menu changes frequently; it includes a superior lamb shank, a country salad with pork confit, or a rare tuna steak with white-bean puree. *218 Lafayette St. (at Spring St.), SoHo, 212/431–7300. Reservations essential. AE, D, DC, MC, V. Closed Sun. No lunch. $$$*

11 *g-1*

CIRCA

Italian-inspired American cooking is served here in a forties-style dining room (brown mohair-covered banquettes and venetian blinds). There are pizzas from a wood-burning brick oven, a raw bar, and terrific ceviche and fried calamari; and the house specialty, pan-roasted cod baked in a terra cotta dish, is exceptional. *103 2nd Ave. (at 6th St.), East Village, 212/777-4137. AE, MC, V. Brunch weekends. Subway: 2nd Ave.; Astor Pl. $–$$*

11 *d-1*

CLEMENTINE

The bar in front is packed; the large, muted-gold dining room is bedecked with brown banquettes and sconces shaped like art deco portholes. The place is very much a scene, but the food *is* superior; chef John Schenk's cooking is bold, vigorous, and unusual. Consider squid stuffed with merguez sausage, couscous, and spicy tomato-cumin broth; fried green tomatoes with barbecued baby-back ribs; and pork loin rubbed with chilis. The terrific desserts include dark-chocolate crepes with tangerine sauce and strawberry-rhubarb pie with coconut sorbet. *1 5th Ave. (at 8th St.), Greenwich Village, 212/253–0003. AE, MC, V. Subway: 8th St.* $$

11 *d-4*

CUB ROOM

A constant, lively bar scene keeps this brick and wood restaurant packed. Make your way to the dining room, in back, for a quieter experience. The menu is far-reaching (sometimes a bit too far) but with some fine dishes, including tuna in a sesame seed crust on soy-flavored Asian greens and pot roast with braised red cabbage and spaetzle. *131 Sullivan St. (at Prince St.), SoHo, 212/677–4100. AE. No lunch Sat., Sun., or Mon. Brunch Sun. Subway: Spring St.; Prince St.* $$$

11 *d-8*

DUANE PARK CAFE

This sleek restaurant has a Japanese chef whose cooking synthesizes Italian, Japanese, Cajun, and Californian styles. Pasta is made on the premises. Try the grilled quail with homemade sausage, the roast leg of lamb with polenta, and the excellent sorbets. *157 Duane St. (between Hudson St. and W. Broadway), Tribeca, 212/732–5555. Reservations essential. AE, DC, MC, V. No lunch weekends. Subway: Chambers St.* $$$

11 *h-1*

FIRST

With huge booths, low lights, professional service, and Sam DeMarco's internationally accented cuisine, First was at first too trendy for words, but it has transcended its own hipness. Open almost until dawn, it's a place to enjoy New York. Check out the creative martini selection, including one flavored with a rose-scented syrup, and, of course, the food—try the Long Island duck marinated in soy honey, the Sunday-night roast suckling pig, and the warm chocolate pudding. *87 1st Ave. (between 5th and 6th Sts.), East Village, 212/674–3823. AE, MC, V. No lunch. Brunch Sun. Subway: Astor Pl.* $$

9 *d-8*

FLOWERS

A new chef from Spain has breathed life into the menu of this former fashion-world haunt. Tapas and other appetizers recall bars in Madrid, and entrées are robust and flavorful. The beautiful rooftop terrace is ideal for cool summer nights. Interestingly, the place still draws a stylish crowd. *21 W. 17th St., Chelsea, 212/691–8888. AE, MC, V. Subway: F to 14th St.* $$

10 *e-1*

GOTHAM BAR & GRILL

After 14 years, this remains one of city's best restaurants, a testament to chef and owner Alfred Portale's many talents. The dining room is a multilevel postmodern brasserie with 17-ft ceilings, soft lighting, and cast-stone ledges that give the sense of a garden courtyard. Portale was the first to serve "architectural" food, and he still does it better than anyone else. Try the chilled seafood salad, the rack of lamb, and all of the desserts. *12 E. 12th St., Greenwich Village, 212/620–4020. Reservations essential. AE, DC, MC, V. Subway: 14th St./Union Sq.* $$$$

9 *e-8*

GRAMERCY TAVERN

Opened by Danny (Union Square Cafe) Meyer (*see below*), this large and attractive restaurant encompasses three dining areas and a tavern room, with a cheaper menu and a bar. Wooden beams, white walls, and country artifacts lend a rustic feel. The food, courtesy of chef Tom Colicchio, is superb: tuna tartare with sea urchin and cucumber vinaigrette; lobster and artichoke salad; roasted sea bass; a fine cheese board. *42 E. 20th St., Gramercy, 212/477–0777. Reservations essential for dining room. AE, DC, MC, V. No lunch weekends.* $$$$

11 *b-3*

THE GRANGE HALL

American farm cooking is served here in a mostly miminalist setting (introduced by an art deco bar) in a quiet section of the West Village. Highlights are the good, hearty breakfasts, organic sandwiches, pork chops with apples, and lamb steak with rosemary. Desserts include coconut cake, pies, and cobblers. *50 Commerce St. (at Barrow St.), 212/924–5246. AE. Subway: W. 4th St./Washington Sq.; Christopher St./Sheridan Sq. $*

9 *e-8*

GRANVILLE

Near Gramercy Park, this cheerful, late-night restaurant looks like a New Orleans bordello and attracts a trendy young crowd. The cooking is modern Creole: crawfish, Louisiana crab cakes, pork with "jerk" spices, bananas foster. There's a lively cigar lounge upstairs. *40 E. 20th St., Gramercy, 212/253–9088. AE, MC, V. Subway: 23rd St. $$$*

10 *d-6*

THE GRILL ROOM

From its clubby, rather corporate perch (wood paneling, marble floors), this restaurant overlooks the yacht marina to New Jersey, the Statue of Liberty, and Ellis Island. Larry Forgione's old-style American cooking is superior: shrimp cocktail, smoked-salmon napoleon with caviar, meltingly tender lamb, and simple, exceptional simple fish. For dessert there is a fine cheesecake and a chocolate pudding. *2 World Financial Center, 225 Liberty St., 2nd floor, Lower Manhattan, 212/945–9400. Reservations essential. AE, DC, MC, V. Closed weekends. Subway: Cortlandt St./World Trade Center. $$$$*

11 *c-2*

HOME

This tiny restaurant's storefront consists of secondhand books in a bay window. Inside, there is always a crowd, with some enjoying the year-round (heated) garden. Chef David Page makes good, seasonal country food: blue-cheese fondue with caramelized shallots, roast chicken with onion rings, excellent fish, and a fine chocolate pudding. *10 Cornelia St. (between Bleecker and W. 4th Sts.), West Village, 212/243–9579. No credit cards. Subway: W. 4th St./Washington Sq. $$*

10 *d-6*

HUDSON RIVER CLUB

The Hudson River Club is one of the prettiest places to dine and imbibe in the Wall Street area. The dining rooms are posh but unpretentious, with views of the yacht marina, the Statue of Liberty, and Ellis Island. Feast on food and wine originating in the Hudson Valley. Sunday brunch is lovely. *4 World Financial Center, 250 Vesey St., 2nd floor, Lower Manhattan, 212/786–1500. Reservations essential. Jacket and tie. AE, MC, V. Brunch Sun. Subway: Cortlandt St./World Trade Center. $$$$*

11 *d-7*

INDEPENDENT

Crowded and trendy, this bilevel bistro has a clubby, turn-of-the-century feel. Downstairs there's a small bar and a row of candlelit tables (where you can smoke); upstairs, a larger dining room. The straightforward American menu includes fried calamari, pork ribs with applesauce, steak with fries, lamb stew with artichokes and thyme, and, for dessert, an excellent thin-crusted apple tart. *179 W. Broadway (between Worth and Leonard Sts.), SoHo, 212/219–2010. Reservations essential. AE, DC, MC, V. Subway: Canal St. $$*

10 *d-1*

INDIGO

This former carriage house in the West Village serves delicious food at budget prices. The eclectic menu includes Thai grilled-beef salad, chicken satay, roast cod with couscous, and pork loin glazed with tamarind; and there is a large, attractive zinc bar. *142 W. 10th St. (between Greenwich Ave. and Waverly Pl.), West Village, 212/691–7757. AE. No lunch. Subway: Christopher St./Sheridan Sq. $$*

11 *e-4*

JERRY'S

This SoHo fixture is busy from breakfast through late night. The downtown decor features zebra prints, tile floors, and red-leather banquettes; daily specials are chalked on a blackboard. The convivial bar is a good meeting place. Try the blackened tuna with orzo or the lamb paillard with fried baby artichokes. Desserts are homey and satisfying. *101 Prince St. (between Greene and Mercer Sts.), SoHo, 212/966–9464. AE, MC, V. No dinner Sun. Subway: Prince St.; Spring St.; Bleecker St.; Broadway–Lafayette St. $$*

7 *f-7*

KINGS' CARRIAGE HOUSE

A perfect spot for a rainy night, this comfortable restaurant inhabits a restored brownstone on a quiet, tree-lined street. The two dining rooms are on separate floors and have different furnishings, both including hand-painted walls and antique tables and chairs. The food is as warm and comforting as the manor-house atmosphere: roasted venison is served with homemade fruit chutney, and wild Alaskan salmon comes perfumed with native herbs. *251 E. 82nd St., Upper East Side, 212/723–5490. AE, DC, MC, V. Closed Sun. Subway: 86th St.* $$

11 *d-3*

LIAM

A deceptively casual bistro, with brick walls, wood floors, and paper tablecloths, Liam serves sophisticated, intelligent food at reasonable prices. Try the saddle of rabbit with figs and port-and–mustard-oil sauce; the oyster stew; or the crisp duck with sweet-and-sour plums. Desserts include fallen chocolate cake and banana pie. *170 Thompson St. (between Houston and Bleecker Sts.), Greenwich Village, 212/387–0666. AE. Closed Mon. No lunch. Subway: West 4th St./Washington Sq.* $$

11 *d-5*

LUCKY STRIKE

A late-night haunt of models and artists, this crowded bistro is adorned with faded silver mirrors with the menu and wine list scrawled on them. Try a hamburger with fries, fried calamari, roast chicken, or steak. *59 Grand St. (at Wooster St.), SoHo, 212/941–0479. AE, MC, V. Subway: Canal St.* $$

9 *c-8*

LUMA

Formerly a pricey Chelsea vegetarian, Luma now serves beef and butter, but the food is organic and very good. Free-range chicken, seared and peppered tuna, excellent salads—this is healthy eating made a pleasure. *200 9th Ave. (between 22nd and 23rd Sts.), Chelsea, 212/633–8033. AE, DC, MC, V. No lunch. Subway: 23rd St.* $$

9 *d-8*

MESA GRILL

Good Southwestern in New York City? Superstar chef Bobby Flay serves up pleasingly spicy fare at this Flatiron destination. The bright, award-winning design offers an amusing counterpoint to the down-home cooking. Try the corn-and-zucchini quesadillas with smoked-tomato salsa and avocado relish; fried, cornmeal-coated oysters; or pan-roasted venison. The blue cornmeal pancakes at Sunday brunch are also delicious. *102 5th Ave. (between 15th and 16th Sts.), Flatiron, 212/807–7400. Reservations essential. Brunch Sun. AE, MC, V. Subway: 14th St./Union Sq.* $$$

11 *d-8*

131 DUANE STREET

This relaxed yet oddly formal restaurant, with its yellow walls and checkerboard floor, has one particularly quirky feature: the picture windows look onto an arched brick wall on the adjacent building, illuminated like an ancient ruin. Seafood is especially good here: oysters, sea scallops on crisp potatoes, bass with scalloped potatoes and black trumpet mushrooms, tuna steak in soy-ginger vinaigrette. For dessert, there's a fine chocolate-soufflé cake with ice cream and an old-fashioned sour-cherry tart. *131 Duane St. (between W. Broadway and Church St.), Tribeca, 212/406–9030. AE, MC. V. Closed Sun. No lunch Sat. Subway: Chambers St.* $$$

11 *d-4*

QUILTY'S

A sleek, off-white storefront named after the character in Nabokov's *Lolita*, Quilty is decorated with butterflies in framed display cases and has, of all things, a New England look. The elegant American cooking has Mediterranean and Asian accents: grilled octopus, Gulf shrimp and shiitake mushrooms, glazed grilled salmon with roast-beet salad, sirloin in balsamic vinegar sauce. *177 Prince St. (between Sullivan and Thompson Sts.), SoHo, 212/254–1260. AE, DC, MC, V. Brunch Sun. Subway: Spring St.* $$$

9 *c-3*

REDEYE GRILL

If America is about size and crowds and money and choice and abundance, than the Redeye Grill is a quintessentially American restaurant. The place is always packed, and the menu offers a little of everything, with an emphasis on seafood: lobster in salad, in pot pie, and grilled; salmon cured like pastrami, smoked, and grilled; sturgeon, sable, pasta, steak, and burgers. It's no wonder the crowd is diverse. Desserts like banana-cream pie and chocolate mousse are crowd-pleasers. Nothing's really great, except maybe the whole idea; but nothing really disappoints, either. *890 7th Ave (at 56th St.), Midtown, 212/541–9000. Reservations essential. AE, DC, MC, V. Subway: 57th St. $$$*

11 *e-4*
SAVOY
Peter Hoffman's cooking has come into its own. Here it's served on two floors of an 1830s red-brick building, with working fireplaces, exposed-brick walls, and a cozy upstairs room (with bar) where you can savor a prix-fixe meal cooked by Hoffman himself Tuesday–Saturday. Try the smoked skate with capers and fries, sea scallops in Riesling sauce, or venison with black beans and swiss chard. *70 Prince St. (at Crosby St.), SoHo, 212/219–8570. Reservations required. AE, DC, MC, V. Closed Sun. No lunch Mon. Subway: Prince St.; 6 to Spring St.; Broadway–Lafayette St. $$$$*

11 *d-4*
SCULLY ON SPRING
Scully serves American food with a Mediterranean bent in a laid-back setting: pressed-tin ceilings, bare brick walls, a long bar at the entrance. Try the interesting pizzas; the baked goat cheese on a bed of eggplant, peppers, and charred tomato coulis; char-grilled octopus salad; and orange ricotta cake with walnut paste, honey, and bitter-orange syrup. *203 Spring St. (at Sullivan St.), SoHo, 212/965–0057. AE, DC, MC, V. Brunch weekends. Subway: Spring St.; Canal St. $$*

11 *e-4*
SOHO KITCHEN & BAR
This cavernous SoHo wine bar boasts a 60-foot-long bar and a long run of popularity, now drawing its share of tourists as well as locals. The city's largest Cruvinet dispenses over 120 choice wines by the glass, including champagnes. Nibbles include pizzas, pasta, salads, and burgers, all available at the bar or at tables. Along for the ride? Draft beer and ales are also available. *103 Greene St. (between Prince and Spring Sts.), SoHo, 212/925–1866. Reservations not accepted. AE, DC, MC, V. Subway: Prince St. $$*

11 *c-7*
TRIBECA GRILL
The flagship venture of the Robert DeNiro–Drew Nieporent partnership, this converted Tribeca warehouse has a consistently charged atmosphere, both at the well-spaced tables and at the exquisite bar in the middle of the dining room. Chef Don Pintabona serves classic American grill food with creative international accents, such as lamb paillard with Israeli couscous or seared tuna with sesame noodles. The wonderful banana tart with chocolate-malt ice cream is a must. *375 Greenwich St. (at Franklin St.), Tribeca, 212/941–3900. AE, DC, MC, V. No lunch weekends. Brunch Sun. Subway: Franklin St. $$$*

9 *e-8*
UNION SQUARE CAFE
One of the city's favorite restaurants, this Flatiron phenom has three dining areas and a long, lively bar where you can also dine. The food, with California/Italian overtones, is superb. Have the black-bean soup; fried calamari with anchovy mayonnaise; marinated filet mignon of tuna; hot garlic potato chips; smoked black-angus shell steak with mashed potatoes and frizzled leeks; and perhaps banana tart with caramel and macadamia nuts. *21 E. 16th St., Flatiron, 212/243–4020. Reservations essential. AE, MC, DC, V. No lunch Sun. Subway: 14th St./Union Sq. $$$$*

9 *e-8*
VERBENA
Refined and romantic, Verbena compliments its large garden with subtle and seasonal cooking by chef and owner Diane Forley. Try her foie gras with salsify, prunes, and pearl onions; homey roast chicken with celery root and wild rice; and créme brûlée scented with verbena. *54 Irving Pl. (at 17th St.), Gramercy, 212/260–5454. AE, DC, MC, V. Brunch weekends. Subway: 14th St./Union Sq. $$$*

9 *c-1*
VINCE & EDDIE'S
Not many restaurants in Manhattan offer a country environment, but sitting among the gingham curtains, exposed brick, and plank floor of this quiet American bistro is truly transporting. Hearty fare such as roasted chicken, veal shank, and mashed potatoes is the perfect antidote to chilly New York winters. The whole package is terrific before or after a Lincoln Center event. *70 W. 68th St., Upper West Side, 212/721–0068. Reservations essential. AE, DC, MC, V. Brunch Sun. Subway: 66th St./Lincoln Center. $$*

10 c-1

YE WAVERLY INN
This 148-year-old Greenwich Village town house has been a restaurant since 1920, always retaining its colonial-tavern feel. The food matches the ambience: simple and comfortable. Look for passable pot pies, Southern fried chicken, and other traditional American dishes. In summer there's a pleasant back garden; in winter, two working fireplaces. *16 Bank St. (at Waverly Pl.), Greenwich Village, 212/929–4377. AE, DC, MC, V. Subway: Christopher St./Sheridan Sq. $*

11 e-4

ZOË
Zoë is a big, very noisy, very SoHo restaurant with an open grill in the back and a long bar up front. Many dishes are wood-grilled or cooked on the rotisserie. Try the salmon tartare with mango-chili salsa, grilled tuna with wok-charred vegetables, grilled buffalo sirloin with garlic-potato cake. *90 Prince St. (between Mercer St. and Broadway),* SoHo, 212/966–6722. AE, DC, MC, V. Closed Mon. Brunch weekends. Subway: Prince St.; Spring St.; Bleecker St./Broadway–Lafayette St. $$

9 b-7

ZUCCA
West Chelsea has become a modified SoHo, with artists moving into local lofts and galleries sprouting up in refurbished buildings. Eminently ready to feed them, Zucca is small and pretty, with tin ceilings, murky mirrors attractively framed in thick dark wood, and a long bar, plus an oyster bar. Try the pumpkin soup with goat cheese, duck confit, roast chicken, strip steak, or grilled salmon. *227 10th Ave. (between 23rd and 24th Sts.), Chelsea, 212/741–1970. AE, DC, MC, V. No lunch weekends. Subway: 23rd St. $$*

AMERICAN CASUAL

11 d-3

AGGIE'S
This updated but still basic luncheonette is a great place for a casual, downtown breakfast or brunch—if you can also stomach the wait and the inflated prices. Hearty and wholesome home cooking is the name of the game. *146 W. Houston St. (at MacDougal St.), SoHo, 212/673–8994. No credit cards. Subway: Christopher St./Sheridan Sq. $*

9 f-3

BILLY'S
In business since 1870, this East Side institution is cherished by the Sutton Place crowd, who enjoy it as a refuge from their more serious dining locales. The old tavern serves steaks and other pub fare from a blackboard menu, and beers and stout on tap. *948 1st Ave. (between 52nd and 53rd Sts.), Midtown, 212/355–8920. Reservations not accepted. AE, DC, MC, V. Subway: 51st St./Lexington–3rd Aves. $*

11 f-2

BOWERY BAR
American food and lots of models are the story of the B Bar, in a former gas station with a velvet rope at the door. Opt for a simple burger or more complex fish and pasta dishes. The scene starts late. *40 E. 4th St. (between Lafayette St. and Bowery), East Village,*

A BREATH OF FRESH AIR

On a sunny day or a sultry night, there's nothing like the great outdoors with your meal.

Bryant Park Grill (Contemporary)
In the summer, this place heaves a collective sigh when the after-work crowds loosen their ties.

Blue Water Grill (Seafood)
Grab a table at Blue Water, and watch others scramble for their leafy greens at the Union Square Greenmarket.

Danal (Tea)
If you missed the train to the Hamptons, get a little country in this homey café's garden.

Flowers (American)
The rooftop terrace lets you enjoy the calm of the city's upper canopy—without getting in trouble with your landlord.

Provence (French)
The SPF-conscious are well protected in this bistro's small, tented garden.

Marichu (Spanish)
When midtown gridlock gets to be too much, duck into the back garden for Basque cooking.

212/475–2220. AE, MC, V. Brunch weekends. Subway: Bleecker St.; Broadway–Lafayette St.; Astor Pl. $$

9 c-3

BROADWAY DINER

These diners don't offer much in ambience or cuisine, but they're good and reliable when you want a fast and inexpensive bite. The typical menu (with a few innovations thrown in) features everything from chef salads to grilled fish. Breakfast and brunch are packed on weekends. Service is nothing to write home about, but your coffee cup is always refilled. 1726 Broadway (at 55th St.), Midtown, 212/765–0909. Reservations not accepted. No credit cards. Subway: 59th St./Columbus Circle. $

9 e-3

590 Lexington Ave. (at 52nd St.), Midtown, 212/486–8838. Subway: 51st St./Lexington–3rd Aves.

9 c-3

BROOKLYN DINER USA

Though less authentic than the name would suggest—where in Brooklyn would your eggs be served with crispy polenta fries instead of potatoes?—this quasi-theme restaurant delivers decent food and good value. Though the large portions of American standbys like burgers and hot dogs make it difficult, try to save room for one of New York's best sundaes. 212 W. 57th St., Midtown, 212/581–8900. Reservations not accepted. AE, DC, MC, V. Subway: N, R to 57th St.; 59th St./Columbus Circle. $$

7 b-7

EJ'S LUNCHEONETTE

The decor invokes the 1950s, when cherry pie and egg creams were the thing, and it somehow persuades crowds to forget their 1990s dietary habits and order enormous omelets or waffles slathered with butter and layered with pecans. The menu has a large selection of retro diner items, from root beer on tap to Salisbury steak and macaroni-and-cheese; but if you'd rather keep your feet on '90s ground, you do have options, like the Cobb salad with balsamic vinaigrette or the grilled vegetable sandwich on seven-grain bread. Steer clear of weekend brunch hours unless you can get there by 10 (AM) or don't mind waiting at least 45 minutes. 447 Amsterdam Ave. (between 81st and 82nd Sts.), Upper West Side, 212/873–3444.

Reservations not accepted. No credit cards. Breakfast daily. Subway: 86th St. $

9 e-1

1271 3rd Ave. (at 73rd St.), Upper East Side, 212/472–0600. Subway: 77th St.

10 d-1

432 6th Ave. (between 9th and 10th Sts.), West Village, 212/473–5555. Subway: W. 4th St./Washington Sq.

9 b-8

EMPIRE DINER

This 24-hour Art Deco diner is a magnet for après-club late-night snacks. Ever stylish, it was here long before Chelsea became trendy. The menu is pricey for diner fare, but the food is generally good. There's live piano music on weekends, and you can sit outdoors in summer. 210 10th Ave. (at 22nd St.), Chelsea, 212/243–2736. Reservations not accepted. AE. Subway: 23rd St. $

11 f-2

GREAT JONES CAFE

Pop into this crowded, down-home Bowery spot for flavorful burgers, chili, red- or bluefish fillets, and the house drink—a jalapeño martini. To top it all off, the jukebox still works. The noise is deafening, but the young crowd doesn't seem to mind. 54 Great Jones St. (between Bowery and Lafayette Sts.), East Village, 212/674–9304. No credit cards. Subway: 8th St.; Astor Pl. $

9 b-1

IT'S A WRAP

Though the wrap sandwich is popping up in fast-food restaurants across the country, It's a Wrap is one of the few places where they actually make their own bread. As opposed to the many wraps about town that resemble glorified burritos, these resemble an Indian naan: chewy flatbread is wrapped around new and classic hot and cold fillings, including curried lentils, turkey and bacon, and roasted lamb. A fresh juice bar and homey desserts like Rice Krispie treats complete the satisfying experience. 2012 Broadway (between 68th and 69th Sts.), Upper West Side, 212/362–7922. Reservations not accepted. No credit cards. Subway: 66th St./Lincoln Center. $

7 f-8

J. G. MELON

J. G. Melon's bar burger has long been called the best on the Upper East Side.

Locals love to hang out and sample the large beer selection while digging into a no-frills burger and a bowl of waffle-cut fries. Red-and-white check tablecloths and sports on the TV complete the aesthetic. *1291 3rd Ave. (at 74th St.), Upper East Side, 212/650–1310. AE, DC, MC, V. Brunch Sun. Subway: 77th St. $*

9 *d-3*

OAK ROOM AND BAR

This traditional wood-paneled restaurant and bar in the famed Plaza is still one of the classiest spots in town for a drink. Order light fare from the bar menu, or sit inside the restaurant for some heartier American food. If you aren't wearing a jacket and tie, you can order from the Oak Room menu and be served in the bar. *Plaza Hotel, 768 5th Ave. (at 59th St.), Midtown, 212/546–5330. AE, DC, MC, V. Subway: 5th Ave./60th St. $$*

9 *f-3*

P. J. CLARKE'S

P. J. Clarke's is the classic Old New York saloon. At lunch and happy hour, Midtown men pack the extremely popular front room for a beer, a burger, or both. If you're more interested in eating than socializing, elbow your way to the dark and atmospheric dining room in the back. Best bites include the burgers, home fries, chili, and spinach salad. *915 3rd Ave. (at 55th St.), Midtown, 212/759–1650. AE, DC, MC, V. Open until 4 (am). Subway: 59th St. $*

9 *e-8*

PETE'S TAVERN

O. Henry, who lived across the street, penned "The Gift of the Magi" in this 1864 tavern. The original bar is quite popular, as is the sunny sidewalk café in summer. The menu mixes old-fashioned Italian food with burgers and Reubens. *129 E. 18th St., Gramercy, 212/473–7676. AE, DC, MC, V. Subway: 14th St./Union Sq. $*

7 *b-7*

POPOVER CAFÉ

The weekend lines outside this Upper West Side brunch spot remind you that the local demand for comfort food far exceeds the supply. Wonderful omelets, cheese grits, and creative pancakes attract families and friends toting the Sunday *Times*. More lunchlike options are sandwiches, hearty burgers, and tasty salads. *551 Amsterdam Ave. (at 87th St.), Upper West Side, 212/595–8555. Reservations not accepted. AE, MC, V. Subway: 86th St. $*

7 *e-6*

SARABETH'S KITCHEN

Sarabeth's is still considered *the* place for brunch on the East Side, so the wait can be torture. But if you get there early, you'll enjoy an elegant country breakfast à la Martha Stewart. Omelets, homemade muffins, potato and cheese blintzes, pancakes with fresh fruit, pumpkin waffles, and other tempting entrées are served all day, every day. Wonderful marmalades, Linzer tortes, and shortbreads are available for takeout. *1295 Madison Ave. (between 92nd and 93rd Sts.), Upper East Side, 212/410–7335. AE, DC, MC, V. Breakfast daily. Subway: 96th St. $*

7 *e-8*

Whitney Museum of American Art, 945 Madison Ave. (at 75th St.), Upper East Side, 212/570–3670. Closed Mon. Subway: 77th St.

7 *b-7*

423 Amsterdam Ave. (between 80th and 81st Sts.), Upper West Side, 212/496–6280. Subway: 79th St.

9 *f-2*

SERENDIPITY 3

For over 35 years this combo ice cream parlor/gift shop has been an inviting spot for lunch, brunch, and late-night snacks. Standing favorites on the menu include a wide range of burgers, footlong hot dogs (with or without chili), French toast, omelets, ice cream, and Serendipity's signature dish, frozen hot chocolate. Lines can be long, but you can divert yourself during the wait with the tchotchkes and novelties for sale. Decor falls into the "whimsical" category, with antiques, flashes of pink, Tiffany lamps, and a general sense of bells and whistles. *225 E. 60th St., 212/838–3531. AE, DC, MC, V. BYOB. Brunch Sun. Subway: 59th St. $*

11 *f-3*

TEMPLE BAR

One of downtown's coolest bars, Temple Bar has lost its trendiness but not its style—which means you can almost always find a seat, and you can hear yourself think. The vodka menu is unmatched; the martinis are gigantic and delicious; and the food is pretty good, too. Try the gourmet pizzas and oysters. *332 Lafayette St. (between Houston and Bleecker Sts.), East Village, 212/925–4242. Subway: Broadway–Lafayette St.; 6 to Spring St. $$*

11 *d-4*

TENNESSEE MOUNTAIN

Feel like ditching the city? This popular SoHo spot could be anywhere in the U.S. Fill up on meaty beef and babyback ribs; fried onion loaf; corn bread; and meat or vegetarian chili. If you still have room, chase it all with a piece of apple-walnut or pecan pie. *143 Spring St. (at Wooster St.), SoHo, 212/431–3993. AE, MC, V. Subway: Spring St. $$*

9 *e-2*

VIAND

This tiny New York coffee shop is famous for its turkey, roasted right before your eyes and carved steaming-hot to order. Have it in sandwiches, chef salads, or with gravy and cranberry sauce. The service is fast, but space is scarce, so expect a wait. Why not enjoy a bit of the killer rice pudding until a table is free? There's also a full diner menu. *673 Madison Ave. (at 61st St.), Upper East Side, 212/751–6622. Reservations not accepted. No credit cards. Subway: 59th St. $*

BARBECUE

11 *b-3*

BROTHERS BBQ

New and spacious digs (nowhere else in Manhattan will you sit so refreshingly far from your neighbors) haven't changed the hearty and satisfying food at this downtown barbecue haven. Ribs, chicken, brisket, and Cajun shrimp come in giant portions, with such appropriate and delicious sides as greens, cornbread, coleslaw, and potato salad. Desserts are simple and rich. The decor is Midwestern kitsch; think traffic lights and memorabilia. *225 Varick St. (between Houston and Clarkson Sts.), SoHo, 212/727–2775. Subway: Houston St. $$*

9 *d-5*

VIRGIL'S REAL BBQ

When you're stuck for a pre-theater meal, remember that there's almost always a free table at this immense barbecue joint—one of the best in the city—where the portions are large, the service is friendly, and the atmosphere is noisy and fun. Highlights are the bar-becued shrimp, chicken, beef, pork ribs, and pulled-pork sandwiches. Sides of cornbread, coleslaw, potato salad, baked beans, and other summertime favorites make dinner here feel like a country picnic year-round. *152 W. 44th St., Theater District, 212/921–9494. AE, DC, MC, V. Subway: 42nd St./Times Sq. $$*

BELGIAN

10 *c-1*

CAFÉ DE BRUXELLES

Bruxelles serves the hearty cuisine of Belgium in a handsome European setting. Classics like waterzooi de poulet, carbonnade flamanade, and boudin blanc are complemented by cones of crisp Belgian frites and an extensive (and pricey) list of imported beers. *118 Greenwich Ave. (at 13th St.), West Village, 212/206–1830. AE, MC, V. Subway: A, C, E to 14th St. $$*

11 *b-3*

PETIT ABEILLE

It's hard to find homestyle European food prepared this well, especially at these prices. In the space where Marnie's Noodle Shop used to be, this tiny Belgian café on Hudson St. serves delicious soupe aux moules (mussel soup), hearty entrées, and, of course, crisp and tasty french fries. The brunch, featuring omelettes and fresh Belgian waffles, is also good. The original store, on 18th Street, serves lunch only—and how. *466 Hudson St. (between Barrow and Grove Sts.), West Village, 212/741–6479. AE, MC, V. Subway: Christopher St./Sheridan Sq. $*

10 *c-1*

400 W. 14th St., West Village, 212/727–1505. Subway: A, C, E to 14th St.

9 *c-8*

107 W. 18th St., Chelsea, 212/604–9350. No dinner. Subway: 1, 2, 3, 9 to 14th St.

BRAZILIAN

9 *c-4*

CHURRASCARIA PLATAFORMA

This New York outpost of a São Paolo favorite so perfectly captures the feeling of a Brazilian barbecue restaurant that you'll be surprised to emerge back into Manhattan. While the jazz trio plays *Joabim* classics, an endless parade of waiters with giant skewers of perfectly grilled meats whizzes by. Chicken, turkey, salmon, lamb, prime rib, top sirloin, and other carnivore favorites, each marinated in different seasonings and grilled to perfection, are deposited on your plate in succession until you say "when" by turning your green chip over to red. You're supposed to begin with the equally impressive salad bar, but be careful not to fill up. The restaurant can easily accommodate large groups. *316 W. 49th St., Theater District, 212/245–0505. AE, D, DC, MC, V. Subway: 50th St.* $$

9 *e-8*

COFFEE SHOP

True, this trendy Brazilian eatery has an unlikely name, but the velvet ropes tell you that it still attracts a stylish crowd. One wonders how all those beautiful people can sit at the sidewalk tables all day long, and how any place can stay so busy until dawn. For all the attitude, the *feijoada* isn't bad, but don't expect any sparks from the kitchen. It's not about food. *29 Union Square West (at 16th St.), Flatiron, 212/243–7969. AE. Subway: 14th St./Union Sq.* $

11 *f-1*

RIODIZIO

The *rodizio*, an all-you-can-eat rotisserie meal for only $21.95, is one reason why this place has been packed since it opened. The restaurant occupies a vast loft space a few doors down from the Public Theater and is huge and noisy, with an enormous bar flanked by an attractive display of seafood. Forget Brazilian samba: your meal is accompanied by thundering disco. *Caipirinhas*, made with lime, sugar, and cachaça (a Brazilian liqueur made from sugar cane), are served by the pitcher. The grilled meats and fish are first-rate, and come with a huge house salad, black beans, collard greens, brown rice, polenta, and fried plantains. *417 Lafayette St. (near Astor Pl.), East Village, 212/529–1313. AE, MC, V. Brunch weekends. Subway: Astor Pl.* $$

CAFÉS

9 *c-3*

CAFE EUROPA

Whether you need a place to refuel after shopping or are meeting an old friend to catch up, this Midtown café is like an oasis in the rendezvous desert—and it has two locations to boot. Simple salads, good sandwiches, a large selection of desserts, and good coffee make it the perfect pit stop. *205 W. 57th St. Midtown, 212/977–4030. Reservations not accepted. AE, D, DC, MC, V. Subway: 57th St.* $

9 *d-4*

1177 6th Ave. (at 46th St.), Midtown, 212/575–7272. Subway: 47th–50th Sts./Rockefeller Center.

11 *d-3*

CAFFÈ DANTE

Frothy cappuccino, bracing espresso, teas, pastries, salads, and little sandwiches make up one of the Village's more inviting Italian cafés. Dante is a throwback to a time before Starbucks, when Mediterranean cooking meant lying in the sun. *79 MacDougal St. (between Bleecker and Houston Sts.), Greenwich Village, 212/982–5275. No credit cards. Subway: Houston St.; W. 4th St./Washington Sq.* $

11 *b-2*

CAFFE VIVALDI

Just off the chaotic runway that is Bleecker Street in these parts, Caffe Vivaldi quietly serves coffees, teas, biscotti, and desserts amid dark wood, old-fashioned sketches and prints, and often a good deal of smoke. In winter, wait for a table near the fireplace; it's worth it. *32 Jones St. (between Bleecker and W. 4th Sts.), 212/929–9384. Reservations not accepted. No credit cards. Subway: W. 4th St./Washington Sq.* $

7 *c-7*

COLUMBUS BAKERY

The open, self-service concept of these stylish bakeries adds to their pleasantly frenetic energy. Make your selection from a counter overflowing with baked goods—quiches, tarts, cakes, pastries, muffins—and very light lunch fare. Though a few things, the breads in particular, look better than they taste, the comfortable chairs, casual service, and neighborhood atmosphere make these places very popular for a quick bite. *474 Columbus Ave. (at 83rd St.), Upper West Side, 212/724–6880. Reservations not accepted. AE, D, MC, V. Subway: 79th St.* $

9 *f-3*

957 1st Ave. (between 52nd and 53rd Sts.), Midtown, 212/421–0334. Subway: 51st St./Lexington–3rd Aves.

7 b-7

DRIP

More than just a coffee bar, this Upper West Side hangout has been called a sociological experiment: young men and women drop in not only for the light fare and coffee-derived drinks, but also to meet each other. Flip through binders of personal profiles of regulars (and some not-so-regulars) to see if your perfect match is about. *489 Amsterdam Ave. (between 83rd and 84th Sts.), Upper West Side, 212/875-1032. Reservations not accepted. MC, V. Subway: 86th St.* $

7 b-7

EDGAR'S CAFÉ

The bright, almost surreal interior of this European-style café is a tribute to its namesake, Edgar Allan Poe. People talk for hours here over light salads, sandwiches, and appealing desserts. A full selection of coffees and teas and pleasant service make this the perfect place to grab a bite and some quality time after a movie—but everyone on the West Side knows it, so you may have to wait for a table. It's worth noting that the place is open 365 days a year. *255 W. 84th St., Upper West Side, 212/496-6126. Reservations not accepted. No credit cards. Subway: 86th St.* $

11 f-5

FERRARA

This famous, lively, very bright café claims to be America's oldest pasticceria, and the honor draws crowds (of tourists) that spill out onto Little Italy's streets in summer. If you can hold out for a seat, you'll enjoy espresso, cappuccino, pastry, and gelati the way they were meant to be. You can also take home boxes of Ferrara's delicious *torrone* candy. *195 Grand St. (between Mulberry and Mott Sts.), Little Italy, 212/226-6150. Reservations not accepted. No credit cards. Subway: Grand St.; Spring St.; Canal St.* $

7 b-3

HUNGARIAN PASTRY SHOP

Cramped, cozy, and timeless, if tired, this Columbia University hangout serves good poppy-seed pastries, Linzer torte, and cappuccino. You can sit for hours with a newspaper or book and nobody will bother you. *1030 Amsterdam Ave. (between 110th and 111th Sts.), Morningside Heights, 212/866-4230. Reservations*

not accepted. No credit cards. Subway: 110th St./Cathedral Pkwy. $

10 f-1

VENIERO'S

A bakery and cafe since 1894, the venerable Veniero's continues to pack 'em in. They come for espresso, cappuccino, and traditional Italian pastry, as well as fresh fruit ices in summer. *342 E. 11th St., East Village, 212/674-4415. No credit cards. Subway: 14th St./Union Sq.* $

CARIBBEAN

10 f-1

BAMBOU

Noel Coward would be quite at home in this attractive and elegant restaurant, which rather resembles a grand old mansion in Jamaica transplanted to a dingy East Village block. "Jerk" pork and chicken—marinated in chilis and spices and smoke-grilled over pimento (allspice) wood fires—are accompanied by bouillabaisse, braised oxtail, and coconut crème brûlée. *243 E. 14th St., East Village, 212/505-1180. Reservations essential. AE, MC, V. Closed Sun. No lunch. Subway: 14th St.* $$

CHINESE

9 f-3

BEIJING DUCK HOUSE

This is the place for those who can't anticipate a craving for Peking duck 24 hours in advance: 20 minutes after you order, a whole duck, perfectly crisp, is carved at your table and presented with all the trimmings (pancakes, scallions, cucumbers, and hoisin sauce). If you're really hungry, start with the duck soup. Don't let the uptown address fool you; the spirit is Chinatown-informal. *236 E. 53rd St., Midtown, 212/759-8260. AE, DC, MC, V. Subway: 51st St./Lexington-3rd Aves.* $$

9 f-4

CHIN CHIN

Jimmy Chin's large and casual but extremely stylish restaurant features imaginatively prepared nouvelle-Chinese offerings, including shredded duck salad, vegetable-duck pie, grilled baby quail, steamed or crispy whole bass, and veal medallions with spicy pepper sauce. The atmosphere, like the food, is contemporary. *216 E. 49th St., Midtown, 212/888–4555. Reservations essential. AE, DC, MC, V. No lunch weekends. Subway: 51st St./Lexington–3rd Aves. $$$*

9 f-2
CHINA FUN
If you just want to satisfy a craving for good, basic Chinese food, head to one of these uptowners, where all of the baking and barbecuing is done on the premises. The menu is filled with Cantonese, Szechuan, and Hunan classics, but the chef also has fun with special entrées and a good selection of dim sum. Though short on atmosphere, these restaurants offer good value. *1239 2nd Ave. (at 65th St.), Upper East Side, 212/752–0810. MC, V. Subway: 68th St. $*

9 c-1
246 Columbus Ave. (at 72nd St.), Upper West Side, 212/580–1516. Subway: 72nd St.

11 g-7
JOE'S SHANGHAI
This Chinatown outpost of the famous Flushing restaurant is every bit as good as the original and a little busier; be prepared to wait. Shanghai cuisine is richer than other Chinese food, so come hungry. For starters, don't miss the steamed soup dumplings pork (or pork with crab) or the turnip shortcakes. Traditional, delicious, and very rich main dishes include lion's head (actually pork meatballs), braised pork shoulder, and homemade Shanghai noodles. The braised bean curd on spinach and eggplant in garlic sauce is also superb. Just stay away from the whole fish. And what's "vegetarian duck"? *9 Pell St. (between Mott. St. and Bowery), Chinatown, 212/223–8888. No credit cards. Reservations not accepted. Subway: 6, N, R, J, M, Z to Canal St. $*

11 g-7
MANDARIN COURT
Though not as impressive in setting or scope as Chinatown's huge dim sum emporia, this small restaurant has a terrific selection of dumplings and other dim-sum favorites. Because the carts have less surface area to cover, the food is often fresher and hotter, too. *61 Mott St. (between Canal and Bayard Sts.), Chinatown, 212/608–3838. AE, MC, V. Subway: 6. N, R, J, M, Z to Canal St. $*

9 f-3
MR. CHOW
As you pass through the Lalique doors, you realize that this restaurant is as much about sleek setting and hip crowd as it is about food—here, Chinese with a touch of French and California thrown into the wok. Overlook the frenetic ambience to enjoy the crispy spinach, gambler's duck, and Grand Marnier shrimp. *324 E. 57th St., Midtown, 212/751–9030. Reservations essential. AE, DC, MC, V. No lunch. Subway: 59th St. $$$*

11 g-7
NY NOODLE TOWN
Open until 3 AM, this humble restaurant has some of the best Chinese food in Chinatown. Order the shrimp-dumpling soup, barbecued duck with flowering chives, and salt-baked softshell crab (in season). Barbecued pork and the other items hanging in the window are also delicious. Oddly enough, the noodles aren't the greatest. *28 Bowery (at Bayard St.), Chinatown, 212/349–0923. No credit cards. Subway: 6, N, R, J, M, Z to Canal St. $*

7 f-8
PIG HEAVEN
The delicious and authentic food is somewhat diminished by the campy swine decor (though some find this part of the charm). While pork is the menu's mainstay, there are plenty of other options for those who'd rather pass. Don't miss the dumplings—they're all winners, fried, steamed, or boiled. Prices are higher than in Chinatown, but still reasonable. *1540 2nd Ave. (at 80th St.), Upper East Side, 212/PIG-4333. AE, DC, V. Subway: 77th St. $$*

9 e-3
SHUN LEE PALACE
Shun Lee offers impeccably prepared Hunan and Szechuan dishes in two of the city's truly plush Chinese settings. There's a low-calorie menu for dieters, but the temptations of the regular menu are so strong—hot-and-sour cabbage, lobster Szechuan, beggar's chicken, crispy whole sea bass, shrimp puffs, spicy Hunan duckling with a smoky flavor. Occasional guest chefs from Hong Kong augment the regular menu. The Lincoln Center location is convenient for pre-concert meals, and the less formal

café there is quicker and more reason-ably priced. *155 E. 55th St., Midtown, 212/371–8844. Subway: 59th St. Reservations essential. AE, DC, MC, V. $$*

9 *c-2*

43 W. 65th St., Upper West Side, 212/595-8895. Subway: 66th St./Lincoln Center.

11 *g-7*

TAI HONG LAU

First-rate seafood, dim sum, and Peking duck in an upmarket setting make Tai Hong Lau one of Chinatown's best restaurants. The flip side: it has some of Chinatown's rudest waiters. *70 Mott St. (between Bayard and Canal Sts.), China-town, 212/219–1431. AE. Subway: Canal St.; Grand St. $*

11 *g-6*

20 MOTT STREET

This three-story Chinatown emporium wins the city's unofficial Best Dim Sum award hands-down. Menu selection is of the point-and-click variety; tasty sur-prises include steamed dumplings and fried eel with orange peel and hot sauce. *20 Mott St. (at Canal St.), 212/964–0380. AE, MC, V. Subway: Grand St.; Canal St. $–$$*

CONTEMPORARY

9 *e-2*

ARCADIA

This is superstar-chef Anne Rosen-zweig's home base, an inviting contem-porary space with a menu to match. Rosenzweig produces wonderfully cre-ative American fare in an attractive, cozy (some say cramped) setting enchanced by Paul Davis murals. The menu is sea-sonal, but Rosenzweig always has an affinity for lobster: try it chimney-smoked or in a seductive crème brûlée. Reserve well in advance, and request the main dining room. *21 E.62nd St., Upper East Side, 212/223–2900. Reservations essential. AE, MC, V. Closed Sun. Subway: 5th Ave. $$$$*

9 *e-2*

AUREOLE

Some of the city's best food is served in the elegant, duplex dining room of this flower-bedecked town house. Chef Charles Palmer prepares an exquisite array of dishes with the freshest sea-sonal ingredients, and New Yorkers con-sistently vote him one of the city's best chefs. The presentations are as startling as the prices, but there's also a reason-ably priced prix-fixe dinner. Decorated with caramel curlicues and tuile trian-gles, the desserts are otherworldly. *34 E. 61 St., Upper East Side, 212/319–1660. Reservations essential. AE, MC, V. Closed Sun. Subway: 5th Ave. $$$$*

9 *d-5*

BRYANT PARK GRILL

It's hard to believe that this immense and stylish restaurant looks out onto the same Bryant Park that used to shel-ter the city's drug dealers and home-less. But once the nearby fashion and publishing industries turned the park into a scoping ground, it seemed only fitting that a decent restaurant follow them. Both the food and the service are competent, and appetizer and entrée portions are huge. The more relaxed, outdoor café, on the restaurant's roof, is idyllic on those rare cool nights in summer. *25 W. 40th St., Midtown, 212/840–6500. Reservations essential for din-ing room. AE, D, DC, MC, V. Subway: 42nd St. $$*

9 *d-3*

CHINA GRILL

Although the atmosphere is corporate—suits and cell phones—the food at this noisy Midtown power-lunch spot is sat-isfying and delicious. Asian-inspired appetizers such as roasted beet dumplings, crunchy calamari salad, and cured salmon rolls are large enough to share, as are most of the entrées. Try the wasabi-crusted cod on mashed pota-toes, the Szechuan spiced beef, or the black pasta with shrimp. Service is friendly, if reserved. *52 W. 53rd St., Mid-town, 212/333–7788. Reservations essen-tial. AE, DC, MC, V. Subway: 5th Ave./53rd St. $$$*

7 *f-7*

ÉTATS-UNIS

As the name implies, this is American cooking from a French perspective, a refreshing twist from the New American trend of rushing toward foreign ingredi-ents at the expense of our native bounty. The results are wonderful: corn soufflé sits on wild greens dressed in a rasp-berry vinaigrette; Colorado beef is coated with peppercorns, simply seared, and served with a potato galette, or whatever potato the chef is in the mood to make that day. The small, cheerful room and exposed kitchen make you feel like you're in the chef's home, and the clientele is so regular that it sometimes seems as if only the restaurant's "family" is allowed in. If you're lucky enough to get a reservation, take it and run. *242 E. 81st. St., Upper East Side, 212/ 517–8826. Reservations essential. AE, MC, V. Closed Sun. No lunch. Subway: 77th St. $$*

9 *d-3*

JUDSON GRILL

With an attractive clientele and an almost banklike feel, this Midtowner has become a favorite meeting place for New York's power brokers. The menu features a wide range of contemporary favorites, from chilled oysters to salmon tartare, grilled foie gras to roasted chicken. The stunning food presentations are almost as high as the ceilings. The impressive wine list with hard-to-find American labels and vintages, and great desserts make the whole experience a fitting tribute to American tastes. *152 W. 52nd St., Midtown, 212/582–5252, Reservations essential. AE, DC, MC, V. Closed weekends in summer. Subway: 49th St.; 50th St. $$$*

7 *f-8*

LENOX ROOM

This is where Upper East Siders come when they're not eating more important meals at Daniel or Le Cirque 2000, but it's good and handsome enough to be a destination in its own right. Charlie Palmer (*see Aureole, above*) oversees the kitchen here, and his influence is palpable—the menu is contemporary American, and features a raw bar and a bold array of flavors. Locals like the fennel, beet, and arugula salad, the roasted lobster, and the sour-lemon custard tart. The bar's comfortable seating and selection of five-dollar tasting plates help make the restaurant a neighborhood hangout. *1278 3rd Ave. (between 73rd and 74th Sts.), Upper East Side, 212/ 772–0404. AE, D, DC, MC, V. Subway: 77th St. $$*

7 *e-8*

LOBSTER CLUB

Everyone loves comfort food, and this is where the Park Avenue crowd goes to get it. Chef Anne Rosenzweig (*see Arcadia, above*) reinterprets the comfort foods of yore to give them a modern spin. Over red-check tablecloths, wealthy locals savor meatloaf with mashed sweet potatoes, fried rock shrimp served in a paper cone, and buttery roast chicken served with Provençal fries. The signature dish is the restaurant's namesake—a lobster club sandwich of Dagwood proportions. The location, in a brownstone on a tree-lined side street near the Metropolitan Museum of Art, adds to the homey atmosphere. Make a reservation or prepare for a long wait. *24 E. 80th St., Upper East Side, 212/249–6500. Reservations essential. AE, D, DC, MC, V. Subway: 77th St. $$*

9 *d-3*

OSTERIA DEL CIRCO

Opened by the three sons of Le Cirque owner Sirio Maccioni, this contemporary Italian eatery comes alive with circus-tent decorations and dancing sculptures. The line of celebrities waiting for tables creates a frenzied atmosphere. Traditional Tuscan specialties such as a 30-vegetable soup and salt cod *alla livornese* go up against contemporary favorites such as tuna carpaccio and lobster salad. Pizzas, pastas, and rotisserie items (particularly the duck) are surprisingly excellent. Save room for dessert: the *bomboloncini*—little Italian donuts filled with chocolate, vanilla, and raspberry—have been voted the best in the city, and the other sweets are pretty spectacular, too. The intelligent and reasonably priced list of Italian wines is also worth checking out. *120 W. 55th St., Midtown, 212/265–3636. AE, DC, MC, V. Subway: 57th St. $$$*

9 *e-3*

VONG

The second of Jean-Georges Vongerichten's three New York restaurants (*see Jo Jo and Jean-Georges, below*), Vong gives life to the man's love of Asian cuisine. Here he fuses French and Thai, and brings peanut sauce to new heights. Presentation is emphasized: food is showcased in dazzling dishes of varying size, color, and shape. The Thai decor is exotic and rich, with a contemporary flair. While some complain about the prices, others say don't sweat it—you're in for the meal of your life. *200 E. 54th St., Midtown, 212/486–9592. AE, DC. MC, V. No lunch weekends. Subway: 51st St. $$$*

9 e-1

WILLOW

The charm of this elegant turn-of-the-century townhouse adds to the food's charisma, which is standard new American: goat cheese, wild greens, duck. The menu is not groundbreaking, but the chef executes it well, and if you factor in the soft lighting and view of the tree-lined street through the lead-glass windows, you end up with a worthwhile experience. The downstairs room has a simpler menu of lighter meals, and on sunny days, lunch is served on lovely sidewalk tables. *1022 Lexington Ave. (at 73rd St.), Upper East Side, 212/717–0703. Reservations essential for dinner. AE, DC, MC, V. Subway: 68th St. $$*

CONTINENTAL

7 c-1

CAFÉ DES ARTISTES

The beautiful, nostalgic ambience, the famous, sweetly naughty murals by Howard Chandler Christy, and the imaginative menu of continental specialties make this West Side classic a favorite for romance. For intimacy in the evening, request one of the nooks surrounding the bar in the rear. The food is not great, but it's not the point. The parlor, adjacent to the main dining room, is easier on the wallet, just as charming, and far more accessible; reservations aren't necessary. *1 W. 67th St., Upper West Side, 212/877–3500. Reservations essential. AE, DC, MC, V. Subway: 66th St./Lincoln Center. $$$*

9 e-3

FOUR SEASONS

Courtesy of Mies van der Rohe, this large, beautiful, modern restaurant is one of the most famous dining destinations in New York, and the city's only restaurant with landmark status. The Grill Room has long been favored for power lunches by publishing, fashion, and financial movers and shakers. The more lavish and romantic Pool Room, centered around an illuminated marble pool, is popular for the prix-fixe pre-theater dinner, as well as post-theater meals. As the name suggests, the menu changes with the seasons. *99 E. 52nd St., Midtown, 212/754–9494. Reservations essential. AE, DC, MC, V. No lunch weekends. Subway: 51st St./Lexington–3rd Aves. $$$$*

7 e-8

MORTIMER'S

Be warned: You may feel out of place at this fashionably clubby Upper East Side restaurant, where the never-too-rich, never-too-thin Ladies Who Lunch lunch. The menu features passable continental fare: rack of lamb, chicken paillard, and twin burgers. Don't expect to sit in the attractive main dining area if you're unknown to owner Glenn Bernbaum. *1057 Lexington Ave. (at 75th St.), Upper East Side, 212/517–6400. Reservations not accepted. AE, DC, MC, V. No lunch weekends. Subway: 77th St. $$*

11 b-2

ONE IF BY LAND, TWO IF BY SEA

If only the food were as appealing as the setting: a roaring fire, fresh flowers, shimmering candlelight, and a live pianist, all in Aaron Burr's former carriage house. The continental entrées, such as beef Wellington and rack of lamb, are nothing more than edible, but the restaurant persists as a favorite spot for intimate dinners. *17 Barrow St. (between W. 4th St and 7th Ave. S.), West Village, 212/255–8649. AE, DC, MC, V. Subway: Christopher St./Sheridan Sq. $$$*

9 d-4

RAINBOW ROOM

To step out of the elevator on Rockefeller Center's 65th floor is to enter another time: The band plays smooth rhythms, elegant couples glide across the dance floor, and waiters in tuxedos weave through tables carrying flaming dishes. The food is standard-to-good, but the Art Deco interior and the fabulous view make the experience worthwhile. For the same effect without the same kind of bill, you can sit at the bar and sip the best Old Fashioneds (made with real muddled fruit) and martinis in town. *30 Rockefeller Plaza (enter on 49th St. or 50th St. between 5th and 6th Aves.), 65th floor, Midtown, 212/632–5000. Reservations essential. AE, D, DC, MC, V. Subway: 47th–50th Sts./Rockefeller Center. $$$$*

9 e-7

SONIA ROSE

Many New Yorkers revere the cozy Sonia Rose as a romantic destination, and it's true that the restaurant's provincial atmosphere offers a change of pace. The three-course prix-fixe menu (with some supplements) is reasonable, but something about the food falls a little short—perhaps it's the fact that the entrées are virtually interchangeable, with similar sauces and the same side dishes. The service is equally unremarkable. Still, if you can get a reservation, you'll have a quiet, pleasant evening. *132 Lexington Ave. (between 28th and 29th Sts.), Murray Hill, 212/545–1777. Reservations essential. AE, MC, V. Subway: 6 to 28th St. $$*

9 *c-1*

TAVERN ON THE GREEN

A celebrity chef, Patrick Clark, has breathed new life into this touristy restaurant, where more than 1,500 diners a day feast on decent shrimp cocktail, crab cakes, grilled swordfish, rotisserie chicken, and other Continental cuisine. Though the paneled hallways and gift shops border on tacky, the views of the park are splendid. A southern grill menu—ribs, chicken, and other favorites—is available on the terrace in the summer. *Central Park West (at 67th St.), Upper West Side, 212/873–3200. AE, D, DC, MC, V. Subway: 66th St./Lincoln Center; B, C to 72nd St. $$$*

STARGAZING

If you keep track of your run-ins, here are some places to up the ante:

Balthazar (French)
You'll be in good company if you can get a reservation, but try not to hurt your neck.

First (American)
Service in the wee hours means that you can watch the stars and see the sun come up.

Indochine (Vietnamese)
If you're a model—or just look like one—or will even settle for watching one, you'll find a glamorous backdrop here.

Nobu (Japanese)
Probably the most imaginative Japanese food in America—with a crowd to match.

Pravda (Russian)
Great appetizers, 65 kinds of vodkas, a fun scene—hey, maybe someone's watching you.

---

9 *e-2*

THE SIGN OF THE DOVE

This beautiful, flower-bedecked restaurant with the look of a romantic indoor garden has had its ups and downs; it's now somewhere in the middle. The menu changes seasonally, and is paired with a well-chosen wine list. For a lighter meal there is an attractive sidewalk café and bar, where you can listen to live piano music. *1110 3rd Ave. (at 65th St.), Upper East Side, 212/861–8080. AE, DC, MC, V. Reservations essential. No lunch Sun. Subway: 68th St./Hunter College. $$$*

9 *d-3*

21 CLUB

Triple-parked limos mark this clubby establishment in a renewed but unchanged turn-of-the-century setting. The noisy and celebrated downstairs bar is where the power folks lunch and sup; the upstairs is quieter, less interesting. Accomplished new chef Erik Blauberg has changed the menu substantially with his light touch and contemporary bent, but you can still order the famous oversized (and pricey) "21" burger or the steak tartare. The wine list is impressive, and if you're someone special (say, Gerald Ford) you can even lay away some special vintages for your next visit. Ask for a tour of the fascinating wine cellar in any case. For a rare treat, splurge on the private dining room near the wine cellar; this special enclave is one of the most beautiful in the city. *21 W. 52nd St., Midtown, 212/582–7200. Reservations essential. AE, DC, MC. Closed weekends in summer. Subway: 5th Ave./53rd St. $$$$*

10 *d-6*

WINDOWS ON THE WORLD

A quarter of a mile in the sky, Windows is quite simply one of the world's most spectacular restaurants. Reopened in 1996 with an exciting new chef, Michael Lomonaco (of 21 Club fame), the restaurant features contemporary continental food, decent service, and an exceptional and unexpectedly affordable wine list. Cocktails and hors d'oeuvres (à la carte) are served every day after 3 (pm), piano music begins at 4, and it's all backed by one of the world's most exciting views. Reserve far in advance and pray for a clear night. *1 World Trade Center, 107th floor, Lower Manhattan, 212/938–1111. Reservations essential. Jacket and tie, no* *denim. AE, DC, MC, V. Subway: Cortlandt St./World Trade Center. $$$*

DELICATESSENS

9 c-3

CARNEGIE DELICATESSEN

With huge portions and prices to match, this famous deli draws chaotic crowds of locals and tourists. The good, Jewish-style dishes are not kosher, but they're about as authentic as you can get short of your grandmother's house. The fatty pastrami and dry corned beef (those are good things) are made on the premises. Don't miss the cheesecake. Be prepared to sit with strangers and to take home the leftovers. *854 7th Ave. (at 55th St.), Midtown, 212/757–2245. No credit cards. Subway: 7th Ave.; N, R to 57th St. $$*

9 e-2

KAPLAN'S AT THE DELMONICO

This informal spot for hearty, Jewish-deli food is convenient to 57th Street shopping. The corned-beef and pastrami sandwiches are the way to go, but the menu offers a full range of options. *59 E. 59th St., Midtown, 212/755–5959. AE, DC, MC, V. Subway: 5th Ave./60th St. $*

10 g-3

KATZ'S DELICATESSEN

A Lower East Side institution, Katz's has terrific hot dogs, inexpensive pastrami, and the best hand-cut, corned-beef sandwiches in town (not kosher). On Sunday it's particularly unbeatable for local color and informality, especially on the part of the waiters; but if you're not in the mood, self-service is always an option. *205 E. Houston St. (at Ludlow St.), Lower East Side, 212/254–2246. No credit cards. Subway: 2nd Ave. $*

10 f-1

SECOND AVENUE KOSHER DELICATESSEN

Bar none, this is the best kosher deli in the city. Though some of the charm was renovated out of the hectic setting, delicious hot Jewish meals still vie aggressively with traditional deli delights for diners' affections (and arteries). A good lunch bet is matzo-ball soup and half a sandwich (the pastrami is to die for); for dinner on cold winter nights, try *cholent* (Jewish cassoulet) or chicken in the pot. You can always take the stuff out, or

have your next event catered—think beautiful platters, and chopped liver in the shape of a heart. *156 2nd Ave. (at 10th St.), East Village, 212/677–0606. Reservations not accepted. No credit cards. Subway: Astor Pl.; 3rd Ave. $*

EASTERN EUROPEAN

7 b-7

BARNEY GREENGRASS

Self-proclaimed "sturgeon king" Barney Greengrass is tops for breakfast and brunch. If you don't like to wake up to orange juice, how about a cold glass of borscht? Order a large platter of smoked salmon and, of course, sturgeon; or try the scrambled eggs with onions and smoked sturgeon. Fresh bagels, bialys, and cream cheese round out the meal. If you still have room, try an individual chocolate babka for dessert. Only complete parties will be seated. *541 Amsterdam Ave. (between 86th and 87th Sts.), Upper West Side, 212/724–4707. Reservations not accepted. No credit cards. Subway: 86th St. $*

10 f-3

SAMMY'S ROUMANIAN

Eating at Sammy's is like attending a bar mitzvah in the Catskills. Rumored to be a favorite hangout of cardiologists, Sammy's serves up Romanian tenderloin steak "with or without garlic," potatoes with gribenes, veal chops, stuffed cabbage, egg creams, and other specialties, all clogging their way to your heart. The pitchers of schmaltz, bottles of seltzer, and bowls of pickles on the table add a certain charm. *157 Chrystie St. (between Delancey and Rivington Sts.), Lower East Side, 212/673–0330. AE, DC. Subway: Grand St. $$*

11 g-1

VESELKA

A better bowl of borscht you will not find; it's served here with slices of delicious homemade egg bread. The pierogis—filled with cheese, mushroom and sauerkraut, or potato—and blintzes aren't bad, either. Renovated in 1996, this 24-hour coffee shop may be the last place in New York where communist intellectuals congregate freely. *144 2nd Ave. (at 9th St.), East Village, 212/228–9682. Reservations not accepted. AE, MC, V. Subway: Astor Pl. $*

ECLECTIC

9 f-4
DELEGATE'S DINING ROOM

Whether or not you're visiting the U.N., this is a fine place to lunch on Midtown's east end. The food is good (representing the many origins of those who dine here), the setting civilized, and the view of the East River wonderful. Your neighbors are ambassadors and attachés. *United Nations, Conference Building, 1st Ave. at 46th St. (visitors' entrance), 4th floor, Midtown, 212/963–7625. Reservations essential. AE, DC, MC, V. Photo ID required. No dinner. Closed weekends. Subway: 42nd St./Grand Central. $*

11 e-4
MATCH DOWNTOWN

A popular place for a drink both early and late at night, this lofty, bilevel restaurant is outfitted with booths, industrial beams, and wood paneling. The food is utterly multicultural—dim sum, sushi, Southwestern, and French—and there's an oyster bar for good measure. *60 Mercer St. (between Houston and Prince Sts.), SoHo, 212/343–0830. AE, DC, MC, V. Brunch weekends. Subway: Prince St.; Bleecker St./Broadway–Lafayette St. $$*

9 e-2
MATCH UPTOWN

What do you call a restaurant that serves sushi, pasta, and spit-roasted baby chicken on one menu? It doesn't really matter, because people aren't here for the food; they're here for each other. The red velvet ropes at the entrance tell you this is a major scene. The bar/lounge area is as big as the dining room, and its din travels throughout the restaurant. Still, the decor is beautiful; a sort of Asia–meets–Park-Avenue library, accented by dramatic flower arrangements. Some call the food "fussy" or "too complicated," but if you stick to the seared peppered tuna, pan-roasted salmon, and chocolate-banana torte, you can't go wrong. *33 E. 60th St., Midtown, 212/906–9173. Reservations essential. AE, DC, MC, V. No lunch weekends. Subway: 59th St. $$$*

FRENCH

11 c-5
ALISON ON DOMINICK STREET

This understated restaurant is worth the trek; wonderful country-French food is served in a romantic, candlelit setting. Try the ragout of mussels, braised lamb shank, or sautéed sea bass in a tarragon-flavored broth; then go for the chocolate-hazelnut ice cream or crème brûlée. *38 Dominick St. (bet. Varick and Hudson Sts.), West Village, 212/727–1188. Reservations essential. AE, MC, V. Subway: 1, 9, A, C, E to Canal St. $$$$*

11 e-5
BALTHAZAR

As we write, Balthazar is a serious scene and virtually impossible to get into. (Just getting them on the phone becomes a crusade.) Keith McNally's recreation of a French brasserie with an adjacent bakery is a smash hit—crowded and noisy, but invigorating. The decor—turn-of-the-century mirrors, tile floor, banquettes—makes the place look a hundred years old. And lo, the food is good: try the *plateau de fruits de mer*, creamy country rillettes of rabbit with marinated mushrooms, warm goat-cheese tart with caramelized onions, duck shepherd's pie, or seared salmon with porcini and polenta. For dessert, there is a wonderful lemon mille-feuille with sorbet and a fine crème brûlée. *80 Spring St. (between Broadway and Crosby St.), SoHo, 212/965–1414. Reservations essential. AE, MC, V. Subway: Spring St.; Prince St. $$$*

10 d-1
BAR SIX

The bar is always packed at this noisy hot spot, which comes complete with a chic and aloof waitstaff and matching clientele. Once you get past the bar, you'll find yourself in an attractively pared-down bistro with decent, inexpensive French-Moroccan dishes such as lamb couscous with preserved lemon. Be prepared for noise at night, when the music pounds and the crowd is in high spirits. *502 6th Ave. (between 12th and 13th Sts.), West Village, 212/691–1363. AE, MC, V. Subway: F to 14th St. $*

11 *f-4*

BISTRO MARGOT

Inexpensive French home cooking is served here in rather cramped but friendly surroundings. *26 Prince St. (between Elizabeth and Mott Sts.), SoHo, 212/274–1027. Subway: Prince St.; Bleecker St./Broadway–Lafayette St. $*

11 *d-8*

BOULEY BAKERY

Who wouldn't want to try a sandwich by the chef once considered the best in this city of great chefs? Walk into the bakery side of this unusual "café" and order away. On the other side, you can sit at one of the 12 coveted elegant tables and enjoy the master in his true form. Table-side bread service—at least 12 varieties are always offered—starts the parade of interesting dishes, most good, some great. But despite the casual-sounding name, you'll pay formal prices in the dining room. *120 W. Broadway (between Duane and Reade Sts.), Tribeca, 212/964–2525. Reservations essential. AE, MC, V. Subway: Chambers St. $$$$*

9 *f-4*

BOX TREE

This art-nouveau town house not only serves classic French food, but has charming rooms upstairs for those interested in spending the night. If that's not romantic, what is? Attentive service and a fireplace help kindle those amorous sparks. It's small and pricey, but no one said love was cheap. *242 E. 49th St., Midtown, 212/758–8320. Reservations essential. AE, MC, V. No lunch weekends. Subway: 51st St./Lexington–3rd Aves. $$$$*

9 *b-1*

CAFÉ LUXEMBOURG

Reminiscent of 1930s Paris, the art deco Luxembourg continues to be one of the most popular late-night see-and-be-seen spots in town, with plenty of stargazing opportunities. Best of all, you can also have a wonderful meal. The menu ranges from simple brasserie fare—steak and pommes frites—to imaginative seasonal creations. Bright and noisy, the restaurant gets so crowded that you'll have to wait a bit even if you have a reservation. *200 W. 70th St., Upper West Side, 212/873–7411. AE, MC, V. Subway: 1, 2, 3, 9 to 72nd St. $$$*

9 *d-5*

CAFÉ UN DEUX TROIS

This large, convivial Parisian brasserie–style eatery is perfect for a quick pre-theater dinner. Leftover Corinthian columns, Crayolas for doodling on the paper tablecloths, and a menu offering moderately priced basic and better French fare attract a diverse and noisy crowd. Service can be dicey, but you'll still leave happy. *123 W. 44th St., Theater District, 212/354–4148. Reservations not accepted. AE, DC, MC, V. Subway: 42nd St./Times Sq. $$*

11 *c-7*

CHANTERELLE

In Tribeca's historic Mercantile Exchange Building, chef David Waltuck serves sublime nouvelle French cuisine in a light, pretty dining room where the service, under the direction of Karen Waltuck, makes everyone feel like a privileged guest. Make tracks for chef Waltuck's signature seafood sausage, rack of lamb, Arctic char, and excellent desserts, and dip into the well-chosen cheese board. The prix-fixe menu, which changes weekly, is expensive but worth it. *2 Harrison St. (at Hudson St.), Tribeca, 212/966–6960. Reservations essential. AE, MC, V. Closed Sun.–Mon. Subway: Franklin St. $$$$*

9 *c-7*

CHELSEA BISTRO AND BAR

One of New York's best neighborhood restaurants, this comfortable bistro with booths and polished mirrors serves high-toned, well-seasoned French food, redolent of fresh herbs and country flavors. Don't miss the fois-gras ravioli. *358 W. 23rd St., Chelsea, 212/727–2026. AE, MC, V. No lunch. Brunch Sun. Subway: 23rd St. $$$*

7 *e-8*

DANIEL

The chef and owner of this four-star establishment first made a name for himself at Le Cirque. Now that he's in his own kitchen, critics and diners flock to his creations, and reservations are tough to get. The atmosphere is warm and understated, the waiters are surprisingly attentive and friendly, the crowd is eclectic, and the food is some of the best in New York. Classic French dishes share the menu with updated versions of more rustic cuisine. Some of the more popular dishes include pumpkin soup, foie gras with quince, and black sea bass wrapped in crisp potatoes. In the ultimate business twist, Daniel will move into the old Le Cirque space (on 65th St.) sometime next year. *20 E. 76th St., Upper East Side, 212/288–0033. Reservations essential. AE, D, DC, MC, V. Closed Sun. No lunch Mon. or Sat. Subway: 77th St. $$$$*

7 e-7
DEMARCHELIER

Both the food and decor of this neighborhood bistro are très French. The menu holds no surprises: steak-frîtes, salmon with beurre blanc, sole meunière, and onion soup. Unfortunately, the service is also authentic. The classic apple tart is a great ending for your meal. *50 E. 86th St., Carnegie Hill, 212/249–6300. AE, MC, V. Subway: 86th St. $$*

11 d-5
FELIX

A lively, neighborhood French bistro with doors that open onto the street in warm weather, this corner restaurant attracts lively, young Europeans, shoppers, and gallery-goers. The food is classic: onion tart, steak-frîtes, and seven-hour braised leg of lamb. *340 W. Broadway (at Grand St.), SoHo, 212/431–0021. AE. No lunch Sun. or Mon. Subway: Canal St. $$*

10 b-1
FLORENT

This gritty storefront in the meatpacking district has become a wee-hours mecca for breakfast and for the crowd—a stylish but egalitarian mixture of up- and downtowners. The reasonably priced dishes include wonderful French onion soup, couscous, sweetbreads, mussels in white-wine broth, duck mousse, and *boudin noir*. Sit at the counter (think diner) or proper tables (think bistro). *69 Gansevoort St. (between Washington and Greenwich Sts.), West Village, 212/989–5779. No credit cards. Open 24 hours. Subway: 14th St. $$*

11 d-4
FRONTIÈRE

Frontière is a pretty, romantic little spot with exposed-brick walls, candles, and a lovely old zinc bar. Try the grilled wild-mushroom salad with warm potatoes, the côte de boeuf for two, or the sautéed salmon with grilled spinach, fried potatoes, and béarnaise sauce. *199 Prince St. (between MacDougal and Sullivan Sts.), SoHo, 212/387–0898. AE, DC, MC, V. Subway: Spring St. $$$*

11 d-4
JEAN CLAUDE

This noisy, crowded, friendly bistro feels strikingly like Paris. The food is highly refined, and the menu changes daily. The fish, leg of lamb with roast-garlic mashed potatoes, and crème brûlée are all excellent. *137 Sullivan St. (between Houston and Prince Sts.), SoHo, 212/475–9232. No credit cards. No lunch. Subway: Spring St. $$*

9 c-2
JEAN GEORGES

Rarely does a new restaurant open to such acclaim. Jean-Georges Vongerichten (of Vong [*see above*] and Jo Jo [*see below*] fame) is back in his haute-French mode: the room is elegantly minimalist, the food formal French. Highlights on one seasonal spring menu include asparagus spears with morel sauce, halibut with tomatoes and zucchini, skate with brown butter, and sweetbreads with demi-glace. Everything in Vongerichten's hands is worth sampling; even the homemade marshmallows that follow dessert will teach you something about fine food. The emphasis is on tableside service, not for show but for pampering. Don't miss the tea selection. For a less expensive, less formal experience you can also try the Mistral Terrace (alfresco) or the Nougatine Room (open for breakfast), each with a different, lighter menu. *Trump International Hotel and Tower, 1 Central Park West, Midtown, 212/299–3900. Reservations essential. AE, DC, MC, V. Subway: 59th St./Columbus Circle. $$$$*

9 e-1
JO JO

While many complain that the space is awkward and somewhat cramped in this Upper East Side brownstone, and some have pronounced the service a bit lacking, no one complains about the food. Jean-Georges Vongerichten still draws a crowd after more than five years of consistently inventive and delicious food, based in his Alsatian roots but influenced by his love for Asian flavors and all sorts of herbs. Try the roasted monkfish with nutmeg and raisins, chicken with coriander and ginger, any of the 27 vegetables, and, for dessert, the apple confit. Ask for a table upstairs; the downstairs can get noisy. *160 E. 64th St., Upper East Side, 212/223–5656. Reservations essential. AE, D, DC, MC, V. Closed Sun. No lunch Sat. Subway: 59th St.; 68th St./Hunter College. $$$*

9 *d-3*
LA CARAVELLE
La Caravelle has been one New York's most fashionable classic-French restaurants for over 30 years. The food has gone up and down during that time, but the restaurant is decidedly riding a crest of its wave now. Nobody does the classics—quenelles, foie gras, terrines—better; innovations are less successful. Service is heavy on the tableside show, but the effect is charming in the amiable setting. *33 W. 55th St., Midtown, 212/586–4252. Reservations essential. AE, DC, MC, V. Closed Sun. and holidays. Subway: 5th Ave./53rd St. $$$$*

11 *f-4*
LA CIGALE
This cozy bistro has a distinctly downtown feel and a pleasant garden. The French-American dishes include salmon ceviche with orange and cilantro; frisée salad; roast cod with fennel and potato salad; thick-cut pork chops; and hanger steak. *231 Mott St. (between Prince and Spring Sts.), SoHo, 212/334–4331. AE. No lunch. Subway: Bleecker St./Broadway–Lafayette St.; Prince St. $$*

9 *e-3*
LA CÔTE BASQUE
Although this venerable institution had to move down the street in 1995, not much has changed. Pushing 40, the restaurant still prepares classic French cuisine as it was meant to be. Oak-smoked salmon, cassoulet, and Dover sole are among the best choices, each skillfully plated tableside by dexterous waiters, who have been known to toss attitude around with the entrées. Prices are high, but portions are large. *60 E. 55th St., Midtown, 212/688–6525. Reservations essential. AE, DC, MC, V. Closed Sun. Subway: 5th Ave./53rd St. $$$$*

9 *e-1*
LA GOULUE
This highly evocative, art-nouveau Parisian setting serves traditional brasserie food and happens to be more comfortable than most of its Madison Avenue French neighbors. True to the neighborhood, sidewalk seating is available for optimal people-watching. *28 E. 70th St., Upper East Side, 212/988-8169. AE, DC, MC, V. Closed Sun. Subway: 68th St./Hunter College. $$$*

9 *e-3*
LA GRENOUILLE
La Grenouille is the grand dame of New York's haute-French cuisine, complete with a lush, floral setting and impeccable service. Enjoy beautifully prepared and perfectly served food among New York's power elite—if you can afford the prix fixe. Not much is original or particularly inspiring, but the quenelles are top-notch. *3 E. 52nd St., Midtown, 212/752-1495. Reservations essential. AE, DC, MC, V. Closed Sun. and Mon. Subway: 5th Ave./53rd St. $$$$*

9 *d-4*
LE BERNARDIN
GQ recently touted this beautiful and spacious French restaurant as the best in the country. The emphasis is on seafood, and in chef Eric Ripert's hands, marine life becomes manna. Scallop ceviche, Spanish mackerel tartare—anything is possible. The service is doting, the wine list extensive, and, for a new taste sensation, the sommelier will recommend some light-bodied reds that go well with creatures of the sea. The bill can be a shock, but what price the food of the gods? *Equitable Building, 155 W. 51st St., Midtown, 212/489-1515. Reservations essential. Closed Sun. No lunch weekends. Subway: 49th St.; 47th–50th Sts./Rockefeller Center. $$$$*

9 *e-2*
LE BILBOQUET
A small, informal, yet fashionable cousin to Madison Avenue's Le Relais, Le Bilboquet is a good place for an alfresco lunch in season, with sidewalk seating and wonderful salads. Evenings inside are filled with joie de vivre—i.e., a lot of ambient noise. *25 E. 63rd St., Upper East Side, 212/751–3036. Reservations essential. AE. No dinner Sun. Subway: 59th St. $$*

9 *e-3*
LE CHANTILLY
The international set has long loved this restaurant, which is pretty, plush, spacious, and serene. Like most of the city's Old World establishments, Le Chantilly

has modernized its French cuisine, emphasizing light flavors and beautiful presentations. The popular prix-fixe pre-theater dinner is slightly easier on the pocket. *106 E. 57th St., 212/751–2931. Reservations essential. AE, DC. MC. V. Closed Sun. Subway: 57th St. $$$$*

9 e-4
LE CIRQUE 2000
Gone are the low ceilings and monkey sconces: picture a spaceship landing in an Italian piazza. From the roller-coaster curves of the futuristic bar to the soaring, gilded, turn-of-the-century ceilings, this dining room of the rich and famous is a study in contrasts. No surprises emerge from the multimillion-dollar kitchen; just straightforward, modern French cooking. Service can be doting or nonexistent, depending on your stature. Love it or hate it, this is a restaurant that must be seen and experienced to be believed. Order the créme brûlée for dessert and you'll leave happy. *New York Palace Hotel, 455 Madison Ave. (between 50th and 51st Sts.), Midtown, 212/794–9292. Reservations essential. AE, DC, MC, V. Subway: E, F to 5th Ave.; 51st St./Lexington–3rd Aves. $$$$*

9 e-2
LE RELAIS
This lovely, bistro-style restaurant features okay French food in a very European atmosphere. The trendy young people at the bar overshadow the food, but the sidewalk is a pleasant place to sit and watch Madison Avenue go by. *712 Madison Ave. (at 63rd St.), Upper East Side, 212/751–5108. AE. Subway: 59th St. $$*

9 d-3
LES CÉLÉBRITÉS
The rich velvets and dark hues of this intimate dining room make this a good place for a (pricey) romantic evening. The extensive menu tempts, with chef Christian Delouvrier's innovations, like his signature foie-gras hamburger—a piece of seared foie gras sandwiched in a baked, miniature Granny Smith apple—and his classics, like civet of rabbit. In fall and winter, a multicourse *menu de la chasse* (hunting menu) offers an array of excellent game dishes. A fine wine list and smooth service round out the indulgence. The name refers to the art on the walls, produced by celebrities such as Phyllis Diller and Tina Turner;

you're better off focusing on the food. *Essex House Hotel, 155 W. 58th St., Midtown, 212/484–5113. Reservations essential. AE, DC, MC, V. Closed Sun. and Mon. Subway: 57th St. $$$$*

9 e-7
LES HALLES
This très Parisian butcher shop and bistro is casual and cacophonous, with a charming, fin-de-siècle decor. Diners pack in like sardines for the *frisée aux lardons* salad with roquefort; authentic cassoulet; boudin noir with apples; terrific steak-frîtes; and the interesting, affordable wine list. *411 Park Ave. S (between 28th and 29th St.), Murray Hill, 212/679–4111. Reservations essential. AE, DC, MC, V. Subway: 33rd St. $$*

9 e-3
LESPINASSE
Only a few years old, this over-the-top formal restaurant has helped revive fine dining in New York and hotel dining everywhere. Celebrity chef Gray Kunz creates food that wallops you with flavor and offers an interesting contrast to the soothing decor and quietly rich ambience. The impeccable wait staff takes care of your every need while you concentrate on the chef's otherwordly creations. If you're lucky, these will include ragout of squab, braised salmon with crispy artichokes, or chocolate-banana soufflé. The large wine selection is made more approachable by an aim-to-please sommelier. *St. Regis Hotel, 2 E. 55th St., Midtown, 212/339–6719. Reservations essential. Closed Sun. Breakfast daily. Subway: 5th Ave./53rd St. $$$$*

10 c-1
LE ZOO
This somewhat cramped yet cozy bistro serves reasonably priced French items that often sound better than they taste. The seasonal, creamless turnip soup is smooth and satisfying, and the chicken breast with chanterelles is moist and flavorful. The adorable French hosts are gracious and attentive, which can make up for the fact that you must climb over a radiator to get to your table. *114 W. 11th St. (at Greenwich St.), West Village, 212/620–0393. Reservations not accepted. AE, MC, V. No lunch. Subway: Christopher St./Sheridan Sq. $$*

9 *f-4*

LUTÈCE

It's hard to believe a company known in New York for its theme restaurants purchased this restaurant from famed French chef André Soltner—but they've installed the competent Eberhard Mueller in the kitchen, and he's turning out fine contemporary-French fare and a few Alsatian classics held over from the Soltner days. The room has been updated, but the staff still won't smile. *249 E. 50th St., Midtown, 212/752–2225. Reservations essential. AE, DC, MC, Closed Sun. Subway: 51st St./Lexington–3rd Aves. $$$$*

9 *f-3*

MARCH

Wayne Nish creates wonderfully imaginative American fare with an Asian twist at this elegant East Side town house. A garden and a fireplace make it an attractive choice year-round. Be prepared, however, for a long and expensive dinner: The new prix-fixe format means you get to sample a variety of dishes—a leisurely process. *405 E. 58th St., Midtown, 212/838–9393. Reservations essential. AE, MC, V. Closed Sun. No lunch. Subway: 59th St. $$$$*

11 *d-7*

MONTRACHET

One of the first restaurants to open in Tribeca, Drew Nieporent's Montrachet remains a fine choice for fine, imaginative French nouvelle cuisine in a spare, high-ceilinged contemporary setting. The prix-fixe menu includes inventive fish choices, such as house lobster salad with asparagus and passion fruit vinaigrette, and truffle-crusted salmon, as well as elegant desserts. Spend some time perusing the award-winning wine list. *239 W. Broadway, between Walker and White Sts., 212/219–2777. AE only. Reservations essential. Open Mon.–Thurs. and Sat. 6–11; Fri. noon–3 and 6–11. Subway: Canal St. $$$*

11 *d-8*

ODEON

This large, '30s-style cafeteria is one of Tribeca's original late-night in spots. The French-bistro food is not terribly ambitious, but it always manages to please. The softly lit, low-frills ambience is timeless, as is the intriguing cast of characters, especially in the wee hours. *145 W. Broadway (at Thomas St.), Tribeca, 212/*

233–0507. AE, DC, MC, V. No lunch weekends. Brunch Sun. Subway: Chambers St. $$

9 *d-3*

PETROSSIAN

The elegant Belle Epoque decor is faded, and the food seems tired, but nowhere is caviar service more elegant than at this posh Parisian palace. The $75 tasting of Beluga, Osetra, and Sevruga caviars arrives in a beautiful, three-sided Christofle holder; the gold-plated paddle pushes the experience over the top. An icy glass of champagne or premium vodka makes this the perfect pit stop on your way to a better dinner. *182 W. 58th St., Midtown, 212/245–2214. AE, MC, V. No lunch Sun. Subway: 57th St. $$$*

9 *c-2*

PICHOLINE

Picholine *is* the French countryside. The chef's Mediterranean state of mind is announced with the bowl of olives (*picholines*) brought to your table with a basket of fresh-baked bread, and dominates the entire enticing menu. Delicate pastas, perfectly cooked whole fish, hearty game dishes . . . everything the kitchen touches is delicious. Don't miss the cheese course; the restaurant actually has a cave, in which they ripen the finest selection of cheeses in the city. The award-winning wine-and-cheese steward will guide you to the best choices. *35 W. 64th St., Upper West Side, 212/724–8585. Reservations essential. AE, DC, D, MC, V. Subway: 66th St./Lincoln Center. $$$$*

11 *d-4*

PROVENCE

This rustic SoHo bistro wins high marks for its authentic Provençal food, moderate prices, and romantic little tented garden, complete with flower-encircled stone fountain. Try the bourride, a garlicky Mediterranean fish stew; steak-frites; braised rabbit; and bouillabaisse. The Provençal wines are well-priced. *38 MacDougal St. (between Prince St. and Houston Sts.), SoHo, 212/475–7500. AE. Subway: C, E to Prince St. $$$*

7 *f-8*

QUATORZE BIS

Uptowners once trekked downtown for this off-the-beaten-track charmer. The downtown location is long closed, but its uptown outpost remains packed. The reasonably priced, reliable bourgeois-French fare, the compatible wine list, and the casual, authentic bistro setting will bring you pretty close to Paris. Have the steak-frites. *323 E. 79th St., Upper East Side, 212/535–1414. Reservations essential. AE, MC, V. Subway: 77th St.* $$

11 *d-4*

RAOUL'S

Raoul's is a permanent fixture in an ever-changing neighborhood. Brave the dark, noisy, and smoky bar, the equally dark front room, and the bustle of the kitchen to get to the somewhat more serene dining room. Stick to the basics—veal chop, the roasted chicken, seared tuna—and enjoy a fine meal. *180 Prince St. (near Sullivan St.), 212/966–3518. Reservations essential. AE, MC, V. No lunch. Subway: C, E to Spring St.* $$$

7 *e-8*

TROIS JEAN

Despite the lackluster service, many consider this the best French bistro in the neighborhood. The two brownstone floors form a double-edged sword: the top floor is quieter, but the service is slower and less attentive; the bottom floor, seemingly reserved for regulars and VIPs, tends to get better service but is much noisier. Locals still come back for the steak tartare with frites, the cassoulet, and the made-to-order warm apple tart. *154 E. 79th St., Upper East Side, 212/988–4858. Reservations essential. AE, DC, MC, V. Closed Sun. in summer. Subway: 77th St.* $$$

GREEK

10 *f-1*

AGROTIKON

Authentic homestyle Greek cooking, including specialities that incorporate goat and octopus, is served in a Mediterranean setting. The salads and whole grilled fish are tops; you'll be surprised not to find a beach outside. *322 E. 14th St., East Village, 212/473–2602. Subway: 14th St.* $

9 *d-3*

MOLYVOS

It's hard to find Greek food this good in Greece, let alone Manhattan. Perfectly prepared *mezedes* (little bites like spinach pie; *tzatziki*, a cucumber-and-yogurt dip;

or roasted eggplant dip), wonderful entrées (marinated lamb shank, stuffed cabbage, and moussaka), and sweet desserts (honey-drenched fritters, custard in phyllo) are lovingly prepared and served in a convivial atmosphere. There are 10 ouzos to choose from, and an interesting selection of Greek wines. *871 7th Ave. (between 55th and 56th Sts.), Midtown, 212/582–7500. AE, DC, MC, V. Subway: 57th St.* $$$

9 *d-8*

PERIYALI

Just about the only thing unusual about the menu at this upscale Greek taverna is that everything tastes so good. Whole grilled fish, lamb on skewers, and other Greek specialites join more contemporary dishes like salmon in phyllo on the menu. Don't leave without sampling the homemade baklava. *35 W. 20th St., Flatiron, 212/463–7890. Reservations essential. AE, MC, V. No lunch weekends. Subway: F, N, R to 23rd St.* $$

HUNGARIAN

7 *f-7*

MOCCA HUNGARIAN

Locals depend on this Old World outpost for hearty and inexpensive Hungarian fare. The goulash and stuffed cabbage may not be gourmet, but they're comforting, filling, and delicious. *1588 2nd Ave. (between 82nd and 83rd Sts.), Upper East Side, 212/734–6470. No credit cards. Subway: 86th St.* $

7 *f-8*

RED TULIP

If you're suddenly craving turn-of-the-century Budapest, this is the spot for you. While some say it's seen its day, many adore the large portions of goulash and schnitzel, the live gypsy violins, and the reasonable prices. *439 E. 75th St., Upper East Side, 212/734-4893. AE. Closed Mon. and Tues.* $

INDIAN

New York's best-known destination for Indian food is Sixth Street between First and Second avenues (map 11/g-1). This short strip packs about twenty Indian restaurants, many festively lit year-round with variously colored Christmas lights. Affectionate (and some not-so-affectionate) rumors circulate about the provenance of the food here; some say that all of these storefronts get their meals from the same giant kitchen under the street. It's not gourmet, but it's tasty, filling, and incredibly cheap, with many entrées under $10; Gandhi and Passage to India are particularly good bets.

Venture beyond Sixth Street for the city's most inspiring Indian cuisine, most of it still reasonably priced.

9 *e-3*

AKBAR

Most diners praise Akbar for its authentic, well-seasoned food in an attractive setting filled with Indian antiques. The prix-fixe lunch is a great buy, considering the neighborhood. *475 Park Ave. (between 57th and 58th Sts.), Midtown, 212/838–1717. Reservations essential for lunch. AE, MC, V. No lunch Sat. Subway: 59th St. $$*

11 *d-4*

BALUCHI'S

Lavishly decorated with Indian artifacts, these inexpensive restaurants offer reliable tandoori food (curries and tasty breads) and good service. *193 Spring St. (between Sullivan and Thompson Sts.), SoHo, 212/226–2828. Subway: Spring St. AE, DC, MC, V. $*

7 *f-7*

1565 2nd Ave. (between 81st and 82nd Sts.), Upper East Side, 212/288–4810. Subway: 86th St.

11 *c-2*

361 6th Ave. (between W. 4th St. and Washington Pl.), Greenwich Village, 212/929–2441. Subway: W. 4th St./Washington Sq.

9 *d-3*

BOMBAY PALACE

Some say this handsomely decorated Midtown restaurant offers some of the best northern Indian cuisine in town. The Tandoori dishes, curries, flat breads, and other traditional specialties are not cheap, but they are skillfully prepared. The reasonably priced lunch buffet offers a wide variety. *30 W. 52nd St., Midtown, 212/541–7777. Subway: 5th Ave./53rd St. $$*

9 *f-3*

DAWAT

When Dawat opened in 1986, the menu (created by actress–food writer Madhur Jaffrey) and the elegant setting made it New York's reigning *rani* of Indian eateries. While some claim the Indian restaurant scene has finally caught up with it, loyalists insist that Dawat makes the most imaginative and best-executed Indian cuisine around. The extraordinary, well-priced lunch makes it a popular Midtown choice. *210 E. 58th St., Midtown, 212/355–7555. Reservations essential. AE, MC, V. No lunch Sun. Subway: 59th St. $$*

9 *d-3*

NIRVANA

Nirvana's claim to fame is its extremely romantic setting, overlooking Central Park. The view is more memorable than the food—decent Indo-Bengali cuisine—but the feeling of being in another world makes the experience pleasant. Dinner is accompanied by live sitar music. *30 Central Park South, 15th floor, Midtown, 212/486–5700. Reservations essential. AE, DC, MC, V. Subway: 57th St. $$*

9 *e-7*

PONGAL

Don't let the fact that it's vegetarian and kosher divert your attention. From the papadams and green-mango relish that arrive when you sit down, to the spicy chopped kachumber salad, to the light and fragrant curries, giant paper-thin dosai, and other specialties from southern India, the food at this quaint restaurant is nothing short of remarkable. Order the Mysore Special or the Gujarati Thali (on the back of the menu) to sample several dishes at one sitting. *110 Lexington Ave. (between 27th and 28th Sts.), Murray Hill, 212/696–9458. AE, MC, V. Subway: 6 to 28th St. $*

ITALIAN

11 *d-7*

ARQUA

This sparse restaurant is lauded for its excellent *cucina nuova*. Pastas are heavenly—the gnocchi is light (!), the daily risotto rich. Other good bets are fish soup; calves' liver with onions and polenta; and grilled chicken. For dessert, the standard ricotta cheesecake and tiramisu are best. *281 Church St. (at White St.), Tribeca, 212/334–1888. AE. Subway: Franklin St. $$$*

9 c-4

BARBETTA

This century-old Italian serves traditional Piedmontese specialties in a sumptuously appointed town house. Stay simple and the food may please—rich *fonduta*, beef braised in Barolo wine, and other regional classics. But in late spring and summer, the real draw is the luxurious outdoor garden, a real oasis in the Theater District; and when white Alba truffles are in season, this is a particularly good place to splurge. Service is madness pre- and post-theater, but indulgent during the show. *321 W. 46th St., Theater District, 212/246–9171. AE, DC, MC, V. Closed Sun. Subway: 42nd St. $$$*

11 d-7

BAROCCO

This casual but trendy Tuscan trattoria remains a Tribeca scene, warehouse dimensions and all. The pastas are wonderful, and so are the breads; don't miss the fettunta and bruschetta. *301 Church St. (between White and Walker Sts.), Tribeca, 212/431–1445. AE, DC, MC, V. Subway: Franklin St. $$$*

11 c-3

BAR PITTI

Here's a friendly Tuscan restaurant with excellent, inexpensive food, an attractive clientele, and outdoor tables in summer. Try the bruschetta; the white-bean salad with tuna, red onions and olive oil; the *panzanella* (bread salad with roast peppers); and the chicken Milanese with arugula. Pastas change daily. *268 6th Ave. (between Bleecker and Houston Sts.), Greenwich Village, 212/982–3300. No credit cards. Subway: W. 4th St./Washington Sq. $$*

9 c-4

BECCO

Though the name is Italian for "little beak," you'll need more than a bird's appetite to enjoy this busy trattoria. Because the menu is prix-fixe, you are presented with an array of antipasti as soon as you sit down, including fried and/or grilled vegetables, white bean spread, fresh breads, and other treats. Waiters roam the room with pans of pasta for you to sample, such as fresh pappardelle with duck ragu, orechiette with broccoli rabe, fresh gnocchi with tomato sauce—the selection changes daily. If you still have room, you can upgrade to an entrée; osso buco, rabbit stew, roasted lamb, suckling pig, and a selection of fish entrées are usually on the list. Still hungry? The bread pudding is fantastic. Wines are all priced at $18 per bottle. The experience is fast, friendly, fun, and delicious. *355 W. 46th St., Theater District, 212/397–7597. Reservations essential. AE, DC, V. Subway: 42nd St. $$*

9 e-3

BICE

This extremely successful Italian bistro was imported from Milan, where the original Bice was founded in 1926. Needless to say, the New York cousin attracts what might be called a Roman crowd—beautiful and fashion-forward. Regulars flock for the heavenly but high-priced Milanese pasta, risotto, grilled dishes, and game (in season). The service can be pretentious to the point of offense. *7 E. 54th St., 212/688–1999. Reservations essential. AE. Subway: E, F to 5th Ave. $$$$*

10 e-1

BUSSOLA BAR AND GRILL

Bussola serves up Sicilian cooking in a cheerful, relaxed setting. The swordfish carpaccio and marinated artichoke hearts are wonderful; salads are generous and fresh; pastas are homemade; and desserts are outstanding. Favorite sweets are the ricotta gelato with preserved orange peel, hazelnut ice cream, and creamy tiramisu dusted with chocolate powder. *65 4th Ave. (near 10th St.), East Village, 212/254–1940. AE, MC, V. Closed Sun. Subway: Astor Pl. $$*

9 e-8

CAMPAGNA

This handsome, country-style trattoria serves earthy Italian food. Try the antipasto (on gleaming display as you enter), gnocchi with wild mushrooms and truffle oil, first-rate pastas, and rib-eye steak with mashed potatoes. *24 E. 21st St. (between Broadway and Park Ave.), Gramercy, 212/460–0900. AE, DC, MC, V. No lunch weekends. Subway: 23rd St. $$$*

7 b-6

CARMINE'S

The portions are huge and the wait is long at these family-style Italian trattorias. Everything, from the spaghetti with red sauce to the fancier veal dishes, satisfies, and sharing is encouraged. The kitchen has a heavy hand with garlic, so don't plan to kiss anyone after dinner. The atmosphere is bustling and loud. *2450 Broadway, Upper West Side, 212/362–2200. Reservations not accepted. AE, MC, V. Subway: 96th St. $$*

9 *c-5*

200 W. 44th St., Theater District, 212/221–3800.

11 *c-3*

CENT'ANNI

This small, crowded, casual West Village trattoria serves simple and very good Florentine food. Try the wonderful seafood salad, grilled veal chop, or pasta, and finish with the zabaglione. *50 Carmine St. (between Bedford and Bleecker Sts.), West Village, 212/989–9494. AE, MC, V. No lunch weekends. Subway: W. 4th St./Washington Sq. $$*

7 *e-8*

COCO PAZZO

Another hit from restaurateur Pino Luongo, this lively, unpretentious, East Side Italian is a good stop for excellent, robust, regional-Italian specialties. The well-dressed local crowd enjoys a nightly array of hot and cold antipasti, as well as risotto, rigatoni with sausage and peas, and a wide array of game choices. The daily specials are always interesting. *23 E. 74th St., Upper East Side, 212/794–0205. Reservations essential. AE, MC, V. Subway: 77th St. $$$*

12 *e-5*

CUCINA

Michael Ayoub has created a Brooklyn haven with this casual trattoria, where the portions are large, the flavors robust, and the prices right. It's hard to get a table in this giant space. Choose from the temptations on the antipasti table, ask for a half-order of pasta, and enjoy the generous entrées, such as succulent osso buco. *256 5th Ave., Park Slope, Brooklyn, 718/230–0711. Reservations essential. AE, MC, V. Subway: N, R to Union St. $$*

11 *g-2*

CUCINA DI PESCE

Hearty portions of inexpensive, Italian-accented fish specialties, served with heaping mounds of pasta, draw a somewhat better-dressed crowd than you might expect. Dip into the mound of free mussels at the crowded bar. *87 E. 4th St., 212/260–6800. Reservations not accepted. No credit cards. Subway: 2nd Ave.; Astor Pl. $*

11 *b-2*

CUCINA STAGIONALE

Despite the name, nothing changes with the seasons at this inexpensive and good Italian eatery. The menu includes myriad pastas and other starters—fusilli with sundried tomato, gorgonzola, and caper sauce is among the best— and equally numerous entrées, including veal and salmon, each ample, tasty, and well prepared. The free antipasto is a welcome touch. *275 Bleecker St. (between 6th and 7th Aves.), West Village, 212/924–2707. Reservations not accepted. No credit cards. BYOB. Subway: W. 4th St./Washington Sq. $*

9 *e-8*

DA VITTORIO

This high-energy, bustling, rather noisy Tuscan trattoria has charming waiters and welcomes you with a selection of colorful antipasti, laid out near the bar. The pasta and polenta are excellent (particularly the ravioli stuffed with mascarpone), as are the osso buco, grilled rabbit, and medallions of venison. Desserts are predictable, handsome, and heavy, and include smooth *panna cotta*, tiramisu, robust apple cake, and good dark-chocolate cake. *43 E. 20th St. (between Broadway and Park Ave. S), Gramercy, 212/979–6532. Reservations essential. AE. Closed Sun. No lunch weekends. Subway: 23rd St.; 14th St./Union Sq. $$$*

11 *e-5*

DOWNTOWN

Downtown attracts the same decadent crowd you see of an evening at Harry's Bar in Venice (and at Harry Cipriani's, uptown—*see below*), knocking back Bellinis at the bar. The stylish food is expensive but good: *vitello tonnato* (cold roasted veal in a sauce of puréed tuna and anchovies), crisp fried calamari with a vivid tomato sauce, ravioli stuffed with veal, grouper *alla carlina* with caper sauce. Desserts are ample, and include lemon and vanilla-cream cakes suffused with frosting and meringue. *376 W. Broadway (near Broome St.), SoHo, 212/343–0999. Reservations essential. AE, DC, MC, V. Subway: Canal St. $$$*

7 f-7
ELIO'S
Woody Allen had a window table here for years, and many less-famous locals have become regulars as well. The star-studded crowd and the chef's admirable northern-Italian fare have made Elio's extremely popular. The handsome, wood-paneled setting is lively and noisy; expect a wait, even with a reservation. The veal Milanese and the basket of fried zucchini are menu favorites. *1621 2nd Ave. (between 84th and 85th Sts.), Upper East Side, 212/772–2242. AE, MC, V. No lunch. Subway: 86th St. $$*

7 f-7
ERMINIA
This family-run restaurant is one of the best-kept secrets on the Upper East Side. Candlelit, cozy (40 seats), and inviting, it's a great place for special occasions. Go for entrées grilled over a Tuscan-style wood fire, tasty pastas, and bruschetta and crostini (toasted bread drenched with olive oil and garlic), or just go because it's one of those intimate, beautiful eateries that you normally find only on small, winding streets in the Village. *250 E. 83rd St., Upper East Side, 212/879–4284. Reservations essential. AE. Closed Sun. Subway: 83rd St. $$$*

9 f-3
FELIDIA
New York's mother of Italian cuisine, Lidia Bastianich, creates a menu of wonderfully original northern-Italian creations for this handsome restaurant. Downstairs, where the exposed brick and wood create a sophisticated warmth, is perfect for dinner, while the painted walls and skylight upstairs make for a cheerful lunch. Don't miss the tasty antipasti, homemade pastas with seasonal ingredients, and rustic regional specialties. An exceptional Italian-wine selection puts the finishing touch on a great meal. *243 E. 58th St., Midtown, 212/758–1479. Reservations essential. AE, DC, MC, V. Closed Sun. No lunch Sat. Subway: 59th St. $$$$*

9 d-7
FOLLONICO
If the dining room had windows overlooking rolling vineyards—or any windows at all, for that matter—Follonico might just be the most effectively Tuscan dining room in the city. Chef Alan Tardi serves contemporary Italian cuisine, much of it prepared in the wood-fired oven visible from the dining room; the menu is heavy on game (in season) and light in texture. Pastas, like the giant open-mushroom raviolo, are all interesting and tasty; the fiorentina steak for two tastes unusually beefy and is cooked just right; and the crisp *grissini* (bread sticks) on the table are addictive. *6 W. 24th St., Flatiron, 212/691–6359. Reservations essential. AE, MC, V. Subway: F, N, R to 23rd St. $$$*

7 b-6
GENNARO
The terrific Italian food at this tiny restaurant draws crowds to an otherwise cuisine-free neighborhood. Both the appetizers, such as *ribollita* (a hearty Tuscan soup), grilled scallops on white beans, and beef carpaccio, and the classic homemade pastas, such as potato gnocchi with fresh tomato sauce and orecchiette with broccoli and provole, have plenty of allure; and entrées like tender osso buco, succulent braised lamb shank, and garlic-perfumed roasted Cornish game hen add to the draw. Perhaps the best reason for the schlepp, however, is the price. All of this means that lots of people wait endlessly for one of the 14 tables. Call before you go, not for a reservation, but to be sure they're open—otherwise, you might arrive to find a handwritten sign saying something like, "Sorry, Gennaro is tired and has stayed home today." *665 Amsterdam Ave. (between 92nd and 93rd Sts.), Upper West Side, 212/665–5348. Reservations not accepted. No credit cards. Subway: 96th St. $$*

9 e-2
HARRY CIPRIANI
An elegant, well-heeled, international set veritably floats through the revolving door, missing nary a beat before grasping a Bellini. As always, Cipriani serves wonderful northern-Italian food to a sophisticated crowd in a sophisticated setting. The atmosphere will make you homesick for Venice, but the bill will make you think, "Maybe next year." *Hotel Sherry-Netherland, 781 5th Ave. (at 59th St.), Midtown, 212/753–5566. Reservations essential. AE, DC, MC, V. Subway: N, R to 5th Ave. $$$$*

10 *e-1*

IL CANTINORI

Il Cantinori is a top-rated Village Italian restaurant known for lovely, uncomplicated Tuscan specialties served in two subtly charming, rustic dining rooms. The front room spills out onto the street in good weather. The wonderful and unusual daily specials, cold antipasti, and grilled meats and vegetables come with wonderfully high prices. *32 E. 10th St., East Village, 212/673–6044. Reservations essential. AE, MC, V. Subway: 8th St.; Astor Pl. $$$*

11 *d-2*

IL MULINO

Some consider this the best Italian restaurant in the city, but *cognoscenti* of Italian food consider it the biggest farce. Glorified Little Italy specialties command prices in the stratosphere—be prepared to pay upwards of $50 for one of the many enticing-sounding specials recited tableside. Do yourself and your wallet a favor, and skip that two-month waiting list altogether. *86 W. 3rd St. (near Sullivan St.), Greenwich Village, 212/673–3783. Reservations essential. AE. Subway: W. 4th St./Washington Sq. $$$$*

9 *e-2*

IL TOSCANACCIO

This beautifully rustic Midtown eatery is another from Pino Luongo (*see Coco Pazzo, above,* and Le Madri, *below*) who seems to lead New York's pack in successful Italian restaurants. This one focuses on Tuscany's home cooking, and its crowd runs the gamut from glamorous models to corporate lawyers wanting a taste of Mama's food. Regulars love the antipasto, which changes according to the chef's whim; the lamb stew, served in a fresh-baked bread bowl; and seasonal pastas. The atmosphere is high-class but casual, so don't be surprised if the table next to you leans over and asks what smells so good. *7 E. 59th St., Midtown, 212/935–3535. Reservations essential. AE, DC, MC, V. No lunch weekends. Subway: 59th St. $$$*

9 *e-7*

I TRULLI

Easily one of the most authentic Italian dining experiences in New York, this charming, casual restaurant (with a beautiful garden in season) is comfortable and welcoming. The warm crusty bread is served with a sinfully good ricotta-and-roasted-garlic spread, and it's all uphill from there. The pastas are all interesting, the entrées flavorful, and the desserts baked fresh each day. *122 E. 27th St., Murray Hill, 212/481–7372. Reservations essential. AE, MC, V. Subway: 6 to 28th St. $$$*

9 *d-8*

LE MADRI

This spacious, high-ceilinged hot spot has died down somewhat since neighboring Barneys closed, but the menu still offers consistently fine and imaginative Tuscan-style cooking. The great pizzas come from a central, wood-burning oven. The outdoor patio is lovely in season. *168 W. 18th St., Chelsea, 212/727–8022. Reservations essential. AE, MC, V. Subway: 14th St. $$$*

10 *d-1*

MARIA ELENA

Old-style Italian food is served here in a West Village brownstone with a garden. The large dining room has exposed-brick walls and—eureka!—well-spaced tables. Try the linguine with lobster, roast pork loin in chianti-and-sage sauce, or veal Milanese topped with tomatoes and arugula. *133 W. 13th St., West Village, 212/741–3663. AE, DC, D, MC, V. Closed Sun. No lunch. Subway: 14th St. $$$*

7 *f-8*

MEZZALUNA

This bustling trattoria drew the in crowd in the '80s. The crowd is less fly today, but the food is just as good. As the name suggests, the decor is celestial, with a cloud-painted ceiling sprinkled with half-moons. Alas, the seating is not so airy; diners sit shoulder-to-shoulder and listen to ear-blasting music. The limited menu includes beef carpaccio with a choice of fixings, main pasta courses that change daily, vegetable and herb pizzas from wood-burning ovens, and cheese, fruit, or sorbet for dessert. *1295 3rd Ave. (between 74th and 75th Sts.), Upper East Side, 212/535–9600. Reservations not accepted. No credit cards. Subway: 68th St. $$*

11 *d-4*

MEZZOGIORNO

From the owners of the miniscule Mezzaluna comes another trendy, very Italian trattoria, this one with a bit more breathing room. Count on an excellent array of carpaccios, thin-crusted brick-oven pizzas (at lunchtime and late at night), pastas, salads, and a great tiramisu for dessert. You can also dine at the long, marble-topped bar. *195 Spring St. (at Sullivan St.), SoHo, 212/334–2112. AE. $$*

11 *e-4*
MONZÙ

Monzù is a corruption of *monsieur*, which is what Sicilians called the French chefs who arrived on their island with King Ferdinand's court after Napoleon invaded Naples in 1798. The resulting cuisine, along with traditional Sicilian peasant dishes of Sicily, is now served beneath the Guggenheim Museum–SoHo in a large basement attractively done up in dark red with wicker chairs, hanging lanterns, and tilted mirrors. Try the antipasto, monkfish-liver pâté, sea urchins on toast with baby chives, foie gras with figs and blood-orange sauce, and pan-roasted quail with figs. *142 Mercer St. (at Prince St.), SoHo, 212/343–0333. AE, DC, MC, V. Brunch weekends. Subway: Prince St.; Bleecker St./Broadway–Lafayette St. $$$*

9 *e-8*
NOVITA

Innovative Italian cooking in a minimalist setting sums up this comfortable, largely yellow Flatiron haunt, lit with Murano glass sconces. It's a favorite with Elite models, who can be seen tucking into red snapper, handmade pasta, and breast of duck with Barolo sauce, pine nuts, and pomegranate seeds. Have the warm chocolate tart for dessert. *102 E. 22nd St., Gramercy, 212/677–2222. AE, DC, MC, V. No lunch weekends. Subway: 23rd St. $$$*

9 *c-4*
ORSO

This casual northern-Italian trattoria on Restaurant Row garners raves for pre- and post-theater pastas, thin-crust pizzas, and tasty grilled entrées. The open kitchen adds to the convivial atmosphere. After the curtain falls, Broadway's show-biz crowd fills the bar and the vaulted, whitewashed, skylit back room. *322 W. 46th St., Theater District, 212/489–7212. MC, V. Subway: 42nd St. $$*

9 *d-4*
PALIO

Wrapped by a striking mural of the Siena Palio by Sandro Chia, the bar at this posh Italian restaurant is the place to be, and you can grab a bite here if you wish. But if you must *dine*, take the elevator to the second-floor dining room, where worn leather banquettes and wood-grained walls make you feel like you're sitting in a boardroom. Though exorbitantly priced, the food is good. Homemade pastas, perfect risottos, seafood, meat, and game dishes recall fine restaurants in northern Italy and are priced to match. *Equitable Center, 151 W. 51st St. Midtown, 212/245–4850. Reservations essential. AE, DC, MC, V. Subway: 49th St.; 47th–50th Sts./Rockefeller Center. $$$$*

7 *e-7*
PARIOLI ROMANISSIMO

Housed in a turn-of-the-century brownstone, this long-standing, luxurious restaurant serves good northern-Italian dishes to a rich and famous clientele. Regulars love the veal and pasta dishes, which some say are unequaled in the city, and the doting, formal service. *24 E. 81st St., Upper East Side, 212/288–2391. Reservations essential. AE, DC, MC, V. Closed Sun. and Mon. Subway: 86th St. $$$$*

9 *d-3*
REMI

The elegant, two-story dining room, dominated by a spectacular mural of Venice and boldly striped banquettes, make dining on Venetian pastas, beef carpaccio, risottos, and wonderful vegetable antipasto even more pleasant. The bar serves far and away the best Bellinis in town. Remi-to-Go, in a glass-enclosed passageway next to the restaurant, serves breakfast and light lunch. *145 W. 53rd St., Midtown, 212/581–4242. Reservations essential. AE, MC, V. Subway: 5th Ave./53rd St. $$$*

11 *d-8*
ROSEMARIE'S

This cozy and comfortable neighborhood trattoria is frequented by artists and Wall Street execs. Good bets are pasta (pappardelle with porcini, tomato, and cream; gnocchi with shrimp), seared tuna with couscous, and osso buco, followed by tiramisu for dessert. *145 Duane St. (between W. Broadway and Church St.), Tribeca, 212/285–2610. AE,*

MC, V. Closed Sun. Subway: Chambers St. $$$

9 *d-3*

SAN DOMENICO NY

Possibly New York's most ambitious Italian restaurant, San Domenico serves beautifully presented traditional and innovative Italian cuisine in luxuriously elegant surroundings. A new chef, known for her homemade pastas, has lightened the menu, but the signature raviolo (with ricotta, egg yolk, butter, Parmesan, and white truffles) is still available. Game is also a specialty. Prices are very high. *240 Central Park S, Midtown, 212/265–5959. Reservations essential. AE, DC, MC, V. Subway: 59th St./Columbus Circle. $$$$*

9 *c-3*

TRATTORIA DELL'ARTE

The amusing decor—oversized proboscises and other body parts—and the lively, upbeat attitude of this casual trattoria make it a best bite pre- or post–Carnegie Hall. Portions, like the noses on the wall, are huge. Antipasto platters for two; thin-crust pizzas; pastas (available in half portions); grilled meats and fish; and other Italian fare are all well prepared. *900 7th Ave. (at 57th St.), Midtown, 212/245–9800. AE, MC, V. Reservations essential. Subway: 57th St. $$$*

10 *e-8*

VIVOLO

This place serves simple, old-fashioned Italian food in a handsome, century-old brownstone with two working fireplaces. You have your choice of atmosphere—dark and clubby downstairs; high, frescoed ceilings upstairs—but either scene is romantic. The friendly service and well-priced early-bird dinner keep the locals coming. *140 E. 74th St., Upper East Side, 212/737–3533. AE, DC, MC, V. Closed Sun. No lunch Sat. Subway: 68th St./Hunter College. $$*

JAPANESE

11 *d-4*

BLUE RIBBON SUSHI

Blue Ribbon Sushi serves excellent fresh sushi and sashimi—with creative twists such as filet-mignon sushi and a delicious lobster hand roll—as well as a decent selection of sake . The waitstaff is efficient, and the decor is stylish Japa-

nese. Be prepared to wait for a table. *119 Sullivan St. (between Spring and Prince Sts.), SoHo, 212/343–0404. Reservations not accepted. AE, MC, V. Closed Mon. No lunch. Subway: Spring St.; Prince St. $$*

11 *f-1*

HASAKI

Wonderfully fresh and artfully presented sushi is your reward for waiting eons for a table. Don't be deterred; the results are worth it, especially if you give the sushi chef the green light to surprise you. *210 E. 9th St., East Village, 212/473-3327. Reservations not accepted. AE, MC, V. No lunch. Subway: Astor Pl. $$*

9 *e-4*

HATSUHANA

While higher marks go to the original (48th St.) for atmosphere and consistency, sushi connoisseurs know that both of these pricey bars are tops in town—that's why they wait so long. The teriyaki isn't bad, either, especially with one of the menu's several Japanese beers. *17 E. 48th St., Midtown, 212/355–3345. Subway: 51st St. Reservations not accepted. AE, DC, MC, V. No lunch Sun. $$*

9 *e-4*

237 Park Ave., Midtown, 212/661–3400. Subway: 42nd St./Grand Central.

11 *e-4*

HONMURA AN

Honmura An is the best place in town for authentic Japanese noodle dishes (which, traditionally, must be slurped). The restaurant makes its own soba noodles daily; you can watch a chef at work in a glassed-in room at the back. Try the seasonal tasting menu and the giant prawn tempura. The dining room, on the second floor of a SoHo warehouse, is spacious and comfortable. *170 Mercer St. (between Prince and Houston Sts.), 212/334–5253. Reservations essential. AE, DC, MC, V. Closed Mon. No lunch Sun. or Tues. Subway: Prince St.; Spring St.; Bleecker St./Broadway–Lafayette St. $$$*

7 *f-8*

ITCHO

It may appear to be a simple room on the Upper East Side, but don't let the atmosphere (or lack thereof) fool you. Look around and you'll see mostly Japanese diners enjoying plates of fresh sushi and other delights—the surest seal of approval. *402 E. 78th St., Upper*

East Side, 212/517–5340. AE, MC, V.
Closed Mon. Subway: 77th St. $$

10 e-1

JAPONICA

This restaurant is always so busy that
you know the sushi is fresh. The sizable
menu—which includes sushi, sashimi,
tempura, and teriyaki—has something
to please every Japanese-food lover. If
you can't decide, economical combo
plates offer a taste of several different
dishes. Be prepared to wait. 90 Univer-
sity Pl. (at 11th St.), Greenwich Village,
212/243–7752. Reservations not accepted.
AE. Subway: Union Sq. $

11 c-7

NOBU

Nobu is one of New York's most exciting
restaurants, and getting a reservation
here can be a frustrating experience. But
the food is sensational, reflecting chef
Nobu Matsuhisa's time in Latin Amer-
ica—think "unusual use of chilis." Try
the glazed black cod, the yellow-tail
sashimi, squid ceviche, or the tartare of
toro (tuna belly), and tuna salad with
ponzu sauce. Best of all, put yourself in
the hands of the chef—but be prepared
to pay. If you can't get a reservation, go
anyway and you will probably be seated
at the sushi bar, which is a show in itself.

FIRESIDE ROMANCE

Romance can be hard enough to find in
New York, let alone a working fireplace.
If you've found the first, here's where
they throw a log on:

Arizona 206 & Café (Southwestern)
Southwestern cuisine in a casual-rustic
Upper East Side setting.

Savoy (American)
This charming and elegant nook on the
edge of SoHo keeps three fires burning
for you.

Verbena (American)
The flickering light is the ornamenta-
tion for this zen-like room.

Vivolo (Italian)
In a late-1800s brownstone, fireplaces
warm both the dimly-lit downstairs and
the frescoed upstairs.

Ye Waverly Inn (American)
Ye olde quaintest tavern in the city, in
the West Village.

---

105 Hudson St. (at Franklin St.), Tribeca,
212/219–0500. Reservations essential. AE,
DC, MC, V. No lunch weekends. Subway:
Franklin St. $$$$

9 d-3

SERYNA

Seryna is a beautiful, serene spot in
Midtown with very good non-sushi Japa-
nese food. Especially popular is the
kobe beef steak (ishiyaki), grilled on a
hot stone at your table and served with
two dipping sauces (accompanied by
french fries!). The shabu-shabu (a sort of
fondue) gets raves. 11 E. 53rd St., Mid-
town, 212/980–9393. AE, DC, MC, V.
Closed Sun. No lunch Sat. Subway: 5th
Ave./53rd St. $$$

11 h-1

TAKAHACHI

The best sushi bargain in town, this no-
frills East Villager in always packed with
a young crowd, hungry for swimmingly
fresh slabs of yellowtail, tuna, and
salmon. Don't expect anything unusual,
and don't demand too much of the frenzied waitstaff; just pray they're not out
of sea urchin. Prepare for a wait. 85 Ave.
A (between 5th and 6th Sts.), East Village,
212/505–6524. No lunch. AE, MC, V. Subway: Astor Place. $

9 e-8

YAMA

Yama is the place to take anyone who
insists that sushi isn't filling. These
huge slabs of sushi and sashimi literally
fall off the plate. Moreover, the fish is
always fresh, tender, and delicious. The
drawbacks are the inevitable wait outdoors and the nonexistent decor. The
original store, on 17th Street, is the one
to hit; the new Houston Street outpost
doesn't measure up. 122 E. 17th St.,
Gramercy, 212/475–0969. Subway: 14th
St./Union Sq. Reservations not accepted.
AE, MC, V. Closed Sun. No lunch Sat. $$

11 d-3

92 W. Houston St. (between LaGuardia
Pl. and Thompson St.), 212/674–0935.
Subway: Broadway–Lafayette St.

KOREAN

11 h-1

DOK SUNI

This tiny storefront has a small, dark
dining room with just a dozen tables,

piped-in rock music, and pleasant service. It serves homestyle Korean cooking—fresh, simple, and, of course, spicy, but never greasy or heavy. The kimchi and spicy broiled pork ribs are great. *119 1st Ave. (between 7th and 8th Sts.), East Village, 212/477–9506. Reservations not accepted. No credit cards. No lunch. Subway: Astor Pl.; 2nd Ave. $*

9 *e-6*

HANGAWI

Everything but the kimchi is bound to baffle the uninitiated in this serene dining room, where you sit shoeless at a sunken table under dark-wood beams. Hangawi specializes in vegetarian Korean mountain cooking, whatever that is; the only way to start is to order a prix-fixe "Emperor's Meal," which translates loosely into a parade of exotic vegetable dishes that are at worst interesting and at best delicious. There are no fewer than ten courses, several of which you may have to assemble yourself; and by the time you hit the last, one your table will be covered with about 20 little bowls of unidentifiable but delicious things. If only the waitstaff could translate the names of the rare wild herbs into English . . .Try one of the many teas—date and citrus are wonderful—and the milky-white Korean sake. *12 E. 32nd St., Garment District, 212/213–0077. AE, MC, V. Reservations essential. Subway: 34th St./Herald Sq.; 33rd St. $$*

KOSHER

10 *g-3*

RATNER'S DAIRY RESTAURANT

This famous kosher-dairy Jewish restaurant offers an extensive range of well-prepared dishes—vegetable goulash, assorted soups, matzo brie, stuffed cabbage, blintzes, mushroom cutlets, and baked stuffed fish. The waiters are straight from Central Casting, and the chef has a traditional heavy hand with the salt. Sundays are hectic. Oddly enough, the back room was recently turned into a tragically hip cocktail lounge with a similar menu and an extensive martini selection; needless to say, it attracts a different sort of Lower East Side crowd. *138 Delancey St. (between Norfolk and Suffolk Sts.), Lower East Side, 212/677–5588. AE, MC, V. Subway: Delancey St. $*

7 *f-7*

TRASTEVERE 83/ TRASTEVERE 84

Two tiny, romantic, candlelit settings showcase the Lattanzi family's hearty (and kosher) Roman specialties. *Pollo alla romana*, veal piccante, and capellini primavera are among the favorites. The wine list is kosher as well. *309 E. 83rd St., Upper East Side, 212/734–6343. Reservations essential. AE. Closed Friday. Subway: 86th St. $$*

7 *e-7*

155 E. 84th St., Upper East Side, 212/744-0210. Subway: 86th St.

7 *f-8*

BISSALEH CLASSIC

This kosher dairy restaurant caters to an Upper East Side crowd, tempting them with the exotic flavors of Egypt and the Middle East. The cool setting is decorated with modern art. Huge portions of terrific hummus and fish appeal to all locals, kosher and otherwise; house specialties include *malwahs*, Yemenite flat bread baked with items such as feta cheese and vegetables. Dessert is more exciting elsewhere. *1435 2nd Ave. (between 74th and 75th Sts.), Upper East Side, 212/717–2333. MC, V. Closed sundown Friday–sundown Saturday. Subway: 77th St. $$*

LATIN

9 *c-3*

BISTRO LATINO

As you climb the narrow, worn staircase to this hidden, second-floor restaurant, you may wonder what you're getting yourself into; after all, you're not that far from Times Square. Rest assured: behind the door is a fun-filled evening of cool rhythms and hot food. Enjoy succulent seafood, ceviche, and paella as you tango and samba the night away; chef Raphael Palomino's contemporary interpretations of South American classics will dance on your tongue. It's part kitsch, part Havana, and all enjoyable. *1711 Broadway (at 54th St.), Midtown, 212/956–1000. AE, D, DC, MC, V. Closed Mon. in Aug. Subway: 57th St. $$*

9 *e-8*

PATRIA

This festive, elegant Flatiron hot spot serves up creative and scrumptious *nuevo latino* fare to excite even the most jaded tongue. Sip a *mojito*, order some plantain chips and salsa, and survey chef Doug Rodriguez's exciting menu. Start with the fire-and-ice, a tuna ceviche, or the super-spicy clam tamale, then move on to the whole red snapper, or the exceptional Patria pork. Be warned that the zing of the flavors is addictive, and that zing costs a helluva lot more than rice and beans. *250 Park Ave. S. (at 20th St.), 212/777–6211. Reservations essential. AE, MC, V. Subway: N, R, 6 to 23rd St. $$$*

9 *c-3*
VICTOR'S CAFE 52
Victor was the pioneer purveyor of Cuban cuisine and atmosphere in his longtime café on Columbus. He's now been firmly ensconced in the Theater District for years, serving hearty paella, *ropa vieja*, grilled pork chops, black bean soup, fried bananas, and strong Cuban coffee, among other delicacies. Nightly entertainment adds to the fun. *236 W. 52nd St., Theater District, 212/586–7714. AE, DC, MC, V. Closed Sun. Subway: 50th St. $$*

MALAYSIAN

11 *g-5*
NYONYA
Filled with Malaysians, which inspires confidence, this noisy and often hectic restaurant serves good food at very low prices. Try the oriental sesame rolls or a whole deep-fried fish. *194 Grand St. (at Mott St.), Little Italy/Chinatown, 212/343–8899. No credit cards. Subway: Grand St.; Spring St.; Bowery. $*

1 *f-3*
PENANG
There are now three Manhattan outposts of this fabulous Flushing restaurant; would that the food at any of them were as good as the original. For an authentic Malaysian experience, make the trip to Queens. Don't miss the coconut shrimp, or the pull-apart roti appetizer with a fragrant chicken-curry dipping sauce. The whole fish and homemade Malaysian noodles are also good. The Manhattan stores, alas, are merely cheap places to eat with attitudinal service and okay food. *38-04 Prince St., Flushing, Queens, 718/321–2078. Reservations not accepted. AE, MC, V. Subway: 7 to Main St./Flushing. $*

7 *f-7*
1596 2nd Ave. (at 83rd St.), Upper East Side, 212/585–3838. Subway: 86th St.

11 *e-5*
109 Spring St. (between Greene and Mercer Sts.), SoHo, 212/274–8883. Subway: Spring St.

9 *b-1*
240 Columbus Ave. (at 71st St.), Upper West Side, 212/769–3988. Subway: 72nd St.

MEDITERRANEAN

9 *d-3*
ESTIATORIO MILOS
The soaring ceilings and stark, neoclassical decor of this new, Greek seafood restaurant at once evoke Santorini, the Acropolis, and a chic Manhattan club. The fish (on display for you to choose, near the open kitchen) is so fresh, you can almost smell the Mediterranean. The special appetizer of paper-thin slices of eggplant and zucchini, fried with saganaki cheese and served with a tzatziki dipping sauce, set the tone for the light, flavorful fare to come. The octopus salad and fried calamari are unbelievably tender. An authentic Greek salad (no lettuce) comes garnished with creamy, goat's milk feta cheese and plump kalamata olives. Gently grilled fish with a drizzle of olive oil and a squirt of lemon is the climax of the ethereal experience. *125 W. 55th St., Midtown, 212/245–7400. AE, DC, MC, V. Subway: 57th St. $$$*

11 *c-8*
SPARTINA
Chef and owner Stephen Kalt has created a relaxed haven in ultrachic Tribeca with this comfortable, unpretentious Mediterranean restaurant; it feels like it's been here forever. The tasty food makes up for the occasionally too-casual service. Try the delicious pizzas, lamb shank Catalan, or black linguini with stewed calamari and chorizo. *355 Greenwich St. (at Harrison St.), Tribeca, 212/274–9310. AE, MC, V. Subway: Franklin St. $$*

MEXICAN

`10` c-1

BENNY'S BURRITOS

For cheap and cheerful Tex/Mex on either end of the Village, head over to cramped and rowdy Benny's, ever popular with the budget crowd. Lava lights, formica, and a jukebox with period tunes form a retro backdrop for the humongous, foot-long burritos. Beware: finish the whole thing and you'll suffer. *113 Greenwich St. (at Jane St.), West Village, 212/633–9210. No reservations. No credit cards. Subway: A, C, E to 14th St. $*

`11` h-1

93 Ave. A (at 6th St.), East Village, 212/254–2054.

`7` b-6

GABRIELA'S

It's not the quietest place, and the service isn't always speedy, but you probably won't find better value at any other Mexican in Manhattan. The flavors are authentic, the corn tacos are fresh, and the *posole* may be the most satisfying soup you've ever tried. The roasted chicken and pork are pretty good, too. Expect an extended wait for a table during peak hours; defuse the waiting experience with a margarita or sangria. *685 Amsterdam Ave. (at 93rd St.), Upper West Side, 212/961–0574. AE, MC, V. Subway: 96th St. $*

`10` c-1

MI COCINA

Authentic regional Mexican cooking (no spicy baby-food pap here) is served here in cramped but convivial surroundings. Try the tamales steamed in Swiss chard; empanadas with beef, raisins, and olives; or shrimp in adobo sauce. *57 Jane St. (at Hudson St.), West Village, 212/627–8273. AE, DC, MC, V. No lunch. Brunch Sun. Subway: 14th St.; Christopher St./Sheridan Sq. $$*

`9` f-3

ROSA MEXICANO

Many hold this festive upscale Mexican restaurant in high esteem, and not only for its wonderful guacamole and signature pomegranate margaritas. The menu features mildly spiced regional dishes, including flaming fajitas served tableside. Try the lamb shank steamed in a parchment pouch with three chilis, or beef tenderloin. *1063 1st Ave. (at 58th St.), Midtown, 212/753–7407. AE, DC, MC, V. Subway: 59th St. $$$*

`9` f-4

ZARELA

Zarela's is one of the more popular spots for "gourmet" Mexican. Renowned Mexican chef Zarela Martinez showcases her zesty, authentic home cooking in an even zestier environment. If you'd rather skip the fiesta atmosphere, opt for the quieter dining area upstairs. *953 2nd Ave. (between 50th and 51st Sts.), Midtown, 212/644–6740. Reservations essential. AE, DC, MC, V. No lunch weekends. Subway: 51st St./Lexington–3rd Aves. $$*

MIDDLE EASTERN

`11` d-7

LAYLA

Layla looks like a Middle East nightspot, with Moroccan tiles and dioramas of belly dancers and pashas (a real-life belly dancer appears once nightly). North African cooking is reinterpreted here, with great success. Try the *meze* (appetizers), including feathery *borek* (phyllo dough filled with sharp feta cheese), fresh sardines, octopus salad, and dips served with pita. The lamb kebabs glazed with pomegranate and the pigeon in vine leaves are also worthwhile. *211 W. Broadway (at Franklin St.), Tribeca, 212/431–0700. AE, DC, MC, V. No lunch. Subway: Franklin St. $$$*

PAN-ASIAN

`10` e-1

MIREZI

The food in this elegant, futuristically decorated restaurant is both comfortable and sophisticated—representing well the sort of eclectic Asian cooking (here, a combination of Korean, Vietnamese, Thai, and Japanese) that didn't exist in the U.S. ten years ago. Try the grilled eggplant folded into a maki roll; the pan-fried beef-and-tofu dumplings; or the Korean barbecued baby-back ribs, falling off the bone. The homemade ice creams are excellent, as is the molten chocolate cake with a dark-chocolate sauce. There is an interesting and well-chosen wine list as well as a wide range of beers. *59 5th Ave. (at 13th St.), Greenwich Village, 212/242–9709. AE, MC, V. Closed Sun. No lunch. $$*

7 *f-8*

ORIENTA

It feels like a SoHo bistro, but this small crowd-pleaser is definitely Uptown, and definitely not a bistro. The kitchen turns out creative and well-presented Thai-Vietnamese cooking for a beautiful crowd that actually comes to eat. Amber lighting and large windows along the street soften the cramped quarters. *205 E. 75th St., Upper East Side, 212/517–7509. Reservations essential. AE, DC, V. No lunch. Subway: 77th St. $$*

11 *h-1*

O.G. (ORIENTAL GRILL)

The decor is minimal: Japanese light fixtures on peach walls (so far as we could tell in the dim lighting), dark-blue banquettes, brown-paper tablecloths, and votive candles. The clever combinations of oriental techniques and ingredients—Japanese, Thai, Chinese, and Indonesian—mean that each dish is well-conceived, not forced or bizarre (despite what you might think about banana wontons flambé). *507 E. 6th St., East Village, 212/477–4649. V, MC. No lunch. Subway: 2nd Ave. $*

7 *c-7*

RAIN

Rain feels like a post-college party on weekend nights, but the food at this contemporary Pan-Asian is skillfully prepared and delicious. The menu reads like the greatest hits of Thai, Vietnamese, and Malaysian cooking. Appetizers of green-papaya salad and summer rolls wrapped in rice paper are cool and refreshing. The coconut chicken soup tastes like the real McCoy. For the main course, try the stir-fried beef in peanut sauce or the Chinese eggplant in bean sauce. Nothing disappoints, though some dishes are more authentic than others. Wash it all down with one of many Asian beers. *100 W. 82nd St., Upper West Side, 212/501–0776. AE, DC, MC, V. Subway: 79th St. $$*

9 *e-8*

REPUBLIC

Republic is noisy, crowded, and doesn't take reservations unless you're having a good-sized party. But it's fun, with a sleek, spare, neo-warehouse design and long, polished, blond-wood tables for food-sharing. This is essentially a sophisticated noodle house. Try curried chicken on skewers; spicy seafood salad; noodle dishes, including curried duck in chicken broth with taro chips; shrimp wontons in chicken broth; and *pad thai*. For dessert, the coconut ice cream is divine. *37 Union Sq. W (between 16th and 17th Sts.), Flatiron, 212/627–7172. AE, DC, MC, V. Subway: 14th St./Union Sq. $*

7 *b-7*

2290 Broadway (between 82nd and 83rd Sts.), Upper West Side, 212/579–5959. Subway: 79th St.

PIZZA

11 *d-3*

ARTURO'S PIZZERIA

Serving what many consider the best coal-oven pizza in town, Arturo's is a popular choice for those who can't get into Lombardi's. Live music starts nightly at 6 PM, and the setting is fun and timeless, if somewhat decrepit. *106 Houston St. (at Thompson St.), West Village, 212/677–3820. AE, MC, V. No lunch. Subway: Houston St.; Broadway–Lafayette St. $*

11 *c-3*

JOE'S PIZZA

If all you want is a slice of thin, crisp New York pizza at its best, drop into Joe's. A sprinkling of hot pepper flakes, garlic powder, oregano, and parmesan cheese will make you think you've died and gone to heaven. Find a place to indulge; there's no seating here. *7 Carmine St. (at Bleecker St.), West Village, 212/255–3946. No reservations. No credit cards. Subway: W. 4th St. $*

11 *c-2*

JOHN'S PIZZERIA

As far as purists are concerned, this longtime Village pizzeria serves the city's only real pizza, baked in stone-floor ovens—thin-crusted, garlicky, and topped with fresh ingredients. Devour your pie (you can't order by the slice) amid old-fashioned, red-check tablecloths, celebrity photos, and painted murals of Italy. The bar serves beer and wine. *278 Bleecker St. (between 6th and 7th Aves.), West Village, 212/243–1680.*

No reservations. No credit cards. Subway: W. 4th St./Washington Sq. $

9 *c-2*

48 W. 65th St., Upper West Side, 212/721–7001. Subway: 66th St./Lincoln Ctr.

9 *c-5*

260 W. 44th St., Theater District, 212/391–7560. Subway: 42nd St./Times Sq.

9 *f-2*

408 E. 64th St, Upper East Side, 212/935–2895. Subway: 68th St./Hunter College.

11 *f-5*

LOMBARDI'S

One of New York's original pizza-making families, the Lombardis have become synonymous with delicious coal-oven pizza. The secret is in the crust, which, according to finicky pizza lovers, has more flavor here than anywhere else. The best salad in any pizza joint and a comfortable, casual atmosphere make the experience a must. *32 Spring St. (between Mott and Mulberry Sts.), Little Italy, 212/941–7994. No reservations. No credit cards. Subway: 6 to Spring St.; Broadway–Lafayette St. $*

9 *e-8*

LA PIZZA FRESCA

Count on this find opposite the glitzy Gramercy Tavern for powerfully flavored pastas and risottos, huge arugula salads sparkling in a dressing of good olive oil and fresh lemon juice, and pizzas whose thin, crisp crusts are blistered and savory from the wood fire in the beehive brick oven at the back of the room. With the wood fire casting its glow on the rear tables and the sponged ochre walls, warm and mellow are the operative words here; La Pizza Fresca is particularly soothing at the end of a long day, or after a movie at the Loews 19th Street Theatre. Moreover, the prices are noticeably reasonable, even if the mostly young waitstaff often needs a gentle nudge. *31 E. 20th St., Flatiron, 212/598–0141. AE, DC, MC, V. No lunch Sun. Subway: 6, N, R to 23rd St. $$*

7 *e-8*

SOFIA FABULOUS PIZZA

There is a full menu at this hip Italian eatery, but pizza is definitely the focus. The menu claims that the water used in the dough is filtered to resemble the water of Naples, but whatever the reason, the pizzas are thin, crispy, and full of flavor. The restaurant occupies the top two floors of a Madison Avenue building, but in summer the ceiling retracts to form a lovely terrace; if you're lucky, you'll sit out here. The hand-painted walls and terra-cotta floors add to the Italian look, as do the Italian accents, which start to fill the restaurant at about 9 PM. *1022 Madison Ave. (at 79th St.), Upper East Side, 212/734–2676. No reservations accepted. AE, DC, MC, V. Subway: 77th St. $*

PORTUGUESE

7 *b-7*

LUZIA'S

Though recently expanded, this neighborhood restaurant has maintained its mom-and-pop charm. Classic dishes such as *caldo verde* (potato and kale soup) and *bacalhau* (salt cod with potatoes and eggs) mingle well with Luzia's other home cooking, such as white-bean salad and peppery chicken legs. Don't miss the flan for dessert. *429 Amsterdam Ave. (between 80th and 81st Sts.), Upper West Side, 212/595–2000. Reservations not accepted. No credit cards. Subway: 86th St. $$*

RUSSIAN

9 *c-4*

FIREBIRD

Prerevolutionary indulgence is the name of the game at this lush dining spot on Restaurant Row, where all of the classics—blini, smoked salmon, caviar, borscht, champagne, frozen vodka—are in fine form. Of the myriad *zakuski* (appetizers), the walnut and chicken *satsivi*, a shredded specialty of Georgia, is particularly good. Other appetizers include baked noodles with poppy seeds, and lamb dumplings with minted sour cream. The entrées run the gamut from a light grilled sturgeon with mustard sauce to a hefty portion of roast goose. Desserts are something of a disappointment, and the service is spotty, but you can't help being pleased, as you sit among the ornate antiques, with the general authenticity. *365 W. 46th St., Theater District, 212/586–0244. AE, D, DC, MC, V. Subway: 42nd St./Times Sq. $$$*

11 *f-4*
PRAVDA
Another lively creation of Keith (Balthazar) McNally (*see above*), Pravda serves 65 different vodkas along with blinis and caviar, French fries wrapped in Russian newspaper, and *zakuski* (appetizers) such as *pirozki* with spinach and cheese or a smoked-fish platter. Popular entrées include chicken Kiev and beef stroganoff. The scene is fun, with some of the most beautiful people in town. *281 Lafayette St. (between Houston and Prince Sts.), SoHo, 212/226–4696. Reservations essential. AE, MC, V. No lunch. Subway: Bleecker St./Broadway–Lafayette St.; Prince St. $$*

SCANDINAVIAN

9 *d-3*
AQUAVIT
This handsome two-level townhouse (formerly owned by Nelson Rockefeller) is the perfect setting for the elegant food of wunderkind Swedish chef Marcus Samuelsson. The more formal dining room, downstairs, offers an array of Swedish specialties (including smoked fish and herring) and some innovative seafood and meat dishes. The soaring atrium and soothing waterfall make the evening relaxing and memorable. Upstairs, the more casual and less expensive bar and café offer lighter fare: Danish open sandwiches, Swedish meatballs, smorgasbord plates, and a variety of aquavits. Aquavit has been called the finest Scandinavian restaurant in the country, though admittedly the competition is not stiff. *13 W. 54th St., Midtown, 212/307–7311. Reservations essential. AE, MC, V. Closed Sun. Subway: 5th Ave./53rd St. $$$*

9 *d-3*
CHRISTER'S
A native Swede, chef Christer Larsson has a flair for seafood, particularly the cold-water fish of his homeland. In the urban lodge setting of his dining room—think Ralph Lauren meets Pee Wee's Playhouse—salmon cookery is elevated to an art form, and herring becomes a noble fish. Whether marinated with lime and ginger or simply cured with sugar and salt to make gravlax, the salmon never bores. Other fish are prepared with equal skill; the

dill pancakes with smoked arctic char have become a signature. Here, Swedish specialties such as *fricadelles* (veal meatballs served on mashed potatoes) have nothing in common with the sickeningly sweet hors d'oeuvres popular in the 1960s. For dessert, try the *pavlova,* an airy meringue confection that sends you floating out the door. *145 W. 55th St., Midtown, 212/974–7224. AE, DC, MC, V. Closed Sun. Subway: 57th St. $$$*

SEAFOOD

11 *c-3*
AQUA GRILL
This cheerful, yellow-and-blue, candlelit fish restaurant is casual and laid-back. It has a first-rate oyster bar and terrific fish dishes, with interesting combinations such as sautéed mussels and snails with potato hash and fried leeks, or grilled salmon in a lovely falafel crust with lemon-coriander vinaigrette. *210 Spring St. (at 6th Ave.), SoHo, 212/274–0505. Reservations essential. AE, MC, V. Closed Mon. Subway: Spring St. $$*

9 *e-8*
BLUE WATER GRILL
Into a former bank with marble floors comes this bustling fish restaurant with a terrific oyster bar and first-rate fish. Try the crab cakes, shrimp wonton, or blackened swordfish with salsa, and for dessert, the strawberry shortcake. Sunday brunch is accompanied by live jazz. *31 Union Sq. W. (between 16th and 17th Sts.), Flatiron, 212/675–9500. AE, MC, V. Subway: 14th St./Union Sq. $$*

7 *b-6*
DOCK'S OYSTER BAR & SEAFOOD GRILL
Both of these restaurants offer fresh, no-nonsense seafood in a stylish, casual, black-and-white setting. Best bites include fried oysters, fried clams, steamed lobsters, and crunchy cole slaw. Save room for the great desserts. *2427 Broadway (between 89th and 90th St.), Upper West Side, 212/724–5588. AE, D, DC, MC, V. Subway: 86th St. $$*

9 *f-5*
633 3rd Ave. (at 40th St.), Midtown, 212/986–8080. Subway: 42nd St./Grand Central.

9 d-4

LE BERNARDIN

See French, *above*.

7 b-8

MAD FISH

The convivial atmosphere and the reasonably priced menu of innovative seafood dishes keep this large, noisy restaurant packed well into the night. For starters, fried baby fish and watercress and squid salad will show you what the kitchen can do with flavor and texture combinations. Not everything on the menu is as it seems; when you order Fish and Chips, for instance, you get a piece of tempura-fried wolffish with a fried spring-roll "chip." Service can be slow, but that seems to be the risk of eating on the Upper West Side. *2182 Broadway (between 77th and 78th Sts.), Upper West Side, 212/787–0202. AE, DC, MC, V. Subway: 79th St. $$*

9 d-3

MANHATTAN OCEAN CLUB

Nothing is great at this Midtown seafood eatery, but the friendly service and contemporary atmosphere keep the dining room filled. Among the myriad dishes, the simplest are best: crab cakes, swordfish en brochette, and blackened redfish, for instance. The wine list is substantial. Don't expect to be out quickly; although congenial, the staff will keep you waiting. *57 W. 58th St., Midtown, 212/371–7777. AE, DC, MC, V. Subway: 57th St. $$$*

9 e-3

OCEANA

Chef Rick Moonen has created the ultimate fish restaurant, right down to the decor: The dining room feels like a private yacht. Nothing on the menu—crab cakes, lobster ravioli, bouillabaisse—disappoints. It's pricey, but most who take the plunge come out knowing that it was worth every penny. *55 E. 54th St., Midtown, 212/759–5941. Reservations essential. AE, MC, V. Closed Sun. Subway: 5th Ave./53rd St. $$$*

9 e-5

OYSTER BAR & RESTAURANT

After a serious fire left part of the dining room under reconstruction, a new chef has breathed life into a spot frequented mainly by commuters and tourists. This Grand Central Station landmark, opened in 1915, claims it serves the most seafood in the world. Go for the wide selection of fresh oysters (flown in daily), six versions of clam chowder, oyster po' boys, and grilled fresh fish. Wines and desserts are equally various. You can sit at the old-fashioned lunch counter or in the dining room proper. *Grand Central Terminal, lower level, 42nd St. at Madison Ave., Midtown, 212/490–6650. AE, DC, MC, V. Closed weekends. Subway: 42nd St./Grand Central. $$*

9 d-4

SEA GRILL

This elegant Rockefeller Center restaurant was designed to draw the sophisticated New Yorker as well as the tourist. The view of the skating rink ensures the happiness of the latter, and chef Ed Brown's cooking takes care of the locals. Although many lay similar claims, Brown's Maryland crab cakes may well be the best in the city. The other seafood options, some classic, some contemporary, aren't bad, either. The wine list is excellent. Complimentary parking is available at the Rockefeller Center Garage from Monday to Saturday after 5:30 PM. *19 W. 49th St., Midtown, 212/246–9201. Reservations essential. AE, DC, MC, V. Closed Sun. Subway: 47th–50th Sts./Rockefeller Center. $$$*

SOUL

6 c-6

COPELAND'S

Though Sylvia's gets all the publicity, many insider's believe this is the only place in Harlem for authentic soul food. From fried chicken to smothered pork chops to ribs, Copeland's has everything your heart desires (especially cholesterol). Put on your best hat for the Sunday Gospel Brunch and dig in. *547 W. 145th St., Harlem, 212/234–2357. AE, MC, V. Closed Mon. Subway: 145th St. $$*

7 d-1

SYLVIA'S

Sylvia Woods is known as the Queen of Soul Food, and her restaurant has been a Harlem institution for more than 30 years. Though there are probably better cooks, you shouldn't hesitate to head uptown for some of Sylvia's down-home Southern specialties, including her braised ribs, fried or smothered chicken with black-eyed peas, collard green, yams, sweet potato pie, and fresh-baked corn bread. Sunday brunch is served to the inspirational tunes of local gospel singers, and two jukeboxes add to the '50s flavor. *328 Lenox Ave. (at 126th St.), Harlem, 212/996–0660. Reservations not accepted. No credit cards. Subway: 125th St.* $

SOUTHERN

11 *e-2*

ACME BAR & GRILL

This funky, garage-like setting is "decorated" with bottles and labels from hot sauce. The homestyle food is well priced and tasty, sometimes tongue-searing. Southern specialties include steamed oysters, fried shrimp, blackened trout, oyster po'boys, grilled pork chops, catfish sandwiches, and sides of corn fritters, hush puppies, and black-eyed peas. *9 Great Jones St. (between Broadway and Lafayette St.), East Village, 212/420–1934. Reservations not accepted. No credit cards. Subway: Astor Pl.* $

9 *e-8*

CAFÉ BEULAH

Beulah has reinvented soul food in a charming setting that evokes a plantation dining room, complete with ceiling fans, old photographs, and creamy yellow walls. After your hearty encounter with country biscuits and corn bread, try the ham in praline bourbon sauce, gumbo, shrimp macaroni, or cheese casserole. For dessert, there's sweet-potato pie and fruit cobbler. *39 E. 19th Sts., Flatiron, 212/777–9700. AE, MC, DC, V. Subway: 23rd St.* $$

9 *c-4*

B. SMITH'S

Run by a model-turned-restaurateur-and-cookbook-author, B. Smith's is a stylish spot for traditional and contemporary Southern cookin' and some of the best people-watching in town. Make a point of the sweet-potato pie. *771 8th Ave. (at 47th St.), Theater District, 212/247–2222. AE, DC, MC, V. Subway: 50th St.* $$

SOUTHWESTERN

9 *f-2*

ARIZONA 206 & CAFÉ

East Siders have become loyal patrons of this Southwestern pair. The menu is inventive (tuna sushi is rolled in flat bread and drizzled with red chili oil and wasabi cream), and the setting is rustic chic. If you're not in the mood for the pricier back room, just order from the tapas-style menu in the café and bar. The fireplace adds to the charm. *206 E. 60th St., Upper East Side, 212/838–0440. AE, DC, MC, V. Subway: 59th St.* $$

9 *c-3*

TAPIKA

The award-winning design of this urban Southwestern is as fanciful as chef David Walzog's innovative cooking. This food is not for the timid. Chilis pop up everywhere, dusted on the fried cornmeal strips and whipped into the Caesar-salad dressing. Other temptations include tequila-cured salmon and vegetable-stuffed chili rellenos with smoked tomato salsa. Steak, pork, and other meats are grilled to perfection and come adorned with an exciting array of sides. The service is friendly, bordering on obtrusive. *950 8th Ave. (at 56th St.), Midtown, 212/397–3737. AE, DC, MC, V. Subway: 59th St./Columbus Circle.* $$$

SPANISH

9 *e-8*

BOLO

Chef Bobby Flay has drawn serious attention to this popular Flatiron restaurant. The food—particularly the lamb shanks and paella—is fine, the decor pretty, and the crowd, well, there. *23 E. 22nd St., Flatiron, 212/228–2200. Subway: N, R to 23rd St.* $$$

10 *c-1*

EL FARO

Redolent with garlic, this small, extremely popular West Villager been serving hearty portions of pungent Spanish food for over 30 years. The decor is appealingly kitschy. Be prepared to wait. *823 Greenwich St. (at Horatio St.), West Village, 212/929–8210. Reservations not accepted. AE, DC, MC, V. Subway: A, C, E to 14th St.* $$

11 *d-4*

ERIZO LATINO

This lively Latin restaurants looks like a Spanish Colonial hacienda and serves the kind of food that first emerged in South Florida. The chef makes liberal use of Hispanic root vegetables and seasonings, tropical fruits, and unusual seafoods. Meals are served tapas-style, in a variety of small dishes intended for sharing. *422 W. Broadway (between Spring and Prince Sts.), SoHo, 212/941–5811. AE, MC, V. Closed Sun. Subway: Spring St. $$*

11 *f-3*
IL BUCO
Il Buco is an antique shop by day, a Mediterranean restaurant by night. The dark, candlelit rooms looks like the setting for a film scene of bohemian Village life in the '50s. The menu consists of tapas, including vigorously seasoned baby eel and octopus; gutsy and very good saffron rice cakes (*arancini*); and grilled sea scallops with capers and olives. *47 Bond St. (betwen Lafayette St. and Bowery), 212/533–1932. Reservations essential. No credit cards. No lunch. Closed Mon. Subway: Bleecker St./Broadway–Lafayette St. $$*

9 *f-4*
MARICHU
Marichu's chef is a former diplomat. Having turned his attentions, he now turns out delicious Basque cooking—particularly seafood—with a contemporary presentation in a classy space. The satisfying combination has hooked those in the U.N. area, and the cheery atmosphere and back garden are helping this relative newcomer gain a wider audience. *342 E. 46th St., Midtown, 212/370–1866. Reservations essential. AE, MC, V. Closed Sun. Subway: 42nd St./Grand Central. $$*

9 *e-4*
PARADIS BARCELONA
This is the only foreign outpost of a Barcelona-based operation. Good Catalonian regional cuisine and a large selection of tapas are presented in a dining room that's distinctly spacious by New York standards. A good selection of Spanish wines and live piano music complete the Spanish mood. *145 E. 50th St., Midtown, 212/754–3333. AE, MC, V. No lunch Sat. Subway: 51st St./Lexington–3rd Aves. $$$$*

9 *f-3*
SOLERA
Authentic Spanish cooking is presented with heart and soul in this delightful little Midtown eatery. The food is seriously

good, and the following is accordingly fierce and loyal, despite the above-average prices for this light, Mediterranean fare. *216 E. 53rd St., Midtown, 212/644–1166. AE, MC, V. Closed Sun. Subway: 51st St./Lexington–3rd Aves. $$*

STEAK

7 *f-6*
DAN MAXWELL'S
If you're in the mood for a big New York steak but not big New York prices, this is the place for you. Rib, skirt, and strip steaks (or salmon and chicken, for the faint of heart) are served with your choice of potatoes and a salad for under $20 a person. Some say the fried onions are "the best ever." As in every steak house, gooey desserts are in order; the triple chocolate-mousse cake is a favorite. The atmosphere is Neighborhood, the service friendly and efficient. *1708 2nd Ave (between 88th and 89th Sts.), Upper East Side, 212/426–7688. AE, D, DC, MC, V. Subway: 86th St. $*

9 *b-8*
FRANK'S
This old Italian steak house opened in 1912 in the Gansevoort meatpacking district. Despite having moved from its original store, a block north, in the mid-1990s due to fire, the place still has plenty of character. Count on good steaks, surf 'n'turf, double-thick lamb chops, and giant salads. The cheesecake is terrific. *85 10th Ave. (at 15th St.), Chelsea, 212/243–1349. Reservations essential. AE, DC, MC, V. Closed Sun. Subway: 14th St. $$$*

10 *c-1*
OLD HOMESTEAD RESTAURANT
Open since 1868—which may be when they last redecorated—this is New York's oldest steak house, appropriately located in the meatpacking district. In addition to the steaks—which include a Japanese Kobe steak, at $100 a serving!—the menu offers generous portions of shrimp, lobster, and prime rib. *56 9th Ave. (between 14th and 15th Sts.), Chelsea, 212/242–9040. AE, DC, MC, V. Subway: A, C, E to 14th St. $$$*

9 *f-4*
PALM RESTAURANT
Sawdusted floors and caricatures on the walls create the nostalgic backdrop

for this very noisy, upbeat steak and lobster house. Once considered the best by many, the Palm has paled with time and the demands of managing its worldwide empire, but its history of famous and powerful famous clients (painted on the walls) still adds flavor to the high-quality steaks and enormous lobsters. Watch the bill add up—cottage fries, onion rings, and vegetables are all à la carte. If the restaurant is too crowded, go across the street to Palm Too. *837 2nd Ave. (between 44th and 45th Sts.), Midtown, 212/687–2953. Reservations essential. AE, DC, MC, V. No lunch weekends. Subway: 42nd St./Grand Central. $$$$*

1 *e-5*
PETER LUGER'S
No one really disputes the idea that this is the best steak you will ever eat. The setting is German beer hall—harsh lights, bare wood tables—rather than gentlemen's steak house, and you'll never see a menu; the friendly waiters know that all you want is shrimp cocktail, tomato-and-onion salad, home fries, creamed spinach, french fries, and a big, beautiful, dry-aged, perfectly cooked porterhouse steak big enough to feed everyone in your party. Save the steak sauce for the fresh onion rolls. If you have room left over, order the pecan pie or the cheesecake—both of which, in case you haven't had enough fat, come with a big bowl of *schlag* (whipped cream). If you arrive in a taxi, the restaurant's own car service will take you home. *178 Broadway (at Driggs Ave.), Williamsburg, Brooklyn, 718/387–7400. Reservations essential. No credit cards. Subway: J, M, Z to Marcy Ave. $$$*

9 *c-5*
PIETRO'S
Regulars still flock to this 50-year-old Italian steak house, now in relatively new quarters. Pietro's serves Italian veal, chicken, and pasta dishes, but is basically known for its porterhouse, served with delicious shoestring, Lyonnaise, or au gratin potatoes. The friendly staff is happy to modify almost anything on the menu to suit your tastes. *232 E. 43rd St., Midtown, 212/682–9760. Reservations essential. AE, DC, MC, V. Closed Sun. Closed Sat. in summer. No lunch Sat. Subway: 42nd St./Grand Central. $$$$*

9 *f-4*
SMITH & WOLLENSKY
Women beware: This is where Midtown business*men* enjoy steak. The clubby atmosphere and extensive wine list speak to a certain clientele that sometimes makes it difficult for women to get the best service. But the steak is well prepared and generous, and the side dishes are good. Limited non–red-meat selections are available, but you're better off eating elsewhere if you're looking for a light meal. Next door to the dining room is Wollensky's Grill, a bit cheaper. *201 E. 49th St., Midtown, 212/753–1530. Reservations essential. AE, DC, MC, V. No lunch weekends in dining room. Subway: 51st St./Lexington–3rd Aves. $$$–$$$$*

9 *f-4*
SPARK'S STEAK HOUSE
If you're missing a macho atmosphere, head over to this informal, clubby restaurant, well known for very fine steaks and lobsters that require a super-human appetite. The double lamb chops also draw raves. An excellent wine list has earned the restaurant several awards. *210 E. 46th St., Midtown, 212/687–4855. Reservations essential. AE, DC, MC, V. Closed Sun. No lunch Sat. Subway: 42nd St./Grand Central. $$$*

SWISS

11 *f-1*
ROETTELLE A. G.
Here's a charming find in (but not of) the East Village for a simple, inexpensive, satisfying Euromeal. German, Swiss, Italian, and French cooking are all represented nightly on the changing menu. Try the smoked, mustard-infused pork chop with spaetzle and red cabbage; the sautéed chicken breast with sun-dried tomatoes and hazelnuts; or the veal in mushroom cream sauce with wonderful Swiss-style *rösti* (potato pancakes). Try to get a seat in the trellised garden. *126 E. 7th St., 212/674–4140. MC, V. Closed Sun. Brunch Sat. Subway: 8th St.; Astor Pl. $$*

TEA

10 *e-1*
DANAL
Whether you're sitting on the sofa, at one of the country tables, or, in fine

weather, in the rear garden, tea in this throwback café is a special treat. The prix-fixe menu offers a selection of fine teas and coffees, dainty sandwiches, homemade scones, and pastries. Brunch is lovely as well. *90 E. 10th St., East Village, 212/982–6930. Reservations essential. AE, MC, V. Subway: 8th St.; Astor Pl.* $

10 *c-1*

TEA & SYMPATHY

This authentic little English tearoom looks rather like your quirky old aunt's apartment. When it isn't teatime, the food is traditional, hearty British fare. No one argues with the tea, but the long wait, cramped space, and worn decor leave some wanting. *108 Greenwich Ave. (between 12th and 13th Sts.), Greenwich Village, 212/807–8329. Reservations not accepted. AE, MC, V. Subway: A, C, E to 14th St.* $

THAI

7 *f-8*

BANGKOK HOUSE

The atmosphere is stark and somewhat dreary, but the restaurant is top-rated for authentic Thai fare, much of which sizzles. Try the "jungle curry," the pork in green curry, or the barbecued chicken (*gai yang*). Wash it down with something from the nice selection of Thai beer. *1485 1st Ave. (at 77th St.), Upper East Side, 212/249–5700. AE, DC, MC, V. No lunch.* $

9 *c-4*

PONGSRI THAI

You'll dine well on spicy Thai specialties both uptown, in the spacious Theater District quarters, or downtown, in the more spartan Chinatown shop. The coconut chicken soup, rich duck curry, and sticky rice are among the highlights. Be prepared to pay more for the same dishes uptown. *244 W. 48th St., Theater District, 212/582–3392. AE, DC, MC, V. Subway: 50th St.* $

11 *f-7*

106 Bayard St. (at Baxter St.), Chinatown, 212/349-3132. Subway: Canal St.

9 *c-8*

ROYAL SIAM

Royal Siam is one of the best restaurants in trendy Chelsea, where the

restaurant scene hasn't quite caught up to everything else. Classic Thai dishes, such as *pad thai* and shrimp in red curry, are well executed, and the service is friendly. The decor recalls suburban Chinese restaurants, complete with lacquered furniture and polyester tablecloths. *240 8th Ave. (between 22nd and 23rd Sts.), Chelsea, 212/741–1732. Reservations not accepted. AE, MC, V. Subway: C, E to 23rd St.* $

9 *e-3*

TYPHOON BREWERY

Its loud, VERY LOUD, but there's a reason: excellent Thai food. There's a slick bar on the first level, with exposed brick, slick black chairs, and an even slicker crowd; upstairs, in the dining room, the room is noisy and it's the food that's slick. Try the Thai vegetables in green curry, sweet-yet-spicy mango-and-grapefruit salad, or basil-topped soft-shell crabs with chili-drenched noodles. With the attentive service (some say too attentive) and fresh-brewed beers, many refuse to eat Thai anywhere else. *22 E. 54th St., Midtown, 212/754–9006. Reservations essential. AE, DC, MC, V. Closed Sun. No lunch Sat. Subway: 5th Ave./53rd St.* $$

TURKISH

9 *e-7*

TURKISH KITCHEN

The food at this comfortable restaurant is like Middle Eastern cooking, only more sophisticated. The traditional salads, such as hummus and baba gahnoush, are good starters, as are the fried cheese and chicken livers with parsley and lemon. For dinner itself, try the lamb or the dumplings in yogurt sauce. *386 3rd Ave. (between 27th and 28th Sts.), Murray Hill, 212/679–1810, AE, MC, V. Subway: 6 to 28th St.* $

VEGETARIAN AND HEALTH FOOD

9 *e-6*

HANGAWI

See Korean, *above.*

7 *b-8*

JOSIE'S

Can you imagine a health-food theme restaurant? Josie's comes pretty close. The food is fresh, much of it is organically grown or raised, and the emphasis is on light, healthy fare. Many of the dishes are vegetarian, and some are dairy-free; not surprisingly, tofu, tempeh, fish, and seafood feature prominently. It's always busy, and the service is always friendly. *300 Amsterdam Ave. (at 74th St.), Upper West Side, 212/769–1212. AE, MC, V. No lunch. Subway: 72nd St. $$*

11 *f-5*

SPRING STREET NATURAL RESTAURANT

This natural eatery spotlights fresh fish, fowl, and seafood while barring chemicals, preservatives, and red meat. Specialties include vegetarian lasagna, sautéed chicken breast with shiitake mushrooms, baked filet of bluefish, and garlic chicken marinated in raspberry vinegar; but alas, most sound better than they taste. *62 Spring St. (at Lafayette St.), SoHo, 212/966–0290. Reservations not accepted. AE, DC, MC, V. Subway: 6 to Spring St.; Broadway–Lafayette St. $*

7 *b-8*

ZEN PALATE

Something like a cross between a Buddhist temple and a coffee bar, this Pan-Asian minichain with a takeout option offers a quick, healthy, vegetarian alternative to the ubiquitous salad bar. To a base of noodles or rice you can add toppings of vegetables, sauces, broths, and other condiments. Dumplings and stir-fries are also available. Though the flavors tend more toward Zen than toward other Asian palates, you always feel good about yourself when you finish a meal here. *2170 Broadway (between 76th and 77th Sts.), Upper West Side, 212/501–7768. AE, DC, MC, V. Subway: 79th St. $*

9 *c-4*

663 9th Ave. (at 46th St.), Theater District, 212/582-1669. Subway: 42nd St.

9 *c-4*

34 Union Sq. E (at 16th St.), Flatiron, 212/614–9291. Subway: 14th St./Union Square.

VIETNAMESE

11 *g-7*

BO KY

Enjoy a terrific lunch for under $5 at this unpretentious (read: down-and-dirty)

soup shop. The rich, spicy, chicken-coconut curry soup with eggplant, potatoes, and egg noodles is absolutely delicious, as is the unfortunately named beef-belly soup with noodles. The other soups are good, too, but you're best off staying away from the barbecued items. To cut the richness, order "vegetable," which inevitably turns out to be Chinese broccoli in oyster sauce. *80 Bayard St. (between Mott and Mulberry Sts.), Chinatown, 212/406–2292. Reservations not accepted. No credit cards. Subway: 6, N, R, J, M, Z to Canal St. $*

11 *d-3*

CAN

The sleek dining room has a skylight in the back, red carpeting, red chairs, and white tablecloths. The French/Vietnamese food is straightforward and consistent. Try the summer rolls, skewers of grilled chicken and beef with peanut-coconut sauce, and whole sea bass fried in a wok. The crème brûlée is first-rate. *482 W. Broadway (at Houston St.), SoHo, 212/533–6333. AE, V, MC. DC. Subway: Bleecker St./Broadway–Lafayette St. $$*

11 *d-3*

EASTERN & ORIENTAL RESTAURANT AND BAR

A young crowd wearing enough black to outfit an army of Vietcong collects in this large restaurant, decorated in red, pale blue, and gold and hung with bird-cage chandeliers. The long bar serves delicious house cocktails and bowlfuls of addictive shrimp chips. Try the Vietnamese ravioli stuffed with shrimp, grilled Asian eggplant, wok-fried Asian vegetables, flounder steamed in a banana leaf, or a green curry. For dessert, it's the coconut-cream black-rice pudding with crème fraîche. The Suzie Wong room, downstairs, is available for parties. *100 W. Houston St. (between Thompson St. and La Guardia Pl.), Greenwich Village, 212/254–7000. AE, MC, V. Open late. Brunch weekends. Subway: Bleecker St./Broadway–Lafayette St. $$*

11 *f-2*

INDOCHINE

On the bones of the old Lady Astor (the bar, not the dowager), Vietnamese/Cambodian cuisine is served in a clamorous, Hollywood-glam setting where it seems like you need a cell phone to get your waiter's attention. You can dine well just by sharing a bunch of appetizers, such as Vietnamese ravioli, stuffed boneless chicken wings, frogs' legs in coconut milk, and scampi *beignet*. Watch out; the tab can add up quickly. Sit up front if you want some peace and quiet. *430 Lafayette St. (between Astor Pl. and 4th St.), East Village, 212/505–5111. AE, DC, MC, V. Subway: Astor Pl. $$*

11 *f-4*
MEKONG
This casual Vietnamese has paper tablecloths, candles, bamboo curtains, and pictures of a Mekong sunset. The cooking is light with clear flavors, and seasoned with fresh mint. Try the sizzling shrimp, barbecued beef in shiso leaves, summer rolls, and curries. *44 Prince St. (near Mulberry St.), SoHo, 212/343–8169. AE, MC, V. Subway: Bleecker St./Broadway–Lafayette St.; Prince St. $*

7 *f-7*
MISS SAIGON
Whatever it lacks in atmosphere, this small but popular restaurant makes up for in tasty Vietnamese cooking. Locals line up out the door to taste the grilled shrimp paste, green papaya and beef salad, and lemongrass pork with garlic and sesame seeds. The moderate prices contribute to the popularity; if you can, try the place at lunchtime, when it's less hectic. *1425 3rd Ave. (between 80th and 81st Sts.), Upper East Side, 212/988–8828. Reservations not accepted. AE, DC, MC, V. Subway: 86th St. $*

7 *b-7*
MONSOON
Among the first restaurants to take authentic Vietnamese food outside Chinatown, Monsoon offers a fast, cheap alternative to Chinese food from its two Upper West Side locations. The menu hides no surprises. The classic rice-paper–wrapped summer rolls and shrimp-wrapped sugarcane are reliable starters; classic beef soups and noodle dishes satisfy; and a crispy, sweet version of Vietnamese barbecued pork chops, sliced extra thin, is delicious. Be prepared to wait. *435 Amsterdam Ave. (at 81st St.), Upper West Side, 212/580–8686. Reservations not accepted. AE, DC, MC, V. Subway: 79th St. $*

7 *b-3*
2850 Broadway (at 110th St.), Upper West Side, 212/655–2700. Subway: 110th St./Cathedral Pkwy.

11 *g-7*
VIET-NAM
It's hard to find, but this cheap, grungy Chinatown dive is the real thing, serving authentic and tasty Vietnamese dishes. Try anything in the pungent black-bean sauce; the green-papaya and beef-jerky salad; and the beef cubes with watercress, exceptional when dipped in tangy lemon-pepper sauce. Go with an adventurous palette, and don't be put off by the cafeteria atmosphere. *11–13 Doyers St. (between Bowery and Pell St.), Chinatown, 212/693–0725. Reservations not accepted. AE. Subway: Canal St. $*

chapter 4

SHOPPING

New York is widely known as a shopper's paradise, and sometimes it is. New Yorkers have discriminating tastes, and they know how to use them; spread these across a complete range of incomes and, of course, zillions of people, and you've got a nearly exhaustive stock of merchandise. Glance through this chapter and you're bound to notice how many stores you've never even seen—or how many you've whizzed past without noticing.

The problem with shopping in New York is really the schlepp factor. You generally have to walk or take a subway or taxi from store to store; you can't just throw your purchases in the back seat of a car. We've all experienced that pang of sympathy when some poor soul who's just bought a new TV steps onto a crowded subway. Is the chase really the most exciting part of the process? Local service can also try your patience; not for New York is the warm-hearted entrepreneur who slowly wraps your items in decorative tissue paper and tells you she hopes you're delighted with your purchase.

It's actually the holes in New York's massive shopping network that make it most interesting. You're better off shopping here for clothing, jewelry, or books than for, say, a truck, or a new set of poolside furniture. The city has not an endless sprawl of goods, but a carefully tailored selection—making it, in the end, just another American city with merchants catering to its population. All the more remarkable.

major destinations

DEPARTMENT STORES

Most department stores and, increasingly, designer boutiques offer the services of personal shoppers. You'll have to schedule an appointment a few days

in advance, but for the price of spontaneity, you get a store-specific guru. The consultant will either walk with you through the store or, if you describe your size, budget, and taste, run off and make the appropriate selections so you can hit the dressing room ASAP. There is no obligation to buy, and the service is free.

9 e-2

BARNEYS NEW YORK

With the sad closing of Barneys' original space in Chelsea, the Madison Avenue store bears most of the responsibility for appearing elegant, cutting-edge, and most of all, innocent of the company's financial woes. Somehow, they pull it off. Having begun life in the men's-suit business, Barneys is still known for its classically tailored and made-to-measure items (for the man's-eye view, see Contemporary in Men's Clothing, below). The women's floors have an amazing range of high-end designers, from the minimalism of Jil Sander to the blue-blood class of Hermès to the extravagance of Vivienne Westwood and Christian Lacroix. Barneys also continues to champion the up-and-coming, such as Isabel Toledo and Martin Margiela. Women's shoes are thick with labels as well (Prada, Dries van Noten), with scads of Manolo Blahniks and some unique numbers like the snub-nose pumps of Philippe Model. The Chelsea Passage level has a small selection of children's clothes plus all of those objets that aren't exactly fashion but still look fabulous: Philippe Starck kitchenware, stationery, vases, crystal, china, beaded cocktail napkins. If the prices and the attitude leave you winded, you can still find something that invokes extravagance; spring for a $15 caviar spoon. And if you can't make it to Kiehl's pharmacy, downtown, the matchless toiletries for both men and women are at the intersection of their respective clothing sections on the ground floor. 660 Madison Ave. (at 61st St.), Upper East Side, 212/826–8900, Subway: 59th St.; World Financial Center, 225 Liberty St., Lower Manhattan, 212/945–1600, Subway: World Trade Center

9 d-3

BERGDORF GOODMAN

With a men's and a women's store facing each other across 5th Avenue, Bergdorf Goodman dominates a solid block of good taste. The atmosphere in both is understated and unmistakably wealthy; the "younger" clothing lines are best suited to teens with a trust fund. But while the building itself whispers "old money," the selections are far from old-fashioned. Fashionistas hone in on the New York–exclusive (or almost) accessories, including Philip Treacy's hats and Samantha Heskia's beaded handbags. Upstairs, many designer labels hold court in separate alcoves: John Galliano, Balenciaga, Guy Laroche, and their four-digit brethren. (With all of these niches, you need a good sense of direction to get back to the escalators.) Bergdorf's own line of sweaters is very sophisticated. The choice of casual clothing is (in this context) happily original, too; familiar brands like Anne Klein are joined by Słowik, Claude Pierlot, and the raucous colors of Voyage. If you pass an abandoned-looking clothes rack on any of the floors, go ahead and riffle—these are normally reduced-price goods. The beauty salon has managed to one-up its competitors by operating in the Goodman family's former penthouse apartment. The home department has roomsful of especially wonderful linens, tableware, and gifts. For Bergdorf Goodman Men, see Clothing for Men—Classic, below. 754 5th Ave. (at 57th St.), Midtown, 212/753–7300. Subway: E, F, N, R to 5th Ave.

1 e-3

BLOOMINGDALE'S

To tourists, Bloomie's is as New York as yellow cabs. To New Yorkers, Bloomie's is a good place to go for a sale on, say, hosiery or bedding. Everyone comes here at some point. The ground floor includes a portion of the menswear collection, mainly ties and shirts for the frantic eleventh-hour shopper. Beyond this relative safety is the mazelike cosmetics area, whose mirrors and shiny black walls can be completely discombobulating. (Enter on 3rd Avenue to avoid this experience.) Clothing for men and women has tended toward the middle-of-the-road; in the past couple of seasons, however, buyers have been reaching out to the more avant-garde (Helmut Lang) and upwardly mobile (Mossimo). As for atmosphere, Bloomie's definitely subscribes to the right-between-the-eyes school of marketing. Theme promotions for movies, music, and Broadway shows can smack of fast-food–style advertising, and the number of people wielding perfume

spritzers is terrifying. 1000 3rd Ave. (at 59th St.), Midtown, 212/355–5900. Subway: 59th St.

9 e-5

LORD & TAYLOR

Once inside this 5th Avenue veteran, you might think the ground floor goes on forever. A trick of mirrors reflecting the arched white ceiling, this impression of cosmetic-department infinity is the store's most overwhelming aspect. For the most part, L&T is a decidedly ladylike experience, with some floors decorated in powder-pink and white. Clothes lean heavily toward conservative American designers; there's more Dana Buchman than Donna Karan, more Tommy Hilfiger than Calvin Klein. For women, you'll also find healthy servings of St. John and Jones New York. 424 5th Ave. (at 38th St.), Midtown, 212/391–3344. Subway: 34th St./Herald Square.

9 d-6

MACY'S

If you don't know the floor plan by heart (many do), Macy's requires the patience of a saint, or a stiff drink. With nine floors (not including the famous Cellar marketplace) and too few signs directing you to either the Broadway building or the 7th Avenue building, you can easily find yourself among the baby booties when you're looking for luggage. Macy's has tons of almost everything: women's shoes eat up an entire floor, with everything from Keds to Candies to Yves Saint Laurent. Major labels often have their own "shop"; the men's section houses Tommy Hilfiger, Calvin Klein, and Nautica shops. What Macy's doesn't have is couture—the swankest it gets is "better sportswear." But while it may not have the clothes to match, it does have fancy accessories, like Louis Vuitton leather and Mont Blanc pens. Service can be amiably casual or surly, but is reliably slapdash. The list of amenities is impressive; there's even a post office. The store has been renovating floor by floor, but you can still ride the old-fashioned wooden escalators. 155 W. 34th St. (Herald Square), Garment District, 212/695–4400. Subway: 34th St./Herald Square.

9 e-4

SAKS FIFTH AVENUE

For his-and-hers takes on Saks, see Clothing for Women—Contemporary and Clothing for Men—Classic, below.

9 *d-6*

STERN'S

The linchpin of the Manhattan Mall (*see* Malls, *below*), Stern's is a very manageable department store. Compared to Manhattan's other mega-emporia, selections here are smaller and more moderately priced. Men's and women's clothes tend to be casual, though there are a few nice suits lying around. Housewares, linen, appliances, and electronics are equally relaxed and reasonably priced. *899 6th Ave. (at 33rd St.), Garment District, 212/244–6060. Subway: 34th St./Herald Square.*

9 *e-3*

TAKASHIMAYA

As Takashimaya sees it, New York is the logical intermediary between Paris and Tokyo. The mingling aesthetics have resulted in a space of impeccable design, and the store has accomplished the unthinkable by creating a perpetually calm atmosphere. The home collection is the most renowned, featuring such finery as delicate tablewares, laquered chopsticks and silverware, and throw pillows covered in patchworks of patterned silks ($75–$365). Some of the larger furniture is antique, such as 19th-century Japanese wooden screens and chests. Clothing for both men and women is limited to what Takashimaya calls "details"—for men: shirts, ties, and the odd coat; for women: jewelry, hats, gauzy scarves, and silk purses. Head up to the 5th floor (loungewear, bedding, baby clothes) for silk robes, Japanese-style velvet thongs, and pale linens that will have you rethinking your bedroom. The ground-floor cosmetics section (don't worry, no one wields a spritzer here) has some extremely rare product lines, including soaps and scents by Santa Maria Novella of Florence. Finally, the beautiful gardening section, visible through the storefront windows, has glazed pots ($10–$35), gardening tools, and a few rather fascinating plants. *693 5th Ave. (between 54th and 55th Sts.), Midtown, 212/350–0100.*

MALLS

A Manhattan mall is nearly an oxymoron, but there are a few, not as intriguing as the prime shopping neighborhoods but easier on the legs.

9 *d-6*

HERALD CENTER

This budget-oriented retail center was hard to get off the ground, but it's braving the traffic well. The main draws are the giant Toys 'R' Us and Kids 'R' Us stores, as well as branches of Daffy's and Payless Shoes. *1 Herald Square (at W. 34th St.), Garment District, 212/634–3883. Subway: 34th St./Herald Square.*

9 *d-6*

MANHATTAN MALL

Like any mall worth its salt, this complex has a skylit atrium, a huge food court, and lots of neon. Stern's anchors the usual bevy of chain and novelty stores—the goofy-tie shop, the candle store, the baseball-cap cart. On the whole, merchandise is low on the price scale; clothing stores include Aéropostale, Express, and Bolton's. There are also branches of yet-larger chains Ann Taylor and Nine West, though, amazingly, there's no Gap . . . yet. *6th Ave. at 33rd St., Garment District, 212/465–0500. Subway: 34th St./Herald Square.*

11 *f-7*

SOUTH STREET SEAPORT MARKETPLACE, PIER 17

In this outdoor mall reminiscent of Boston's Quincy Market, you'll find three clusters of stores: one on a pedestrians-only extension to Fulton Street; one in the Fulton Market building, the original home of NYC's fish market; and one at Pier 17. Squint at the old buildings and you can still make out a few painted signs from the old fish merchants. Many of the stores along the cobbled streets are chains, such as Ann Taylor, Victoria's Secret, and Liz Claiborne; Manhattan's first J. Crew store is in one of the Seaport's historic waterfront hotel buildings. Pier 17 is also dominated by retail giants like The Gap, but there are a few unusual boutiques, such as Mariposa, which sells brilliantly colored butterflies encased in Lucite. *Fulton and Water Sts., Lower Manhattan, 212/732–7678. Subway: 2, 3 to Fulton St.*

9 *e-3*

TRUMP TOWER

The soaring marble atrium, with its wall of water and bronze tones at every turn, makes this place unmistakably Trump. Finding a knockout gem here is no trouble; Cartier, Harry Winston, and Asprey all have branches on site. The glamour quotient is further upped by such vendors as Salvatore Ferragamo and Caviar Direct. Since the sprawling Abercrombie & Fitch decamped in 1997, the most youth-accessible place is probably the Tower Records outpost in the basement. *725 5th Ave. (at 56th St.), Midtown, 212/832–2000. Closed Sun. Subway: E, F to 5th Ave.*

specialist shops

ANTIQUES

Nearly every neighborhood in New York has its own array of antiques stores, but there are some well-known pockets. These include SoHo (especially Lafayette St. south of Houston St.); 9th to 13th streets between Broadway and 2nd Avenue; and Madison and Lexington avenues from 72nd to 86th streets.

New York also has several flea markets, antiques centers, and seasonal antique shows. The Manhattan Art & Antiques Center (1050 2nd Ave, between 52nd and 53rd Sts.) is a Midtown classic. The 26th Street Flea Market (6th Ave. from 24th to 27th Sts.) is open for mass consumption on weekends, and its organizer, the Annex Antiques Fair & Flea Market, also maintains an indoor venue on 25th Street between 6th and 7th avenues.

Call Stella Management (212/255–0020) for information on the Triple Pier Expo, Coliseum, and 7th Regiment Armory shows; call Sanford Smith Associates (212/777–5218) for information on the Fall Antiques, Pier, and Modernism shows. Metropolitan Art and Antiques (212/463–0200) also produces several shows a year. For a full review of the Armory show, *see* Events–January *in* Chapter 2.

auction houses

9 e-2

CHRISTIE'S AND CHRISTIE'S EAST
New York's branches of the famed London house hold auctions of fine art, furnishings, tapestries, books, and manuscripts and appraise art at no charge. "Low-end" antiques and col-

lectibles are often up for grabs. *502 Park Ave. (at 59th St.), Midtown, 212/546–1000, subway 59th St.; 219 E. 67th St. Upper East Side, 212/606–0400, subway 68th St./Hunter College. Information on current sale, 212/546–1178. 24-hr auction line, 212/371–5438. Information on lectures and courses, 212/546–1092.*

10 e-1

GREAT GATSBY'S
Just off the East Village's beaten antiques path, Gatsby's deals in American and European antiques and decorative arts. Estate auctions are held every other Tuesday at 11 AM; viewing begins four days in advance. *91 University Pl. (near 12th St.), Greenwich Village, 212/260–2000. Subway: 8th St.*

9 e-7

HARMER
Harmer specializes in stamps: They auction, appraise, and arrange private treaties. They also auction coins and antiquities three or four times a year. *3 E. 28th St., Murray Hill, 212/532–3700. Subway: N, R, 6 to 28th St.*

9 d-7

LUBIN GALLERIES
Estates of varying quality go on this block every other Saturday, though holiday weekends bring the best buys. Items sell for as little as $5 to as much as $5,000; view the wares on the preceding Thursday and Friday. *110 W. 25th St., Chelsea, 212/924–3777. Subway: F, 1, 2, 3, 9 to 23rd St.*

7 f-8

PHILLIPS
Founded in London in 1796, Phillips still holds fine art and estate sales. Items are displayed two or three days before the auction. Watch the paper for Phillips' ads. *406 E. 79th St., Upper East Side, 212/570–4830. Subway: 77th St.*

9 g-1

SOTHEBY'S
Appraiser and auctioneer since 1744, the world-famous Sotheby's sells paintings, jewelry, furniture, silver, books, porcelain, Orientalia, rugs, and more. The house is exciting to visit even if you won't be buying. Sotheby's Arcade, a sort of junior Sotheby's, sells more affordable pieces. *1334 York Ave. (at 72nd St.), 212/606–7000. Subway: 77th St. 24-*

hr auction and exhibition line, 212/606–7245. Sotheby's Arcade, 212/606–7409 or 800/444–3709 outside NYC.

7 f-8

411 E. 76th St., Upper East Side

9 e-7

TEPPER GALLERIES

Large and lively, Tepper is popular with collectors for its fine furniture, paintings, rugs, accessories, and jewelry. Auctions are every other Saturday; viewing is on Thursday and Friday. 110 E. 25th St., Gramercy, 212/677–5300. Subway: 6 to 23rd St.

7 e-7

WILLIAM DOYLE GALLERIES

Estates are the specialty here, particularly 18th- and 20th-century decorative and fine arts including furniture, paintings, rugs, and accessories. Auctions are held every other Wednesday; viewing runs from Saturday through Tuesday. The tag sale next door can yield bargains. 175 E. 87th St., Upper East Side, 212/427–2730. Subway: 4, 5, 6 to 86th St.

flea markets and antiques centers

With escalating rents chasing many small businesses out, flea markets are becoming the last bastion of affordable goods.

9 d-7

ANNEX ANTIQUES FAIR & FLEA MARKET

Year-round, in nearly every kind of weather, the Annex draws the curious. A serious dealers' market with quality antiques and collectibles, the market is particularly strong on silver, jewelry, vintage clothing, glass, Americana, Victoriana, and ephemera, but there's much more. The stock varies from week to week, as most of the dealers are itinerant; they go where the action is. One block south of the Annex is a more chaotic lot with a preponderance of junk; it's also worth a look for good vintage clothing and the occasional quilt. On Sundays, yet more dealers set up shop in a garage on 25th Street between 6th and 7th avenues. Parking for all Annex events is free. 6th Ave. and 26th St., Chelsea, 212/243–5343. Admission. Subway: F to 23rd St.

9 f-1

ANTIQUES, FLEA, & FARMER'S MARKET

With both indoor and outdoor venues, this Saturday market is a friendly place to scout good-quality antiques and collectibles, including jewelry and linens. New goods and fresh produce round out the shopping experience. P.S. 183 (1st Ave. and 67th St.), Upper East Side, 212/737–8888. Subway: 68th St./Hunter College.

9 d-7

CHELSEA ANTIQUES BUILDING

For antiques shopping in a conveniently mall-like setting, hit these 12 floors of antiques any day of the week. 110 W. 25th St., Chelsea, 212/929–0909. Subway: F, 1, 2, 3, 9 to 23rd St.

7 b-8

GREENFLEA'S MARKET ON COLUMBUS

Greenflea's now rivals 26th Street as the Sunday flea market, though it's dark the rest of the week. Two hundred vendors offer antiques, collectibles, old clothes, jewelry, and new merchandise in both indoor and outdoor venues. Columbus Ave. and 76th St., Upper West Side, 212/316–1088. Subway: 79th St.

9 f-3

MANHATTAN ART & ANTIQUE CENTER

This is a class act. Under one roof, over 100 shops and galleries sell a great selection of antiques and fine-art objects from around the world. Prices range impressively from $10 to $300,000. 1050 2nd Ave. (near 56th St.), Midtown, 212/355–4400. Subway: 59th St.

11 e-2

TOWER FLEA MARKET

These mainly young and earnest artisans and designers sell T-shirts, clothes, jewelry, hats, and other adornments every weekend. Broadway and 4th St., Greenwich Village, no phone. Subway: 8th St.; Astor Pl.

collectibles specialists

7 b-8

MORE & MORE ANTIQUES

Steve Mohr has one of the best eyes in the business, and his wonderful shops are brimming over with late-19th- to early-20th-century French and English decorative antiques, with a bent toward the Victorian. Offerings include paisleys, wonderful hand-painted china, bead-work, bamboo furnishings, rugs, screens, and an eclectic selection of jewelry, from 1840–1940. *360 Amsterdam Ave. (at 78th St.), Upper West Side, 212/580–8404. Subway: 79th St.*

9 *e-2*

A LA VIEILLE RUSSIE

This exquisite collection of Russian art and antiques includes clocks and art objects—especially icons, Fabergé, silver and porcelain, antique jewelry, and snuff boxes. *781 5th Ave. (at 59th St.), Midtown, 212/752–1727. Subway: N, R to 5th Ave.*

9 *e-1*

AMDUR ANTIQUES

A treasure trove of decorative antiques and accessories, Amdur sells antique bamboo, beaded footstools, Victorian picture frames, match strikers, and more. *1026–28 Lexington Ave. (near 73rd St.), Upper East Side, 212/472–2691. Subway: 77th St.*

9 *e-2*

AMERICA HURRAH

Here's your source for Americana, with magnificent patchwork quilts and textiles, weathervanes, folk sculpture, painted American country furniture, and American Indian art. *766 Madison Ave. (at 66th St.), Upper East Side, 212/535–1930. Closed Sun.–Mon. Subway: 68th St./Hunter College.*

11 *e-4*

BACK PAGES

Back Pages is a center for antique amusement and slot machines, Wurlitzer jukeboxes, Coca-Cola vending machines, player pianos, and other large items. They also restore. *125 Greene St. (near Prince St.), SoHo, 212/460–5998. Subway: Prince St.*

7 *e-7*

BERNARD & S. DEAN LEVY, INC.

This lovely town-house gallery has top-quality late-17th- to early-19th-century

American antiques, furniture, silver, paintings, and decorative wares. *24 E. 84th St., Upper East Side, 212/628–7088. Subway: 4, 5, 6 to 86th St.*

11 *d-4*

BERTHA BLACK

A tiny SoHo shop with antique American painted furniture, folk art, and country dining accessories, Bertha Black also carries an extensive collection of Mexican *retablos* and *santos*, 1820–1900. *80 Thompson St. (near Spring St.), 212/966–7116. Closed Mon.–Tues. Subway: C, E to Spring St.*

9 *f-2*

CHICK DARROW'S FUN ANTIQUES

For the Peter Pan in your family, hit Chick Darrow's, with antique toys of every description: automobiliana, wind-ups, mechanical banks, carousel animals, toy soldiers, gambling devices, arcade machines. Prices range widely, from $2 to $5,000. *309 E. 61st St., Upper East Side, 212/838–0730. Closed Sun. except by appt. Subway: 59th St.*

10 *f-1*

COBBLESTONES

The best word for this stuff is *stuff*—a lot of fun old *stuff*. Kitchen utensils, costume jewelry, books, glassware, sunglasses, hats, cigarette cases, evening bags . . . you never know what you'll find. *314 E. 9th St., Greenwich Village, 212/673–5372. Closed Mon. Subway: 8th St.; Astor Pl.*

7 *e-8*

D. LEONARD & GARY TRENT

Specializing in the 20th-century decorative arts, Leonard and Trent concentrate on Art Nouveau and Art Deco: Tiffany lamps, glass, posters, bronzes, and mirrors, and English and French cameo glass. *950 Madison Ave. (near 75th St.), Upper East Side, 212/737–9511 or 212/879–1799. Subway: 77th St.*

10 *e-1*

DULLESVILLE

Jewelry, pottery, and decorative objects from 1900 through the 1960s—including one of the largest collections of Bakelite in the country—are joined by a good deal of Russell Wright. *143 E. 13th St., Greenwich Village, 212/505–2505. Subway: 14th St./Union Square.*

11 *d-5*

ECLECTIQUES

This aptly named shop carries an interesting mix: Art Deco, Art Nouveau, 1920s Mica lamps, Mission furniture, 20th-century oils and illustrations, paisley shawls, and vintage Vuitton luggage. *55 Wooster St. (at Broome St.), SoHo, 212/966–0650. Subway: Canal St.*

7 *e-7*

HUBERT DES FORGES

Forges can be counted on for lovely French and English antiques and decorative accessories. *1193 Lexington Ave. (near 81st St.), Upper East Side, 212/744–1857. Closed weekends. Subway: 77th St.*

11 *g-3*

IRREPLACEABLE ARTIFACTS

Head to the East Village for original, spectacular architectural ornamentation for interior and exterior use—stained glass, mantel pieces, fountains, wrought iron, paneling, and much, much more. *14 2nd Ave. (at Houston St.), East Village, 212/777–2900; 259 Bowery (near Houston St.), East Village, 212/982–5000. Open by appt. only. Subway: 2nd Ave.*

9 *f-8*

IRVING BARBER SHOP ANTIQUES

These cramped quarters overflow with glassware, costume jewelry, beaded evening bags, prints, and sometimes antique linens, quilts, and vintage cloths. Browse—gingerly—at 210 E. 21st St., Gramercy, no phone. Closed weekends. Subway: 6 to 23rd St.

7 *f-8*

JANA STARR–JEAN HOFFMAN ANTIQUES

Focusing on the period 1900–1930, Starr-Hoffman is jam-packed with wedding dresses from the turn of the century to the 1950s, but also manages to stuff into its tight quarters beautiful embroidered table and bed linens, jewelry, hats,

gloves, dressing-table items, bags, antique laces and textiles, walking sticks, all obviously gathered with care. They also rent period props. *236 E. 80th St., Upper East Side, 212/861–8256 or 212/535–6930. Closed Sun. Subway: 77th St.*

10 *c-1*

LE FANION

Feel like Provence? Peruse French country antiques and contemporary ceramics in a shop with a deliciously country atmosphere. *299 W. 4th St. (at Bank St.), West Village, 212/463–8760. Closed Sun. Subway: Christopher St./Sheridan Square.*

7 *e-8*

LEO KAPLAN LTD.

Leo Kaplan has an extensive selection of French and American modern paperweights; 18th-century English pottery and porcelains; Russian enamels; English and French cameo glass of the Art Nouveau period; and contemporary studio glass. *967 Madison Ave. (near 75th St.), Upper East Side, 212/249–6766. Subway: 77th St.*

9 *f-3*

LILLIAN NASSAU

This is *the* place for Art Nouveau and Art Deco pieces, especially Tiffany glass and rare art glass as well as furniture and sculpture. *220 E. 57th St., Midtown, 212/759–6062. Subway: 4, 5, 6 to 59th St.*

7 *e-8*

LINDA HORN

Linda has quite an eye for the unusual. Check out her opulent treasures from the 18th and 19th centuries in a setting to match. *1015 Madison Ave. (near 78th St.), Upper East Side, 212/772–1122. Subway: 77th St.*

11 *d-4*

MOOD INDIGO

The 1930s and '40s get their due in this inviting shop full of Russell Wright, Fiesta, and Harlequin ware, Art Deco chrome accessories, and a wonderful selection of Bakelite jewelry. *181 Prince St. (near Thompson St.), SoHo, 212/254–1176. Closed Mon. Subway: Prince St.*

9 *e-2*

MORIAH

Antique Judaica, prints, engravings, and curios make up this unique mix. *699*

Madison Ave. (near 62nd St.), Upper East Side, 212/751–7090. Closed weekends. Subway: 59th St.

9 f-2

OLD VERSAILLES, INC.

The specialty here is, *bien sûr*, French and continental antiques and furniture. 315 E. 62nd St., Upper East Side, 212/421–3663. Closed weekends. Subway: 4, 5, 6 to 59th St.

7 e-8

PRICE GLOVER, INC.

English pewter, pottery, and brass, circa 1690–1820, are joined by early-19th-century English brass light fixtures, and Chinese furniture, 1600–1700. 59 E. 79th St., 3rd floor, Upper East Side, 212/772–1740. Closed weekends. Subway: 77th St.

9 e-1

PRIMAVERA GALLERY

These decorative arts include paintings, furniture, glass, and jewelry from the turn of the century to the 1950s. 808 Madison Ave. (near 68th St.), Upper East Side, 212/288–1569. Subway: 68th St./Hunter College.

11 e-4

SARAJO

Sarajo's large and impressive selection of textiles, antique furniture, and objects comes from Central Asia, Africa, the Far East, and Central and South America. 98 Prince St. (near Mercer St.), SoHo, 212/966–6156. Subway: Prince St.

9 e-1

THOS. K. WOODARD

This prime selection of Americana includes antique quilts, country furniture, and folk art. Rag rugs, both originals and wood-weave reproductions, are an interesting sub-specialty. 835 Madison Ave. (near 73rd St.), 2nd floor, Upper East Side, 212/794–9404 or 212/988–2906. Subway: 77th St.

7 e-7

TROUVAILLE FRANÇAISE

Muriel Clark collects and purveys treasures from France and Belgium with loving care: antique bed and table linens, laces, curtains, christening gowns, and much more. 212/737–6015. Open by appt. only. Subway: 4, 5, 6 to 86th St.

11 f-4

URBAN ARCHAEOLOGY

The name is literal: all of these gargoyles and other grand bygone architectural embellishments were saved from the wrecking ball. With a focus on New York City, this shop carries Americana from the 1880s to 1925, antique slot and arcade machines, and a celebrated collection of Art Deco interiors and exteriors. Displays spill outdoors. 285 Lafayette St. (between Prince and Houston Sts.), SoHo, 212/431–6969. Subway: Broadway–Lafayette St.

11 g-5

210 Elizabeth St. (near Spring St.), SoHo/Little Italy, 212/941–4800. Subway: 6 to Spring St.

11 d-7

143 Franklin St. (between Varick and Hudson Sts.), Tribeca, 212/431–4646. Subway: Franklin St.

9 f-3

239 E. 58th St., Midtown, 212/371–4646. Subway: 59th St.

7 e-8

VITO GIALLO

Tastefully chosen antiques from the 18th and 19th centuries fill this tiny shop and turn over very quickly: quilts, paisleys, Staffordshire china, fountain pens, and assorted small treasures. 966 Madison Ave. (near 76th St.), 212/535–9885. Subway: 77th St.

10 e-1

WAVES

Vintage radios, wind-up phonographs, old telephones, and neon clocks are sold, repaired, and rented; other communications memorabilia include old advertisements and 78-rpm records. 32 E. 13th St., Greenwich Village, 212/989–9284. Closed Sun.–Mon. Subway: 14th St./Union Square.

furniture specialists

11 c-4

CARPE DIEM ANTIQUES

This excellent cache of '50s and '60s furniture includes a particularly notable collection of lamps. 187 6th Ave. (between Spring and Prince Sts.), SoHo, 212/337–0018. Closed Mon. Subway: C, E to Spring St.

11 d-3
COBWEB
Cobweb has a good selection of ethnic antique furniture and accessories from Europe and the Middle East. *116 W. Houston St. (at Sullivan St.), West Village, 212/505–1558. Subway: Houston St.*

11 d-4
EILEEN LANE ANTIQUES
Spacious quarters show off a lovely and well-priced selection of Swedish and Viennese Biedermeier and Art Deco furniture, as well as period art glass and alabaster lighting. *150 Thompson St. (between Prince and Houston Sts.), SoHo, 212/475–2988. Subway: C, E to Spring St.*

9 f-1
EVERGREEN ANTIQUES
Some of this rustic, 18th- and 19th-century Scandinavian pine furniture has its original hand-painted finishing. Accents include rag rugs, pottery, and wooden boxes. *1249 3rd Ave. (at 72nd St.), Upper East Side, 212/744–5664. Subway: 72nd St.*

7 e-8
FLORIAN PAPP
Since 1900, Papp has been a source for antiques from the William and Mary, Sheraton, and other periods of fine English and European furniture, and the store now carries Victorian items as well. *962 Madison Ave. (near 76th St.), Upper East Side, 212/288–6770. Subway: 77th St.*

11 e-4
GALLERY 532
Original furniture and ceramic pieces will delight the Arts & Crafts lover. *117 Wooster St. (between Prince and Spring Sts.), SoHo, 212/219–1327. Subway: Spring St.*

11 f-3
GUÉRIDON
The name means "side table" in French, and the store boasts a wide array of these and other funky modern pieces at a range of prices to suit almost any budget. The owners are highly knowledgeable and equally charming. *359 Lafayette St. (between Bond and Bleecker Sts.), 212/677–7740. Subway: Bleecker St.; Broadway–Lafayette St.*

10 e-1
HOWARD KAPLAN ANTIQUES
An early purveyor of the Rustic French look, Howard Kaplan now carries a broader range of French (including country) and 19th-century English furnishings and a luscious group of decorative accessories, all in a beautiful shop. *827 Broadway (near 12th St.), Greenwich Village, 212/674–1000. Closed weekends. Subway: 14th St./Union Square.*

11 e-4
INTÉRIEURS
Alas, this truly choice contemporary furniture, along with lighting, tabletop items, and other accessories from France, comes with equally choice prices. Be prepared to drool, and bring the platinum card. *114 Wooster St. (between Spring and Prince Sts.), SoHo, 212/343–0800. Subway: Spring St.*

11 f-4
LOST CITY ARTS
Architectural antiques and Americana join advertising icons and Art Deco. *275 Lafayette St. (between Prince and Houston Sts.), SoHo, 212/941–8025. Subway: Broadway–Lafayette St.; Prince St.*

9 f-3
NEWEL ART GALLERIES
It takes six stories to house this supreme collection of antique furnishings from the Renaissance to Art Deco, with an emphasis on the unusual and whimsical. They cater to those in the trade, stylists scouting props, and those who know *exactly* what they want. *425 E. 53rd St., Midtown, 212/758–1970. Closed weekends. Subway: 51st St./Lexington–3rd Aves.*

11 a-1
PIERRE DEUX ANTIQUES
Pierre Deux specializes in exquisite 18th- and 19th-century country French furniture and accessories. *369 Bleecker St. (at Charles St.), West Village, 212/243–7740. Subway: Christopher St./Sheridan Square.*

10 e-1
RETRO MODERN STUDIO
The collection centers on European and American designer Art Deco furniture, lighting, and fine-art objects. *58 E. 11th St. (between Broadway and University*

Pl.), 2nd floor, Greenwich Village, 212/674–0530. Closed Sun. Subway: 8th St.; Astor Pl.

10 c-2
THE RURAL COLLECTION
You *can* go home again: finds from the farm, old cupboards, and weather-worn painted furniture from the Midwest are priced very reasonably here. 117 Perry St. (between Greenwich and Hudson Sts.), West Village, 212/645–4488. Subway: Christopher St./Sheridan Square.

11 e-3
SECONDHAND ROSE
The focus here is twentieth-century American decorative arts: Donald Desky, Gilbert Rohde, R. T. Frankl, Paul Evans, Charles Eames. Also on hand are antique wallpaper and fabrics. A splendid collection, if it's your cup of tea. 138 Duane St. (between Church and Broadway), Tribeca, 212/393–9002. Subway: Chambers St.

7 f-8
TREILLAGE
Owned by Bunny Williams and John Rosselli, Treillage has made its name with furniture and accessories for the garden, but it now features an interesting selection of tableware and lighting as well. 418 E. 75th St., Upper East Side, 212/535–2288. Subway: 77th St.

11 d-7
WYETH
Come here for steel furniture and other stylish Americana. 151 Franklin St. (between Hudson and Varick Sts.), West Village, 212/925–5278. Subway: Franklin St.

quilt specialists
Most antiques stores have a few quilts in stock, but these shops have built collections of outstanding quality, originality, and quantity.

9 f-2
AMERICA HURRAH
This shop specializes in American textile folk art: hooked rugs, samplers, and the largest, finest selection of quilts anywhere, not to mention 19th-century American Indian rugs, blankets, weavings, and beadwork. They offer expert restoration and mounting. 766 Madison Ave. (at 66th St.), Upper East Side, 212/

535–1930. Closed Sun.–Mon. Subway: 68th St/Hunter College.

9 e-3
GAZEBO
A must for the hearth-and-home enthusiast, this Midtown shop features American quilts mainly from the 1920s and '30s, and new ones in traditional patterns. They're happy to take custom orders. Vintage wicker furnishings and accessories, old and new baskets, silk flowers, and other accessories round out the beautiful displays. 114 E. 57th St., Midtown, 212/832–7077. Subway: 59th St.

10 b-1
KELTER-MALCE ANTIQUES
Kelter and Malce have a very large, very fine collection of antique American quilts along with folk art, rag rugs, antique American Indian textiles, and pottery. 74 Jane St. (near Washington St.), West Village, 212/989–6760. Open by appt. only. Subway: A, C, E to 14th St.

9 f-3
LAURA FISHER
Fisher has an exciting collection of pieced and appliquéd quilts, circa 1830–1930, including Amish and crib quilts. The wares extend to paisley shawls, woven coverlets, Marseilles bedspreads, hooked and American Indian rugs, needlework, and decorative Victorian accessories. Manhattan Art & Antiques Center, 1050 2nd Ave. (at 55th St.), Midtown, 212/838–2596. Closed Sun. Subway: 59th St.

11 a-1
SUSAN PARRISH ANTIQUES
Knowledgeable and caring, Susan Parrish has a lovely selection of pretty quilts, original 18th- and 19th-century painted American country furniture, and American Indian weavings. 390 Bleecker St. (near Perry St.), West Village, 212/645–5020. Closed Sun. Subway: Christopher St./Sheridan Square.

7 e-6
SWEET NELLIE
This charming Carnegie Hill shop specializes in American country, mainly originals: quilts, pillows made from antique paisleys, new game boards, crib quilts, and hooked rugs. 1262 Madison Ave. (near 90th St.), Upper East Side, 212/876–5775. Subway: 4, 5, 6 to 86th St.

7 g-8

WOODARD & GREENSTEIN
A known and respected source for
American quilts from the 1850s on,
Woodard & Greenstein also carry
hooked rugs, samplers, game boards,
baskets, and much more—mint Americana. 506 E. 74th St., Upper East Side,
212/988–2906. Subway: 77th St.

ART SUPPLIES

9 d-4

ARTHUR BROWN & BROS.,
INC.
Long established, this superior art- and
drafting-supply store has a fantastic pen
department. 2 W. 46th St., Midtown, 212/
575–5555. Subway: B, D, F, Q to 42nd St.

9 e-6

CHARRETTE
A favorite with students, Charrette discounts its incredible selection of art
supplies 20%. The custom framing is
top-quality. 215 Lexington Ave. (at 33rd
St.), Murray Hill, 212/683–8822. Subway:
33rd St.

11 e-4

KATE'S PAPERIE
See Stationery, below.

10 d-1

See Stationery, below.

9 c-3

LEE'S ART SHOP
Right across the street from the Art Students' League, Lee's caters to both professional and amateur artists. The large
inventory includes stationery, pens,
gifts, paint and brushes, and architectural and drafting supplies, and they're
happy to frame your masterpiece once
you're finished. 220 W. 57th St., Midtown, 212/247–0110. Subway: N, R to 57th
St.; 59th St./Columbus Circle.

10 e-1

NEW YORK CENTRAL
Serving New York's artists for over 80
years, New York Central has the finest
of everything: handmade papers,
parchment, 3,000 different pastels,
200 different canvases, and much
more, all for 20%–40% less than elsewhere. They specialize in finding the
"impossible." 62 3rd Ave. (near 11th

St.), East Village, 212/473–7705. Subway:
3rd Ave.; Astor Pl.

11 e-6

PEARL
With nine floors of art supplies, Pearl is
the world's largest art, craft, and graphics discount center—no mean feat. It's a
wonderful source for this stuff, as well
as house and industrial paints at 20%–
50% off. 308 Canal St. (between Church
and Broadway), SoHo, 212/431–7932.
Subway: Canal St.

9 d-8

SAM FLAX, INC.
Sam Flax adds school and office supplies to its admirably complete selection
of art materials. 12 W. 20th St., Chelsea,
212/620–3038. Subway: F to 23rd St.

9 e-3

425 Park Ave. (at 55th St.), Midtown, 212/
620–3060. Subway: 59th St.

10 e-1

UTRECHT ART AND
DRAFTING SUPPLIES
Utrecht makes its own huge stock of
paint, art, and drafting supplies right
down the road in Brooklyn. Prices are reasonable, and quality is high. Other manufacturers' supplies are discounted as
well. 111 4th Ave. (at 11th St.), East Village,
212/777–5353. Subway: 8th St./Astor Pl.

BASKETS

While home stores like Pier 1, Hold
Everything, Pottery Barn, and Crate &
Barrel will always carry some baskets,
your best bet for an inspired creation is
to cruise the Flower District, on 28th
Street between 6th and 7th Avenues.
While it's technically a wholesale market, you'll be surprised at the bargains
you can score if you look like you know
what you're doing—and pay in cash.

BEAUTY

fragrances & skin products
All major department stores have a full
line of fragrances for both men and
women on their main floor, often with
live representatives ready and eager to
spray you. Be warned that counterfeit
fragrances, packaged to look like the
real thing, are showing up all over

town; to avoid getting fooled, buy in reputable shops.

9 c-8

ALCONE

Although primarily a supplier of theatrical makeup, Alcone has become popular with models, actresses, and makeup artists, who come for brands not found in other stores. *235 W. 19th St., Chelsea, 212/633–0551. Subway: C, E to 23rd St.*

11 c-4

AVEDA

Aveda offers European hair and skin-care products, makeup, bath preparations, and home fragrance, all made with natural ingredients. Tired of shopping? The Spring Street and West Broadway stores also offer massages and facials. *233 Spring St. (between 6th Ave. and Varick St.), West Village, 212/807–1492. Subway: C, E to Spring St.*

11 d-4

456 W. Broadway (between Prince and Houston Sts.), SoHo, 212/473–0280. Subway: Broadway–Lafayette St.

9 d-8

140 5th Ave. (at 19th St.), Flatiron, 212/645–4797. Subway: N, R to 23rd St.

9 e-3

509 Madison Ave. (between 52nd and 53rd Sts.), Midtown, 212/832–2146. Subway: E, F to 5th Ave.

11 e-1

THE BODY SHOP

This hugely successful toiletry chain now has cheery shops worldwide. The fragrant, all-natural products come in biodegradable or recyclable packaging, do not pollute the water, and have not been tested on animals—and in addition to saving the earth, they cleanse, polish, and protect the skin and hair, though they make no promises about beauty. It's great stuff if you don't have oily skin. For a full list of locations in New York City and elsewhere, call 800/541–2535. *747 Broadway (near Astor Pl.), East Village, 212/979–2944. Subway: 8th St.; Astor Pl.*

9 d-6

Manhattan Mall, 901 6th Ave. (at 33rd St.), Garment District, 212/268–7424. Subway: 34th St./Herald Square

9 e-2

773 Lexington Ave. (at 61st St.), Upper East Side, 212/755–7851. Subway: 59th St.

7 b-8

2159 Broadway (at 76th St.), Upper West Side, 212/721–2947. Subway: 79th St.

10 d-1

C. O. BIGELOW CHEMISTS

A pharmacy the way they used to be, Bigelow's has been in the same place since 1838, but its stock has changed with the times. Besides the usual items, the store has a huge selection of homeopathic remedies, various cosmetics (especially European), a variety of toiletries, and makeup accessories. *414 6th Ave. (between 9th and 10th Sts.), Greenwich Village, 212/533–2700. Subway: W. 4th St./Washington Square.*

9 e-2

CAMBRIDGE CHEMISTS

These fine British toiletries include Floris of London, Penhaligons, Cyclax, Innoxa, Sabona of London, and Simpson (shave brushes), and extend to French, Swiss, and German items. *21 E. 65th St., Upper East Side, 212/734–5678. Subway: 68th St./Hunter College.*

9 e-4

CASWELL-MASSEY CO.

Settle your bets now—in business since 1752, Caswell-Massey is the oldest apothecary in the United States. (The original store was in Newport, Rhode Island.) The cologne specially blended for George and Martha Washington and Lafayette, the cold cream made for Sarah Bernhardt, and the world's largest collection of imported soaps—including pure Castile by the pound—are all for sale in this pretty and fragrant shop. Also on offer: one-of-a-kind silver jars and wood and faux-ivory brushes. *518 Lexington Ave. (at 48th St.), Midtown, 212/755–2254. Subway: 42nd St./Grand Central*

10 d-6

World Financial Center, Battery Park City (West and Liberty Sts.), Lower Manhattan, 212/945–2630. Subway: World Trade Center.

9 e-4

COSMAIR BEAUTY RESPONSE CENTER

Anyone willing to test new fragrances and cosmetics from well-known manufacturers can get free products here. Make an appointment, fill out a profile, and, if accepted, go home to evaluate the products and come back to report the results. Guinea pigs receive a gift after each visit. *575 5th Ave. (at 47th St.), 8th floor, Midtown, 212/984–4164. Subway: B, D, F, Q to 42nd St.; E, F to 5th Ave.*

9 *f-3*

COSMETIC SHOW

This shop is a true find—if you can find it, as there are no obvious signs. Go to the building entrance, but don't go inside; look left and you'll see some doors, one with a sign reading "Cosmetics." Voilà! Inside, bargains abound on name-brand products. *919 3rd Ave. (at 56th St.), Midtown, 212/750—8418. Subway: 59th St.*

9 *d-5*

COSMETICS PLUS

Cosmetics Plus has the largest selection of cosmetics and fragrances in the city, all at discounted prices. *518 5th Ave. (near 43rd St.), Midtown, 212/221–6560. Subway: B, D, F Q to 42nd St.*

9 *d-7*

275 7th Ave. (at 26th St.), Chelsea, 212/727–0705. Subway: 1, 9, C, E to 23rd St.

9 *e-3*

515 Madison Ave. (near 53rd St.,), Midtown, 212/644–1911. Subway: 51st St./Lexington–3rd Aves.

9 *d-3*

666 5th Ave. (between 52nd and 53rd Sts.), Midtown, 212/757–2895. Subway: E, F to 5th Ave.; and other locations.

9 *d-4*

CRABTREE & EVELYN

England's famed all-natural toiletries and comestibles are beautifully packed and presented for a touch of luxury. Gift baskets can be made to order. *Rockefeller Center Promenade (620 5th Ave., between 49th and 50th Sts.), Midtown, 212/581–5022. Subway: 47th–50th Sts./Rockefeller Center*

9 *e-3*

520 Madison Ave. (at 53rd St.), Midtown, 212/758–6419. Subway: E, F to 5th Ave.

10 *e-6*

151 World Trade Center (Church and Vesey Sts.), concourse level, Lower Manhattan, 212/432–7134. Subway: World Trade Center

7 *e-6*

1310 Madison Ave. (at 93rd St.), Upper East Side, 212/289–3923. Subway: 6 to 96th St.

9 *d-7*

FIFTH AVENUE PERFUMES, INC.

Make the trip for discounted prices—in the 50% range!—on popular fragrances normally found in high-end stores. *246 5th Ave. (at 28th St.), Murray Hill, 212/213–9321. Subway: N, R to 28th St.*

9 *e-8*

JAY'S PERFUME BAR

This stretch of 17th Street has several small, no-frills, down-and-dirty discount fragrance shops. Don't expect great service, but do expect great deals. *14 E. 17th St., Flatiron, 212/243–7743. Subway: N, R to 23rd St.; F to 14th St.*

10 *f-1*

KIEHL'S PHARMACY

Since 1851 this fascinating pharmacy, now a New York institution, has carried a large selection of pure essences (including one called Rain), perfumes, homeopathic remedies, and cosmetics (foundation and lip color only, filled with vitamins and sunscreen), and all-natural ingredients for remedies to cure whatever ails you. The store makes all of its own products on the premises, including the "Age Deterrent" cream. Alas, they no longer carry leeches, but they do stock over 300 different treatments for hair, body, skin, and nails. The staff is knowledgeable and helpful. *109 3rd Ave. (near 13th St.), East Village, 212/677–3171 or 212/475–3698. Subway: 3rd Ave.*

11 *d-4*

ORIGINS

This user-friendly SoHo store features exclusively Origins products: soaps, oils for massage and bath, lotions, aromatherapy, skin treatments, and related accessories. *402 W. Broadway (at Spring St.), SoHo, 212/219–9764. Subway: C, E to Spring St.*

11 *e-1*

PERFUMANIA

The nationwide chain stocks hundreds of fragrances, from high-end designer scents to the more obscure. They promise an average discount of 70%. *755 Broadway (at 8th St.), Greenwich Village, 212/979–7674. Subway: 8th St.*

9 *d-6*

20 W. 34th St., Garment District, 212/736–0414. Subway: 34th St./Herald Square

9 *e-2*

782 Lexington Ave. (between 60th and 61st Sts.), Upper East Side, 212/750–2810. Subway: 59th St.

7 *b-7*

2321 Broadway (at 84th St.), Upper West Side, 212/595–8778. Subway: 1, 9 to 86th St.; other locations.

hair

New Yorkers know that hair is an important accessory, and that it can cost a fortune in upkeep. What many don't know is that almost every high-end salon has a training night at least once a month, when haircuts and color are either greatly discounted or free. The catch is that a student cuts your hair, but the proceedings are highly supervised, and you never know who that student will be in three years.

Note that many salons are closed on Monday.

11 *e-1*

ASTOR PLACE BARBER STYLIST

Success story: A family-owned 1940s barbershop finds new life as the in place to have your tresses trimmed—if you're young or adventuresome. Choose from the Guido, Detroit, Little Tony, Punk, Mohawk, James Dean, Fort Dix, Sparkle Cut, What-the-Hell, Spike, Spina di Pesce . . . It's cheap and fun, but you may have to wait up to two hours on weekends. The street scene is interesting in itself. They still give shaves, and now have an annex for perms, manicures, pedicures, facials, and all the rest. *2 Astor Pl., East Village, 212/475–9854 or 212/475–9790. Subway: Astor Pl.*

9 *e-3*

BRAD JOHNS

Specializing in blond color, Brad Johns is extremely opinionated but really quite fabulous. He tends to the locks of editors and celebs alike. *693 5th Ave. (between 54th and 55th Sts.), Midtown, 212/583–0034. Subway: E, F to 5th Ave.*

9 *e-3*

FREDERIC FEKKAI BEAUTÉ DE PROVENCE

A fashion-world darling, Fekkai now reigns in his own wonderful salon in the Chanel building, creating elegant, feminine looks in quiet private rooms. Clients include Cindy Crawford, Sigourney Weaver, and Kelly McGillis. Pampering options include massage. *Frederic Fekkai Beauté de Provence, 15 E. 57th St., Midtown, 212/753–9500. Subway: E, F, N, R to 5th Ave.*

9 *d-3*

GARREN NEW YORK AT HENRI BENDEL

A fashion-world favorite—he made over Lisa Marie Presley for her *Vogue* cover shoot—Garren recently opened a full-service salon at Henri Bendel. *712 5th Ave. (at 56th St.), Midtown, 212/841–9400. Subway: E, F, N, R to 5th Ave.*

9 *b-1*

GEMAYEL SALON

Gemayel is the Upper West side choice for fun, trendy cuts at reasonable prices. *2030 Broadway (at 70th St.), Upper West Side, 212/787–5555. Subway: 1, 2, 3, 9 to 72nd St.*

9 *b-1*

HAROLD MELVIN BEAUTY SALON

Specializing in African-American hair, Melvin has built quite a reputation among celebrities, and has done hair for magazine shoots and movie sets. *137 W. 72nd St., Upper West Side, 212/724–7700. Subway: 1, 2, 3, 9 to 72nd St.*

9 *e-7*

JEAN LOUIS DAVID

Drop in here for the streamlined, quick-service approach. Designer cuts, styles, perms, and colors take less than an hour and are very reasonably priced. They don't make appointments, but you can wait for your favorite stylist if you want an ongoing relationship. *303 Park Ave. S (at 23rd St.), Gramercy, 212/260–3920. Subway: 6 to 23rd St.*

9 *e-4*

367 Madison Ave. (at 46th St.), Midtown, 212/808–9117. Subway: 42nd St./Grand Central

9 *d-4*

1180 6th Ave. (at 46th St.), Midtown, 212/944–7389. Subway: 47th–50th Sts./Rockefeller Center

9 *b-1*

2113 Broadway (at 73rd St.), Upper West Side, 212/873–1850; other locations.

173

10 *e-7*

JOHN ALLAN'S

A respite for busy Wall Streeters, John Allan is a full-service salon for men only. Between haircuts and manicures, you can mess around with the pool table, drum set, and requisite humidor. *95 Trinity Pl. (at Thames St.), Lower Manhattan, 212/406–3000. Subway: Wall St.*

11 *d-4*

JOHN DELARIA

This busy SoHo salon has three floors of stylists trained in every look from classic to *au moment*. Walk-ins are usually accomodated, and prices are reasonable. *433 W. Broadway (between Prince and Spring Sts.), SoHo, 212/925–4461. Subway: C, E to Spring St.*

11 *d-6*

JOHN MASTERS ORGANIC HAIRCARE

Masters and his colleagues specialize in color, using only plant- and vegetable-based dyes. *79 Sullivan St. (near Canal St.), SoHo, 212/343–9590. Subway: A, C, E to Canal St.*

9 *d-3*

LINDA TAM SALON

Chosen for "Best Hair Coloring" by *New York Press*, Linda Tam is not cheap, but followers swear to a no-nonsense color job that won't fade after a few washes. *680 5th Ave. (between 53rd and 54th Sts.), Midtown, 212/757–2555. Subway: E, F to 5th Ave.*

9 *e-1*

LOUIS LICARI COLOR GROUP

For blended tone-on-tone coloring and a beautifully healthy, natural look, he's the tops—just ask Christie Brinkley, Ellen Barkin, or Jessica Lange. Ask also about training nights, for huge discounts on cut or color. Come in for a free consultation weekdays 9–5. *797 Madison Ave. (near 67th St.), Upper East Side, 212/517–8084. Subway: 68th St./Hunter College.*

9 *e-2*

MARSHALL KIM

Kim is a favorite neighborhood barber with Upper East Siders. *788 Lexington Ave. (at 61st St.), Upper East Side, 212/486–2453. Subway: 59th St.*

9 *e-3*

ORIBE SALON LTD.

Now firmly ensconced behind Elizabeth Arden's red door, Oribe is booked months in advance. He's usually at photo shoots—you know, tending the models' tresses. This is the trendiest salon in town for individual, feminine-sexy looks like those of Kelly Klein, Darryl Hannah, and Linda Evangelista. *691 5th Ave. (at 54th St.), Midtown, 212/319–3910. Subway: E, F to 5th Ave.*

11 *a-1*

PERRY WEST

There's always a wait—but a fun one—for chatty and fun owner Bentley Rand, formerly of Bumble & Bumble, who gives cuts and colors in a cozy West Village setting. *55 Greenwich Ave. (at Perry St.; enter on Perry), West Village, 212/463–0387. Subway: Christopher St./Sheridan Square.*

9 *e-3*

PIERRE MICHEL COIFFEUR

A longtime specialist in the treatment and styling of long hair, Pierre Michel is also a full-service beauty salon for both men and women. *Trump Tower (725 5th Ave., at 56th St.), Midtown, 212/593–1460. Subway: E, F to 5th Ave.*

9 *d-3*

Plaza Hotel, 5th Ave. and 59th St., Midtown, 212/593–7930. Subway: N, R to 5th Ave.

11 *a-1*

ROBERT KREE

This light, airy, open West Village salon gives "cuts so good we actually go back." It looks trendy, but there's no attitude. *375 Bleecker St. (between Charles and Perry Sts.), West Village, 212/989–9547. Subway: Christopher St./Sheridan Square.*

11 *c-4*

SPACE

Very stylish, very unpretentious, and very new, Space has already won design awards for its interior, and is bound to be a haircut hot spot soon. *155 6th Ave. (at Spring St.), SoHo, 212/647–8588. Subway: C, E to Spring St.*

9 *e-2*

VIDAL SASSOON

The man who liberated hair now has 32 stylists and a helpful staff, providing cuts, color, and perms for both men and women. *767 5th Ave. (at 59th St.), Midtown, 212/535–9200. Subway: N, R to 5th Ave.*

10 *d-1*

90 5th Ave. (at 15th St.), Flatiron, 212/229–2200. Subway: 14th St./Union Square

9 *d-3*

WARREN TRICOMI

Downtown comes uptown in this full-service salon, with a regular clientele including many celebs. *16 W. 57th St., Midtown, 212/262–8899. Subway: E, F, N, R to 5th Ave.*

massage

11 *e-4*

BLISS SPA

Chosen by *New York Press* as having the "Best Gift Certificate," Bliss is the hot spa of the moment. With friendly staff and a wide range of massage options, it books up weeks in advance, so call ahead. *See* Skin Care & Day Spas, *below. 568 Broadway (at Prince St.), SoHo, 212/219–8970. Subway: Prince St.; Broadway–Lafayette St.*

9 *d-8*

CARAPAN

Decorated to look and feel like New Mexico, Carapan specializes in Swedish massage but offers seven other kinds, as well as facials, craniosacral therapy, and other healing measures. It's a treasure. *5 W. 16th St., Chelsea, 212/633–6220. Subway: F to 14th St.*

7 *b-8*

CYNTHIA CRISP

A licensed massage therapist, Cynthia Crisp is trained in everything from acupuncture to lymph drainage to Mongolian bone massage. Her fans include Donna Karan and Lou Reed. *127 W. 79th St., Upper West Side, 212/228–0900. Subway: 79th St.*

9 *d-3*

DORIT BAXTER

Facials, body scrubs and treatments, and a full-service salon are wrapped up in a convenient Midtown location. *47 W. 57th. St., Midtown, 212/371–4542. Subway: B, Q to 57th St.*

9 *d-3*

ELIZABETH ARDEN

See Skin Care & Day Spas, *below.*

9 *e-3*

GEORGETTE KLINGER

See Skin Care & Day Spas, *below.*

7 *e-8*

See Skin Care & Day Spas, *below.*

11 *d-7*

MILLEFLEURS

Patterned after an Egyptian temple, Millefleurs offers herbal wraps, scrubs, massages, facials, reflexology, acupuncture, and even colonics in an incredible setting complete with waterfalls. *6 Varick St. (at Franklin St.), West Village, 212/966–3656. Subway: Franklin St.*

9 *d-7*

OHASHI INSTITUTE

This spa offers Ohashi Shiatsu, a form of traditional bodywork created by Japanese healer Ohashi. The environment is low-key; clients lie on soft mats surrounded by Japanese paper screens. *12 W. 27th St., Chelsea, 212/684–4190. Subway: N, R to 28th St.; F to 23rd St.*

9 *a-7*

ORIGINS FEEL-GOOD SPA

Origins offers so many services, including a variety of full-day packages and any fraction thereof, that they're almost too numerous to mention: massage, reflexology, facials, acupressure, mud and seaweed treatments . . . call for a brochure. *The Sports Center, Pier 60, Chelsea Piers (12th Ave. and 23rd St.), Chelsea, 212/336–6780. Subway: C, E to 23rd St.*

9 *d-3*

PENINSULA SPA

Tucked in the Peninsula Hotel, this truly deluxe facility provides all the expected treatments plus a full gym, a salon, and an incredible outdoor pool by which to take in the equally incredible view. *700 5th Ave. (at 55th St.), 21st floor, Midtown, 212/903–3910. Subway: E, F to 5th Ave.*

9 *e-2*

THE STRESS LESS STEP

This no-nonsense massage center—note the "Talking Discouraged" signs—offers Swedish, shiatsu, and reflexology. Celebrities drop in from the Regency

Hotel, across the street. *48 E. 61st St., Upper East Side, 212/826–6222. Subway: 59th St.*

11 *c-7*

ULA SKIN CARE SALON

See Skin Care & Day Spas, *below.*

skin care & day spas

Each of the major department stores devotes a chunk of its main floor to cosmetics. All of the big names are represented, and there are often sample demonstrations, free makeovers, and promotional gifts.

11 *e-4*

BLISS SPA

This full-service SoHo salon is frequented by models and celebs, who love the trendy Oxygen facials and the various massage options (*see* Massage, *above*). *568 Broadway (at Prince St.), 212/219–8970. Subway: Broadway–Lafayette St.; Prince St.*

9 *e-2*

BOYD CHEMISTS

Boyd sells a dazzling array of European makeup and treatment products in addition to their own line. Experts-in-residence give beauty advice, makeup demonstrations, lessons, and encouragement. It's a mecca for beautiful people and wannabes alike, and now also has a salon facility for haircuts, facials, and waxing. Oh, and they still fill prescriptions. *655 Madison Ave. (near 60th St.), Upper East Side, 212/838–6558. Subway: 59th St.*

9 *d-3*

CHRISTINA & CARMEN

This Romanian mother-and-daughter team uses traditional techniques in their deep pore-cleansing facials, body-sloughing with paraffin, and stress-relieving shiatsu massage. They also sell holistic plant-based products for the road. *128 Central Park S, Midtown, 212/757–5811. Subway: B, Q, N, R to 57th St.*

9 *e-3*

CHRISTINE VALMY

Renowned skin-care expert Christine Valmy helped American women discover skin care. Using Swiss fresh-cell therapy, she gives both men and women two-hour facials and offers post–plastic surgery care, makeup, and foot massage. A special pretheater package includes facial, manicure, shampoo, and blow-dry. Weekdays you can opt for a lower-price facial by a supervised student at the Valmy School for Aestheticians (212/581–1520 for appt.). *767 5th Ave. (at 58th St.), Midtown, 212/752–0303. Subway: N, R to 5th Ave.*

9 *d-3*

101 W. 57th St., Midtown, 212/581–9488. Subway: B, Q to 57th St.

9 *d-3*

DIANE YOUNG

Come here for holistic skin care in a beautiful setting. Young offers facials, treatments, herbal aromatherapy, expert nutritional advice, makeup lessons, manicures, pedicures, Swedish massage, waxing, and electrolysis (with disposable needles). Day of Beauty packages are available, as is the Ultimate Makeover. *38 E. 57th St., Midtown, 212/753–1200. Subway: E, F, N, R, to 5th Ave.*

9 *e-1*

ELENA POCIU

Romanian-born Pociu runs a full-service skin-care salon, specializing in facials. Her masks are made on the premises. *23 E. 67th St., Upper East Side, 212/717–5543. Subway: 68th St./Hunter College.*

9 *e-3*

ELIZABETH ARDEN/ THE SALON

Just knock on the red door for head-to-toenail pampering in this Midtown mini-spa. Expert facials and free makeup applications are among the many highlights. Treat yourself or a loved one to a Miracle Morning or a Main Chance Day: You get a spell in the sauna followed by massage, haircut and styling, facial, manicure and pedicure, eyebrow shaping, and makeup. *691 5th Ave. (near 54th St.), 212/486–7900. Subway: E, F to 5th Ave.*

11 *d-4*

ERBE

A favorite with SoHo denizens, Erbe offers facials and a legendary line of skin products. *196 Prince St. (near MacDougal St.), SoHo, 212/966–1445. Subway: Prince St.*

9 c-1

FACE STOCKHOLM

A household name in Sweden, Face offers fabulous makeup at great prices. Creative director and makeover whiz Gary Greco can usually be found at the SoHo store, throwing together fresh looks for the likes of Winona Ryder or Carolyn Bessette Kennedy. *224 Columbus Ave. (at 71st. St.), 212/769–1420. Subway: 72nd St.*

11 e-4

110 Prince St. (at Greene St.), SoHo, 212/334–3900. Subway: Prince St.

9 e-3

GEORGETTE KLINGER SKIN CARE

Klinger's famously expert skin treatments include surface peeling, deep-pore cleansing, and scalp care for both women and men. Take advantage of the new full-day, full-body "Intensive Curriculum," also for both sexes, at 978 Madison. The only drawback is a hard sell of the product line. *501 Madison Ave. (near 52nd St.), Midtown, 212/838–3200. Subway: 51st St./Lexington–3rd Aves.*

7 e-8

978 Madison Ave. (near 77th St.), Upper East Side, 212/744–6900. Subway: 77th St.

9 e-2

IL MAKIAGE

An Upper East Side trendsetter, Il Makiage has over 200 eye and cheek colors and updates them seasonally. Makeover programs range from an elementary eye primer to a full makeup consultation and are really quite special. *107 E. 60th St., Upper East Side, 212/371–3992. Closed Sat. Subway: 59th St.*

9 e-3

JANET SARTIN

Come in for a consultation and get a product-and-treatment prescription from a world-famous skin expert—Sartin herself charges $400 for a 90-minute pore-cleansing facial. The staff is well trained, and the clientele is high on the social registry. *480 Park Ave. (near 58th St.), Midtown, 212/751–5858. Subway: 59th St.*

10 f-1

KIEHL'S PHARMACY

See Fragrance & Skin Products, *above.*

7 e-8

LAURA GELLER MAKEUP STUDIOS

A former makeup artist on Broadway, Geller will make you up, give you a makeup lesson, sell you her own products, and make up your wedding party when the time comes. *1044 Lexington Ave. (at 74th St.), Upper East Side, 212/570–5477. Subway: 77th St.*

9 e-3

LIA SCHORR SKIN CARE

Ms. Schorr analyzes every client's skin prior to treatment, resulting in sensible care, especially for sensitive and acne-plagued skin. Her restorative Day of Beauty includes a facial, body massage, manicure, pedicure, makeup and snack. Men are welcome, too. *686 Lexington Ave. (near 57th St.), Midtown, 212/486–9670. Subway: 59th St.*

11 c-1

M.A.C

M.A.C. stands for Make-Up Art Cosmetics, created by makeup artist Frank Toskan in 1984. The popular products are vitamin-enriched, contain no mineral oil or fragrance, are not tested on animals, and come in a variety of textures as well as tints—and the store recycles the containers. It's geared toward makeup professionals, but clients include Cher, Madonna, Gloria Estefan, and Paula Abdul. *14 Christopher St. (near 6th Ave.), West Village, 212/243–4150. Subway: Christopher St./Sheridan Square*

11 d-4

113 Spring St. (near Wooster St.), SoHo, 212/334–4641. Subway: Spring St. Closed Mon.

9 d-8

THE MAKEUP SHOP

Led by makeup artist Tobi Britton, The Makeup Shop offers makeovers, makeup lessons, eyebrow shaping, and a whole line of products. *131 W. 21st St., Chelsea, 212/807–0447. Subway: F, 1, 9 to 23rd St.*

9 f-3

MARIO BADESCU SKIN CARE

Sadly, Mario is gone, but his expert analyses and natural-formula skin products for women and men still have a loyal following. Other options include manicures, pedicures, massage, waxing, and electrolysis. *320 E. 52nd St., Midtown, 212/758–1065. Subway: 51st St./Lexington–3rd Aves.*

11 *d-4*

MAKE-UP FOREVER

Hip and happening makeup keeps downtowners happy—even if they now live uptown. *Pierre 409 W. Broadway (between Spring and Prince Sts.), SoHo, 212/941–9337. Subway: C, E to Spring St.*

9 *e-3*

Michel Beauty Salon, Trump Tower (725 5th Ave., at 56th St.) Midtown, 212/757–5175. Subway: E, F to 5th Ave.

11 *d-1*

PATRICIA FIELD

These are the raw materials for the downtown avant-garde look—non-smudge matte liners, matte lipsticks and lip pencils, lip paint from Japan. Even your mother won't recognize you. Note: The SoHo store is called Hotel Venus. *10 E. 8th St., East Village, 212/254–1699. Subway: 8th St., Astor Pl.*

11 *d-5*

382 W. Broadway (between Broome and Spring Sts.), SoHo, 212/966–4066. Subway: C, E to Spring St.

9 *e-2*

PETER COPPOLA SALON

A solid hour of old-fashioned pampering, using hypo-allergenic Italian products, cleans your skin without the usual squeezing. *746 Madison Ave. (between 64th and 65th Sts.), Upper East Side, 212/988–9404. Subway: 68th St./Hunter College.*

9 *e-2*

TRISH MCEVOY

McEvoy gives deep pore-cleansing facials, body buffs, and waxing, and makeup application and lessons to the likes of Madonna and Kim Alexis. *800A 5th Ave. (near 61st St.), Upper East Side, 212/758–7790. Subway: N, R to 5th Ave.*

11 *c-7*

ULA SKIN CARE SALON

In a discreet Tribeca location, Ula offers nine different facials and seven different body treatments plus waxing, electrolysis, manicures, and pedicures in a highly relaxing setting. *22 Harrison St.*

(between Hudson and Greenwich Sts.), 212/343–2376. Subway: Franklin St.

11 *c-3*

YANA HERBAL BEAUTY SALON

Fans of Yana's have raved about her relaxing herbal facials for years. A little-known fact is that Yana also waxes; using the ancient Middle Eastern technique that involves sugar instead of wax. *270 6th Ave. (between Houston and Bleecker Sts.), West Village, 212/254–6200. Subway: W. 4th St./Washington Square.*

BICYCLES

9 *c-7*

DIFFERENT SPOKES

A fireman and a tie salesperson teamed up with one of New York's best bike mechanics to open this crackerjack shop. Ask any bike messenger about the quality of the repairs. You get all the best brands, great service, and generous opening hours. *240 7th Ave. (at 24th St.), Chelsea, 212/727–7278. Subway: 1, 9 to 23rd St.*

10 *h-4*

FRANK'S BIKE SHOP

Frank sells and repairs. The stock includes Schwinn, GT, Giant, Ross, Bianchi, Mongoose, Raleigh, and Diamond. *533 Grand St. (near Lewis St.), Lower East Side, 212/533–6332. Subway: Grand St.; Delancey St.*

10 *f-1*

METRO BICYCLE STORES

Metro sells a complete line of performance parts, accessories, and clothing for racing, touring, and road, mountain, and city biking. They also rent bikes and do expert repairs. *332 E. 14th St., East Village, 212/228–4344. Subway: 1st Ave.*

9 *c-4*

360 W. 47th St., Theater District, 212/581–4500. Subway: 49th St.

7 *e-6*

1311 Lexington Ave. (at 88th St.), Upper East Side, 212/427–4450. Subway: 4, 5, 6 to 86th St.

7 *b-5*

231 W. 96th St., Upper West Side, 212/663–7531. Subway: 1, 2, 3, 9 to 96th St.; other locations.

BOOKS

general

11 c-1

B. DALTON

The national chain has a reliable selection of popular books, magazines, and calendars. 369 6th Ave. (at 8th St.), West Village, 212/674–8780. Subway: W. 4th St./Washington Square.

9 e-8

BARNES & NOBLE, INC.

Long a downtown institution, Barnes & Noble has lately sprouted walnut-and-pine-green superstores all over the city, not to mention a few smaller shops. Some branches have specialties; the store that started it all, on lower 5th Avenue, has an excellent selection of textbooks, and the Lincoln Square emporium keeps its eye on the performing arts. B&N now has a few branches in Queens and a store in literary Park Slope, Brooklyn, so watch for more stores in the boroughs. The tolerant attitude toward browsing is a pleasure, as are the bountiful magazine racks and bookshelves, and the smell of fresh cappuccino in the aisles can be nearly irresistible. 105 5th Ave. (at 18th St.), Flatiron, 212/807–0099. Subway: N, R to 23rd St., F to 14th St.

9 d-4

600 5th Ave. (at 48th St.), Midtown, 212/765–0590

9 f-3

Citicorp Center (3rd Ave. and 54 St.), Midtown, 212/750–8033. Subway: 51st St./Lexington–3rd Aves.

9 b-2

1960 Broadway (at 66th St.), Upper West Side, 212/595–6859. Subway: 66th St./Lincoln Center, B, C to 72nd St.; and other locations.

9 e-3

BORDERS BOOKS & MUSIC

What was once a cozy Ann Arbor independent is now very much a part of the New York landscape. The World Trade Center store is a hive of activity downtown, and the newer branch on Park Avenue adds some literary interest to an otherwise quiet stretch. The selections are vast and dense, the chain's resources excellent. As long as you've got stamina, it's hard to beat Borders for a healthy mixture of quantity and quality. 461 Park Ave. (at 57th St.), Midtown, 212/980–6785. Subway: 59th St.

10 d-6

5 World Trade Center (Church and Vesey Sts.), Lower Manhattan, 212/839–8049. Subway: Cortlandt St./World Trade Center.

9 c-3

COLISEUM BOOKS, INC.

Large, well-located, well-stocked, and well-run, Coliseum is great for current paperbacks, hardcovers, reference books, and a good variety of remainders, including many for $1 from March through November. 1771 Broadway (at 57th St.), Midtown, 212/757–8381. Subway: 59th St./Columbus Circle.

7 e-6

THE CORNER BOOKSTORE

This welcoming Carnegie Hill shop specializes in literature, art, architecture, and children's books. They'll fill special orders in one day, search for out-of-print titles, and gift-wrap your choices for free. An Upper East Side perk: house accounts, even for kids. 1313 Madison Ave. (at 93rd St.), Upper East Side, 212/831–3554. Subway: 6 to 96th St.

9 d-4

GOTHAM BOOK MART AND GALLERY

Once a literary mecca, the Gotham Book Mart endures. It's particularly strong in theater, general literature (especially fiction and classics), 20th-century first editions, film, and philosophy, and has the city's largest selection of poetry. For those with arcane requirements, the store gets a whopping 250 literary and small-press magazines. 41 W. 47th St., Midtown, 212/719–4448. Subway: 47th–50th Sts./Rockefeller Center.

9 d-3

RIZZOLI

Rizzoli is famously strong in art, architecture, photography, and university-press titles, but people of letters can also pick up French, Italian, and German books; translations; foreign magazines and newspapers; and classical recordings. 31 W. 57th St. (Sohmer Bldg.), Midtown, 212/759–2424. Subway: B, Q to 57th St., N, R to 5th Ave.

11 d-4

454 W. Broadway (near Prince St.), SoHo, 212/674–1616. Subway: C, E to Spring St.

10 *d-6*

3 World Financial Center, Battery Park City (West and Liberty Sts.), Lower Manhattan, 212/385–1400. Subway: World Trade Center.

11 *e-1*

SHAKESPEARE & COMPANY

This next-generation favorite has a great selection of literature and general fiction. 716 Broadway (at Washington Pl.), Greenwich Village, 212/529–1330. Subway: 8th St.

9 *e-1*

939 Lexington Ave. (between 68th and 69th Sts.), Upper East Side, 212/570–0201. Subway: 68th St./Hunter College.

10 *f-1*

ST. MARK'S BOOKSHOP

One of the hippest bookstores in the city, St. Mark's focuses on the humanities of the moment, including literature, poetry, drama, criticism, women's studies, contemporary theory, foreign titles, and small-press offerings. Spoken-word records and tapes are also on hand. 31 3rd Ave. (at 9th St.), East Village, 212/260–7853. Subway: Astor Pl.

10 *e-1*

THE STRAND

America's largest secondhand bookstore has eight miles of books (that's 2 million titles)—in appropriately dusty quarters, at the Broadway store. Head downstairs for review copies of new books at 50% off. History, art, and Americana are particular strengths, both new and used. Warning: You'll spend more time and money than you intended. 828 Broadway (at 12th St.), Greenwich Village, 212/473–1452. Subway: 14th St./Union Square

10 *f-7*

South Street Seaport, 159 John St., Lower Manhattan, 212/809–0875. Subway: 2, 3 to Fulton St.

10 *d-1*

THREE LIVES & CO.

Three women own this lovely bookshop, named for the Gertrude Stein work and dedicated to literature. Salon readings by noted authors are a special feature. 154 W. 10th St., West Village, 212/741–2069. Subway: Christopher St./Sheridan Square.

11 *f-2*

TOWER BOOKS

Well stocked in every area, Tower is a good downtown browsing spot (the store stays open very late) and holds the usual author readings, signings, and special events. The discount scheme is very competitive. 383 Lafayette St. (at 4th St.), Greenwich Village, 212/228–5338. Subway: 8th St.

10 *e-7*

WALDENBOOKS

You know Waldenbooks—there's one in that mall you grew up in. 57 Broadway (near Rector St.), Lower Manhattan, 212/269–1139. Subway: Rector St.

antiquarian

9 *d-8*

ACADEMY BOOK STORE

This Chelsea shop specializes in art, literature, history, photography, the social sciences, and out-of-print books. 10 W. 18th St., 212/242–4848. Subway: F to 14th St.

7 *b-7*

GRYPHON BOOK SHOP

Gryphon concentrates on used and rare paperbacks, particularly on the performing arts. There's an interesting collection of pre-1940s children's books. 2246 Broadway (between 80th and 81st Sts.), Upper West Side, 212/362–0706. Subway: 79th St.

9 *d-3*

J.N. BARTFIELD

Bartfield has one of the most impressive collections of leather-bound books, rare books, and first editions in the city, and will appraise collections. 30 W. 57th St., 3rd floor, Midtown, 212/245–8890. Subway: B, Q to 57th St.; N, R to 5th Ave.

9 *d-8*

LARRY LAWRENCE RARE SPORTS

Larry specializes in rare sports books and ephemera. 150 5th Ave. (at 20th St.), Flatiron, 212/362–8593. Open by appt. only. Subway: F, N, R to 23rd St.

7 *b-3*

NATURALIST'S BOOKSHELF

Out toward the Hudson, the store has rare, antique, and just plain used books on natural history and the outdoors.

540 W. 114th St., Morningside Heights, 212/865–6202. Subway: 116th St./Columbia Univ.

9 d-7

OLD PAPER ARCHIVE

It's as quaint as it sounds, specializing in antique books on the performing arts: theatre, film, opera, and ballet. 122 W. 25th St., Chelsea, 212/645–3983. Subway: F, 1, 9 to 23rd St.

10 e-1

PAGEANT BOOK & PRINT SHOP

Literature, fiction, Americana, and used books mix well with an extensive selection of old prints and engravings. Film buffs will recognize the setting from Woody Allen's Hannah and Her Sisters. 109 E. 9th St., East Village, 212/674–5296. Subway: 8th St.; Astor Pl.

9 e-1

STUBBS BOOKS AND PRINTS

This uptown antiquarian leans toward architecture and the decorative arts, fashion, and literature. The gallery has original prints and illustrations. 153 E. 70th St., Upper East Side, 212/772–3120. Subway: 68th St./Hunter College.

special interest

9 b-1

APPLAUSE BOOKS

Applause concentrates on the performing arts, particularly drama, and reaches out toward film, video, radio, TV, and general pop culture. 211 W. 71st St., Upper West Side, 212/496–7511. Subway: 1, 2, 3, 9 to 72nd St.

10 c-1

BIOGRAPHY BOOKSHOP

True to its name, this appealing West Village shop specializes in biographies, diaries, and autobiographies as well as select fiction. 400 Bleecker St. (at 11th St.), West Village, 212/807–8655. Subway: Christopher St./Sheridan Square.

7 b-6

BLACK BOOKS PLUS

African-American history, art, literature, and general studies prevail. 702 Amsterdam Ave. (at 94th St.), Upper West Side, 212/749–9632. Subway: 1, 2, 3, 9 to 96th St.

9 d-8

BOOKS OF WONDER

This is the largest collection of children's books in the city—new, used, and out-of-print. The 19th- and early-20th-century picture books are very special, as are the book-related toys, and it's all knowledgeably purveyed. 16 W. 18th St., Chelsea, 212/989–3270. Subway: F to 14th St.

11 e-3

CENTER FOR BOOK ARTS

It's kind of meta: Here are books on the book arts, including binding and printing, and classes teaching the techniques. 626 Broadway (between Bleecker and Houston), 2nd floor, 212/460–9768. Subway: Broadway–Lafayette St.; Bleecker St.

10 d-6

CIVILIZED TRAVELLER

Everything you might need for a civilized trip, beginning with videos, maps, and guidebooks and moving on to irons, coffeemakers, security devices, converters, binoculars, games, and specialty luggage. 2 World Financial Center, 225 Liberty St., Lower Manhattan, 212/786–3301. Subway: World Trade Center.

9 b-1

2003 Broadway (at 68th St.), Upper West Side, 212/875–0306. Subway: 66th St./Lincoln Center.

9 e-2

864 Lexington Ave. (at 65th St.), Upper East Side, 212/288–9190. Subway: 68th St./Hunter College.

9 e-2

1 E. 59th St., lower level, Midtown, 212/702–9502. Subway: N, R to 5th Ave.

9 d-4

COMPLEAT STRATEGIST

The stock covers military and war games, science fiction, and fantasy. 630 5th Ave. (between 50th and 51st. Sts.), Midtown, 212/265–7449. Subway: E, F to 5th Ave.

9 e-6

THE COMPLETE TRAVELLER BOOKSTORE

This attractive Murray Hill shop is devoted to travel. In the first room, pick up guidebooks, maps, and dictionaries for the destination of your choice; in the second, browse hungrily among the used and rare travel books, including well-loved, yellowing travelogues and original WPA guides. New travel literature, posters, and art books round out the mix. It's worth a trip. *199 Madison Ave. (at 35th St.), Murray Hill, 212/685–9007. Subway: 33rd St.*

9 *d-8*

A DIFFERENT LIGHT BOOKSTORE

These books were written by and for gays and lesbians, covering everything from gay and lesbian studies and the social sciences to erotica and travel. *151 W. 19th St., Chelsea, 212/989–4850. Subway: 1, 9 to 23rd St.*

9 *d-6*

DOG LOVER'S BOOKSHOP

What's next? This shop sells both new and antique volumes on Person's Best Friend. *9 W. 31st St., Garment District, 212/594–3601. Subway: 34th St./Herald Square.*

9 *d-4*

DRAMA BOOK SHOP

The Drama Book Shop is well known for its extensive and well-organized selection of theater (especially criticism), film, and TV titles and published plays. You can also hunt down vocal scores and sheet music from Broadway musicals. *723 7th Ave. (near 48th St.), 2nd floor, Theater District, 212/944–0595. Subway: N, R to 49th St.*

10 *d-1*

EAST-WEST BOOKS

Inspired by Eastern religion and philosophy, these books focus on mental and physical well-being. *78 5th Ave. (near 14th St.), Flatiron, 212/243–5994. Subway: F to 14th St.*

7 *b-6*

568 Columbus Ave. (between 87th and 88th Sts.), Upper West Side, 212/787–7552. Subway: 1, 9 to 86th St.

10 *e-2*

EL CASCAJERO

Books on all things Hispanic: history, culture, language, and the arts. *506 La Guardia Pl. (between Bleecker and Houston Sts.), Greenwich Village, 212/254–0905. Subway: Bleecker St.*

9 *c-7*

FASHION INSTITUTE OF TECHNOLOGY BOOKSTORE

The bookstore of the prestigious fashion college covers all aspects of the industry, including design and marketing. *227 W. 27th St., Garment District, 212/564–4275. Subway: 9 to 28th St.*

9 *d-3*

HACKER ART BOOKS

This large specialty shop has old, new, and rare titles on art, architecture, and crafts, and reprints of important art books. *45 W. 57th St., 5th floor, Midtown, 212/688–7600. Subway: B, Q to 57th St.*

7 *e-6*

JEWISH MUSEUM BOOKSHOP

Selections cover all aspects of Jewish life and culture. *1109 5th Ave. (at 92nd St.), Upper East Side, 212/423–3211. Subway: 96th St.*

9 *d-4*

KINOKUNIYA BOOKSTORE

Kinokuniya is one of the largest bookstore chains in Japan. These two floors of books in Japanese cover every topic imaginable; you'll also find books about Japan in English. *10 W. 49th St., Midtown, 212/765–1461. Subway: 47th–50th Sts./Rockefeller Center.*

7 *e-6*

KITCHEN ARTS & LETTERS

For the cook in your life, Kitchen Arts & Letters has books from all over on food, cooking, and wine; food ephemera; original art and photography of food; and stationery items with a culinary theme. *1435 Lexington Ave. (near 93rd St.), Upper East Side, 212/876–5550. Closed Sun. Subway: 6 to 96th St.*

7 *b-3*

LABYRINTH BOOKS

This newcomer to New York's dwindling roster of independent bookshops opened to some fanfare in 1997. Its 100,000 titles are scholarly and academic, many from university presses; there's fiction as well. *536 W. 112th St., Morningside Hts., 212/865–1588. Subway: 110th St./Cathedral Pkwy.*

9 *d-7*

MILLER'S

Miller's has been a leading source of equestrian books for 75 years. *117 E. 24th St., Gramercy, 212/673–1400. Subway: 6 to 23rd St.*

7 *e-6*

THE MILITARY BOOKMAN

Sure enough, the selection focuses on military, naval, and aviation history, including out-of-print and rare books. *29 E. 93rd St., Upper East Side, 212/348–1280. Closed Sun.–Mon. Subway: 96th St.*

9 *f-2*

MORTON BOOKS

All the current books and periodicals on design, decorating, gardening, and architecture, all in one place. *989 3rd Ave. (near 59th St.), Midtown, 212/421–9025. Subway: 59th St.*

7 *b-6*

MURDER INK

If you can't get enough of mystery and suspense novels, Murder Ink has them new, used, and out-of-print. *2486 Broadway (between 92nd and 93rd Sts.), Upper West Side, 212/362–8905. Subway: 1, 2, 3, 9 to 96th St.*

9 *d-3*

MYSTERIOUS BOOKSHOP

New, used, and out-of-print murder, mystery, and mayhem are the selling points; the staff will also search for rare books. Mystery paraphernalia adds a graphic touch. *129 W. 56th St., Midtown, 212/765–0900. Subway: B, Q, N, R to 57th St.*

9 *e-5*

NEW YORK ASTROLOGY CENTER

A complete line of astrology books is supplemented by titles on acupuncture and the healing arts. *124 E. 40th St., Suite 402, Midtown, 212/949–7211. Subway: 42nd St./Grand Central.*

11 *e-5*

NEW YORK OPEN CENTER BOOKSHOP

New Age topics are the main thrust, including holistic medicine, health and nutrition, and meditation. *83 Spring St. (between Broadway and Lafayette Sts.), SoHo, 212/219–2527. Subway: 6 to Spring St.*

11 *a-2*

OSCAR WILDE MEMORIAL BOOKSHOP

Specializing in gay and lesbian titles, this shop also sells stationery, cards, records, T-shirts, and jewelry. *15 Christopher St. (near Greenwich Ave.), West Village, 212/255–8097. Subway: Christopher St./Sheridan Square.*

10 *d-1*

PARTNERS & CRIME MYSTERY BOOKSELLERS

For the serious aficionado, this downtown shop has new, used, and antique books, magazines, and other periodicals on crime, mystery, espionage, and the like. *44 Greenwich Ave. (between 6th and 7th Aves.), West Village, 212/243–0440. Subway: F, 1, 2, 3, 9 to 14th St.*

11 *d-4*

PERIMETER

Perimeter's collection focuses on architecture and design. *146 Sullivan St. (between Houston and Prince Sts.), SoHo, 212/529–2275. Subway: C, E to Spring St.*

11 *e-4*

A PHOTOGRAPHER'S PLACE

This may be the city's best selection of photography books, both new and used. *133 Mercer St. (between Prince and Spring Sts.), SoHo, 212/431–9358. Subway: Prince St.; 6 to Spring St.*

11 *d-3*

SCIENCE FICTION SHOP

Longtime source in larger quarters, filled with books on science fiction, fact, and fantasy; new and old. *214 Sullivan St. (between Bleecker and W. 3rd Sts.), Room 2D, Greenwich Village, 212/473–3010. Subway: W. 4th St./Washington Sq.*

10 *f-6*

SOUTH STREET SEAPORT BOOK & CHART STORE

In keeping with the nautical theme in these parts, this charming shop stocks nautical and New York books joined by maritime periodicals, posters, prints, and charts. *209 Water St. (near Fulton St.), Lower Manhattan, 212/669–9455. Subway: 2, 3 to Fulton St.*

9 *d-3*

TRAVELLER'S BOOKSTORE

An oasis for travel buffs, these intelligently organized shelves are stuffed with guidebooks, fiction, and nonfiction on every country under the sun—okay, every country on earth. The wonderful travel merchandise includes diaries, currency converters, electrical converters, ponchos, bags, and flashlights. The staff is friendly and interested. *22 W. 52nd St. (lobby), Midtown, 212/664–0995. Subway: E, F to 5th Ave.*

10 *e-7*

TRINITY BOOKSHOP

Come here for a good selection of technical and financial books. *74 Trinity Pl. (near Rector St.), Lower Manhattan, 212/349–0376. Closed weekends. Subway: Rector St.*

9 *e-4*

URBAN CENTER BOOKS

Run by the Municipal Art Society, Urban Books specializes in architecture, urban design and planning, and historic preservation. *457 Madison Ave. (near 51st St.), Midtown, 212/935–3595. Closed Sun. Subway: 51st St./Lexington–3rd Aves.*

10 *e-1*

FRED WILSON BOOKS

Yes, it's an entire store full of new and used books on chess. You can even sign up for a seminar. *80 E. 11th St., Suite 334, Greenwich Village, 212/533–6381. Subway: 8th St.; Astor Pl.*

BUTTONS

Most button and notions shops are in the West 30s between 5th and 6th avenues, and on 6th Avenue between 34th and 39th streets.

9 *c-5*

GORDON BUTTON CO.

Think about it: Ten million buttons and buckles in 5,000 varieties, from classic to novelty, from 10¢ to $2 each—and lo, service with a smile. *222 W. 38th St., Garment District, 212/921–1684. Closed weekends. Subway: 34th St./Herald Square.*

9 *e-2*

TENDER BUTTONS

This special shop displays every kind of button imaginable, including sets of old and rare buttons and antique buckles and cufflinks. Prices range from 25¢ to

$3,500. *143 E. 62nd St., Upper East Side, 212/758–7004. Subway: 59th St.*

CANDLES

Candles have become so popular that almost every gift, home-furnishings, or department store has a selection. These stores sell candles exclusively.

11 *b-2*

CANDLE SHOP

It's the best, with candles in every color, shape, and size for every occasion, and holders in which to plunk them. *118 Christopher St. (near Bleecker St.), West Village, 212/989–0148. Subway: Christopher St./Sheridan Square.*

9 *d-8*

CANDLESHTICK

If you can picture it, they carry it. Feast your nose on the scented candles, and your eyes on the candlesticks and decorative votives. *181 7th Ave. (between 20th and 21st Sts.), Chelsea, 212/924–5444. Subway: 1, 9 to 23rd St.*

7 *b-6*

2444 Broadway (between 90th and 91st Sts.), Upper West Side, 212/787–5444. Subway: 1, 9 to 86th St.

10 *f-1*

ENCHANTMENTS, INC.

This is the best selection of specifically inexpensive candles downtown, from votives to tapers to columns to those already poured into a jar. *341 E. 9th St., East Village, 212/228–4394. Subway: 8th St./Astor Pl.*

COINS

9 *d-3*

COEN-BLUM, INC.

They buy and sell rare coins both foreign and domestic; gold and silver; and Franklin Mint collections. *39 W. 55th St., Midtown, 212/246–5025. Subway: E, F to 5th Ave.*

9 *f-3*

PAUL J. BOSCO

Bosco specializes in coins from around the world, circa 1500–1900, and also has medals and tokens. *1050 2nd Ave. (at 55th St.), Midtown, 212/758–2646. Subway: 59th St.*

9 e-2

SPINK AMERICA

A member of the Christie's group, Spink America deals and auctions rare coins and bank notes. *502 Park Ave. (at 59th St.), Midtown, 212/546–1056. Subway: 59th St.*

9 d-3

STACK'S

America's oldest and largest coin dealer, Stack's deals in rare coins (U.S. and foreign) and sells ancient gold, silver, and copper coins at retail. The house holds eight auctions a year. *123 W. 57th St., Midtown, 212/582–2580. Closed weekends. Subway: B, Q, N, R to 57th St.*

COMPUTERS & SOFTWARE

10 e-6

J&R MUSIC & COMPUTER WORLD

It's chaos in here, but J&R is staffed with savvy salespeople who are far more patient than you'd think, if you can only flag one down. You'll find all the major brands: Apple, AT&T, Brother, Compaq, Epson, HP, IBM, Intel, NEC, Panasonic, Sony, Texas Instruments, and more. *15 Park Row (between Ann & Beekman Sts.), Lower Manhattan, 212/238–9100. Subway: Brooklyn Bridge/City Hall.*

9 d-7

TEKSERVE

It's almost quaint, their nickname: "The Old Reliable Mac Service Shop." True, Mac sales are secondary to service and repair at this haven for Mac users, but these salespeople are some of the most knowledgeable in New York, and they're incredibly honest and friendly. Doubts? Check out the line in their hallway at 8:55 a.m. This writer once spilled a beer on her PowerBook, and Tekserve was entirely sympathetic—said a Diet Coke would have been worse. *155 W. 23rd St., 4th floor, Chelsea, 212/929–3645. Subway: 1, 9, F to 23rd St.*

COSTUME RENTAL

All of these companies rent costumes to both consumers and folks in the trade. Note that you will be allowed to take Polaroids when you try the costumes on, but will probably be charged a fee for each picture, as companies don't want their costumes to be copied. You may want to call ahead for the company's policy.

11 a-2

ABRACADABRA

Here's a huge inventory of costumes, with masks, magic, and makeup to top them off. *10 Christopher St. (near Greenwich Ave.), West Village, 212/627–5745. Subway: Christopher St./Sheridan Square.*

3 c-4

EAVES-BROOKS COSTUME CO.

A longtime renter of theatrical costumes, Eaves-Brooks has thousands in very good condition and can also manufacture to your specifications. *21–07 41st Ave. (near 21st St.), Long Island City, Queens, 718/729–1010. Closed weekends; longer hours around Halloween. Subway: B, Q to 21st St./Queensbridge.*

9 c-7

ODD'S COSTUME RENTALS

This huge loft area is filled with costumes and associated props. *231 W. 29th St., Garment District, 212/268–6227. Open by appt. only. Subway: 34th St./Penn Station.*

9 d-7

SOURCE III

Dress up the whole family in vintage, character, and contemporary clothing for men, women, and children. *49 W. 24th St., Chelsea, 212/243–2164. Subway: F to 23rd St.*

4 f-5

ZAK'S FUN HOUSE

Zak's rents and sells costumes, wigs, masks, makeup, and props. *2214 86th St., Bay Ridge, Brooklyn, 718/373–4092. Subway: R to 86th St.*

CRAFTS & HOBBIES

10 f-1

CLAYWORKS POTTERY

Clayworks is a retail shop by day and a studio in the evening, with classes in stoneware and earthenware. *332 E. 9th St., East Village, 212/677–8311. Hours vary; call first. Subway: Astor Pl.; 1st Ave.*

9 e-2

THE WOMAN'S EXCHANGE

Sixty percent of each sale goes to the consigner, who is generally a craftsperson in need. Wares include hand-smocked clothing for children, sweaters, toys, quilts, homemade jams, and chocolates. *149 E. 60th St., Upper East Side, 212/753–2330. Closed Sun. Subway: 59th St.*

CLOTHING FOR WOMEN/GENERAL

conservative

9 e-2

AQUASCUTUM OF LONDON

The funny name derives from the Latin for "water shield," and that's what this very British firm does best. A lined raincoat—trench-style, of course—can run over $600. There are also exceedingly proper long pleated skirts, traditional blazers, and knitwear. Triple-digit price tags are the norm. *714 Madison Ave. (between 63rd and 64th Sts.), Upper East Side, 212/753–8305. Subway: 59th St.*

9 e-5

BROOKS BROTHERS

The women's clothes in this menswear bastion are often variations on old-boy standards. Women can snag loafers, double-breasted navy wool blazers (a little under $200), and men's-style, French-cuff, cotton button-downs ($48). The Madison Avenue branch has a larger selection. *346 Madison Ave. (at 44th St.), Midtown, 212/682–8800. Subway: 42nd St./Grand Central.*

10 e-6

1 Church St. (Liberty Plaza), Lower Manhattan, 212/267–2400. Subway: World Trade Center.

9 e-3

BURBERRYS

The signature Burberrys plaid appears in most Americans' image of classic British clothing, and so it appears to handsome effect here on nasty-weather gear: umbrellas, scarves, and trench-coat linings. *9 E. 57th St., Midtown, 212/371–5010. Subway: E, F, N, R to 5th Ave.*

9 d-3

ESCADA

Everything in this store appears to have a high-gloss polish, from the gold-tone railings to the buttons and sequins to the bright colors on the racks. Suits are nicely shaped, and skirts are normally just above the knee; even the few denim items look tailored. No high-tech fabrics here: blazers of 100% camel hair run about $1,650. *7 E. 57th St., Midtown, 212/755–2200. Subway: E, F, N, R to 5th Ave.*

9 e-1

JAEGER INTERNATIONAL

Jaeger's classic English sportswear is very well made; it goes beyond trench coats to dresses, vests, and sweater sets. *818 Madison Ave. (at 69th St.), Upper East Side, 212/628–3350. Subway: 68th St./Hunter College.*

9 d-3

LOUIS FÉRAUD

These suits hint at their Parisian roots; jackets sometimes have a ruffle at the neck, or are shown with one of those oh-so-Euro short capes tossed around the shoulders. Some of the summer clothes, on the other hand, scream for a cruise. *3 W. 56th St., Midtown, 212/956–7010. Subway: B, Q to 57th St.: N, R to 5th Ave.*

7 e-8

NORIKO MAEDA

This ultrafeminine store—perfumed air, silver tea service—is the designer's only post outside Japan. Some suits seem to be nodding to Audrey Hepburn, with their three-quarter-length sleeves and round-brimmed hats. Most start around $1,000 and can go up to more than double that. *985 Madison Ave. (between 76th and 77th Sts.), Upper East Side, 212/717–0330. Subway: 77th St.*

9 e-3

ST. JOHN

This designer's 5th Avenue outpost caters to the silk-scarf-and-pearls set. Many of the suits owe more than a little to Chanel; others have a whiff of the nautical about them. *665 5th Ave. (at 53rd St.), Midtown, 212/755–5252. Subway: E, F to 5th Ave.*

contemporary

10 f-7

ABERCROMBIE & FITCH

Wholesome and urbanely rugged (corduroy jumpers with a slightly curved waist, woolly sweaters, flannel shirts), this chain has the audacity to make a point of not producing any all-black clothes. *110 Water St. (at Fulton St.), Lower Manhattan, 212/809–9000. Subway: 2, 3 to Fulton St.*

11 f-4

ABOUT TIME

Frankly, it's about time this place got some more attention. The stock includes dramatic ensembles by Victor de Souza and M. Yoko and some vintage wear, from leopard-print slips à la Mrs. Robinson to demure black suits. *13–15 Prince St. (at Elizabeth St.), SoHo/Little Italy, 212/941–0966. Closed Mon. except by appt. Subway: Prince St.*

11 e-4

AGNÈS B.

These stores feel more authentically French than a squashed beret. The French adoration for the "7th art," i.e., the movies, is indulged with posters (Godard, not Spielberg) and the occasional T-shirt proclaiming "j'aime le cinéma". The separates are low-key but flatteringly cut; seasonal staples are, naturally, in black and white. With its small but choice range of shoes, filmy scarves, and even makeup, this line could outfit you completely, without making you a cookie cutter. Just remember not to pronounce the "g" when you tell people where you got those trim pants. *116 Prince St. (between Greene and Wooster Sts.), SoHo, 212/925–4649. Subway: Prince St.*

7 e-7

1063 Madison Ave. (between 80th and 81st Sts.), Upper East Side, 212/570–9333. Subway: 77th St.

9 d-8

13 E. 16th St., Chelsea, 212/741–2585. Subway: F to 14th St.

9 e-2

AGNONA

Having had enough of subcontracting its fabrics to other makers, this Italian wool company started at the top of the retail world—an exclusive Madison Avenue boutique. They continue to mill their own phenomenally soft wools and cashmeres, and now produce a smallish (though expensive) ready-to-wear line. Sweaters run about $400–$975; there are also long coats (in the thousands of dollars), bathrobes, pajamas, and even cashmere teddy bears. Don't come here for tropical colors: the color palette is strictly neutral. *744–748 Madison Ave. (between 64th and 65th Sts.), Upper East Side, 212/452–2119. Subway: 68th St./Hunter College.*

7 e-8

ALICIA MUGETTI

This store gives new meaning to the concept of the flowered silk dress. The softly hued silk, often crinkled, is embroidered or exquisitely hand-painted. Many of the gauzy items need to be layered. *999 Madison Ave. (between 77th and 78th Sts.), Upper East Side, 212/794–6186. Subway: 77th St.*

11 d-4

186 Prince St. (at Sullivan St.), SoHo, 212/226–5064. Subway: Prince St.

9 e-2

ANN TAYLOR

Like a good hardware store, Ann Taylor has nearly everything on hand for a quick fix-it. You can put together a very presentable boardroom outfit in no time, from crisp white blouse to hose; all you need to bring from home are your skivvies. A tidy skirt suit runs about $300, and utilitarian bodysuits are circa $50. Many items are dosed with rayon, but those that aren't, like the silk blouses, are still reasonably priced. The shoe selection is stuffed with stacked-heel loafers, and if you truly want head-to-toe AT, there's even cologne. The tailored look infuses the casual clothes, too, resulting in navy-blazer-and-khaki combos and oxford-style shirts. The Madison Avenue location is the biggest; four stories tall, it's got an entire floor for petites. *645 Madison Ave. (at 60th St.), Upper East Side, 212/832–2010. Subway: 59th St.*

9 b-1

2015–2017 Broadway (at 69th St.), Upper West Side, 212/873–7344. Subway: 72nd St.

9 e-4

850 3rd Ave. (at 52nd St.), Midtown, 212/308–5333. Subway: 51st St./Lexington–3rd Aves.; other locations.

11 *e-4*
ANNA SUI
Anna Sui is not a designer opposed to rhinestones. Her purple-and-black SoHo boutique is bedecked with neon posters of alternative bands (Beck, the Beastie Boys) to match the rock-star clothes. Fringe, glitter, and suede make regular appearances; the rocker look was cemented by the arrival of Hanes underwear printed with the faces of KISS. *113 Greene St. (between Spring and Prince Sts.), SoHo, 212/941–8406. Subway: Prince St.*

11 *d-5*
ANTHROPOLOGIE
You won't be surprised to hear that this store is a corporate sibling of Urban Outfitters. It lures those who have outgrown patchouli oil and butterfly chairs with the same basic layout: not-too-serious housewares, not-too-fancy clothes. As the name implies, things here are down-home—the prices are moderate, the sweaters slouchy, the skirts often drapey, and tags rarely read "Dry Clean Only". Even the labels sound crunchy or all-American: Pulp, Buffalo, Lucky Brand. *375 W. Broadway (between Broome and Spring Sts.), SoHo, 212/343–7070. Subway: 6 to Spring St.*

11 *e-4*
A.P.C.
This place is for dressed-down starlets on a first-name basis with Sophia Coppola. Make your way across the rough-hewn, slightly warped floorboards to the hanging racks of ultracool French simplicity: straight-leg pants (starting around $110), classic shirts (some with buttons to keep rolled-up sleeves in place), and, as the store puts it, the "Permanents—If it ain't broke, don't fix it," i.e., jeans, khakis, and the like. Every season the store features a small line by a guest designer, such as Milk Fed. *131 Mercer St. (between Prince and Spring Sts.), SoHo, 212/966–0069. Subway: Prince St.*

11 *e-4*
ARMANI EXCHANGE
This "casual essentials" fiefdom of the Armani empire provides the requisite blond-wood, high-ceiling environment. The beige, black, and denim staples are occasionally punctuated with an interesting green or blue. Those anxious to donate free chest advertising will find plenty of A/X-logo T-shirts. At press time, a construction site at 5th Avenue and 51st Street had the A/X name on it. *568 Broadway (at Prince St.), SoHo, 212/431–6000. Subway: Prince St.*

11 *d-5*
BAGUTTA
The labels sound like Barneys: Dolce & Gabbana, John Galliano, Alexander McQueen, Costume National, Ann Demeulemeester, Hervé Leger. But you won't have to rack-rake so strenuously in this SoHo space, dominated by a curvaceous staircase—you can practice your grand entrance on the salespeople, who will probably be unimpressed. The upstairs is even more lofty, with the choice bits displayed in a high-ceiling, wood-floor, large-windowed room. *402 W. Broadway (between Spring and Broome Sts.), SoHo, 212/925–5216. Subway: 6 to Spring St.*

9 *e-4*
BANANA REPUBLIC
England and France may still be balking, but Banana Republic has fully embraced the Euro. The rhino T-shirts are fully extinct; look instead for slim black suits and filmy little neck scarves. As the most sophisticated sector of the Gap enterprise, Banana Republic gets to dabble in black-and-white photos and curvy cologne bottles; the latter even won a design award. Technofibers may come and go, but you can depend on lightweight, wool houndstooth trousers (about $130), velvet tops (polyester), and little-boy tees for $20. The khaki selection is blessedly less complicated than the Gap's; the fabric has a tad more heft, as does the price tag. Rounding out the now-I'm-grown-up look, there's a smattering of suede and leather jackets at $200–$400. If this keeps up, the store may have to change its name to something in a romance language. *655 5th Ave. (at 52nd St.), Midtown, 212/644–6678. Subway: E, F to 5th Ave.*

7 *e-7*
1136 Madison Ave. (between 84th and 85th Sts.), Upper East Side, 212/570–2465. Subway: 4, 5, 6 to 86th St.

9 *e-3*
130 E. 59th Street (at Lexington Ave.), Midtown, 212/751–5570. Subway: 59th St.; and other locations.

9 *e-2*

BCBG

This French acronym for "*bon chic bon genre*" is almost the equivalent of WASP—but there's nary an oxford shirt in sight. BCBG was one of the first "casual" designers to crash the couture-show circuit with catwalks of its own. The store's address may be Madison Avenue, but BCBG is far from snobby; the closest thing to tailoring is a body-hugging material. It's a great place to pick up a dress (short or ankle-length) for around $100. *770 Madison Ave. (at 66th St.), Upper East Side, 212/717–4225. Subway: 68th St./Hunter College.*

11 *d-4*

BETSEY JOHNSON

These stores retain their sense of humor as well as their hot-pink interiors. Clingy fabrics, quirky patterns (cherries, pinup girls), faux fur, and the occasional crino-line often point to those who still need to tote their IDs around, but the spring-summer collections normally have a few more (dare we say?) sedate dresses in fabrics like linen and seersucker. *130 Thompson St. (near Prince St.), SoHo, 212/420–0169. Subway: C, E to Spring St.*

9 *c-1*

248 Columbus Ave. (between 71st and 72nd Sts.), Upper West Side, 212/362–3364. Subway: 72nd St.

9 *f-2*

251 E. 60th St., Upper East Side, 212/319–7699. Subway: 59th St.

7 *e-7*

1060 Madison Ave. (between 80th and 81st Sts.), Upper East Side, 212/734–1257. Subway: 77th St.

10 *g-2*

BLUE

Blue is a godsend for those whose bud-get doesn't quite equal their taste: it has simple and classy cocktail dresses, more-formal styles, and even bridal gowns. Each design has a *Vogue*-ish name, like "Nadja" or "Claudia," and you can have anything made to order—all this without a stuffy attitude or a hefty price tag. *125 St. Mark's Pl., East Village, 212/228–7744. Subway: Astor Pl.*

11 *e-4*

BLUE FISH

"Beauty, quality, soul, meaning"—Blue Fish gives its clothes a tall order. The block-printed fabrics are all unique; at the counter you can check out a display of the artists' signature wooden blocks and find out just who put the interesting mauve whorls on the hem of that skirt. Cuts tend to be generous, and most items are made of cotton or linen. *150 Greene St. (at Houston St.), SoHo, 212/925–3775. Subway: Broadway–Lafayette St.*

11 *f-4*

CALYPSO

Born on St. Barthélemy, Calypso has found a cozy niche in NoLita. There's lots by Tracy Feith; fringe peeks out from under the hem of a mid-length plaid skirt, appliqué flowers crawl up skirts, and tissue-thin, long paisley silk dresses beg you to take them back to the Caribbean. *280 Mott St. (between Prince and Houston Sts.), East Village/Little Italy, 212/965–0990. Subway: Bleecker St.*

9 *d-3*

CHARIVARI

Barneys isn't the only business making cutbacks. Since 1995 Charivari has folded its stores one by one; now there's just a single holdout. But despite shed-ding addresses, Charivari still has notable merchandise. Nicole Farhi has plenty of rack space, as do the ethnically inspired silks of Dries van Noten and the avant-garde looks of Martin Margiela. *18 W. 57th St. (between 5th and 6th Aves.), Midtown, 212/333–4040. Sub-way: B, Q to 57th St.: N, R to 5th Ave.*

9 *d-8*

CLUB MONACO

With the reasonable prices and trendy-but-not-garish clothes, Club Monaco won't break your wallet or make your mother cringe. Clothes are often grouped by color, great for the match-ing-impaired; brown, beige, and cream; black and white. Even the dress clothes are affordable—black-silk slip dresses are only about $80, while tux-style trousers run around $120. *160 5th Ave. (between 20th and 21st Sts.), Chelsea, 212/352–0936. Subway: F to 23rd St.*

9 *f-2*

1111 3rd Ave. (at 65th St.), Upper East Side, 212/355–2949. Subway: 68th St./Hunter College

7 *b-7*

2376 Broadway (at 87th St.), Upper West Side, 212/579–2587. Subway: 1, 9 to 86th St.

11 *e-4*

COSTUME NATIONAL

This dark store is lightened by a glowing white display case that separates the men's and women's racks. It may be the *only* separation—the same nightcrawler mix of velvet pants and shirts, itchy faux fur, and translucent blouses sells to both sexes. *108 Wooster St. (between Spring and Prince Sts.), SoHo, 212/431–1530. Subway: C, E to Spring St.*

11 *d-4*

COUNTRY ROAD

This clean-cut Australian line is a good resource for casual-Friday career clothes: button-downs, long skirts, and the like. Colors are nonconfrontational. *411 W. Broadway (between Prince and Spring Sts.), SoHo, 212/343–9544. Subway: Prince St.*

9 *f-2*

1130 3rd Ave. (at 66th St.), Upper East Side, 212/744–8633. Subway: 68th St./Hunter College

10 *f-7*

South Street Seaport, Lower Manhattan, 212/248–0810. Subway: 2, 3 to Fulton St.

9 *e-5*

335 Madison Ave. (at 43rd St.), Midtown, 212/949–7380. Subway: 42nd St./Grand Central.

9 *f-2*

CP SHADES

This company is particularly vocal about using nothing but "natural fibers" for all their clothes, and so it does—if you consider chemically processed wood pulp (a.k.a. rayon) natural. Linen and cotton crop up on the labels too, though, and the stock turnover is brisk. Styles tend to be loose and drapey, colors subdued. *1119 3rd Ave. (between 65th and 66th Sts.), Upper East Side, 212/759–5710. Subway: 68th St./Hunter College*

11 *d-4*

154 Spring St. (between Wooster St. and W. Broadway), SoHo, 212/226–4434. Subway: Spring St.

11 *d-4*

CYNTHIA ROWLEY

This is not Fran Liebowitz territory. Cynthia Rowley's feminine little shop is lined with simply cut dresses, both short and long, often in silk, eyelet lace, or mildly retro prints. There are pants, too, but you're more likely to find cigarette or capri cuts than classic trousers. Prices generally fall in the $100–$250 range. *112 Wooster St. (between Prince and Spring Sts.), SoHo, 212/334–1144. Subway: Prince St.*

11 *d-4*

D&G

You could go snow-blind at this "Young Collection" by glamour-pusses Dolce & Gabbana. Squint against the glare of the ultrabright lights trained on white-white surfaces, and you'll find spin-offs of the luxe look. (Relax: the lights in the dressing rooms are not so merciless.) Leopard prints, lingerie straps, crochet, and black are as present here as at the designer store, but with less detail and a lower (if not exactly *low*) price tag. *434 W. Broadway (between Spring and Prince Sts.), SoHo, 212/965–8000. Subway: C, E to Spring St.*

11 *f-1*

DARYL K

This designer's goal is to make your sit-down look good in a pair of jeans. This may well happen if you have the hips of a 12-year-old boy. The signature jeans ($120–$130) tend to have a short rise and skinny legs; try the slacks if you need something higher-waisted. For something cheaper, like a waitressy white blouse, look for the K-189 label. *208 E. 6th St., East Village, 212/475–1255. Subway: Astor Pl.*

11 *f-3*

21 Bond St. (between Lafayette St. and Bowery), East Village, 212/777–0713. Subway: Bleecker St., 2nd Ave.

9 *e-2*

DIESEL SUPERSTORE

With the washing machine–like windows, an in-house DJ, and even a video game or two near the café, Diesel pitches to the hip. At $100, the jeans may give you pause, but the short dresses and mildly clublike gear are more fun anyway. *770 Lexington Ave. (at 60th St.), Upper East Side, 212/308–0055. Subway: 59th St.*

11 d-4

DOSA

This store's modest size actually works for it, and it's in keeping with the serene, Eastern-influenced designs. Flourishes are kept to a minimum, but not a bare minimum—an indigo silk blouse (say, $200) may have sharp rows of frogging or a crisp Nehru collar. *107 Thompson St. (at Spring St.), SoHo, 212/431–1733. Subway: C, E to Spring St.*

11 d-5

EILEEN FISHER

Cinched waists will never happen at Eileen Fisher. Her comfortably fluid dresses and skirts are lifesavers during a New York summer. Alas, chalk-tone simplicity does not come cheap. *395 W. Broadway (between Broome and Spring Sts.), SoHo, 212/431–4567. Subway: Spring St.*

9 e-3

521 Madison Ave. (at 53rd St.), Midtown, 212/759–9888. Subway: E, F to 5th Ave.

7 e-8

1039 Madison Ave. (at 79th St.), Upper East Side, 212/879–7799. Subway: 77th St.

7 c-8

341 Columbus Ave. (at 76th St.), Upper West Side, 212/362–3000. Subway: 72nd St.

9 e-8

103 5th Ave. (at 17th St.), Chelsea, 212/924–4777. Subway: F to 14th St., N, R to 23rd St.

9 e-2

EMILIO PUCCI

Yes, it's the original. Ring the bell, walk up the pink-carpet stairs, and you'll find yourself surrounded by the timelessly psychedelic swirls of Pucci's dresses, scarves, blouses, even bikinis. The color palette is often a late-'60s time capsule: pink-and-purple combinations, or yellow-and-almost-avocado. *24 E. 64th St., Upper East Side, 212/752–4777. Subway: 68th St./Hunter College.*

9 e-3

EMPORIO ARMANI

It's funny how after half an hour here, you start thinking of white as a dazzling color. Somber tones dominate just about

every season's palette, but think of it this way: dark colors hide spots, so they'll make great traveling clothes. Armani's way with a suit jacket is still obvious in this midrange label; the soft shoulders and plush fabrics are hard to resist, though you'll pay for the privilege of giving in. Fittingly discreet handbags, shoes, and accessories are also available. *601 Madison Ave. (between 57th and 58th Sts.), Midtown, 212/317–0800. Subway: 59th St.*

9 d-8

110 5th Ave. (at 16th St.), Chelsea, 212/727–3240. Subway: F to 14th St.

7 e-8

EN SOIE

Come here when you need an immediate pick-me-up. The playfulness of the interior (colorful bibelots everywhere, small, fanciful antlered heads in the dressing rooms) belies a very serious raison d'être: exquisite silk. There are blouses, scarves, even bolts of it, all beautifully textured; the original Swiss house provided fabric to Dior. A hand-woven silk blouse with real brass buttons can run $300. *988 Madison Ave. (at 77th St.), Upper East Side, 212/717–7958. Subway: 77th St.*

9 e-2

ETRO

When this store opened in 1996, the windows were striking even for Madison Avenue—they were filled with knee breeches, tailcoats, and corseted dresses. The company's antique outfits aren't just curios, though; their cuts, colors, and fabrics have a palpable influence on today's designs. Wool blazers can have velvet trim and nipped-in waists; sometimes blouses are layered three deep. Keep your eyes peeled for the rich tones of the trademark paisley, and if you're into vests, be sure to check out the men's selection. *720 Madison Ave. (between 63rd and 64th Sts.), Upper East Side, 212/317–9096. Subway: 68th St./Hunter College.*

9 d-3

FELISSIMO

Felissimo's selection is as memorable as it is limited. Two recent finds: a brocade Nehru jacket ($1,250) and a short jacket with the eyes of peacock feathers trapped between layers of black tulle ($445). *10 W. 57th St., Midtown, 212/247–5656. Subway: B, Q to 57th St.: N, R to 5th Ave.*

9 *d-4*

FRENCH CONNECTION

A mix of lightning-speed runway steals and wardrobe staples in vivid hues, the (British) French Connection is at best a quick fix. Sweaters are reasonably priced, at about $50 for a boxy, wool V-neck and roughly $100 for a chenille cardigan; but the cuts generally leave something to be desired—a little too short here, a little too tight there. Still, they'll jump on and pump out a high-fashion trend in a matter of weeks, like the short-short skirts (one in polyester "suede") for $66 to $88. *1270 6th Ave. (at 51st St.), Midtown, 212/262–6623. Subway: 47th–50th Sts./Rockefeller Center.*

11 *e-2*

700 Broadway (at E. 4th St.), Greenwich Village, 212/473–4486. Subway: 8th St.

11 *d-4*

435 W. Broadway (at Prince St.), SoHo, 212/219–1197. Subway: Prince St.

7 *c-8*

304 Columbus Ave. (between 74th and 75th Sts.), Upper West Side, 212/496–1470. Subway: 72nd St.

9 *e-3*

GAP

It's hard to go six blocks without running into one of these lookalike student-wardrobe warehouses. Lately the Gap has hit a new high: khakis now scramble into no less than 100 combinations. Sizes 1 to 16, three lengths (ankle, regular, long), quasidifferent colors, and urban-evocative names (Palisades, Newsstand, City Park). All this can translate into 45 minutes in the dressing room, but tenacity should result in something that fits for a little under $40. Jeans (about $30 to $60) are a similar dizzy spell. Luckily, the rest of the selection is much less complex: button-down shirts; long, patterned rayon skirts and dresses; ribbed T-shirts and turtlenecks. The larger stores have pajamas, underwear, sweats, and other dorm staples. At press time, Gap had a huge construction site on a prime 5th Avenue space at 54th Street; it had to happen sometime. *60 W. 34th Street (Herald Square), Garment District, 212/643–8960. Subway: 34th St./Herald Square*

9 *d-6*

734 Lexington Ave. (at 59th St.), Midtown, 212/751–1543. Subway: 59th St.

9 *e-2*

1131–1149 3rd Ave. (between 66th and 67th Sts.), Upper East Side, 212/472–5559. Subway: 68th St./Hunter College; and other locations.

9 *e-2*

HENRY LEHR

The casual clothes are worth a stop, but the notably flattering jeans deserve most of your browsing time (even if they are more expensive than custom-fit Levi's). *772 Madison Ave. (between 66th and 67th Sts.), Upper East Side, 212/535–1021. Subway: 68th St./Hunter College.*

7 *e-8*

ISSEY MIYAKE

You'll never look at polyester the same way again. The bare bones of this shop focus all attention on the uncommon clothes, whose ultratight pleats either cling to the body or form geometric shapes. *992 Madison Ave. (at 77th St.), Upper East Side, 212/439–7822. Subway: 77th St.*

9 *e-8*

J. CREW

Ever the purveyors of rugged East Coast chic, this trio of stores now sells everything from the ubiquitous rollneck sweaters and flannels to evening wear. The Prince Street and 5th Avenue stores carry the Collection, an exclusive, Calvin Klein–ish women's line not available from those catalogs you've been getting every three weeks. *91 5th Ave. (at 17th St.), Chelsea, 212/255–4848. Subway: F to 14th St, N, R to 23rd St.*

11 *e-4*

99 Prince St. (between Mercer and Greene Sts.), SoHo, 212/966–2739. Subway: Prince St.

10 *f-7*

203 Front St. (South Street Seaport), Lower Manhattan, 212/385–3500. Subway: 2, 3 to Fulton St.

9 *e-1*

JOSEPH

Some people call this place "the pants store," and that's not far from the truth.

Pants practically dominate the window displays and sprawl their skinny legs on the walls. Most have a certain amount of stretch, and there are a few unconventional fabrics (polyurethane was listed on one tag). The 804 Madison Avenue store has tops, too—jackets and shirts with trim lines to match. *804 Madison Ave. (at 68th St.), Upper East Side, 212/570–0077. Subway: 68th St./Hunter College*

9 *e-1*

796 Madison Ave. (at 67th St.), Upper East Side, 212/327–1773. Subway: 68th St./Hunter College

11 *e-4*

115 Greene St. (between Prince and Spring Sts.), SoHo, 212/343–7071. Subway: Spring St.

9 *e-2*
KENAR
What with Kenar's high-profile, supermodel ad campaigns, you may be surprised at the relative accessibility of these clothes. The Madison Avenue boutique tries for cinematic appeal, with a movie playing in the front window and the Kenar name lit up in the floor, but the suits and dresses aren't too much of a stretch: You can get a pretty, short-sleeved blouse for about $40. The West Side boutique is significantly smaller. *755 Madison Ave. (between 65th and 66th Sts.), Upper East Side, 212/517–7520. Subway: 68th St./Hunter College.*

7 *c-8*

303 Columbus Ave. (between 74th and 75th Sts.), Upper West Side, 212/874–9766. Subway: 72nd St.

9 *e-1*
KENZO BOUTIQUE
You don't have to wait for spring to find flowery clothes at Kenzo. The cheerful colors of the knits and blouses run year-round; suits are usually a bit more subdued. *805 Madison Ave. (between 67th and 68th Sts.), Upper East Side, 212/717–0101. Subway: 68th St./Hunter College.*

11 *f-4*
LABEL
The clothes here have subversion in their seams—whether the designer's messing with popular logos or printing "Revolution series" T-shirts (about $20)

with Che's face or Patty Hearst's FBI file. Riot grrrls will have a field day. *265 Lafayette St. (between Prince and Spring Sts.), East Village, 212/966–7736. Subway: Prince St.; 6 to Spring St.*

9 *e-3*
LACOSTE
The preppy alligator now has a fitting lair. Women's clothes are in the back and, naturally, feature stacks of those brightly colored polo-style cotton shirts (nearly $60). Lacoste is strictly sporty; there are tennis-appropriate whites and even a few black items. *543 Madison Ave. (between 54th and 55th Sts.), Midtown, 212/750–8115. Subway: E, F to 5th Ave.*

7 *c-8*
LAURA ASHLEY
The Upper West Side shop is the last New York bastion of this squeaky-clean clothier. Downstairs are the mother-and-child lines and home furnishings; upstairs is a small selection of casual clothes, often in—yes—floral patterns. But this isn't a merciless flood of old-world cabbage roses; some prints are stylized to the point of abstraction, and you can buy versatile dresses in solids or subdued stripes. Still, a straw hat would go well with almost anything except the nightgowns. *398 Columbus Ave. (at 79th St.), Upper West Side, 212/496–5110. Subway: 79th St.*

11 *e-3*
LE CHÂTEAU
An excellent place for an unabashed knockoff, or something to wear below 14th Street. They cadge from the best: a Prada-esque leaf pattern here, a touch of Dolce & Gabbana in a leopard print there. It's hardly verisimilitude, and prices are low; as an extra wink, there's some vinyl and marabou around the edges. *611 Broadway (at Houston St.), Greenwich Village, 212/260–0882. Subway: Broadway–Lafayette St.*

9 *d-6*

34 W. 34th St., Garment District, 212/967–0025. Subway: 34th St./Herald Square.

9 *e-1*
LES COPAINS
The day and evening wear here is so high-quality it's practically old-world. Trouser pockets are perfectly placed, wool is blended with cashmere or silk so

it's not itchy—the attentive details add up. (As will the bill; one outfit can break $1,000.) Bear in mind that the cuts run a bit small. For something more casual, seek out the Trend Les Copains line. *807 Madison Ave. (between 67th and 68th Sts.), Upper East Side, 212/327–3014. Subway: 68th St./Hunter College.*

9 *e-3*
LEVI'S
For once, women's jeans have one-upped men's. At these two Levi's stores, you can actually have a pair tailored to just the right length, width, or slouch; they cost only $15 more than a regular pair and take three weeks to produce. You can even have them shipped to your door. *3 E. 57th St., Midtown, 212/838–2188. Subway: E, F, N, R to 5th Ave.*

7 *f-7*
1492 3rd Ave. (at 84th St.), Upper East Side, 212/249–5045. Subway: 1, 9 to 86th St.

11 *f-4*
LIQUID SKY D-SIGN
A haven for club kids, this narrow store-front has a mild mishmash of camouflage, clever computer graphics, and pop-culture references like that almond-eyed alien face (a fine excuse for a $25 T-shirt). Brave the steep, winding, metal staircase at the back of the store and you'll find a cache of basement music—trip-hop, ambient, electronica, and Liquid Sky's own label. *241 Lafayette St. (between Prince and Spring Sts.), SoHo, 212/343–0532. Subway: 6 to Spring St.*

9 *e-2*
LUCA LUCA
A perfect antidote for the black-and-beige blahs. Instead of serving as the be-all and end-all, black is used to offset vibrant colors, like fuschia or kelly green. *690 Madison Ave. (at 62nd St.), Upper East Side, 212/755–2444. Subway: 59th St.*

7 *e-8*
1011 Madison Ave. (at 78th St.), Upper East Side, 212/288–9285. Subway: 77th St.

11 *f-4*
LUCIEN PELLAT-FINET
It's high time this neighborhood got a cashmere shop, particulary one this great. The sweaters here are lusciously colored and tend to be smallish and refined rather than bulky or baggy.

Warmer-weather knits are mixed with silk. *226 Elizabeth St. (between Prince and Houston Sts.), SoHo/Little Italy, 212/343–7033. Subway: Broadway–Lafayette St.*

9 *e-1*
MALO
Chiseled stone floors are in clever contrast to the plush cashmere sweaters. The color schemes are beautiful, and you'll occasionally find something unusual, like a knit cashmere blazer. *814 Madison Ave. (at 68th St.), Upper East Side, 212/585–4243. Subway: 68th St./Hunter College.*

11 *e-4*
MARC JACOBS
Ah, another bare-bones boutique, this one with men's and women's wear in two separate straight lines. It's hard not to warm to the fabrics, though: silk, cashmere, soft wool. Instead of fashion histrionics, you'll find a few quiet quirks, like a discreetly asymmetrical seam or cashmere in thermal-style waffle-weave. *163 Mercer St. (between Prince and Houston Sts.), SoHo, 212/343–1490. Subway: Prince St.*

9 *e-1*
MAXMARA
One of the best "bridge" designers, MaxMara tends to show monochromatic suits enlivened with texture, like a nubbly tweed or openwork stockings. Most pieces are in blacks, browns, and grays, but a lipstick-red suit isn't out of the question. *813 Madison Ave. (at 68th St.), Upper East Side, 212/879–6100. Subway: 68th St./Hunter College.*

9 *e-1*
MISSONI
This boutique is almost entirely devoted to knits—the distinctive, multicolored stripes zigzag through mohair, rayon, and wool in scarves, sweaters, and even long sparkly dresses. The few nonknit items (you could dredge up a button-down shirt) are patterned similarly. *836 Madison Ave. (at 69th St.), Upper East Side, 212/517–9339. Subway: 68th St./Hunter College.*

9 *e-1*
MÉNAGE À TROIS
Look up at this store's second-story window to catch a glimpse of some very

feminine trappings, like bias-cut skirts or airy ruffled sleeves. In some cases you can custom mix-and-match a particular fabric and dress pattern. *799 Madison Ave. (between 67th and 68th Sts.), Upper East Side, 212/396–2514. Subway: 68th St./Hunter College.*

11 *e-4*
MIU MIU
New Yorkers' insatiable hunger for Miuccia Prada's designs won the city the first Miu Miu boutique in North America. The basic premise of slip dresses, sheer fabrics, and high wedge shoes is intact, but you can get it here for a bit less filthy lucre. *100 Prince St. (between Mercer and Greene Sts.), SoHo, 212/334–5156. Subway: Prince St.*

9 *e-2*
MORGANE LE FAY
Many of the dresses here have great swaths of skirt under a high waist. The strongest influences are not from this century; it helps to have perfect posture and a European accent. *746 Madison Ave. (between 64th and 65th Sts.), Upper East Side, 212/879–9700. Subway: 68th St./Hunter College*

11 *d-4*
152 Spring St. (between Wooster St. and W. Broadway), SoHo, 212/925–0144. Subway: C, E to Spring St.

11 *d-4*
NANA
Having made its name (in California anyway) with kick-'em-in-the-shins, thick-soled shoes, NANA now has the clothes to go with 'em: bowling-style shirts, hats straight out of *Swingers*, and T-shirts emblazoned with "This is Spinal Tap" or pictures from *Faster Pussycat, Kill Kill!* *138 Prince St. (between Wooster St. and W. Broadway), SoHo, 212/274–0749. Subway: Prince St.*

11 *d-4*
NICOLE MILLER
Instant recognition of a Miller design is almost guaranteed. The designer made her name with funny silk prints: bamboo, cocktails, even sports gear. On the flip side of the coin are some simple dresses in solids. *134 Prince St. (between Wooster St. and W. Broadway), SoHo, 212/343–1362. Subway: Prince St.*

9 *e-2*
780 Madison Ave. (between 66th and 67th Sts.), Upper East Side, 212/288–9779. Subway: 68th St./Hunter College.

11 *e-5*
NOVOBATZKY
This name might not be the first to jump to mind under "SoHo couture," but the quasi-dressy clothes are very well made, and some come in some rather theatrical fabrics. *65 Mercer St. (between Spring and Broome Sts.), SoHo, 212/431–4120. Subway: 6 to Spring St.*

9 *d-8*
OLD NAVY
Cotton is king here—and cheap. The Chelsea space is a behemoth, and judging from the big, black supermarket shopping carts, they assume you'll be buying in bulk. Old Navy's own fashion timeline puts them somewhere between the '40s and '50s, but there's scant evidence of this beyond the retro (though multiculturally correct) edge to the mannequins and advertising. Instead, clothes are functional, casual, and vaguely trendy—stretch pants and faux-snakeskin bags have rack space alongside the jumpers. Here's a sampling of what $30 will get you: a velour top, a lambswool sweater, a pair of jeans (some under $25!), a couple of thermal shirts, an Old Navy disco-mix CD, or half a dozen tubes of body glitter. Shoes, unfortunately, are generally unexciting. The bath supplies may lure you, with their cutesy names and spare packaging, but the body-wash container bears a strong resemblance to an IV bag. There's also a (comparatively) small outlet in South Street Seaport. *610 6th Ave. (at 18th St.), Chelsea, 212/645–0663. Subway: F to 14th St.*

10 *f-7*
Pier 17, South Street Seaport, Lower Manhattan, 212/571–6159. Subway: 2, 3 to Fulton St.

11 *d-1*
PATRICIA FIELD
A club kid's answer to the invading SoHo boutiques, Patricia Field's is crammed with marabou, kitsch accessories, feather boas, drag-queen makeup, and skin-tight anything. The clothes aren't as cheap as you might wish; the best or craziest stuff (tube tops, high-slit skirts) always seems to be

way over $50. On the other hand, the beauty salon (212/598–0395) turns out some awesome dye jobs; leopard-spot is popular. *10 E. 8th St., Greenwich Village, 212/254–1699. Subway: 8th St.; Astor Pl.*

11 *f-4*
POP SHOP
Nothing says "New York" like a messenger-style bag covered with Keith Haring's interlocking babies. This place hawks nothing but Haring; every surface is crawling with his grafitti-style figures. If you can't resist one of these T-shirts, sweatshirts, or jackets, you'll have to decide whether to pretend you bought it long before the renewed Haring craze. *292 Lafayette St. (between Houston and Prince Sts.), East Village, 212/219–2784. Subway: Broadway–Lafayette Sts.*

9 *e-1*
POLO/RALPH LAUREN
Lauren's flagship store, ensconced in a grand, beautifully renovated turn-of-the-century town house, is one of New York's most distinctive shopping experiences. The atmosphere is scrupulously groomed; portraits are clustered over heavily carpeted stairs, and you'll come across salespeople wearing jodhpurs or carrying cups of tea on a silver tray. The women's clothes run from casual madras shorts (perfect for the East-hampton bungalow) to glimmering, silk evening gowns (perfect for the Academy Awards). Across the street is another Ralph Lauren boutique, this one modern and glossy, with chiseled, tough-jawed mannequins in the windows; it features casual clothes, sports gear, and an apparent overflow of old-money accessories, like antique pocket watches. *867 Madison Ave. (at 72nd St.), 212/606–2100; 888 Madison Ave. (at 72nd St.), 212/434–8000. Subway: 68th St./Hunter College.*

11 *e-4*
REPLAY COUNTRY STORE
This store carries a mishmash of styles, all under the umbrella-guise of a country store (wood floors, Old West lettering). Women's clothes run from sporty, tennis-type skirts to '70s-inspired tops to rockabilly glittery jeans. *109 Prince St. (at Greene St.), SoHo, 212/673–6300. Subway: Prince St.*

9 *e-4*
SAKS FIFTH AVENUE
The line of flags along Saks' façade is enough to rally the most exhausted shopper. Saks is a fashion-only department store, and several top-flight designers have their own, rarefied micro-environments here. The women's designer sections form an excellent range of international labels (Thierry Mugler, Sonia Rykiel, Moschino, Dolce & Gabbana) as well as American standards (Calvin Klein, Donna Karan, Ralph Lauren). Many of these names reappear in the casual line. As for women's shoes, Saks has one of the biggest selections of Ferragamos outside, well, Ferragamo. *611 5th Ave. (at 50th St.), Midtown, 212/940–2455. Subway: E, F to 5th Ave.*

7 *e-7*
SEARLE
Searle is an exclusively East Side phenomenon. The knits are covetable—there's lots of chenille—but most outstanding are the coats. Wool, leather, shearling, pea coats, reversible coats . . . to get your foot in the door, go to a trunk show at the 605 Madison Avenue branch. *605 Madison Ave. (at 58th St.), Midtown, 212/753–9021. Subway: 59th St.*

9 *e-2*
1051 3rd Ave. (at 62nd St.), Upper East Side, 212/838–5990. Subway: 59th St.

9 *e-1*
860 Madison Ave. (at 70th St.), Upper East Side, 212/772–2225. Subway: 68th St./Hunter College

7 *e-8*
1035 Madison Ave. (at 79th St.), Upper East Side, 212/717–4022. Subway: 77th St.

7 *e-8*
1124 Madison Ave. (at 84th St.), Upper East Side, 212/988–7318. Subway: 4, 5, 6 to 86th St.

11 *f-3*
SPOOLY D'S
New clothes look retro and vintage clothes look fresh in this little boutique a skip away from the going-uptown Bleecker Street subway stop. Most items would look quite at home in a pool hall or bowling alley, especially if you could zoom back a few decades. *51 Bleecker St. (at Lafayette St.), East Village, 212/598–4415. Subway: Bleecker St.*

11 *d-5*

STEVEN ALAN

Clothes are often coy but not necessarily cheap in these cramped quarters. Short-in-the-tooth designers include Milk Fed, Built by Wendy, Shackleford, and the downtown denim diva, Daryl K, for pants. The clothes on display tend to be in small sizes; you may have to ask them to bring out anything larger than a 6. Dodge the three-digit prices by heading to the outlet store at 330 East 11th Street (212/982–2881). *60 Wooster St. (at Broome St.), SoHo, 212/334–6354. Subway: Spring St.*

11 *e-4*

TEHEN

According to Tehen's business cards, Greene Street is the store's only branch outside Paris. Invest in some French flair; the low scoop necks and wrap tops are body-conscious but not too body-revealing. *122 Greene St. (at Prince St.), SoHo, 212/431–5045. Subway: Prince St.*

11 *e-4*

TOCCA

Feeling feminine? Float down to Tocca for a liberal dose of slip dresses, cap sleeves, embroidered flowers, and dangling beaded necklaces. The slightly retro aspect makes the merchandise hip, though the $180–$350 price tags make it perhaps tragically so. *161 Mercer St. (between Houston and Prince Sts.), SoHo, 212/343–3912. Subway: Prince St.*

11 *e-4*

TODD OLDHAM STORE

Compared to this store's decor, the clothes are practically sedate. Tie-dye velvet drapes the dressing rooms, and the floor is a crazy quilt of colored tiles. Sequins, satin, and spandex all emerge from Oldham's creative Cuisinart. It's fun, without a doubt—if your sense of humor extends to paying $100 for a bright-orange lycra shirt. *123 Wooster St. (between Spring and Prince Sts.), 212/219–3531. Subway: Prince St.; Spring St.*

11 *g-1*

TRASH AND VAUDEVILLE

True to its St. Mark's form, Trash and Vaudeville is a good source of club wear. Lou Reed reportedly trolls for tight jeans here. *4 St. Mark's Pl., East Village, 212/982–3590. Subway: Astor Pl.*

9 *e-1*

TSE CASHMERE

Good-girl cardigans aren't the only things on TSE's mind; recent collections have shown cobwebby cashmere dresses, boiled cashmere blends, and tiny tank tops. There are also forays outside the realm of cashmere—stretch wool pants, a leather coat or two, even a little angora. But don't move too far past those sweater sets, whose soft colors and stitching make them endlessly desirable—even at $1,000 a pop. *827 Madison Ave. (at 69th St.), Upper East Side, 212/472–7790. Subway: 68th St./Hunter College.*

9 *e-4*

UNITED COLORS OF BENETTON

Benetton has firmly joined the flagship ranks. Its latest real-estate coup is the historic Scribner building at 5th Avenue and 48th Street, which it has stocked with slick sports goods and an espresso bar as well as those candy-colored separates. Question is, do the clothes match the new digs? Some of the suits are office-ready, but the overall feel is still casual. Benetton is still a good place to find sweaters in a wide range of colors; you won't be deciding between blue and green but between sky, robin's egg, royal, and navy. For relative sophistication, drop in on one of the readings the store hosts in the espresso bar—not the 92nd St. Y, but if you sharpen your elbows you can behold the likes of Martin Amis. This reference to the building's literary pedigree may have you waxing nostalgic for the building's prior tenant, Brentano's, or seething at Benetton's condescension. *542 5th Ave. (between 48th and 49th Sts.), Midtown, 212/398–1205. Subway: E, F to 5th Ave.*

9 *f-2*

805 Lexington Ave. (at 62nd St.), Upper East Side, 212/752–5283. Subway: 59th St.

11 *e-1*

749 Broadway (at 8th St.), Greenwich Village, 212/533–0230. Subway: 8th St.; and other locations.

11 *e-3*

URBAN OUTFITTERS

This funky chain rides trends hard and long. Street penchants for the '60s have produced not only clogs and beaded jewelry but bushels of peasant blouses. They've also got intriguing housewares (often dorm-friendly), books (most not entirely serious), cards, and toys (voodoo doll, anyone?). *628 Broadway (between Houston and Bleecker Sts.), Greenwich Village, 212/475–0009. Subway: Bleecker St.*

11 *c-1*

Broadway–Lafayette St.; 394 6th Ave. (at Waverly Pl.), West Village, 212/677–9350. Subway: W. 4th St./Washington Square

9 *e-3*

127 E. 59th St., Midtown, 212/688–1200. Subway: 59th St.

11 *d-3*

VERONICA BOND

An unexpected bolt of couture just north of Houston. The dimpled Veronica (sweeter than Archie's) creates some mighty enticing clothes: jackets with glossy feather collars, tummy-baring gowns, svelte coats. Prices are very reasonable considering the workmanship; you'll never find a mismatched stripe here. *171 Sullivan St. (between Houston and Bleecker Sts.), West Village, 212/254–5676. Subway: W. 4th St./Washington Square.*

11 *e-4*

VIVIENNE TAM

Embroidered flowers and koi fish aren't just for Chinatown anymore. Tam's designs are often a cultural grab bag; Mao Zedong's face shows up in the darndest places. Go to the back, past the huge carved screens, to find the casual (and cheaper) Vivienne Tam Sport line, including Buddha T-shirts. *99 Greene St. (between Prince and Spring Sts.), SoHo, 212/966–2398. Subway: Prince St.*

11 *f-4*

WANG

One of the new rash of Mott Street boutiques, Wang shows a keen eye for detail. Edged and contrast-stitched pockets show up in unexpected places, or a small line of ruffle suddenly flirts with your shoulder. Best of all, prices are relatively low—$170 for a nonubiquitous black dress. *219 Mott St. (between Prince and Spring Sts.), SoHo/Little Italy, 212/941–6134. Subway: Broadway–Lafayette St.*

11 *d-4*

WEARABLE ENERGY

A lot of these clothes seem destined for a night out: clingy velvet tanks,

stovepipe pants, and sub-$100 little black dresses. And at these prices, you'll have enough money left over for an overpriced drink. *73 W. Houston St. (between W. Broadway and Wooster St.), SoHo, 212/475–0026. Subway: W. 4th St./Washington Square.*

designer

9 *e-2*

CALVIN KLEIN

This pared-down store is no catch-all CK emporium; it skims the cream of the designer's collections. Most of the women's collection is on the first floor, as are the shoes and accessories (divinely simple jewelry). Upstairs on the mezzanine are the bathing suits, lingerie, and evening wear—though more than one customer has been overheard mistaking the unadorned, long, thin-strapped silk dresses for nightgowns. The neighboring evening accessories should have been a tip-off; the tiny, box-like purses are hopelessly refined. *654 Madison Ave. (at 60th St.), Upper East Side, 212/292–9000. Subway: 59th St.*

9 *e-3*

CHANEL

When the new Chanel building opened in 1996, just a few doors down from its old location, rumors abounded that the hautest of haute couture couldn't handle the Warner Bros. store as a neighbor. Whatever the motivation, the building is a true Chanel temple, where even the doorknobs (modeled after the bottle stoppers on No. 5 perfume) pay homage. The interior glitters with black lacquer and mirrors, and a grand double staircase leads you upstairs. The irreverent touches come from longtime house designer Karl Lagerfeld, who puts the famous interlocking Cs on everything from sneakers to bathing suits. Okay, it isn't *really* Paris, but Provence has touched down in the form of Frédéric Fekkai's five-story beauty salon. *15 E. 57th St., Midtown, 212/355–5050. Subway: E, F, N, R to 5th Ave.*

9 *e-3*

CHRISTIAN DIOR

This two-story boutique is decorated in the soft dove gray preferred by Dior himself, and the day and evening wear are perfectly tailored, often in girlish pastels. Funny, considering that the wild John Galliano now heads the house. *703*

5th Ave. (at 55th St.), Midtown, 212/223–4646. Subway: E, F to 5th Ave.

11 e-4

COMME DES GARÇONS

Long before Calvin Klein stripped his interiors, this store was an audaciously minimalist retail space. The bare white walls and cement floors haven't changed, but now it's Rei Kawakubo's designs that break new ground. In recent collections, Kawakubo overthrows conventional ideas of beauty (not to mention posture) by adding padded "body bumps" under tightly wrapped dresses. It takes serious presence to carry these off, but they are certainly unforgettable. They can also spark some hot debates. 116 Wooster St. (between Prince and Spring Sts.), SoHo, 212/219–0660. Subway: Prince St.; Spring St.

9 e-1

DOLCE & GABBANA

Somewhere among the buzzing synapses of Domenico Dolce and Stefano Gabbana, Sicilian widows became founts of sex appeal. The combination of bosomy black and movie-star flair is intoxicating, and all the more so when you're let loose in two stories of it. The leopard-print chiffon, impeccable embroidery, bustiers, faux-fur-collared suits, and sweeping coats are unfailingly cinematic. The store itself keeps the number of baroque-Italian references down, but the dressing rooms are swathed in lush ruby velvet, and there's a lovely little terrace upstairs on the men's floor. 825 Madison Ave. (between 68th and 69th Sts.), Upper East Side, 212/249–4100. Subway: 68th St./Hunter College.

9 e-1

EMANUEL UNGARO

This store isn't nearly as staid as you might think. Granted, the heavily beaded evening jackets haven't changed a bit, but the suits come in nicely textured fabrics or fun prints—one summer pants suit was covered with giant strawberries. 792 Madison Ave. (at 67th St.), Upper East Side, 212/249–4090. Subway: 68th St./Hunter College.

9 e-2

GEOFFREY BEENE

This small boutique, tucked near the entrance to the Sherry-Netherland hotel, may not pack the floor space of the Madison Avenue flagships, but it's got an enviable stable of curvaceous evening dresses. The day wear is no slouch, either. 783 5th Ave. (between 59th and 60th Sts.), Midtown, 212/935–0470. Subway: N, R to 5th Ave.

9 e-1

GIANFRANCO FERRE

A shiny, steely decor is Ferre's backdrop for extravagant women's prêt-à-porter. There's a bit of old Hollywood in the giant collars, the oversized buttons, and the sometimes revealing ensembles. 845 Madison Ave. (at 70th St.), Upper East Side, 212/717–5430. Subway: 68th St./Hunter College.

9 e-4

GIANNI VERSACE

With his trademark blend of deference and rebelliousness, Versace restored this turn-of-the-century 5th Avenue building, inlaid his Medusa-head logo on the sidewalk out front, and limned the interior with neon lights. The five floors encompass all of Versace's designs, from housewares to $150 jeans to couture. It's possible to find perfectly proper suits and daring evening dresses on the same floor. At press time, the Madison Avenue store was being joined by a Versus boutique, carrying ever more street-inspired fashion. 647 5th Ave. (between 51st and 52nd Sts.), Midtown, 212/317–0224. Subway: E, F to 5th Ave.

9 e-1

817 Madison Ave. (between 68th and 69th Sts.), Upper East Side, 212/744–6868. Subway: 68th St./Hunter College; Versus: 815 Madison Ave. (between 68th and 69th Sts.), Upper East Side. Subway: 68th St./Hunter College.

9 e-2

GIORGIO ARMANI

Armani managed to top them all with his molto minimalist flagship store. Yet it's far from hard-edged; the muted tones and inviting fabrics make you want to whisper. The clothes are reverentially displayed, from the Black Label couture (up to five figures) to the shoes and sportswear. Who else could make a svelte ski jacket? 760 Madison Ave. (between 65th and 66th Sts.), Upper East Side, 212/988–9191. Subway: 68th St./Hunter College.

7 *e-8*

GIVENCHY

Givenchy has managed to keep this boutique intimate. There are no towering structure, no espresso bars . . . instead the clothes are sometimes guarded by sleek white dog figures (and can look a little crowded on the rack). There are ladies-who-lunch day suits, some beautiful purses and accessories, and formal gowns in the back. *954 Madison Ave. (at 74th St.), Upper East Side, 212/772–1040. Subway: 77th St.*

9 *e-3*

GUCCI

Tom Ford's design revamp has made Gucci one of the most gawked-at stores in the city. Sexy, decadent-rocker clothes (tight shimmery pants, loose velvet shirts, thongs . . . and those were for men) have transformed Gucci's name from stale to edgy. Along with the outré are some perfectly wearable suits and dresses, plus the oft-copied shoes and accessories. Take a ride in the elevator for a glimpse of the Gucci past—the brown leather panels still have a stripe of that red-and-green ribbon. *685 5th Ave. (at 54th St.), Midtown, 212/826–2600. Subway: E, F to 5th Ave.*

9 *e-3*

HENRI BENDEL

In the summer of 1997, Bendel unveiled some surprising new collections—its own. After years in the backseat, Henri Bendel has put the efforts of its own design team front and center with three new lines: Henri Bendel Body, Henri Bendel New York, and Henri Bendel Spa. The first New York line (fall/winter 1997) showed simple cuts in luscious fabrics and colors—inky blue-black stretch velvet (pants near $150), grape chenille, mossy cashmere (a sweater for $398). Body includes basic microfiber bodysuits, tanks, and T-shirts, while the Spa section carries loungewear. Bendel will still carry other designers, such as Michael Kors, Jean-Paul Gaultier, and Zoran, on its upper floors. The first-floor cosmetics continue to be very select (M.A.C. is perched in the Gilded Cage). Alas, there's no shoe department, but there is a serene and modern tea room on the second floor. *712 5th Ave. (at 56th St.), Midtown, 212/247–1100. Subway: E, F to 5th Ave.*

9 *e-2*

KRIZIA

Look through the pieces and you'll notice a certain animal figure cropping up—a jaguar, or perhaps an eagle. This is the "protector" of that particular collection, something that began as a whim and is now a Krizia signature. This is a good place to go suit shopping; the jackets are often more interesting than the standards. *769 Madison Ave. (at 66th St.), Upper East Side, 212/879–1211. Subway: 68th St./Hunter College.*

9 *e-8*

MATSUDA

High ceilings, rows of smooth wood columns, and an expectant hush make this store seem more Madison Avenue than lower 5th. The clothes are cool and clever—the stripes on a multicolored sweater might recall barbed wire—but, of course, this sort of thing comes at a price. A sundress could easily set you back $700. *156 5th Ave. (at 20th St.), Chelsea, 212/645–5151. Subway: N, R to 23rd St.*

9 *e-1*

MOSCHINO

Moschino's flagship is crazy, silly, and a helluva good time. Once drawn in by the tongue-in-cheek window displays, you'll be adrift in smiley faces, bright mosaic floors, and murals trumpeting maxims like "It's Better to Dress As You Wish Than As You Should!" The women's Cheap and Chic line is on the ground floor (more teasing sayings on the T-shirts); women's couture is up the curving staircase, with its question-mark shaped bars. Don't worry, things don't get serious even when the price tags hit four figures—chairs in the couture area are upholstered with red-check tablecloth fabric, and there's a sculpted bowl of spaghetti on a table. Make sure you visit the "Toy-lette," which has walls of Lego and a Monopoly-board mirror. *803 Madison Ave. (between 67th and 68th Sts.), Upper East Side, 212/639–9600. Subway: 68th St./Hunter College.*

9 *d-3*

OMO NORMA KAMALI

One thing this store doesn't have to worry about is being run-of-the-mill. The dun interior, with its blocky, disjointed stairways and mysterious corners, looks like a cross between an army bunker and a set from the *Star Wars* trilogy.

Against this grim background, the gleaming satin and beads of the evening dresses or the shirring of a white bathing suit may be something of a shock. Kamali is unfailingly creative, dreaming up everything from parachute-ready olive-green outfits to sky-blue, Eastern-influenced cotton tunics. *11 W. 56th St., Midtown, 212/957–9797. Subway: E, F to 5th Ave.*

9 *e-1*
PRADA
It's a dream come true for the status-hawks: three spacious floors of the unmistakeable Miuccia. Within the Madison Avenue store's pale-green walls (they call the color "verdolino"; keep this in mind if you think you're getting land-bound *mal de mer*) is one of the biggest Prada selections outside Milan. The women's collections include pale gossamer dresses, occasional flashes of brightly colored trim, and stark black technofabric suits. Naturally, you'll also find plenty of the items that fueled the frenzy: sleek black nylon bags and thick-soled shoes. The 57th Street store is much smaller, but at press time Prada had started construction on a new shrine in the former Doubleday book-store at 5th Avenue and 52nd Street. *841 Madison Ave. (at 70th St.), Upper East Side, 212/327–4200. Subway: 68th St./Hunter College*

9 *e-3*
45 E. 57th St., Midtown, 212/308–2332. Subway: E, F, N, R to 5th Ave.

9 *e-1*
SPAZIO ROMEO GIGLI
This Italian designer has a way with rich colors, opulent textures, and exotic touches—he's even designed kilims. Here are velvets, moiré fabrics, shirts with stripes in dark jewel tones, and even cutaway coats invoking the 19th century. *21 E. 69th St., Midtown, 212/744–9121. Subway: 68th St./Hunter College.*

9 *e-1*
YVES SAINT LAURENT
Seemingly frozen in their black, purple, and orange moment, the clothes here are eternally theatrical. Heavy velvets appear in the women's section year-round. *855 Madison Ave. (at 71st St.), Upper East Side, 212/988–3821. Subway: 68th St./Hunter College.*

9 *e-1*
SONIA RYKIEL BOUTIQUE
Malcolm McLaren once wrote a song called "Who the Hell Is Sonia Rykiel?" Now that Rykiel has a boutique on Madison, there's no excuse for asking the question. The grande dame of French knitwear creates lovely sweaters, often in black, orange, and red. *849 Madison Ave. (between 70th and 71st Sts.), Upper East Side, 212/396–3060. Subway: 68th St./Hunter College.*

9 *e-1*
VALENTINO
The latest Valentino incarnation has true cinematic appeal. Dresses and coats often have fur or feather collars (hope you have a long neck . . .); fabrics can be enticingly sheer or softly weighty. The store is serene, with smooth marble, the occasional well-placed orchid, and a courtyard garden. *747 Madison Ave. (between 68th and 69th Sts.), Upper East Side, 212/772–6969. Subway: 68th St./Hunter College.*

7 *e-8*
VERA WANG
Justly famous for her bridal gowns, Wang also has a stunning selection of made-to-order evening wear. Choosing one of these gowns is an event in itself, and happens by appointment only, so call a few days in advance. A shimmering footwear collection was added in fall 1997; the shoes are dyed to match whichever showstopper you choose. *991 Madison Ave. (at 77th St.), Upper East Side, 212/628–3400. Subway: 77th St.*

11 *e-5*
YOHJI YAMAMOTO
These designs aren't always as severe as they seem. The silk can be rough, but some of the wool sweaters are so fine they're translucent. *103 Grand St. (at Mercer St.), SoHo, 212/966–9066. Subway: N, R to Canal St.*

discount & off-price
Though discount designer clothes can now be found all over town, the traditional bargain-hunting area is the Lower East Side. Orchard Street has the highest concentration of shops, with everything between chic and schlock. Sunday is a hectic but very New York experience, not to be missed; Orchard Street itself

becomes a pedestrian mall. If you can, leave your car at home.

10 e-6
CENTURY 21

Century 21 still claims to be "New York's best-kept secret" despite numerous breathlessly enthusiastic articles exposing it. True, it's a bit out of the way (down in the financial district), but don't let that stop you. You'll find three vast floors of in-season name-brand and designer fashions (Donna Karan, Calvin Klein, even the odd Lacroix) at a quarter to a third off. The crowds can induce heart palpitations in the uninitiated. *22 Cortlandt St. (at Trinity Pl.), Lower Manhattan, 212/227–9092. Subway: Cortlandt St./World Trade Center.*

9 d-6
DAFFY'S

The Daffy's experience can fluctuate, from depressing racks of lurid polyester (Herald Center) to well-tended cruise wear (57th Street). You may have to wander through racks of undesirables to hit upon something, but you'll know it when you do: Cynthia Rowley dresses at one-third the list price, Calvin Klein bathing suits at half, or maybe a coup from a store closing, like $400 Susan Bennis Warren Edwards shoes for $40. Be sure to inspect the more delicate items, as they can be manhandled beyond repair. *1311 Broadway (at 34th St.), Garment District, 212/736–4477. Subway: 34th St./Herald Square*

9 e-8
111 5th Ave. (at 18th St.), Flatiron, 212/529–4477. Subway: F to 14th St., N, R to 23rd St.

9 e-5
335 Madison Ave. (at 44th St.), Midtown, 212/557–4422. Subway: 42nd St./Grand Central.

9 e-3
135 E. 57th St., Midtown, 212/376–4477. Subway: 59th St.

9 d-8
FILENE'S BASEMENT

This longtime Boston tradition now has a few branches in New York. The stock leans heavily toward American casual and business wear like Jones New York and CK Calvin Klein, but you can also get a good deal on a London Fog trench coat during most of the year. Another key area is lingerie—a few half-price pairs of Calvin Klein briefs never hurt anyone, and you may even find a La Perla bra for under $100. *620 6th Ave. (between 18th and 19th Sts.), Chelsea, 212/620–3100. Subway: F to 14th or 23rd Sts.*

7 b-8
2220–26 Broadway (at 79th St.), Upper West Side, 212/873–8000. Subway: 79th St.

9 c-8
LOEHMANN'S

Bargain hunters throughout Manhattan pinched themselves when the legendary Loehmann's finally opened here in fall 1996—in Barneys' former Chelsea space, of all places. They pinched themselves yet again when, after 75 years, Loehmann's broke down and decided to offer men's clothing. Oddly enough, brand names in the men's section are more impressive than those in the famous Back Room—besides $40 Ralph Lauren chinos, you can even find Donna Karan and Dolce & Gabbana suits. For women, the most fashionable clothing is concentrated in the Back Room, upstairs, where you'll find things like Isaac by Isaac Mizrahi separates. Stock quality varies, but it's replenished quickly. Old-guard Loehmann's fans may feel a bit disappointed in the new store; designer clothes are diluted with dozens of unknown labels. Thanks to the quantities alone, the shoe selection is great, though the system for finding your size is confusing. *101 7th Ave. (at 16th St.), Chelsea, 212/352–0856. Subway: 1, 2, 3, 9 to 14th St.*

9 e-3
SYMS

Syms' educated consumers have enabled the store to snag a Park Avenue address, and while there might be more floor space for men's clothes than for women's, you won't feel neglected. Skip the dubious racks of shorts sets and head to the humble, hand-lettered signs marked "couture," where the range of designers is far from shabby: Yves Saint-Laurent, Guy Laroche Couture, Romeo Gigli, even Gianni Versace. Granted, the wares may be a collection or two old, but a cool beige silk blouse won't tell. Prices are normally slashed about 50%, though recently a few minutes at the rack turned up a gorgeous, black-wool Calvin Klein Collection coat slashed from $1,200 to $490. Compared to these riches, the jeans rack is a little paltry, but denim's not the most exhilarating deal anyway. The shoe selection may require a little more weeding, but finds like $48 Delman flats are standard. And don't forget the accessories, like Echo silk scarves and Mark Cross handbags. *400 Park Ave. (at 54th St.), Midtown, 212/317–8200. Subway: 51st St./Lexington–3rd Aves.*

10 *e-7*

42 Trinity Pl. (at Rector St.), Lower Manhattan, 212/797–1199 subway: Rector St.

plus sizes

Among the department-store selections, Macy's has one of the most extensive large-size collections, called Macy Woman. Saks' Salon Z has some great designer lines, such as Dana Buchman, plus a special intimate-apparel area.

9 *e-2*

ASHANTI LARGER SIZES

These unique styles in large sizes (14–30) are often made of handwoven and hand-dyed fabrics. *872 Lexington Ave. (between 65th and 66th Sts.), Upper East Side, 212/535–0740. Subway: 68th St./Hunter College.*

7 *b-7*

DAPHNE

There's an ethnic twist to most of the clothes here—batik-style prints, chunky jewelry. *467 Amsterdam Ave. (between 82nd and 83rd Sts.), Upper West Side, 212/877–5073. Subway: 79th St.*

9 *e-2*

FORGOTTEN WOMAN

A great resource for designer clothes in sizes 14–24, this store carries such lines as Tomatsu, Givenchy, and Anne Klein, and occasionally daywear by Marina Rinaldi. *880 Lexington Ave. (at 66th St.), Upper East Side, 212/535–8848. Subway: 68th St./Hunter College.*

7 *c-1*

LANE BRYANT

One of the spearheading mass-marketers for larger sizes (going back to 1916!), Lane Bryant carries both casual and moderately dressy lines in sizes 14–28. *222–224 W. 125th St., Harlem, 212/678–0546. Subway: 2, 3, A, B, C, D to 125th St.*

resale

7 *e-7*

ENCORE RESALE DRESS SHOP

This sophisticated recycler carries designer outfits and couture, including Chanel, Armani, and Ungaro. Because it's a consignment shop and new stuff turns up daily, you may have to make a few trips to find that must-have. *1132 Madison Ave. (between 84th and 85th Sts.), 2nd floor, Upper East Side, 212/879–2850. Subway: 4, 5, 6 to 86th St.*

11 *f-4*

INA

This pair of resale shops focuses on the more casual designer lines—Calvin Klein blouses or Ralph Lauren cotton sundresses rather than full-blown, four-figure suits. Rifle through the choice shoes and you just may stumble upon Gucci loafers or Stephane Kélian sandals. *21 Prince St. (between Mott and Elizabeth Sts.), SoHo/Little Italy, 212/334–9048. Subway: Prince St.*

11 *d-4*

101 Thompson St. (between Prince and Spring Sts.), SoHo, 212/941–4757. Subway: C, E to Spring St.

7 *e-8*

MICHAEL'S

A small black sign near the entrance reminds you, "The treasure you see today may not be here tomorrow." The women who shop here take this to heart: there's an air of unusual seriousness to the browsing. Classic Chanel suits go for a cool $1,000. *1041 Madison Ave. (at 79th St.), Upper East Side, 212/737–7273. Subway: 77th St.*

vintage

Most vintage-clothing shops have a final-sale policy, so purchase carefully and wisely. East 7th Street is a good place to start.

ABOUT TIME

See Contemporary, *above.*

11 *e-5*

ALICE UNDERGROUND

Having shuffled locations over the past few years, Alice's latest store is the brightest and least crowded. (Being above ground will do that to you.) While the thrift-store standards—denim, leather coats—have a decent amount of rack space, they don't overwhelm the cashmere sweaters ($45–$85), filmy nightgowns, and well-preserved beaded tops. Linens and lots of crocheted doilies are in the back room. Scout around for the store's own label on bowling shirts with atmospheric slogans like "Laverne's Cocktail Lounge." *481 Broadway (between Broome and Grand Sts.), 212/431–9067. Subway: 6 to Spring St.; N, R to Canal St.*

10 *g-2*
ANNA
The selection here is choice—merchandise moves fast (painful for the indecisive), but they save you from doing the digging yourself. *150 E. 3rd St., East Village, 212/358–0195. Subway: 2nd Ave.*

11 *e-1*
ANTIQUE BOUTIQUE
This is some of the most trodden vintage ground in New York, but with thousands of items, the pickings are rarely slim. Retro wear includes party dresses, polyester pants, and leather motorcycle jackets. There's some brand-new and appropriately transitory club wear, too. *712 Broadway (between Astor Pl. and 4th St.), Greenwich Village, 212/460–8830. Subway: Astor Pl.*

11 *e-5*
CANAL JEAN COMPANY
A yawning expanse of dusty duds, this is one of downtown's best pawing-around spots. House dresses and bowling shirts, tuxedo coats and plaid flairs cram the racks, and there are some new threads (CK, French Connection) as well, if you're feeling flush. Downstairs are discounted shoes and army-navy camouflage stuff. *504 Broadway (between Spring and Broome Sts.), SoHo, 212/226–3663. Subway: 6 to Spring St.; N, R to Canal St.*

10 *e-1*
CHEAP JACK'S
The ordinary size of this store's entrance belies the huge amount of clothes-jammed space upstairs, downstairs, and in between. There are enough bomber jackets to outfit a few squadrons, old Izod madras shirts, bell bottoms, track suits, and the odd fur-trimmed wool suit with that authentic

naphthalene smell. However, sometimes Jack isn't as cheap as you'd like him to be. *841 Broadway (between 13th and 14th Sts.), Flatiron, 212/777–9564. Subway: 14th St./Union Square.*

11 *d-5*
THE 1909 COMPANY
These classy two-piece suits and cashmere sweaters look like they once belonged to a *dame d'un certain âge.* The scarves and gloves are appropriately dainty. *63 Thompson St. (between Spring and Broome Sts.), SoHo, 212/343–1658. Subway: A, C, E to Canal St.*

10 *d-1*
REMINISCENCE
Breeze past the tchotchkes (remember Garbage Pail Kids?) to the rows of '70s prom dresses, halter tops, Hawaiian shirts, and golf pants. This kitsch tends to be relatively cheap. *74 5th Ave. (between 13th and 14th Sts.), Greenwich Village, 212/243–2292. Subway: N, R, F to 14th St.*

11 *h-1*
RESURRECTION
The shoe selection here is generally far superior to that in most vintage shops, ranging from blunt-nosed pumps to knee-high boots. Dresses range from full-skirted to that narrow early-'60s look. *123 E. 7th St., East Village, 212/228–0063. Subway: Astor Pl.; 2nd Ave.*

11 *h-1*
ROSE IS VINTAGE
This store's promise of new merchandise daily makes for a lot of repeat customers. Short coats can be good buys (faux Persian lamb or nubbly wool), as can some of the old-fashioned, square-cut bathing suits. *145 1st Ave. (at 9th St.), East Village, 212/533–8550*

11 *h-1*
96 E. 7th St., East Village, 212/533–8550. Subway: 1st Ave.; Astor Pl.

11 *f-2*
SCREAMING MIMI'S
Vintage here doesn't go too far back—mostly to the '60s and '70s. But the finds (soccer shirts, short kilts, velveteen dresses) repeatedly end up in fashion spreads. If you can squeeze into the narrow loft, you might find some Mai Tai glasses among the housewares.

382 Lafayette St. (at E. 4th St.), East Village, 212/677–6464. Subway: Astor Pl.; Broadway–Lafayette St.

11 *f-5*

SMYLONYLON

If you're into man-made, make tracks. Polyvinyl, polyester, pleather, and more—prices start around $10. *222-B Lafayette St. (between Spring and Broome Sts.), SoHo, 212/431–0342. Subway: 6 to Spring St.*

11 *d-3*

THE STELLA DALLAS LOOK

Barbara Stanwyck would be perfectly happy here. Specializing in '40s clothes, this Village boutique has some swell dresses, generally of high quality. *218 Thompson St. (between W. 3rd and Bleecker Sts.), West Village, 212/674–0447. Subway: W. 4th St./Washington Square.*

11 *g-1*

TOKIO 7

Japanese Kewpie dolls beckon from the display windows; inside are crowded racks of clothes a few seasons old. Betsey Johnson and Cynthia Rowley labels are common. There's the odd and inexplicable early-'90s Jean-Paul Gaultier item, too. *64 E. 7th St., East Village, 212/353–8443. Subway: 1st Ave.; Astor Pl.*

11 *d-5*

WHAT GOES AROUND COMES AROUND

This is no fly-by-night operation; What Goes Around Comes Around is known for its collectible denim and high-quality pickings, like $45 Pucci halters. They're quick to jump on trends, like beaded purses and running pants, and sometimes, as in the case of old Nikes, they catch them good and early. *351 W. Broadway (between Broome and Grand Sts.), SoHo, 212/343–9303. Subway: N, R to Canal St.*

CLOTHING FOR WOMEN/ SPECIALTY

furs

New York's wholesale, and to some extent retail, fur district is centered around 7th Avenue and 30th Street. On weekdays the area bustles with activity as merchandise is carted or carried through the streets; on weekends many places are closed, or open by appointment only. Besides the individual storefronts, there are a few tall buildings filled with furriers; if you're curious, just go in and look at the directory. Remember that some furriers close for part of August.

9 *e-3*

FENDI

Animal products (fur and leather) being the Fendi backbone, you'll find extremely high quality, and prices, in their second-floor salon. Fendi specializes in furs other than the serviceable mink: sable, chinchilla, lynx. Styles are extravagant, even in mink—huge collars and interesting piecing. *720 5th Ave. (at 56th St.), Midtown, 212/767–0100. Subway: E, F to 5th Ave.*

9 *d-3*

THE FUR VAULT

Make tracks here for incredible variety and some of the lowest prices in town. *41 W. 57th St., Midtown, 212/754–1177. Subway: B, Q to 57th St.*

9 *d-7*

FURS BY DIMITRIOS

The salespeople here are more than happy to help out a fur novice. Coat designs are straightforward, and the company believes staunchly in American mink. Dimitrios is one of the few storefronts in the 30th Street area that's open on Saturdays. *130 W. 30th St., Garment District, 212/695–8469. Subway: 34th St./Penn Station; 1, 9 to 28th St.*

9 *e-2*

J. MENDEL

This Parisian firm has impeccable coats. They're often in mink, or in thick cashmere with fur trim, and you can easily find a slim style that's not overwhelming. There are some hard-to-resist fur accessories, too, like a mink muff that converts to backpack. *723 Madison Ave. (between 63rd and 64th Sts.), Upper East Side, 212/832–5830. Subway: 59th St.*

9 *e-3*

MAXIMILIAN FUR COMPANY

New York's longtime society furrier now has a special salon in Bloomingdale's. *1000 3rd Ave. (at 59th St.), 4th floor, Midtown, 212/705–3335. Subway: 59th St.*

9 d-7
150 WEST 30TH STREET
This towering building is heavy with fur-riers, including the traditional craftsman Ben Kahn (212/279–0633), and George Mamoukakis Furs (212/564–2976), which carries mainly mink. *150 W. 30th St., Garment District. Subway: 34th St./Penn Station; 1, 9 to 28th St.*

9 e-3
REVILLON
Another Parisian firm, Revillon is luxuri-ous without being old-fashioned. Besides the dignified minks and foxes, there are some brightly dyed fur vests (one, in orange, looks like a hunting vest . . . hmmm . . .) and short, zip-pered jackets. For something less con-spicuous, there are fur-lined coats in wool or water-resistant microfiber. *717 5th Ave. (at 56th St.), Midtown, 212/317–0039. Subway: E, F to 5th Ave.*

9 d-3
RITZ THRIFT SHOP
This is an excellent place to try for a "gently worn" fur. You can get a basic mink for around $700, though prices go up to about $5,000 (with a few $10,000-plus beauties thrown in). Everything is cleaned and glazed, and your purchase comes with free alterations and free storage. *107 W. 57th St., Midtown, 212/265-4559. Subway: 57th St.*

9 d-7
345 7TH AVENUE
With 25 floors filled predominantly with furriers, you can hardly go wrong. The Antonovichs are all here: Antonovich Ah! Furs (fax only: 212/244–2362), David A. Furs (212/244–0666), and Daniel A. Furs (212/244–3161). There are plenty of other glamorous names, like Furs by Frederick Gelb (212/239–8787) and Furs by Steven (212/244–2360). *345 7th Ave. (between 29th and 30th Sts.), Garment District. Subway: 1, 9 to 28th St.; 34th St./Penn Station.*

gloves

9 e-6
LACRASIA
The practice of wearing gloves for fash-ion or propriety instead of just warmth may be history, but LaCrasia is a won-derful holdout. Do your hands a favor and have them fitted for a custom pair. LaCrasia's work goes far beyond the short, everyday variety—for a heady dose of elegance, try the elbow-length or long gloves. Diehards can make an appointment to see the Glove Museum. *304 5th Ave. (between 32nd and 31st Sts.), Garment District, 212/594–2223. Subway: 33rd St.*

handbags
New York's department stores have large selections of handbags in all price ranges. Chain stores can be good resources for decent knockoffs; Banana Republic has gotten quite good at faux Kate Spades and Guccis. For something even cheaper (because you can always bargain down to $20), hit Canal Street. You may even be able to watch them stapling on your Prada logo. *See* Leather Goods, *below.*

9 e-1
ALAIN MIKLI OPTIQUE
Granted, this is an eyewear store; but alongside those funky frames are some killer handbags and totes—pearlized plastic on the outside, leather on the inside. In fact, the bags are made of the same material as some of the frames, so obsessive accessory-matchers can let loose. *880 Madison Ave. (between 71st and 72nd St.), Upper East Side, 212/472–6085. Subway: 68th St./Hunter College.*

9 e-2
ARTBAG
Besides selling new bags, this store is essential for those who can't part with their old ones: they arrange expert, albeit expensive, handbag repairs, plus custom jobs, alterations, and reconditioning. While they inspect your scruffy tote, check out the gleaming wares, some in alligator or ostrich. *735 Madison Ave. (at 64th St.), Upper East Side, 212/744-2720. Subway: 68th St./Hunter College.*

9 e-2
COACH
See Leather Goods, *below.*

9 e-3
See Leather Goods, *below.*

9 e-5
See Leather Goods, *below.*

10 d-6
See Leather Goods, *below.*

11 h-4
FINE & KLEIN

One of the best Lower East Side discount anythings, Fine & Klein sells chichi day and evening bags at great discounts. If you have your heart set on something in particular, come with a picture and style number; often they can track it down or order it. Sunday is a feeding frenzy, so try to come on a weekday. *119 Orchard St. (between Delancey and Rivington Sts.), Lower East Side, 212/674–6720. Subway: Delancey St.*

9 c-1
FURLA

This Italian firm specializes in smooth, classic shapes—but not too classic. Some purses are elongated, others have a bold clasp. Accessories include some adorable coin purses shaped like fruit. *159A Columbus Ave. (at 67th St.), Upper West Side, 212/874–6119. Subway: 66th St./Lincoln Center.*

9 e-2

727 Madison Ave. (between 63rd and 64th Sts.), Upper East Side, 212/755–8986. Subway: 59th St.

9 e-3
HERMÈS

Once a saddler, always a saddler. After well over a century, Hermès still has beautiful saddles and bridles (upstairs), as well as the famous scarves (about $275) and trim "Kelly" bags designed for Grace herself. *11 E. 57th St., Midtown, 212/751–3181. Subway: E, F to 5th Ave.*

7 e-8
JUDITH LEIBER

Judith Leiber's small, sparkling cases are meant to be cradled in the palm rather than slung over the shoulder. The bejeweled shapes include fruit, animals, and even seashells—beautiful, certainly, but you may have to ask your escort to carry your wallet. *987 Madison Ave. (between 76th and 77th Sts.), Upper East Side, 212/327–4003. Subway: 77th St.*

11 e-5
KATE SPADE

There's very little leather here, and no attitude from either the stock or the salespeople. Instead, you'll find the original satin-finish microfiber handbags and totes (even one for baby gear) that are copied high and low, plus the same pared-down designs in various textiles—pinstripes, velvet, faux leopard. You could also come away with scarves, a blouse, or some wonderfully simple pajamas. The clothes and accessories, though, are in exclusively short supply. Of course, "simple" doesn't mean "cheap." *454 Broome St. (at Mercer St.), 212/274–1991. Subway: C, E to Spring St.*

9 e-3
LOUIS VUITTON

Vuitton's famous monogram adorns everything from wallets to steamer trunks, plus an extremely exclusive line of travel gear dreamt up by designers like Vivienne Westwood. Besides the brown-on-brown LVs, there's the Epi leather line, with a striated texture and fun colors (blue, rain-slicker yellow). A new and larger store, on East 57th Street, was under construction at press time. *49 E. 57th St., 212/371–6111. Subway: E, F to 5th Ave.*

hats

Handmade hats can be expensive accessories (we're talking the same price arena as Hermès scarves), but the attention they draw can be well worth it. For the caviar of the hat world, otherwise known as designer Philip Treacy, head to Bergdorf's—or London.

11 d-4
THE HAT SHOP

Hats climb the walls, inviting a try-on (as do the friendly salespeople). Traditional shapes are often tweaked; a fedora, for example, might have a lengthened, perforated front brim. The cocktail hats are tiny, Dr. Seuss–like things with a precarious plume or two. Everything can be made to order at no extra charge. *120 Thompson St. (between Prince and Spring Sts.), SoHo, 212/219–1445. Subway: Prince St.*

11 f-4
KELLY CHRISTY

Woven berets, wide-brims, and other confections can be made to order; you can even custom-pick the colors. Prices start around $200. *235 Elizabeth Street (between Houston and Prince Sts.), SoHo/Little Italy, 212/965–0686. Subway: Broadway–Lafayette St.*

9 *e-8*

LOLA

Classy straw hats are joined by some whimsical shapes—including hats that look like soccer balls. *2 E. 17th Street, Flatiron, 212/366–5708. Subway: L, N, R to 14th St.*

11 *e-4*

RODRIGUEZ

Don't let the two steep flights of stairs come between you and this funky work-shop-cum-store. Hats come in all kinds of fabrics: velvet, faux fur, even burlap. There are riding hats, floppy hats, even structured head scarves with ties. *150 Spring St. (between Wooster St. and W. Broadway), SoHo, 212/965–1927. Subway: C, E to Spring St.*

lingerie & nightwear

For sheer volume and selection, department stores are dependable standbys. Macy's has a massive selection, and Bloomingdale's still makes those days-of-the-week underpants. In most small boutiques the focus is on fancier, pricier, more decorative lingerie.

9 *e-1*

BRA SMYTH

This dedicated shop really knows its inventory; it's even got a bra hot line (800/BRA–9466). Lacy, expensive European imports predominate (some of the simplest and cheapest are by Hanro), but they've also got a great selection of minimizers, uplift bras, and seamless underwear. *905 Madison Ave. (between 72nd and 73rd Sts.), Upper East Side, 212/772–9400. Subway: 77th St.*

9 *e-2*

FOGAL

Fogal carries Swiss-made pantyhose, stockings, and bodysuits in more than 100 colors. And then there's "bal paré," a sheer mesh stocking with a stripe of diamond-shape crystals up the back seam. *680 Madison Ave. (between 61st and 62nd Sts.), Upper East Side, 212/759–9782. Subway: 59th St.*

9 *e-3*

510 Madison Ave. (at 53rd St.), Midtown, 212/355–3254. Subway: E, F to 5th Ave.

11 *d-4*

JOOVAY

This store is so petite that it literally has underwear up to the ceiling. There's a good price range, though not much on the low end: Rigby & Peller, with Queen Elizabeth II's seal of approval (and a royal price tag), La Perla, Mystère, and Josie by Natori (bras about $25). *436 W. Broadway (between Prince and Spring Sts.), SoHo, 212/431–6386. Subway: Prince St.; 6 to Spring St.*

9 *e-1*

LA PERLA

The Italian sizing might take some getting used to; bras are sized 1, 2, 3, and so on instead of having cup sizes. (The cups are approximately B to C.) But the styles are beautiful—shirred silk bras edged in creamy lace (about $200), form-fitting shapers, and delicate camisoles. *777 Madison Ave. (between 66th and 67th Sts.), Upper East Side, 212/570–0050. Subway: 68th St./Hunter College.*

10 *e-1*

LA PETITE COQUETTE

The autographed photos on the walls have extra cachet here; one thank-you came from Frederique, longtime Victoria's Secret model. (If she's spent that much time in just her underwear, she must know whereof she speaks.) The silky stuff is on the ground level—some Aubade (about $150 for a stunning bustier), and La Petite Coquette's own rainbow selection of silk slips, camisoles, and nightgowns (around $70 for a chemise). Downstairs are cotton nightgowns and a few children's items. *52 University Pl. (between 9th and 10th Sts.), Greenwich Village, 212/473–2478. Subway: 8th St.*

11 *d-5*

LE CORSET

Besides the usual underwear, this small boutique carries some of its namesake, including gorgeous Vivienne Westwood bustiers (about $375). *80 Thompson St. (between Spring and Broome Sts.), SoHo, 212/334–4936. Subway: C, E to Spring St.*

9 *e-3*

WOLFORD

Hosiery here runs about $25 and up, but if you invest in "Individual 10," a sheer stocking with a high percentage of Lycra, you stand a good chance of wearing it several times. There are also short- and long-sleeved bodysuits, at roughly double the price of hosiery. *619 Madison Ave. (between 58th and 59th Sts.), Midtown, 212/688–4850. Subway: 59th St.*

7 *e-8*
996 Madison Ave. (between 78th and 77th Sts.), Upper East Side, 212/327–1000. Subway: 77th St.

maternity wear

All of New York's department stores have maternity departments; but only Bloomingdale's and some specialty boutiques carry Belly Basics, a boxed set of supremely comfortable, stretchy clothes like leggings and tunics. The combination of nonelastic waistbands and flattering fabrics and styles made these mix-and-match kits quick sellouts.

9 *f-1*
MOM'S NIGHT OUT
This second-floor boutique fills a small but crucial niche: it specializes in maternity evening wear and cocktail-dress rentals. Renters can choose from over 300 styles and colors; a 3- to 4-day rental can run anywhere from $95 to $220. If you're thinking of investing in four-months-at-a-time evening wear, you can browse through the styles, create a design, and have an outfit custommade. There's also a small ready-to-wear selection. Call ahead; you may need to make an appointment. *970 Lexington Ave. (between 70th and 71st Sts.), Upper East Side, 212/744–6667. Subway: 68th St./Hunter College.*

7 *e-7*
MOTHERHOOD MATERNITY
A less-expensive chain, these stores concentrate on casual items such as denim overalls or jumpers and T-shirts. *1449 3rd Ave. (at 82nd St.), Upper East Side, 212/734–5984. Subway: 86th St.*

9 *d-8*
641 6th Ave. (at 20th St.), Chelsea, 212/741–3488. Subway: F to 23rd St.

9 *d-6*
Manhattan Mall (see Malls, above), 212/564–8170.

9 *f-2*
MOTHERS WORK MATERNITY
Mothers Work provides businesslike suits and dresses for those settings

where leggings and an oversized oxford shirt won't pass muster. *1021 3rd Ave. (between 60th and 61st Sts.), Upper East Side, 212/832–2667. Subway: 59th St.*

9 *e-3*
PEA IN THE POD
Though the name is lighthearted, the clothing is in all seriousness: comfortable and well-made casual and career clothes, even bathing suits. *625 Madison Ave. (between 58th and 59th Sts.), Midtown, 212/826–6468. Subway: 59th St.*

shoes & boots

The crowded stretch of 8th Street between 5th and 6th Avenues is commonly known as Shoe Street. And so it is—especially for those who have yet to hit the corporate hamster wheel. The stores lining this block specialize in mean-looking boots, outrageous platforms, and skateboard-worthy sneakers.

9 *e-1*
ANDREA CARRANO
This store has a laser-specific, perfectly fulfilled purpose: ballerina flats in every color imaginable, from simple black suede to half a dozen blues to metallic bronze. *850 Madison Ave. (at 70th St.), Upper East Side, 212/570–1443. Subway: 68th St./Hunter College.*

9 *e-3*
BALLY OF SWITZERLAND
The delicately tapered toes and beautiful leathers of these conservative shoes will never change. *628 Madison Ave. (at 59th St.), Midtown, 212/751–9082. Subway: 59th St.*

9 *e-3*
BELGIAN SHOES
If you'd like a real touch of Henri Bendel, you'll visit this modest store instead of the namesake emporium on 5th. Bendel sold the big store decades ago, then kept his hand in with these soft-soled, loaferlike flats. (The tiny-bow-on-the-vamp style is originally his.) The premise might be casual, but the materials (raspberry velvet, black suede) and the price tag (a few hundred) certainly aren't. Don't save this store for the weekend; it's open weekdays only, and still closes a little earlier than most. *60 E. 56th St., Midtown, 212/755–7372. Subway: E, F to 5th Ave.*

11 *d-1*
BOOTÉRO
A quintessential West 8th Street store, Bootéro carries high platforms, plastic sandals, thick heels, and even Tevas. *10 5th Ave. (at 8th St.), Greenwich Village, 212/529–7515. Subway: 8th St.*

9 *e-2*
BOTTEGA VENETA
These shoes would look right on Ginger Rogers or Rita Hayworth—satin open-toe sandals, rough-silk slides, ankle-strap pumps with heels little wider than cigarettes. The cost of such sophistication is in the multi-hundreds, but the twice-a-year sales are phenomenal. *635 Madison Ave. (between 59th and 60th Sts.), Midtown, 212/371–5511. Subway: 59th St.*

9 *e-1*
CHARLES JOURDAN
French to their soles, these shoes often have a coquettish detail, like a low vamp or a slight platform. "Bis" on the label means more casual/less expensive. There's also a small selection of Karl Lagerfeld shoes. *777 Madison Ave. (between 66th and 67th Sts.), Upper East Side, 212/486–2350. Subway: 68th St./Hunter College.*

11 *d-4*
CHUCKIES
Don't let the name fool you; this is no Buster Brown outlet. Chuckies has a dashing selection of designer shoes—lots of Dolce & Gabbana (at the 3rd Avenue store), some Sonia Rykiel, and Chuckies' own line of cool pumps and boots. *399 W. Broadway (between Prince and Spring Sts.), 212/343–1717. Subway: Prince St.*

9 *f-2*
1073 3rd Ave. (between 63rd and 64th Sts.), Upper East Side, 212/593–9898. Subway: 59th St.

9 *e-2*
COLE-HAAN
Cole-Haan's woven, moccasin, and loafer styles go through endless permutations and combinations. The shelves are filled with versatile brown or black—not adventurous, but very well made. Moccasins average around $165. *667 Madison Ave. (at 61st St.), Upper East Side, 212/421–8440. Subway: 59th St.*

9 *e-4*
620 5th Ave. (at 50th St.), Midtown, 212/765–9747. Subway: E, F to 5th Ave.

9 *e-3*
EASY SPIRIT
Built for comfort, these shoes still sometimes manage to look sharp. *555 Madison Ave. (at 56th St.), Midtown, 212/715–0152. Subway: E, F to 5th Ave.*

9 *e-5*
437 5th Ave. (at 39th St.), Midtown, 212/725–5901. Subway: B, D, F, Q to 42nd St.

7 *b-7*
2251 Broadway (at 81st St.), Upper West Side, 212/875–8146. Subway: 79th St.

7 *e-7*
1518 3rd Ave. (between 85th and 86th Sts.), Upper East Side, 212/828–9593. Subway: 86th St.; other locations.

9 *e-1*
JOAN & DAVID
Stylish but never trendy, Joan & David always manage to produce a perfect brown wingtip for fall and a lovely, strappy sandal for summer. They also make some graceful clothes and substantial pendant necklaces. *816 Madison Ave. (at 68th St.), Upper East Side, 212/772–3970. Subway: 68th St./Hunter College.*

9 *e-8*
104 5th Ave. (at 16th St.), Chelsea, 212/627–1780. Subway: F to 14th St.

11 *e-4*
JOHN FLUEVOG SHOES
Inventor of the Angelic sole (protects against most earthly liquids "and Satan"), Fluevog carries big, thick shoes and boots. These are no Doc Martens knockoffs, though—the liberal use of platforms, curvaceous heels, and extremely pointy toes on the various styles take them far beyond the yellow-stitched standard. Black leather occasionally makes way for gem-colored suede or pearlescence. *104 Prince St. (between Mercer and Greene Sts.), SoHo, 212/431–4484. Subway: Prince St.*

11 *e-4*
KENNETH COLE
Posters on the walls trumpet clever, liberal sayings ("Shoes shouldn't stay in the closet either") to match the clever, liberal shoes. *567 Broadway (between*

Houston and Prince Sts.), SoHo, 212/965–0283. Subway: Broadway–Lafayette St.

7 *b-8*

353 Columbus Ave. (between 76th and 77th Sts.), Upper West Side, 212/873–2061. Subway: 79th St.

9 *e-8*

95 5th Ave. (at 17th St.), Chelsea, 212/675–2550. Subway: F to 14th St.; N, R to 23rd St.

11 *d-1*

KINWAY INDUSTRIES LTD.

Nothing dainty here (including the decor)—it's crammed with well-priced Converse, Airwalk, and Simple sneakers plus Sketchers, Doc Martens, and Frye boots. 5 W. 8th St., Greenwich Village, 212/777–3848. Subway: 8th St.; W. 4th St./Washington Square.

11 *d-1*

LUICHINY

This little store holds the fleeting title of Biggest Shoes on West 8th Street. With platforms and towering heels, the stock defies anything under six inches tall. 21 W. 8th St., Greenwich Village, 212/477–3445. Subway: 8th St.; W. 4th St./Washington Square.

9 *d-3*

MANOLO BLAHNIK

Blahnik's spindly-heel, pointy-toe shoes are the last word in luxury. Society dames swear by them, Hollywood types teeter in them, and Tori Amos loves them—all with good reason. The vamps are the shoe equivalent of a well-cut low neckline, making the foot a sensual thing indeed. A simple satin evening pump is roughly $400; prices can sky-rocket to over $2,000. 15 W. 55th St., Midtown, 212/582–3007. Subway: E, F to 5th Ave.

9 *e-2*

MARAOLO

Midtown Manhattan is crawling with Maraolo-shod cubicle farmers. This is the place to go for a shiny moc-croc or trim pump. The West 72nd Street location is a factory outlet, with shoes priced between $19 and $99. 782 Lexington Ave. (at 61st St.), Upper East Side, 212/832–8182. Subway: 59th St.

9 *b-1*

131 W. 72nd St., Upper West Side, 212/787–6550. Subway: 72nd St.

9 *e-3*

551 Madison Ave. (at 55th St.), Midtown, 212/308–8794. Subway: E, F to 5th Ave.; other locations.

10 *e-1*

99x

These Brits have an enviably encyclopedic selection of Doc Martens and creepers. 84 E. 10th St., East Village, 212/460–8599. Subway: Astor Pl.

11 *d-4*

OMARI

The selection's not substantial, but no one's complaining as long as they keep turning out the sly pumps and flats. The sale rack in the back is excellent hunting territory. 132 Prince St. (between Wooster St. and W. Broadway), SoHo, 212/219–0619. Subway: Prince St.

9 *e-2*

PATRICK COX

Cox's Wannabe line is typical—a retro edge on desperately hip styles. 702 Madison Ave. (between 62nd and 63rd Sts.), Upper East Side, 212/759–3910. Subway: 59th St.

9 *e-1*

PETER FOX

It's hard to pin down the lavish, offbeat look of these English shoes—at first glance, the window displays look rather vintage. That's until you notice the little platforms or curvy heels. Part of the Thompson Street store is for bridal shoes only; prepare for lots of lustrous satin and bows. 806 Madison Ave. (at 68th St.), Upper East Side, 212/744–8340. Subway: 68th St./Hunter College.

11 *d-4*

105 Thompson St. (between Prince and Spring Sts.), SoHo, 212/431–6359 or 212/431–7426 (bridal). Subway: C, E to Spring St.

11 *d-1*

PETIT PETON

These shoes are very cutting-edge, even for the West 8th Street corridor; they include rarities like the club-envy, Belgian-made Stéphan BXL. 27 W. 8th St., Greenwich Village, 212/677–3730. Subway: 8th St.; W. 4th St./Washington Square.

9 e-2
ROBERT CLERGERIE
These classy French shoes make their own fun: thick-sole slides are stitched with white, pumps have a triangular heel, chunky loafers sidle up to velvet tie-up sandals. Most pairs run in the hundreds of dollars. *681 Madison Ave. (between 61st and 62nd Sts.), Upper East Side, 212/207–8600. Subway: 59th St.*

9 e-4
SALVATORE FERRAGAMO
Giant photos of happy customer Audrey Hepburn beam down on the gorgeous goods. These shoes know how to flatter a woman's foot—molded insteps, heels just the right height. Famous Ferragamo touches, like the scalloped heel, are re-invented in elegant ways. *661 5th Ave. (between 52nd and 53rd Sts.), Midtown, 212/759–3822. Subway: E, F to 5th Ave.*

9 e-5
SELBY FIFTH AVENUE
One of them's not on 5th Avenue, but no matter. You'll never have to worry about pinched toes with this selection, which includes Easy Spirit, Mephisto, Nickels, and Clarks. Selby's own line is both cheaper and sleeker. *417 5th Ave. (at 38th St.), Garment District, 212/328–1020. Subway: B, D, F, Q to 42nd St.*

9 e-2
1055 3rd Ave. (between 62nd and 63rd Sts.), Upper East Side, 212/328–1001. Subway: 59th St.

11 d-1
SEVER BOUTIQUE LTD.
Cowboy boots and (almost) nothing but—they come in ostrich, snakeskin, and over a dozen colors. *19 W. 8th St., Greenwich Village, 212/533–5909. Subway: 8th St.; W. 4th St./Washington Square.*

11 f-4
SIGERSON MORRISON
Shoe boxes line the walls of this tiny boutique; peer down and you'll find deli-cate leather shoes at your feet. Pay close attention to the details, like tiny buckles or interesting hues. Prices generally hover a bit above $200. *242 Mott St. (between Houston and Prince Sts.), SoHo/Little Italy, 212/219–3893. Subway: Broadway–Lafayette St.*

11 d-4
STEPHANE KÉLIAN
Kélian's woven beauties are a Euro-hound's favorite; they do wonders to an all-black outfit. Often the woven leather uppers are laced with a hard-to-match but too-chic color, like ochre or burnt orange. *120 Wooster St. (between Spring and Prince Sts.), SoHo, 212/925–3077. Subway: Spring St.*

9 e-2
717 Madison Ave. (between 63rd and 64th Sts.), Upper East Side, 212/980–1919. Subway: 68th St./Hunter College.

9 e-3
STEWART WEITZMAN
Never let it be said that these guys don't love their shoes. Besides those (from no-nonsense pumps to lime-green pumps), they have cards, wrapping paper, nap-kins, and other shoe-oriented accessories peeking from the corners. *625 Madison Ave. (between 58th and 59th Sts.), Mid-town, 212/750–2555. Subway: 59th St.*

9 e-8
TOOTSI PLOHOUND
An essential part of many downtown closets, these shoes are often chunky-soled and somewhat heftily priced. You'll find Costume National, Freelance, and Miu Miu, plus plenty of cheaper Miu Miu knockoffs with weird Italianate labels. During sales, you can get some good stompers for about $80. *137 5th Ave. (between 20th and 21st Sts.), Chelsea, 212/460–8650. Subway: F to 23rd St.*

11 d-4
413 W. Broadway (between Prince and Spring Sts.), SoHo, 212/925–8931, C, E to Spring St.

9 e-2
1116 3rd Ave. (between 65th and 66th Sts.), Upper East Side, 212/249–0671. Subway: 68th St./Hunter College.

9 e-2
UNISA
This is a fantastic place to get a lower-priced take on a trend. Thick-soled slides are under $50, while grown-up pumps and loafers are just under $60. *701 Madison Ave. (at 62nd St.), Upper East Side, 212/753–7474. Subway: 59th St.*

9 *e-1*

VARDA

These handmade Italian shoes are worth every penny. The exclusive designs often have softly rounded toes, T-straps, or even patent-leather–trimmed zippers. You can have most styles in any color you want—as long as it's black. *786 Madison Ave. (between 66th and 67th Sts.), Upper East Side, 212/472–7552. Subway: 68th St./Hunter College.*

11 *d-4*

149 Spring St. (between W. Broadway and Wooster St.), SoHo, 212/941–4990. Subway: Spring St.

9 *e-2*

VIA SPIGA

The first U.S. branch of this Italian shoemaker has wooed the city with just what it likes—mostly black shoes and low boots, many in buffed-to-a-shine calfskin or soft-as-butter suede. *765 Madison Ave. (between 65th and 66th Sts.), Upper East Side, 212/988–4877. Subway: 68th St./Hunter College.*

9 *e-2*

WALTER STEIGER

Following trends from a discreet distance, Walter Steiger makes lovely pumps (about $300), some in textured leather or patterned fabric. There's also quite a range of golf shoes—those white leathers and cleats can come spiked with snakeskin or shiny primary colors. *739 Madison Ave. (between 65th and 66th Sts.), Upper East Side, 212/570-1212. Subway: 68th St./Hunter College.*

swimsuits

Most department stores have year-round swim- and cruisewear departments. If you need a workhorse suit, try a sporting-goods store (*see* Sporting Goods & Clothing, *below*).

7 *e-8*

WATER WEAR

No matter what time of year your cruise departs, Water Wear is waiting with a full selection of swimsuits. You may have to duck some garish getups, but there's almost always something acceptable. Big bonus: Bikini tops and bottoms can be bought separately. *1349 3rd Ave. (at 77th St.), Upper East Side, 212/570–6606. Subway: 77th St.*

11 *e-5*

KEIKO

Tug no more on the back end of your bathing suit—here you can have it customized to fit. Keiko herself once worked for Warner Bros., which may have something to do with the kapow! primary-color palette. *62 Greene St. (between Spring and Broome Sts.), SoHo, 212/226–6051. Subway: Spring St.*

CLOTHING FOR MEN/GENERAL

classic

ALFRED DUNHILL TAILORS OF LONDON

See Custom, *below*.

9 *e-2*

AQUASCUTUM OF LONDON

This is the New York home of an English clothing firm famed for its trench coats and luxurious tailoring. Highlights are cashmere sweaters, tweed coats, and snappy London pinstripes that would make a Lloyds adjuster weep with pleasure. *714 Madison Ave. (between 63rd and 64th Sts.), Upper East Side, 212/753–8305. Subway: 59th St.*

9 *d-8*

BANANA REPUBLIC

You can't swing a dead cat in any of these graceful, jazz-addled stores without hitting a slumming European sifting through the lambs-wool polo sweaters and pillars of shirts. Shoppers who recall BR as a safari-style catalog outfit trying to dress everyone like the cast of *Out of Africa* will be refreshed by the stores' about-face toward urban casual chic of a decidedly Italian stripe. Yeah, they still have khakis and jeans, but what about that black-wool crepe suit? Three buttons and four-inch side vents! Hermès and Gucci knockoff ties and a footwear section that combines the latest looks with loafer/oxford classics are shelved in pale-pine bays alongside leather jackets and bathing bibelots. Irritants include the store's habit of precuffing every pair of trousers (alterations are free) and a misguided foray into golf equipment. Since 1996, BR has plunged into a design ideology heavy on the sleek, neo-mod styles that have been dominating the runways, leading to piping, ribbing, and cabling that only *Sein-*

feld's Kramer could get away with; still, almost no one makes a nicer long-sleeve French-blue shirt. Almost. *655 5th Ave. (at 52nd St.), Midtown, 212/644–6678. Subway: E, F to 5th Ave.*

9 *e-4*

89 5th Ave. (at 18th St.), Flatiron, 212/366–4630. Subway: F to 14th St., N, R to 23rd St.

7 *e-7*

1136 Madison Ave. (at 84th St.), Upper East Side, 212/570–2465. Subway: 4, 5, 6 to 86th St.; and other locations.

9 *d-3*

BERGDORF GOODMAN MEN

Once revolutionary—a throwback to the refined era of clubby gentleman's haberdashery with curveballs such as Prada, Dolce & Gabbana, and Gaultier tossed in—this spectacular emporium across the street from the Plaza Hotel has lately retrenched, aiming to garner "serious" dressers and leave the friskier stuff (Gucci thongs, Matsuda sarongs) to the boutiques stretching north on Madison Avenue. Featured are Romeo Gigli, Georgio Armani, and Guccis as well as perhaps the best shoe selection in Manhattan, with To Boot and J.P. Tod anchoring the high end. Pampering for the affluent executive includes custom tailoring, a concierge, a café, a penthouse hair salon, the use of cellular phones, and a putting green. *745 5th Ave. (at 58th St.), Midtown, 212/753–7300. Closed Sun. Subway: N, R to 5th Ave.*

9 *e-3*

BIJAN

If you have extravagant taste and a bankroll to match—oh, and an appointment—this haute haberdasher from Rodeo Drive offers, among other frills, shirts that start at $240 and ties at $110(!). *699 5th Ave. (between 54th and 55th Sts.), Midtown, 212/758–7500. Closed Sun. Subway: E, F to 5th Ave.*

9 *e-4*

BRIONI

Elegant Italian men's clothing, featuring sumptuous fabrics and classic European styling and cut, sells for appropriately high prices at this luxurious, inviting boutique. Suits can be made to measure. *55 E. 52nd Street, 212/355–1940. Subway: E, F to 5th Ave.*

9 *d-5*

BROOKS BROTHERS

For any man who reveres classic, unforced, American unforced style—the gray-wool sack suit, the navy blazer, seersucker, repp ties, chinos, dignified formal wear, and, above all else, the best damn shirt money can buy—this institution is a shrine, a mecca, a solace in dark times, a bastion since 1818. No one has been clothing American men longer, under the discreet "Brooks Brothers, Makers" label, and the confidence that comes with that kind of history shows on all four menswear floors. Lately, a minor Euro vibe has crept in (some of the tweed jackets lack back vents; and can someone explain those merino-wool polo sweaters?), but this has only served to spark new life in some sections, notably shirts, available in a myriad of patterns and colors, from a bucolic tattersall to deep blue end-on-end. And what a shirt! Brooks' oxford-cloth button-down, in pale blue or white with a single cuff button and a collar that rolls just so, has been imitated by every clothier and designer on the planet, but at $48, there remains no substitute. It is the shirt perfected. There are four or five sales a year, with special discounts extended to frequent shoppers. *346 Madison Ave. (at 44th St.), Midtown, 212/682–8800. Subway: 42nd St./Grand Central; 1 Church St. (Liberty Plaza), Lower Manhattan, 212/267–2400. Subway: World Trade Center.*

9 *b-8*

CAMOUFLAGE

These Chelsea specialty shops feature classic, American-made menswear with an upbeat, imaginative feel, plus more-casual threads at No. 139. Don't miss the elaboarate selection of ties. *141 8th Ave. (at 17th St.), Chelsea, 212/741–9118; 139 8th Ave. (at 17th St.), Chelsea, 212/691–1750. Subway: A, C, E to 14th St.*

9 *e-1*

DAVID CENCI

This dignified shop is a handsome setting for an expensive but outstanding selection of impeccably tailored classics, showcasing wonderful fabrics in everything from suits and sportswear to coats and formal wear. *801 Madison Ave. (near 67th St.), Upper East Side, 212/628–5910. Closed Sun. Subway: 68th St./Hunter College.*

9 e-8

EMPORIO ARMANI

Against a mellow Milanese backdrop (blond wood, stainless steel, pale-cream lampshades) in a Stanford White building, the oft-imitated but rarely equaled Italian master showcases his "mid" range: slightly less expensive, sportier, and more experimental than the Collezioni. If you're out to see what Gio has on his mind, this is the place to witness his ever-changing moods. They're generally arrayed around a basic theme—a concoction of Indian motifs, gray, corduroy, tweed, and red, each depending on the season—and take shape in classic separates, casual sweaters, trousers, ties, shoes, belts, and accessories—and formal wear! This store is something of a touchstone; stroll by each season to take stock of menswear and to be entertained by the always-inventive and frequently modified window displays. *110 5th Ave. (at 16th St), Chelsea, 212/727–3240. Subway: F to 14th St.*

9 e-3

FAÇONNABLE

A limber, sporty, Mediterranean mood dominates this unimposing two-story shop in the middle of Manhattan's poshest shopping strip. The clothes are simple, French interpretations of American classics: button-down check shirts, khakis, windbreakers, lightweight cotton sweaters, fun-in-the-sun accessories, colorful ties, and conservatively tailored suits and separates. Frenchmen can't get enough of this stuff; it combines the European flair for relaxed elegance with durable fabrics that can wear several hats. Perfect threads for a weekend jaunt to Sag Harbor, or a late weekday lunch at Balthazar. *689 5th Ave. (at 54th St.), Midtown, 212/319–0111. Subway: E, F to 5th Ave.*

9 e-3

GAP

Why shop anywhere else, right? The megaGap at Herald Square breaks clothes down into several categories for guys who really don't like clothes very much: jeans, T-shirts, sporty separates, athletic wear, and haberdashery. This last is the most notable. For young men with light wallets, it's possible to get done up at the Gap's larger stores in updated Ivy League style—khakis, oxfords, blazers, sweater-vests, cheap ties—for a casual yet professional look that constitutes a leap from standard post-college attire. The secret to shopping the Gap is to stop in every few weeks; if you see something you like, it's a lock that it will go on sale within a month, so determined is the Gap to keep its mix moving. Secret number two is the shoes, which are cheap, simple, and well-made. *60 W. 34th Street (Herald Square), Garment District, 212/643–8960. Subway: 34th St./Herald Square.*

9 d-6

734 Lexington Ave. (at 59th St.), Midtown, 212/751–1543. Subway: 59th St.

9 e-2

1131–1149 3rd Ave. (between 66th and 67th Sts.), Upper East Side, 212/472–5559. Subway: 68th St./Hunter College; and other locations.

9 d-3

HARRISON JAMES

This brand-new menswear emporium stresses exquisite Italian tailoring and personal service. The store itself is remarkable—it's in a townhouse across the street from the MoMA sculpture garden, in a building whose first floor once served as Cary Grant's office. The spirit of Grant's debonair ease dominates this clubby store, not to mention its movie-star prices (think nothing of spending $1000 on a sport coat, or $400 on a pair of loafers). There are almost no salespeople; instead, customers are greeted in the store's lobby and assigned a "guide" who provides a tour of the shop, including a glimpse at the tailoring room and the cigar humidor. The philosophy is snooty, but it doesn't overwhelm the store's understanding that fine menswear should be comfortable and basically conservative. Also available are formal wear, custom shirtings, a bar, and a barber shop whose waiting area contains a pool table, on which customers can, as the management says, "pay off their bills" by wagering. *5 W. 54th St., Midtown, 212/541–6870. Subway: E, F to 5th Ave.*

9 e-3

HERMÈS

East 57th Street is home to some of the most exclusive boutiques this side of the Rive Gauche, but the French import that has made the biggest splash, particularly in the wake of the runaway bull market on Wall Street, is this longtime

French saddlemaker and purveyor of ultrafine silk prints. A fashionable man will tell you that if you have $1000 to spend on your whole ensemble, this is the place to buy that tie that you'll pass down to your grandson. The average price for a whimsical bridle-tack print? $120. Also on the block are Hermès suits, jackets, leather goods, and, of course, saddles. Don't forget to save the boxes! They're the best in retailing, and their signature color is now commonly known as "Hermès Orange." *11 E. 57th St., Midtown, 212/751–3181. Subway: E, F to 5th Ave.*

9 *d-8*

J. CREW

This catalog-retailing phenom recently crept north from its rather stolid Seaport digs to a pair of splendidly stark shops in SoHo and the Flatiron District. While at one time the best that could be said for Crew was that it gave men another place to buy khakis and polos, things have changed with the advent of haberdashery designed to challenge the uptown supremacy of Brooks Brothers and Paul Stuart in the hearts of boys who like to dress conservatively, but with panache. Success? Well, sort of. The basics are commendable, and the underwear unbeatable, but the suits are sloppily tailored, and the ties, while they knot just right, don't seem to be catching on. What works? Shirts, of course, in dozens of patterns and colors—from lime gingham to architectural checks—that move effortlessly from office to gallery opening. For those who want to emulate that particular brand of Los Angeles–New York casual cool favored by Flatiron copywriters and Santa Monica art dealers, J. Crew wallops the competition. *91 5th Ave. (between 16th and 17th Sts.), Chelsea, 212/255–4848, F to 14th St., N, R to 23rd St.*

10 *f-7*

99 Prince St. (between Mercer and Greene Sts.), SoHo, 212/966–2739. Subway: Prince St.

11 *e-4*

203 Front St. (South Street Seaport), Lower Manhattan, 212/385–3500. Subway: 2, 3 to Fulton St.

9 *e-5*

J. PRESS

It's been almost a hundred years since this store opened its doors in New Haven, Connecticut, ready to serve the basic sartorial needs of Yalies. In New York the stock has gone through precious few changes since the '60s—lapels and ties have gotten wider, maybe a few more belts have been added to the mix, but Press still delivers that natural-shouldered, hyperpreppy, button-down look for new generations determined to perpetuate Ivy League style (even if most people at the Ivies have moved on). If you've just gotten into Skull and Bones, this is where you go to buy your club tie. *16 E. 44th Street, Midtown, 212/687–7642. Closed Sun. Subway: 42nd St./Grand Central.*

11 *e-4*

NEW REPUBLIC CLOTHIERS

This rinky-dink boutique has for nearly 20 years offered an idiosyncratic take on classic British menswear. Superb shoes, high-quality straw hats, old-boy ties, and regimental scarves are on offer, plus a variety of skillfully cut and tailored suits, jackets, and trousers, along with belts, socks, and some of the finest—and liveliest—shirtings this side of London's Turnbull & Asser. Don't miss the biannual sales, when much of the stock is discounted 50%–75%. *93 Spring St. (between Broadway and Mercer St.), 212/219–3005. Subway: 6 to Spring St.*

9 *e-4*

PAUL STUART

The mood here is natty, dashing, conservative but unstuffy, with an emphasis on variety where it counts; hence the tiny shoe section adjacent to the largest selection of *good* ties in the city (including more bows and knitteds than you've ever seen under a single glass display). Men who buy here spend huge amounts on few choice items, don't noodle with the basics, and know that this is the place to come for, bar none, the best fedora in the Big Apple. Sales do happen, but they seem to be advertised by ESP; those who benefit are those who drop in often. *10 E. 45th St., Midtown, 212/682–0320. Closed Sun. Subway: 42nd St./Grand Central.*

9 *e-1*

POLO/RALPH LAUREN/ POLO SPORT

Ah, what a pompous paean to the vanished days of merrie olde England, all jammed into the Rhinelander Mansion amid more mahogany and green baize than anyone should ever see in one place. Trimmings include dog prints, and plenty of them; images of blue-bloods on horseback in red hunting jackets; weathered leather; and scads of clean-cut, impeccably bronzed employees, buzzing around attending to every imaginable (or imagined) need. What Bronx-born Lauren has done is out-WASP those WASPs whose casual, hale-and-hearty, outdoorsman style inspired his designs. Frugality, however, is not one of the things he has borrowed from the Old Newport crowd: Everything he sells is of obsessively high quality, maybe too high if you're not sure you need flannels designed for Arctic conditions or herringbone tweeds that weigh more than the average beagle. The khakis, signature polo shirts, shoes, sport coats, and other preppy staples are all here, but so is Lauren's new Purple Label line of English suits, something he's lately been passionately promoting after decades of showing up everywhere in jeans and a bomber jacket. *867 Madison Ave. (at 72nd St.), Upper East Side, 212/606–2100. Closed Sun. Subway: 68th St./Hunter College.*

9 *d-4*

SAKS FIFTH AVENUE

Once perhaps the most fabled store in town, Saks has in recent years seen its thunder stolen by a host of competitors, everyone from Barneys to The Gap. However, for a clean, well-mannered menswear experience, and one that suits most fellas head-to-toe, Saks continues to sustain enormous snob appeal, if limited hipness. All of the usual suspects can be found on the 6th floor: Armani Collezioni, Calvin Klein, Versace Versus, Donna Karan. However, where Saks really shines is in the classic arena. Oxford Clothes, the nearly century-old Savile Row–style clothier, delivers that Prince of Wales look—snugly tailored conservative suits in dashing pinstripes and sturdy flannels—while across the aisle is Alan Flusser's shop, a Saks exclusive. Flusser's business went belly-up several years back, but he's maintained a presence at Saks, where his clothes never really went away. This remains one of the few places in town where you can buy Flusser's indispensable menswear guide. *611 5th Ave. (at 50th St.), Midtown, 212/940–2455. Subway: E, F to 5th Ave.*

9 *e-1*

YVES SAINT LAURENT RIVE GAUCHE FOR MEN

Saint Laurent's high-priced high fashion is worn by almost no one. Cowards. There are few other places in town to obtain a correctly cut, side-vented navy blazer, a Parisian standby. *859 Madison Ave. (between 70th and 71st Sts.), Upper East Side, 212/517–7400. Closed Sun. Subway: 68th St./Hunter College.*

contemporary

9 *e-2*

BARNEYS NEW YORK

Oh, how the mighty have fallen! With the close of Barneys' flagship store on 17th Street and the Pressman family's resolution of their battle with Japanese investors over the fate of the uptown palace (they've been bailed out by Hong Kong financier Dickson Poon), it's beginning to look as if this New York institution, started three generations ago as a discount menwear shop, is going to go the way of B. Altman. For the time being, however, this is *the* place to go for that quintessentially snotty Manhattan shopping experience. From the supple staples of Georgio Armani and Calvin Klein to the vanguard fantasies of Helmut Lang, Paul Smith, and Dries van Noten—not to mention the sticker shock supplied by Hermès—the Madison Avenue store sells merchandise that's available in plenty of other places, but not in the über-stylish, *forward* gestalt that Barneys has built its reputation on. For a more egalitarian vibe, there's always the annual downtown warehouse sale, which finds Gotham's male population lined up for hours to snare deeply discounted suits, acres of shirts, yards of designer ties, and avant-garde items that just didn't move on the main floor, like that Comme des Garçons linen jacket with seven pockets, marked down from $1200 to a tidy $600. Alterations are free. *660 Madison Ave. (at 61st St.), Upper East Side, 212/826–8900, Subway: 59th St.; World Financial Center, 225 Liberty St., Lower Manhattan, 212/945–1600, Subway: World Trade Center.*

11 *e-4*

AGNÈS B. HOMME

Taking its cue from the early 1960s, this medium-sized SoHo shop—bedecked with old French New Wave cinema posters and such baubles as postcards of *Psycho*'s Tony Perkins grinning in blue gingham and tweed—is perhaps the finest example anywhere of the Parisian take on American Rat Pack style. Suits, stacks of exquisite shirts, leather porkpie chapeaux (for that Dean Martin snap), dozens of ties no wider than two inches, leather car coats, striped boatsman T-shirts, and an assortment of witty accessories make Agnès B. Homme a must-stop for any cat infatuated with the Sands Hotel heyday of Old Blue Eyes, or the Cold War irreverence of Goddard and Truffaut. *79 Greene St. (at Spring St.), SoHo, 212/431–4339. Subway: Spring St.*

11 *e-4*
A.P.C.

This store resembles a cross between an American barn and a French farmhouse, yet the clothes are anything but country. Anything but cheap, either. The style tends to be nerdish urban slacker, drawing heavily on the aesthetic of thrift-store finds from the '70s: fuzzy wool sweaters, in colors like aqua and avocado; narrow-wale corduroy jeans; velvet jackets with trousers to match, in chocolate; white shirts. All very Beck, circa 1996. It's not for everybody, but A.P.C. can generally be counted on for comfortable, unforced threads that mine current fringe trends in a high-quality manner (no one really *wants* to wear some moth-eaten mohair cardigan from Cheap Jack's, anyway). *131 Mercer St. (between Prince and Spring Sts.), SoHo, 212/966–9685. Subway: 6 to Spring St.; Prince St.*

11 *e-4*
A/X (ARMANI EXCHANGE)

Perhaps a bit more Euro than absolutely necessary (What's up with those enormous belt buckles? And really, who wears indigo denim besides Italian photojournalists?), but nevertheless a commendable distillation of the Milanese Master's easy, fluid, and in this case even colorful sportswear designs, meant to compete with The Gap and J. Crew. "A/X" is meant to recall the buy-everything U.S. Army "P/X" (Post Exchange) of the Gomer Pyle era; truth is, if you don't mind shelling out some heavy dollars for a shirt (say, $100), there's scant reason to shop anywhere

else, so comprehensive is the A/X selection. The stuff—jeans, jackets, outerwear, T-shirts, and so on—is superbly made, beautifully textured and styled, and comfortable. Some of the sales are succulent. *568 Broadway (between Houston and Prince Sts.), SoHo, 212/431–6000. Subway: Prince St.; Broadway–Lafayette St.*

11 *e-4*
BEAU BRUMMEL

This is shopping for the confused: The store's own line shares space with no-brainer professional standbys, such as Hugo Boss, but the whole affair exudes a dated, overly flashy vibe that looks more discount than upscale, despite the steep prices. *421 W. Broadway (between Prince and Spring Sts.), SoHo, 212/219–2666. Subway: C, E to Spring St.*

9 *e-2*
CALVIN KLEIN

The boutique-as-art-gallery metaphor flourishes at this multifloor architectural promo for America's prime minimalist. You name it, CK's got it: sportswear, the drapey suits, the textured, monochrome ties, socks, and, of course, scads of that scanty underwear. The place is a real Madison Avenue scene on a Saturday afternoon in early spring or fall. *654 Madison Ave. (at 60th St.), Upper East Side, 212/292–9000. Subway: 59th St.*

9 *d-3*
CHARIVARI

A pioneer with forward-looking European and American fashions, this family-owned shop was right there with Barneys in promoting Giorgio Armani and Gianni Versace. It's well stocked and well run. *18 W. 57th Street, Midtown, 212/333–4040. Closed Sun. in summer. Subway: B, Q to 57th St.*

11 *d-4*
COMME DES GARÇONS

Astoundingly expensive avant-garde designs (multifabric jackets, innovative textures, tricks with linings, funky shoes, $60 socks) from Japanese fashion radical Rei Kawakubo are austerely displayed in a vaguely penal setting. *116 Wooster St. (between Prince and Spring Sts.), SoHo, 212/219–0660. Subway: Spring St.*

9 *d-4*

FRENCH CONNECTION

Okay, okay; the colors and styles aren't for everybody, and unless you're in entertainment or advertising, it might be tough to get away with some of the four-button Euro-casual suits and separates in which this pseudo-Gallic, slightly libertine version of Banana Republic specializes. They deliver big, though, on the inventory-clearing sales. *1270 6th Ave. (at 51st St.), Midtown, 212/262–6623. Subway: 47th–50th Sts./Rockefeller Center.*

11 *e-4*

435 W. Broadway (at Prince St.), SoHo, 212/219–1197. Subway: Prince St., Broadway–Lafayette St.

7 *a-7*

FRANK STELLA

Stella offers super men's fashions, including silk shirts in solids and stripes along with the more common, 100-percent-cotton variety; sweaters; hundreds of ties; and accessories. *440 Columbus Ave. (at 81st St.), Upper West Side, 212/877–5566. Subway: 79th St.*

0 *e-2*

GIORGIO ARMANI/ EMPORIO ARMANI

Nearly across the street from his snazzier main boutique, Armani has opened a second store to sell his midprice Emporio line. While the older shop is a spiritual cousin of Calvin Klein's (white, open, airy), the Emporio resembles a pre–World War I Berlin department store. It's funky, but certainly not excessive, and it's hard to beat either location for high-quality, supremely reserved, and ever-so-inhabitable styles for everyone from lawyers to Indian chiefs with a thing for beige. *760 Madison Ave. (between 65th and 66th Sts.), Upper East Side, 212/988–9191. Subway: 68th St./Hunter College*

9 *e-3*

Emporio, 601 Madison Ave. (between 57th and 58th Sts.), Midtown, 212/317–0800. Subway: 59th St.

11 *e-4*

LAUNDRY INDUSTRY

You have three color choices at this Amsterdam import: white, beige, and black—lots and lots of black. The clothes are nothing complicated, just reliable SoHo casual stuff with an eye toward body-consciousnesss that will carry the unflappable wearer from office to event to late-night bistro. *122 Spring St. (at Greene St.), SoHo, 212/343–2225. Subway: Spring St.*

11 *e-8*

PAUL SMITH

Smith's ideas of menswear are a bit much for some. He adores pattern clash, is addicted to a slim, mod silhouette that hefty guys might not cotton to, and is excessively buffeted by the winds of change. Still, for top-flight duds, glibly designed accessories (the best watch, cufflink, and eyeglass styles going), supremely slick, wanna-be Italian suits, nifty ties, and shoes to die for—not to mention biannual seasonal sales (75% off during their final days)—Paul Smith continues to dazzle. Celebrity customers include David Hockney, which should reveal something about Smith's fearless attitude toward color. Not for the monochrome set. *108 5th Ave. (at 16th St.), Chelsea, 212/627–9770. Subway: F to 14th St.*

9 *e-3*

PRADA

This very expensive, very Italian, very minimal boutique delivers the styles of the moment amid lime walls and chrome railings: slim, neo-mod suits in charcoal and black, chunky shoes, exquisite leathers, and no small measure of attitude. Absolutely the current It Store, the place to see and be seen. *45 E. 57th St., Midtown, 212/308–2332. Subway: E, F to 5th Ave. Closed Sun.*

9 *e-1*

841 Madison Ave. (at 70th St.), Upper East Side, 212/327–4200. Subway: 68th St./Hunter College.

11 *d-4*

SEAN

Amid the black-and-white boxes that litter SoHo is this warm little boutique that quietly yet gleefully out-Euros them all. It's the only U.S. store to carry the understated, carefully crafted clothes of French designer Pierre Emile Lafaurie, and it quietly lays on its Continental hands with such gems as a corduroy "painter's jacket" (about $100) and multi-hued dress shirts. *132 Thompson St. (between Prince and Houston Sts.), SoHo, 212/598–5980. Subway: Prince St.*

custom

9 e-3

ALFRED DUNHILL TAILORS OF LONDON

Dunhill supplies old-school British tailoring perfection in the form of custom men's suits and shirts (remarkably, they'll come to you for a fitting) and off-the-peg imports. The facade is suitably imposing, as the wares are very luxurious and very expensive; secondary treats include sweaters, custom-made shoes, ties, scarves, leather goods, jewelry, writing instruments, fine gifts, and smokers' accessories. *450 Park Ave. (at 57th St.), Midtown, 212/753–9292. Subway: N, R to 5th Ave.*

9 e-4

CHIPP

Custom tailoring rules here. The high-quality, bespoke suits, plus ready-to-wear suits, jackets, and trousers, are very expensive. *11 E. 44th St., Midtown, 212/687–0850. Closed Sun.; also closed Sat. in summer. Subway: 42nd St./Grand Central.*

9 e-6

CHRIS-ARTO CUSTOM SHIRT COMPANY

Take your pick of nearly 500 natural fabrics in this Garment District shirt shop. The minimum order is six shirts; delivery takes four weeks. Other custom options are pajamas and boxers. *39 W. 32nd St., 6th floor, Garment District, 212/563–4455. Closed weekends. Subway: 34th St./Herald Square.*

9 e-2

CUSTOM SHOP

These stores are clearinghouses for custom-made shirts. Shoppers can choose from over 300 cotton and cotton-blend fabrics and a variety of collar and cuff styles, as well as ready-to-wear. Delivery takes six weeks. *618 5th Ave. (at 50th St.), Midtown, 212/245–2499. Subway: E, F to 5th Ave.*

9 e-5

338 Madison Ave. (between 43rd and 44th Sts.), Midtown, 212/867–3650. Subway: 42nd St./Grand Central.

10 d-7

115 Broadway (between Cedar and Pine Sts.), Lower Manhattan, 212/267–8535. Subway: Rector St.

10 e-7

60 Wall St. (at Hanover St.), Lower Manhattan, 212/480–2954. Subway: Wall St. Closed Sun.

9 e-3

SULKA

Custom-made shirts and such trifles as silk pajamas are the order of the day at this perennial *GQ* favorite, which caters to both rich tastes and deep pockets. The off-the-peg selection features English-style suits, sport jackets, and slacks. *430 Park Ave. (at 55th St.), Midtown, 212/980–5200. Subway: 59th St.*

9 e-4

301 Park Ave. (at 50th St., in the Waldorf-Astoria), Midtown, 212/872–4592. Subway: 51st St./Lexington–3rd Aves. Closed Sun.

discount & off-price

10 e-6

CENTURY 21

It's combat shopping, but where else are you going to score that Gaultier or Gigli suit at half price? They sell absolutely everything here, and they sell it cheap; but they don't have fitting rooms, so the idea is to grab, grab, grab and return later. The store's a favorite of the nearby Wall Street broker crowd, who hit the gigantic cut-rate department store's racks regularly to load up on Gene Meyer ties, underwear, socks, and Ralph Lauren suits. There's also an enormous selection of dress shirts, and a bevy of shoes (including Bruno Magli) downstairs. *22 Cortland St. (between Broadway and Church St.; near World Trade Center), Lower Manhattan, 212/227–9092. Subway: Cortlandt St./World Trade Center.*

9 e-5

DOLLAR BILL'S GENERAL STORE

This well-located, well-stocked, well-priced menswear store sells many designer names. Low frills, high savings. *32 E. 42nd St., Midtown, 212/867–0212. Subway: 42nd St./Grand Central.*

9 e-8

DAFFY'S

Like Century 21, Daffy's is an endurance test, full of as much garbage as gold; it rewards the diligent shopper who visits often enough to recognize the dandy stuff. Recent gems have included Industria jackets and sportswear by Les Copains, a popular French purveyor of simple, slightly dressy casual duds including jackets, sweaters, and suits. Don't miss the oceans of ties and socks, not to mention suits and formal wear from countries you didn't know were in the rag trade. *111 5th Ave. (at 18th St.), Chelsea, 212/529–4477. Subway: F to 14th St., N, R to 23rd St.*

9 *e-5*

335 Madison Ave. (at 44th St.), Midtown, 212/557–4422. Subway: 42nd St./Grand Central.

9 *d-6*

1311 Broadway (at 34th St.), Garment District, 212/736–4477. Subway: 34th St./Herald Square.

10 *e-6*
GORSART
This no-frill Manhattan standby offers classic, natural-shoulder clothing. Prices are low, and alterations are free. *9 Murray Street (between Broadway and Church St.), 2nd floor, Lower Manhattan, 212/962–0024. Closed Sun. Subway: 2, 3 to Park Pl.; N, R to City Hall.*

9 *e-8*
MOE GINSBURG
Need a suit? Why not get four? Along with, say, Filene's Basement, this is the place to go if you've just landed an entry-level job at Merrill Lynch and need something to wear for the first week. Slicker than Brooks Brothers, Moe provides a shot at some flash (read: designer) clothing for less than you would pay at a fine department store. The suits are many, and the salespeople are low-pressure, honest fellas who deliver competent advice on fit and alterations. *162 5th Ave. (at 21st St.), 2nd to 5th floors, Chelsea, 212/242–3482. Subway: F to 23rd St.*

11 *b-2*
NEW YORK ARMY & NAVY
The rule here is inexpensive outdoor clothes, shoes, and equipment for active types. *328 Bleecker St. (at Christopher St.), West Village, 212/242–6665. Subway: Christopher St./Sheridan Square.*

9 *b-8*

110 8th Ave. (between 15th and 16th Sts.), Chelsea, 212/645-7420. Subway: A, C, E to 14th St.; 221 E. 59th St., Midtown, 212/755–1855. Subway: 59th St.

9 *e-8*
ROTHMAN'S
Rothman's is a reliable source of quality men's clothing, though the overall sportswear look is stuck in the '80s, with lots of too-slick Italianate stuff upstairs. Belts and ties (some of the ugliest prints in town) are particularly lost in a vanished moment. A more businesslike demeanor reigns downstairs on the suit racks, which feature Perry Ellis, Alexander Julian, and Ralph Lauren as well as deep discounts on Hickey Freeman and Norman Hilton. *200 Park Ave. S (at 17th St.), Flatiron, 212/777–7400. Closed Sun. Subway: 14th St./Union Square.*

9 *e-4*
SAINT LAURIE, LTD.
The specialty here is well-tailored business suits in fine fabrics, supplemented by sport coats, overcoats, and slacks. The huge selection is discounted 30%. Alterations are free, and custom tailoring is available by appointment. *350 Park Ave. (between 51st and 52nd Sts.), Midtown, 212/317–8700. Closed Sun. Subway: 51st St./Lexington–3rd Aves.*

9 *e-3*
SYMS
This mondo-store offers three floors of off-price (30%–50%) men's apparel from shoes and socks to hats and coats to swimsuits and tuxes. Designers include Blass, Cerruti, Cardin, Hechter, and After Six. The specialty? Shirts, and they leave the original labels on, an uncommon practice at the city's other discount centers. Avoid lunch hour here; it's madness. *400 Park Ave. (at 54th St.), Midtown, 212/317–8200. Subway: 51st St./Lexington–3rd Aves.*

10 *e-7*

42 Trinity Place (at Rector St.), Lower Manhattan, 212/797–1199. Subway: Rector St.

9 *d-8*
TODAY'S MAN
You'll have no trouble finding a suit here, even if the selection is sort of crummy. Today's Man is one of the superstores (along with Barnes & Noble and Bed, Bath, & Beyond) that led to the dazzling revival of a desolate stretch of 6th Avenue below 23rd Street, a turf

once ruled by bike messengers. It aims to appeal to Everyman, a guy who might have any job or any budget, but who in any case dislikes shopping enough to cleave to the promise that he can yank out his Visa once a year and stock up for the next 12 months. The stock includes the full upscale monty: easy, Italian threads alongside more traditional button-down styles as well as accessories, shoes, and underwear. *625 6th Ave. (at 18th St.), Chelsea, 212/924–0200. Subway: F to 14th St.*

9 *e-5*

529 5th Ave. (at 44th St.), Midtown, 212/557–3111. Subway: 42nd St./Grand Central.

RESALE, VINTAGE, SURPLUS

10 *e-6*

CHURCH STREET SURPLUS

New and used government-issue, civilian surplus, and vintage clothing fill this store and the overflowing bins on the street, making for a candy store of dusty bargains. *327 Church Street (between Canal and Lispenard Sts.), Lower Manhattan, 212/226–5280. Closed Sun. Subway: Canal St.*

10 *d-1*

REMINISCENCE

The best deals here are modern translations of vintage vests, linen and wool pleated trousers, and Hawaiian and silk collarless shirts. Bottom them off with antique and surplus shoes. *75 5th Ave. (between 13th and 14th Sts.), Greenwich Village, 212/243–2292. Subway: F to 14th St.*

11 *e-4*

UNIQUE CLOTHING WAREHOUSE

This is street-chic headquarters for war surplus, new and renewed; athletic wear; industrial uniforms; and colorfully dyed stuff, all fairly priced. *118A Greene St. (between Prince and Spring Sts.), SoHo, 212/431–8210. Subway: Spring St.*

9 *e-8*

WEISS & MAHONEY

Here's an authentic army-navy surplus shop from the pre–cheap chic era (est. 1924). It bills itself as "peaceful" and delivers good buys on fatigues, pea coats, jumpsuits, sweaters, and leather flight jackets. *142 5th Ave. (at 19th St.), Chelsea, 212/675–1915. Subway: F, N, R to 23rd St.*

unusual sizes

9 *d-4*

IMPERIAL WEAR

Imperial stocks a large selection of quality clothing and accessories for the big or tall man, including Burberry's, Adolfo, Halston, Izod LaCoste, Perry Ellis, Bill Blass, and London Fog. Alterations are free. *48 W. 48th St., 212/719–2590. Subway: E, F to 5th Ave.*

9 *d-3*

ROCHESTER BIG & TALL

Yes, the large man can obtain a styling look in the Big Apple without having to slunk into the tailoring nether-regions of the outer boroughs. This store, which stocks XL sizes from such formidable sources as Zegna, Canali, and Burberrys plus shoes from Bally, has branches in both Midtown and Wall Street, both territories where giants stride the earth. And giants need sharp clothes. *1301 6th Ave. (at 52nd St.), Midtown, 212/247–7300.*

10 *f-6*

67 Wall St. (at Pearl), 212/952-8500.

CLOTHING FOR MEN/SPECIALTY

formal wear

9 *e-4*

HARRISON FORMAL WEAR

Harrison can always be counted on for the latest styles, including After Six, Adolfo, Bill Blass, Yves Saint Laurent, and Lord West. The shop provides same-day service, along with free delivery and pickup. Sundays are by appointment only. *560 5th Ave. (at 46th St.), Midtown, 212/302–1742. Closed Sun. in summer. Subway: 42nd St./Grand Central.*

9 *e-3*

ZELLER TUXEDOS

The penguin suits range from traditional to trendy at this Upper East Side shop. Makers include Ungaro, Ferragamo, Valentino, Bally, and Canali, and the selection includes formal accessories. Alterations are free with a purchase. *201*

E. 56th St., 2nd floor, Midtown, 212/355–0707. Closed Sun. Subway: 59th St.

hats

11 *a-1*

CHAMPION SHOES AND HATS

This wide variety of headgear includes Borsalino, Stetson, and Van Dyke's own brand, plus cleaning and blocking. *94 Greenwich Ave. (W. 12th St.), West Village, 212/929–5696. Closed Sun.; also closed Sat. in summer. Subway: F, 1, 2, 3, 9 to 14th St.*

9 *e-5*

WORTH & WORTH LTD.

The complete hatter for men, Worth & Worth specializes in fedoras by Borsalino, Cavanagh, Stetson, and Christy's of London. Equally worthy are caps and walking hats in cashmere, shetland, viyella, and Harris tweed, as well as a variety of straw summer lids. There's even a catalog. *331 Madison Ave. (at 43rd St.), Midtown, 212/867–6058. Closed Sun. Subway: 42nd St./Grand Central.*

shirts

9 *e-2*

ADDISON ON MADISON

This small shop sells private-label, French-made cotton shirts and silk ties. *698 Madison Ave. (between 62nd and 63rd Sts.), Midtown, 212/308–2660. Closed Sun. Subway: 59th St.*

9 *e-3*

ASCOT CHANG

The only games at this prestigious address are the ready-to-wear and custom shirts from the renowned Hong Kong shirtmaker. The vast selection of glorious fabrics, along with 12 different collar styles, amounts to a guarantee that the shirt will, after multiple fittings, feel like you were born in it. Chang also sells made-to-measure suits, dressing gowns, PJs, and handcrafted umbrellas. *7 W. 57th St., Midtown, 212/759–3333. Closed Sun. Subway: E, F to 5th Ave.*

9 *e-2*

TURNBULL & ASSER

London's legendary haberdasher, T & A has supplied candy-stripe shirts to everyone from Dominick Dunne to those media divas who started *Spy Magazine. 745 5th Ave. (at 58th St., in Bergdorf Goodman Men), Midtown, 212/753–7300. Subway: N, R to 5th Ave.*

10 *f-7*

VICTORY, THE SHIRT EXPERTS

Victory sells its own 100% cotton shirts, comparable in quality to the clubwear uptown. Ready-to-wear shirts range from sizes 14/32 to 18½/36, but if nothing fits, they'll make to measure. Also on sales are silk ties, "braces," and other accessories. *125 Maiden Lane (between Water and Pearl Sts.), Lower Manhattan, 212/480–1366. Closed Sun.; also closed Sat. from Jan.–Sept. Subway: Wall St.*

shoes & boots

ATHLETE'S FOOT

See Sporting Goods & Clothing–Running, *below.*

9 *e-5*

BALLY OF SWITZERLAND

This is the place to come for high-quality, classic yet stylish shoes, all imported from Switzerland. *628 Madison Ave. (at 59th St.), Midtown, 212/751–9082. Subway: 59th St.; 347 Madison Ave. (at 44th St.), Midtown, 212/986–0872. Subway: 42nd St./Grand Central.*

9 *e-3*

BOTTICELLI

This store's cachet has fallen somewhat since the return to tailoring and a trimmer cut in the mid-'90s, American men's newfound preference for English rather than Italian styles, and the general disdain for flash. But the shoes are as sleek and soft as ever. *666 5th Ave. (at 53rd St.), Midtown, 212/582–2984. Subway: E, F to 5th Ave.*

9 *e-4*

CHURCH'S ENGLISH SHOES

Fast by Brooks Brothers, Paul Stuart, and J. Press, this is New York's best alternative to Weston and Cole-Haan for elegant, conservative footwear. Regular Joes can exploit the great sales. *428 Madison Ave. (at 49th St.), Midtown, 212/755–4313. Subway: 51st St./Lexington–3rd Aves.*

9 *e-3*

GUCCI

It's not just for shoes anymore, though you can still get the classic horsebit loafer in brown or black, a true barefoot-preppie standard. Lately, with the appointment of designer Tom Ford to run the label, Gucci has mined its '70s heyday, pillaging styles that run a gamut from slick to slicker. If you're beginning to crave gloss, and a tone of overt sexiness, you may want to chuck your Weejuns and head for this joint. *689 5th Ave. (at 54th St.), Midtown, 212/826–2600. Subway: E, F to 5th Ave.*

7 *b-8*

HARRY'S SHOES

At some point in the life of every New Yorker comes a pilgrimage to Harry's Shoes, shoe mecca of the Upper West Side. The shopping is full-contact, but the salepeople know their way around every style, from suede Hush Puppy loafers to rugged Timberland boots. They even print a catalog. *2299 Broadway (at 83rd St.), Upper West Side, 212/874–2035. Subway: 79th St.*

9 *e-1*

J. M. WESTON

Exclusive bootmakers in Paris since 1865, this establishment makes the best penny loafer known to man or beast. Weston is renowned for styling and fit; 80% of each shoe is made by hand, and you can choose from among 60 styles in 24 sizes and five widths. *812 Madison (at 68th St.), Upper East Side, 212/535–2100. Subway: 68th St./Hunter College.*

9 *e-3*

J. P. TOD'S

Audrey Hepburn wore 'em; so did Steve McQueen. And they are way expensive, averaging around $400 for the coveted butter-soft driving loafer. Lately, this purveyor of premium casual footwear has captivated the Hamptons set, displacing Gucci and Belgian Shoes as the maker of choice for Ladies Who Lunch in jeans and khakis. Airs aside, however, these are absolutely fabulous shoes. *41 E. 57th St., Midtown, 212/644–5945. Closed Sun. Subway: N, R to 5th Ave.*

9 *e-8*

KENNETH COLE

Cole provides a steady supply of fresh, never over-the-top, shoe styles to younger customers. Accoutrements include ties, leather goods, jackets, and socks. Those who care will notice that Cole also runs one of footwear's more clever ad campaigns, and that the stores sponsor seasonal (predatory) sales. *95 5th Ave. (at 17th St.), Chelsea, 212/675–2550. Subway: F to 14th St., N, R to 23rd St.*

11 *e-4*

597 Broadway (between Houston and Prince Sts.), SoHo, 212/965–0283. Subway: Broadway–Lafayette St.

7 *b-8*

353 Columbus Ave. (between 76th and 77th Sts.), Upper West Side, 212/873–2061. Subway: 79th St.

9 *d-4*

MCCREEDY & SCHREIBER

This longtime emporium has one of New York's best selections of boots (including Lucchese) and shoes for both casual and dress wear. Pick up Frye, Timberland, Cole-Haan, Sperry, Rockport, Sebago, Alden, Allen Edmonds, Dan Post, Justin, Tony Lama, and Larry Mehan at competitive prices. *37 W. 46th St., Midtown, 212/719–1552. Subway: B, D, F, Q to 42nd St.*

9 *e-2*

213 E. 59th St., Midtown, 212/759–9241. Subway: 59th St.

9 *b-1*

TO BOOT

The famed boot selection, including handmade exotic leathers, has been joined by men's casual, leisure, business, and formal footwear. The entire Columbus Avenue stock is To Boot's own design and manufacture; the Bergdorf store also carries an exclusive line by Italy's Cesare Paciotti. *256 Columbus Ave. (at 72nd St.), 212/724–8249. Subway: 72nd St.*

9 *d-3*

745 5th Ave. (at 58th St., in Bergdorf Goodman Men), Midtown, 212/339–3335. Subway: N, R to 5th Ave.

ties

Allen Street between Delancey and Houston streets on the Lower East Side has several necktie stores featuring nice, inexpensive ties.

7 *e-6*

SEIGO

Atop the haughty shopper's miracle row that is Madison Avenue resides this small, exquisite shop, literally stuffed with neckwear style. The only place with a more intriguing selection is Paul Stuart. The hook at Seigo is the marriage of East and West: the four-in-hands and bows are all classically English, the patterns borrow something from Italy, France, and the U.S., but the printing process is the same one the Japanese use to create kimonos. The results, which begin around $50, are lovely. As if that weren't enough, the owners have divided the store in half, with one side devoted to more fragile, textured fabrics, the other to smoother, sturdier prints. *1248 Madison Ave. (at 90th St.), Upper East Side, 212/987–0191. Closed Sun. Subway: 4, 5, 6 to 86th St.*

9 *e-7*

TIECRAFTERS

A sort of tie hospital, Tiecrafters will remove even the most difficult stains. For fussy stylists, they'll also narrow, widen, and shorten ties. *116 E. 27th St., 6th floor, Murray Hill, 212/867–7676. Closed weekends. Subway: 6 to 28th St.*

9 *e-3*

TIE RACK

There's something for just about every guy in these bevies of reasonably priced ties. *599 Lexington Ave. (between 52nd and 53rd Sts.), Midtown, 212/355–0656. Subway: 51st St./Lexington–3rd Aves.*

9 *e-5*

200 Park Ave. (at 45th St., in MetLife building), 212/697–0337. subway: 42nd St./Grand Central.

10 *d-6*

World Trade Center, concourse level, Lower Manhattan, 212/432–7074. Subway: World Trade Center.

DISCOUNT

These stores make it easy to go broke saving money. There's a heavy concentration of thrift shops from 75th Street between 2nd and 3rd avenues to 89th St. and 3rd Avenue; all offer secondhand and some new merchandise of varying quality. Patience can yield bargains, and the proceeds do go to charity. *Caveat emptor:* not all shops with "thrift" in their names are charity stores.

10 *e-6*

CENTURY 21

These three chaotic floors of discounted merchandise include name-brand clothing, electronics, toys, and more. *See also* Discount & Off-Price *in* Clothing for Women *and* Clothing for Men, *above. 22 Cortlandt St. (between Broadway and Church St.), Lower Manhattan, 212/227–9092. Closed Sun. Subway: Cortlandt St./World Trade Center.*

10 *g-4*

DEMBITZER BROS.

Small and large appliances both sell for small prices here, but it's hectic, so you'd best know what you want. *5 Essex St. (at Canal St.), Lower East Side, 212/254–1310. Closed Sat. Subway: Delancey St.*

11 *e-3*

NATIONAL WHOLESALE LIQUIDATORS

You name it, it's here at a super-discounted price. These two floors are stuffed with home furnishings, electronics, clothing, cleaning supplies, storage bins and other plastic items, art supplies, and more. It's a bit of a mishmash, but savvy downtowners swear by it. *632 Broadway (between Houston and Bleecker Sts.), Greenwich Village, 212/979–2400. Subway: Bleecker St.; Broadway–Lafayette St.*

10 *e-6*

ODD JOB TRADING CORP.

Come here for closeouts of brand-name consumer goods. The best buys are in sports gear and small appliances. *10 Cortlandt St. (at Broadway), Lower Manhattan, 212/571–0959. Subway: Cortlandt St./World Trade Center.*

9 *d-6*

390 5th Ave. (at 36th St.), Garment District, 212/239–3336. Subway: 34th St./Herald Square.

9 *d-6*

149 W. 32nd St., Garment District, 212/564–7370. Subway: 34th St./Herald Square; other locations. Closed Sat.

ELECTRONICS

`10` *g-4*

ABC TRADING COMPANY

They stock most major brands and will order what they don't have. Discounts are deep. *31 Canal St. (near Essex St.), Lower East Side, 212/228–5080. Closed Sat. Subway: E. Broadway.*

`9` *e-5*

FORTY-SECOND STREET PHOTO

Despite the name, Forty-Second Street Photo has more electronic equipment then photography equipment: VCRs, computers, fax machines, phones, CD and cassette players, and so forth, all at discount prices. *109 E. 42nd St., Midtown, 212/490–1994. Subway: 42nd St./Grand Central; 11 W. 42nd St., Midtown, 212/730–8325. Subway: B, D, F, Q to 42nd St.*

`9` *d-6*

378 5th Ave. (at 35th St.), Garment District, 212/594–6565. Subway: 34th St./Herald Square.

`10` *g-4*

GOODMAN ELECTRONICS

Goodman offers substantial discounts on Sony, Panasonic, KLH, Fisher, and Garrard products. Call with the model number for details. *37 Essex St. (near Grand St.), Lower East Side, 212/673–3220. Closed Sat. Subway: Grand St.*

`9` *d-4*

HARVEY

Harvey has sold and installed fine audio and video systems since 1927. Current features include home-theater components from Adcom, Infinity, McIntosh, and other high-end brands. *2 W. 45th St., Midtown, 212/575–5000. Subway: B, D, F, Q to 42nd St.; ABC Carpet & Home, 888 Broadway (at 19th St.), Flatiron, 212/473–3000. Subway: 14th St./Union Square; N, R to 23rd St.*

`10` *e-6*

J&R MUSIC & COMPUTER WORLD

J & R may well have the most complete selection of electronic products anywhere, which, happily, assures that all budgets can be accommodated. The sales staff is knowledgeable, prices are competitive, and crowds are here in force. Be patient; it's worth it in the end.

23 Park Row (between Ann and Beekman Sts.), Lower Manhattan, 212/238–9000 or 800/221–8180. Subway: Brooklyn Bridge/City Hall.

`9` *d-8*

RADIOSHACK

RadioShack carries mainly its own brand of consumer electronics, including stereos, telephones, and pagers, and has a handy stash of electrical converters for travel abroad. Fans swear by the service and maintenance follow-up, not to mention the prices. It's worth a look if you're not a label snob. *641A 6th Ave. (at 20th St.), Chelsea, 212/604–0695. Subway: F to 23rd St.*

`9` *e-5*

287 Madison Ave. (at 41st St.), Midtown, 212/682–9309. Subway: 42nd St./Grand Central.

`7` *f-7*

1477 3rd Ave. (at 84th St.), Upper East Side, 212/327–0979. Subway: 4, 5, 6 to 86th St.

`7` *b-4*

2812 Broadway (at 108th St.), Upper West Side, 212/662–7332. Subway: 110th St./Cathedral Pkwy.

`9` *e-3*

SONY PLAZA

Sony has cleverly designed a consumer-friendly atrium in the heart of Midtown and filled it with the latest Sony products. The expert yet no-pressure sales approach means that many people just hang out here for hours. *550 Madison Ave. (between 55th and 56th Sts.), Midtown, 212/833–8830. Subway: 59th St.*

`9` *e-8*

SOUND BY SINGER

Singer's sales and service get consistently high reviews from serious audiophiles, but the great sales staff will also work with tight budgets. *18 E. 16th St., Flatiron, 212/924–8600. Subway: 14th St./Union Square.*

`10` *e-4*

UNCLE UNCLE ELECTRONICS

Head to Canal for these low prices on stereo equipment, TVs, and VCRs. You can try the stuff out in the sound room. *343 Canal St. (near Church St.), Lower Manhattan, 212/226–4010. Subway: A, C, E to Canal St.*

10 *g-3*

VICMARR AUDIO

Vicmarr is one of very few electronics stores that will give prices over the phone, indicating its uncommonly low-pressure sales approach. The store's well-organized shelves are packed with well-priced merchandise from brands like JVC, Alpine, and Panasonic. *88 Delancey St. (at Orchard St.), Lower East Side, 212/505–0380. Subway: Delancey St.*

FABRIC

Orchard Street south of Houston Street is New York's center for discounted fabric. Be prepared to pick through roll after roll; you'll find major manufacturers' overstock at about 40% off the retail price.

9 *c-5*

ART MAX FABRICS

The fashion fabrics include full lines of linens, English wool suitings, domestic and imported wools, cotton prints and solids, cashmere coatings, and silks. Bridal fabrics are a particular specialty. *250 W. 40th St., Garment District, 212/398–0755. Closed Sun. Subway: 42nd St./Times Square.*

9 *c-5*

B & J FABRICS

Family-owned since 1940, B & J is three floors of fashion fabrics, many imported. *263 W. 40th St., Garment District, 212/354–8150. Closed Sun. Subway: 42nd St./Times Square.*

9 *f-2*

BARANZELLI SILK SURPLUS

Designer silk, velvet, and brocades for draperies, upholstery, and slipcovers join Scalamandre closeouts and seconds in a shop popular with the trade as well as retail customers. *1127 2nd Ave. (between 59th and 60th Sts.), Midtown, 212/753–6511. Subway: 59th St.*

10 *g-3*

BECKENSTEIN HOME FABRICS

It's got a lot of competition, but this store has the widest variety of well-priced fabrics on the Lower East Side. *130 Orchard St. (near Delancey St.), Lower East Side, 212/475–4887. Closed Sat. Subway: Delancey St.*

10 *g-3*

BECKENSTEIN MEN'S FABRICS

Some say this is the finest men's-fabric store in the United States. The nation's custom tailors, top men's-clothing manufacturers, and a who's-who list of clients shop here for the finest quality in every type of men's fashion fabric. *121 Orchard St. (near Delancey St.), Lower East Side, 212/475–6666. Closed Sat. Subway: Delancey St.*

12 *f-5*

FABRIC ALTERNATIVE

Pick up high-quality fabrics at a discount—home decor, children's fabrics, imported laces, Schumacher, Waverly, and Riverdale. They'll do the sewing, too. *78 7th Ave., Park Slope, Brooklyn, 718/857–5482. Subway: D, Q, F to 7th Ave.*

11 *h-5*

FABRIC WORLD

Fabric World offers a lovely line of fabrics at discount prices, with a bonus if you're renovating: they'll convert your chosen fabric into wallpaper. *283 Grand St. (near Eldridge St.), Lower East Side, 212/925–0412. Closed Sat. Subway: Grand St.*

11 *e-6*

ISLAND FABRIC WAREHOUSE

Three floors of every conceivable type of fabric include designer, upholstery, and some imports and a good selection of notions, all at fantastic savings. Custom service is available. *406 Broadway (near Canal St.), Lower Manhattan, 212/431–9510. Subway: N, R to Canal St.*

7 *b-8*

LAURA ASHLEY

The finest purveyor of the English country-house look, good old Laura Ashley creates ever-delicate floral and geometric prints on natural cotton fabrics, with wallpapers and furnishings to match. *398 Columbus Ave. (at 79th St.), Upper West Side, 212/496–5110. Subway: 79th St.*

9 *e-1*

PIERRE DEUX

Pierre Deux is the exclusive American outlet for hand-screened Souleiado print fabric from Provence; the store also has reproduction furniture and beautiful accessories. They custom-design window and bed treatments. *870 Madison Ave. (at*

71st St.), Upper East Side, 212/570–9343.
Subway: 68th St./Hunter College.

FLOWERS & PLANTS

For the freshest flowers, go to the wholesale flower market on and around 28th Street between 6th and 7th avenues, where New York's florists buy their flowers. Wholesalers will often sell at retail if you're willing to pay cash.

9 *d-8*

BLOOM FLOWERS HOME GARDEN

Bloom Flowers does everything from weddings to private and corporate parties to individual arrangements and fresh cut flowers. There's also a small selection of home furnishings. *16 W. 21st St., Chelsea, 212/620–5666. Closed Sun. Subway: F to 23rd St.*

9 *e-7*

PRESTON BAILEY FLORAL & EVENT DESIGN

Preston Bailey has 15 years experience designing floral arrangements for big events. Corporate clients include Tiffany & Co., Christie's, and Disney; weddings and large parties are a specialty. *88 Lexington Ave. (near 26th St.), Murray Hill, 212/683–0035. Open by appt. only. Subway: 6 to 28th St.*

9 *e-2*

RENNY

This well-known floral designer doesn't kid around; clients include some serious society, and prices can reflect that. The handiwork is extraordinary. *505 Park Ave. (between 59th and 6oth Sts.), Midtown, 212/288–7000. Subway: 59th St.*

7 *e-8*

Carlyle Hotel, 35 E. 76th St., Upper East Side, 212/988–5588. Subway: 77th St. Closed weekends.

10 *b-1*

ROBERT ISABELL

Isabel is famous for decorating over-the-top society parties on big budgets. *410 W. 13th St. (near Washington St.), West Village, 212/645–7767. Subway: A, C, E to 14th St.*

9 *e-1*

RONALDO MAIA LTD.

These expensive and inventive floral creations come in natural cachepots or baskets and make elegant, simple centerpieces. The potpourri and candles are wonderful. *27 E. 67th St., Upper East Side, 212/288–1049. Subway: 68th St./Hunter College.*

11 *d-4*

SPRING ST. GARDEN

Order personalized floral arrangements, wreaths, garlands, or whatever strikes you. The small retail area includes plants, fresh cut flowers, and gardening *objets. 1861–62 Spring St. (near Thompson St.), SoHo, 212/966–2015. Closed Sun.–Mon.; closed Aug. Subway: C, E to Spring St.*

7 *b-8*

SURROUNDINGS

These West Side floral designers have a satisfied following. *224 W. 79th St., Upper West Side, 212/580–8982. Subway: 79th St.*

10 *c-1*

VSF

A-list clients hire this designer for English-country–style weddings, special events, holiday decorations, or just the perfect flower arrangement. *204 W. 10th St. (near Bleecker St.), 212/206–7236. Closed Sun.; closed Sat. in summer. Subway: Christopher St./Sheridan Square.*

9 *f-3*

ZEZÉ

Known for its dramatic arrangements, ZeZé specializes in exotic orchids. *398 E. 52nd St., Midtown, 212/753–7767. Closed weekends except holiday weekends. Subway: 51st St./Lexington–3rd Aves.*

FOOD

baked goods

9 *b-4*

AMY'S BREAD

Choose from sourdough, semolina, rosemary, black olive, organic whole wheat, and rye breads, as well as specialty breads, sandwiches, and sweets. All breads are made with a natural starter, quality ingredients, and no preservatives; the most popular are sourdough and semolina with golden raisins and fennel. *672 9th Ave. (at 46th St.), Hell's Kitchen, 212/977–2670. Subway: 42nd St./Port Authority*

10 *b-1*

75 9th Ave. (at 15th St.), Chelsea, 212/462–4338. Subway: A, C, E to 14th St.

11 *e-5*

BALTHAZAR BAKERY

The hottest of hot restaurants also has a storefront patisserie with an amazing array of French-style breads. Try chocolate, rye, multigrain, olive, cranberry-raisin-pecan, potato-onion, and the signature *"pain de seigle"* of rye and wheat. You can also pick up tarts, sandwiches, salads, soups, and delicious coffee by the cup. The decor is so Parisian, it's almost Disneyesque—almost. *80 Spring St. (at Broadway), 212/965–1785. Subway: 6 to Spring St.*

10 *f-1*

BLACK FOREST

These wonderful European confections include a rum truffle and an excellent Black Forest cake. *177 1st Ave. (at 11th St.), East Village, 212/254–8181. Subway: 1st Ave.; Astor Pl.*

7 *e-8*

BONTE PATISSERIE

These popular French pastries never fail to please. Check out the seasonal specialties. *1316 3rd Ave. (at 75th St.), Upper East Side, 212/535–2360. Subway: 77th St.*

9 *e-8*

THE CITY BAKERY

The City Bakery adds stylish and beautiful tarts to its exceptional selection of cookies, brownies, desserts, and breads. *22 E. 17th St., Flatiron, 212/366–1414. Subway: 14th St./Union Square.*

7 *f-8*

CREATIVE CAKES

Here's the deal: you name a person, pet, building, car, or any other shape or design you fancy, and they create a "portrait-likeness" three-dimensional cake—buttercream outside, chocolate fudge inside. It's expensive, but delicious and most impressive. Call two weeks in advance. *400 E. 74th St., Upper East Side, 212/794–9811. Subway: 77th St.*

9 *b-5*

CUPCAKE CAFÉ

This funky store offers very pretty cupcakes in addition to cakes, pies, doughnuts, muffins and more. All cakes are made to order. *522 9th Ave. (at 39th St.), Hell's Kitchen, 212/465–1530. Subway: 42nd St./Port Authority.*

11 *e-4*

DEAN & DELUCA

The city's finest gourmet shop has a magnificent selection of breads, desserts and pastries. The gingerbread makes a delicious energizer during a SoHo shopping trip. *560 Broadway (at Prince St.), SoHo, 212/431–1691 or 800/221–7714. Subway: Prince St.*

7 *e-8*

E.A.T.

The home of Eli's famous sourdough *ficelles* and raisin-nut bread also supplies bread to most of New York's restaurants. The terrific holiday gift baskets can be shipped anywhere. *1064 Madison Ave. (at 80th St.), Upper East Side, 212/772–0022. Subway: 77th St.*

9 *e-2*

ECCE PANIS

The aroma makes it difficult to pass this place by; and why should you? Ecce Panis serves glorious bread—light and dark sourdough, double-walnut, plain or rosemary neo-Tuscan, chocolate—from the same ovens that supply the Sign of the Dove. Also on offer are various foccaccia, biscotti, fresh pastas, and specialty items. *1120 3rd Ave. (at 65th St.), Upper East Side, 212/535–2099. Subway: 68th St./Hunter College.*

9 *b-5*

LITTLE PIE COMPANY

This gourmet bakery specializes in delicious all-American pies—just like Grandma used to make, only better. The ever-popular Sour Cream Apple Walnut Pie is legendary. *424 W. 43rd St., Hell's Kitchen, 212/736–4780. Subway: 42nd St./Port Authority.*

11 *b-1*

MOISHE'S HOMEMADE KOSHER BAKERY

Moishe's is one of New York's oldest and finest kosher Jewish bakeries, serving very special corn bread, egg challah, homemade bagels (some call them the only authentic bagels in the city), rugelach, and hamentaschen. *115 2nd Ave. (between 6th and 7th Sts.), East Village, 212/505–8555. Subway: 2nd Ave.*

11 *h-3*

181 E. Houston St. (near Orchard St.), Lower East Side, 212/472–9624

7 *f-8*

ORWASHER'S

Certified kosher, Orwasher offers 35 varieties of handmade breads and rolls, baked on the premises in hearth ovens using no preservatives or additives. Specialties include Hungarian potato bread and Vienna twists; inventions include raisin pumpernickel and marble bread. Pick up cheeses, coffees, teas, and condiments while you're here. *308 E. 78th St., Upper East Side, 212/288–6569. Subway: 77th St.*

10 *b-1*

PATISSERIE LANCIANI

These beautiful baked goods include a great sacher torte, over which you can linger in the adjoining café. *414 W. 14th St., West Village, 212/989–1213. Subway: A, C, E to 14th St.*

9 *c-5*

POSEIDON CONFECTIONERY CO.

Serving the best in Greek pastries, Poseidon also offers spinach-and-cheese pies and stuffed vine leaves. *629 9th Ave. (at 44th St.), Hell's Kitchen, 212/757–6173. Subway: 42nd St./Port Authority.*

9 *b-1*

SOUTINE

A full-service neighborhood bakery, Soutine makes American and French-style bread, croissants, and brioche. Birthday cakes and holiday goodies are specialties, and the store will ship them anywhere. *104 W. 70th St., Upper West Side, 212/496–1450. Subway: 72nd St.*

9 *c-8*

TAYLOR'S

Taylor's accompanies its sandwiches and salads with old-fashioned comfort food—huge fudge brownies, oversize muffins, and homey pies. *228 W. 18th St., Chelsea, 212/366–9081. Subway: A, C, E to 14th St.*

10 *c-1*

523 Hudson St. (near W. 10th St.), West Village, 212/645–8200. Subway: Christopher St./Sheridan Square.

10 *f-1*

175 2nd Ave. (near 11th St.), East Village, 212/674–9501. Subway: Astor Pl.; 3rd Ave.

10 *f-1*

VENIERO'S PASTICCERIA

In business since 1894, Veniero's makes Italian sweets as tasty as they are beautiful, including cannoli, fogliatelle, gelato, and marzipan. The café serves old-fashioned espresso and cappuccino. *342 E. 11th St., East Village, 212/674–7264. Subway: 1st Ave.*

11 *d-4*

VESUVIO

White, whole-wheat, and seeded Italian breads are baked in coal-fired ovens in the basement, without sugar, fat, or preservatives. Just follow your nose. *160 Prince St. (near W. Broadway), 212/925–8248. Subway: Prince St.*

7 *e-7*

WILLIAM GREENBERG, JR., BAKERY

Greenberg is said to make the best brownies in the city, and whips up spectacular custom cakes. *1100 Madison Ave. (at 82nd St.), Upper East Side, 212/744–0304. Subway: 4, 5, 6 to 86th St.*

7 *b-8*

2187 Broadway (at 77th St.), Upper West Side, 212/580–7300. Subway: 79th St.

9 *e-6*

518 3rd Ave. (near 34th St.), Murray Hill, 212/686–3344. Subway: 33rd St.

11 *e-1*

60 E. 8th St. (near Broadway), East Village, 212/995–9184. Subway: 8th St.

11 *b-2*

ZITO & SONS

Zito's best seller is a delicious, crusty whole-wheat loaf, followed closely by a Sicilian loaf. Frank Sinatra used to have this stuff delivered fresh to the Waldorf. *259 Bleecker St. (near 7th Ave.), West Village, 212/929–6139. Subway: W. 4th St./Washington Square.*

candy

9 *e-2*

AU CHOCOLAT

Boxed, loose, solid, filled, domestic, European—it's all here, from such makers as Godiva, Perugina, Laderach, Lindt, Corne, Dalloyen, and Bloomie's own. Custom gift baskets are available. *Bloomingdale's, 1000 3rd Ave. (at 59th St.), Midtown, 212/705–2953. Subway: 59th St.*

10 *f-1*

BLACKHOUND

The elegant packages of chocolates and truffles in Shaker boxes make perfect gifts. Cookies, cakes, and pies are also available. *149 1st Ave. (at 9th St.), East Village, 212/979–9505 or 800/344–4417. Subway: Astor Pl.*

7 *f-7*

ELK CANDY

Elk's specialty is delicious homemade marzipan, coated with chocolate or otherwise flavored. *240 E. 86th St., Upper East Side, 212/650–1177. Subway: 4, 5, 6 to 86th St.*

10 *e-6*

GODIVA

Eighty years old and justly famous, these Belgians proffer elaborately boxed sweets for spontaneous consumption or carefully meditated gifts. *33 Maiden Lane (near Nassau St.), Lower Manhattan, 212/809–8990. Subway: Broadway–Nassau St.*

9 *e-3*

701 5th Ave. (near 54th St.), Midtown, 212/593–2848. Subway: E, F to 5th Ave.

9 *e-1*

793 Madison Ave. (near 67th St.), Upper East Side, 212/249–9444. Subway: 68th St./Hunter College.

9 *c-1*

245 Columbus Ave. (near 71st St.), Upper West Side, 212/787–5804. Subway: 72nd St.; other locations.

9 *e-1*

LA MAISON DU CHOCOLAT

Parisian chocolatier Robert Linxe whips up expensive, exquisitely flavored chocolate morsels filled with cinnamon, honey, mint, lemon, marzipan, kirsch, and more. Snap them up by the piece or the pound. *25 E. 73rd St., Upper East Side, 212/744–7117. Subway: 77th St.*

11 *b-2*

LI-LAC CHOCOLATES

These homemade chocolates include French mint patties, hazelnut truffles, almond bark, and highly edible, hand-molded milk, dark, and white Empire State Buildings and Statues of Liberty. The goods have been made on the premises since 1923. *120 Christopher St. (at Bleecker St.), West Village, 212/242–7374. Subway: Christopher St./Sheridan Square.*

9 *d-6*

MACY'S MARKETPLACE

This place is a dream—or a nightmare, depending on how you look at it. You'll find every boxed chocolate on the market, plus loose samples from Michel Guerard, Godiva, Neuhaus, and Perugina. It all adds up to over 2,000 square feet of candy. *Macy's, 155 W. 34th St. (Herald Square), The Cellar (lower level), Garment District, 212/695–4400. Subway: 34th St./Herald Square.*

9 *d-3*

MANON, LE CHOCOLATIER

Shopping on Fifth tiring you out? Duck into Bergdorf and choose from over 30 varieties of high-quality chocolate to nibble on the spot or ship to a friend. *Bergdorf Goodman, 754 5th Ave. (at 57th St.), 7th floor, Midtown, 212/753–7300. Closed Sun. Subway: E, F, N, R to 5th Ave.*

7 *b-3*

MONDEL CHOCOLATES

This family business has produced an amazing array of naturally flavored chocolates with little fat for over 45 years—mint, orange, coffee, amaretto, and more. Beautiful boxes and baskets make presentation a snap. *2913 Broadway (at 114th St.), Morningside Heights, 212/864–2111. Subway: 116th St./Columbia University.*

9 *d-3*

NEUCHATEL CHOCOLATES

Chocolatier to the stars, in business for five generations, Neuchatel has over 60 different Swiss-European chocolates, truffles, and treats, with a specialty in champagne truffles. Other truffle options include Grand Marnier, Espresso, and white chocolate. *Plaza Hotel, 5th Ave. and 59th St., Midtown, 212/751–7742. Subway: N, R to 5th Ave.*

9 *e-3*

PERUGINA

Pick up Italian chocolate *baci* and lovely gift-packaged candies at the company's own store. *520 Madison Ave. (at 53rd St.), Midtown, 212/688–2490. Subway: 51st St./Lexington–3rd Aves.*

9 *e-3*

RICHART DESIGN ET CHOCOLAT

Many different collections of boxed chocolates with art as theme, in a store that resembles a gallery. Signature Petits Richart Collection of miniature chocolates that resemble jewelry, are embellished with modern abstract designs. The Children's Design collection features winning designs from an art contest. All made in France, flown in weekly, made with the finest cocoa available. *7 E. 55th St., Midtown, 212/371–9369. Closed Sun. Subway: E, F to 5th Ave.*

9 *e-2, d-4*

TEUSCHER CHOCOLATES OF SWITZERLAND

The ultimate Swiss-chocolate treats are flown in weekly from Switzerland. Try the champagne truffles—happily, you can buy just one. *25 E. 61st St., Upper East Side, 212/751–8482. Subway: 59th St.; 620 5th Ave. (at 50th St.), Midtown, 212/246–4416. Subway: E, F to 5th Ave.*

cheese

7 *f-8*

AGATA & VALENTINA

This Italian gourmet shop has an outstanding international selection of cheeses. *1505 1st Ave. (at 79th St.), Upper East Side, 212/452–0690. Subway: 77th St.*

10 *d-1*

BALDUCCI'S

Balducci's is especially well known for Italian cheeses, but the cheese lover's selection is unbeatable all around. Pop in for a free sample. *424 6th Ave. (at 9th St.), Greenwich Village, 212/673–2600 or 800/BALDUCCI. Subway: F to 14th St.*

10 *g-3*

BEN'S CHEESE SHOP

Ben is renowned for his homemade farmer cheese, baked with vegetables, scallions, raisins, blueberries, strawberries, or pineapple. The homemade cream cheese is enhanced by chives, caviar, lox, or herbs and garlic. *181 E. Houston St. (near Orchard St.), Lower East Side, 212/254–8290. Closed Sat. Subway: 2nd Ave.*

9 *b-7*

CHEESE UNLIMITED

The name's no joke: you'll find 400 varieties of cheese from the world over. *240 9th Ave. (at 24th St.), Chelsea, 212/691–1512. Subway: C, E to 23rd St.*

11 *e-4*

DEAN & DELUCA

Cheese from all over the world are (like everything else) beautifully displayed here, and the knowledgeable staff will help you explore unfamiliar varieties. *560 Broadway (at Prince St.), SoHo, 212/431–1691 or 800/221–7714. Subway: Prince St.*

11 *f-5*

DI PALO'S DAIRY STORE

In the heart of Little Italy, Di Palo's offers fresh-ground Parmesan cheese, smoked mozzarella, and homemade ricotta-filled ravioli. *206 Grand St. (at Mott St.), 212/226–1033. Subway: Bowery.*

10 *f-1*

EAST VILLAGE CHEESE STORE

The prices in this neighborhood shop can't be beat. People file in for the weekly specials (with a half-pound minimum purchase). Domestic and imported cheese are joined by cold cuts, pâtés, coffees, crackers, jams, and condiments. *34 3rd Ave. (at 9th St.), East Village, 212/477–2601. Subway: Astor Pl.*

7 *b-8*

FAIRWAY

Fairway has one of the best cheese selections in the city, including an extensive array of goat cheese. *2127 Broadway (at 75th St.), Upper West Side, 212/595–1888. Subway: 79th St.*

6 *c-8*

133rd St. at West Side Hwy, Harlem, 212/234–3883. Subway: 137th St./City College.

9 *f-1*

GRACE'S MARKETPLACE

The upscale clientele has its pick of many fine domestic and imported cheese. The staff is happy to fix you up with samples. *1237 3rd Ave. (at 71st St.), Upper East Side, 212/737–0600. Subway: 68th St./Hunter College.*

11 *e-5*
GOURMET GARAGE
Both locations have wide and well-priced cheese selections. *453 Broome St. (at Mercer St.), SoHo, 212/941–5850. Subway: 6 to Spring St.*

9 *f-2*
301 E. 64th St., Upper East Side, 212/535–6271. Subway: 68th St./Hunter College.

9 *f-2*
IDEAL CHEESE
This top-rated cheese shop has over 300 varieties of domestic and imported cheese, and adds pâtés to the mix. *1205 2nd Ave. (at 63rd St.), Upper East Side, 212/688–7579. Subway: 59th St.*

9 *e-8*
LA MARCA CHEESE SHOP
Choose from a wide variety of cheeses cut to order, plus fresh-baked farmer cheese with various fruit fillings, and good croissants. *161 E. 22nd St., Gramercy, 212/673–7920. Subway: 6 to 23rd St.*

7 *f-6*
THE VINEGAR FACTORY
Owned by Eli Zabar, of E.A.T. fame, this gourmet grocery store carries a large array of domestic and imported cheeses. *431 E. 91st St., Upper East Side, 212/987–0885. Subway: 4, 5, 6 to 86th St.*

coffee & tea
Zabar's and Macy's Cellar have a variety of fresh and packaged teas and coffees. The two used to go head-to-head in their own little coffee price wars.

10 *e-1*
DANAL
In this charming café and gift shop are over 32 teas (in bulk or gift-boxed): aromatics from France (try the four red-berries), classics from India and China, decaf varieties, herbal infusions, and more. Highlights include Taganda, an exclusive from Zimbabwe; packaged teas by G. Ford; and Barrow's unblended Darjeeling. The only coffee in stock is the high-quality Sumantra blend served in the café, also available in decaf. *90 E. 10th St., East Village, 212/*

982–6930. Closed Mon. Subway: 8th St.; Astor Pl.

9 *d-3*
FELISSIMO
The Japanese-owned boutique has a top-floor tea room, where you can sip tea between shopping spells or choose from over 50 varieties of loose tea to take home. *10 W. 57th St., Midtown, 212/247–5656. Closed Sun. Subway: E, F to 5th Ave.*

11 *b-2*
MCNULTY'S TEA & COFFEE COMPANY
Established in 1895, this well-known Village shop sells rare teas and over 200 choice imported coffees, straight or custom-blended. Imported jams and jellies are tempting accompaniments. *109 Christopher St. (near Bleecker St.), 212/242–5351. Subway: Christopher St./Sheridan Square.*

11 *d-1*
OREN'S DAILY ROAST
The widespread Oren's serves and scoops a wide selection of coffee from around the world. *31 Waverly Pl. (near University Pl.), Greenwich Village, 212/420–5958. Subway: 8th St.*

9 *e-6*
434 3rd Ave. (near 31st St.), Murray Hill, 212/779–1241. Subway: 33rd St.

9 *e-3*
33 E. 58th St., Midtown, 212/838–3345. Subway: N, R to 5th Ave.

7 *e-8*
1144 Lexington Ave. (near 79th St.), Upper East Side, 212/472–6830. Subway: 77th St.; other locations.

11 *c-3*
PORTO RICO IMPORTING CO.
Porto Rico has sold high-grade teas and coffees since 1907, and now roasts 50 different coffees each week. Options include custom blends, Jamaican Blue Mountain, decaffeinated espresso, 120 kinds of tea, and every conceivable coffee and tea accessory at 30%–50% off the list price. *201 Bleecker St. (near 6th Ave.), Greenwich Village, 212/477–5421. Subway: W. 4th St./Washington Square*

11 *g-1*
40½ St. Mark's Pl., East Village, 212/533–1982. Subway: Astor Pl.

10 *d-1*

SCHAPIRA COFFEE COMPANY

Since 1903, this coffee source has roasted coffee and blended tea. Try the coveted and expensive Jamaica Blue Mountain, or pick up that sorely needed hand grinder or espresso pot. *117 W. 10th St., West Village, 212/675–3733. Subway: Christopher St./Sheridan Square.*

9 *c-1*

SENSUOUS BEAN

The friendly folks who run this pretty shop will blend from a wide variety of coffees. *66 W. 70th St., Upper West Side, 212/724–7725. Subway: 72nd St.*

11 *e-1*

STARBUCKS

Exported from Seattle, Starbucks' name has become synonymous with delicious coffee. Choose from the now-classic café mix of coffee-based drinks, baked goods, small lunch menu, and several fresh coffees by the pound. *13–25 Astor Pl., East Village, 212/982–3563. Subway: Astor Pl.*

9 *c-3*

1656 Broadway (at 52nd St.), Theater District, 212/397–7124. Subway: 1, 9 to 50th St.

7 *e-8*

1290 3rd Ave. (at 74th St.), Upper East Side, 212/772–6903. Subway: 77th St.

7 *b-4*

2681 Broadway (at 102nd St.), Upper West Side, 212/280–1811; other locations.

9 *e-3*

TAKASHIMAYA

Fifth Avenue has the flagship American store for this 160-year-old Japanese company. The Tea Box, downstairs, serves lunch and afternoon tea and sells about 40 varieties of loose tea by the ounce. You'll find excellent, domestically grown black and herbal teas as well as green teas from Japan and a beautiful variety of teacups, teapots, and accessories. *693 5th Ave. (between 54th and 55th Sts.), Midtown, 212/350–0100. Closed Sun. Subway: E, F to 5th Ave.*

9 *f-2*

TIMOTHY'S COFFEES OF THE WORLD

This local chain sells passable coffee, cappuccino, iced tea, lemonade, baked goods, and fresh coffee by the pound. The stores are quite cozy, even if the mulled cider (in fall) is a bit of a sham. *1033 3rd Ave. (at 61st St.), 212/755–6456. Subway: 59th St.*

9 *f-1*

1296 1st Ave. (near 69th St.), 212/794–7059. Subway: 68th St./Hunter College

7 *e-7*

1188 Lexington Ave. (at 81st St.), 212/879–0384. Subway: 77th St.; other locations.

ethnic foods

New York's food markets reflect the diversity of the city's population—unbeatable for variety, vitality, and, in most cases, authenticity.

12 *b-4*

ATLANTIC AVENUE (MIDDLE EASTERN)

Dodge the traffic for such Mediterranean delights as Turkish coffees, Lebanese pita breads, hummus, stuffed grape leaves, halvah, and baklava. *Atlantic Ave. from Henry to Court Sts., bordering Brooklyn Heights. Subway: Borough Hall.*

5 *h-5*

BELMONT (ITALIAN)

Belmont is still good for homemade pasta, pepperoni, bread, pastries, and espresso cafés. *Arthur Ave. and E. 187th St., Bronx. Subway: 182nd–183rd Sts.*

4 *f-5*

BENSONHURST (ITALIAN)

The shops teem with salamis, sausages, cheeses, prosciutto, and *pizza rustica.* *18th Ave. from 61st to 86th St., Brooklyn. Subway: 18th Ave.*

10 *f-4*

CHINATOWN

Chinatown's main artery is Mott Street, but it takes the whole neighborhood to produce such a wealth of Chinese restaurants, tea parlors, bakeries, and gift shops. *Bordered by Canal, Worth, and Mulberry Streets, the Bowery, and Chatham Square. Subway: 6, N, R, J, M, Z to Canal St.; Grand St.*

3 *f-3*

JACKSON HEIGHTS (INDIAN)

Shop for Indian spices, condiments, sweets, and saris and stop for a breathtaking meal at one of several unassuming Indian restaurants in this melting pot of a neighborhood. *74th St. from 37th to Roosevelt Aves. Subway: 7 to 74th St./Broadway.*

7 *e-3*

LA MARQUETA
East Harlem has its own, *muy* aromatic Latin American market, with over 250 stalls displaying exotic fruits and vegetables; grains, spices, hot sauces, smoked meats, and fish. *Park Ave. from 110th to 116th St. Subway: 6 to 116th St. Subway: 6 to 116th St.*

8 *d-4*

LITTLE ATHENS
Fact of the day: Astoria houses the largest Greek community outside Greece. Explore Greek tavernas, coffeehouses (*raffenion*), restaurants, and churches to the tunes of bouzouki music, baklava, and thick, rich Greek coffee. *Ditmars Blvd. from 31st to 38th Sts., Astoria, Queens. Subway: Ditmars Blvd./Astoria.*

11 *f-5*

LITTLE ITALY
Little Italy has more or less dwindled away as an Italian residential neighborhood, but its restaurants, pastry and espresso cafés, cheese and pasta shops live on. You won't find cannolis like these uptown. The Feast of San Gennaro packs the streets each fall (*see* Events *in* Chapter 2). *Mulberry St. between Houston and Canal Sts. Subway: 6, N, R, J, M, Z to Canal St.*

3 *c-7*

LOWER EAST SIDE
Okay, so it's becoming an extension of the East Village, but the Lower East Side retains a few vestiges of its Jewish era. Knishes, barreled schmaltz herring, pastrami, corned beef, pickles, and bagels share this neighborhood with the discount shops. *Roughly Houston–Canal Sts. from Bowery to East River. Subway: Delancey St.; Grand St.*

9 *c-5*

PADDY'S MARKET
Stores with sidewalk stands have replaced the pushcarts of yore, but the atmosphere's gone nowhere. Once predominantly Italian and Greek, Hell's Kitchen is now a United Nations of food. The 9th Avenue International Food Festival celebrates this rather cool and obscure fact in May (*see* Events *in* Chapter 2). *9th Ave. from 37th to 42nd St., Hell's Kitchen. Subway: 42nd St./Port Authority.*

10 *f-1*

UKRAINIAN AND POLISH AREA
Emerge from that dive bar and check out the East Village's *first* cultural legacy: wonderful pierogi, blintzes, kielbasa, headcheese, babka, and black bread. If you need an excuse, the Ukrainian Festival shows them all off every May (*see* Events *in* Chapter 2). *1st Ave. near 7th St. Subway: 2nd Ave.*

7 *f-7*

YORKVILLE
The German area has nearly disappeared, but a few restaurants still serve hearty, home-style foods and bock beer; a few *Konditorei* serve exquisite pastries; and a few shops sell specialty foods. There's still a small Hungarian enclave within this district. *Lexington Ave. to York Ave., mainly on East 86th St. Subway: 4, 5, 6 to 86th St.*

fish & seafood

10 *d-1*

BALDUCCI'S
Like most foods in this gourmet bastion, the seafood is high-quality and creatively selected. *424 6th Ave. (at 9th St.), West Village, 212/673–2600 or 800/BALDUCCI. Subway: W. 4th St./Washington Square.*

9 *c-5*

CENTRAL FISH COMPANY
True, it's not centrally located, but the selection of fresh fish is enormous. *527 9th Ave. (at 39th St.), Garment District, 212/279–2317. Subway: 42nd St./Port Authority.*

7 *f-8*

CITARELLA
Citarella's Upper West Side store was so successful that the owners opened up shop on the East Side, offering much more than just fish. The West Side shop has long been cherished for its amazing window displays of fresh seafood sculptures, and, of course, its superior selec-

tion of fresh fish. *2135 Broadway (at 75th St.), Upper West Side, 212/874–0383. Subway: 79th St.*

7 *f-8*

1313 3rd Ave. (at 75th St.), Upper East Side, 212/452–2780. Subway: 77th St.

7 *b-6*

JAKE'S FISH MARKET
Everyone seems to love this shop for its fresh fish and savvy staff. Prices are high, but the quality and variety are beyond dispute. *2425 Broadway (at 89th St.), Upper West Side, 212/580–5253. Subway: 1, 9 to 86th St.*

10 *d-1*

JEFFERSON MARKET
This neighborhood West Village shop has a good selection of fresh fish and is particularly appreciated for its friendly staff and personal service. *450 6th Ave. (near W. 10th St.), 212/533–3377. Subway: F to 14th St.*

9 *f-1*

LEONARD'S
The exquisite selection includes smoked or poached salmon; caviar; crabmeat; and boiled lobster. Delivery is free. *1241 3rd Ave. (between 71st and 72nd Sts.), Upper East Side, 212/744–2600. Subway: 68th St./Hunter College.*

9 *f-4*

PISACANE
Here in U.N. territory is a good general selection of high-quality fish. *940 1st Ave. (between 51st and 52nd Sts.), Midtown, 212/355–1850. Subway: 51st St./Lexington–3rd Aves.*

7 *e-8*

ROSEDALE
You can't beat Rosedale for quality and selection, but you can definitely beat its prices. This shop is known for delicious soft-shell crabs and superior salmon. *1129 Lexington Ave. (at 78th St.), Upper East Side, 212/288–5013. Closed Sun. Subway: 77th St.*

gourmet goodies

10 *d-1*

BALDUCCI'S
This New York institution is a foodie destination for natives and tourists alike. Inhale olives, vinegars, cheeses, paté, breads and pastries, chocolates, meats, desserts, and coffees. *424 6th Ave. (at 9th St.), West Village, 212/673–2600 or 800/BALDUCCI. Subway: W. 4th St./Washington Square.*

9 *f-3*

CALL CUISINE
Don't feel like cooking? Choose from about 15 different gourmet dinners, each prepared daily. The retail shop clues you in to the ingredients. *1032 1st Ave. (between 56th and 57th Sts.), Midtown, 212/752–7070. Subway: 59th St.*

9 *e-2*

CAVIARTERIA
Eight varietes of fresh caviar and six varieties preserved are the raison d'être, but you can also buy foie gras and Scotch and Nova Scotia salmon. *29 E. 60th St., Upper East Side, 212/759–7410. Subway: 59th St.*

11 *e-4*

DEAN & DELUCA
Who doesn't love this fabulous food emporium? A well-edited department in every food category means you'll find only the best of the best. The quality and beauty of the food are matched only by the quality and beauty of the clientele. To prepare your purchase in style, head to the back of the store, where great-looking kitchenware and cookbooks are temptingly displayed. *560 Broadway (at Prince St.), SoHo, 212/431–1691 or 800/221–7714. Subway: Prince St.*

7 *e-8*

E.A.T.
Ah, such lovely imports at such breathtaking prices! The handsome E.A.T. offers daily specials on its excellent assortment of pâtés, cheeses, coffees, and breads. The chocolate roulade cake is particularly magnificent. *1064 Madison Ave. (at 80th St.), Upper East Side, 212/772–0022. Subway: 77th St.*

11 *e-5*

GOURMET GARAGE
Known for such staples as fresh produce, pastas, breads, oils, and vinegars, Gourmet Garage sells a fine selection of quality goods at reasonable prices. *453 Broome St. (near Mercer St.), SoHo, 212/941–5850. Subway: 6 to Spring St.*

9 *f-2*

301 E. 64th St., Upper East Side, 212/535–6271. Subway: 68th St./Hunter College.

9 *f-1*

GRACE'S MARKETPLACE

This upscale store has a loyal neighborhood following and is always busy. Pick up fresh produce, pasta, oils and vinegars, fresh dairy products and cheeses, sliced meats, olives, baked goods, candy, desserts, fresh coffee, prepared foods, sandwiches and more. 1237 3rd Ave. (at 71st St.), Upper East Side, 212/737–0600. Subway: 68th St./Hunter College.

9 *e-3*

MAISON GLASS

Maison Glass is a good general store for smoked Scotch and Nova Scotia salmon, Smithfield ham, foie gras, cheese, and canned and packaged gourmet food. 111 E. 58th St., Midtown, 212/755–3316. Subway: 59th St.

10 *c-1*

MYERS OF KESWICK

It may be a stretch to call it "gourmet," but anglophiles will love this charming grocer. Knock yourself out with sausage rolls, kidney pies, pork pies, Scotch eggs, Stilton cheese, and Aberdeen kippers, along with packaged British cookies, candy, and other foods. Yes—they do have HobNobs! 634 Hudson St. (near Jane St.), West Village, 212/691–4194. Subway: A, C, E to 14th St.

7 *f-6*

THE VINEGAR FACTORY

Eli Zabar, the founder of both Zabar's and E.A.T., has another big, bustling shop in a converted turn-of-the-century vinegar factory. The great selection of everything from prepared foods to produce means you'll find whatever you need. The Factory sells Eli's famous bread for less than you'd pay at E.A.T. Bonus: there's free parking nearby. 431 E. 91st St., Upper East Side, 212/987–0885. Subway: 4, 5, 6 to 86th St.

9 *d-3*

PETROSSIAN BOUTIQUE

Indulge in the world's finest caviar, and try the delicious buckwheat blinis, sturgeon, pâté, and prepared foods. Prices are not low. 182 W. 58th St., Midtown, 212/245–2217. Subway: N, R to 57th St.

7 *e-8*

WILLIAM POLL

This Upper East Side caterer and store has undoubtedly made many a society dinner party. They're known for delicious hors d'oeuvres, thin sandwiches, prepared foods, spreads, and specialty items. 1051 Lexington Ave. (between 74th and 75th Sts.), Upper East Side, 212/288–0501. Closed Sun. Subway: 77th St.

7 *b-8*

ZABAR'S

From its humble beginnings as a deli and cheese shop, Zabar's has become the king of New York's gourmet stores. Its mind-boggling array of cheeses, meats, smoked fish, coffees, teas, and prepared entrées has won the city over. Kitchenwares are discounted 20–40% on the mezzanine. Go just for the sights, sounds, smells, and social life. 2245 Broadway (at 80th St.), Upper West Side, 212/787–2000. Subway: 79th St.

health foods

11 *c-7*

COMMODITIES NATURAL

With over 5,000 square feet to play with in its Tribeca store, this supermarket has 24 kinds of granola, 50 kinds of honey, 125 kinds of tea, 30 bins of grains, and, well, tons of fresh organic produce. 117 Hudson St. (at N. Moore St.), Tribeca, 212/334–8330. Subway: Franklin St.

10 *f-1*

165 1st Ave. (at 10th St.), East Village, 212/260–2600. Subway: 1st Ave.; Astor Pl.

10 *e-1*

HEALTHY PLEASURES

The feature presentations are an organic salad bar and a selection of healthy prepared foods. Other health- and environment-conscious products include vitamins, personal-care items, and cleaning products. 93 University Pl. (near 11th St.), Greenwich Village, 212/353–3663. Subway: 8th St.

10 *c-1*

INTEGRA YOGA NATURAL FOODS

Health-food enthusiasts flock here for the wide selection, including freshly made prepared foods. 229 W. 13th St., West Village, 212/243–2642. Subway: A, C, E to 14th St.

11 e-4

WHOLE FOODS

Whole Foods is a complete natural-food market, with specialties in produce, chicken, and fish. There's a large bulk department, many fresh herbs, and a selection of gourmet takeout meals. Natural cosmetics and vitamins wrap your personal package nicely. *117 Prince St. (between Wooster and Greene Sts.), SoHo, 212/982–1000. Subway: Prince St.*

7 b-6

2421 Broadway (at 89th St.), Upper West Side, 212/874–4000. Subway: 1, 2, 3, 9 to 96th St.

herbs & spices

11 c-2

APHRODISIA

This inviting Villager has an interesting selection of herbs at reasonable prices. *264 Bleecker St. (near 6th Ave.), West Village, 212/989–6440. Subway: W. 4th St./Washington Square.*

11 e-4

DEAN & DELUCA

Image is everything: Dean & DeLuca's immense variety of spices are, upon purchase, packaged in signature round tins. They look so spiffy in the kitchen that you may want to start collecting them. *560 Broadway (at Prince St.), SoHo, 212/431–1691 or 800/221–7714. Subway: Prince St.*

11 g-2

MEADOWSWEET HERBAL APOTHECARY

Here's your source for herbs, herbal medicines, essential oils, ointments, liniments, and Bach flower remedies. You can also sing up for herbology classes. *77 E. 4th St., East Village, 212/254–2870. Closed Mon.–Tues. Subway: Astor Pl.*

12 c-4

SAHADI IMPORTING CO.

This exotic market is well worth the trip for its great selection of spices and Middle Eastern food at excellent prices. Bulk purchases offer even more savings. *187–89 Atlantic Ave. (near Court St.), Brooklyn Heights, 718/624–4550. Closed Sun. Subway: Borough Hall.*

meat & poultry

New York's meatpacking district is otherwise known as Washington Market, spanning Ninth and Tenth Avenues from Gansevoort Street to West Fourteenth Street. From here, wholesale meat distributors supply hotels and restaurants. Many of these outlets sell retail as well, providing a mighty colorful experience and incomparable selection and savings.

11 c-2

FAICCO'S PORK STORE

In business since the exact turn of the century, Faicco's has become a New York institution, renowned for its delicious sausages. *260 Bleecker St. (near 6th Ave.), West Village, 212/243–1974. Subway: W. 4th St./Washington Square.*

4 e-4

6511 11th Ave. (at 65th St.), Bay Ridge, Brooklyn, 718/236–0119. Subway: Fort Hamilton Pkwy. Closed Mon.

10 d-1

JEFFERSON MARKET

Jefferson's fans prefer it to neighboring Balducci's for meat. Don't hesitate to ask questions; the friendly staff is into customer service. *450 6th Ave. (near W. 10th St.), West Village, 212/533–3377. Subway: F to 14th St.*

11 h-1

KUROWYCKY MEATS

This family-run shop has been in business for nearly 40 years, preparing and purveying some of the city's finest smoked (on the premises) and cured meats. Look for baked hams, unusual sausages (including sausage with caraway seeds, or the spicy Ukrainian kielbasa). Top off your purchase with dark Lithuanian bread, homemade Polish mustard, and sauerkraut. *124 1st Ave. (near 7th St.), East Village, 212/477–0344. Subway: Astor Pl.*

9 e-7

LES HALLES

The popular French bistro (*see* French *in* Chapter 3) also has a highly regarded butcher shop for French cuts of meat. *411 Park Ave. S (between 28th and 29th Sts.), Murray Hill, 212/679–4111. Subway: 6 to 28th St.*

7 b-5

OPPENHEIMER PRIME MEATS

The butcher and owner of this old-fashioned shop carries a top selection of meats, game, and poultry. *2606 Broadway (at 99th St.), Upper West Side, 212/662–0246. Closed Sun. Subway: 1, 2, 3, 9 to 96th St.*

7 *g-7*
OTTOMANELLI BROS.
Catch prime cuts and fresh game in season. They'll deliver to nearby addresses. *1549 York Ave. (at 82nd St.), Upper East Side, 212/772–7900. Subway: 4, 5, 6 to 86th St.*

nuts & seeds

11 *c-8*
A. L. BAZZINI
Since 1886 Bazzini has served up dried fruit, nuts, coffees, candies, chocolates, gourmet cookies, specialty sandwiches and more. Try their famous pistachios and nut crunches. *339 Greenwich St. (at Jay St.), Tribeca, 212/334–1280. Closed Sun. Subway: Chambers St.*

7 *b-7*
BROADWAY NUT SHOPPE
The name is no joke: this store has Georgia pecans, black walnuts in season, pignoli nuts, Indian nuts, macadamias, cashews, almonds, pistachios, and filberts roasted on the premises. Add imported candies and dried fruit to your mix. *2246 Broadway (at 81st St.), Upper West Side, 212/874–5214. Subway: 79th St.*

12 *c-4*
SAHADI IMPORTING CO.
Purveyors of nuts and dried fruit since 1895, Sahadi has nearly 100 varieties between the two. *See Herbs & Spices, above. 187–89 Atlantic Ave. (near Court St.), Brooklyn Heights, 718/624–4550. Closed Sun. Subway: Borough Hall.*

7 *f-7*
TREAT BOUTIQUE
Treat stocks candy, nuts, dried fruit, and assorted gourmet items, and makes fudge on the premises. *200 E. 86th St., Upper East Side, 212/737–6619. Subway: 4, 5, 6 to 86th St.*

pasta

9 *c-4*
BRUNO RAVIOLI CO.
What more can we say? Pasta makers since 1905, Bruno supplies many restaurants and caterers with its fresh manicotti; tortellini; vegetable lasagna; egg fettuccine; and ravioli with sun-dried tomato, shiitake mushrooms, or pesto. Pick up a homemade sauce, too. *653 9th Ave. (near 45th St.), Hell's Kitchen, 212/246–8456. Subway: 42nd St./Port Authority*

9 *c-8*
249 8th Ave. (near 22nd St.), Chelsea, 212/627–0767. Subway: C, E to 23rd St.

7 *b-8*
2204 Broadway (near 78th St.), Upper West Side, 212/580–8150. Subway: 79th St.

11 *f-5*
PIEMONTE HOMEMADE RAVIOLI COMPANY
In the heart of Little Italy, Piemonte makes a variety of fresh pastas daily, including gluten-free macaroni for those with an allergy. *190 Grand St. (near Mulberry St.), 212/226–0475. Closed Mon. Subway: 6, J, M, N, R, Z to Canal St.*

11 *d-3*
RAFFETTO'S CORPORATION
This longstanding Village shop (est. 1906) cuts fresh pasta and egg or spinach noodles to your specifications as you watch. Every day brings new batches of ravioli stuffed with cheese or meat. Nobody does it better, or for less. *144 W. Houston St. (near Sullivan St.), West Village, 212/777–1261. Closed Sun.–Mon. Subway: Houston St.*

produce

10 *d-1*
BALDUCCI'S
Balducci's is known for many things, but everyone loves the place for its amazing and delicious variety of fresh fruits and vegetables. For custom baskets, call 212/206–4600. *424 6th Ave. (at 9th St.), West Village, 212/673–2600 or 800/BALDUCCI. Subway: W. 4th St./Washington Square.*

11 *e-4*
DEAN & DELUCA
It is, after all, the strikingly colorful array of fresh produce that entices passers-by into this gourmet nirvana. The stuff is pricey, but people pay—for the pleasure of shopping here. Stylists and still-life photographers sometimes drop in, looking for the perfect fruit or veggie for that day's shoot. *560 Broadway (at Prince*

St.), SoHo, 212/431–1691 or 800/221–7714. Subway: Prince St.

7 *b-8*

FAIRWAY

Famous for good produce at low prices, Fairway goes further by stocking an unbelievable selection—every conceivable fruit and vegetable, from A to Z, include seasonal specialties and baby vegetables. Deliveries arrive daily, so there's never an "off" day, though weekends can be unpleasantly hectic. *2127 Broadway (at 75th St.), Upper West Side, 212/595–1888. Subway: 79th St.*

6 *c-8*

133rd St. at West Side Hwy, Harlem, 212/234–3883. Subway: 137th St./City College.

11 *e-5*

GOURMET GARAGE

Fear not, family shoppers: here you'll find fruit and vegetables both basic and rarefied, to satisfy both the discerning gourmand and the average Joe (or child). Prices are generally reasonable, but keep an eye on them. *453 Broome St. (at Mercer St.), SoHo, 212/941–5850. Subway: 6 to Spring St.*

9 *f-2*

301 E. 64th St., Upper East Side, 212/535–6271. Subway: 68th St./Hunter College.

9 *f-1*

GRACE'S MARKETPLACE

The exotic selection of fresh produce includes hard-to-find seasonal specialties from around the world, including Kiwano and Pepino melons, loquats, white Queene Anne cherries, and Ceremoya fruit. Apricots, plums, peaches, nectarines, and cherries are available year-round.*1237 3rd Ave. (at 71st St.), Upper East Side, 212/737–0600. Subway: 68th St./Hunter College.*

GREENMARKETS

New York's year-round greenmarkets give the city a breath of fresh air, with the help of area farmers. Produce is often cheaper than at grocery stores and gourmet shops; and it's sold by the grower, so freshness is guaranteed. In addition to local seasonal fruits and vegetables, you'll find fresh-cut wildflowers, baked goods, cheeses, fresh milk, and apple cider in season. Ask around in your neighborhood; major squares throughout the five boroughs (such as Union Square) have the most abundant markets.

7 *e-7*

PARADISE MARKET

Indeed, it's Eden for fresh produce, with a wide selection of exotic yet (may we hope?) permissible fruits and vegetables. The prices, alas, are postlapsarian. *1100 Madison Ave. (at 83rd St.), Upper East Side, 212/737-0049. Subway: 4, 5, 6 to 86th St.*

7 *e-8*

1080 Lexington Ave. (at 76th St.), Upper East Side, 212/57–1190. Subway: 77th St.

7 *f-6*

THE VINEGAR FACTORY

Not surprisingly, they've got a wide selection of fresh fruits and veggies, including hard-to-find items. *431 E. 91st St., Upper East Side, 212/987–0885. Subway: 4, 5, 6 to 86th St.*

FRAMING

9 *d-8*

A. I. FRIEDMAN

Over 2,000 styles of ready-made wood, plexi, and metal frames go for 20% off the list price, and the staff will custom-frame as well. *44 W. 18th, Chelsea, 212/243–9000. Closed weekends. Subway: F to 14th St.*

7 *e-8*

A.P.F., INC.

This company's own factory makes a variety of custom frames, museum-quality reproductions, and contemporary styles. *172 E. 75th St., Upper East Side, 212/988–1090. Subway: 77th St.*

9 *f-2*

231 E. 60th St., Upper East Side, 212/223–0726. Subway: 59th St.

11 *e-5*

BARK FRAMEWORKS

Bark has specialized in archivally correct framing for over 20 years. The service doesn't come cheap, but it's worth it for fine works of art and photography that you want to last a lifetime. *85 Grand St. (at Greene St.), SoHo, 212/431–9080. Subway: N, R to Canal St.*

9 *c-8*

CHELSEA FRAMES

This shop concentrates on custom and archival framing of everything from posters to conservation pieces. The staff is helpful, turnaround is fast, and prices are reasonable. *207 8th Ave. (between 20th and 21st Sts.), Chelsea, 212/807–8957. Subway: C, E to 23rd St.*

7 *g-8*

HOUSE OF HEYDENRYK

Heydenryk has sold, repaired, and restored antique frames since 1935; the company now also sells reproduction frames, made by a staff of craftsmen who work above the showroom. Repros take four weeks. *417 E. 76th St., Upper East Side, 212/249–4903. Subway: 77th St.*

9 *e-2*

J. POCKER & SON

Expert framers since 1926, J. Pocker & Son provide custom work, including conservation, in a wide range of styles, from ornate, hand-carved gilt to plexi. They'll even pick up and deliver your piece. Drop into the gallery to browse prints and posters. *135 E. 63rd St., Upper East Side, 212/838–5488 or 800/782–8434. Subway: 59th St.*

4 *d-2*

YALE PICTURE FRAME & MOULDING CORP.

This estimable firm imports and manufactures picture frames; discounts over 400 moldings for custom-made frames by 25%; and offers over 20,000 ready-made frames. *770 5th Ave. (at 28th St.), Sunset Park, Brooklyn, 718/788–6200. Closed Sat. Subway: 25th St.*

GIFTS

11 *c-1*

AMALGAMATED HOME

As the name implies, Amalgamated Home is devoted to chic and sleek home furnishings, with an emphasis on funky, ultramodern designs and unusual materials. Traditionalists may cringe, but others find the mix fresh and pleasingly cutting-edge. *9 Christopher St. (between 6th Ave. and Gay St.), West Village, 212/255–4160. Subway: Christopher St./Sheridan Square.*

11 *d-5*

ANTHROPOLOGIE

Now a national chain, Anthropologie features an interesting mix of both new and antique home furnishings, including upholstered pieces, smaller decora-

tive items, clothing, and accessories. Both the home and the fashion selections are basic, but they're very well-edited, and prices are fairly reasonable for this trendy shopping site. *375 W. Broadway (at Broome St.), SoHo, 212/343–7070. Subway: C, E to Canal St.*

9 *d-8*

APARTMENT 48

The genius of this store is that it really does look like an apartment, but almost everything in it is for sale. In the living room, you'll find furniture and books; in the kitchen, a variety of kitchen utensils; in the bath, everything from rubber duckies to soap; and so on. It's probably the most comfortable shopping experience in the city. *48 W. 17th St., Chelsea, 212/807–1391. Subway: F to 14th St.*

7 *e-8*

E.A.T. GIFTS

Here lie thousands of super-cute little gifts and favors for children's parties, many of which would make great stocking stuffers. *1062 Madison Ave. (at 80th St.), Upper East Side, 212/861–2544. Subway: 77th St.*

9 *d-3*

FELISSIMO

An oasis of quiet in mid-Midtown, the whole of Felissimo is configured according to *feng shui*, the Eastern art of placement, so you've *got* to feel harmonious. The first floor features gardening accessories; the second floor has clothing, accessories, and a beautiful bedroom area, with fine linens and bath products; the third floor covers the dining-room table; and once you've made it to the fourth floor, you can plop elegantly down in the Tea Room (*see* Food–Coffee & Tea, *above*). *10 W. 57th St., Midtown, 800/565–6785. Subway: E, F to 5th Ave.*

10 *d-1*

GALILEO

This small but extremely stylish store is devoted to the home, packing its shelves with new and vintage ceramics, linens, lighting, and other trimmings, including furniture by Heywood Wakefield. *167½ 7th Ave. S (at 12th St.), West Village, 212/243–1629. Subway: Christopher St./Sheridan Square.*

7 *e-8*

IL PAPIRO

Direct from Italy, this charmer carries delightful gifts and stationery, all made with hand-marbled Florentine papers: picture frames, desk accessories, decorative boxes, albums, and more. *1021 Lexington Ave. (between 73rd and 74th Sts.), Upper East Side, 212/288–9330. Subway: 77th St.*

11 *d-5*

JAMSON WHYTE

Imported from Singapore, Whyte showcases antiques, artifacts and home furnishings that either come from Asia or look like they might have. It's so well styled as to be slightly intimidating, but don't be; just look at the prices, which are extremely reasonable for SoHo. Whether you have $20 or $2,000 to spend, you'll find something here. *47 Wooster St. (at Broome St.), SoHo, 212/965–9405. Subway: A, C, E, N, R to Canal St.*

9 *e-1*

LEXINGTON GARDENS

Always brimming with interesting new items, Lexington Gardens features English-country–style accessories and furniture for the home and garden, including fabulous dried-flower arrangements and topiaries. *1011 Lexington Ave. (at 73rd St.), Upper East Side, 212/861–4390. Closed Sun. Subway: 77th St.*

9 *d-3*

MOMA DESIGN STORE

The Museum of Modern Art's retail showroom sells modern furniture, home accessories, kitchenware, tools, desk accessories, jewelry, children's toys, and books, all with a nod toward good design. *44 W. 53rd St., Midtown, 212/708–9800. Subway: E, F to 5th Ave.*

11 *e-4*

MOSS

Moss is heaven for anyone into very, very modern, European-designed furnishings and accessories. Think Alessi, Kartell, Starck . . . it's like the MOMA Design Store downtown, but more heavily edited. If it's new and cool, or not-so-new but classically modern, it's here. *146 Greene St. (between Prince and Houston Sts.), SoHo, 212/226–2190. Subway: Prince St.*

10 *c-1*

MXYPLYZYK

Don't even try to pronounce the name; just try to stop by this beautiful West Village store, a favorite of editors and stylists alike. Mxy focuses on high-style, but not high-priced, home furnishings and gifts, including books, jewelry, and pet accessories. *125 Greenwich Ave. (between Jane and Horatio Sts.), West Village, 212/989–4300. Subway: 1, 9, C, E to 14th St.*

11 *f-4*

POP SHOP

Yes, it's an entire store devoted to the designs of Keith Haring: T-shirts for the whole family, games, bags, and, of course, posters. Hours can be erratic; call first. *292 Lafayette St. (between Prince and Houston Sts.), SoHo, 212/219–2784. Subway: Broadway–Lafayette St.; Prince St.*

9 *d-3*

THE SHARPER IMAGE

The gadget-filled catalog comes to life: Here are all those intriguing items you know you can live without but aren't sure you want to. Fall for a massage chair, a robot that serves hors d'oeuvres, a safari hat with a built-in fan, a talking scale . . . *4 W. 57th St., Midtown, 212/265–2550. Subway: E, F to 5th Ave.; Pier 17, South Street Seaport, Lower Manhattan, 212/693–0477. Subway: 2, 3 to Fulton St.*

9 *e-1*

SLATKIN & COMPANY

This jewel box of a decorator-owned shop features private-label traditional English-country–style accessories. *131 E. 70th St., Upper East Side, 212/794–1661. Closed Sun.; closed Sat in July and Aug. Subway: 68th St./Hunter College.*

7 *f-8*

TREILLAGE LTD.

This unusual and stylish mix of antique and reproduction garden furniture and accessories encompasses English terracotta pots and plants, gardening tools, watering cans, gloves, candles, home- and garden-design books, and interesting Christmas decorations in season. *418 E. 75th St., Upper East Side, 212/535–2288. Closed Sun.; closed Sat. in July and Aug. Subway: 77th St.*

11 *e-4*

TROY

Yes, there is a Troy, and he has great taste. Expensive taste. This store is an incredibly chic mixture of contemporary home furnishings and accessories, both new and antique, and the only retail source in the city for ICF furniture. You're bound to fall in love with something here, so come in a generous mood. *138 Greene St. (between Prince and Houston Sts.), 212/941–4777. Subway: Broadway–Lafayette St.; Prince St.*

9 *e-2*

WILLIAM WAYNE & COMPANY

With a pair of shops on Lexington and an offshoot downtown, this store divides its stock between gardening wares and a traditional mix of home accessories, including well-chosen *objets*, lamps, furniture, and gifts. Monkeys are a favored motif. *846 Lexington Ave. (at 64th St.), Upper East Side, 212/737–8934. Subway: 68th St./Hunter College.*

9 *e-2*

850 Lexington Ave. (at 64th St.), Upper East Side, 212/288–9243. Subway: 68th St./Hunter College.

10 *e-1*

40 University Pl. (at 9th St.), Greenwich Village, 212/533–4711. Subway: 8th St.; Astor Pl.

HOME

bedroom & bath

9 *e-8*

HASTING TILE & IL BAGNO

The whole store is a knockout, with bold designs for bathrooms and all the fittings, including artful designer tiles. They do kitchens, too. *230 Park Ave. S (at 19th St.), Gramercy, 212/674–9700. Subway: N, R, 6 to 23rd St.*

11 *g-3*

IRREPLACEABLE ARTIFACTS

Mixed into this well-known stash of architectural miscellany (*see* Antiques–Collectibles Specialists, *above*) is a collection of antique bathroom fixtures and accessories. *14 2nd Ave. (at Houston St.), East Village, 212/777–2900. Subway: 2nd Ave.*

9 *f-2*

KRAFT HARDWARE

Kraft is an Upper East Side source for high-end fixtures and bath accessories. *306 E. 61st St., 212/838–2214. Subway: 59th St.*

9 *e-8*

NEMO TILE

Finish off your bath project with these medicine cabinets, bath fixtures, porcelain and glass tiles, mosaics, and accessories. Nemo is a full-line distributor and importer of ceramic tile. *48 E. 21st St., Gramercy, 212/505–0009. Subway: N, R, 6 to 23rd St.*

9 *e-3*

SHERLE WAGNER INTERNATIONAL

Here they are: the world's most elegant and expensive bathroom fixtures. *60 E. 57th St., Midtown, 212/758–3300. Closed weekends. Subway: E, F to 5th Ave.*

9 *f-7*

SIMON'S HARDWARE

Simon's has everything for the bath, including an impressive line of tile in marble, granite, stone, and slate. *421 3rd Ave. (between 29th and 30th Sts.), Murray Hill, 212/532–9220. Closed Sun. Subway: 6 to 28th St.*

9 *f-3*

WATERWORKS

This pair of shops carries classic, elegant, British-inspired bath fixtures plus a full line of tiles and stones. *237 E. 58th St., Midtown, 212/371–9266. Subway: 59th St.; 469 Broome St. (at Greene St.), SoHo, 212/966–0605. Subway: 6 to Spring St.; N, R to Canal St.*

carpets & rugs

New York's rug district spans 30th–33rd Streets between 5th and Madison Ave.s, where you'll find a particular concentration of Orientals and Persians. Bloomingdale's and Macy's also carry Oriental rugs.

9 *e-8*

ABC CARPET & HOME

Opened in 1897, this amazing emporium boasts two of the largest carpet showrooms anywhere. The holdings include

Oriental, designer, area, scatter, rag rugs, and over 5,000 rolls of national brands plus (downstairs at no. 881), a large selection of remnants in a variety of fibers, colors, and sizes. You can arrange for immediate delivery and installation. *881 and 888 Broadway (at 19th St.), Flatiron, 212/473–3000. Subway: 14th St./Union Square; N, R to 23rd St.*

11 *e-3*
A. BESHAR & CO.
Beshar has been selling handsome Oriental rugs, as well as cleaning and repairing them, since 1898. *611 Broadway (near Bleecker St.), rm. 405, Greenwich Village, 212/529–7300. Subway: Bleecker St.*

9 *d-8*
ARONSON'S
This floor-covering supermarket meets all your flooring needs with carpet remnants, closeouts, or custom cuts; tile; and linoleum. *135 W. 17th St., Chelsea, 212/243–4993. Subway: F, 1, 2, 3, 9 to 14th St.*

7 *b-7*
CENTRAL CARPET
Come here first! Central Carpet is a great source for low-priced (they guarantee New York's lowest) antique, semi-antique, and new handmade Chinese, Persian, and Caucasian rugs. There's a large selection of Art Deco Chinese rugs and flat-weave Indian dhurries, as well as modern Belgian rugs—a total of over 5,000 rugs on two floors. Prices range from $19 to $10,000. *426 Columbus Ave. (near 81st St.), Upper West Side, 212/787–8813. Subway: 79th St.; 81 8th Ave. (at 14th St.), Chelsea, 212/741–3700. Subway: A, C, E to 14th St.*

9 *e-3*
EINSTEIN-MOOMJY
This oddly named carpet department store features new Orientals, broadlooms, and area rugs. *150 E. 58th St., Midtown, 212/758–0900. Subway: 59th St.*

11 *e-4*
MODERN AGE
Modern Age is New York City's only retail outlet for Christine Van Der Hurd rugs, with their uniquely beautiful contemporary designs. *102 Wooster St. (between Spring and Prince Sts.), SoHo,*

212/966–0669. Subway: Spring St.; Prince St.

7 *b-8*
RUG WAREHOUSE
For over 50 years this store has maintained a best-price guarantee on its Caucasians, Persians, Art Deco Chinese, dhurries, and kilims, both antique and modern. *220 W. 80th St., Upper West Side, 212/787–6665. Subway: 79th St.*

9 *e-8*
SAFAVIEH CARPETS
A reputable source for new and antique Oriental rugs, Safavieh will also buy, wash, appraise, and restore old rugs. *902 Broadway (between 20th and 21st Sts.), Flatiron, 212/477–1234. Subway: N, R to 23rd St.*

9 *e-6*
153 Madison Ave. (at 32nd St.), Murray Hill, 212/683–8399. Subway: 33rd St.

9 *f-2*
238 E. 59th St., Midtown, 212/888–0626. Subway: 59th St.

ceramic tiles
See Housewares & Hardware, *below.*

9 *e-8*
ANN SACKS TILE & STONE
Ann Sacks will fit limestone, slate, terracotta, marble mosaics, handcrafted tile, and stone antiquities to your commercial or residential specifications. *5 E. 16th St., Gramercy, 212/463–8400. Subway: 14th St./Union Square.*

9 *f-8*
COUNTRY FLOORS
This appealing shop specializes in fine hand-painted tiles, both antique and modern; most are imported from Italy, France, Holland, Peru, Finland, Spain, and Portugal. Sinks can be designed to match tiles. *315 E. 16th St., Gramercy, 212/627–8300. Closed weekends. Subway: 14th St./Union Square.*

9 *e-8*
HASTING TILE & IL BAGNO
See Bedroom & Bath, *above.*

9 *f-4*
IDEAL TILE
These importers of Italian ceramic tiles will provide expert installation or a do-it-

yourself guide. *405 E. 51st St., Midtown, 212/759–2339. Subway: 51st St./Lexington–3rd Aves.*

9 *e-8*

NEMO TILE

See Bedroom & Bath, *above.*

9 *e-6*

THE QUARRY

New York's largest stock of reasonably priced Spanish, Dutch, French, Portuguese, and Mexican tiles comes mainly in bright colors and patterns. The Quarry will install your choices or provide do-it-yourself guidance and supplies. Also on sale are bathroom and kitchen accessories and a complete line of wallpaper. *128 E. 32nd St., Murray Hill, 212/679–8889. Closed Sat. after 3 PM. Subway: 33rd St.*

china, glassware, porcelain, pottery

You can buy fine china in any of the large department stores, and even finer china at Tiffany's and Cartier (*see* Jewelry–Contemporary, *below*).

7 *b-7*

AVVENTURA

This wide selection of glassware and tabletop contains china, serving pieces, and flatware. The stock is heavy on Italian manufacturers and hard-to-find pieces. *463 Amsterdam Ave. (near 83rd St.), Upper West Side, 212/769–2510. Subway: 1, 9 to 86th St.*

9 *e-3*

BACCARAT, INC.

Baccarat sells its own famed and expensive French crystal plus china by Limoges, Ceralene, and Raynaud; pewter by Etains du Manoir; and silver by Christofle and Puiforcat. *625 Madison Ave. (near 58th St.), Midtown, 212/826–4100. Subway: 59th St.*

9 *e-3*

CARDEL

Cast your eye on all major brands of high-end china, crystal, and silver in one location. This stuff makes great wedding gifts. *621 Madison Ave. (near 58th St.), 212/753–8690. Closed Sun. Subway: 59th St.*

11 *f-6*

CERAMICA

Hand-painted ceramics and reproduction majolica are imported straight from Italy to these cheerful, charming, chock-full-of-china shops. New shipments arrive every three months. *182 Hester St. (near Mulberry St.), Little Italy, 212/966–3170. Subway: 6, N, R, J, M, Z to Canal St.*

11 *d-4*

59 Thompson St. (near Spring St.), SoHo, 212/941–1307. Subway: C, E to Spring St. Closed Mon.

9 *e-2*

CHRISTOFLE

Here you'll find Christofle's full line of sterling, silver-plate, and stainless tableware and home accessories in addition to crystal by Baccarat and St. Louis, china by Haviland and Ceralene, and private-label linens. *680 Madison Ave. (near 62nd St.), Upper East Side, 212/308–9390. Closed Sun. Subway: 59th St.*

9 *e-8*

FISHS EDDY

These highly whimsical shops sell 1930s and '40s china and glassware that once belonged to corporations, restaurants, hotels, private clubs, and the government—making for some fascinating logos. Sugar bowls, creamers, and other vintage kitchen and dining accessories join the tableware. There are always some interesting collectibles here, and their prices are low; the shop is highly browsable. *889 Broadway (near 19th St.), Flatiron, 212/420–9020. Subway: 14th St./Union Square, N, R to 23rd St.*

11 *a-1*

551 Hudson St. (near Perry St.), West Village, 212/627–3956. Subway: Christopher St./Sheridan Square.

9 *e-2*

HOYA CRYSTAL GALLERY

Here is the world's largest collection of this respected Japanese firm's art and functional pieces. Hoya is known for its low iron content, which results in glass with no discolorations or bubbles. Prices range from $30 to $30,000. *689 Madison Ave. (at 62nd St.), Upper East Side, 212/223–6335. Subway: 59th St.*

11 e-4

THE L.S. COLLECTION

A large selection of unique and stylish giftware including china, handblown crystal, glasses, and sterling. *469 W. Broadway (between Prince and Houston Sts.), SoHo, 212/673–4575. Subway: C, E to Spring St.; Prince St.*

9 e-2

LALIQUE

Lalique's posh shop sells its own rightly famous, incredibly beautiful French crystal. *680 Madison Ave. (between 61st and 62nd Sts.), Upper East Side, 212/355–6550. Subway: 59th St.*

11 h-6

LANAC SALES COMPANY

Imported and domestic china and crystal goes for a discount here, as does sterling and stainless flatware. *73 Canal St. (at Allen St.), Lower East Side, 212/925–6422. Closed Sat. Subway: Canal St.*

9 e-1

LA TERRINE

Concoct wonderful house presents or special accent pieces from the hand-painted Portuguese, Italian, and French ceramics in this neighborhood shop. Complementary table linens from Provence and India complete the international look. *1024 Lexington Ave. (at 73rd St.), Upper East Side, 212/988–6550. Closed Sun. Subway: 77th St.*

9 e-1

MACKENZIE-CHILDS LTD.

Here's the flagship New York store for MacKenzie-Childs' whimsical line of hand-painted ceramics, glassware, and furniture. It is, shall we say, not the place to bargain-hunt. *824 Madison Ave. (near 69th St.), Upper East Side, 212/570–6050. Closed Sun. Subway: 68th St./Hunter College.*

10 d-1

MAD MONK

This shop is a longtime Village source for interesting handmade pottery and mirrors. *500 6th Ave. (near 13th St.), West Village, 212/242–6678. Subway: F to 14th St.*

9 d-7

MIKASA

Mikasa's contemporary dinnerware, crystal, flatware, table linens, and tea sets may become widely popular thanks, oddly enough, to a blitz of subway advertising beginning in 1997. *30 W. 23rd St., Chelsea, 212/206–3766. Subway: F to 23rd St.*

9 e-3

ORREFORS CRYSTAL GALLERY

This shop is one of very few that stock the entire collection of this world-renowned Swedish crystal. *58 E. 57th St., Midtown, 212/753–3442. Subway: N, R to 5th Ave.*

9 b-1

POTTERY BARN

How many catalogs do they print a year, anyway? Pottery Barn's everyday dishes, mugs, glasses, flatware, serving platters, bowls candlesticks, pitchers, and vases combine with furniture, accent lighting, rugs, candles, and decorative accessories for a useful, if sometimes bland, contemporary collection. *2109 Broadway (near 73rd St.), Upper West Side, 212/595–5573. Subway: 1, 2, 3, 9 to 72nd St.*

9 c-8

100 7th Ave. (near 16th St.), Chelsea, 212/633–8405. Subway: 1, 2, 3, 9 to 14th St.

11 e-3

600 Broadway (near Houston St.), SoHo, 212/505–6377. Subway: Broadway–Lafayette St.

7 f-8

1451 2nd Ave. (near 76th St.), Upper East Side, 212/988–4228. Subway: 77th St.; other locations.

9 e-2

ROYAL COPENHAGEN PORCELAIN

Danish china and Orrefors and Kosta Boda crystal join Georg Jensen silver flatware and jewelry. *683 Madison Ave. (near 61st St.), Upper East Side, 212/759–6457. Subway: 59th St.*

9 e-1

SARA

Sara focuses on imported Japanese ceramics of fine handcrafted quality. *953 Lexington Ave. (near 69th St.), Upper East Side, 212/772–3243. Closed Sun. Subway: 68th St./Hunter College.*

11 *d-4*

SIMON PEARCE

All of these simple and elegant hand-blown glasses, pitchers, candlesticks, and vases are made in Vermont. *120 Wooster St. (near Spring St.), SoHo, 212/334-2393. Subway: Spring St.*

9 *e-2*

500 Park Ave. (near 59th St.), Midtown, 212/421-8801. Subway: 59th St.

9 *e-3*

STEUBEN GLASS

Steuben's showroom is like a museum, its pieces both beautiful and precious. Make time to browse both the unique glass sculptures and the functional pieces. *715 5th Ave. (at 56th St.), Midtown, 212/752-1441. Subway: E, F to 5th Ave.*

9 *e-3*

TIFFANY & CO.

The jeweler of renown sells its own china, crystal, and sterling tableware on the third floor, at surprisingly reasonable prices. *727 5th Ave. (at 57th St.), Midtown, 212/755-8000. Closed Sun. Subway: E, F, N, R to 5th Ave.*

7 *e-8*

VILLEROY & BOCH

The German tabletop company's entire line is here, in its flagship New York store. Compare retail prices on this fine china, silver flatware, crystal, and art glass to the company's many outlet stores, which sell virtually indistinguishable seconds at roughly 40% off. The outlets are, of course, a day trip away. *974 Madison Ave. (near 76th St.), Upper East Side, 212/535-2500. Closed Sun. Subway: 77th St.*

9 *c-8*

WILLIAMS-SONOMA

In addition to the famous cookware, you'll find a stylish, well-priced selection of china, pottery, wine glasses, bistroware, flatware, and serving pieces. As one fan put it, Williams-Sonoma stores are not about cooking; they're about lifestyle. Both camps are happy here. *110 7th Ave. (near 17th St.), Chelsea, 212/633-2203. Subway: 1, 2, 3, 9 to 14th St.*

9 *e-2*

20 E. 60th St. (near Madison Ave.), Upper East Side, 212/980-5155. Subway: 59th St.

9 *f-1*

1309 2nd Ave. (near 69th St.), Upper East Side, 212/288-8408. Subway: 68th St./Hunter College.

7 *e-7*

1175 Madison Ave. (near 86th St.), Upper East Side, 212/289-6832. Subway: 4, 5, 6 to 86th St.

11 *e-4*

WOLFMAN GOLD & GOOD

Assemble a stylish, well-groomed, mainly all-white look for your table in this appealing rustic setting. The dinnerware, glassware, linens, stainless flatware, tabletop gifts, oddities, and collectibles can all be adorned with dried floral topiaries. *116 Greene St. (at Prince St.), SoHo, 212/410-7000. Subway: Spring St.*

10 *d-1*

WOODEN INDIAN

Glassware in every shape and size is laid out in a low-frills space with prices to match. There are a few old pieces in the china collection. The management is friendly and helpful. *60 W. 15th St., Chelsea, 212/243-8590. Closed Sun.-Mon. Subway: F to 14th St.*

furniture & accessories

In addition to these specialist shops, Bloomingdale's and Macy's have extensive collections of home furnishings, mostly contemporary and traditional. Bloomingdale's model rooms are always well designed. You may not get the personal service you need, though, at these retail behemoths.

9 *e-8*

ABC CARPET & HOME

The heartwarming ABC is a wonderful source for antique furniture and accessories as well as contemporary linens. On the second floor you'll find Herman Miller, vintage stainless steel, and traditional furniture. *888 Broadway (at 19th St.), Flatiron, 212/473-3000. Subway: 14th St./Union Square; N, R to 23rd St.*

11 *d-4*

AERO

Aero sells highly chic furniture of its own design as well as vintage pieces. *132 Spring St. (near Wooster St.), SoHo, 212/966-1500. Closed Sun. Subway: Spring St.*

9 *e-8*

THE BOMBAY COMPANY

Butler's tray tables, Biedermeier consoles, tole lamps, Verona mirrors—the Bombay Company sells an heirloom look in home furnishings, accessories, and wall decor at good prices. Okay, so it isn't heirloom *quality*, but that's for your heirs to worry about. *900 Broadway (at 20th St.), Flatiron, 212/420–1315. Subway: N, R to 23rd St.*

9 *e-2*

1062A 3rd Ave. (at 63rd St.), Upper East Side, 212/759–7217. Subway: 59th St.

9 *b-1*

2001 Broadway (at 68th St.), Upper West Side, 212/721–7701. Subway: 66th St./Lincoln Center.

9 *f-4*

BRANCUSI

Choose from a large selection of modern tables in glass, chrome, brass, stainless steel, and forged iron. *938 1st Ave. (near 51st St.), Midtown, 212/688–7980. Subway: 51st St./Lexington–3rd Aves.*

9 *e-3*

CASSINA USA

Cassina is the licensed representative for classic modern furniture, including pieces by Frank Lloyd Wright, Le Corbusier, Charles Rennie Macintosh, and Gerrit Rietveld. *155 E. 56th St., Midtown, 212/245–2121. Closed weekends. Subway: 59th St.*

9 *d-7*

CASTRO CONVERTIBLES

This chain has one of New York's largest selections of sofabeds, recliners, and wall units. *43 W. 23rd St., Chelsea, 212/255–7000. Subway: F to 23rd St.; other locations.*

9 *e-2*

CRATE & BARREL

Crate & Barrel has become an all-American favorite for first-time furniture buyers, with a variety of styles in both traditional and modern silhouettes. You get good quality at a reasonable price. *650 Madison Ave. (at 59th St.), Midtown, 212/308–0011. Subway: 59th St.; N, R to 5th Ave.*

9 *e-7*

DEVON SHOP

Formerly for decorators only, the Devon Shop now offers its beautiful custom-made, hand-carved traditional furniture, as well as all of its design services, to the public. *111 E. 27th St., Murray Hill, 212/686–1760. Subway: 6 to 28th St.*

11 *d-5*

DIALOGICA

This duo is known for brightly colored velvet upholstery pieces in bold designs. *484 Broome St. (near Wooster St.), SoHo, 212/966–1934. Subway: Spring St.*

7 *e-7*

1070 Madison Ave. (near 81st St.), Upper East Side, 212/737–7811. Subway: 77th St.

9 *f-1*

DOMAIN

Domain specializes in European-country oversized upholstery pieces, reproduction painted farmtables, and armoires. *1179 3rd Ave. (at 69th St.), Upper East Side, 212/639–1101. Subway: 68th St./Hunter College.*

9 *e-8*

938 Broadway (at 22nd St.), Flatiron, 212/228–7450. Subway: N, R to 23rd St.

9 *d-8*

DOOR STORE

This local chain tends toward reasonably priced contemporary furniture, with some traditional looks mixed in. There's an extensive chair selection. It's a solid option for the first-time apartment-filler. *123 W. 17th St., Chelsea, 212/627–1515. Subway: F, 1, 2, 3, 9 to 14th St.*

9 *e-6*

1 Park Ave. (at 33rd St.), Murray Hill, 212/679–9700. Subway: 33rd St.

9 *e-3*

599 Lexington Ave. (at 53rd St.), Midtown, 212/832–7500. Subway: 51st St./Lexington–3rd Aves.

9 *f-1*

1201 3rd Ave. (at 70th St.), Upper East Side, 212/772–1110. Subway: 68th St./Hunter College.

9 *e-8*

GOTHIC CABINET CRAFT

Gothic shops are sprouting up all over the place—and a good thing, too. The store sells both unpainted stock and custom-built furniture; one handy option is to pick an unfinished piece and have it finished in your choice of hue. They're fast and reliable, and the prices are great. *909 Broadway (between 20th and 21st Sts.), Flatiron, 212/673–2270. Subway: N, R to 23rd St.*

10 *f-1*

104 3rd Ave. (at 13th St.), Murray Hill, 212/420–9556. Subway: 3rd Ave.

7 *f-7*

1655 2nd Ave. (at 86th St.), 212/288–2999; other locations.

10 *c-1*

JENSEN-LEWIS

This low-key Chelsea store started out featuring the director's chair in every possible shape, height, and color—and personalized if desired. You'll now find a roomy display of contemporary furniture and accessories, and canvas by the yard, in 34 colors. *89 7th Ave. (at 15th St.), Chelsea, 212/929–4880. Subway: 1, 2, 3, 9 to 14th St.*

11 *e-4*

KNOLL

Modern office furniture is mixed with residential furniture and textiles. Construction is high-quality, and prices are stiff. *105 Wooster St. (near Prince St.), SoHo, 212/343–4000. Closed Sun. Subway: Prince St.*

9 *e-2*

LIGNE ROSET

Crafted in France, this modern furniture by top European designers is both understated and distinctive. *1090 3rd Ave. (near 64th St.), Upper East Side, 212/794–2903. Subway: 68th St./Hunter College.*

9 *e-6*

MAURICE VILLENCY

High-quality contemporary furniture fills model rooms in this commodious Murray Hill store. *200 Madison Ave. (at 35th St.), 212/725–4840. Subway: 33rd St.*

11 *e-4*

MODERN AGE

Come here for contemporary European furniture. *102 Wooster St. (near Prince St.), SoHo, 212/966–0669. Closed Sun. Subway: Prince St.*

9 *e-3*

PALAZZETTI

Palazzette has faithful reproductions of 20th-century classic furniture, including licensed copies of styles by Eames, Breuer, Le Corbusier, and Mies van der Rohe. *515 Madison Ave. (near 53rd St.), Midtown, 212/832–1199. Subway: 51st St./Lexington–3rd Aves.*

11 *e-4*

152 Wooster St. (near Prince St.), SoHo, 212/260–8815. Subway: Prince St.

11 *d-4*

PORTICO HOME

Simple French-country furniture is mixed with a good deal of Shaker-inspired and cherry pieces. *379 W. Broadway (near Spring St.), SoHo, 212/941–7800. Subway: C, E to Spring St.*

11 *f-4*

SALON MODERNE

These styles are either contemporary or '40s- and '50s-inspired, with a certain flair; most are new, but a few antiques are mixed in. *281 Layfayette St. (near Prince St.), SoHo, 212/219–3439. Subway: Prince St.; Broadway–Lafayette St.*

9 *e-8*

SEE LTD.

SEE, or Spatial Environmental Elements, sells the work of over 70 avant-garde designers of European and contemporary furniture, lamps, lighting, and accessories. *920 Broadway (near 21st St.), Flatiron, 212/228–3600. Subway: N, R to 23rd St.*

11 *e-4*

SHABBY CHIC

The name says it all: this custom-slip-covered furniture has a homey, lived-in look. Interesting throw pillows, linens, and period accessories follow through on the lovably scruffy theme. *93 Greene St. (between Spring and Prince Sts.), SoHo, 212/274–9842. Subway: Spring St.*

9 *e-6*

WORKBENCH

This attractive American and European contemporary furniture is reasonably priced, and the sales are excellent. The overall look is somewhat minimal. *470 Park Ave. S (near 32nd St.), Murray Hill, 212/481–5454. Subway: 33rd St.*

11 *c-4*

161 6th Ave. (at Spring St.), SoHo, 212/675–7775. Subway: C, E to Spring St.; other locations.

HOUSEWARES & HARDWARE

The large department stores have good selections of kitchenware. Restaurant suppliers are clustered on the Bowery, near Cooper Square and below Grand Street; travel here for good buys on practical, no-frills, professional cooking implements. Hardware buffs should wander over to the stretch of Canal Street from Lafayette to West Broadway.

9 *d-8*

BED, BATH & BEYOND

This Chelsea emporium has billions and billions of kitchen appliances, gadgets, and accessories, plus a good selection of linens, tabletop, and general home stuff. *620 6th Ave. (at 19th St.), Chelsea, 212/255–3550. Subway: F to 23rd St.*

9 *f-3*

BRIDGE KITCHENWARE

No-nonsense Bridge has best-quality professional equipment for the home at great prices: copperware (and retinning), earthenware, woodware, French porcelain baking supplies, restaurant-size stockpots, and more. Know what you want before you go—they have over 40,000 items—but do go. Julia Child does. *214 E. 52nd St., Midtown, 212/688–4220. Subway: 51st St./Lexington–3rd Aves.*

11 *e-5*

BROADWAY PANHANDLER

This roomy and attractive SoHo store carries an extensive collection of top-notch gourmet cookware, cutlery, and gadgets at low prices. Check out the huge stock of bakeware; cake molds and decorating implements are a specialty. *477 Broome (between Wooster and Greene Sts.), SoHo, 212/966–3434. Subway: Spring St.*

10 *f-6*

BROOKSTONE

The famed New Hampshire purveyor of hard-to-find tools and gadgets displays a sample of every item it sells. Pick up a clipboard upon entering—it's your order form. *South Street Seaport, Schermerhorn Row, 18 Fulton St., Lower Manhattan, 212/344–8108. Subway: 2, 3 to Fulton St.*

9 *e-1*

GRACIOUS HOME

Anything and everything you can think of for the home: custom kitchens, appliances, wall coverings, bath accessories, brass hardware, lighting, tableware, paint, and all the rest. *1220 3rd Ave. (at 70th St.), Upper East Side, 212/517–6300. Subway: 68th St./Hunter College.*

9 *e-3*

HAMMACHER SCHLEMMER

Established on the Bowery in 1848, Hammacher Schlemmer has been on 57th Street since 1926, filling its six floors with unique gadgets, conveniences, and indulgences for every room in the home; the car; the sauna; the yacht; or the private airplane. *147 E. 57th St., Midtown, 212/421–9000. Subway: 59th St.*

9 *d-6*

HENRY WESTPFAL & CO.

This legendary cutlery shop will also sharpen your tired knives. *105 W. 30th St., Garment District, 212/563–5990. Subway: 34th St./Herald Square.*

9 *e-5*

HOFFRITZ

The most impressive selection of cutlery and gadgetry in town. *Madison Ave. (near 43rd St.), Midtown, 212/697–7344. Subway: 42nd St./Grand Central.*

9 *c-3*

203 W. 57th St., Midtown, 212/757–3431. Subway: 59th St./Columbus Circle; other locations.

9 *c-8*

HOLD EVERYTHING

What a great idea! This division of Williams-Sonoma sells the means for you to store almost anything neatly and attractively. *104 7th Ave. (near 16th St.), Chelsea, 212/633–1674. Subway: 1, 2, 3, 9 to 14th St.*

9 *f-1*

1311 2nd Ave. (at 69th St.), Upper East Side, 212/535–9446. Subway: 68th St./Hunter College.

11 *a-2*

KITSCHEN

Here is the kitchenware our parents grew up with: Kitschen is chockablock with vintage (circa 1920–60) mixing bowls, cookie jars, pitchers, waffle irons, salt and pepper shakers, corn-on-the-cob plates, and other dedicated nostalgia, all displayed in color-coordinated tableaux. *15 Christopher St. (near Greenwich Ave.), West Village, 212/727–0430. Subway: Christopher St./Sheridan Square.*

9 *f-2*

KRAFT HARDWARE

With over 12,000 square ft of basic hardware, Kraft is the largest store of its kind in Manhattan (*see Home—Bedroom & Bath, above*). *306 E. 61st St., Upper East Side, 212/838–2214. Closed weekends. Subway: 59th St.*

9 *d-7*

LAMALLE KITCHENWARE

One of the city's best high-end kitchenware stores, LaMalle's got pots and pans by Sitram, Paderno, and Mauviel Copperware; knives by Wusthof and Dexter-Russell; baking supplies; and every imaginable gadget. *36 W. 25th St., 6th floor, Chelsea, 212/242–0750. Subway: F, N, R to 23rd St.*

11 *e-1*

LECHTER'S HOUSEWARES & GIFTS

The ubiquitous Lechter's has a conveniently large selection of basic kitchen, bath, and home items at very reasonable prices. Only the posh brands are missing. There's not much for the trousseau, but a lot for the teeny apartment. *55 E. 8th St., East Village, 212/505–0576. Subway: 8th St.; Astor Pl.*

9 *c-3*

250 W. 57th St., Midtown, 212/956–7290. Subway: 59th St./Columbus Circle

9 *f-1*

1198 3rd Ave. (at 69th St.), Upper East Side, 212/744–1427. Subway: 68th St./Hunter College

7 *b-8*

2151 Broadway (at 75th St.), Upper West Side, 212/580–1610. Subway: 1, 2, 3, 9 to 72nd St.; other locations.

9 *d-6*

MACY'S—THE CELLAR

A Shangri-La for cooks, Macy's beautifully stocked series of "shops" is dedicated to both housewares and food. Wander through mazes of gourmet foods and baked goods; coffees and

teas; and utensils and equipment for creative cookery. This floor always has a festive atmosphere. *155 W. 34th St. (Herald Square), Garment District, lower level, 212/695–4400. Subway: 34th St./Herald Square.*

10 *c-1*

P. E. GUERIN

This importers and manufacturer of decorative hardware and bath accessories is actually the oldest American firm of its kind. *23 Jane St. (near Greenwich St.), West Village, 212/243–5270. Open by appt. only. Subway: 1, 2, 3, 9 to 14th St.*

9 *d-4*

RIO TRADING INTERNATIONAL

Rio Trading is an authorized dealer of Henckels, Swiss Army, Gerber, and Buck knives. *10 W. 46th St., Midtown, 212/819–0304. Subway: B, D, F, Q to 42nd St.*

9 *e-7*

SIMON'S HARDWARE & BATH

This busy, highly regarded shop has ample decorative hardware plus tools and supplies. Trust them; they're problem-solvers. *421 3rd Ave. (near 30th St.), Murray Hill, 212/532–9220. Closed Sun. Subway: 6 to 28th St.*

9 *c-8*

WILLIAMS-SONOMA

The famed San Francisco kitchen-supply company is on fertile ground in New York, with attractive, sturdy wares, well-stocked stores, and a total understanding of the yuppie aesthetic. There's a culinary consultant on hand, and the occasional cooking demonstration. For bargain-bin discounts, *see Williams-Sonoma Outlet Center, below*. *110 7th Ave. (near 17th St.), Chelsea, 212/633–2203. Subway: 1, 2, 3, 9 to 14th St.*

9 *e-2*

20 E. 60th St. (near Madison Ave.), Upper East Side, 212/980–5155. Subway: 59th St.

9 *f-1*

1309 2nd Ave. (near 69th St.), Upper East Side, 212/288–8408. Subway: 68th St./Hunter College.

7 *e-7*

1175 Madison Ave. (near 86th St.), Upper East Side, 212/289–6832. Subway: 4, 5, 6 to 86th St.

9 *b-7*

WILLIAMS-SONOMA OUTLET CENTER

Pinch us, we must be dreaming—outlet shopping in Manhattan? Now that West Chelsea's become an art lair, you have a reason to trek out here and examine the excess and marked-down merchandise from Williams-Sonoma's mail-order catalogs and stores: Williams-Sonoma (cookware), Chambers (bed and bath linens), Gardener's Eden (garden implements), Hold Everything (storage and organization), and Pottery Barn (tabletop and decorative accessories). The huge inventory fills three floors of this bare-bones warehouse and sells for 30%–70% off. *231 10th Ave. (near 24th St.), Chelsea, 212/206–8118. Subway: C, E to 23rd St.*

7 *b-8*

ZABAR'S

The gourmet giant's housewares department is on the mezzanine. *2245 Broadway (near 80th St.), Upper West Side, 212/787–2000. Subway: 79th St.*

lamps & lighting

Department stores stock both modern and traditional lamps, and many neighborhood houseware and hardware stores carry inexpensive modern fixtures. The Bowery from Delancey to Grand Streets is the city's cash-and-carry district for discounted lamps and light fixtures; shop after shop offers what's new and modern or—in most cases—what's tacky and tasteless, all below list prices.

11 *e-5*

ARTEMIDE

Artemide's very modern line of Italian lighting—tabletop, floor, hanging, and wall-mounted—includes the now-classic Tizio desk lamp. *46 Greene St. (near Broome St.), SoHo, 212/925–1588. Subway: Spring St.; A, C, E, N, R to Canal St.*

9 *c-8*

BARRY OF CHELSEA

Here's an antique twist: Barry specializes in original American lighting from 1880 to 1940. *154 9th Ave. (near 19th St.), Chelsea, 212/242–2666. Closed Sun.–Mon. Subway: C, E to 23rd St.*

9 *e-8*

JUST BULBS

Just Bulbs is just that—nearly 3,000 light bulbs of every description, for every need. This Flatiron shop is great for the hard-to-find. *938 Broadway (at 22nd St.), 212/228–7820. Closed weekends. Subway: N, R to 23rd St.*

11 *g-5*

JUST SHADES

Look no further for that elusive dream shade: SoHo has New York's largest selection of lampshades. Every size and material is discounted 20%–30%. If you're still attached to the old girl, Just Shades can help you re-cover her. *21 Spring St. (at Elizabeth St.), 212/966–2757. Closed Wed. Subway: 6 to Spring St.*

9 *c-3*

LEE'S STUDIO

Lee specializes in designer lighting from such makers as Halo, Lightolier, Kovacs, Artemide, Flos, and from smaller firms. There's a good selection of bulbs, and the studio will install, rent, and repair your lighting after helpful consultations. *1755 Broadway (at 56th St.), Midtown, 212/581–4400. Subway: 59th St./Columbus Circle; 1069 3rd Ave. (at 63rd St.), Upper East Side, 212/371–1122. Subway: 59th St.*

11 *g-5*

LIGHTING BY GREGORY

An almost overwhelming shopping experience, this store carries everything a body needs in residential and stage lighting. Rentals are available. *158 Bowery (between Delancey and Broome Sts.), Lower East Side, 212/226–1276. Subway: Grand St.*

9 *f-2*

THE LIGHTING CENTER

The Lighting Center has a generous selection of domestic and imported lighting and a critical mass of bulbs. *111 2nd Ave. (at 59th St.), Midtown, 212/888–8383. Subway: 59th St.*

9 *c-8*

LIGHTFORMS

The mostly modern, groovy lighting by a variety of U.S. and foreign designers is accompanied by a full line of bulbs, shades, and dimmers. Repairs are made on-site. *168 8th Ave. (between 18th and*

19th Sts.), Chelsea, 212/255–4664. Subway: C, E to 23rd St.

7 *b-7*

509 Amsterdam Ave. (between 84th and 85th Sts.), Upper West Side, 212/875–0407. Subway: 1, 9 to 86th St.

paint & wallpaper

Hardware stores carry basic paints and supplies; the extent of the stock depends mainly on the size of the shop. The stores below are specialists.

11 *c-4*

JANOVIC/PLAZA

This wholesale and retail paint-and-wallpaper center has 15,000 wallpaper patterns and will mix paint to match any one of them. Bath, fabric, and window departments keep your imagination whirring. The professional staff is expert, and delivery is free. *161 6th Ave. (near Spring St.), SoHo, 212/627–1100. Subway: Spring St.*

9 *c-7*

213 7th Ave. (near 23rd St.), Chelsea, 212/243–2186. Subway: 1, 9 to 23rd St.

9 *e-1*

1150 3rd Ave. (at 67th St.), Upper East Side, 212/772–1400. Subway: 68th St./Hunter College.

9 *b-1*

159 W. 72nd St., Upper West Side, 212/595–2500. Subway: 72nd St.

pillows

Most department stores and home-furnishing stores carry decorative pillows.

9 *e-8*

ABC CARPET & HOME

This may be the largest selection of decorative and throw pillows in New York. *888 Broadway (at 19th St.), Flatiron, 212/473–3000. Subway: 14th St./Union Square; N, R to 23rd St.*

11 *c-1*

AMALGAMATED HOME

Amalgamated has a small selection of well-chosen, highly funky pillows in interesting materials. *Christopher St. (between Greenwich Ave. and Gay St.), West Village, 212/255–4160. Subway: 1, 2, 3, 9 to 14th St.*

9 *d-8*

BANANA REPUBLIC HOME

The new home collection in this popular clothing chain features many pillows as well as sheets, tabletop items, and other accessories. *128 5th Ave. (at 16th St.), Flatiron, 212/366–4630. Subway: F to 14th St.*

9 *d-3*

BERGDORF GOODMAN

The 7th-floor home-furnishing department stocks classic high-end pillows. *754 5th Ave. (at 57th St.), Midtown, 212/753–7300. Subway: E, F, N, R to 5th Ave.*

11 *h-3*

ECONOMY FOAM & FUTON CENTER

Foam is cut to size and shape while you wait, or shredded by the pound for "piller filler." Fiberfill is another option. The Center also sells ready-made decorative and bed pillows, foam mattresses, designer sheets and spreads, and futons, all closing out at 30%–50% off retail. Accompaniments include custom covers, wall coverings, and upholstery fabric and vinyl. *173 E. Houston St. (at 1st Ave.), East Village, 212/473–4462. Closed Sat. Subway: 2nd Ave.*

11 *e-8*

IZ DESIGN

These chenille and velvet throw pillows are designed by Elizabeth Tapper. *92 Reade St. (near Broadway), Tribeca, 212/608–4223. Subway: Chambers St.*

7 *b-7*

LAYTNER'S LINEN & HOME

Laytner's West Side branch has throw pillows ranging from classic to corduroy, damask to down. *2270 Broadway (at 81st.St.) Upper West Side, 212/724–0180. Subway: 79th St.*

11 *h-3*

PILLOW TALK

Head over to Ludlow Street for custom-made seat cushions, decorative pillows, and sleeping pillows in every shape and size; you pick the filling. *See also Linens–Quilts & Duvets, below. 174 Ludlow St. (near Houston St.), 212/477–1788. Closed Sat. Subway: 2nd Ave.*

`9` e-1

THE PILLOWRY

Start thinking now; many of the Pillowry's unusual pillows come from antique textiles and rugs, including kilims from Persia, Afghanistan, Turkey, Russia, and Romania. Other decorative options are old silk, needlepoint, damask, ikat, homespun, Aubusson, and lace. Tapestries and rugs frame your pillows in style, and expert restoration ensures that they'll outlive you. *19 E. 69th St., 3rd floor, Upper East Side, 212/628–3844. Closed Sat. except by appt. Subway: 68th St./Hunter College.*

`9` e-3

PORTANTINA

This small shop carries a beautiful line of pillows in velvet, silk, and satin, all designed by Susan Unger. *895 Madison Ave. (at 55th St.), Upper East Side, 212/472–0636. Subway: 59th St.*

wicker

`11` C-2

BAZAAR

Vaguely chaotic in appearance, Bazaar is nonetheless a solid option for wicker (and other) furnishings at reasonable prices. There's also a full line of housewares, which accost you visually as you approach the store. *125 W. 3rd St. (between 6th Ave. and MacDougal St.), Greenwich Village, 212/673–4138. Subway: W. 4th St./Washington Square.*

`9` f-7

501 2nd Ave. (near 28th St.), Murray Hill, 212/683–2293. Subway: 6 to 28th St.

`7` c-7

540 Columbus Ave. (near 86th St.), Upper West Side, 212/362–7335. Subway: 1, 9 to 86th St.; other locations. Closed Sun.

`11` e-4

COCONUT COMPANY

High-style furniture and decorative *objets* for the home come in wicker and rattan—not to mention wood. Many of the pieces are from Bali and Indonesia. *129 Greene St. (between Houston and Prince Sts.), SoHo, 212/539–1940. Subway: Prince St.*

`7` e-6

PAMELA SCURRY'S WICKER GARDEN

Pamela Scurry specializes in antique wicker furniture for both adults' and children's rooms. *1318–27 Madison Ave. (between 93rd and 94th Sts.), Upper East Side, 212/348–1166. Open by appt. only. Subway: 6 to 96th St.*

`7` e-7

PIER 1 IMPORTS

Widely popular for its attractive and affordable furnishings, Pier 1 is a main source for contemporary wicker furniture and accessories. *1550 3rd Ave. (at 87th St.), Upper East Side, 212/987–1746. Subway: 4, 5, 6 to 86th St.*

`10` e-1

71 5th Ave. (between 14th and 15th Sts.), Flatiron, 212/206–1911. Subway: 14th St./Union Square.

`9` e-5

461 5th Ave. (at 40th St.), Midtown, 212/447–1610. Subway: B, D, F, Q to 42nd St.

JEWELRY

New York's wholesale and retail jewelry center, also known as the Diamond District, is West 47th Street between 5th and 6th avenues. Taken together, these stores offer a dazzling selection of gold, silver, and precious stones in antique, traditional, and modern designs. The proximity of shops and stalls makes comparison shopping easy, pleasant, and—since prices are not necessarily firm—eminently practical. *See* Historic Buildings & Areas *in* Chapter 2.

The large department stores have basic but attractive collections of gold and silver jewelry (*see* Silver, *below*).

antique & collectible

`9` e-3

ALICE KWARTLER

Kwartler has amassed one of the city's largest collections of cufflinks, supplemented by such Victorian items as lockets and cameos. *123 E. 57th St., Midtown, 212/752–3590. Subway: 59th St.*

`9` e-3

ARES RARE

The time line here is very long: Ares has jewelry from antiquity through the 1940s, though the focus does fall in the 19th and early 20th centuries. The store will appraise any piece, and offers a selection of books on jewelry. *605 Madison Ave. (between 57th and 58th Sts.), 4th floor, Midtown, 212/758–5340. Subway: 59th St.*

CAMILLA DIETZ BERGERON

Bergeron deals in period jewelry from all over the world, including a good selection of cufflinks, from her Upper East Side apartment. *212/794–9100. Open by appt. only.*

9 e-1

DECO DELUXE

Specializing in jewelry from the Art Deco period, Deco Deluxe also has a good selection of Bakelite. *993 Lexington Ave. (between 71st and 72nd Sts.), Upper East Side, 212/472–7222. Subway: 68th St./Hunter College.*

10 e-1

DULLSVILLE

Bakelite, Bakelite, Bakelite, in all of its adornment forms. *143 E. 13th St. East Village, 212/505–2505. Subway: 3rd Ave.*

7 e-8

EDITH WEBER & ASSOCIATES

This period jewelry includes pieces formerly owned by such luminaries as Andy Warhol, Queen Victoria, and even Napoleon. *994 Madison Ave. (at 77th St.), Upper East Side, 212/570–9668. Subway: 77th St.*

10 e-1

FICHERA & PERKINS

We can't resist calling this a gem of a place; it has a fine variety of vintage pieces at prices to suit almost anyone's budget. *50 University Pl. (between 9th and 10th Sts.), Greenwich Village, 212/533–1430. Subway: 8th St.*

9 e-1

FRED LEIGHTON, LTD.

Devoted exclusively to luxurious and rare antique and estate jewelry, Leighton emphasizes the 1920s, particularly extravagant Cartier pieces. Other chronological concentrations are the 1800s and the 1950s. *773 Madison Ave. (at 66th St.), Upper East Side, 212/288–1872. Subway: 68th St./Hunter College.*

9 e-3

Trump Tower (725 5th Ave., at 56th St.), 3rd floor, Midtown, 212/751–2330. Subway: E, F to 5th Ave.

ILENE CHAZENOF

Jewelry and *objets* from the late 19th to mid-20th centuries range across the Victorian, Art Deco, Art Nouveau, and Retro Moderne styles and are priced very reasonably. Add to this Arts-and-Crafts jewelry, metalwork, and furniture, and 1950s Scandinavian and Italian glass. The proprietor is knowledgeable and lovely, and her services include research, shipping, appraisal, and rental. Prices range from $1–$5,000. *212/254–5564. Open by appt. only. Closed Sun.*

9 e-3

JAMES II GALLERIES

Victorian jewelry is a focus here, as is fin-de-siècle agate jewelry. *11 E. 57th St., 4th floor, Midtown, 212/355–7040. Subway: N, R to 5th Ave.*

7 e-8

J. MAVEC & CO.

Mavec carries a wonderful selection of stick pins and other unique pieces, and hosts occasional exhibits of unusual items with an animal or garden theme. *946 Madison Ave. (between 74th and 75th Sts.), Upper East Side, 212/517–7665. Subway: 77th St.*

9 e-2

JULIE ARTISANS' GALLERY

This Madison Ave. standby draws you in with a window full of Bakelite; inside are vintage designer pieces and some contemporary baubles as well. The owner, Julie Schafler Dale, is the author of *Wearable Art. 687 Madison Ave. (at 60th St.), Upper East Side, 212/688–2345. Subway: 59th St.*

9 e-2

A LA VIEILLE RUSSIE

Focuses here are authentic Fabergé jewelry and accessories and American and European period jewelry, especially Victorian pieces. *781 5th Ave. (at 59th St.), Midtown, 212/752–1727. Subway: N, R to 5th Ave.*

9 e-2

MACKLOWE GALLERY

Impressive and expensive, this jewelry hails mainly from the Art Deco, Georgian, Victorian, and Art Nouveau periods. Repairs are made on the premises. *667 Madison (between 60th and 61st Sts.), Upper East Side, 212/517–7665. Subway: 59th St.*

11 *d-4*
MULLEN & STACY
Mullen & Stacy is for the serious Bakelite collector, ready to pay serious prices. *98 Thompson (between Spring and Prince Sts.), SoHo, 212/226–4240. Subway: C, E to Spring St.*

9 *e-1*
PRIMAVERA GALLERY
Elegant Primavera has a stellar selection of Art Deco, Art Nouveau, and Victorian jewelry. *808 Madison Ave. (near 68th St.), Upper East Side, 212/288–1569. Subway: 68th St./Hunter College.*

7 *e-8*
SYLVIA PINES UNIQUITIES
The name is clever, no? Sylvia Pines has a truly exquisite array of antique and estate jewelry—from Victorian to Deco, with some Georgian pieces thrown in. Deco marquisite is a particular strength, and the collection of beaded and jeweled bags, bronzes, picture frames, and enameled boxes is spectacular. *1102 Lexington Ave. (near 77th St.), Upper East Side, 212/744–5141. Subway: 77th St.*

contemporary

9 *d-3*
AARON FABER
Imaginative contemporary designs in gold join a fine collection of vintage wristwatches. Every eight weeks the upstairs gallery showcases a particular artist. Custom work, repairs, and restoration are available. *666 5th Ave. (between 52nd and 53rd Sts.), Midtown, 212/586–8411. Subway: E, F to 5th Ave.*

11 *e-1*
BIJOUX
French-born Sophie Pujebet's jewelry comes in gold and silver. Look into custom wedding rings. *127 E. 7th St., East Village, 212/777–1669. Subway: Astor Pl.; 2nd Ave.*

9 *e-3*
BUCCELLATI
Each piece from this renowned Milanese silver- and goldsmith is uniquely handcrafted. Peruse finely created artisan pieces with precious stones and gold pieces in the medium range (a relative term). *Trump Tower (725 5th Ave., at 56th St.), Midtown, 212/308–5533. Subway: E, F to 5th Ave.; 46 E. 57th St., Midtown, 212/308–2900. Subway: N, R to 5th Ave.*

9 *e-2*
BULGARI
Carving its name in distinctive Roman caps, this firm is internationally known for fine precious jewels. *730 5th Ave. (at 57th St.), Midtown, 212/315–9000*

9 *e-2*
Pierre Hotel, 2 E. 61st St., Upper East Side, 212/486–0326. Subway: N, R to 5th Ave.

9 *e-3*
CARTIER
One of Cartier's main attractions is its shell: the store is in a beautiful former mansion traded to Cartier for two strands of Oriental pearls. Inside you'll find jewelry, silver, fine porcelain, picture frames, and all the other prestige items that have become modern classics. *653 5th Ave. (at 52nd St.), Midtown, 212/753–0111. Subway: E, F to 5th Ave.*

9 *e-3*
Trump Tower (725 5th Ave., at 56th St.), Midtown, 212/308–0840. Subway: E, F to 5th Ave.

9 *e-1*
Westbury Hotel (Madison Ave. and 69th St.), Upper East Side, 212/249–3240. Subway: 68th St./Hunter College.

9 *e-3*
FORTUNOFF
The self-appointed "Source" is four floors of contemporary and antique gold, silver, diamonds, watches, flatware, and pewter, all at very special prices. You'll find Georg Jensen, Oneida, Reed & Barton, and Dansk, and others. *681 5th Ave. (near 54th St.), 212/758–6660. Subway: E, F to 5th Ave.*

9 *d-3*
HARRY WINSTON
The largest, rarest, finest gems in the world are behind these lovely locked doors. The wealthy don't just buy Harry Winston jewelry; they invest in it. *718 5th Ave. (at 56th St.), Midtown, 212/245–2000*

9 *e-3*
Trump Tower (725 5th Ave., at 56th St.), 2nd level, Midtown, 212/245–2000. Subway: E, F to 5th Ave.

9 e-2

MICHAEL DAWKINS
Many of these well-priced silver and gold pieces have pearl accents. *33 E. 65th St., Upper East Side, 212/639–9822. Subway: 68th St./Hunter College.*

9 e-1

MISHON MISHON
Here is the latest designer jewelry, in precious metals with precious and semiprecious stones. It's expensive, but the best sales can yield a buy. *899 Madison Ave. (near 72nd St.), Upper East Side, 212/288–7599. Subway: 68th St./Hunter College.*

9 e-1

REINSTEIN/ROSS
Much of this handmade jewelry has a medieval feel, often with cabochon stones. It's all designed by Susan Reinstein. *29 E. 73rd St., Upper East Side, 212/772–1901. Subway: 77th St.*

11 e-4

122 Prince St. (between Greene and Wooster Sts.), SoHo, 212/226–4513. Subway: Prince St.

11 d-5

ROBERT LEE MORRIS
Each one made by Morris himself, these adornments —necklaces, bracelets, earrings, belt buckles, hair ornaments—are really works of art. *400 W. Broadway (between Broome and Spring Sts.), 212/431–9405. Subway: C, E to Spring St.*

11 e-5

TED MUEHLING
These special pieces are designed by Muehling and other artists, including Gabriella Kiss. Owning one is worth the investment. *47 Greene St. (between Grand and Broome Sts.), SoHo, 212/431–3825. Subway: A, C, E, N, R to Canal St.*

9 e-3

TIFFANY & CO.
Now over a century old, the beloved treasure house still makes an elegant ground zero for fine gold and silver jewelry, including the designs of Jean Schlumberger, Elsa Peretti, and Paloma Picasso; diamond engagement rings; famous-name watches; gems; crystal, china, and sterling; clocks; and stationery. The newest additions are Tiffany's own scarves and perfume.

Don't be intimidated; there are some very reasonably priced items here. The windows are almost as famous as the interior—have a look at both. *727 5th Ave. (at 57th St.), Midtown, 212/755–8000. Subway: E, F, N, R to 5th Ave.*

9 d-3

VAN CLEEF & ARPELS
The name is synonymous with price and perfection. The Bergdorf Goodman setting is tiny, but it easily packs a king's ransom of diamonds, rubies, emeralds, pearls, and platinum. *744 5th Ave. (at 57th St.), Midtown, 212/644–9500. Subway: E, F, N, R to 5th Ave.*

costume
The large department stores and many boutiques have plenty of au courant costume jewelry.

11 d-4

AGATHA
Agatha's fun French jewelry encompasses everything from classic to kitsch, at good prices. *158 Spring St. (at W. Broadway), SoHo, 212/925–7701. Subway: C, E to Spring St.*

9 d-4

Rockefeller Center (Promenade, 5th Ave. between 49th and 50th Sts.), Midtown, 212/586–5890. Subway: E, F to 5th Ave., 47th–50th Sts./Rockefeller Center.

9 e-1

19 E. 69th St., Upper East Side, 212/535–7500. Subway: 68th St./Hunter College.

9 e-1

611 Madison Ave. (at 58th St.), Upper Midtown, 212/758–4301. Subway: N, R to 5th Ave.

9 e-1

DIAMOND ESSENCE
All of these fantastic faux diamonds are set in 14K gold, and the faux pearls are attractive as well. Only you will know they're not real. *784 Madison Ave. (between 66th and 67th Sts.), Upper East Side, 212/472–2690. Subway: 68th St./Hunter College.*

9 e-3

ERWIN PEARL
This store is by no means just pearls, but it must be said that the big draw is the replica of Jackie O's famous triple-strand pearl necklace. You'll pay some-

what less than that piece fetched at auction. *677 5th Ave. (between 53rd and 54th Sts.), Midtown, 212/207–3820. Subway: E, F to 5th Ave.*

9 *e-3*

697 Madison Ave. (at 62nd St.), Upper East Side, 212/753–3155. Subway: 59th St.

9 *e-4*

GALE GRANT

Grant specializes in reproductions of such high-priced originals as Chanel and Tiffany. *485 Madison Ave. (between 51st and 52nd Sts.), 212/752–3142. Subway: 51st St./Lexington–3rd Aves.*

9 *b-1*

SAVAGE

Here's a motley crew: jewelry from hip to ethnic to kitsch to classic, plus a good many watches. *267 Columbus Ave. (at 72nd St.), Upper West Side, 212/724–4662. Subway: 72nd St.*

KITES

7 *e-7*

BIG CITY KITES

Your spirits will soar in this joyful venue, with 200 varieties of colorful kites for every level of expertise and aspiration. Accessories include kite-making supplies and air toys. Prices range from $2 to $200. *1201 Lexington Ave. (near 81st St.), Upper East Side, 212/472–2623. Subway: 77th St.*

LINENS

Barneys New York, Bergdorf Goodman, Bloomingdale's, and Macy's all have fine linen departments; hit them up for discounts during the January and August white sales. Year-round bargains are available on the Lower East Side, specifically Grand Street from Allen to Forsyth Streets for first-quality seconds and discontinued designer lines. The Lower East Side shops are closed on Saturday; just remember that when they open again on Sunday, they fill with crowds.

9 *e-8*

ABC CARPET & HOME

This ever-exciting gallery of shops has a fine selection of imported and domestic bed and bath linens, as well as custom services. *888 Broadway (at 19th St.), Flatiron, 212/677–6970. Subway: 14th St./Union Square; N, R to 23rd St.*

11 *d-4*

AD HOC SOFTWARES

Creative and intriguing, this selection of sheets, blankets, bath towels, kitchen towels, and table linens ranges from tradtional to funky. It's always fun to see how they throw things together. *410 W. Broadway (at Spring St.), SoHo, 212/925–2652. Subway: C, E to Spring St.*

9 *d-8*

BED, BATH, & BEYOND

This store is the size of an airplane hangar. Grab a shopping cart and fill it from the hundreds of options in discounted bedding. *620 6th Ave. (at 19th St.), Chelsea, 212/255–3550. Subway: F to 14th St.*

11 *h-5*

EZRA COHEN

Known far and wide for its splendid selection of discount merchandise, Cohen carries the latest in sheets from every brand plus famous-maker bedspreads. Down comforters come both ready- and custom-made. Cover your bed and soften your bathroom for 15%–30% off retail. *275 Grand St. (near Eldridge St.), Lower East Side, 212/431–9025 Closed Sat. Subway: Grand St.*

9 *e-1*

FRETTE

Frette makes Italian bed and table linens and lingerie of very fine quality. It's expensive, but still cheaper than Porthault (*see below*). *799 Madison Ave. (near 67th St.), Upper East Side, 212/988–5221. Closed Sun. Subway: 68th St./Hunter College.*

9 *e-1*

GRACIOUS HOME

If it's quality and good taste you want, Gracious Home has linens for every room in your house. The sizable stock of high-end bed linens includes makers like Peter Reed, Designer's Guild, and Palais Royal; top them off with bed blankets, decorative throws, and baby bedding. Designer table linens for both everyday use and special occasions come in every price range. The folks over in bathroom linens make a point of stocking towels to match any bathroom color. The staff is knowledgeable and helpful. *1220 3rd Ave. (near 70th St.), Upper East Side, 212/517–6300. Subway: 68th St./Hunter College.*

11 *h-5*
HARRIS LEVY
It's hectic, but this Lower East Side experience is worth the trouble for 20%–40% discounts on name-brand bed linens, bathroom linens, and imported tablecloths. The second floor features custom- and ready-made curtains, bedspreads, dust ruffles, throw pillows, lamp shades, and draperies. *278 Grand St. (near Eldridge St.), Lower East Side, 212/226–3102. Closed Sat. Subway: Grand St.*

7 *f-7*
LAYTNER'S LINEN
East and west, Laytner's delivers high-quality designer linens for the bed, bath, and table. *237 E. 86th St., Upper East Side, 212/996–4439. Subway: 4, 5, 6 to 86th St.*

7 *b-7*
2270 Broadway (near 81st St.), Upper West Side, 212/724–0180. Subway: 79th St.

9 *e-2*
LERON
Beautiful hand-sewn linens and lingerie can be matched here with Old World handmade lace and appliquées. Leron will custom-embroider table linens and towels to match any fabric. *750 Madison Ave. (near 65th St.), Upper East Side, 212/753–6300. Closed Sun.; closed Sat in July and Aug. Subway: 68th St./Hunter College.*

9 *e-1*
POLO/RALPH LAUREN
Ascend to the fourth floor for a wide selection of bedding, including sheets, wool and cotton blankets, decorative comforters, down pillows, and duvets. The "White Label" bedding features an astonishing thread count of 350. Ample towels come in bath, hand, and beach sizes; table linens come in popular patterns. They will match department-store prices if you ask. *867 Madison Ave. (at 72nd St.), Upper East Side, 212/606–2100. Closed Sun. Subway: 68th St./Hunter College.*

9 *e-1*
PORTHAULT
Porthault makes the Rolls-Royce of sheets. The store's exclusive and extravagantly expensive line of 100%-cotton bed linens come in 600 prints in a variety of colors. You can also shop for table and bath linens, exquisite children's clothes, and gift items. *18 E. 69th St., Upper East Side, 212/688–1660. Subway: 68th St./Hunter College.*

11 *d-4*
PORTICO BED & BATH
A discerning eye creates this special mix of fine domestic and imported linens for the bed and bath. Portico also has a wide array of cast- and wrought-iron beds. The abundance of bath and body products makes shopping here a sensual experience. *139 Spring St. (at Wooster St.), SoHo, 212/941–7722. Subway: Spring St.*

9 *e-8*
903 Broadway (at 20th St.), Flatiron, 212/328–4343. Subway: N, R to 23rd St.

7 *c-7*
450 Columbus Ave. (near 81st St.), Upper West Side, 212/579–9500. Subway: 79th St.

9 *e-1*
PRATESI
Pratesi has been manufacturing fine bed, bath, and table linens in Florence since the turn of the century, as well as linens and clothing for infants. It's all mighty expensive. *829 Madison Ave. (at 69th St.), Upper East Side, 212/288–2315. Subway: 68th St./Hunter College.*

7 *e-7*
SCHWEITZER LINEN
An established purveyor of fine imported linens, Schweitzer specializes in sleeping pillows, custom-made to odd sizes in both down and poly. *1132 Madison Ave. (near 84th St.), Upper East Side, 212/249–8361. Subway: 4, 5, 6 to 86th St.*

quilts & duvets
Most major department stores carry ready-made quilts with a variety of fillings and prices.

7 *e-6*
DOWN & QUILT SHOP
These folks will custom-design your bedroom. They've got plenty to work

with: private-label down quilts and down pillows; downlike polyester fiberfill quilts and pillows (for customers with allergies); antique iron beds; hundreds of sheets and duvet covers; patchwork quilts; floor coverings; and probably whatever else you've dreamed up. *1225 Madison Ave. (near 88th St.), Upper East Side, 212/423–9358. Subway: 4, 5, 6 to 86th St.*

7 *c-7*

518 Columbus Ave. (near 85th St.), Upper West Side, 212/496–8980. Subway: 4, 5, 6 to 86th St.

11 *h-3*

I. ITZKOWITZ

Itzkowitz is the best quilt man in America, and, alas, the last of a breed. You pick the filling and the covering, and he'll make you a new quilt or refurbish your old one. Go for a custom-made sleeping pillow, too. *174 Ludlow St. (near Houston St.), Lower East Side, 212/477–1788. Closed Sat. Subway: 2nd Ave.*

10 *g-3*

J. SCHACHTER

This longtime Lower East Side source has new digs from which to wow you with their custom- and ready-made comforters and quilts. Choose a new filling, design, and covering, or have your favorite old patchwork quilt made into a comforter. Schachter will also re-cover and sterilize your down comforters and pillows. Current domestic and imported linens are 25%–40% off. *85 Ludlow St. (near Delancey St.), Lower East Side, 212/533–1150 or 800/468–6233. Closed Sat. Subway: Delancey St.*

LEATHER GOODS

11 *h-5*

BRIDGE MERCHANDISE CORPORATION

This substantial store substantially discounts its substantial selection of leatherwear. *100 Orchard Street (between Delancey and Broome Sts.), Lower East Side, 212/674–6320. Closed Fri. and Sat. Subway: Delancey St.*

9 *e-3*

COACH

Coach legend holds that the founders were inspired by the sturdy yet supple leather of a baseball glove. Now hand-bags and accessories come in the classic glove-tanned leather plus some textured leathers (the pebbly Madison line, the Berkeley suede) and a water-resistant leather. All bags come in a range of colors, some including the likes of russet or pale blue as well as warm browns and black. In the past few years, Coach has expanded its wares into dressy shoes and even men's clothing. The 342 Madison Avenue store carries exclusively business accessories. *595 Madison Ave. (at 57th St.), Midtown, 212/754–0041. Subway: 59th St.*

9 *e-2*

710 Madison Ave. (at 63rd St.), Upper East Side, 212/319–1772. Subway: 59th St.

9 *e-5*

342 Madison Ave. (at 44th St.), Midtown, 212/599–4777. Subway: 42nd St./Grand Central.

10 *d-6*

The Mall at the World Trade Center (Church and Vesey Sts.), Lower Manhattan, 212/488–0080. Subway: World Trade Ctr.; other locations.

9 *f-3*

LEATHERCRAFT PROCESS

Since 1919 these specialists have been treating shearlings, sheepskins, suede, and leather garments. Drop your cargo at Meurice Cleaners. *245 E. 57th St., Midtown, 212/564–8980. Subway: 59th St.*

11 *b-2*

LEATHER MAN

An emporium for custom-designed leather jackets, pants, vests, tees, and briefs, many of which lean toward the homoerotic, is perfectly understandable on this block, only a few doors from the site of the Stonewall Riot and the beginnings of Gay Lib. Prices are moderately high, the quality first-rate. *111 Christopher Street (between Bleecker and Hudson Sts.), West Village, 212/243–5339. Subway: Christopher St./Sheridan Square.*

10 *2-f*

TRASH & VAUDEVILLE

They've worked hard, here in the guts of Lou Reed and Ramones territory, to perfect the punk look in leather: jackets, boots, and accessories that will help you to pass as a native east of Avenue A. *4 St. Mark's Pl., East Village, 212/982–3590. Subway: Astor Pl.*

LUGGAGE

11 *h-4*

ALTMAN LUGGAGE

Come down east for luggage, trunks and other leather goods from American Tourister, Travelpro, Andiamo, Delsey, Kenneth Cole, Briggs & Riley, Samsonite, and Halliburton. *135 Orchard St. (near Rivington St.), Lower East Side, 212/ 254–7275. Subway: Delancey St.*

10 *e-1*

THE BAG HOUSE

Well placed in a university neighborhood, The Bag House has a huge selection of soft luggage: backpacks and duffels from brands like Jansport, Manhattan Portage, Tumi, Gregory, Club USA, Le Sportsac, Kipling, EastPak, and Temba. The service isn't always as sweet as the selection. *797 Broadway (between 10th and 11th Sts.), Greenwich Village, 212/260–0940. Subway: 8th St.; Astor Pl.*

10 *e-7*

INNOVATION LUGGAGE

This chain has everything from the hardy to the hip, at not-bad prices. Service is not always savvy about the merchandise, but Innovation's best when you've got a flight the next morning and have just discovered a tear in your favorite garment bag. *83 Maiden Lane (at William St.), Lower Manhattan, 212/ 509–0258. Subway: Wall St.*

9 *e-5*

10 E. 34th St., Murray Hill, 212/685–4611. Subway: 33rd St.

9 *f-5*

300 E. 42nd St., Midtown, 212/599–2998. Subway: 42nd St./Grand Central.

9 *c-3*

1755 Broadway (at 57th St.), Midtown, 212/582–2044. Subway: 59th St./Columbus Circle.

MAPS

9 *e-2*

ARGOSY BOOK STORE

Argosy has been known for its fine maps and atlases since 1924. *116 E. 59th St., Midtown, 212/753–4455. Subway: 59th St.*

11 *f-5*

DOWN EAST ENTERPRISES

This store deals primarily with books on outdoor travel, so within its solid selection of maps are those of our National Parks. *50 Spring St. (between Lafayette and Mulberry Sts.), SoHo/Little Italy, 212/ 925–2632. Subway: 6 to Spring St.*

9 *d-5*

HAGSTROM MAP AND TRAVEL CENTER

Makers of the familiar yellow-and-green city maps, Hagstrom specializes, of course, in cartography, globes, and atlases. *57 W. 43rd St., Midtown, 212/ 398–1222. Subway: B, D, F, Q to 42nd St.*

9 *d-3*

RAND MCNALLY—THE MAP AND TRAVEL STORE

A household name in travel aids, Rand sells guidebooks, maps, travel literature, luggage, gifts, and accessories in its own, peaceful Midtown store. There's even a children's section. *150 E. 52nd St., 212/758–7488. Subway: 51st St./Lexington–3rd Aves.*

MEMORABILIA

9 *c-2*

BALLET COMPANY

Ballet memorabilia abounds here, including rare programs, signed books both in and out of print, autographs, records, art, and sculpture. Peer at the opera and theater ephemera, too. *1887 Broadway (near 63rd St.), Upper West Side, 212/581–7990. Subway: 66th St./Lincoln Center.*

10 *e-5*

COLLECTOR'S STADIUM

This is your best bet for trading cards and sports-related memorabilia. *17 Warren St. (between Church St. and Broadway), Lower Manhattan, 212/353–1531. Subway: Chambers St.*

10 *c-1*

JERRY OHLINGER'S MOVIE MATERIAL STORE

Ohlinger's stocks still photos from every movie and TV show ever made, as well as movie posters. The shop is a great aid to research. *242 W. 14th St., Chelsea, 212/989–0869. Subway: 1, 2, 3, 9, A, C, E to 14th St.*

9 *d-8*

MOVIE STAR NEWS

Another New York superlative: this is one of the world's largest collections of movie-star photos, both originals and reissues. Check out the posters, too. *134 W. 18th St., Chelsea, 212/620–8160. Subway: F, 1, 2, 3, 9 to 14th St.*

11 *f-4*

NEW YORK FIREFIGHTER'S FRIEND

Clothing, accessories, and toys celebrate the fire-slayers of yore. *265 Lafayette St. (between Spring and Prince Sts.), SoHo, 212/226–3142. Subway: Prince St.; 6 to Spring St.*

9 *e-8*

RICHARD STODDARD PERFORMING ARTS BOOKS

Everything in this great selection of old, rare, and out-of-print books and ephemera relates to the performing arts. Vintage playbills, autographs, original costume and scene designs, photographs, and memorabilia keep the glamorous past alive. *18 E. 16th St., Flatiron, Room 305, 212/645–9576. Closed Wed. and Sun. Subway: 14th St./Union Square.*

MINIATURES

9 *e-8*

B. SHACKMAN & COMPANY

See Toys–New, below.

7 *e-6*

DOLLHOUSE ANTICS, INC.

Head here for your next dollhouses and all of its miniature furnishings, including fine hand-painted pieces by Natasha; accessories; and, of course, occupants. The store can provide electrification and (whoa) interior decoration. *1343 Madison Ave. (at 94th St.), Upper East Side, 212/876–2288. Subway: 6 to 96th St.*

7 *e-8*

TINY DOLL HOUSE

Tiny Doll House has everything conceivable, but in miniature. They can wire and wallpaper the house before you start tinkering—or after you're done. *1146 Lexington Ave. (between 79th and 80th Sts.), Upper East Side, 212/744–3719. Subway: 77th St.*

MUSIC BOXES

9 *c-2*

RITA FORD MUSIC BOXES

Rita Ford's is the best collection of working antique music boxes (circa 1830–1910) in the world, and it includes contemporary specimens, too. Some of the handcrafted carousels and other unique items are made expressly for this shop. The price range is wide, and the store restores and repairs as well. *19 E. 65th St., Upper East Side, 212/535–6717. Subway: 68th St./Hunter College.*

MUSIC & MUSICAL INSTRUMENTS

9 *c-2*

BROWN'S MUSIC CO.

Formerly Schirmer's, this venue is a long-established source for sheet music (new and used), books, musical gifts, instruments, and accessories. *44 W. 62nd St., Upper West Side, 212/541–6236. Subway: 59th St./Columbus Circle.*

9 *d-3*

HAVIVI VIOLINS

These folks sell and appraise violins, cellos, violas, and bows, strings, and accessories as well as repair all of the above. *881 7th Ave. (at 56th St.), Midtown, 212/265–5818. Closed weekends. Subway: N, R to 57th St.*

9 *d-3*

JOSEPH PATELSON'S MUSIC HOUSE

Patelson's is one of those rare stores whose bag you're proud to carry. This quiet, wood-floored shop near Carnegie Hall is the classical musician's haven for sheet music and scores, with an exhaustive, meticulously organized stock (both new and used), knowledgeable staff, and serious atmosphere. Your purchase is slipped into a delightfully unnecessary gray envelope adorned with Patelson's name dancing across a lute, and off you go to finger your cargo fondly before attempting to play it. *160 W. 56th St., Midtown, 212/582–5840. Subway: N, R, B, Q to 57th St.*

11 *b-2*

MATT UMANOV GUITARS

Umanov has a fine selection of new and used guitars in a wide price range, and an excellent repair department. *273*

Bleecker St. (near 7th Ave S), West Village, 212/675–2157. Subway: W. 4th St./Washington Square.

11 *c-2*

MUSIC INN

Come here for less classical instruments, such as banjos, mandolins, dobros, dulcimers, sitars, balalaikas, ethnic flutes, tabla drums, zithers, and more. Guitars are a specialty; they're sold new and used, and expertly repaired. Browse ethnic art on the side. *169 W. 4th St. (near 6th Ave.), 212/243–5715. Closed Sun.–Mon. Subway: W. 4th St./Washington Square.*

9 *d-4*

SAM ASH

If you're coming here for the first time, prepare to be whisked back to your days with the high-school band. In business since 1924, Sam Ash is popular with professional musicians for its wide inventory, good prices, and savvy staff. The wares are divided between a cluster of shops and include wind instruments and supplies; electronic keyboards, guitars, and amplifiers; and drums. Some instruments can be rented. Sheet music, scores, and books on music give you something to play. *155, 160, 166 W. 48th St., Theater District, 212/719–2299, –2625, or –5109. Closed Sun. Subway: 47th–50th Sts./Rockefeller Center.*

9 *d-3*

STEINWAY & SONS

Steinway's longtime home, this elegant showroom has soundproof rooms for practice. Appropriately, it's within whistling distance of Carnegie Hall. *109 W. 57th St., Midtown, 212/246–1100. Subway: B, Q to 57th St.*

NEEDLEWORK

9 *e-2*

ERICA WILSON NEEDLEWORKS

This store is a real resource for needle arts and supplies, including gear for knitting, embroidery, needlepoint, and crewel, and custom canvases. *717 Madison Ave. (near 63rd St.), 2nd floor, Upper East Side, 212/832–7290. Subway: 59th St.*

7 *b-7*

THE YARN COMPANY

Somebody's sewing on the Upper West Side; this shop has yarn, needles, patterns, buttons, needlepoint canvases, and kits. *2274 Broadway (near 82nd St.), 212/787–7878. Closed Sun.–Mon. Subway: 79th St.*

NEWSPAPERS & MAGAZINES

Street-corner newsstands are all over the city, most with such local essentials as *New York* and such national nonessentials as *People*. For indoor magazine browsing, try Barnes & Noble or Borders (*see Books, above*), neither of which seems to care if you hang out all day.

9 *e-4*

EASTERN NEWSSTAND

Try to imagine the better part of 3,000 different magazine titles, including many from abroad. Then come here, and live the dream. *345 Park Ave. S (between 50th and 51st Sts.), Midtown, 212/838–7081. Subway: 51st St./Lexington–3rd Aves.*

9 *d-5*

HOTALING'S NEWS AGENCY

With over 200 out-of-town newspapers and 35 foreign-language newspapers, Hotaling's is like a down-market university library. The scale of the magazine selection isn't far behind, and they throw in state maps for good measure. *142 W. 42nd St., Theater District, 212/840–1868. Subway: 42nd St./Times Square.*

11 *e-1*

HUDSON NEWS COMPANY

Hudson News is all over town, but this branch has a gratifyingly huge selection of magazines, both domestic and foreign, inspiring uptowners to make special trips. The biggest bonus: There's room to turn around, making browsing extra-pleasant. *753 Broadway (at 8th St.), Greenwich Village, 212/674–6655. Subway: 8th St.*

9 *d-7*

JAY BEE MAGAZINES

Some of these back-dated magazines and periodicals go back as far as 1888— Jay Bee has over 2 million lying around.

(Isn't that a fire hazard?) The *TV Guide* holdings go back to 1953. The setting is cluttered, but the store is now fully computerized, making it a great source for research. *134 W. 26th St., lower level, 212/675–1600. Closed weekends. Subway: F, 1, 9 to 23rd St.*

9 *c-3*

UNIVERSAL NEWS & MAGAZINE

If they don't have it, it may not exist. Universal stocks over 7,000 titles, including foreign newspapers and magazines. *977 8th Ave. (between 57th and 58th Sts.), Hell's Kitchen, 212/459–0932. Subway: N, R to 57th St.; 59th St./Columbus Circle.*

NOTIONS

Some large stores have small notions departments, but this city has a notions *street:* On West 38th Street between 5th and 6th avenues, there are 20 stores full of trimmings. Here are some of the best.

9 *d-5*

HYMAN HENDLER & SONS

It's filled to the brim with ribbons: satin, grosgrain, velvet, silk, you name it, in every color, size, and width. *67 W. 38th St., Garment District, 212/840–8393. Closed weekends. Subway: 34th St./Herald Square.*

9 *d-5*

M & J TRIMMING

All you need supply is the idea. M & J has the trimmings for any day's fashion accessories: rhinestones, studs, feathers, cords, buttons, bindings, satin ribbons, lace, eyelets, embroidered trim, silk ropes, even large feather boas. A few doors up 6th Avenue, at No. 1014, the same folks sell home-decorating accessories. *1008 6th Ave. (near 37th St.), Garment District, 212/391–9072. Closed Sun. Subway: 34th St./Herald Square.*

9 *d-5*

TINSEL TRADING COMPANY

Bring a pair of shades: this place specializes in metallic yarns, threads, lamés, gauzes, tassels, fringe, rosettes, buttons, antique ribbons, embroideries, and fabrics. There's much from the '20s and '30s. *47 W. 38th St., Garment District, 212/730–1030. Subway: 34th St./Herald Square.*

OFFICE SUPPLIES

With the recent boom in home offices, almost every home-furnishing or gift shop has its own take on office supplies or accessories (*see* Stationery, *below*).

9 *e-5*

AIRLINE STATIONERY COMPANY, INC.

Long-established and reputable, Airline is bound to have what you need. *284 Madison Ave. (at 40th St.), Midtown, 212/532–6525; 155 E. 44th St., Midtown, 212/532–9410. Subway: 42nd St./Grand Central.*

9 *e-3*

KROLL STATIONERS, INC.

This fine stationery and office-supply store also sells computer supplies and office furniture and arranges fine printing and engraving. *145 E. 54th St., Midtown, 212/750–7720. Subway: 51st St./Lexington–3rd Aves.*

9 *c-6*

STAPLES

The office-supply megastore carries everything from paper clips to paper to printers to furniture. For a full list of locations, call 800/237–0413. *1 Penn Plaza (34th St. between 7th and 8th Aves.), Garment District, 212/629–3990. Subway: 34th St./Penn Station.*

9 *e-6*

16 E. 34th St., Murray Hill, 212/683–8003. Subway: 33rd St.

9 *d-5*

1075 6th Ave. (between 40th and 41st Sts.), Midtown, 212/944–6744. Subway: B, D, F, Q to 42nd St.

7 *e-7*

1280 Lexington Ave. (between 86th and 87th Sts.), Upper East Side, 212/426–6190. Subway: 4, 5, 6 to 86th St.

PENS

9 *d-4*

ARTHUR BROWN & BROS., INC.

Arthur Brown has one of the world's largest pen selections. Every brand you can name is here—from Anson to Waterman by way of Garland, Mont Blanc, Staedtler, and everyone else—in a wide variety of styles. The store also arranges repairs. *2 W. 46th St., Mid-*

town, 212/575–5555. *Subway: B, D, F, Q to 42nd St.*

9 *d-3*

AUTHORIZED SALES AND SERVICE

This shop sells and repairs electric shavers, fine cigarette lighters, and vintage and contemporary pens. *30 W. 57th St., Midtown, 212/586–0947. Closed Sun. Subway: E, F to 5th Ave.; B, Q to 57th St.*

9 *e-8*

BERLINER PEN

Jeffrey Berliner is an true pen historian, and his shop reflects his taste in both the new and the old. Brands include Waterman, Mont Blanc, and Omas. *928 Broadway (near 22nd St.), Flatiron, 212/614–3020. Closed weekends. Subway: N, R to 23rd St.*

10 *e-5*

FOUNTAIN PEN HOSPITAL

Collectors swear by this out-of-the-way shop, to the extent that its clientele extends nationwide. Bill Cosby is a regular. You'll find all major brands, limited editions, and collectible pens, and, true to the name, they'll fix what you already own if it's ailing. *10 Warren St. (across from City Hall), Lower Manhattan, 212/964–0580. Closed weekends. Subway: Chambers St.*

9 *e-3*

MONT BLANC BOUTIQUE

The famous pen maker has a whole store for its "snow-capped" creations. *595 Madison Ave. (between 57th and 58th Sts.), Midtown, 212/223–8888. Subway: N, R to 5th Ave.*

9 *e-3*

REBECCA MOSS

Three successive generations of Mosses have run this Midtown shop; they know their high-end writing instruments. *510 Madison Ave. (at 53rd St.), Midtown, 212/832–7671. Subway: 51st St./Lexington–3rd Aves.*

9 *d-8*

SAM FLAX, INC.

Sam Flax adds school and office supplies to its admirably complete selection of art materials. *12 W. 20th St., Chelsea, 212/620–3038. Subway: F to 23rd St.*

9 *e-3*

425 Park Ave. (at 55th St.), Midtown, 212/620–3060. Subway: 59th St.

PHOTO EQUIPMENT

If you're shopping mainly for the best price, check "Arts and Leisure" in Sunday's *New York Times*, where camera stores advertise their weekly specials.

9 *c-6*

B & H PHOTO & ELECTRONICS

You may want to read up before you come: B & H stocks over 200 camera styles from top manufacturers, as well as professional photo and video equipment. *429 9th Ave. (near 33rd St.), Hell's Kitchen, 212/807–7474. Closed Sat. Subway: 34th St./Penn Station.*

10 *d-1*

CAMERA DISCOUNT CENTER

These folks will meet or beat any advertised price with these discounts on name-brand cameras. They also repair. *45 7th Ave. (near 14th St.), Chelsea, 212/206–0077. Closed Sat. Subway: 1, 2, 3, 9 to 14th St.*

9 *e-5*

FORTY-SECOND STREET PHOTO

See Electronics, above.

9 *d-6*

See Electronics, above.

9 *d-6*

WILLOUGHBY'S

This longtime top shop for cameras and audio carries a complete range of cameras, lighting, and darkroom equipment. There's even a secondhand department. *136 W. 32nd St., Garment District, 212/564–1600. Subway: 34th St./Penn Station.*

9 *e-5*

50 E. 42nd St., Midtown, 212/681–7844. Subway: 42nd St./Grand Central.

POSTCARDS

11 *c-3*

ARTFUL POSTERS LTD

Stands and stands of postcards spill onto the sidewalk in front of this tiny shop. Inside you'll find more cards, mostly photographic variety, plus a wide selection of photographic posters. Think New York City views, celebrities, and classic black-and-white photography. *194 Bleecker St. (between 6th Ave. and Mac-Dougal St.), Greenwich Village, 212/473–1747. Subway: W. 4th St./Washington Square.*

POSTERS

Most museum gift shops have some high-quality posters of art from their permanent collections, as well as banner posters from special exhibitions. *See also* Galleries–Prints & Original Posters *in* Chapter 2.

9 e-3
MOTION PICTURE ARTS GALLERY

Original movie posters take you from the silent era to the present, with the emphasis on older material, both American and European. Prices range from $20 to $10,000. *133 E. 58th St., 10th floor, Midtown, 212/223–1009. Closed Sun.–Mon. Subway: 59th St.*

9 d-8
POSTER AMERICA

These original American and European posters range from 1890 to 1960; you'll also find a few advertising graphics. The staff is friendly and knowledgeable, and will arrange custom framing. *138 W. 18th St., Chelsea, 212/206–0499. Closed Sun.–Mon. Subway: F, 1, 2, 3, 9 to 14th St.*

7 e-8
REINHOLD-BROWN GALLERY

Expect fine posters of works by Bayer, the Beggarstaffs, Bradley, Cassandre, Hohlwein, Klimt, Lautrec, Lissitzky, Macintosh, Mucha, Tschichold, Van de Velde. *26 E. 78th St., Upper East Side, 212/734–7999. Closed Sun.–Mon. Subway: 77th St.*

9 c-4
TRITON GALLERY

Triton has a huge inventory of posters featuring Broadway, Off-Broadway, and Off-Off-Broadway shows; West End productions; and dance. In much smaller form, they make nice note cards, also on sale. Custom framing is available. *323 W. 45th St., Theater District, 212/765–2472. Subway: A, C, E to 42nd St.*

RECORDS, TAPES & CDS

11 d-2
BLEECKER BOB'S GOLDEN OLDIES

Bleecker Bob specializes in New Wave music, independent labels, and British imports. The hip staff knows what's up with today's music, and the hip opening hours last well beyond midnight. *118 W. 3rd St., West Village, 212/475–9677. Subway: W. 4th St./Washington Square.*

11 c-2
BLEECKER STREET RECORDS

Billing itself as the world's largest oldies shop, this Village standby carries rock, blues, reggae, jazz, and soundtrack LPs, 45s, and CDs. *239 Bleecker St. (between 6th and 7th Aves.), 212/255–7899. Subway: W. 4th St./Washington Square.*

9 c-4
COLONY RECORDS

A Broadway institution, Colony carries the latest releases but specializes in hard-to-find items: rare and out-of-print LPs, cassettes, and CDs. *1619 Broadway (at 49th St.), 212/265–2050. Subway: N, R to 49th St.*

11 c-2
DISCORAMA

Choose from a large selection of discounted CDs; 12-inch dance records; cassettes; and videos. *186 W. 4th St. (between 6th Ave. and Christopher St.), West Village, 212/206–8417. Subway: Christopher St./Sheridan Square.*

11 c-2

Classical and clearance titles, 146 W. 4th St. (between 6th Ave. and MacDougal St.), Greenwich Village. Subway: W. 4th St./Washington Square.

9 e-8

Annex, 40 Union Square (between 16th and 17th Sts.), Flatiron, 212/260–8616. Subway: 14th St./Union Square.

9 d-5
DOWNSTAIRS RECORDS

Downstairs specializes in the hard-to-find and stocks a robust, well-organized selection of oldies. There's even a phonograph on which to give things a whirl. The helpful, music-lovin' staff brings it all together. *1026 6th Ave. (near*

38th St.), Garment District, 212/354–4684. Subway: 34th St./Herald Square.

11 *f-1*

FINYL VINYL

This amply stocked and well-organized shop features the sounds of the '30s to the '70s—everything from Robert Johnson to Bootsy Collins. They're open "8 days a week." *204 E. 6th St., East Village, 212/533–8007. Subway: 8th St.; Astor Pl.*

10 *e-1*

FOOTLIGHT RECORDS

Footlight's an excellent East Village outpost for out-of-print and hard-to-find Broadway cast albums, movie soundtracks, big bands, jazz, and vocals from the 1940s–'60s. *113 E. 12th St., East Village, 212/533–1572. Subway: 14th St./Union Square; 3rd Ave.*

9 *b-1*

GRYPHON RECORD SHOP

Within its book shop on Broadway, Gryphon has amassed scores of thousands of jazz, rock, folk, and spoken-word recordings. Down on 72nd Street, they're selling rare and out-of-print LPs, mainly classical with some soundtracks, vocals, and jazz thrown in. Prices are reasonable, and they welcome "want" lists. *251 W. 72nd St., Upper West Side, 212/874–1588. Subway: 1, 2, 3, 9 to 72nd St.*

7 *b-7*

2246 Broadway (between 80th and 81st Sts.), Upper West Side, 212/362–0706. Subway: 79th St.

9 *d-6*

HMV

With over 300,000 recordings, this English chain is giving Tower a run for its money. It's well stocked in all areas, and puts unusually appealing titles on sale up near the cash registers; have a peek. *57 W. 34th St., Garment District, 212/629–0900. Subway: 34th St./Herald Square.*

9 *e-4*

565 5th Ave. (at 46th St.), Midtown, 212/681–6700. Subway: B, D, F, Q to 42nd St., 47th–50th Sts./Rockefeller Center.

9 *b-1*

2081 Broadway (at 72nd St.), Upper West Side, 212/721–5900. Subway: 72nd St.

7 *e-7*

1280 Lexington Ave. (at 86th St.), Upper East Side, 212/348–0800. Subway: 4, 5, 6 to 86th St.

10 *e-6*

J&R MUSIC WORLD

J & R inspires faith by dividing its stock among different storefronts: classical CDs are at No. 33, jazz is at No. 25, and the rest is at No. 23. Selections are comprehensive, and, of course, you can also walk out with new equipment to play yours on (*see Electronics, above*). *23, 25, 33 Park Row (between Ann and Beekman Sts.), Lower Manhattan, 212/732–8600 (212/349–8400 for jazz, 212/349–0062 for classical). Subway: City Hall.*

11 *c-2*

MUSIC INN

Don't give up on that obscure international or ethnic title, on record, tape, *or* CD—Music Inn specializes in African music and in English, Irish, and Celtic folk. Jazz, blues, folk, and comedy are also well represented. *169 W. 4th St. (near 6th Ave.), West Village, 212/243–5715. Closed Sun.–Mon. Subway: W. 4th St./Washington Square.*

11 *d-3*

NOSTALGIA AND ALL THAT JAZZ

Recordings of jazz, movie soundtracks, and early radio broadcasts are surrounded by posters and movie stills. *217 Thompson St. (near Bleecker St.), Greenwich Village, 212/420–1940. Subway: Broadway–Lafayette St.*

11 *c-1*

SAM GOODY

Goody has a large and standard stock and offers excellent weekly sales on current recordings. Sales on specific labels pop up as well; check "Arts and Leisure" in Sunday's *New York Times* for detailed advertisements. *390 6th Ave. (between 8th St. and Waverly Pl.), West Village, 212/674–7131. Subway: W. 4th St./Washington Square.*

9 *f-5*

230 E. 42nd St., Midtown, 212/490–0568. Subway: 42nd St./Grand Central.

9 *f-2*

1011 3rd Ave. (at 60th St.), Upper East Side, 212/751–5809. Subway: 59th St.; other locations.

9 b-1

TOWER RECORDS

With over 500,000 titles, Tower is a classic New York record giant. It's all here, from current hits to obscure imports in rock, r&b, jazz, world, show tunes, and so forth. The classical section uptown may be the best anywhere, though service seems to have gone downhill since the store's high-tech makeover. Check out the downtown store's annex for bargains. *1961 Broadway (at 66th St.), Upper West Side, 212/799–2500. Subway: 66th St./Lincoln Center*

11 e-2

692 Broadway (at 4th St.), Greenwich Village, 212/505–1500. Subway: 8th St.

11 f-1

VENUS RECORDS

The stock's time line runs from the late '50s to current American and imported rock. *13 St. Mark's Pl., East Village, 212/598–4459. Subway: Astor Pl.*

11 c-3

VINYLMANIA

This never-say-die shop has used records, collector's items, LPs, and 45s, with a specialty in the 12-inch dance record. CDs and cassettes are also available. *60 Carmine St. (between 6th and 7th Aves.), West Village, 212/924–7223. Subway: W. 4th St./Washington Square.*

9 c-4

VIRGIN MEGASTORE

The largest retail music and entertainment center in the world, the looming Virgin stocks 1 million CDs in stock, including a 12,000-square-ft classical section. You feel rather like Jonah in the whale's belly. *1540 Broadway (near 45th St.), Theater District, 212/921–1020. Subway: 42nd St./Times Square.*

SILVER

See Antiques *and* Jewelry: Antique & Collectible.

9 e-3

ASPREY & CO., LTD.

This prestigious London firm is known for its exclusive silver patterns, both antique and modern, as well as crystal and china. Consider one of the luxurious gift items, such as a hand-bound book, rare first edition, or 18K-gold beard comb. *Trump Tower (725 5th Ave., at 56th St.), Midtown, 212/688–1811. Subway: E, F to 5th Ave.*

10 g-4

EASTERN SILVER CO.

Eastern carries a large general selection of silver items, and will repair and replate. *54 Canal St. (near Orchard St.), 2nd floor, Lower East Side, 212/226–5708. Closed Sat. Subway: E. Broadway.*

9 e-3

FORTUNOFF

The impressive antique-silver department at the jewelry giant has American, Georgian, Russian, and Chinese silverware; tea services and various *objets* as well as contemporary flatware in sterling, plate, and stainless. *681 5th Ave. (near 54th St.), Midtown, 212/758–6660. Subway: E, F to 5th Ave.*

9 e-3

JAMES ROBINSON

For over 70 years Robinson has purveyed fine 17th- to 19th-century English hallmark silver, rare porcelain dinner sets, and antique jewelry. The store is also known for its own hand-forged silver flatware. Upstairs, the less-formal, less-expensive James II Galleries (*see* Jewelry, *above*) have 19th-century bibelots. *480 Park Ave. (at 58th St.), Midtown, 212/752–6166. Subway: 59th St.*

9 d-4

JEAN'S SILVERSMITHS

Dropped that gravy dish? Jean's has the city's largest selection of discontinued silver patterns—over 900—plus new flat- and holloware at winning prices. *16 W. 45th St., Midtown, 212/575–0723. Closed weekends. Subway: B, D, F Q to 42nd St.*

9 d-4

MICHAEL C. FINA

This well-known store features an extensive stock of silver at substantial savings. Jewelry, sterling silver flatware, tea sets, giftware, clocks, and more. *3 W. 47th St., Midtown, 212/869–5050. Subway: 47th–50th Sts./Rockefeller Center.*

9 e-3

S. J. SHRUBSOLE

A trove of antique English and early American silver and jewelry, this is the best selection of silver in New York. *104*

E. 57th St., Midtown, 212/753–8920. Subway: 59th St.

9 *e-1*

S. WYLER, INC.

Established in 1890, S. Wyler is the oldest silver dealer in the U.S., with antique and modern silver, fine porcelain, antiques, and a replating service. *941 Lexington Ave. (at 69th St.), Upper East Side, 212/879–9848. Subway: 68th St./Hunter College.*

SPORTING GOODS & CLOTHING

general

9 *e-3*

GYM SOURCE

The largest exercise-equipment dealer in the area, Gym Source has bikes, stair and weight machines, rowers, and treadmills for rent or sale. *40 E. 52nd St., Midtown, 212/688–4222. Closed Sun. Subway: 51st St./Lexington–Park Aves.*

10 *e-5*

MODELL'S SPORTING GOODS

Family-run since 1889, Mo's has a variety of sporting goods and footwear, particularly team wear. *280 Broadway (near Chambers St.), Lower Manhattan, 212/962–6200. Subway: Chambers St.*

10 *e-6*

200 Broadway (near Fulton St.), Lower Manhattan, 212/964–4007. Subway: Fulton St.

9 *e-5*

51 E. 42nd St., Midtown, 212/661–4242. Subway: 42nd St./Grand Central.

7 *f-7*

1535 3rd Ave. (near 86th St.), Upper East Side, 212/996–3800. Subway: 4, 5, 6 to 86th St.

9 *e-8*

PARAGON SPORTING GOODS

Almost 100 years old, Paragon has the city's most impressive collection of clothes and equipment for every imaginable sport. The deep stock contains down jackets, track shoes, and shorts; baseball, football, lacrosse, golf, and hockey equipment; skates, skis, and swimwear; and camping, fishing, and

backpacking paraphernalia. Values can be excellent. *867 Broadway (at 18th St.), Flatiron, 212/255–8036. Subway: 14th St./Union Square.*

9 *e-8*

PRINCETON SKI SHOP

Make tracks here for ski equipment and apparel and the ever-important custom boot-fitting. Other specialized departments cater to tennis and in-line skating. *21 E. 22nd St., Flatiron, 212/228–4400. Subway: N, R to 23rd St.*

10 *e-6*

SPIEGEL

Spiegel has carried a good selection of sporting goods at discounted price since 1916. The staff is knowledgeable and helpful. *105 Nassau St. (at Ann St.), Lower Manhattan, 212/227–8400. Closed Sun. Subway: Fulton St.; Broadway–Nassau St.*

9 *d-6*

THE SPORTS AUTHORITY

Departments include tennis, golf, skiing, camping, footwear, apparel, and excercise. *401 7th Ave. (at 33rd St.), Garment District, 212/563–7195. Subway: 34th St./Penn Station.*

9 *f-4*

845 3rd Ave. (at 51st St.), Midtown, 212/355–9725. Subway: 51st St./Lexington–3rd Aves.

9 *d-3*

57 W. 57 St., Midtown, 212/355–6430. Subway: E, F, N, R to 5th Ave.; B, Q to 57th St.

boating

9 *d-6*

GOLDBERG'S MARINE

Head straight here for marine supplies at a discount; they've got all the necessities, finished off by foul-weather apparel. *12 W. 37th St., Garment District, 212/594–6065. Subway: 34th St./Herald Square.*

camping & climbing

11 *e-3*

EMS—THE OUTDOOR SPECIALISTS

This familiar, ruggedly spiffy chain specializes in backpacking and climbing, and is also well stocked for downhill and cross-country skiing, tennis, and running. *611 Broadway (between Houston* and Bleecker Sts.), Greenwich Village, 212 505–9860. Subway: Broadway–Lafayette St., Bleecker St.

9 c-2

20 W. 61st St., Upper West Side, 212/397–4860. Subway: 59th St./Columbus Circle.

10 e-6

TENTS & TRAILS
Top-quality camping supplies are for sale or rent next to apparel and footwear for adults and children. 21 Park Pl. (near Broadway), Lower Manhattan, 212/227–1760. Subway: Park Pl.

fishing

9 c-7

CAPITOL FISHING TACKLE CO.
A fisherman's friend since 1897, Capitol Fishing Tackle can equip you for freshwater, saltwater, deep-sea, and big-game fishing, all at ample discounts. 218 W. 23rd St., Chelsea, 212/929–6132. Closed Sun. Subway: 1, 9, C, E to 23rd St.

9 e-3

HUNTING WORLD
The Angler's World department has a fine selection of fly-fishing equipment. 16 E. 53rd St., Midtown, 212/755–3400. Subway: E, F to 5th Ave.

9 e-4

ORVIS NEW YORK
Peruse a complete line of fly rods, reels, and accessories from the oldest rod-building company in the country. 355 Madison Ave. (at 45th St.), Midtown, 212/697–3133. Subway: 42nd St./Grand Central.

9 e-7

URBAN ANGLER
True to the charming name, this Gramercy shop features fly-fishing rods and reels and the attention of a caring specialist. 118 E. 25th St., 3rd floor, 212/979–7600. Closed weekends. Subway: 6 to 23rd St.

golf

9 e-4

AL LIEBER'S WORLD OF GOLF
Lieber has the latest in well-priced golf equipment. 147 E. 47th St., 2nd floor,

Midtown, 212/755–9398. Subway: 51st St./Lexington–3rd Aves.

9 e-4

RICHARD METZ GOLF STUDIO
Richard Metz sells golf equipment and supplies for both men and women, and offers expert instruction. 425 Madison Ave. (near 49th St.), Midtown, 212/759–6940. Subway: 51st St./Lexington–3rd Aves.

riding

9 e-3

HERMÈS
Though most New Yorkers associate Hermès with chic silk items (for the horsey set), the French firm has in fact made saddles and bridle equipment for over 150 years. 11 E. 57th St., Midtown, 212/751–3181. Subway: E, F to 5th Ave.

9 e-7

MILLER HARNESS COMPANY
This informed source has everything for the horse and rider: equipment, clothing, and accessories. Hey, it's the official outfitter of the U.S. equestrian team. 117 E. 24th St., Gramercy, 212/673–1400. Closed Sun. Subway: 6 to 23rd St.

running

11 e-2

ATHLETE'S FOOT
This national outfit offers an incredible selection of moderately priced athletic footwear—by Reebok, Nike, Adidas, New Balance, Avia, Converse, et. al.—as well as related accessories and clothing. 2563 Broadway (at 96th St.), Upper West Side, 212/961–9556. Subway: 1, 2, 3, 9 to 96th St.

9 e-5

390 5th Ave. (at 36th St.), Midtown, 212/947–6972. Subway: 34th St./Herald Square.

9 e-4

41 E. 42nd St., Midtown, 212/867–4599. Subway: 42nd St./Grand Central.

9 e-3

NIKETOWN
In a high-tech setting inspired by sports arenas and old school gyms, this relatively new Midtown monster has five floors of footwear and apparel for tennis, golf, basketball, football,

baseball, team sports (pro and college), running, and cross-training for men, women, boys, and girls. 6 E. 57th St., Midtown, 212/891–6453. Subway: E, F to 5th Ave.

9 e-7

SUPER RUNNER'S SHOP

A complete running store, this chain has shoes, gear, and accessories from all the big names. 416 3rd Ave. (at 29th St.), Murray Hill, 212/213–4560. Subway: 6 to 28th St.

9 e-1

1246 3rd Ave. (at 72nd St.), Upper East Side, 212/249–2133. Subway: 68th St./Hunter College.

7 b-8

360 Amsterdam Ave. (at 77th St.), Upper West Side, 212/787–7665. Subway: 79th St.

7 e-6

1337 Lexington Ave. (at 89th St.), Upper East Side, 212/369–6010. Subway: 4, 5, 6 to 86th St.

skating

9 a-7

BLADES BOARD & SKATE

These folks sell, rent, and repair in-line, ice, and hockey skates; snowboards; and skateboards, and sell related clothing and accessories. They also arrange bus trips to Hunter Mountain every Thursday, Friday, and Sunday in season. For general information, call 888/55–BLADES. Chelsea Piers (12th Ave. and 23rd St.), 212/336–6299. Subway: C, E to 23rd St.

11 e-3

659 Broadway (near Bleecker St.), Greenwich Village, 212/477–7350. Subway: Broadway–Lafayette St., Bleecker St.

9 b-1

120 W. 72nd St., Upper West Side, 212/787–3911. Subway: 1, 2, 3, 9 to 72nd St.

9 f-1

1414 2nd Ave. (near 73rd St.), Upper East Side, 212/249–3178. Subway: 77th St.; other locations.

9 c-3

PECK & GOODIE SKATES

Some say Peck & Goodie is New York's finest skate shop. Family-owned since 1940, it's in any case the city's original in-line and roller skate dealer. In addi-

tion to an excellent selection of in-line skates, you'll find a complete line of figure and hockey skates and equipment, and can bring your old stuff in for sharpening or repair. 919 8th Ave. (near 54th St.), Hell's Kitchen, 212/246–6123. Subway: C, E to 50th St.

skiing

9 e-1

BOGNER

These are the people who revolutionized the ski slopes with stretch pants in the 1950s. Ski fashions and Bogner ready-to-wear are imported from Germany. 821 Madison Ave. (near 68th St.), Upper East Side, 212/472–0266. Subway: 68th St./Hunter College.

9 d-3

SCANDINAVIAN SKI & SPORTS SHOP

This top city source for ski equipment fills three floors with it, and throws in brand-name ski wear to boot. They also sponsor a ski clinic in late October. 40 W. 57th St., Midtown, 212/757–8524. Subway: B, Q to 57th St.

tennis

9 d-3

MASON'S TENNIS MART

Shop for rackets, balls, bags, high-fashion European tennis wear, and, in season, ski wear. They'll restring your racket, as well. 911 7th Ave. (near 57th St.), Midtown, 212/757–5374. Subway: N, R to 57th St.

STATIONERY

Tiffany, Cartier, and the major department stores sell fine stationery. See also Art Supplies and Office Supplies, above.

9 e-3

DEMPSEY & CARROLL

These folks know their business, having been at it since 1878. They create fine, hand-engraved stationery from over 200 monogram styles. 110 E. 57th St., Midtown, 212/486–7508. Subway: 59th St.

10 f-1

JAM PAPER & ENVELOPE

This store is a terrific source for both basic and unusual-hued stationery; they have over 150 colors in stock. Try the map stationery for overseas mail. Try to stop in at the warehouse outlet store, on lower 5th Ave. *111 3rd Ave. (near 13th St.), East Village, 212/473–6666. Subway: 3rd Ave.*

9 *d-8*

661 6th Ave. (near 17th St.), Chelsea, 212/255–4593. Subway: F to 14th St. Closed weekends.

9 *e-8*

Warehouse outlet store: 125 5th Ave. (near 19th St.), Flatiron, 212/388–9189. Subway: N, R to 23rd St.

9 *e-1*

JAMIE OSTROW

Ostrow creates custom invitations, holiday greeting cards, and personalized stationery with a contemporary edge. *876 Madison Ave. (near 71st St.), Upper East Side, 212/734–8890. Closed Sun. Subway: 68th St./Hunter College.*

11 *e-4*

KATE'S PAPERIE

Kate's is beloved for its handmade fine-art papers for artists, photographers, and mere mortals who just can't walk past them. The wonderfully spacious store is worth the trip to SoHo, with exquisite paper in all of its varieties: for writing, wrapping, and making collages or matting pictures. The gorgeous desk accessories are just as compelling, as are the handmade greeting cards and the diaries, photo albums, storage boxes—we could go on and on. The creative wedding invitations are fun to look at even if you're not planning a wedding, and the Christmas-card selection is one of the finest in town. *561 Broadway (at Prince St.), SoHo, 212/941–9816. Subway: Prince St.*

10 *d-1*

8 W. 13th St., Greenwich Village, 212/633–0570. Subway: F to 14th St.

9 *e-2*

MRS. JOHN L. STRONG

The original stationer to the Duke and Duchess of Windsor, Mrs. Strong provides hand-engraved invitations, announcements, and social stationery on the company's own, 100%-cotton paper. Motifs are whimsical and interesting, and the matching envelopes are hand-lined. The boxed cards are also

sold at Barneys (*see* Department Stores, *above*). *699 Madison Ave. (near 62nd St.), Upper East Side, 212/838–3775. Open by appt. only. Subway: 59th St.*

9 *e-2*

PAPYRUS CARDS & STATIONERY

Contemplate personalized stationery, wrapping paper, photo albums, cards, stickers, frames, address books, and the like. *852 Lexington Ave. (at 65th St.), Upper East Side, 212/717–0002.*

9 *e-1*

1270 3rd Ave. (at 73rd St.), Upper East Side, 212/717–1060. Subway: 77th St.

THEATRICAL

See Books, Costume Rental, *and* Memorabilia.

9 *c-4*

ONE SHUBERT ALLEY

It's a tourist's dream, but natives may also find themselves charmed amid these posters, buttons, T-shirts, sweatshirts, theatrical-theme jewelry, duffel bags, and soundtracks to past and present Broadway and off-Broadway shows. *1 Shubert Alley (between 44th and 45th Sts., west of 7th Ave.), Theater District, 212/944–4133. Subway: 42nd St./Times Square.*

TOBACCO

9 *e-3*

ALFRED DUNHILL OF LONDON

The esteemed tobacconist produces custom-blended tobaccos, pipes, humidors, cigars, and gifts, including, of course, their own renowned and pricey lighters. *450 Park Ave. (near 57th St.), Midtown, 212/753–9292. Subway: 59th St.*

9 *e-4*

Saks Fifth Ave., 611 5th Ave. (at 50th St.), Midtown, 212/940–2455. Subway: E, F to 5th Ave.

9 *d-4*

CONNOISSEUR PIPE SHOP

Established in 1917, the Connoisseur offers unique custom- and handmade pipes—including one-of-a-kind unstained, unvarnished, natural-finish pipes—and skillful pipe repairs. Fill them with hand-blended tobacco mixtures and choose from a full range of tobacco pouches, humidors, racks, and accessories. Prices range from $27.50 to $4,200. *1285 6th Ave. (at 51st St.), concourse level, Midtown, 212/247–6054. Closed weekends. Subway: 47th–50th Sts./Rockefeller Center.*

9 *e-3*

/ **DAVIDOFF OF GENEVA**
Davidoff sells fine tobaccos and a variety of smoking accessories. *535 Madison Ave. (near 54th St.), Midtown, 212/751–9060. Subway: 51st St./Lexington–3rd Aves.*

9 *e-4*

/ **J & R TOBACCO CORPORATION**
The world's largest cigar store stocks over 2,800 different sizes, shapes, and colors, from nickel cigars to the rare and expensive. *11 E. 45th St., Midtown, 212/983–4160, closed Sun. Subway: 42nd St./Grand Central.*

10 *e-6*

219 Broadway (near Barclay St.), Lower Manhattan, 212/233–6620, closed weekends. Subway: World Trade Center.

9 *e-8*

MAY ROSE
Billing itself as "no-frills," this unassuming store has long been quietly run by a little old Cuban man who personally rolls the cigars he sells. The shop is a favorite with those who understood cigars before they became au courant. *866 Broadway (between 17th and 18th Sts.), Flatiron, 212/475–7080. Subway: 14th St./Union Square.*

9 *d-5*

/ **NAT SHERMAN CIGARS**
Choose from pipe tobacco, an imported selection of cigars in a walk-in humidor, and 30 blends of cigarette tobacco—wrapped in your choice of colored paper, with your name or company's name imprinted if you wish. Pipes and cigarette lighters are also in good supply. *711 5th Ave. (at 42nd St.), Midtown, 212/751–9100. Subway: E, F to 5th Ave.*

9 *c-8*

/ **TOBACCO PRODUCTS**
A longstanding family-run operation, Tobacco Products custom-blends cigars

using tobaccos from Brazil, the Dominican Republic, Nicaragua, and Mexico and sells pipes and lighters. *137 8th Ave. (near 16th St.), Chelsea, 212/989–3900. Subway: A, C, E to 14th St.*

TOYS & GAMES

collectible

11 *c-3*

ALPHAVILLE
Check out vintage toys, posters, magic, TV memorabilia, comics, and games from the American past. *226 W. Houston St. (between Varick St. and 6th Ave.), West Village, 212/675–6850. Subway: Houston St.*

7 *e-7*

BURLINGTON ANTIQUE TOYS
These miniature fighter planes, wooden boats, racing cars, and die-cast model cars are both new and collectible. There's a fine selection of tin soldiers (circa 1900–60). *Burlington Books, 1082 Madison Ave. (near 81st St.), downstairs, Upper East Side, 212/861–9708. Subway: 77th St.*

11 *d-3*

CLASSIC TOYS
The mix is both new and antique, including military miniatures; a wonderful collection of old matchbox and other collectible cars; and zoo, farm and prehistoric animals. *218 Sullivan (between Bleecker and W. 3rd Sts.), Greenwich Village, 212/674–4434. Subway: W. 4th St./Washington Square.*

9 *f-2*

DARROW'S FUN ANTIQUES
Founded in 1964 by Chick Darrow (see Antiques–Collectibles Specialists, above), this longtime mecca for nostalgia is now lovingly tended by Chick's son. The stock includes vintage windup toys, rare robots, tiny trucks and cars, vending machines, arcade games, carousel figures, character watches, and campaign buttons. *1101 1st Ave. (near 60th St.), Upper East Side, 212/838–0730. Subway: 59th St.*

new

11 h-1

ALPHABETS

These fun stores sell small toys and novelty items for both kids and adults. There's a good selection of Hello Kitty items (remember them?), kitschy T-shirts, cards, games, books, and gag gifts. It's a great stop for affordable last-minute gifts. *115 Ave. A (between 7th and 8th Sts.), East Village, 212/475–7250. Subway: Astor Pl.*

11 a-1

47 Greenwich Ave. (between Perry and Charles Sts.), West Village, 212/229–2966. Subway: Christopher St./Sheridan Square.

7 b-7

2284 Broadway (between 82nd and 83rd Sts.), Upper West Side, 212/579–5702. Subway: 1, 9 to 86th St.

9 e-8

B. SHACKMAN AND COMPANY

Fun is serious business, of course, and B. Shackman has been at it since 1898, specializing in Victorian-style toys, including miniatures; other whimsical novelties; and cards. It's a treasure, and a must for toy enthusiasts. *85 5th Ave. (at 16th St.), Flatiron, 212/989–5162. Subway: 14th St./Union Square.*

7 b-6

CHILDREN'S GENERAL STORE

Conveniently located at Playspace, this shop focuses on classic, wooden, educational toys. *Playspace, 2473 Broadway (at 92nd St.), Upper West Side, 212/580–2723. Subway: 96th St.*

10 f-1

DINOSAUR HILL

Dinosaur Hill specializes in toys from around the world, plus children's clothing. *306 E. 9th St., East Village, 212/473–5850. Subway: 8th St.; Astor Pl.*

11 e-5

ENCHANTED FOREST

This shop is SoHo's own wonderland, with an interior created by a professional set designer. It's a magical place, with books and toys that will appeal to adults as well as kids. *85 Mercer St. (between Broome and Spring Sts.), SoHo, 212/925–6677. Subway: Spring St.*

9 e-3

F.A.O. SCHWARZ

It's a kid's idea of heaven, a parent's idea of sensory overload. F.A.O. Schwarz has three floors absolutely packed with toys and tourists. The Madison Avenue entrance is the secret way to slip in during the busy holiday season, albeit through the Barbie Shop. Can't deal? Hire one of the store's personal shoppers. *767 5th Ave. (between 58th and 59th Sts.), Midtown, 212/644–9400. Subway: N, R to 5th Ave.*

10 d-1

GEPPETTO'S TOY BOX

This fairly new West Villager has become very popular. The selection is small, but it's well edited to include puppets, stuffed animals, books, and even jack-in-the-boxes. *161 7th Ave. S (between Waverly Pl. and Perry St.), West Village, 212/620–7511. Subway: Christopher St./Sheridan Square.*

11 d-8

JUST JAKE

Voted the "Best Downtown Toy Store" by *New York Press,* Just Jake's is full of such brainy toys as ant farms, books, and—well—small, quirky stuff. There's even a personal-shopping service. *40 Hudson St. (between Duane and Thomas Sts.), Tribeca, 212/267–1716. Subway: Chambers St.*

11 h-2

LITTLE RICKIE

This small store is packed with wacky, whimsical gifts and novelty items; many go for $2–$5. Fidget with games, Elvis paraphernalia, T-shirts, religious candles and artifacts, books, and the ever-popular photo booth. *49 1st Ave. (at 3rd St.), East Village, 212/505–6467. Subway: 2nd Ave.*

UMBRELLAS

Department stores and many handbag shops and boutiques carry umbrellas. If you forget yours on a rainy day, however, you're bound to find someone hawking $4 umbrellas on the next street corner. They're guaranteed to last—through that particular shower.

11 h-5

SALWEN

This friendly, well-established shop sells Knirps and designer umbrellas, including Givenchy, at a minimum of 25% off. There's also a fine diverse line of handbags and small leather goods. *45 Orchard St. (near Grand St.), 212/226–1693. Closed Sat. Subway: Grand St.; Delancey St.*

9 d-3

UNCLE SAM

Uncle Sam's been in business since 1866, and now stocks 50,000 umbrellas and 1,000 walking canes in every color, size, and description, including beach and garden umbrellas. The store performs expert, reasonably priced restorations and repairs, too. *161 W. 57th St., Midtown, 212/582–1976. Subway: B, Q, N, R to 57th St.*

VIDEOS

BLOCKBUSTER VIDEO

The national video megachain has a store in virtually every neighborhood in Manhattan and many 'hoods in the neighboring boroughs. Most stores are open until midnight and handle both rentals and sales. Check the business listings in your White Pages for the location nearest you.

11 f-2

TOWER VIDEO

Never to be outdone, Tower has thousands of music and film video titles for rent or sale, and the Village and Upper West Side stores are open until midnight. *383 Lafayette St. (at 4th St.), East Village, 212/505–1166. Subway: Astor Pl., 8th St.*

9 b-1

1961 Broadway (at 66th St.), Upper West Side, 212/799–2500. Subway: 66th St./Lincoln Center.

9 e-3

Trump Tower (sales only: 725 5th Ave., at 56th St.), Midtown, 212/838–8110. Subway: E, F to 5th Ave.

WATCHES & CLOCKS

The large department stores stock a variety of watches in the inexpensive and moderate ranges, with the accent on fashion.

antique

9 d-3

AARON FABER

Faber carries a sizable selection of antique and vintage wristwatches from the turn of the century to the 1960s, by such makers as Elgin, Hamilton, Patek Philippe, Rolex. *666 5th Ave. (between 52nd and 53rd Sts.), Midtown, 212/586–8411. Subway: E, F to 5th Ave.*

9 e-1

FANELLI ANTIQUE TIMEPIECES

This large selection of antique timepieces includes pocket- and wristwatches, wall clocks, shelf clocks, tall case clocks, and carriage clocks. The quality is high, and rare pieces abound. Prices range from $225 to $50,000. Expert appraisals and repairs are available. *790 Madison Ave. (between 66th and 67th Sts.), Upper East Side, 212/517–2300. Subway; 68th St./Hunter College.*

7 e-8

TIME WILL TELL

This shop is full of beautiful, one-of-a-kind classic timepieces from the 1920s–1950s. Brands include Audemars Piguet, Cartier, Hamilton, Bulova, Rolex, Tiffany, and Patek Philippe; bands are made of alligator, ostrich, and lizard. Pocket-watch lovers, you have some choices here, too. Prices range from $300–$40,000. Repairs are available. *962 Madison Ave. (near 75th St.), Upper East Side, 212/861–2663. Subway: 77th St.*

contemporary

9 e-3

CELLINI

Known as one of the best high-end watch shops in town, Cellini carries such exclusive brands as Frank Mueller and Cartier. *509 Madison Ave. (between 52nd and 53rd St.), Midtown, 212/888–0505. Subway: E, F, to 5th Ave.*

9 e-4

Waldorf-Astoria Hotel (Park Ave. and 50th St.), Midtown, 212/751–9824. Subway: 51st St./Lexington–3rd Aves.

`9` d-8

CHELSEA WATCH OUTLET

Sift through a good selection of brand names for real bargains. *62 W. 22nd St., Chelsea, 212/627–0130. Subway: F to 23rd St.*

`9` e-2

EXCLUSIVELY BREITLING

It's an exclusive address for an exclusive line of superb Swiss watches, which start at about $900 and top out over $100,000. *740 Madison Ave. (between 64th and 65th Sts.), Upper East Side, 212/628–5678. Subway: 68th St./Hunter College.*

`9` d-5

JOSEPH EDWARDS

The new and used watches include Omegas, Tags, Citizen, and Hamiltons. Repairs are done on-site. *500 5th Ave. (between 42nd and 43rd Sts.), Midtown. Subway: B, D, F, Q to 42nd St. 800/833–1195.*

`9` e-5

323 Madison Ave. (between 42nd and 43rd Sts.), Midtown. Subway: 42nd St./Grand Central.

`9` e-3

GEORGE PAUL JEWELERS

George Paul sells not watches, but a large selection of fine leather watchbands, including alligator, lizard, crocodile, pig, buffalo, snake, and bird. If they don't stock it, they'll make it to order. *51 E. 58th St., Midtown, 212/308–0077. Closed Sun. Subway: 59th St.*

`9` d-3

MOSTLY WATCHES

The small storefront hides a good selection of Omega, Swiss Army, and other watches, including both new and collectible Swatches. Repairs are done on-site. *200 W. 57th St., Midtown, 212/265–7100. Subway: B, Q, N, R to 57th St.*

`9` d-4

MOVADO

Movado is the home of the famous Museum Watch, as well as several other watch styles and a selection of jewelry. *630 5th Ave. (at 51st St.), Midtown, 212/262–2059. Subway: E, F to 5th Ave.*

`9` d-3

SWATCH STORE

Each Swatch store is independently owned and operated, so selections may vary, but prices should be consistent for these high-design but well-priced cult icons. *5 W. 57th St., Midtown, 212/317–1100. Subway: E, F to 5th Ave.*

`9` d-5

500 5th Ave. (at 42nd St.), Midtown, 212/730–7530. Subway: B, D, F, Q to 42nd St.

`10` f-6

Pier 17, South Street Seaport, Lower Manhattan. Subway: 2, 3 to Fulton St.

`9` e-3

TOURNEAU

Tourneau specializes in handsome, elegant, and famous watches for the fashion-conscious. Choose from Rolex, Cartier, Piaget, Omega, Corum, Patek Philippe, Baume & Mercier, Vaucheron Constantin, and many more; they're expensive, but battery replacements are free for life. (Let's see, where's my calculator . . .) There's also a fine selection of vintage watches. *500 Madison Ave. (at 52nd St.), Midtown, 212/758–6098. Subway: 51st St./Lexington–3rd Aves.*

`9` e-3

635 Madison Ave. (at 59th St.), Midtown, 212/758–6688. Subway: 59th St.

`9` c-6

200 W. 34th St., Garment District, 212/563–6880. Subway: 34th St./Penn Station.

`10` f-6

VINCENT GERARD

Gerard carries a good selection of both low- and high-priced brands, such as Fossil, Gruen, Tissot, Omega, and Longines. *Pier 17, South Street Seaport, Lower Manhattan, 212/732–6400. Subway: 2, 3 to Fulton St.*

`9` e-3

WATCH WORLD

As the name suggests, this shop carries a wide variety of watches for kids and adults. Brands include Guess, Citizen, Timex, Boy London and designer brands like Skagen and M & Co. *Trump Tower (725 5th Ave., at 56th St.), Midtown, 212/755–2090. Subway: E, F to 5th Ave.*

`11` e-3

649 Broadway (at Bleecker St.), Greenwich Village, 212/475–6090. Subway: Bleecker St.

WINES & SPIRITS

11 *f-1*

ASTOR WINES & SPIRITS

The largest liquor store in New York State is a must for bargain-hunting oenophiles. Selections are well-chosen, and the store's own label is well-priced and of competitive quality. Get yourself on the mailing list for special values. *12 Astor Pl. (at Lafayette St.), East Village, 212/674–7500. Closed Sun. Subway: Astor Pl.*

10 *d-1*

CROSSROADS

It's cramped, and not always cheap, but they have wines you won't find anywhere else. *55 W. 14th St., Chelsea, 212/924–3060. Closed Sun. Subway: F to 14th St.*

9 *e-1*

GARNET WINES & LIQUORS

For selection and price, this is the best all-around wine store in town. *929 Lexington Ave. (between 68th and 69th Sts.), Upper East Side, 212/772–3211. Closed Sun. Subway: 68th St./Hunter College.*

9 *e-3*

MORRELL & COMPANY

This beautiful, well-run wine shop features a large collection of port and an excellent selection of California wines.

Wine catering is available. *535 Madison Ave. (near 54th St.), Midtown, 212/688–9370. Subway: 51st St./Lexington–3rd Aves.*

9 *e-2*

SHERRY LEHMANN, INC.

One of the best liquor stores around, Sherry Lehmann has a comprehensive stock and knowledgeable staff. *679 Madison Ave. (near 61st St.), 212/838–7500. Closed Sun. Subway: 59th St.*

11 *d-4*

SOHO WINES AND SPIRITS

This attractive, spacious, well-organized SoHo shop is particularly strong in Bordeaux and has what may be the city's largest selection of single-malt Scotch whiskey. *461 W. Broadway (between Prince and Houston Sts.), SoHo, 212/777–4332. Closed Sun. Subway: Prince St.*

ZIPPERS

Most notions purveyors (*see* Notions, *above*) also carry zippers.

11 *h-6*

A. FEIBUSCH ZIPPERS

Feibusch has zippers in every length and every color, with thread to match. If they don't, they'll cut it to order. *27 Allen St. (between Hester and Canal St.), Lower East Side, 212/226–3964. Closed Sat. Subway: Canal St.*

chapter 5

ARTS, ENTERTAINMENT & NIGHTLIFE

arts

New York has always been a center for the arts, but at century's end, it really is more dynamic than ever. Purveyors and producers must compete frantically for the attention of increasingly savvy and voracious audiences. Who has not been warned about the long lines for Rent or free Shakespeare in the Park tickets; the all-night queues of audience hopefuls for The Rosie O'Donnell Show; or the agitated crowds outside the Metropolitan Opera House moments before curtain time, offering ticketholders a small fortune to see Die Walküre? These fans know exactly what they want, and pleasing them has become a real challenge—not least because of enormous production costs.

In each of the arts, there is a palpable sense of rising standards. As the Times Square renaissance continues, Broadway's musicals get more rewarding every year, both financially and (many agree) artistically. The Metropolitan Opera and its magnificent orchestra have not been this consistently exciting in decades. Kurt Masur has brought the New York Philharmonic back into top form; the art-gallery scene is flourishing; and film types throng to the Film Forum to catch movies they aren't likely to see anywhere else in the world.

CONCERT HALLS

9 *b-2*
ALICE TULLY HALL
Many have declared the acoustics in this medium-sized auditorium the fairest of them all, including a great many international soloists. The Chamber Music Society of Lincoln Center performs here, and the New York Film Festival takes over in late September. *1941 Broadway (at 65th St.), Upper West Side, 212/875–5050. Subway: 66th St./Lincoln Center.*

7 *b-1*
APOLLO THEATER
Ever since it opened in 1913, this legendary Harlem high point has been everything from a burlesque hall to a showcase for the ongoing Wednesday Amateur Nights. Ella Fitzgerald, Duke Ellington, Billie Holiday, Count Basie, Bill Cosby, and Aretha Franklin are only a few of those who have lit the place up. *253 W. 125th St., Harlem, 212/749–5838. Subway: 125th St.*

9 *b-2*
AVERY FISHER HALL
Well-worn as the home of the New York Philharmonic from September to June, this austere modern hall also hosts the beloved Mostly Mozart festival in summer and all sorts of other special events, from superstar recitals to the annual American Film Institute salutes. *Lincoln Center Plaza (Broadway at 64th St.), Upper West Side, 212/875–5030. Subway: 66th St./Lincoln Center.*

1 *a-1*
BARGEMUSIC LTD.
Against the incomparable skyline of lower Manhattan and the Brooklyn Bridge, Bargemusic presents chamber music year-round on an enclosed former coffee barge. The attractive performance space is paneled in cherry and backed by a glass wall onto the view. *Fulton Ferry Landing, Brooklyn Heights, 718/624–4061. Subway: High St. (Fulton exit); Clark St.*

7 *b-8*
BEACON THEATER
This huge theater has a wildly diverse history, but it currently tends toward pop and rock concerts. *2124 Broadway (near 74th St.), Upper West Side, 212/496–7070. Subway: 72nd St.*

1 *e-3*
BROOKLYN ACADEMY OF MUSIC (BAM)
Home to the Brooklyn Philharmonic, BAM also presents important, often innovative operatic and theatrical performances, as well as experimental and established dance companies (see Dance, below). *30 Lafayette Ave., Downtown Brooklyn, 718/636–4100. Subway: Atlantic Ave.; Pacific St.; BAM Bus to and from Manhattan.*

9 *c-3*

CARNEGIE HALL/ WEILL RECITAL HALL

Carnegie Hall's acoustics are as legendary as the musicians who have enjoyed them over the last 100 years. Orchestras sound their very best here, but so do solo pianists; something about the place inspires all kinds of performers to outdo themselves. The hall still looks fresh from its total renovation in 1986. Intimate Weill Recital Hall is wonderfully unpretentious, with clean acoustics and a no-nonsense atmosphere. *154 W. 57th St., Midtown, 212/ 247–7800. Subway: 57th St.*

7 *e-7*

GRACE RAINEY ROGERS AUDITORIUM

The Met presents classical music, mostly chamber, in the glorious surroundings of one of the world's greatest art museums. Concerts run from early October to late May, with a concurrent lecture series. *Metropolitan Museum of Art, 1000 5th Ave. (at 82nd St.), Upper East Side, 212/570–3949. Subway: 86th St.*

9 *b-8*

THE KITCHEN

This diminutive space is currently the epicenter of performance art—but it highlights dance, video, and music as well. *512 W. 19th St., Chelsea, 212/255– 5793. Subway: 23rd St.*

9 *c-6*

MADISON SQUARE GARDEN

Where else can 20,000 people see Barbra Streisand, Phish, or the New York Knicks? The Garden complex now includes the new, 5,600-seat Paramount Theater, where megamusical versions of *A Christmas Carol* and *The Wizard of Oz* make annual appearances. *7th Ave. at 31st–33rd Sts., Midtown, 212/465–6741. Subway: 34th St.*

9 *b-1*

MERKIN CONCERT HALL

This relative newcomer to the concert-hall pantheon gained rapid prestige with its ambitious programming: the smallish auditorium is almost entirely devoted to 20th-century chamber music. *Abraham Goodman House, 129 W. 67th St., Upper West Side, 212/362–8719. Subway: 66th St./Lincoln Center.*

9 *d-4*

RADIO CITY MUSIC HALL

Still breathtaking after all these years, Radio City's 6,000-seat auditorium features two-ton chandeliers, a 60-ft-high Art Deco lobby and foyer, and some of the glitziest acts ever concocted. The resident Rockettes still kick higher than any chorus line, and their Christmas and Easter performances will curl your toes. Pop stars from Bette Midler to k.d. lang to Tony Bennett also pack the house. *1260 Ave. of the Americas (at 50th St.), Midtown, 212/247–4777. Subway: 47th– 50th Sts./Rockefeller Center.*

7 *b-6*

SYMPHONY SPACE

Formerly a movie theater, this enormous auditorium now functions as a life-size multimedia venue. Symphony Space boasts the most varied programs in town—all-day readings of *Ulysses*, zither recitals, gospel, Gershwin—and the friendly flavor of its neighborhood. *2737 Broadway (at 95th St.), Upper West Side, 212/864–5400. Subway: 96th St.*

7 *e-6*

TISCH CENTER FOR THE ARTS

The Tisch Center at the 92nd Street Y offers an endless, fascinating, and fairly affordable array of readings, lectures, and concerts—classical, pop, and jazz. Most series take a breather in summer, but the jazz plays on. *92nd Street Y, 1395 Lexington Ave. (at 92nd St.), Upper East Side, 212/996–1100. Subway: 86th St.; 96th St.*

9 *d-5*

TOWN HALL

This low-key historic beauty quietly hosts an eclectic mix of chamber music, staged readings, stand-up comedy, high-end cabaret acts, and pop. *123 W. 43rd St., Theater District, 212/840–2824. Subway: 42nd St.*

CONCERTS IN CHURCHES

Churches play a quiet but crucial role in New York's classical scene, allowing both amateur and professional performers to find their own audiences. See Saturday's *New York Times* for additional venues and specific programs.

7 *b-3*

CATHEDRAL CHURCH OF ST. JOHN THE DIVINE

Huge, dark, and majestic, to say the least, St. John has the acoustics and atmosphere to make any musical event a stirring experience. *1047 Amsterdam Ave. (at 112th St.), Upper West Side, 212/316–7449. Subway: 110th St./Cathedral Pkwy.*

7 *e-7*

CHURCH OF ST. IGNATIUS LOYOLA

The acclaimed "Sacred Music in a Sacred Space" concert series uses this lush Italianate setting to showcase the church's own professional choir and fabulous organ as well as visiting artists. Solemn mass, every Sunday at 11 AM, features Gregorian chant and a new musical program each week. *980 Park Ave. (at 84th St.), Upper East Side, 212/288–3588. Subway: 86th St.*

10 *e-1*

GRACE CHURCH

Further downtown, this magnificent church sponsors frequent concerts and recitals, usually in early evening. *802 Broadway (at 10th St.), Greenwich Village, 212/254–2000. Subway: 8th St.; 14th St./Union Sq.*

9 *e-4*

ST. BARTHOLOMEW'S CHURCH

This Byzantine-style church has been making and sponsoring great music for 100 years. *109 E. 50th St., Midtown, 212/378–0200. Subway: 51st St.*

9 *e-3*

ST. PETER'S CHURCH AT CITICORP CENTER

Stop by on your lunch hour (or just peer through the street-level windows) for midday jazz or an organ recital on this innovative stage, or check out the unique Jazz Vespers on Sunday. Weekend evenings see choral action. *619 Lexington Ave. (at 54th St.), Midtown, 212/935–2200. Subway: 51st/Lex. Ave.*

9 *d-3*

ST. THOMAS CHURCH

New York's most famous men-and-boys choir works magic in this soaring Episcopal space. *1 W. 53rd St., Midtown, 212/757–7013. Subway: 5th Ave.*

9 *e-2*

TEMPLE EMANU-EL

The world's largest Reform synagogue offers regular recitals, organ and otherwise. *1 E. 65th St., Upper East Side, 212/744–1400. Subway: 59th St.*

DANCE

Ballet and modern dance flourish year-round in New York. Check the *New Yorker, New York* magazine, the *New York Times,* and *TimeOut* for current programs. Before you let anyone sound the death knell for New York dance—a noise some fans made when the Joffrey Ballet moved to Chicago in 1995—let 'em know that over 150 dance companies are alive and well in this town, not counting the steady flow of world-famous troupes that leap through every year. You have more than one performance option almost any night of the year.

1 *e-3*

BROOKLYN ACADEMY OF MUSIC (BAM)

Every fall, BAM's three-month Next Wave Festival features cutting-edge dance groups from the U.S. and abroad. Classical dance companies perform in the spring. *30 Lafayette Ave., Downtown Brooklyn, 718/636–4100. Subway: Atlantic Ave.; Pacific St.; BAM Bus to and from Manhattan.*

9 *d-3*

CITY CENTER

This busy ballet and modern dance theater hosts the Paul Taylor Dance Company and the Alvin Ailey American Dance Theater on a regular basis. It's also New York's most popular stop with touring international companies. *131 W. 55th St., Midtown, 212/581–1212. Subway: 57th St.*

9 *c-8*

DANCE THEATER WORKSHOP (DTW)

DTW is one of the country's most ambitious and successful laboratories for modern dance and performance art. *Bessie Schoenberg Theater, 219 W. 19th St., 2nd floor, Chelsea, 212/924–0077. Subway: 23rd St.*

10 *f-1*

DANSPACE PROJECT

This hallowed space, once graced by Isadora Duncan and Martha Graham, presents some of the most adventurous dance of the moment. *St. Mark's Church, 2nd Ave. at 10th St., East Village, 212/674–8194. Subway: Astor Pl.; 2nd Ave.*

9 *c-8*

THE JOYCE THEATER

A fine, highly eclectic modern-dance venue, the Joyce is the permanent home of the Feld Ballets/NY and features several other modern companies, including Pilobolus, Lar Lubovitch Dance Company, and Ballet Hispanico. It's medium-sized and unusually comfortable. *175 8th Ave. (at 18th St.), Chelsea, 212/242–0800. Subway: 14th St.*

9 *b-2*

METROPOLITAN OPERA HOUSE

The renowned American Ballet Theater presents a new season each year from April to June. In summer the hopping Lincoln Center Festival features visiting national ballet companies, including the Royal Ballet. *Lincoln Center Plaza (Broadway at 64th St.), Upper West Side, 212/362–6000. Subway: 66th St./Lincoln Center.*

9 *b-2*

NEW YORK STATE THEATER

The famed New York City Ballet holds court April–June and November–February. From Thanksgiving through the New Year, the company stages its legendary production of George Balanchine's *Nutcracker* (*see* Events *in* Chapter 2). *Lincoln Center Plaza (Broadway at 64th St.), Upper West Side, 212/870–5570. Subway: 66th St./Lincoln Center.*

10 *f-1*

P.S. 122

Very obviously a tumble-down public school, this fascinating and idiomatic experimental dance/performance space operates year-round. *150 1st Ave. (at 9th St.), East Village, 212/477–5288. Subway: Astor Pl.; 2nd Ave.*

9 *d-7*

GRAMERCY ARTS THEATER

Gramercy Arts Theater's Repertorio Español is best known as the frequent host of Spanish choreographer Pílar Rioja, who recently celebrated her 25th anniversary at this space. *138 E. 27th St., Gramercy, 212/889–2850. Subway: 23rd St.*

9 *e-1*

SYLVIA AND DANNY KAYE PLAYHOUSE

A frequent host to upwardly mobile dance companies, this space is notable for its comfortably small audience capacity, paired with a stage that accommodates good-sized productions. *Hunter College, 68th St. between Park and Lexington Aves., Upper East Side, 212/772–4448. Subway: 68th St./Hunter College.*

7 *b-6*

SYMPHONY SPACE

Watch this space for varied and electrifying ethnic dance. *2537 Broadway (at 95th St.), Upper West Side, 212/864–5400. Subway: 96th St.*

11 *c-8*

TRIBECA PERFORMING ARTS CENTER

Catch fine international dance troupes at this versatile space with two theaters, one intimate, the other more substantial. Tickets are an encouraging $7–$20. *199 Chambers St. (between Greenwich Ave. and West Side Hwy.), Tribeca, 212/346–8500. Subway: Chambers St.*

FREE ENTERTAINMENT

Call 212/360–1333 daily for a list of the day's free events in city parks, and check Events (*see* Chapter 2) for special annual happenings, especially summer festivals.

MOVIE THEATERS WORTH NOTING

Due mainly to the invention of the VCR, most of the fabled movie-repertory houses of the 1960s and '70s are gone now (the 80 St. Mark's, the Elgin, the Regency). Their absence makes the independent theaters listed here that much more valuable (and popular)—their programming not only supports the work of indy filmmakers but also keeps repertory fare alive, including films unavailable on video. Meanwhile, first-run movie theaters have proliferated wildly throughout Manhattan, with multiscreen complexes sprouting in every neighborhood, most owned by Sony, Cineplex Odeon, or City Cinemas. Alas, while the theaters are more numerous, the screens have shrunk, the prices have skyrocketed, and there are actually fewer films playing at any given time. For current listings, check any daily newspapers, the *New Yorker*, *New York* Magazine, or *Time Out* (particularly good on art-house listings).

8 *c-5*
AMERICAN MUSEUM OF THE MOVING IMAGE
36–01 35th Ave. (at 36th St.), Astoria, Queens, 718/784–0077. Subway: Steinway St.

10 *e-1*
CINEMA VILLAGE
E. 12th St. (between 5th Ave. and University Pl.), Greenwich Village, 212/924–3363. Subway: 14th St.; 8th St.

10 *c-3*
FILM FORUM
209 W. Houston St., West Village, 212/727–8110. Subway: Houston St.

9 *d-3*
MUSEUM OF MODERN ART
11 W. 53rd St., Midtown, 212/708–9480. Subway: 5th Ave.

9 *d-3*
MUSEUM OF TELEVISION AND RADIO
25 W. 52nd St., Midtown, 212/621–6600. Subway: 5th Ave.

9 *b-2*
WALTER READE THEATER/ FILM SOCIETY OF LINCOLN CENTER
165 W. 65th St., Upper West Side, 212/875–5600. Subway: 66th St./Lincoln Center.

OPERA

11 *f-2*
AMATO OPERA
Since 1947 this tiny theater has provided a unique showcase for some thrilling singing. Where else can you see and hear 50 (usually young) singers on a 20-ft stage, performing Verdi's *Falstaff* with real passion? Repertory standards are performed on varying weekends from September through June. *319 Bowery (at 2nd St.), East Village, 212/228–8200. Subway: Bleecker St./Broadway–Lafayette St.*

1 *e-3*
BROOKLYN ACADEMY OF MUSIC (BAM)
BAM has hosted several of the most important operatic premieres of the last decade (including the brilliant *Nixon in China*), and several august companies, including the Welsh National Opera, have performed brilliantly here. *30 Lafayette Ave., Downtown Brooklyn, 718/636–4100. Subway: Atlantic Ave.; Pacific St.; BAM Bus to and from Manhattan.*

9 *b-2*
METROPOLITAN OPERA COMPANY
Tickets are pricey, to say the least, but most agree that the Met is the finest opera company in the country—the finest in the world, on some nights. The company's hefty season runs from September to April. *Metropolitan Opera House, Lincoln Center Plaza (Broadway and 64th St.), Upper West Side, 212/362–6000. Subway: 66th St./Lincoln Ctr.*

9 *b-2*
NEW YORK CITY OPERA
This courageous and remarkable company performs standards (*Carmen*, *Traviata*), Broadway musicals with operatic aspirations (*Street Scene*, *A Little Night Music*), and, best of all, new works (*Malcolm X*, *The Times of Harvey Milk*) and unforgivably neglected masterpieces (*The Cunning Little Vixen*, *The Makropulos Case*). Ticket prices are decidedly more welcoming than those across the plaza. The season runs from September to November and from March to April. *New York State Theater, Lincoln Center Plaza (Broadway at 64th St.), Upper West Side, 212/870–5570. Subway: 66th St./Lincoln Center.*

9 *c-3*
OPERA ORCHESTRA OF NEW YORK
Under the intrepid guidance of Eve Queler, OONY performs concert versions of (usually) rarely performed works by major composers, often featuring star soloists and always furnishing libretti for the audience (the lights are kept up). *Carnegie Hall (see Concert Halls, above).*

TELEVISION SHOWS

Getting free tickets to television tapings is trickier than it used to be. Most shows require a postcard—with your name, address, phone number, and the number of tickets requested—at least a month in advance. But standby (same-day) tickets are available to those willing to spend several hours standing in line.

9 d-4

LATE NIGHT WITH CONAN O'BRIEN

Same-day standby tickets are available after 10 AM at the NBC Page Desk in the lobby of 30 Rockefeller Plaza—but you're better off writing in advance. *NBC Tickets, Late Night with Conan O'Brien, 30 Rockefeller Plaza, New York, NY 10112. Information: 212/664–3056. Subway: 47th–50th Sts./Rockefeller Center.*

9 c-3

THE LATE SHOW WITH DAVID LETTERMAN

Standby tickets go on sale weekdays at noon in front of the Ed Sullivan Theater (Broadway at 54th Street), but you need to get there good and early. Better yet, write in advance. You must be over 16. *Late Show Tickets, 1697 Broadway, New York, NY 10019. Information: 212/975–1003. Subway: 50th St.*

9 c-1

LIVE WITH REGIS AND KATHY LEE

You need to be over 18 to watch this one live. Standby tickets go on sale weekdays at 8 AM at the ABC headquarters; line up at the corner of 67th Street and Columbus Avenue. Otherwise, write a full year in advance. *Live Tickets, Ansonia Station, Box 777, New York, NY 10023-0777. Information: 212/456–3537. Subway: 66th St./Lincoln Center.*

9 d-4

THE ROSIE O'DONNELL SHOW

Highly coveted standby tickets go on sale Monday–Thursday at 8 AM, at the 49th Street entrance to 30 Rockefeller Plaza. There is currently a 9–12-month wait for tickets requested by postcard; if you can plan ahead, write *during April, May, or June.* Only two tickets are allotted per postcard, and children under five are not permitted. Call 212/506-3288 for all sorts of information on Rosie's show, including recipes, internships, and how to apply for a guest appearance. *ABC Studios, Rosie O'Donnell Show, 30 Rockefeller Plaza, New York, NY 10112.*

9 d-4

SATURDAY NIGHT LIVE

Standby tickets go on sale at 9:15 AM, at the 49th Street entrance to 30 Rockefeller Plaza. Advance tickets for performances and dress rehearsals are available by lottery; postcards are accepted during August only. You must be over 16. *NBC Tickets, Saturday Night Live, 30 Rockefeller Plaza, New York, NY 10112. Information: 212/664–4000. Subway: 47th–50th Sts./Rockefeller Center.*

9 d-7

THE VICKI LAWRENCE SHOW

Call Fox before 1 PM for ticket information. *Fox TV, 212 5th Ave. (at 26th St.), Gramercy, 212/802–4200. Subway: 23rd St.; 28th St.*

9 c-3

WNET (CHANNEL 13)

There are no regular tapings with a live audience, but the network offers periodic tours. *356 W. 58th St., Midtown, 212/560–2000. Subway: 59th St./Columbus Circle.*

THEATERS & THEATER COMPANIES

Until fairly recently, "theater" in New York City meant "Broadway." Today, Off-Broadway drama is just as vital and important as the blockbuster musicals. At this point more than a few Tony Award–winning megahits can claim to have originated Off-Broadway, where ticket prices are usually about half of those on the well-traveled Great White Way. An Off-Off-Broadway experience may involve sitting on a folding chair in a church basement or at the back of a coffeehouse, but many feel that the true pulse of American theater beats most steadily in these settings, where actors often work for free, runs are limited, and admission amounts to little more than a donation.

For current theater information, call New York City Onstage (*see* Tickets, *below*), or consult the *New Yorker, New*

York magazine, the *New York Times*
(especially Friday's "Weekend" and Sunday's "Arts and Leisure" sections), or
Time Out. For off- and off-off-Broadway,
Time Out is best.

Note that few Broadway box offices
accept phone calls; Telecharge and TicketMaster field the thousands of calls for
Broadway shows. The phone numbers
below will lead you to the appropriate
ticket vendor.

broadway

9 *c-4*
AMBASSADOR THEATER
219 W. 49th St., 212/239–6200. Subway:
49th St.; 50th St.

9 *c-4*
**BROOKS ATKINSON
THEATER**
256 W. 47th St., 212/719–4098. Subway:
49th St.; 50th St.

9 *d-4*
BELASCO THEATER
111 W. 44th St., 212/239–6200. Subway:
42nd St.

9 *c-4*
BOOTH THEATER
222 W. 45th St., 212/239–6200. Subway:
42nd St.

9 *c-4*
BROADHURST THEATER
235 W. 44th St., 212/239–6200. Subway:
42nd St.

9 *c-3*
BROADWAY THEATER
1681 Broadway (at 53rd St.), 212/239–
6200. Subway: 50th St.; 7th Ave.

9 *c-4*
CIRCLE IN THE SQUARE
235 W. 50th St., 212/239–6200. Subway:
50th St.

9 *d-4*
CORT THEATER
138 W. 48th St., 212/239–6200. Subway:
49th St.; 50th St.

9 *c-4*
CRITERION CENTER
1514 Broadway (at 45th St.), 212/764–
7902. Subway: 42nd St.

9 *c-4*
**ETHEL BARRYMORE
THEATER**
243 W. 47th St., 212/239–6200. Subway:
49th St.; 50th St.

9 *c-4*
EUGENE O'NEILL THEATRE
230 W. 49th St., 212/246–0220. Subway:
49th St.; 50th St.

9 *c-4*
GERSHWIN THEATER
222 W. 51st St., 212/307–4100. Subway:
50th St.

9 *c-4*
GOLDEN THEATER
252 W. 45th St., 212/239–6200. Subway:
42nd St.

9 *c-4*
HELEN HAYES THEATRE
240 W. 44th St., 212/307–4100. Subway:
42nd St.

9 *c-4*
IMPERIAL THEATER
249 W. 45th St., 212/239–6200. Subway:
42nd St.

9 *c-4*
LONGACRE THEATER
220 W. 48th St., 212/239–6200. Subway:
49th St.; 50th St.

9 *c-4*
LUNT-FONTANNE THEATRE
205 W. 46th St., 212/307–4100. Subway:
42nd St.

9 *c-4*
LYCEUM THEATER
149 W. 45th St., 212/239–6200. Subway:
42nd St.

9 *c-4*
MAJESTIC THEATER
247 W. 44th St., 212/239–6200. Subway:
42nd St.

9 *c-4*

MARQUIS THEATER
211 W. 45th St., 212/307–4100. Subway: 42nd St.

9 *c-4*

MARTIN BECK THEATER
302 W. 45th Street, 212/246–6363. Subway: 42nd St.

9 *c-4*

MINSKOFF THEATER
200 W. 45th St., 212/307–4100. Subway: 42nd St.

9 *c-4*

MUSIC BOX THEATER
239 W. 45th Street, 212/239–6200. Subway: 42nd St.

9 *c-5*

NEDERLANDER THEATER
208 W. 41st St., 212/307–4100. Subway: 42nd St.

9 *c-3*

NEIL SIMON THEATRE
250 W. 52nd St., 212/757–8646. Subway: 50th St.

9 *c-5*

NEW AMSTERDAM THEATER
214 W. 42nd St., 212/307–4100. Subway: 42nd St.

9 *c-4*

PALACE THEATER
1564 Broadway (at 47th St.), 212/307–4100. Subway: 49th St.; 50th St.

9 *c-4*

PLYMOUTH THEATER
236 W. 45th St., 212/239–6200. Subway: 42nd St.

9 *c-4*

RICHARD RODGERS THEATRE
226 W. 46th St., 212/221–1211. Subway: 42nd St.

9 *c-4*

ROUNDABOUT THEATER COMPANY
1530 Broadway (at 45th St.), 212/869–8400. Subway: 42nd St.

9 *c-4*

ROYALE THEATRE
242 W. 45th St., 212/239–6200. Subway: 42nd St.

9 *c-4*

ST. JAMES THEATRE
246 W. 44th St., 212/239–6200. Subway: 42nd St.

9 *c-4*

SHUBERT THEATER
225 W. 44th St., 212/239–6200. Subway: 42nd St.

9 *c-3*

VIRGINIA THEATRE
245 W. 52nd St., 212/239-6200. Subway: 50th St.

9 *b-2*

VIVIAN BEAUMONT THEATER
Lincoln Center, 150 W. 65th St., Upper West Side, 212/239–6200. Subway: 66th St./Lincoln Center.

9 *c-4*

WALTER KERR THEATER
219 W. 48th St., 212/239-6200. Subway: 49th St.; 50th St.

9 *c-4*

WINTER GARDEN THEATER
1634 Broadway (at 50th St.), 212/239-6200. Subway: 50th St.

off broadway

11 *b-2*

ACTORS' PLAYHOUSE
100 7th Ave. S. (between Bleecker and Christopher Sts.), West Village, 212/239-6200. Subway: Christopher St./Sheridan Sq.

9 *c-7*

AMERICAN JEWISH THEATER
307 W. 26th St., Chelsea, 212/633–9797. Subway: 23rd St.

9 *d-4*

AMERICAN PLACE THEATER
111 W. 46th St., Theater District, 212/840–3074. Subway: 42nd St.

11 *e-2*

ASTOR PLACE THEATER
434 Lafayette St., East Village, 212/254–4370. Subway: Astor Pl.; 8th St.

9 *d-8*

ATLANTIC THEATER COMPANY
33 W. 20th St., Chelsea, 212/645–1242. Subway: 23rd St.

11 *f-2*

BOUWERIE LANE THEATER
330 Bowery (at 2nd St.), East Village, 212/677–0060. Subway: 2nd Ave.; Bleecker St.

10 *d-1*

CENTURY THEATER CENTER
111 E. 15th St., Flatiron, 212/239–6200. Subway: 14th St.

11 *a-1*

CHERRY LANE THEATER
38 Commerce St. (between Bedford and Barrow Sts.; off 7th Ave. S.), West Village, 212/989–2020. Subway: Christopher St./Sheridan Sq.

9 *d-3*

CITY CENTER, I & II
131 W. 55th St., 212/581–1212. Subway: 57th St.

10 *e-1*

CSC REPERTORY
136 E. 13th St., East Village, 212/677–4210. Subway: 14th St.

9 *b-5*

DOUGLAS FAIRBANKS THEATER
432 W. 42nd St., 212/239–6200. Subway: 42nd St.

9 *c-4*

DUFFY THEATER
1553 Broadway (at 46th St.), 212/695–3401. Subway: 42nd St.

9 *a-3*

ENSEMBLE STUDIO THEATER
549 W. 52nd St., 212/247–3405. Subway: 50th St.

9 *b-4*

47TH STREET THEATER
307 W. 47th St., 212/239–6200. Subway: 49th St.; 50th St.

9 *b-5*

HAROLD CLURMAN THEATER
412 W. 42nd St., 212/594–2826. Subway: 42nd St.

9 *b-7*

HUDSON GUILD THEATER
441 W. 26th St., Chelsea, 212/760–9810. Subway: 23rd St.

9 *b-5*

INTAR THEATER
420 W. 42nd St., 212/279–4200. Subway: 42nd St.

9 *a-3*

IRISH ARTS CENTER
553 W. 52nd St., Midtown, 212/757–3318. Subway: 50th St.

9 *d-8*

IRISH REPERTORY THEATER
132 W. 22nd St., Chelsea, 212/727–2737. Subway: 23rd St.

7 *e-6*

JEWISH REPERTORY THEATER
316 E. 91st St., Upper East Side, 212/831–2000. Subway: 86th St.

9 *b-5*

JOHN HOUSEMAN THEATER
450 42nd St., 212/967–9077. Subway: 42nd St.

11 *f-2*

JOSEPH PAPP PUBLIC THEATER
425 Lafayette St. (near Astor Pl.), East Village, 212/598–7150. Subway: Astor Pl.; 8th St.

11 *g-2*

LA MAMA E.T.C.
74A E. 4th St. (between Bowery and 2nd Ave.), East Village, 212/475–77 10. Subway: 2nd Ave.; Astor Pl.; Bleecker St.

9 d-4
LAMBS THEATER
130 W. 44th St., Theater District, 212/239–6200. Subway: 42nd St.

9 c-4
LAURA PELS THEATER
1530 Broadway (at 45th St.), 212/869–8400. Subway: 42nd St.

11 a-2
LUCILLE LORTEL THEATER
121 Christopher St. (between Bleecker and Hudson Sts.), West Village, 212/239–6200. Subway: Christopher St./Sheridan Sq.

1 d-3
MAJESTIC THEATER
651 Fulton St. (2 blocks from Brooklyn Academy of Music), Downtown Brooklyn, 718/636–4100. Subway: Atlantic Ave.; Pacific St.

9 d-3
MANHATTAN THEATER CLUB
131 W. 55th St., Midtown, 212/581–1212. Subway: 57th St.

11 c-2
MINETTA LANE THEATER
18 Minetta La. (between Bleecker and W. 3rd Sts.; off 6th Ave.), Greenwich Village, 212/420–8000. Subway: W. 4th St.

9 b-2
MITZI E. NEWHOUSE THEATER
Lincoln Center, 150 W. 65th St., Upper West Side, 212/239–6200. Subway: 66th St./Lincoln Center.

9 b-3
NEGRO ENSEMBLE COMPANY
424 W. 55th St., Midtown, 212/246–8545. Subway: 57th St.

11 g-2
NEW YORK THEATER WORKSHOP
79 E. 4th St. (between Bowery and 2nd Ave.), East Village, 212/460–5475. Subway: 2nd Ave.; Bleecker St.

11 e-4
OHIO THEATER
66 Wooster St. (between Broome and Spring Sts.), SoHo, 212/966–2509. Subway: Spring St.

11 g-1
ORPHEUM THEATER
126 2nd Ave. (at 8th St.), East Village, 212/307–4100. Subway: 2nd Ave.

9 b-4
PAN ASIAN REPERTORY THEATER
423 W. 46th St., Theater District, 212/245–2660. Subway: 42nd St.

11 g-1
PEARL THEATER COMPANY
80 St. Mark's Pl., East Village, 212/598–9802. Subway: Astor Pl.

11 d-2
PLAYERS THEATER
115 MacDougal St. (at Minetta La., between Bleecker and W. 4th Sts.), Greenwich Village, 212/254–5076. Subway: W. 4th St.

7 f-6
PLAYHOUSE 91
316 E. 91st St., Upper East Side, 212/207–4100. Subway: 86th St.

9 b-5
PLAYWRIGHTS HORIZONS MAIN STAGE
416 W. 42nd St., Theater District, 212/279–4200. Subway: 42nd St.

9 c-4
PRIMARY STAGES
345 W. 45th St., Theater District, 212/333–4052. Subway: 42nd St.

7 b-8
PROMENADE THEATER
2162 Broadway (at 76th St.), Upper West Side, 212/239–6200. Subway: 72nd St.

9 d-7
REPERTORIO ESPAÑOL
138 E. 27th St., Gramercy, 212/889–2850. Subway: 23rd St.

9 *b-5*

SAMUEL BECKETT THEATER

410 W. 42nd St., Theater District, 212/594–2826. Subway: 42nd St.

11 *a-3*

ST. JOHN'S CHURCH

81 Christopher St., West Village, 212/239–6200. Subway: Christopher St./Sheridan Sq.

9 *c-4*

ST. LUKE'S CHURCH

308 W. 46th St., Theater District, 212/239–6200. Subway: 42nd St.

7 *b-8*

SECOND STAGE

2162 Broadway (76th St.), Upper West Side, 212/239–6200. Subway: 72nd St.

11 *b-4*

SOHO PLAYHOUSE

15 Vandam St. (between 6th Ave. and Varick St.), SoHo, 212/691–1555. Subway: Spring St.

9 *c-3*

STARDUST THEATER

1650 Broadway (at 51st St.), 212/239–6200. Subway: 49th St.; 50th St.

11 *d-3*

SULLIVAN STREET PLAYHOUSE

The world's longest-running musical, *The Fantasticks*, is now in its 37th year here. *181 Sullivan St. (between Houston and Bleecker Sts.), Greenwich Village, 212/674–3838. Subway: Bleecker St./Broadway–Lafayette St.*

11 *c-1*

THEATER OFF PARK

224 Waverly Pl. (between 11th and Perry Sts.; west of 7th Ave.), West Village, 212/627–2556. Subway: 14th St..

10 *d-1*

THE 13TH STREET THEATER

50 W. 13th St., Greenwich Village, 212/627–2556. Subway: 14th St.

9 *f-8*

UNION SQUARE THEATER

100 E. 17th St., 212/307–4100. Subway: 14th St./Union Sq.

10 *f-1*

VARIETY ARTS

110 3rd Ave. (betwen 13th and 14th Sts.), East Village, 212/239–6200. Subway: 14th St./Union Sq.

9 *c-4*

VILLAGE GATE

240 W. 52nd St., Midtown, 212/307–5252. Subway: 50th St.

10 *e-1*

VINEYARD THEATER

108 E. 15th St., Flatiron, 212/353–3366. Subway: 14th St./Union Sq.

10 *b-2*

WESTBETH THEATER CENTER

151 Bank St. (between Hudson St. and 12th Ave.), West Village, 212/741–0391. Subway: 14th St.

9 *b-5*

WESTSIDE ARTS THEATER

407 W. 43rd St., Theater District, 212/239–6200. Subway: 42nd St.

9 *b-7*

WPA THEATER

519 W. 23rd St., Chelsea, 212/206–0523. Subway: 23rd St.

9 *e-3*

YORK THEATER COMPANY

St. Peter's Church at Citicorp Center, 619 Lexington Ave. (at 54th St.), 212/935–5820. Subway: 51st St./Lexington Ave.

TICKETS

You can buy advance tickets to most arts presentations at full price by mail, in person at the box office, or by phone (with a credit card). Buying tickets directly from the theater by mail (using a certified check or money order) is the charmingly old-fashioned way, but you may end up in old-fashioned seats under the overhang in the side-rear orchestra—at $75 a pop. Your best bet for choice seats is to go to the box office well in advance of your preferred date; box-office personnel usually know the theater and its current production very well, and if they're in a good mood, they'll help you nab the best of what's available. Of course, this process can be physically inconvenient, so Telecharge (212/239–6200) and Ticket-

Master (212/307–7171) have learned to describe seat locations upon request. Newspaper and magazine listings for each show will tell you which service to use. The catch is that you pay a $2–$5 surcharge on each ticket when you order by phone. If you call well in advance of the performance, your tickets can be mailed to you; otherwise they'll be held at the box office until just before curtain time. If you need to pick up held tickets to a very popular show, be sure to arrive at the theater in plenty of time and bring your credit card. Less-expensive tickets to off- and off-off-Broadway shows (no less exciting than the biggies) may be similarly obtained through a kind of joint box office called Ticket Central (416 W. 42nd St, 212/279–4200; open daily 1 PM to 8 PM).

The following two discount ticket booths sell half-price or ¾-price tickets (for cash or traveler's checks only) for same-day Broadway and off-Broadway shows, as well as some music and dance performances. Be prepared to stand in line after checking the board for available shows and performances, and be sure to have alternate selections; shows may sell out as the line proceeds. Be prepared for the $2.50 service charge. TKTS makes a dizzying two transactions per minute, but you'll still have to queue outdoors here, so remember your umbrella if necessary.

If you can afford to lose, wait until just before curtain time (half an hour or less), when some shows release unclaimed or unsold tickets; lines are much shorter at that point.

9 *c-4*

TIMES SQUARE THEATER CENTER (TKTS)
Broadway at 47th St., Theater District. Subway: 49th St.; 42nd St. Open for same-day evening performances Mon.–Sat. 3–8; for matinee performances Wed. and Sat. 10–2; for Sunday matinee and evening performances 11 AM to closing.

3 *b-8*

LOWER MANHATTAN THEATER CENTER
2 World Trade Center, Mezzanine, Lower Manhattan. Subway: Cortlandt St./World Trade Center. Open for same-day evening performances weekdays 11–5:30; Sat. 11–3:30. Matinee and Sunday performances: sold one day before performance.

NEW YORK CITY ONSTAGE
Here's a phone number well worth memorizing: 212/768-1818. Courtesy of the Theater Development Fund (TDF), this touch-tone menu gives you an impressive array of accurate recorded information, in English or Spanish, on theater, dance, and music events, cancelled performances, and arts events in other boroughs, including subway directions.

STUBS AND PLAYBILL ONLINE
The glossy pamphlet *Stubs* gives detailed seating plans for all of New York's Broadway theaters and major off-Broadway theaters; stadiums; and concert halls. You can pick it up for $9.95 at many newsstands and bookstores. If you have access to the World Wide Web, check out *Playbill*'s Web site at www.Playbill.com, where you'll find a wealth of resources: links to seating charts for all Broadway theaters and quite a few others, including those on London's West End; access to Telecharge services; feature articles on Broadway and off-Broadway happenings; dozens of daily news items; listings for American regional theaters; and links to a dizzying 650 other theater-oriented sites.

nightlife

New York's nightlife has been shaken up in the past few years, as Mayor Rudy Giuliani's crackdown on "quality-of-life" issues has grown to include nightspots that disturb their neighbors. Peter Gatien (owner of the Limelight and Tunnel clubs) having been arrested for profiting from drug dealing at his venues, Limelight was closed at press time, but by the time you read this it should be up and running again. Save the Robots, another beloved after-hours spot, also closed its doors. The seamy, gritty meatpacking district, north of the West Village, has become a hot new nightspot area thanks to low rents and a paucity of residents (and thus of noise complaints). Midtown West has also seen the opening of two big new dance clubs. SoHo continues to attract the velvet-rope crowd.

The trends these days are lounges and cigars, often together. Many nightspots and restaurants have jumped on the bandwagon, offering cigar-friendly areas and even cigar menus.

All nightspots stop serving alcohol at 4 AM, but Energizer bunnies keep dancing at clubs that stay open. You can always recharge at an all-night diner and move on to the after-hours clubs.

BARS

7 *e-8*

AMERICAN TRASH

Bikers, slackers, and yuppies mix well at this divey bar with a pool table and a good jukebox. *1471 1st Ave. (between 76th and 77th Sts.), Upper East Side, 212/988–9008. Subway: 77th St.*

10 *f-1*

BEAUTY BAR

Get a happy-hour manicure at this kitschy space with an old-time beauty-parlor vibe but an East Village clientele. *231 E. 14th St., East Village, 212/539–1389. Subway: 14th St/Union Sq.*

11 *f-2*

BOILER ROOM

A relaxed, dark gay bar with cheap drinks, a pool table, and an '80s-theme jukebox, this hot spot attracts Village dudes rather than Chelsea muscle boys. Girls take over one Sunday a month. *86 E. 4th St., East Village, 212/254–7536. Subway: Astor Pl.*

11 *f-2*

BOWERY BAR

Although it's been replaced as *the* place to be seen, B Bar still has a cool vibe and a huge and wonderful outdoor patio. *358 Bowery (at 4th St.), East Village, 212/475–2220. Subway: Astor Pl.*

11 *d-5*

CHAOS

At press time this was one of the three hottest spots in the city. The door is tough here; the clientele beautiful, hip, and often famous; and the smoke sometimes unbearable (the cigars, you know). *23 Watts St. (off W. Broadway/Broome Sts.), SoHo, 212/925–8966. Subway: Canal. St.*

9 *f-4*

DIVINE BAR

On the forefront of a welcome Midtown East resurgence, this popular, SoHo-esque bar and tapas lounge has a large selection of and wines and beers plus

zebra-striped bar chairs, a cigar area, and velvet couches upstairs. It's packed after work. *244 E. 51st St., Midtown, 212/319–9463. Subway: 51st St.*

11 *b-3*

HENRIETTA HUDSON

The best lesbian bar in town, this pick-up joint with two huge rooms and a pool table attracts all types of women. Some nights feature comedy or live music. *438 Hudson St. (off Martin St.), West Village, 212/924–3347. Subway: Houston St..*

10 *b-1*

HOGS & HEIFERS

Drew Barrymore and Julia Roberts have added their bras to the moose-head collection, and Harrison Ford and JFK, Jr., have stopped in. Why? They needed a break from the slick-n-trendy in spots where one is *expected* to hang out. This

---

BREW PUBS

Tired of drinks that take as long to order as they do to make? Do you just want a beer? An interesting, freshly brewed beer?

Chelsea Brewing Co. (Chelsea Piers)
Hudson views and homemade brews, including a nut-brown.

Heartland Brewery (35 Union Sq. W)
Farmer Jon's oatmeal stout is a blue-ribbon favorite at this packed post-collegiate bar.

Park Slope Brewing Co. (Brooklyn)
Supremely mellow in Park Slope; a smoky pub in Brooklyn Heights.

Times Square Brewery and Restaurant (160 W. 42nd St.)
To everyone's surprise, both the brews and the menu have garnered praise.

Typhoon Brewery (22 E. 54th St.)
As much about scene and satay as suds (carbonated and cold).

Westside Brewing Co. (340 Amsterdam Ave.)
Upper West Siders and other yuppies slurp the four hit-or-miss beers on tap.

Yorkville Brewery (1359 1st Ave.)
This handsome hangout changes its special house brews every few weeks.

is a pseudo-redneck dive, plain and simple. Leave your politically correct friends at the door, order a domestic beer, and dance on the bar. *859 Washington St. (at 13th St.), West Village, 212/929–0655. Subway: 14th St.*

10 e-2
LOUISIANA COMMUNITY BAR & GRILL
The energy level is high at this swinging New Orleans roadhouse with Mardi Gras float decorations and free live Cajun or zydeco music every night. *622 Broadway (between Houston and Bleecker Sts.), East Village, 212/460–9633. Subway: Astor Pl. or Houston St.*

11 f-1
MCSORLEY'S OLD ALE HOUSE
Established in 1854, McSorley's is one of New York's oldest watering holes. The epitome of a saloon, it's dark, cramped, and dusty around the edges, but the old Irish barkeeps serve McSorley's own excellent dark and pale brews. *15 E. 7th St., 212/473–9148. Subway: Astor Pl.*

9 e-8
OLD TOWN BAR AND RESTAURANT
The name is accurate: this classic, wood-paneled, New York bar has been around since 1892 and still serves a great burger. *45 E. 18th St., Gramercy, 212/529–6732. Subway: 14th St./Union Sq.*

9 f-7
PADDY REILLY'S MUSIC BAR
This Irish hole-in-the-wall launched the rocking-roots band Black 47, which plays here most Saturday nights. Live music is frequent, including a regular Irish jam session on Thursday nights. Grab a Guinness and pogo with the crowd. *519 2nd Ave. (between 28th and 29th Sts.), Gramercy, 212/686–1210. Subway: 28th St.*

11 f-4
PRAVDA
The martinis are divine at this trendy but friendly Russian-themed lounge with a tiny upstairs bar. If yours is an obscure brand of vodka, this is the place to track it down: there are more than 70 brands behind the bar. The street entrance is difficult to find; look for stairs going down. Tip: Brush up on your Russian before you venture into the loo. *281 Lafayette St. (between Prince and Houston Sts.), East Village, 212/226–4696. Subway: Houston St.*

9 d-4
THE ROYALTON
The lobby of this modern, Phillipe Starck–designed hotel is a cool and relaxed place to sip a tall drink and keep an eye on the parade of hip celebrities and guests coming to dine at 44. Everything, including the entrance to the hotel (look for the curved silver railings) is hidden, so you have to be adventurous. The tiny, ultra-cool Vodka Bar is behind the dipped sunken table and chairs on the right as you enter from the street. Dress: sleek. *44 W. 44th St., Midtown, 212/768–5000 or 212/869–4400. Subway: 42nd St./Grand Central.*

7 b-8
SHARK BAR
Anyone who wants to eat at this fantastic Southern restaurant has to make it through the slick but friendly yuppie crowd at the bar. *307 Amsterdam Ave. (between 73rd and 74th Sts.), Upper West Side, 212/874–8500. Subway: 72nd St.*

11 e-4
SOHO KITCHEN AND BAR
Bartenders behind this big, paper-clip–shaped bar can pour you from an enormous selection of beers and wines by the glass or the flight—for example, a tasting of three South American reds. People who aren't always comfortable in SoHo will feel just fine here—there's none of that black-clothing-only vibe. *103 Greene St. (between Spring and Prince Sts.), SoHo, 212/925–1866. Subway: Spring or Prince St.*

11 e-4
SPY
If you can get past the velvet rope, settle into a plush couch and enjoy the baroque parlor setting and pretty people. Opened in 1995, Spy was a setter of the lounge trend. *101 Greene St. (between Spring and Prince Sts.), SoHo 212/343–9000. Subway: Spring or Prince St.*

11 b-1

STONEWALL

This unpretentious gay bar, the site of the Stonewall riot, attracts a mix of tourists and neighborhood regulars. *53 Christopher St. (between 7th Ave. S. and Waverly Pl.), West Village, 212/463–0950. Subway: Christopher St.*

10 f-1

TELEPHONE BAR

Look for the red English telephone booths out front and join the handsome, polite crowd at this welcoming spot, more a bar and restaurant than a pub. *149 2nd Ave. (between 10th and 11th Sts.), East Village, 212/529–5000. Subway: Astor Pl.*

11 f-3

TEMPLE BAR

Look for the painted iguana skeleton (there's no sign) and walk past the slim bar to the back, where, in near-total darkness, you can lounge on a plush banquette surrounded by velvet drapes. *332 Lafayette St. (at Bleecker St.), East Village, 212/925–4242. Subway: Houston St.*

9 d-3

21 CLUB

Long a haunt for power suits toasting their latest M&A, the bar in this dark bastion is staid and discreet, and attracts more than its share of recognizable faces. (*See* Continental *in* Chapter 3.) *21 W. 52nd St., Midtown, 212/582–7200. Subway: 50th St.; 47–50th Sts./Rockefeller Center.*

9 d-5

THE VIEW LOUNGE

This large, bilevel, slowly revolving lounge has a phenomenal view of the city's landmark buildings. You'll be glad you fought the tourist hordes when you sink into a banquette and notice how serene the city looks from the 48th floor. *Marriott Marquis, 1700 Broadway (at 44th St.), Theater District, 48th floor. 212/398–1900. Subway: 42nd St./Times Sq.*

9 g-7

WATER CLUB

You'll feel like you're in a private club in Darien, but you're actually on a docked barge on the East River. On one side is a polished wood bar accented by floral arrangements and framed prints; on the other is the lovely dining room, with New York's version of a water view. But if you hit the weather and the timing right (call ahead), you can slouch in a director's chair at the open-deck bar upstairs and pretend you're on a tropical island. *500 E. 30th St., Murray Hill, 212/683–3333. Subway: 28th St.*

BLUES

10 c-1

CHICAGO BLUES

This new club has quickly become an institution, with open jam nights about once a week. *73 8th Ave. (between 12th and 13th Sts.), West Village, 212/924–9755. Subway: 14th St.*

7 e-7

MANNY'S CAR WASH

Think straight white men don't dance? Come here in the wee hours and watch 'em bop. A rowdy Upper East Side audience, average age 30, flocks to this rectangular semi-dive for Chicago-style blues and one another. *1558 3rd Ave. (between 87th and 88th Sts.), Upper East Side, 212/369–2583. Subway: 86th St.*

10 f-6

SEAPORT LIBERTY CRUISES

Every Wednesday in the summer, these boats circle Manhattan accompanied to the tunes of a live blues band. *Pier 16, South Street Seaport, Lower Manhattan, 888/322–2583. Subway: Fulton St.*

11 c-2

TERRA BLUES

Smokin' local blues bands as well as traveling names take the stage here in New York's blues district. *149 Bleecker St. (between Thompson St. and LaGuardia Pl.), West Village, 212/777–7776. Subway: Bleecker St.*

CABARET

7 d-8

CAFE CARLYLE

See Piano Bars, *below.*

9 c-4

DON'T TELL MAMA

Catch singers, comedians, and female impersonators in the long-running backroom cabaret. Extroverts will be tempted by the open mike at the piano bar up front. *343 W. 46th St., Theater District, 212/757–0788. Subway: 42nd St./Times Sq.*

9 *b-5*

DOWNSTAIRS AT THE WEST BANK CAFE
Below a restaurant across from Theater Row, this club makes the most of its surroundings, serving up plays, cabaret, and musical revues. *407 W. 42nd St., Theater District, 212/695–6909. Subway: 42nd St./Times Sq.*

11 *b-1*

THE DUPLEX
Opened in 1951, this gay, campy cabaret near Sheridan Square claims to be New York's oldest. Upstairs you might find a singer, comedian, or rock band (or, on open-mike night, folks who fancy themselves any of the above); downstairs, a piano bar. *61 Christopher St. (at 7th Ave.), West Village, 212/255–5438. Subway: Christopher St.*

10 *c-1*

EIGHTY EIGHTS
Original musical revues and comedy are on tap in the intimate, inviting Cabaret Room; downstairs at the piano bar, the sing-alongs can get raucous. *228 W. 10th St., West Village, 212/924–0088. Subway: 14th St.*

11 *b-2*

55 GROVE STREET
Above Rose's bar, this landmark cabaret offers a piano bar, singers, celebrity impersonators, and sketch comedy. *55 Grove St. (between Bleecker St. and 7th Ave. S.), West Village, 212/366–5438. Subway: Christopher St.*

11 *h-3*

LUCKY CHENG'S
Drag queens strut their stuff to taped music in front of a goldfish pond. Lucky Cheng's is more a restaurant (serving Asian fare) than a bar, but if you just want to see the shows, hang out at the bar and wait until your bartender disappears for a costume change. *24 1st Ave. (between 4th and 5th Sts.), East Village, 212/473–0516. Subway: Broadway-Lafayette or Bleecker St.*

9 *d-5*

OAK ROOM
Gifted song stylists like Andrea Marcovicci draw crowds at this sophisticated, long and narrow club-cum–watering hole. One of the great classic cabarets, the Oak Room is formal (jacket and tie for men) and offers pre-theater dining; diners get better tables. *Algonquin Hotel, 59 W. 44th St., Midtown, 212/840–6800. Subway: 42nd St./Grand Central.*

9 *d-4*

RAINBOW AND STARS
Around the bend from the Rainbow Room, this smart, Art Deco supper club overlooking Central Park presents the greats—Maureen McGovern, Rosemary Clooney—against the twinkling lights of the city. *30 Rockefeller Plaza, 65th floor, Midtown, 212/632–5000. Subway: 47th–50th Sts./Rockefeller Center.*

COMEDY

9 *c-4*

CAROLINE'S
This high-gloss stand-up club features established names as well as those on the brink; Joy Behar, Sandra Bernhard, and Gilbert Gottfried have appeared. Head downstairs when you arrive; the entrance to the show area is to the right of the bar. *1626 Broadway (between 49th and 50th Sts.), Midtown, 212/757–4100. Subway: 50th St.*

9 *c-7*

CATCH A RISING STAR
You might catch a rising comedy star here, but you might also catch headliners like Janeane Garofalo, Denis Leary, or *Saturday Night Live* cast members. R&B, jazz, and cabaret are other possibilities; the schedule is a toss-up. *253 W. 28th St., Chelsea, 212/462–2824. Subway: 28th St.*

9 *f-2*

CHICAGO CITY LIMITS
This improv troupe has been doing what they describe as "comedy without a net" for almost 20 years. They're big on audience participation. *1105 1st Ave. (between 58th and 59th Sts.), Upper East Side, 212/888–5233. Subway: 59th St.*

11 *c-3*

THE COMEDY CELLAR

Beneath the Olive Tree Café, this long-standing, tightly packed club has had consistently good bills for nearly twenty years and shows no sign of slowing down; it's open nightly until 2:30 AM. *117 MacDougal St. (between Bleecker and W. 3rd Sts.), West Village, 212/254–3480. Subway: West 4th St.*

7 *f-8*

COMIC STRIP

This classic comedy showcase is packed, yet it feels like a corner bar. Eddie Murphy got some of his first laughs here. *1568 2nd Ave. (between 81st and 82nd Sts.), Upper East Side, 212/861–9386. Subway: 77th St.*

9 *f-2*

DANGERFIELD'S

Comedian Rodney Dangerfield owns this club, an important stand-up show-case since 1969. *1118 1st Ave. (between 58th and 59th Sts.), Upper East Side, 212/593–1650. Subway: 59th St.*

9 *c-6*

IMPROVISATION

Lots of now-famous comedians, including Richard Pryor and Bette Midler, got their first laughs here. It's the oldest (1963) and most famous of the show-case spots, and draws a huge crowd on weekends. *433 W. 34th St., Garment District, 212/279–3446. Subway: 34th St.*

7 *a-8*

STAND-UP NEW YORK

If you're on the West Side and need some comic relief, make tracks to this club—the stage gets some recognizable faces. *236 W. 78th St., Upper West Side, 212/595–0850. Subway: 79th St.*

COUNTRY & WESTERN

9 *e-4*

DENIM AND DIAMONDS

Break out your boots and hit the dance floor for country line-dancing seven nights a week. If you need help strutting your stuff, come between 7 and 8 PM for lessons. A DJ spins country and western on the main floor; upstairs in the Roadhouse, there's live music (c&w, rocka-billy, cowpunk, electrocountry, the Charlie Daniels Band) Fridays and Saturdays. You can also play pool and scarf Southwestern meals. *511 Lexington Ave. (between 48th and 49th Sts.), Midtown, 212/371–1600. Subway: 51st St.*

DANCE CLUBS

9 *b-3*

COPACABANA NEW YORK

A well-dressed (by club law) Latino crowd comes to salsa to a live orchestra at this legendary club on Tuesdays, Fridays, and Saturdays. *617 W. 57th St., Midtown, 212/582–2672. Subway: 57th St.*

9 *b-3*

LE BAR BAT

Yes, there are fake bats and a Halloween feel at this flashy monster on Theme Restaurant Row, but don't expect to find Goths. There's no Bauhaus; just upbeat, danceable tunes you can probably sing along to. Preppies come here to pick up. *311 W. 57th St., Midtown, 212/307–7228. Subway: 57th St.*

9 *d-8*

LIMELIGHT

At press time, it looked as though the beloved dance club and performance space was reopening its doors. You never know what you'll find in the dark corners of this labyrinthine space in a former church, but it's always fun to explore. *660 Sixth Ave. (between 20th and 21st Sts.), Chelsea, 212/807–7850. Subway: 23rd St.*

10 *b-1*

MOTHER

This small, gay club in the meatpacking district is home to the legendary Tuesday-night party Jackie 60, at which flamboyance rules. The theme changes each week; call ahead and dress appropriately. Saturday night's new, cyber-themed Click & Drag party is also popular, but you might not make it past the door without thigh-high silver platform boots and some S&M gear. The DJ spins mainly industrial and hard house, and there are live performances late in the evening. Fridays draws lipstick lesbians to the Clit Club party. *432 W. 14th St. (at Washington St.), West Village, 212/366–5680. Subway: 14th St.*

11 *e-2*
POLLY ESTHER'S
The walls of these clubs (which are really more like bars) look like suburban teenage bedrooms, circa 1977: posters and pinups of Charlie's Angels, Cheryl Tiegs, Leif Garrett, and Shaun Cassidy cover every inch. Young yups make new friends as they catch disco fever on the small dance floors. *186 W. 4th St., West Village, 212/924–5707, Subway: W. 4th St.*

7 *f-8*
1487 1st Ave. (between 77th and 78th Sts.), Upper East Side, 212/628–4477, Subway: 77th St.

11 *h-1*
PYRAMID
Relive the '80s—in all of their New Wave glory—on Friday nights at this quintessential East Village club. On other nights you'll find kitsch art shows, avant-garde theme parties, and a highly unpredictable assortment of live performances. *101 Avenue A (between 8th and 9th Sts.), East Village, 212/473–7184. Subway: Astor Pl.*

9 *c-3*
ROSELAND
They're serious about ballroom dancing here. It's no longer ten cents a dance, but this enormous space still recalls another time. Dancing happens Thursdays (with a DJ) and Sundays (with an orchestra *and* a DJ). The average age of the patrons nosedives the rest of the week, when bands like the Foo Fighters and GWAR fill the space with distinctly modern music. *239 W. 52nd St., Midtown, 212/247–0200. Subway: 50th St.*

9 *b-8*
ROXY
Roxy's 5,000-square-ft dance floor turns into a chaotic, pulsating roller disco on Tuesday (gay night) and Wednesday and a multiborough dance club Friday and Saturday. *515 W. 18th St., Chelsea, 212/645–5156. Subway: 14th St.*

11 *c-4*
S.O.B.'S
The name stands for Sounds of Brazil, and this club feels like a night in Rio. The decor is tropical, and a joyful carnival atmosphere prevails year-round. Regional Brazilian food is served, and there's live, spirited Brazilian, Caribbean, African, and Latin music and dancing on the small dance floor. *200 Varick St. (at W. Houston St.), West Village, 212/243–4940. Subway: Houston St.*

10 *d-1*
SYSTEM
If you just want to dance and perhaps make some new Eurofriends, System is your place. Door policy is laid-back at this one-room club with a strong sound system and a glassed-in lounge with trees. *76 E. 13th St., East Village, 212/388–1060. Subway: 14th St.*

9 *a-7*
TUNNEL
This laser-lit megaclub has about a million rooms, with about a million DJs spinning about a million types of music. Be prepared for the unisex bathroom, with its own bar and lounge. *220 12th Ave. (at 27th St.), Chelsea, 212/695–4682. Subway: 23rd St.*

10 *e-1*
WEBSTER HALL
A fave with NYU students and similar species, Webster Hall has four floors, five eras of music, trapeze artists, and occasionally live bands. *125 E. 11th St., East Village, 212/353–1600. Subway: 14th St. or Astor Pl.*

DINING & DANCING

9 *d-4*
RAINBOW ROOM
Dust off your ostrich-trimmed gown, or your top hat and tails, for this Art Deco supper club in the sky. The celebrated Rainbow Room has 24 floor-to-ceiling windows with stunning city views north, east, and south and a revolving dance floor surrounded by three levels of tables. The music comes, of course, from a 12-piece orchestra, and the menu features classic and contemporary dishes. Be prepared to shell out $100 per person. Isn't it romantic? *30 Rockefeller Plaza, 65th floor, Midtown, 212/632–5000. Subway: 47th–50th Sts./Rockefeller Center.*

9 *c-4*
SUPPER CLUB
This is exactly what a supper club should look like: a true ballroom, two levels to explore, and plush banquettes

to hide away in. A full orchestra plays cheek-to-cheek big-band sounds on Friday and Saturday nights. You won't recognize the place the rest of the week, when touring alternative and rock-and-roll bands take the stage. *240 W. 47th St., Theater District, 212/921–1940. Subway: 42nd St/Times Square.*

JAZZ

9 *b-5*
BIRDLAND
Originally Charlie Parker's place on 57th Street, this club was one of the centers of jazz's golden age, with everyone up to Miles Davis and the Bird himself taking the stage. The venue moved to 105th Street for a while, but it's back in Midtown now, making good use of a huge space. From 5 PM to midnight you'll find up-and-coming groups and occasionally a known performer, plus dinner. *315 W. 44th St., Theater District, 212/581–3080. Subway: 42nd St./Times Square.*

11 *c-2*
BLUE NOTE
This large and respected jazz club presents well-known jazz, Latin, and blues artists. Ticket prices dive on Monday, when record labels promote their artists' new releases. *131 W. 3rd St. (between 6th Ave. and MacDougal St.), West Village, 212/475–8592. Subway: W. 4th St.*

10 *c-1*
CAJUN
This landlocked Chelsea restaurant with a riverboat feel dishes New Orleans–style jazz alongside Cajun-Creole grub. Live music from the likes of former Louis Armstrong clarinetist Joe Muranyi makes you feel like you've ducked in off Bourbon Street. Dixieland is the fare every night save Wednesday, when modern swing takes over. *129 8th Ave. (between 14th and 15th Sts.), Chelsea, 212/691–6174. Subway: 14th St.*

11 *d-7*
KNITTING FACTORY
The bar is laid-back, and the three small performance spaces often showcase avant-garde jazz artists. On May 17, 1997, Czech President Vaclav Havel and Secretary of State Madeleine Albright

hung here with Lou Reed and Laurie Anderson. *74 Leonard St., Tribeca, 212/219–3055. Subway: Franklin St.*

9 *c-3*
MICHAEL'S PUB
New York's worst-kept secret: Woody Allen moonlights as a clarinetist here on Monday nights, with his New Orleans Jazz Band. Tuesday–Saturday, the Eddie Davis Dixieland Jazz Band has a standing gig. The crowd is monied, uptown. *Hotel Le Parker Meridien, 118 W. 57th St., Upper West Side, 212/758–2272. Subway: 57th St.*

10 *d-1*
SMALL'S
If you're hankering for a jazz jam at 5 AM, head to this pocket-sized club, where the jam sessions run literally all night long. The look is exposed brick and low lighting. The low prices attract lots of NYU students. *183 W. 10th St., West Village, 212/929–7565. Subway: 14th St.*

11 *b-2*
SWEET BASIL
Sweet Basil is a little ritzier than most dark jazz spots. It's a popular eatery and bar with mainstream jazz in comfortable, brick-and-wood surroundings. There are three shows nightly and a Sunday brunch. *88 7th Ave. S. (between Grove and Bleecker Sts.), West Village, 212/242–1785. Subway: Christopher St.*

10 *c-1*
VILLAGE VANGUARD
Since 1935 this renowned New York jazz institution has featured all the greats—Monk, Coltrane, Charles Mingus, Gordon, Marsalis, and so on. It's a quintessentially noisy, smoky, no-frills, Greenwich Village basement club. Get there early if you want a good seat. *178 7th Ave. S. (between 11th and Perry Sts.), West Village, 212/255–4037. Subway: 14th St.*

10 *c-1*
ZINNO
This great Italian restaurant morphs into a mellow jazz club every night. Oenophiles will be thrilled by the outstanding wine list. *126 W. 13th St., West Village, 212/924–5182. Subway: 14th St.*

NIGHTCLUBS

9 *f-2*

DECADE

This smart dance club draws a fortyish crowd—hence, perhaps, the tame music. There's a serious pick-up scene at the bar and, of course, a cigar lounge. The decor is spare and funky, and the food is passable. *1117 1st Ave. (between 58th and 59th Sts.), Midtown, 212/835–5979. Subway: 59th St.*

10 *d-6*

GREATEST BAR ON EARTH

DJ Lucien has enticed hip youngsters not only to party in the Financial District (!) but to stand in line at a tourist attraction. Kate Moss and other such celebs help form the Strato Lounge party on Wednesdays; other nights, DJs and live bands play swing, funk, and blues. Of course, some people just come for the extraordinary views. *1 World Trade Center, 107th floor, Lower Manhattan, 212/524–7000. Subway: World Trade Center.*

11 *c-2*

LIFE

Wednesday night is salsa night, with a diverse, smartly dressed crowd; other nights, drag queens, Europoseurs, and SoHo types groove to house at this glamorous club-of-the-moment in the former Village Gate space. *158 Bleecker St. (at Thompson St.), West Village, 212/420–1999. Subway: W. 4th St.*

10 *c-1*

NELL'S

It's *intime* with all the trappings of a time past—overstuffed seating, subdued lighting, wood paneling, gilt mirrors, and quiet places to drink, dine, and talk. Downstairs you can dance to house, hip-hop, or whatever the DJ decrees. *246 W. 14th St., Chelsea, 212/675–1567. Subway: 14th St.*

9 *e-4*

TATOU

Dine, dance, and enjoy jazz and cabaret under one stylish roof. The decor is all cherubs, gilt, and red velvet. Dress: smart. *151 E. 50th St., Midtown, 212/753–1144. Subway: 51st St.*

PIANO BARS

Of the cabarets listed above, Don't Tell Mama, Duplex, Eighty Eights, and the Oak Room have piano bars as well.

7 *e-7*

BRANDY'S PIANO BAR

Every night finds this small, convivial neighborhood spot packed with smiling people. There's piano entertainment nightly and sometimes other fare as well, such as folk or swing. *235 E. 84th St., Upper East Side, 212/650–1944. Subway: 86th St.*

7 *d-8*

CAFÉ CARLYLE AND BEMELMANS BAR

The unpretentiously elegant Café Carlyle is a must, especially when witty, urbane entertainer Bobby Short is in residence (September–December and April–June); he's as New York as Gershwin. The rest of the year you might find Barbara Cook or Eartha Kitt purring by the piano. The dining is intimate, especially if you're on a comfy banquette, basking in a romantic glow. You can dine at the bar for a fraction of the price. Right next door, sophisticated Bemelmans Bar is perfect for a cocktail or cognac, with murals by the author of the *Madeline* books as a backdrop. *Carlyle Hotel, 35 E. 76th St. (enter through main hotel or at 981 Madison Ave.), Upper East Side, 212/744–1600. Subway: 77th St.*

9 *d-2*

CAFÉ PIERRE

The dressy (jacket required), upscale international crowd in this classy venue hears piano music nightly. *2 E. 61st St., Upper East Side, 212/838–8000. Subway: 59th St.*

9 *g-4*

TOP OF THE TOWER

This seductive, 26th-floor, penthouse cocktail lounge is filled with romantic duos gazing at one another and the twinkling city lights. The atmosphere is elegant and subdued. There's piano music every night save Monday. *Beekman Tower, 3 Mitchell Pl. (off 1st Ave./49th St.), Midtown, 212/355–7300. Subway: 51st St.*

POP/ROCK

11 *c-2*

THE BITTER END

Once upon a time Bob Dylan, Lisa Loeb, and Warren Zevon played The Bitter End, a Village standby for middle-of-the-road rock, fusion, folk, and blues. Moral: You never know which of this week's unknowns will be accepting a Grammy a few years hence. *147 Bleecker St. (between Thompson St. and LaGuardia Pl.), West Village, 212/673–7030. Subway: W. 4th St.*

11 *e-2*

BOTTOM LINE

A warm and intimate space built mainly of wood, this granddaddy of clubs has showcased such budding talents as Stevie Wonder and Bruce Springsteen. Buster Poindexter works the room regularly; other recent headliners include the Jazz Passengers and Cherish the Ladies. When there's a crowd, patrons are packed like sardines at mostly long, thin tables; but most don't mind, as there's not a bad seat in the house, and, remarkably, smoking is not allowed. *15 W. 4th St., West Village, 212/228–7880. Subway: W. 4th St.*

11 *f-3*

CBGB AND OMFUG/CB'S 313 GALLERY

Punk was born at CB's, a long, dark tunnel of a club featuring bands with inventive names like Shirley Temple of Doom and Reuben Kincaid (hey—who had heard of Blondie or the Ramones in 1976?). Next door, 313 attracts a quieter crowd with mostly acoustic music. *313–315 Bowery (between 1st and 2nd Sts.), East Village, 212/982–4052 (CBGB), 212/677–0455 (CB's 313 Gallery). Subway: Bleecker St.; Astor Pl.*

10 *e-1*

IRVING PLAZA

The perfect size for general-admission live music, Irving Plaza serves up everything from Marilyn Manson to Oasis to Better Than Ezra. There's a small balcony with a bar and an even smaller lounge. *17 Irving Pl. (at E. 15th St.), Gramercy, 212/777–1224. Subway: 14th St./Union Sq.*

11 *d-7*

THE KNITTING FACTORY

See Jazz, *above.*

9 *d-8*

TRAMPS

A small club with a lot of energy, Tramps has hosted a range of rockabilly, blues, zydeco, alternative, and country acts for over twenty years. Anyone from Merle Haggard to Betty Seveert to Steel Pulse might drop in. *45 W. 21st St., Chelsea, 212/727–7788. Subway: 23rd St.*

11 *c-3*

ROCK 'N' ROLL CAFÉ

Nostalgic for the Doors, Led Zep, Hendrix, or Clapton? Choose a night and the appropriate sleeveless concert T, and rock out to a cover band. *149 Bleecker St., West Village, 212/677–7630. Subway: Bleecker St.*

11 *c-7*

WETLANDS

Rescue your favorite tie-dye from the laundry pile (or the attic) and slink over to this ode to the '60s—VW bus and everything—with an environmental-'90s bent. The live music, often psychedelic and often danceable, ranges from reggae and grass-roots rock to bluegrass and folk. Dave Matthews and Hootie and the Blowfish used to play this small space, known as the Sweatlands when it's packed. *161 Hudson St. (at Laight St.), Tribeca, 212/966–4225. Subway: Canal St.*

chapter 6

PARKS, GARDENS, AND SPORTS

I t may seem counterintuitive, but New York is and always has been a great place for sports. It all goes back to why the city sprang up here in the first place—lots of water, a strong rock foundation, forests, marshlands, and proximity to other areas of commercial interest. Over the years, New Yorkers have made the most of their natural environment and created their own exercise options indoors as well. Pick any block (well, almost any block . . .), and what do you see walking down the street but gorgeous bodies, young and old. Then look at the facilities—the city with the biggest and best of everything is never willing to be outdone. Lured by the vast market potential and capital resources, sports outfitters will launch just about anything here, hence the endless cycle of fitness trends—roller basketball, a new brand of aerobics every month, even such seemingly rural pastimes as rock climbing and kayaking. It's hard to find a better combination of natural and man-made facilities—and if anyone tries to argue about that, you can just remind them that another popular New York exercise is kvetching.

parks

It's easy to get frustrated in a city where green signs that say PARK point you to a garage rather than a green space. But New York has its share of parks, large and small, teeming and tranquil— 26,220 acres at last count. From the seemingly endless Pelham Bay Park and the Staten Island Greenbelt to midtown's vest-pocket delights, parks have saved the soul of many a harried New Yorker. One recent survey found that almost two-thirds of all New Yorkers visit a park more than once a week.

Landscape architects Frederick Law Olmsted and Calvert Vaux come up again and again in New York City—and American—park history, as they designed a number of the city's most impressive "natural" spaces and introduced concepts that now seem essential to our enjoyment of parks. They sought to enhance the natural topography of their sites, focusing on "turf, wood, and water," and they felt that different types of park users—such as walkers, horseback riders, and (then) carriage users— needed separate paths. Central Park, Prospect Park, and several other parks and parkways are some of Olmsted and Vaux's lasting gifts to New York. A survey of New York's natural history also includes Robert Moses, who held various city positions from the WPA era through the 1960s, including parks commissioner (he united what had been five independent agencies) and chair of the Triborough Bridge and Tunnel Authority. Though he's responsible for the creation and rehabilitation of some treasured parks, Moses eventually grew more interested in building highways than parks, so he's also responsible for much of New York's isolating asphalt.

When visiting a park, use common sense: After dark, you're probably safer with other people. During the day, try not to interfere with activities, whether it's a ball game or a skater whizzing by. Motor vehicles are allowed on some park roads, so watch out for those, too.

PARK INFORMATION

The City of New York/Parks and Recreation, also known as the Parks Department or the Department of Parks and Recreation, is responsible for the vast majority of parks, beaches, malls, playgrounds, and woodlands within city limits. The department offers a number of phone information lines, provide permits for games and events in parks, and staff Urban Park Ranger programs. Much of their work is handled by individual borough offices. The general **parks hot line,** for information and emergencies, is 800/201–PARK. For recorded information pertaining to **special events** in the city's parks, call 212/ 360–3456. **Borough headquarters offices** have information about the parks in their respective boroughs and can help you locate sporting facilities near you: **Bronx** (718/430–1868), **Brooklyn** (718/ 965–8900), **Manhattan** (212/408– 0100), **Queens** (718/520–5900), and **Staten Island** (718/390–8000).

The New York State Department of Parks, Recreation and Historic Preservation (NYC Region 212/387–0271) also manages some of the city's outdoor spaces, including Staten Island's Clay Pit Ponds Preserve and Manhattan's

Riverbank State Park. Gateway National Recreation Area, formed as the first urban national recreation area in 1972, consists of National Park Service parklands spread out over waterfront districts in Queens, Brooklyn, and Staten Island/New Jersey, Together, these spits of land form a natural gateway (get it?) to New York's great harbor. Among its treasures are a wildlife refuge, historic forts and airfields, and beaches. Headquarters are at Brooklyn's Floyd Bennett Field (718/338–3338).

PERMITS

For details and permits for use of city ball fields, call or stop by the Parks Department's permit office (16 W. 61st St., 6th floor, Manhattan, 212/408–0209). Other borough offices are: Bronx (718/430–1840), Brooklyn (718/965–8919), Queens (718/520–5933), and Staten Island (718/816–6529). There's nothing to stop you from using an open field, but if someone with a permit and field reservation shows up, you'll have to leave. For tennis permits, *see* Tennis, *below.*

URBAN PARK RANGERS

Trained in the history, landscape design, geology, wildlife, and botany of the city's parks, these uniformed officers guide tours and lead workshops to help visitors better understand and appreciate the parks. Topics include everything from horseshoe-crab mating habits to the buildings surrounding Central Park; all are free and fascinating. For program information call the appropriate number: **Bronx** (718/430–1832), **Brooklyn** (718/438–0100), **Manhattan** (212/427–4040), **Queens** (718/699–4204), and **Staten Island** (718/667–6042).

bronx

2 *d-4*

BRONX PARK

Laid out in the 1880s, this 718-acre park became the home of the city's zoo and botanical gardens in 1899 (*see* Gardens *and* Zoos & Aquariums, *below*). *Bronx Park East at Brady Ave., Bronxdale.*

2 *c-6*

CROTONA PARK

Formerly the estate of the Bathgate family and known as Bathgate Woods, it was renamed after the ancient Greek city of Croton. The 128-acre park contains a bathhouse and pool dating back to the 1930s. *Fulton Ave. at E. 175th St., Claremont Village.*

2 *g-2*

PELHAM BAY PARK

This 2,764-acre park is one of the city's most versatile. It was named after Englishman Thomas Pell, who bought land in the area in 1654. Fish, egret, frogs, raccoons, owls, fox, ospreys, and even seals share the land with New Yorkers. Habitats of the last group include tennis courts, baseball diamonds, a track, a playground, golf courses, and a stable. Some relics of the past include the Bartow-Pell Mansion (see Chapter 2). **Orchard Beach,** a crescent-shaped Robert Moses creation, is one highlight (see Beaches, below). Southeast of here, **Rodman's Neck** is a meadow-and-scrub area where the NYPD practices shooting. The **Thomas Pell Wildlife Refuge and Sanctuary,** established in 1967, contains wetlands and woodlands. **Split Rock,** a massive glacier-split boulder, is where poet Anne Hutchinson died in 1643 at the hands of the Siwanoy Indians. **Hunter Island** is a coastal area full of tidal wetlands and the park's largest continuous forest. The 6-mi Siwanoy Trail runs through the entire park. *Bruckner Blvd. and Middletown Rd., 718/430–1890. Pelham Bay Park Environmental Center (near Orchard Beach), 718/885–3466. Subway: Pelham Bay Park.*

2 *b-2*

VAN CORTLANDT PARK

Despite the intrusion of various parkways, this park's more than 1,000 acres of wetlands and woodlands are home to a remarkable variety of critters. The **Parade Ground** is the most popular area for people, featuring several fields and the **Van Cortlandt House** (*see* Chapter 2), the oldest building in the Bronx. The Van Cortlandt family burial, **Vault Hill,** has fine views from its perch 169 ft above sea level. **Tibbets Brook** flows through marshy areas into the 13-acre **Van Cortlandt Lake.** Hikers have plenty of options: the **John Kieran Nature Trail** runs alongside the lake, the **Aqueduct Trail** follows the route of the Croton Aqueduct, and the **Cass Gallagher Nature Trail** winds its way through the **Northwest Forest.** Summer brings New York Philharmonic concerts and many other events. *W. 242nd Street to city line, between Broadway and Jerome Ave., 718/430–1890. Subway: 242nd St./Van Cortlandt Park.*

brooklyn

4 *d-6*

DYKER BEACH PARK

This 217-acre park, adjacent to the Fort Hamilton Military Reservation, has beautiful views of Gravesend Bay and the Verrazano Narrows Bridge. Fine expanses of lawn, sea breezes, and good fishing make it a relaxing place to spend a few hours. *Shore Pkwy., east of the Verrazano Narrows Bridge, Fort Hamilton. Subway: B, M to 18th Ave.*

12 *b-1*

EMPIRE FULTON FERRY STATE PARK

New York City needs more parks like this one—a grassy area right on the waterfront. The views of Manhattan from between the Manhattan and Brooklyn bridges are spectacular, the breezes keep summer sunbathers cool, and the out-of-the-way location means it's terribly underappreciated. *Plymouth St. at Main St., Brooklyn Heights. Subway: York St.; High St./Brooklyn Bridge.*

12 *e-2*

FORT GREENE PARK

The site of Fort Putnam during the Revolutionary War and Fort Greene during the War of 1812, this 30-acre hill was turned into Brooklyn's first major park by Olmsted and Vaux in 1848. (Then called Washington Park, it was renamed in 1897.) Pretty paths meander up and down the park's hills, past tennis courts, playgrounds, and harbor views. In the center, stands Prison Ship Martyrs' Monument, designed in 1908 by architect Stanford White. *Myrtle to DeKalb Aves.; St. Edward to Washington Park Ave. Subway: Atlantic Ave.*

1 *f-7*

MARINE PARK

This 1,024-acre expanse borders Gateway National Recreation Area and includes several scenic coves as well as trails, fields, and a golf course. *Inlet between Gerritsen and Flatbush Aves., inland to Fillmore Ave., between Burnet and E. 32nd Sts.*

1 *h-6*

PROSPECT PARK

Olmsted and Vaux's ode to Brooklyn covers 526 acres, and its designers liked it better than Central Park. Though Brooklynites first planned to have their park designed around Flatbush Avenue by Egbert Viele, chief engineer of Central Park, the Civil War gave them time to reconsider. In an act that would surely be criticized today as a bureaucratic delay tactic, the park commissioners had Calvert Vaux reexamine the proposal. Vaux quickly realized that a highway bisecting a park would greatly detract from the greenery, and instead suggested a layout west of Flatbush Avenue. Starting in 1865, he and Olmsted designed the park's broad meadows, gardens, terraces, and landscaped walks.

Like many large city parks, this one has endless recreational possibilities. Joggers and people on wheels seem to circle the loop road endlessly, yet other paths through woods and fields are barely touched. Boats float around in summer near where skaters spin in winter. The playgrounds are alive with children's squeals, the fields with ballgames and barbecues. Prospect Park's roadways are closed to motor vehicles the same hours as Central Park's (*see* Manhattan, *below*).

The main entrance to the park is **Grand Army Plaza,** planned in the spirit of Paris's L'Etoile (a.k.a. Place Charles-de-Gaulle, home of the Arc de Triomphe). The neo-Roman Soldiers and Sailors Memorial Arch is a memorial to the Union Army (open to climbers mid-May–early July weekends and holidays 1–5). This grandiose structure and most of the other entrance gates were added after Olmsted and Vaux had finished their work, much to their chagrin. Just inside the park, along the footpath to the east of the roadway, **Endale Arch** beautifully frames your view of **Long Meadow,** whose crescent shape makes its 90 acres seem even bigger. Frisbee, volleyball, soccer, and lounging are popular on this luxurious expanse; it's also the site of summer Philharmonic concerts. Other concert venues are the **Bandshell** at 9th Street, which hosts "Celebrate Brooklyn" festivities of all kinds, and the **Music Pagoda,** designed to resemble a traditional Chinese gateway (just north of Lullwater, a kind of feeder to Prospect Lake). Between Long Meadow and Flatbush Avenue toward the northern end of the park, the **Vale of Cashmere** is a natural amphitheater and a refuge for small birds. The **Prospect Park Wildlife Center** (*see below*), **Lefferts Homestead Children's Museum** (*see*

Chapter 2), and the restored 1912
Carousel (weekends and holidays noon–
5, additional hours and days in summer)
comprise the most child-friendly section
of the park, right off Flatbush Avenue.
Prospect Park Alliance offices are in the
red-brick 1929 **Picnic House,** near 7th
Street and Prospect Park West. Woods,
rocky hills, and a small stream distinguish the **Ravine,** the rugged central
area. The 60-acre **Prospect Lake** is the
main body of water in the park; its water
is delivered through a complicated
plumbing and water-recycling system.
Vaux's **Terrace Bridge,** added in 1890,
gives a good view of the lake and Lullwater. You can rent boats from the breathtaking Italian-style **Boathouse** on
Lullwater, which stands practically in the
shadow of the wonderfully gnarled
Camperdown Elm. A snack bar and skating rink abut Prospect Lake, nearby. *Bordered by Flatbush Ave., Ocean Ave.,
Parkside Ave., Prospect Park Southwest,
and Prospect Park West, 718/965–8999.
Subway: Grand Army Plaza; D, Q to
Prospect Park; F to 15th St./Prospect Park.*

manhattan

10 *e-8*
BATTERY PARK

Jutting out as if it were Manhattan's
green toe, this verdant landfill is loaded
with monuments and sculpture.
Because it's at the junction of the Hudson and East rivers, it has a great view
of New York Harbor: Governors Island,
Brooklyn, the Verrazano Narrows
Bridge, Staten Island, the Statue of Liberty, Ellis Island, and New Jersey. The
park's name refers to a line of cannons
once mounted here to defend the shoreline, which ran along what is currently
State Street. Castle Clinton, first known
as the West Battery, was erected off-
shore on a pile of rock for the War of
1812 (nary a shot was ever fired). Landfill later joined it to the mainland, and it
has since served as an entertainment
and concert facility (Castle Garden), a
federal immigration center, and the New
York City Aquarium. Robert Moses tried
to knock it down after forcing the aquarium out in the early 1940s—claiming
that its 8-ft-thick walls weren't stable—
but he lost that battle (*see Zoos and
Aquariums, below*). Now slated for yet
another renovation, Castle Clinton sits
squarely in Battery Park and is home to
the ticket booth for the Statue of Liberty
and Ellis Island ferries. Greenery, sea

breezes, and great vistas draw mainly
bankers and brokers at noon on sunny
days, but tourists come to catch the ferries no matter what the weather. *State
St. and Battery Pl., Lower Manhattan.
Subway: 1, 9 to South Ferry.*

10 *c-6*
BATTERY PARK ESPLANADE

This 1.2-mi linear park, running along
the perimeter of Battery Park City, is one
of the city's newest and best. Old-fashioned lampposts, shade trees, well-
maintained lawns, and benches facing
unimpeded Hudson River views make
this an inviting spot. *Enter at West and
Liberty streets, Lower Manhattan. Battery
Park City Parks Corporation, 212/267–
9700. Subway: Cortlandt St.; World Trade
Center.*

10 *e-8*
BOWLING GREEN

Rented out to local residents for the outrageous price of one peppercorn a year
starting in 1733, this park was not fully
available to everyone until 1850, but it's
still the city's oldest extant public park.
The British erected its simple iron fence
in 1771 to protect a statue of George III,
but on July 9, 1776 the statue was top-
pled. The fence still stands. *Broadway
and Battery Pl., Lower Manhattan. Subway: Bowling Green.*

9 *d-5*
BRYANT PARK

In 1823, these nine acres were set aside
as a potters' field, but they became a
public park (called Reservoir Square,
after the drinking-water reservoir that lay
where the library is now) in 1847. New
York's version of London's Crystal
Palace was erected here in 1853, but it
burned down five years later. The land
was renamed for poet and editor
William Cullen Bryant in 1884. It degen-
erated into a good place to buy and sell
drugs in the 1970s, but, having been
renovated and restored in the late
1980s, it now teems with well-dressed
professionals who snatch up the lawn
chairs for their brown-bag power
lunches. Weekday and evening concerts
and an outdoor movie festival (Monday
nights in summer) help keep it hopping.
The **Bryant Park Dance and Music Ticket
Booth** sells discounted tickets for music
and dance performances throughout the
city. *6th Ave. between 40th and 42nd Sts.,
behind New York Public Library Center for*

the Humanities, Midtown. Subway: B, D, F, Q to 42nd St.

7 *g-7*

CARL SCHURZ PARK

During the American Revolution, a house on this promontory was used as a fortification by the Continental Army, then taken over as a British outpost. Later, in more peaceful times, the land became known as East End Park. It was renamed in 1911 to honor Carl Schurz, a prominent 19th-century German immigrant who had been a senator and secretary of the interior. A curved stone staircase leads up to John Finley Walk, lined with wrought-iron railings, which overlooks the East River. The view—of the Triborough, Hell's Gate, and Queensboro bridges; Wards, Randalls, and Roosevelt islands; and Astoria, Queens—is so tranquil that you'd never guess you're directly above the FDR Drive. Behind you, along the walk, are raised flower beds as well as some enclosed dog runs. Other popular hangouts are the hill at the north end (for sledding in winter and sunning in summer) and the playground. The city's first family—the mayor's—lives behind the high fence in **Gracie Mansion,** at the north end of the park. *East End Ave. to East River, between 84th and 90th Sts., Upper East Side. Subway: 4, 5, 6 to 86th St.*

1 *d-4*

CENTRAL PARK

America's premier urban park, this 840-acre oasis is 2½ mi long, ¾ mi wide, and smack in the middle of Manhattan. Every day, thousands of joggers, cyclists, skaters, and walkers make their daily jaunts about "the loop," the reservoir, and the rest of the park. Sunseekers crowd the grassy lawns in summer, and athletes of all stripes make use of the fields, trails, courts, and other facilities year-round. In fall, the foliage is magnificent and the air is crisp. Ice skaters come out for the rinks and frozen lakes in winter, while cross-country skiers and sledders hit the fields and trails. In spring, blooming flowers turn the park into a scented wonderland. Summer especially sees a crowded calendar of concerts, readings, and theater and opera performances. All told, some 15 million users take advantage of the park each year.

Although it appears to be nothing more than a swatch of rolling countryside excused from urban development, Central Park is an artificial landscape. After the city acquired the land for the park, it held a competition for the park's design. Park superintendent Frederick Law Olmsted and landscape architect Calvert Vaux beat the nearly three dozen other entries with their "Greensward Plan"—part formal, part pastoral, part picturesque, it skillfully blends man-made lakes and ponds, hills and dales, secluded glens, wide meadows, a bird sanctuary, bridle paths, and nature trails. Four transverse roads were designed to carry crosstown traffic beneath the park's hills and tunnels without disturbing those at play, and 40 bridges were conceived—each with a unique design and name—to give people easy access to various areas.

Construction was a monumental task. Entire communities were displaced, swamps were drained, millions of cubic yards of soil were removed, walls of schist were blasted, and hundreds of thousands of trees and shrubs were planted. Almost a century and a half later, we can see ongoing construction, restoration, and maintenance. In the mid-1990s alone, the Turtle Pond has been enlarged, the Great Lawn has been completely revamped, and entrance gates have been remodeled.

Those who wish to stroll unharassed by traffic should bear in mind that the circular drive through the park is closed to auto traffic on weekdays 10 AM to 3 PM (except the southeastern portion of the road, below 72nd Street, which remains open) and 7 to 10 PM, and on weekends and holidays. Nonautomotive traffic on the road is often heavy and sometimes fast-moving, so always be careful when you're crossing the road, and stay toward the inside when you're walking. Tip: The first two digits of the number plate of each lamppost in the park indicate the nearest cross street.

For the classic old-fashioned indulgence, you can glide gently through the park on a horse-drawn carriage (operated by Chateau Stables, 212/246–0520, or Hansom Cabs). It's the perfect way to amuse visiting relatives from out of town. Just walk up to any carriage along Central Park South, especially near 5th Ave.; the rates, which are reasonable, should be posted on each one. Only on extremely hot days do the horses take a break.

Whole volumes have been filled by writers extolling Central Park and its landmarks. In the southeast corner, the **Pond,** dominated by Overlook Rock, is home to swans and ducks. Picturesque **Gapstow Bridge** gives you a good view of midtown and leads to **Wollman Rink,** a popular ice- and roller-skating rink. **The Dairy** (mid-park at 64th St., 212/794–6564, closed Mon.) is to the north, with its pointed eaves, steeple, and high-pitched roof; once a working dairy, it's now the park information center. In what was planned as a Children's District is an antique-horse **Carousel;** the **zoo** (*see* Zoos and Aquariums, *below*) is to the east. The expansive field in the southern section of the park is **Sheep Meadow,** once frequented by sheep but now a favorite of picnickers and sunbathers. The sheep who did graze here lived in what is now **Tavern on the Green** (*see* chapter 3). East of Sheep Meadow is the **Mall,** a formal promenade lined by elms and statues of literary figures in a section called the Literary Walk. At the north end of the Mall, across the 72nd Street transverse, is **Bethesda Terrace** and **Bethesda Fountain,** the latter built in 1863. Willows, rhododendrons, and cherry trees surround the magnificent staircase. If you continue west on 72nd Street you'll come to **Strawberry Fields,** 2½ landscaped acres that form an "International Peace Garden" in memory of John Lennon. Follow the water northwest from Bethesda Terrace and you'll cross **Bow Bridge** into **The Ramble,** a heavily wooded, wild 37-acre area laced with twisting, climbing paths. This is prime bird-watching territory. The neo-Victorian **Loeb Boathouse,** on the lake, has boats and bikes for rent and a waterside cafe. On the east side of the park at 74th Street is **Conservatory Water** (commonly known as the Sailboat Lake), a symmetrical stone basin where model yachts race Saturday mornings near statues of the fanciful Hans Christian Andersen and Alice in Wonderland. Midpark at 79th Street, **Belvedere Castle** towers above the **Turtle Pond** and the outdoor **Delacorte Theater,** where the Public Theater stages plays in the summer. On the castle's ground floor, the **Henry Luce Nature Observatory** (212/772–0210, closed Mon.) has nature exhibits, children's workshops, and educational programs. To its west is the dark-wood **Swedish Chalet,** a marionette theater. Behind all this are the newly restored **Turtle Pond** and the **Great Lawn,** 13 acres of Kentucky bluegrass, ball fields, and courts. Between the Great Lawn and the Metropolitan Museum of Art, which encroaches on park territory, stands **Cleopatra's Needle,** an Egyptian obelisk given to the city in 1881. The **Jacqueline Kennedy Onassis Reservoir** (midpark, 85th to 96th Sts.) is a 106-acre lake that is *not* used for drinking water—thus the ceaseless rumors that it might be drained. The path around it makes for great running. Further north, at 105th Street, the formal **Conservatory Garden** (*see* Gardens, *below*) presides over Fifth Avenue. **Harlem Meer** is another striking body of water—the adjacent **Charles A. Dana Discovery Center** (212/860–1370, closed Mon.) runs many nature programs for families. *Bordered by Central Park West, 59th St., 5th Ave., and 110th St. General information 212/360–3444. Subway: 59th St./Columbus Circle; N, R to 5th Ave.; B, C to 72nd–110th Sts.*

10 *e-6*
CITY HALL PARK
Known in colonial times as the Fields or the Common, this green spot has hosted hangings, riots, and demonstrations. Now City Hall's front yard, schoolchildren with picnic lunches and office workers with sun visors fill the park in good weather. *Between Broadway, Park Row, and Chambers St., Lower Manhattan. Subway: Brooklyn Bridge/City Hall.*

3 *c-1*
EAST RIVER ESPLANADE
You have to stretch your imagination to call this a park, but any long stretch of water with pedestrian access bears mentioning. This one starts near the heliport at East 59th Street—to reach the promenade, take the funky pedestrian suspension bridge at 60th Street. The paved strip, lined by benches, patches of grass, and the occasional small tree, continues to a staircase at 80th Street. Up the steps is the lovely Carl Schurz Park (*see above*), and the esplanade continues past Gracie Mansion all the way to 125th Street. There's usually a crew of fishermen near 100th Street, but most other people on the path remain in motion. *East River from 59th St. to 125th Sts., Upper East Side/East Harlem. Subway: 6 to 59th St.–125th Sts.*

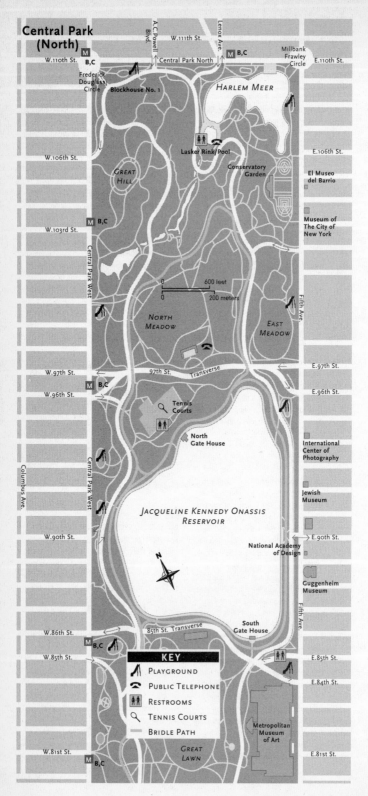

Central Park
(North)

W.111th St.
A.C.Powell Blvd.
Lenox Ave.
Central Park North
Millbank
Frawley Circle
E.110th St.

W.110th St.
M B,C
M B,C

Frederick
Douglass
Circle
Blockhouse No. 1

HARLEM MEER

Lasker Rink/Pool

Conservatory
Garden

W.106th St.
E.106th St.

GREAT
HILL

El Museo
del Barrio

W.103rd St.
M B,C

Museum of
The City of
New York

Central Park West

0   600 feet
0   200 meters

NORTH
MEADOW

EAST
MEADOW

Fifth Ave.

W.97th St.
97th St. Transverse
E.97th St.

M B,C
W.96th St.
E.96th St.

Tennis
Courts

North
Gate House

International
Center of
Photography

Jewish
Museum

Columbus Ave.

JACQUELINE KENNEDY ONASSIS
RESERVOIR

W.90th St.
E.90th St.

National Academy
of Design

N

Guggenheim
Museum

85th St. Transverse

South
Gate House

Fifth Ave.

W.86th St.
M B,C

W.85th St.
E.85th St.

KEY
E.84th St.

Playground
Public Telephone
Restrooms
Tennis Courts
Bridle Path

Metropolitan
Museum
of Art

W.81st St.
M B,C

GREAT
LAWN

E.81st St.

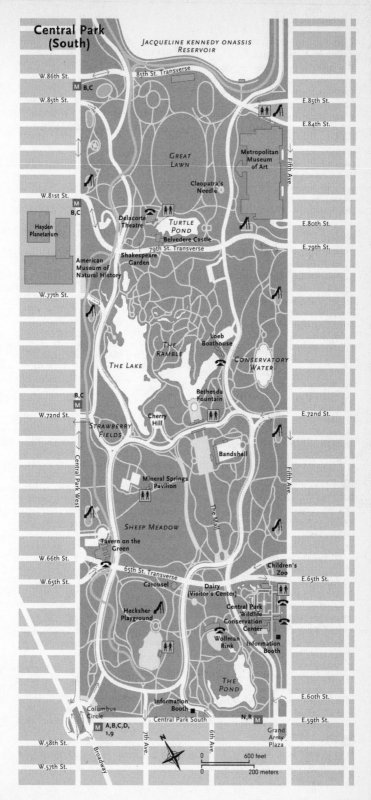

Central Park (South)

W.86th St. Ⓜ B,C
W.85th St.

Jacqueline Kennedy Onassis Reservoir

85th St. Transverse

E.85th St.
E.84th St.

Fifth Ave.

Great Lawn

Cleopatra's Needle

Metropolitan Museum of Art

W.81st St. Ⓜ B,C

Hayden Planetarium

Delacorte Theatre

Turtle Pond

Belvedere Castle

79th St. Transverse

E.8oth St.
E.79th St.

Shakespeare Garden

American Museum of Natural History

W.77th St.

Loeb Boathouse

The Ramble

Conservatory Water

The Lake

Bethesda Fountain

B,C Ⓜ

W.72nd St.

Cherry Hill

E.72nd St.

Strawberry Fields

Bandshell

Mineral Springs Pavilion

Central Park West

Sheep Meadow

The Mall

Children's Zoo

Tavern on the Green

W.66th St.

65th St. Transverse

Carousel

W.65th St.

Dairy (Visitor's Center)

E.65th St.

Central Park Wildlife Conservation Center

Heckscher Playground

Wollman Rink

Information Booth

The Pond

E.6oth St.

Columbus Circle

Information Booth

Ⓜ A,B,C,D, 1,9

Central Park South

N,R

E.59th St.

W.58th St.

Grand Army Plaza

Broadway

7th Ave.

6th Ave.

W.57th St.

N

0   600 feet
0   200 meters

10 *h-2*

EAST RIVER PARK

This park is wider and greener than its newer cousin on the Hudson, but it doesn't draw half as many people. The facilities—tennis courts, a track, fields, a playground, basketball courts—aren't all in the best condition, but that's no reason to stay away. Look forward to the renovation of the decrepit theater—the original home of "Shakespeare in the Park"—by 1999. *East River Dr. between 14th and Delancey Sts., East Village/Lower East Side. Subway: Delancey St.*

5 *b-7*

FORT TRYON PARK

Named after New York's last English governor, William Tryon, Fort Tryon Park occupies the site of Fort Washington, the last holdout against the British invasion of Manhattan (it fell November 16, 1776). Capping a hill 250 ft above the river, these 66 acres of wooded hills and dales overlooking the Hudson were a gift to the city from the Rockefeller family. The beautiful flower gardens and terracing, and the view of the Palisades across the Hudson, make you feel miles away from the city. The **Cloisters** museum (*see* Chapter 2) is in the middle of the park. *Between Riverside Dr. and Broadway from 192nd to Dyckman Sts., Washington Heights. Subway: A to 190th St.*

9 *e-8*

GRAMERCY PARK

This tiny patch of land, originally swamp, is New York's only surviving private square. It was bought and drained by early real-estate developer Samuel B. Ruggles, who then created a park (in 1831) for the exclusive use of those who would buy the surrounding lots. Sixty-six of the city's fashionable elite did just that, and no less than golden keys were provided for them to penetrate the park's 8-ft-high fence. Although no longer golden, keys are still given to residents only. The rest of us can only gaze at the pristine park and the landmark 19th-century row houses that surround it; still, the pretty square is refreshing to look at. *Lexington Ave. between 20th and 21st Sts. Subway: 6, N, R to 23rd St.*

6 *d-3*

HIGH BRIDGE PARK

High Bridge, built as Aqueduct Bridge between 1837 and 1848 to carry upstate reservoir water to the city, is the oldest remaining bridge connecting Manhattan to the mainland. The landmark **Water Tower** on the Manhattan side was once in use. The forested terraces and rocky ledges here have good views across the Harlem River. *Between Harlem River Dr. and Edgecombe and Amsterdam Aves., from 155th to Dyckman Sts., Washington Heights. Subway: A, B to 155th St. or 163rd St.*

1 *c-5*

HUDSON RIVER PARK

Though plans involving design and funding for this park probably won't be settled until the park is completed years from now, we will someday have a waterfront walking, cycling, and blading path and more than 10 public piers stretching from 59th Street all the way down the West Side. The park is already a reality up to 14th Street, where bladers and Village people convening at all hours attest to how sorely New Yorkers need more waterfront space. The southern end of the park, now called **Nelson A. Rockefeller Park,** has expansive green lawns and the Lilliputian, cast-bronze "Real World" sculptures by artist Tom Otterness. (Kids love these; you can climb on them and play in the water that surrounds some of them.) Piers 25 and 26, at North Moore Street, have summertime activities for kids, including fishing, games, and environmental education. Pier 84, at West 44th Street, isn't yet connected to the rest of the "park," but it's open to the public and has a small community garden and activities organized by Floating the Apple (*see* Boating, *below*). Piers 45 (Christopher St.), 54 (13th St.), and 62 (W. 23rd St.) also allow public access. The Hudson River Parks Conservancy, the group working to realize the park, sponsors activities such as outdoor movies, regattas, and even swims. *Battery Park to 59th St. along the Hudson River, 212/533– PARK for event information. Subway: 1, 9 to Canal–14th Sts.; A, C, E, L to 14th St.*

5 *b-5*

INWOOD HILL PARK

The Hudson and Harlem rivers meet at the tip of this unbelievably quiet, scenic park. Its 196 acres of hill-climbing woods are laced with hidden paths and contain Manhattan's only remaining natural forest. Its history is rich, too:

Algonquin Indians once dwelled in caves on this site, and British and Hessian troops were quartered here during the American Revolution. *Dyckman St. to the Harlem River, from Seaman to Payson Aves, Inwood. Subway: A to Dyckman St./200th St. or 207th St./Inwood.*

7 *h-7*
LIGHTHOUSE PARK
This lovely green area has views you'd otherwise need a boat to admire—Manhattan's Upper East Side, Ward's Island, Long Island City, and Astoria, Queens, and a few bridges, all from water level. It's named for the 50-ft stone lighthouse, vintage 1872, that used to help sailors navigate the East River. *Northern tip of Roosevelt Island. Subway: B, Q to Roosevelt Island.*

9 *e-7*
MADISON SQUARE PARK
At various times in its history the area was a potter's field, the site of the city's first baseball games (1845), a luxurious residential area, and the location of the original Madison Square Garden. Now there are small flower plantings and several splendid sculptures here, including a statue of Alaska buyer William H. Seward. The park is now used mainly by office workers and dog owners. *23rd to 26th Sts. between 5th and Madison Aves., Murray Hill. Subway: 6, N, R to 23rd St.*

7 *d-2*
MARCUS GARVEY PARK
As the city pushed northward, it didn't want Harlem to be without a park, so it built one around this 70-ft-high rocky eminence in the middle of Fifth Avenue. From the street on the park's southern side, you can see the three-tiered, cast-iron fire tower (1856), the only remaining tower in a now-defunct citywide network. First called Mt. Morris Park, it was renamed in 1973 after Marcus Garvey, who led the back-to-Africa movement. It's not known for being safe. *120th to 124th Sts. at 5th Ave, Harlem. Subway: 2, 3 to 125th St.*

7 *b-2*
MORNINGSIDE PARK
Sadly, this 1887 Olmsted and Vaux gem in Morningside Heights is another park that's just not safe. It follows the crest of the cliffs above Harlem, pressing up to the Columbia University campus. *110th to 123rd Sts. from Morningside Dr. to Manhattan and Morningside Aves. Subway: B, C to 110th–125th Sts.*

9 *d-3*
PALEY PARK
A boon to midtown's weary, this memorial to former CBS executive Samuel Paley is remarkable not so much for its features but for its historical status as one of the first of New York's "vest-pocket parks" to be inserted into the concrete canyons. A recycling waterfall blocks out traffic noise, and feathery honey-locust trees provide shade. The snack bar opens in warm weather. *3 E. 53rd St., Midtown. Subway: E, F to 5th Ave.*

1 *c-3*
RIVERSIDE PARK
In the tradition of English landscaping, Frederick Law Olmsted met the challenge of this sloping terrain to provide a playground along and above the Hudson River for Upper West Siders. Its various promenades make for usually uncrowded walking, especially beautiful in spring when crab apple and cherry trees are in bloom. The **79th Street Boat Basin** is home for those who live in its flotilla of houseboats. The **Rotunda,** behind it, occupies a wonderful circular space punctuated by a fountain. The park holds several important monuments, including the **Soldiers' and Sailors' Memorial** and **Grant's Tomb** (*see* Chapter 2) The **Eleanor Roosevelt statue,** at the 72nd Street entrance, is the park's latest addition. *72nd to 159th Sts. between Riverside Dr. and the Hudson River, Upper West Side. Subway: 1, 9 to 72nd St.–157th St.*

6 *b-7*
RIVERBANK STATE PARK
This unlikely 28-acre park opened in 1993 atop a sewage treatment plant. Elevated as high as 69 ft above the Hudson, it's not at all marred by its neighbor below, and its facilities—including indoor and outdoor pools, an outdoor track, a skating rink, numerous playing fields, and a playground—are state-of-the-art. Just being cooled by the breeze and admiring the view is rewarding, too. *Entrances: Riverside Dr. at 138th and 145th Sts., Harlem, 212/694–3600. Subway: 1, 9 to 137th St./City College or 145th St.*

7 *b-3*

ST. NICHOLAS PARK

Like Morningside Park, this thin green strip climbs a steep hill and backs up to a college—in this case, City College. Its designer, Frederick Law Olmsted, feared that its narrowness and difficult terrain would make it unsafe, and he was right. The playgrounds and courts that edge the park see a lot of use, but the interior is desolate and poorly maintained. If the National Park Service moves Hamilton Grange (*see* Chapter 2) here from its location just around the corner, per the rumors, the park might get some needed help. *128th to 141st. between St. Nicholas Ave. and St. Nicholas Terr., Harlem. Subway: B, C to 135th St.*

10 *f-1*

STUYVESANT SQUARE

This historic square, now full of flower plantings, was once part of Peter Stuyvesant's farm but was ceded to the city in 1836 by his great-great-grandson. It comprised the core of fashionable New York in the late 19th century. *2nd Ave. from 15th to 17th Sts., Gramercy. Subway: 3rd Ave.*

10 *g-2*

TOMPKINS SQUARE PARK

Named after one-time New York State Governor Daniel P. Tompkins, this 16-acre park looks better than it has in years. The oldest park on the Lower East Side, its post-1960s troubles have included violent clashes between city officials and the park's permanent residents, and its reputation as a drug center. None of those who now use it for basketball, dog walking, relaxing, and other park activities seems to care. *7th to 10th Sts. betweem Avenues A and B, East Village. Subway: Astor Pl.; 2nd Ave.*

10 *e-1*

UNION SQUARE

Though its name comes from its function as a transportation nexus, the square has been the site of many union protests, and several radical groups once had their headquarters nearby. At that time—the late 19th century—the surrounding neighborhood was a commercial area, with fine shops such as Tiffany's, but by World War I it had turned shabby. The park was refurbished in the 1980s and now has a colorful **Greenmarket** at its western and north-

ern edges every Monday, Wednesday, Friday, and Saturday. Manicured lawns and flowerbeds and numerous trendy restaurants around and even in the park prove that happy days are here again. *14th to 17th Sts. between Broadway and Park Ave. S., Flatiron. Subway: 14th St./Union Square.*

9 *g-5*

UNITED NATIONS

Adjacent to the UN headquarters are lovely lawns and trees, full of happy squirrels, and a small formal rose garden, all overlooking the East River. *Main public entrance, 1st Ave. at 46th St., Midtown. Open weekdays 9 AM–4:45 PM, weekends 9:15–4:45. Subway: 42nd St./Grand Central.*

1 *d-3*

WARD'S AND RANDALL'S ISLANDS

Formerly separate pieces of land, these East River islands have been joined by landfill. Downing Stadium, on Randall's Island, hosts concerts and sporting events, including rugby games and track-and-field meets (*see* Sports Stadiums, *below*). Both islands have parklands and playing fields used by many community groups. Picnicking and fishing East Harlemites stream across the footbridge at 104th Street in good weather, but the islands remain uncrowded. The roads are good for running, skating, and biking. *Junction of East and Harlem rivers. Enter via Triborough Bridge or footbridge from East River Esplanade, 104th St. Subway: 6 to 103rd St.*

11 *g-8*

WASHINGTON MARKET PARK

This former vacant lot has been turned into a 1½-acre park with a Victorian gazebo and an adventure playground. *Greenwich St. between Chambers and Duane Sts., Tribeca. Subway: Chambers St.*

11 *d-2*

WASHINGTON SQUARE PARK

Once marshy area favored by duck hunters, then a potter's field, then the site of hanging gallows, this square became a public park in 1828 and a fashionable residential area shortly thereafter (Edith Wharton and Henry James lived nearby). At the park's center is its landmark arch, designed by Stanford

White in 1892. Though it sometimes feels like NYU is trying to claim the park as its yard, Washington Square is the emotional, if not geographical, heart of Greenwich Village. Park goers include playground-happy children, chess players, Frisbee throwers, skilled skaters, dog walkers, guitar strummers, folk singers, and magicians. *W. 4th St. to Waverly Pl. (at the foot of 5th Ave.) between MacDougal St. and University Pl., Greenwich Village. Subway: W. 4th St./Washington Square.*

queens

1 *g-3*
ALLEY POND PARK
Alley Pond was named after a row of 18th-century commercial buildings, including a gristmill and a general store. The buildings and the pond are long gone (the latter disappeared when the LIE was built), but the parkland retains the name—and its 655 acres of highlands, ponds, marshes, creeks, trees, and an amazing array of wildlife, including rabbits, muskrats, and opossums. Bisected by the LIE, it has meadowlands to the north and woodlands to the south. Pitobik Trail is a 2-mi walk through a former Mattinecock Indian camp, and Turtle Pond Trail takes you through dense vegetation past glacial kettles. The **Alley Pond Environmental Center** (228–06 Northern Blvd., 718/229–4000) has live animals, offers trail walks, and hosts lively children's programs on weekends (registration required). *Grand Central Pkwy. at Winchester Blvd., Bayside.*

3 *d-2*
ASTORIA PARK
This waterfront park, opened in 1913, provides great vistas of several bridges and the Manhattan skyline. Facilities include tennis courts and a large outdoor pool. *Hoyt Ave. to Ditmars Blvd. between 19th St. and the East River. Subway: Ditmars Blvd./Astoria.*

1 *g-3*
CUNNINGHAM PARK
This large park, seemingly an endless array of fields, courts, and picnic grounds strung together, is all over the Queens outdoor-event calendar. In the summer it hosts the New York Philharmonic, opera, and jazz. *193rd to 210th*

Sts. between Long Island Expressway and Grand Central Pkwy., Fresh Meadows. Subway: 179th St./Jamaica.

3 *h-2*
FLUSHING MEADOWS–CORONA PARK
Queens's largest park (1,257 acres) has a Cinderella history: Originally a swamp, then a garbage dump, the area was the site of the 1939–40 World's Fair, the meeting ground of the nascent United Nations 1946 to 1950, and the host of another World's Fair in 1964–65. Structures we now know as the **Queens Museum of Art, Shea Stadium,** the **United States Tennis Association (U.S.T.A.) National Tennis Center,** the **New York Hall of Science,** the **boathouse,** and the **Flushing Bay marina** are all remnants of the world's fairs, as is the steel **Unisphere,** the symbol of the later one. Smaller remnants from the fairs, such as salt shakers, ties, pins, programs, silverware, and general kitsch are on display in the Queens Museum (*see* Chapter 2) along with a history of the land. The park's wide range of activities means you're bound to find something to do. Families enjoy the **Queens Wildlife Center** and the newly renovated **Playground for All Children** (718/699–8283), which was the first in the country to include facilities for both able and disabled children. Athletes have overwhelming options—tennis, golf, swimming, boating, bicycling, ice skating, and lots of playing fields. The **Theater-in-the-Park** (718/760–0064) hosts performances with particular appeal to immigrants from the surrounding neighborhoods. *Union Tpke. from 111th St. and Grand Central Pkwy. to the Van Wyck Extension, Flushing, 718/699–4209. Subway: 7 to 111th St. or Willets Point/Shea Stadium; Union Tpke./Kew Gardens.*

1 *f-5*
FOREST PARK
This 538-acre park is another Olmsted treasure. Its roads, trails, and dense forests are well traveled by hikers, bikers, and bird-watchers; other draws are a golf course, tennis courts, fields, a carousel, a model-airplane field, and a bandshell. *Union Ave. and Union Tpke. to Park Lane S, between Park Lane and Cypress Hill Cemetery, 718/520–5900. Subway: J, Z to Woodhaven Blvd.; Union Tpke./Kew Gardens.*

1 g-6

JAMAICA BAY WILDLIFE REFUGE

Though departing planes from JFK command aural attention, it's the smaller aviators that are worth noting here. These 9,155 acres of salt marshes, fresh and brackish ponds, and open bay attract hundreds of species of shorebirds and constitute a major stop on the Atlantic Flyway. It's most exciting in spring, when hundreds of thousands of birds are nesting—including the great egret, snowy egret, and glossy ibis—and during the fall migratory season. Now that Jamaica Bay is part of Gateway National Recreation Area, and cleaner thanks to pollution-control efforts, we can hope for even more avian action. There are over 5 mi of trails, and rangers guide tours regularly. *Broad Channel, 718/338–4340. Subway: Broad Channel.*

1 f-3

KISSENA PARK

A pretty landscape of hills, trees, and water, along with tennis courts and a golf course, are expected and appreciated at this 235-acre park. More unusual is a grove of exotic trees, many of them Asian imports, planted in the 19th century by Parsons Nursery. Long forgotten, the grove was rediscovered only in 1981. *Nature Center: Rose Ave. and Parsons Blvd., Kissena, 718/353–2460. Subway: Main St./Flushing.*

staten island

1 a-4

CLAY PIT PONDS STATE PARK PRESERVE

This 260-acre former clay mine is unique for its location at the terminal point for some northern and southern plant species, which live in its swamps, bogs, spring-fed streams, sandy barrens, wetlands, and woodlands along with numerous species of birds, reptiles, amphibians, and mammals. Birders, horseback riders, and hikers are welcome on trails during daylight hours, and the nature center leads weekend programs (advance registration required) year-round. An interesting novelty is the composting toilet, which you will use if nature calls. *Entrance off Carlin St., Charleston, 718/967–1976. Nature center open Mon.–Sat. 9–5.*

4 a-7

CLOVE LAKES PARK

Bucolic pleasures at this popular and picturesque park, created by the damming of an ancient glacial valley, include a brook, waterfalls, a quartet of lakes, forests of oaks and beeches, and picnic grounds. The more active might enjoy ice skating, horseback riding, football, softball, jogging, and fishing. *Clove Rd. near Victory Blvd., Sunnyside, 718/390–8000.*

1 b-3

EVERGREEN PARK

Rare ferns and orchids grow in Staten Island's newest park. *Greaves St. between Dewey Ave. and Evergreen St., Great Kills.*

1 d-8

FORT WADSWORTH

First used during the Revolutionary War, this military installation was an active part of the harbor defense system up until the 1970s. Because of its location just off the Verrazano Narrows Bridge, it's tromped on by thousands of runners (and becomes the site of the world's longest urinal) at the start of the New York City Marathon. Now part of Gateway National Recreation Area and newly open to the public, the place has a 1½-mi self-guided trail around its fortifications. Other ranger-led tours can be reserved in advance. *Bay St. at Wadsworth Ave., Shore Acres, 718/354–4500. Open Sun.*

1 b-2

GREENBELT

One of New York's newer large parks (land acquisition began in 1964), Greenbelt is also one of the best. Designed by the last of the great glaciers, its nearly 2,000 contiguous acres comprise linked woodlands, meadows, ponds, wetlands, golf courses, and cemeteries, all forming a green ring in the center of Staten Island. The rambling woods, teeming with plant and animal wildlife, are all the more remarkable given the developed lands—including the Fresh Kills landfill—that border them. The park protects five kinds of owls, shelters the most northerly example of the sweetbay magnolia tree, is home to more than 50 species of birds, and grows such rare wildflowers as blue cohosh and Virginia waterleaf. Hikers have 28 mi of trails to cover, so it's a good idea to carry a map (available at the main office). Urban

Park Rangers lead hikes, bird walks, and other nature activities. *Office: 200 Nevada Ave., Egbertville, 718/667–2165. Office open weekdays 9–4.*

1 *b-2*

HIGH ROCK PARK IN THE GREENBELT

Bird-watching is especially good in this 86-acre section of peaceful woods. A visit to the environmental education center is on many schools' calendars, but it offers walks, talks, and exhibits to all. *200 Nevada Ave., Egbertville, 718/ 667–2165. Center open weekdays 9–4.*

1 *b-2*

LA TOURETTE PARK IN THE GREENBELT

This 511-acre park features a beautiful golf course and clubhouse—once the farmland and mansion of the La Tourette family—as well as wooded and uninterrupted wetland trails popular with cross-country skiers in winter. The best trail is Buck's Hollow. *Forest Hill and Richmond Hill Rds., Richmondtown.*

1 *c-2*

MILLER FIELD

Like Fort Wadsworth, this is a former military base (U.S. Army) that's now part of Gateway National Recreation Area, and tours sometimes focus on its military history (it has two post–World War I hangars). It's Staten Island's host for summer opera and Philharmonic concerts. *Between New Dorp and Elmtree Sts., New Dorp, 718/351–6970.*

1 *d-8*

VON BRIESEN PARK

A small but meticulously groomed city park, Von Briesen somehow doesn't attract many people. Its elevated, harbor-front location provides a stunning panorama of lower Manhattan, the Upper and Lower New York bays, and Brooklyn. *Bay St. and Wadsworth Ave., Shore Acres.*

1 *a-2*

WILLIAM T. DAVIS WILDLIFE REFUGE

Named for noted Staten Island naturalist William Thompson Davis, these 260 acres of dry and wetland attract many birds rarely seen in this area, and the wide variety of habitats makes for an ideal sanctuary. *Travis Ave. off Richmond Ave., New Springville, 718/667–2165.*

1 *a-2*

WILLOWBROOK PARK IN THE GREENBELT

American soldiers called it the Great Swamp when they hid here during the Revolutionary War, but Willowbrook is now one of Staten Island's more popular parks. Picnic tables, a fishing lake, athletic fields, an archery range, horseshoe pitches, a playground, and a kite-flying area are spread throughout the 164 acres. *Victory Blvd. and Richmond Ave., New Springville, 718/698–2186.*

other green spaces

BEACHES

Though Manhattan lacks a sandswept beach, that doesn't stop anyone from sunbathing—on rooftops ("tar beaches"), river piers ("splinter beaches"), and parks ("Manhattan Rivieras"). The other boroughs, however, are blessed with miles and miles of beaches, all easily accessible by bus, subway, or car. City beaches are officially open from Memorial Day weekend to Labor Day, sunrise to midnight, with swimming allowed when lifeguards are on duty (usually 10 AM to 6 PM).

bronx

2 *g-2*

ORCHARD BEACH

For sun, sand, and salsa, this section of Pelham Bay Park is the place. A white-sand, crescent-shaped beauty on the Long Island Sound, Orchard Beach was one of Robert Moses's pride and joys. It draws crowds, largely from the Bronx's Latino population. *Shore Rd. and City Island Rd., Eastchester, 718/885–2275. Subway: Pelham Bay Park.*

brooklyn

4 *h-6*

BRIGHTON BEACH

Brighton Beach is actually the "beginning" of the beach that becomes Coney Island further west. At this end you'll find locals: mothers with children, older retired folks, and Russians who have emigrated to this shore, commonly called "Odessa by the Sea." The board-walk has little but benches, so bring your lunch or buy it on your way. *15th St. to Ocean Pkwy., Brighton. Subway: Brighton Beach; Ocean Pkwy.*

4 *g-7*

CONEY ISLAND BEACH

Named for the rabbits that were once its main inhabitants (from the Dutch *Konijn Eiland*), Coney Island began its resort days in the 1830s, when elegant hotels drew the elite. Railroads were eventually built to connect it with other parts of Brooklyn, carting in people attracted to its increasing array of entertainment: horse races, sporting events, amuse-ment parks, and, of course, beaches. The first roller coaster opened in 1884, and by 1904 there were three amuse-ment parks. It's now a mere shadow of its early-twentieth-century self, but Coney Island still has a fine 2½-mi sandy beach and a 2-mi boardwalk with every-thing you'd expect to find at a beach resort (cotton candy, soft ice cream) plus a few unique extras—Nathan's hot dogs, bona fide freak shows, and a land-mark roller coaster (the Cyclone). Hot summer days have brought as many as a million people to Coney Island at once, which at times makes it a bit diffi-cult to find a place in the sun without stepping on someone else's blanket. *Ocean Pkwy. to 37th St., 718/946–1350. Subway: Stillwell Ave./Coney Island.*

1 *f-8*

MANHATTAN BEACH

This small beach draws a young crowd and is a nice place for sunning and swimming. Adjacent to the beach is a park, with barbecue facilities as well as handball, tennis, and basketball. *Ocean Ave. between Oriental Blvd. and MacKen-zie St., 718/946–1373. Subway: Brighton Beach.*

queens

1 *g-7*

JACOB RIIS PARK

Just over the Marine Parkway Bridge from Brooklyn, this mile-long stretch of Rockaway beach was named for the Danish reformer-photographer and is part of the Gateway National Recreation Area. There is a concrete "boardwalk" for strolling and a wide, sandy beach. Sports facilities include softball fields and paddle-tennis courts. Though it

draws crowds, the less central areas are usually peaceful enough. *Beach 149 to Beach 169 St., 718/318–4300. Access: Flat-bush Ave. to Marine Pkwy/Gil Hodges Memorial Bridge.*

1 *h-7*

ROCKAWAY BEACH

Nearly 10 mi of glorious sandy beach and 7½ mi of boardwalk fronting the Atlantic form the core of this recre-ational area, with surfable waves and rel-atively clean water adding to the appeal. Best of all, the A train can get you—and everyone else—here. Due to lifeguard shortages, beach erosion, and plover nestings, parts of the strand were closed in summer 1997 and may be closed in 1998 as well. *Beach 1st to Beach 149 St., 718/318–4000. Subway: Rockaway Park/Beach 116 St.*

staten island

1 *c-3*

GREAT KILLS PARK

Built on landfill, with a major recent cleanup and renovations to the actual beach as well as public buildings, Great Kills offers surfable waves, a marina, fields, a public boat ramp, a model-air-plane flying field, fishing, and trails. Migrating monarch butterflies stop here in late summer and fall. *Hylan Blvd. and Hopkins Ave., 718/351–6970.*

4 *d-8*

MIDLAND AND SOUTH BEACH

Connected by the **Franklin D. Roosevelt Boardwalk,** which starts at Miller Field and continues for 7,500 ft, these two beaches are sandy and attractive. Mid-land is somewhat cleaner, though South Beach has been improved in recent years. You can fish off the boardwalk until 1 PM, except in summer. Even if you don't want to swim, you might enjoy the view of lower New York Bay. *From Miller Field to Fort Wadsworth, parallel to Fr. Capodanno Blvd., 718/987–0709 (Mid-land), 718/816–6804 (South).*

1 *b-4*

WOLFE'S POND PARK

This 312-acre park has saltwater swim-ming and surfing, a large wooded area, a freshwater lake, and rustic picnic set-tings. *Holton to Cornelia Ave. on Raritan Bay, Prince's Bay, 718/984–8266.*

long island

New York's Atlantic beaches don't stop at the city line, but extend out past Rockaway along Long Island all the way to The End (Montauk). Several are popular among New York City day-trippers. **Long Beach**—a unique community in that its street plan discourages cars—has a mile-long boardwalk. **Jones Beach,** built by Robert Moses, has beautiful bathhouses and teems with happy crowds, though it's big enough that if you're willing to walk, you can escape the densely packed bodies. **Robert Moses State Park,** on the westernmost tip of Fire Island, is also easy to reach from New York, but it draws more of a Long Island crowd. The Long Island Rail Road offers package day trips to all three beaches, and others, for under $15; call 718/217–LIRR.

BOTANICAL GARDENS

New York City's first botanical garden opened in 1801, covering 20 acres that is now Rockefeller Center; it was the first public garden in the country. (Sorry, Boston.) Today, each borough has its own public botanical garden and many smaller horticultural delights as well.

bronx

2 *c-4*

NEW YORK BOTANICAL GARDEN

This 250-acre garden, founded in 1891, was patterned after the Royal Botanical Gardens at Kew, England. Every season is spectacular. The **Peggy Rockefeller Rose Garden** has 2,700 bushes of 230 different varieties; the **Arlow B. Stout Daylily Garden** glows in July; and there is an herb garden, an azalea glen (spectacular in May), a pine grove, a newly restored rock garden (admission $1, open Apr.–Oct.), 40 acres of trails through natural forest, and much more. The 11 interconnecting galleries of the **Enid A. Haupt Conservatory** (which closes an hour earlier than the garden grounds), including a striking, Victorian glasshouse that reopened in 1997 following a $25 million restoration, showcase plant life around the world and seasonal flower shows. A restored 1840 **Snuff Mill** overlooking the Bronx River and a stone cottage from the same year are other man-made treasures. Narrated

tram tours (tickets $4; every 30 min) run every 30 minutes and can transport you across the immense grounds, while walks and self-guided tours focus on topics and areas of special interest. A children's adventure garden (opening spring 1998), a maze made of hedges, hands-on gardening, and other discovery activities, indoors and out, are great fun for kids. *Bronx Park at 200th St. and Southern Blvd., Bronx Pkwy, 718/817–8700, 718/817–8779 for directions. Admission: garden $3, conservatory $3.50, Garden Passport (all admissions and tram tour) $8. Free Wed., Sat. 10–noon. Open Apr.–Oct., Tues.–Sun. and Mon. holidays 10–6, Nov.–Mar. 10–4. Subway: Bedford Park Blvd.*

2 *a-3*

WAVE HILL

A nonprofit environmental center, these 28 acres overlook the Hudson and the Palisades from their Riverdale location. The former estate of conservation-minded financier George Perkins, rented at various times rented to Theodore Roosevelt, Mark Twain, and Arturo Toscanini, Wave Hill was donated to the city in 1960. With 18 acres of gardens, it has greenhouses (open limited hours) and exquisite herb, wildflower, and aquatic gardens. Directors of other public gardens come from all over the country to admire the plants and their unusual juxtapositions, which change from year to year. Family art projects, guided garden walks, an art museum, and concerts round out the possibilities. *Main entrance: 249th St. and Independence Ave., Riverdale, 718/549–3200. Admission: $4; free Nov. 16–Mar. 14. Open Tues.–Sun. 9–4:30. Metro-North: Harlem Line to Riverdale.*

brooklyn

4 *e-1*

BROOKLYN BOTANIC GARDEN

Founded in 1910 on the site of a city dump, Brooklyn's garden is just one-fifth the size of its Bronx cousin, but within its 52 acres are more than enough wonders to fill a day. Spring flowers include Japanese cherry trees along the **Cherry Esplanade,** magnolias in **Magnolia Plaza,** lilacs in the **Louisa Clark Spencer Lilac Collection,** and daffodils on **Daffodil Hill.** More than 5,000 varieties of roses bloom through the summer in the **Cranford Rose Garden.** The **Shakespeare Gar-**

den contains 80 plants mentioned by the playwright in his works. Lots of giant carp and turtles call the **Japanese Hill-and-Pond Garden** home, and the lily pools are another unusual delight. Other green attractions include the **Fragrance Garden**, designed for the blind but a pleasure for all; an herb garden; a rock garden; and a garden planted only with flora from the metropolitan region. While most of the **Steinhardt Conservatory** follows the "Trail of Evolution," one room has dozens of bonsai plants. Free guided tours leave from the conservatory at 1 PM on weekends. *1000 Washington Ave. (at Carroll St.), Park Slope, 718/622–4433. Admission: $3, free Tues. Open Apr.–Sept., Tues.–Fri. 8–6, weekends and Mon. holidays 10–6; Oct.–Mar., Tues.–Fri. 8–4:30, weekends and holidays 10–4:30. Subway: Eastern Pkwy./Brooklyn Museum.*

manhattan

5 *a-7*

THE CLOISTERS GARDEN
Green-thumbed monks from the 15th century would be right at home with the 250 species of plants and flowers planted among the cloisters here. The **Gothic Trie Cloister** houses the 50 species identified in the museum's *Unicorn Tapestries.* Flowering bulbs are displayed year-round in the skylighted **St. Guilhem Cloister**. *Fort Tryon Park (see Parks, above). Subway: A to 190th St.*

7 *d-4*

CONSERVATORY GARDEN
Established in 1937, this formal, six-acre garden is almost secretly ensconced in a forgotten corner of Central Park. Named for the elegant old greenhouses that stood here before the Depression, the garden is a lavishly landscaped conglomerate: an ornate and manicured French garden, a classic Italian garden flanked by crab-apple *allées,* and a densely planted perennial garden. Opening onto the main lawn is the handsome wrought-iron Vanderbilt Gate, a popular spot for wedding portraits. *5th Ave. and 105th St., Central Park, 212/360–2766. Open daily 8 AM–dusk. Subway: 6 to 103rd St.*

11 *g-3*

LIZ CHRISTY MEMORIAL GARDEN
Planted in 1972 by the Green Guerrillas, this tiny but lush garden is an unlikely rest stop. Since its creation, hundreds of other community gardens have sprung up in vacant lots around the city. *Northeast corner of Houston St. and Bowery, East Village. Open May–Sept., daily noon–4. Subway: 2nd Ave.*

7 *c-8*

SHAKESPEARE GARDEN
This garden grew from seeds and cuttings of the same mulberry and hawthorn trees Shakespeare himself once tended. The lushly landscaped terraced hill provides a peaceful setting. *Central Park near W. 81st St., south of Delacorte Theater. Subway: B, C to 81st St.*

queens

1 *f-3*

QUEENS BOTANICAL GARDEN
Originally created for the 1939–40 World's Fair, held at Flushing Meadows, and later transplanted here, the garden is now 39 acres of specialized plantings. Stepping in here from Main Street feels like entering someone's backyard. Then, though, you see the bridal parties traipsing through to pose in the gazebo in the Wedding Garden. The best green attraction here is the rose garden, the city's largest. Other treats include bird and bee gardens, pine cove, and formal flower plantings along the center mall. *43–50 Main St., Flushing, 718/886–3800. Open Tues.–Fri. 8–6, weekends 8–7. Subway: Main St./Flushing.*

staten island

4 *a-6*

STATEN ISLAND BOTANICAL GARDEN
Visit the Snug Harbor Cultural Center and you can't help but stumble upon this garden, a newcomer to the outer-borough botanical-garden scene (established 1977) and a trove of English perennials. Other highlights are a Chinese garden, a pond garden, special plants meant to attract butterflies, and a greenhouse that houses the Neil Vanderbilt Orchid Collection. *Richmondtown Terr. from Tysen St. to Kissel Ave., Snug Harbor, 718/273–8200. Open daily dawn–dusk.*

zoos & aquariums

Haven't you heard? It's no longer politically correct to call them zoos—"wildlife conservation centers" more accurately describes their missions, and all but the Staten Island Zoo are run by the Wildlife Conservation Society (718/220–5100), headquartered at the Bronx Zoo. But no matter the name, these great centers of animal life draw millions of New Yorkers every year. Most were completely renovated in the late 1980s and early '90s to better serve both inhabitants and admirers.

bronx

2 b-3

BRONX ZOO/WILDLIFE CONSERVATION PARK

Who knew you could visit a baboon reserve, smell a skunk, watch sea lions laze around on a simulation of the rocky California coastline, and penetrate the world of animal nightlife, all in the Bronx? Opened in Bronx Park in 1899, this 265-acre behemoth is the world's largest urban zoo. About 4,000 animals of 560 species live here, mainly in realistic habitats and often separated from you by no more than a moat—accommodations include Himalayan highlands (snow leopards, red pandas, and cranes), the rugged Patagonian coast (penguins, terns, and cormorants), and African plains (lions, gazelles, zebras, among others). The Beaux Arts **Keith W. Johnson Zoo Center**'s elephants and rhinos, the **World of Reptiles'** crocs, snakes, and turtles, and separate giraffe, mouse, monkey, ape, and aquatic bird houses are among the popular indoor exhibits. Bats, moles, porcupines, and other nocturnal critters are fooled into thinking it's night—which means they're awake for you—in the **World of Darkness.** In season, you can perambulate via shuttle and skyfari through the entire zoo, take the **Bengali Express Monorail** through **Wild Asia,** or opt for a leisurely camel ride. Children are encouraged to act out their animal instincts, whether it's sitting in a nest, wearing a turtle shell, or outfoxing a fox at the **Children's Zoo** (Apr.–Oct., $2 adults; $1.50 children 2–12); they can also pet or feed domestic animals. *Fordham Rd. at Bronx River Pkwy., Bronx Park, 718/367–1010. Admission: Apr.–Oct. $6.75, Nov.–Mar. $3, free Wed. year-round. Open Apr.–Oct., weekdays 10–5, weekends 10–5:30; Nov.–Mar., daily 10–4:30. Subway: Pelham Pkwy.*

brooklyn

4 h-7

AQUARIUM FOR WILDLIFE CONSERVATION

The New York Aquarium was immensely popular at its Castle Clinton, Manhattan, location from its inception in 1896 until its closing (by Robert Moses) in 1941. After moving temporarily to the Bronx, the aquatic creatures found a new home in Coney Island in 1957. Inside this 14-acre complex you can hear beluga whales whistle and moan, look massive sharks in the eye, and drool over the walrus's 400-pound weekly ration of shrimp, smelt, and herring. All told, the aquarium has about 7,500 residents, including mammals (otters, dolphins, whales, seals), birds (penguins), reptiles (sea turtles), cartilaginous fish (sharks, rays, skate), bony fish (tarpon, eels, trout, cod, piranhas, puffers), and invertebrates (jellyfish, sea urchins, lobsters, mollusks), some of them lucky enough to live in beachside outdoor pools. Dolphins and sea lions perform in a new Aquatheater, and penguins, sharks, sea otters, seals, walruses, and other creatures don't mind if you watch them eat. Curious children can get zapped by electric fish, walk under a crashing wave, and touch crabs and sea urchins in the Discovery Cove. *W. 8th St. and Surf Ave., Coney Island, 718/265–FISH. Admission: $7.75. Open Memorial Day–Labor Day, weekdays 10–5, weekends and holidays 10–7. Subway: W. 8th St./NY Aquarium.*

4 3-1

PROSPECT PARK WILDLIFE CENTER

Reopened after a complete reconstruction in 1993, this small zoo focuses on small animals, such as prairie dogs, wallabies, baboons, and capybaras. "The World of Animals," "Animal Lifestyles," and "Animals in our Lives" exhibit areas help children learn by observing, mimicking, and touching. *450 Flatbush Ave., Prospect Park, 718/399–7339. Admission: $2.50. Open Apr.–Oct., weekdays 10–5, weekends and holidays 10–5:30; Nov.–Mar. daily 10–4:30. Subway: D, Q to Prospect Park.*

manhattan

9 *d-2*

CENTRAL PARK WILDLIFE CENTER

Much of New York's oldest zoo has been demolished (though several of the WPA-era buildings have been restored), and a more modern, more humane, 5½-acre habitat has taken its place. Clustered around the central **Sea Lion Pool** are separate exhibits for each of the earth's major environments: the **Polar Circle** features a huge penguin tank and polar-bear ice floe; the open-air **Temperate Territory** is highlighted by a pit of chattering monkeys; and the **Tropic Zone** contains the flora and fauna of a miniature rain forest. The **Tisch Children's Zoo,** on the north side of Denesmouth Arch, reopened in fall 1997 after a complete reconstruction. In its Enchanted Forest, small animals such as rabbits, frogs, and free-flying birds are all at home; kids learn to relate to their fellow creatures by hopping on lily pads, peering underwater through a fish's-eye lens, and fidgeting with other interactive amusements. *Entrance: 5th Ave. and 64th St., Central Park, 212/439–6500. Admission: $2.50. Open Apr.–Oct., weekdays 10–5:00, weekends and holidays 10:30–5:30; Nov.– Mar., daily 10–4:30. Subway: N, R to 5th Ave.*

queens

3 *h-2*

QUEENS WILDLIFE CENTER

About 340 animals of just over 50 North American species live in this lightly populated, 11-acre zoo. Strolling through treetops amid free-flying birds in the aviary is a highlight. Outside, elk are at home on the range, black bears play in their pseudo-Adirondack territory, and sea lions swim off a faux Pacific Coast. You can paw domesticated plants and animals in the petting zoo. *53–51 111th St., Flushing Meadows–Corona Park, 718/271–7761. Admission: $2.50. Open Apr.–Oct., weekdays 10–5, weekends and holidays 10–5:30; Nov.–Mar. daily 10–4:30. Subway: 7 to 111th St.*

staten island

1 *c-8*

STATEN ISLAND ZOO

Operated by its own Staten Island Zoological Society, this small zoo (established 1936) is known for its reptiles, especially rattlesnakes, who slither through the **Serpentarium.** Shrimp and sharks jockey for position in the aquarium, flamingos wade in an outdoor pool, and endangered South American plants and animals live in an indoor re-creation of a tropical forest. Leopards and tigers lurk in the new **African Savannah at Twilight** exhibit. The feeding schedule isn't for the weak of heart— mealtimes for reptiles, sharks, piranha, and bats are scheduled for your visiting pleasure. If you're weak-kneed, you might find the domesticated farm animals at the outdoor children's center more enjoyable. *614 Broadway, Barrett Park, 718/442–3100. Admission: $3, free Wed. after 2. Open daily 10–4:45.*

sports & outdoor activities

With nearly eight million people living within city limits, New York could field a winning team in just about any sport. Organized amateur options range from casual leagues and clubs, where socializing is as important as the game, to extremely competitive teams with die-hard coaches. If you can't find exactly what you're looking for, ask your friends, check the Yellow Pages, or call the Parks Department (*see* Parks Information, *above*); it's got to be around here somewhere. Ongoing leagues abound, especially for popular sports like basketball and softball; check with your employer, school, or local gym for information. Chelsea Piers (*see* Fitness Centers, *below*) and the Yorkville Sport Association (212/645–6488), for example, arrange many.

If your idea of a good workout is *watching* a great game, you're still in luck. New York's professional baseball, basketball, football, hockey, and soccer teams play in local stadiums, and these same arenas host a full calendar of various sporting events year-round.

BASEBALL

Many places in and around New York claim an important role in baseball's history, and the sport remains one of New York's favorite pastimes. You're either a Mets fan or a Yankees fan, period; and you'd better choose your friends carefully, because allegiances run deep. Since 1997 the Mets and the Yankees have played each other a few times a year during the regular season, but fans continue to hope the teams will meet again in a subway series. The professional baseball season runs from early April through September, a few weeks longer if your team is lucky. Tickets are usually available both in advance and at the stadium on game day.

where to watch

6 *f-5*

NEW YORK YANKEES

Home games for this much beloved yet oft maligned American League team are at **Yankee Stadium** (*see* Sports Stadiums, *below*). The Bronx Bombers' petulant owner, George Steinbrenner, keeps threatening to pick up and move his boys into New Jersey—or, heaven forbid, Manhattan—but ever since they won the World Series in 1996, bigger crowds have been returning to the South Bronx. *718/293–6000.*

3 *h-1*

NEW YORK METS

It's not easy being a Mets fan these days, what with all the attention paid to the Yankees' playing acceptably and threatening to leave the city. Let them go! Still, the National League Mets have a large and spirited following. Home games are at **Shea Stadium** (*see* Sports Stadiums, *below*), in Flushing, Queens. *718/507–8499.*

where to play

There are hundreds of municipal baseball facilities in the city, but many of them are reserved by softball and baseball leagues. For details on permits, *see* Permits, *above*.

BASKETBALL

The regular men's professional season (NBA) runs in the winter, from November to April. Women (WNBA) have been slotted into the traditionally slow summer season, mid-June–August. In addition to teams listed below, **Madison Square Garden** (*see* Sports Stadiums, *below*) often hosts college games in winter.

where to watch

NEW JERSEY NETS

The up-and-coming Nets can be seen at the Continental Airlines Arena. *Meadowlands Sports Complex, East Rutherford, NJ, 201/935–3900.*

9 *c-6*

NEW YORK KNICKS

Patrick Ewing and Co. play to intense sell-out crowds at Madison Square Garden. *7th Ave. between 31st and 33rd Sts., Midtown, 212/465–JUMP. Subway: 34th St./Penn Station.*

9 *c-6*

NEW YORK LIBERTY

They play halves instead of quarters and use a smaller ball than the men, but the Women's National Basketball Association (WNBA) attracted a lot of attention and respect in its inaugural 1997 season. Olympic champ Rebecca Lobo is the center for New York's team, which plays at Madison Square Garden. *7th Ave. between 31st and 33rd Sts., Midtown, 212/564–WNBA.*

where to play

Call the Parks Department (*see* Parks Information, *above*) for the basketball court nearest you—in some neighborhoods they're on almost every corner. Hoops on Manhattan's West 4th Street (at 6th Ave.) often have lively games complete with spectators. Other popular pickup locations in Manhattan are on West 76th Street (at Columbus Ave.), at Asphalt Green (90th St. at York Ave.), and at Riverbank State Park (*see* Parks, *above*).

BICYCLING

With all of its long, flat, paved stretches, New York City should be a biker's dream. Unfortunately, motor vehicle traffic, potholes, and pollution make it otherwise, but there are still some good recreational routes, especially in parks and along the waterfront, and biking is often the fastest and most convenient

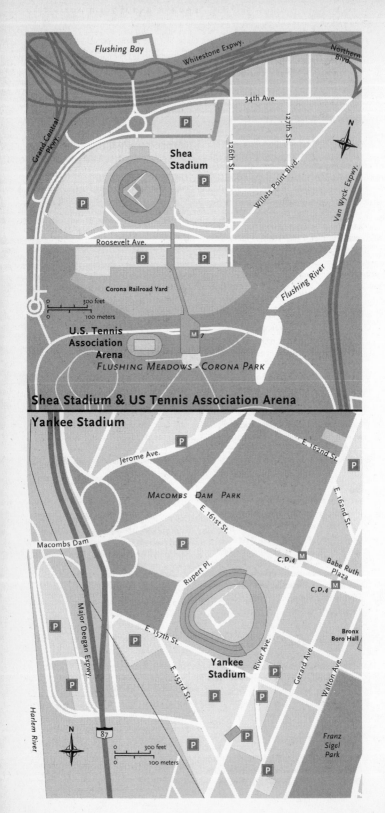

Shea Stadium & US Tennis Association Arena

Yankee Stadium

The Meadowlands

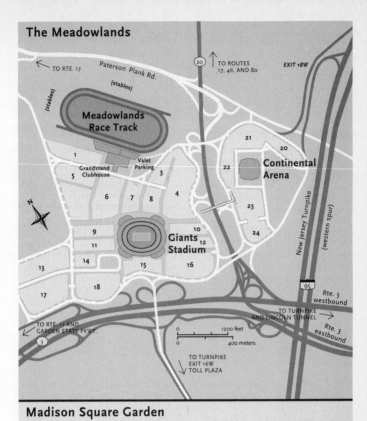

Madison Square Garden

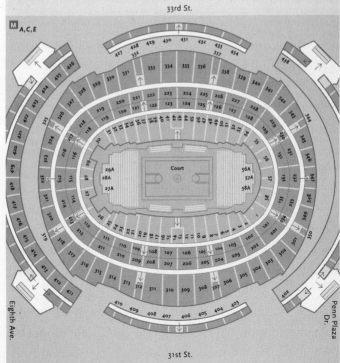

way to get around town. The Department of Transportation (Bicycle Program, 212/442–9890) and **Department of City Planning** (Bicycle Network Development Program, 212/442–4640) produce bicycle maps for each borough; in addition to showing recommended routes (greenways and paths as well as street routes), these pinpoint bike shops and explain cycling regulations. Even if you read up, though, navigating roads and figuring out how to access bridges can be challenging, so ride with someone who's experienced before setting out on your own.

Bicycles are considered vehicles, which means they have to stop at red lights, obey speed limits, stay off sidewalks (if over 13 years old), and ride in the direction of traffic. Children under 14 must wear helmets. Bikes are permitted on the subway and the Staten Island ferry without a permit, and most other regional mass transport allows them with a free or inexpensive permit; **Transportation Alternatives** (see below) can provide details. The city's bike clubs send out calendars to their members, who generally pay a modest annual fee, but welcome everyone on rides.

FIVE BOROUGH BICYCLE CLUB
The 5BBC has road and all-terrain bike (ATB) rides for all levels year-round, with many especially suited to cyclists not used to heavy mileage. Its parent organization, American Youth Hostels, is also the parent of **Bike New York,** which puts on an annual mass tour of the five boroughs in early May (see Sports Events, below). 891 Amsterdam Ave. (at 103rd St.), 212/932–2300.

NEW YORK CYCLE CLUB
Rides are classified by average speed, and the calendar has trips for everyone from beginners to pace-line racers, but this group tends to be heavy on competitive riders. The summer **Bicycle Beach Bum** series, organized in conjunction with the 5BBC (see above), is popular and social. 212/886–4545.

STATEN ISLAND BICYCLING ASSOCIATION
Staten Island and New Jersey are the usual focus for this group's day rides. They're categorized by level and include additional weekly on-island spins on Wednesday and Saturday. 517 Jewett Ave., 718/815–9290.

TIME'S UP
Time's Up promotes environmental awareness through biking. Rides are generally just one or two hours, but offer unique glimpses of the city. The monthly Central Park Moonlight Ride, for example, travels the scenic paths. Other regular rides are the critical-mass attempt and historic tours. Though the club produces a free calendar every once in a while, you're better off calling for upcoming events. 212/802–8222.

TRANSPORTATION ALTERNATIVES
The city's bicycle-and-pedestrian advocacy group gets its members discounts at several bike stores and can help you decrease the amount of pollution in your life. Its bimonthly newsletter, **"City Cyclist,"** available in bike stores throughout the city, lists rides and events of interest to cyclists. Every September TA organizes a century (100-mi) ride within city boundaries. 115 W. 30th St., Suite 1207, 212/629–8080.

bronx
Moshulu Parkway and **Pelham Parkway** are paralleled by scenic bike routes for miles; Moshulu goes to City Island Road and over to City Island. The **Grand Concourse** is a good route on weekends because it has a separate service road in each direction, and has been closed to auto traffic on summer Sundays for a few years.

brooklyn
The 3½-mi loop road in **Prospect Park** provides excellent cycling, especially when the park is closed to cars (see Parks, above). Beware a short strip on the eastern side of the park near the boathouse and skating rink—cars can access the parking lot at all times. The **Ocean Parkway** bike path, which turned 100 in 1995, starts just outside the southwest exit of Prospect Park and ends about 6 mi later, near Coney Island, where the boardwalk is open to cyclists before 10 AM. Along the parkway, you ride on elevated medians in the shade of trees. The **Shore Parkway Path** goes from Owl's Head Park, in Bay Ridge, under the Verrazano Narrows Bridge to Bay 8th in Bensonhurst, and picks up again off Emmons Avenue in Sheepshead Bay. From here you can connect to a path that runs parallel to **Flatbush Avenue** and brings you

to Rockaway, or continue to Kennedy Airport.

manhattan

The 6-mi loop road in **Central Park** probably logs the most cycler miles in the city, but it's often crowded (sometimes with cars, when they're allowed in, forcing bikers, bladers, and joggers to share a narrow lane) and requires adept navigation skills. Always beware other park users. Bike rentals are available at the boathouse (212/861–4137). Leaving Central Park, the **Broadway/St. Nicholas Avenue** bike lane brings you nearly to the **George Washington Bridge,** whose pedestrian crossway gives cyclists spectacular views up and down the Hudson and easy access to Palisades Interstate Park (River Road, left off the bridge and then left again, is a hilly favorite) and Route 9W in New Jersey. Lower Manhattan is surrounded by greenways—**Hudson River Park** from Battery Park to West 14th Street gets crowded with cruising bikers and skaters; the path along **East River Park** is much greener and less congested. Uptown, you can bike right along the water in the West Side's **Riverside Park** and from Carl Schurz Park up to 125th Street on the **East River Esplanade.**

The south outer roadway of the **Queensboro Bridge** is open to cyclists (except for a temporary closing during afternoon rush hour, when bikes must be carted in a free shuttle bus), and cyclists and skaters split the spectacular elevated roadway/boardwalk on the **Brooklyn Bridge.** All of the Manhattan-Bronx bridges accommodate cyclists as well.

queens

Rockaway Peninsula is a long, flat strip crying out for your cruiser on either the road or the boardwalk; take the Marine Parkway Bridge from Brooklyn's Flatbush Avenue bike path. In **Forest Park,** near the Brooklyn border, take the main road or bike trails for a gorgeous ride through the woods. **Flushing Meadows–Corona Park** has lakeside routes as well as plenty of pavement separating playing fields and attractions. The lack of hills makes it popular with families, and rentals are available by the tennis stadium (718/699–9598). The few miles of bike path on the west edge of **Little Neck Bay** have great views of the Long Island Sound.

staten island

Staten Island's traffic often seems less threatening than that of other boroughs—which helps make up for the lack of separate bike paths on this park-filled island. Despite typical hiker-biker disagreements, **High Rock Park** is the best place for mountain biking in the entire city. The **Franklin D. Roosevelt Boardwalk,** which connects several beaches on the eastern shore, is relaxing and scenic. The **Bayonne Bridge,** with its narrow pedestrian crossway separated from the main part of the bridge, makes for an exhilarating trip into New Jersey.

BILLIARDS

Every sport has to catch on among the trendsetters sooner or later, and billiards finally has. Tables usually cost $10–$15 per hour, many halls have lounges and/or snack bars attached, and most operate around-the-clock.

manhattan

7 b-8
AMSTERDAM BILLIARD CLUB
This upscale club, partly owned by comedian David Brenner, has 31 tables. The newer East Side location is equally well-equipped. *344 Amsterdam Ave. (at 77th St.), Upper West Side, 212/496–8180. Subway: 79th St.*

7 f-7
210 E. 86th St., Upper East Side, 212/570–4545. Subway: 86th St.

9 c-8
THE BILLIARD CLUB
High ceilings, velvet curtains, and pseudo-Victorian decor give this place class. The 33 tables help, too. *220 W. 19th St., Chelsea, 212/206-7665. Subway: C, E to 23rd St.*

9 d-8
CHELSEA BILLIARDS
Crowds fill the two floors, looking to play pool or snooker (50 pool tables, 8 snooker tables). *54 W. 21st St., 212/989-0096. Subway: F to 23rd St.*

10 e-1
CORNER BILLIARDS
East Village yuppies congregate around the 28 tables. *85 4th Ave. (at 11th St.),*

212/995-1314. Subway: 14th St./Union Square.

10 e-1
LE Q
These 30 tables are among the cheapest in town: $3 per person, per hour. 36 E. 12th St., East Village, 212/995-8512. Subway: 14th St./Union Square.

11 f-3
SOHO BILLIARDS
These 28 tables have a choice NoHo location for after-hours action. 298 Mulberry St. (at Houston St.), Greenwich Village, 212/925-3753. Subway: Bleecker St.; Broadway–Lafayette St.

9 a-4
WEST SIDE BILLIARD AND TABLE TENNIS CLUB
Several Ping-Pong tables complement the pool offerings (13 tables) at this western outpost. 601 W. 50th St., Hell's Kitchen, 212/246-1060. Subway: C, E to 50th St.

BIRD-WATCHING

Pigeons (rock pigeons, if you're in the know) may be the first species that comes to mind when you think about avian life in the city, but New York City's parks, marshes, and woodlands are home to thousands of species of birds, including Canada geese, Kentucky warblers, fork-tailed flycatchers, downy woodpeckers, barn owls, dark-eyed juncos, and glossy ibises. The city is also on the Atlantic Flyway, a major spring and fall migratory route; birds heading to or from as far away as the High Arctic pass through. May is the best season for bird-watching, since the songbirds are in their freshest colors; the fall migration is less concentrated and less colorful. As the local chapter of our nation's premier birding organization, the New York City Audubon Society (71 W. 23rd St., room 606, 691-7483) can fill you in on area bird walks and help you with your watching. Rare Bird Alert (212/979-3070) has up-to-the-minute news on what's been seen where. In addition to the sources below, check with the Urban Park Rangers (see Parks, above) for information on walks.

bronx

2 c-4
NEW YORK BOTANICAL GARDEN
Many species of birds live on garden grounds year-round or stop by seasonally. Great horned owls are most likely found in the grove of evergreen trees, while ring-necked pheasants prefer the wetlands, daffodil hill, and rose garden. There are bird walks every Friday at 1:30 and Saturday at 12:30, and there's an annual bird count in late December. Bronx Park at 200th St. and Southern Blvd., Bronx Pkwy, 718/817-8700, 718/817-8779 for directions. Admission: garden $3, conservatory $3.50, Garden Passport (all admissions and tram tour) $8. Free Wed., Sat. 10-noon. Open Apr.-Oct., Tues.-Sun. and Mon. holidays 10-6, Nov.-Mar. 10-4. Subway: Bedford Park Blvd.

2 g-2
PELHAM BAY PARK
The saltwater marsh and the lagoon have been known to attract bald eagles, ospreys, and great horned owls. Bruckner Blvd. and Middletown Rd., 718/430-1890. Pelham Bay Park Environmental Center (near Orchard Beach), 718/885-3466. Subway: Pelham Bay Park.

brooklyn

1 f-7
MARINE PARK
A springtime warbler watch is part of each year's birding highlights at the marsh. Inlet between Gerritsen and Flatbush Aves., inland to Fillmore Ave., between Burnet and E. 32nd Sts.

1 h-6
PROSPECT PARK
Birds similar to those in Central Park (see below) settle in Prospect Park's lakes and hills. The Rose Garden, Midwood, Prospect Lake, and Lookout Hill are good viewing spots. Park bordered by Flatbush Ave., Ocean Ave., Parkside Ave., Prospect Park Southwest, and Prospect Park West, 718/965-8999. Subway: Grand Army Plaza; D, Q to Prospect Park; F to 15th St./Prospect Park.

manhattan

1 *d-4*

CENTRAL PARK

The Pond near East 59th Street, the Reservoir, the Ravine, and especially the Ramble are prime birding areas. Species that nest in the park include cardinals, gray catbirds, and mallard ducks; among those that pass through (typically March–mid-May) are blue-gray gnatcatchers, brown creepers, orioles, and warblers. The **Henry Luce Nature Observatory,** at Belvedere Castle (212/772–0210), loans out the *Discovery Kit* to help mainly (but not exclusively) children learn about park wildlife. The **Dana Discovery Center** (212/860–1370) invites families to learn birding basics while exploring northern sections of the park with the Family Bird Watching Club, a free program that meets Saturdays at 11 AM in spring. *Park bordered by Central Park West, 59th St., 5th Ave., and 110th St. General information 212/360–3444. Subway: 59th St./Columbus Circle; N, R to 5th Ave.; B, C to 72nd–110th Sts.; for Dana Discovery Center, 2, 3 to 110th St./Central Park North.*

queens

1 *g-3*

ALLEY POND PARK

Shorebirds and small birds live in abundance in Alley Pond's woodlands and wetlands. The active **Queens County Bird Club** (718/939–6224) meets at the environmental center on the third Wednesday of every month. The club welcomes new birders and arranges slide programs and monthly trips (though fewer in July and August). *Grand Central Pkwy. at Winchester Blvd., Bayside.*

1 *g-6*

JAMAICA BAY WILDLIFE REFUGE

Ten percent of the bird species known to live in the continental United States have been spotted here. It's a prime habitat for waterfowl and shelters migrating shorebirds and wading birds such as herons, plovers, and sandpipers. The visitor center (Broad Channel island, 718/318–4340) has more details. *Broad Channel, 718/338–4340. Subway: Broad Channel.*

staten island

1 *a-4*

CLAY PIT PONDS STATE PARK PRESERVE

More than 40 species of birds breed in the preserve's fields, wetlands, barrens, and streams, and about 170 species live here. The visitor center has a checklist of birds you might see, and when you might see them. *Entrance off Carlin St., Charleston, 718/967–1976. Nature center open Mon.–Sat. 9–5.*

1 *a-2*

WILLIAM T. DAVIS WILDLIFE REFUGE

A variety of birds live here due to the luxurious position between salt marshes and hardwood forests. It's an especially good place to sight hawks. *Travis Ave. off Richmond Ave, New Springville, 718/667–2165.*

1 *b-4*

WOLFE'S POND PARK

Duck, geese, herons, and cormorants are some of the water birds that like the mix of saltwater and freshwater here. *Holton to Cornelia Ave. on Raritan Bay, Prince's Bay, 718/984–8266.*

BOATING

Water, water, everywhere, but not as many boating options as we'd like (unless you own your own craft). Look for more operators as the city better utilizes its waterways. Most renters require identification and/or a deposit in addition to an hourly rental charge (usually $10–$20).

bronx

2 *h-3*

CITY ISLAND

From here you can row to your heart's content in Pelham Bay and the Long Island Sound. *Boat Livery, 663 City Island Ave., 718/885–1843. Subway: 6 to Pelham Bay Park, then BX29 bus to City Island Ave.*

2 *g-2*

PELHAM BAY PARK

This is the only regatta course in the city for both canoeing and rowing, but you have to bring your own boat. *Bruckner Blvd. and Middletown Rd. Hunter Island*

Lagoon: 718/430–1890. Subway: Pelham Bay Park.

brooklyn

1 h-6

PROSPECT PARK

You and up to three friends can rent a pedal boat to tool around Prospect Lake and Lullwater. *Boat rentals: Kate's Corner (at the Wollman Center), off East Lake Dr. (near Flatbush Ave. and Empire Blvd.), 718/282–7789. Subway: D, Q to Prospect Park.*

manhattan

9 d-1

CENTRAL PARK

Row around the 18-acre lake under gorgeous arched bridges in fine view of some of Manhattan's most beautiful apartment buildings. *Enter park at 5th Ave. and 72nd St., Upper East Side, 212/517–2233. Subway: 77th St.*

11 b-7

DOWNTOWN BOATHOUSE

Free kayaking lessons on summer weekends, a boat launch for human-powered watercraft, and friendly, informative people make this new spot inviting. *Hudson River Park, Pier 26, North Moore St., Tribeca, no phone. Subway: Franklin St.*

9 b-5

FLOATING THE APPLE

Comprised of maritime historians, boat-builders, and the interested public, this group is dedicated to keeping New York's small-craft history alive. From their boathouse on Pier 84 (W. 44th St.), they have weekly public rows and sails on boats made by community groups, and they also organize reenactments of important boating events. *Boatbuilding storefront: 330 W. 42nd St., Hell's Kitchen, 212/564–5412. Subway: 42nd St./Port Authority.*

9 a-8

MANHATTAN KAYAK COMPANY

Kayak owners can keep their equipment here, and newbies can learn paddling basics. Statue of Liberty and nighttime tours depart regularly. *Chelsea Piers (23rd St. and 12th Ave.), Pier 60, 212/336–6068. Subway: C, E to 23rd St.*

queens

3 h-2

FLUSHING MEADOWS–CORONA PARK

Rent rowboats on Meadow Lake. *Park: Union Tpke. from 111th St. and Grand Central Pkwy. to the Van Wyck Extension, Flushing, 718/699–9596. Subway: 7 to 111th St. or Willets Point/Shea Stadium; Union Tpke./Kew Gardens.*

BOCCIE

New York has about 100 boccie courts; here are a few choice options.

manhattan

7 f-1

CULLIVER PARK

There are eight courts near the East River at 125th St. *East Harlem. Subway: 4, 5, 6 to 125th St.*

9 g-5

EAST RIVER DRIVE AT 42ND STREET

There are two courts here, near the UN building. *Midtown. Subway: 42nd St./Grand Central.*

10 h-2

EAST RIVER PARK

Like most facilities in this neglected park, the three boccie courts are under-utilized but perfectly good. *East River Dr. between 14th and Delancey Sts., East Village/Lower East Side. Subway: Delancey St.*

11 g-3

HOUSTON STREET AND 1ST AVENUE

This playground has five courts. *East Village. Subway: 2nd Ave.*

BOWLING

For a few decades, bowling just *wasn't* cool in certain crowds; but it's been revitalized thanks to the retro-chic craze of the '90s. It must be the fab shoes and glow-in-the-dark lanes. Of course, for many it never lost its attraction. Call before you go to make sure a league isn't camped out on your lane.

bronx

`2` f-4

FIESTA LANES

Open bowling times in these 28 lanes are mainly during the day. *2826 Westchester Ave. (near Middletown Rd.), Pelham Bay, 718/824–2600. Subway: Middletown Rd.*

brooklyn

`4` d-3

MELODY LANES

Bumper bowling (with guard rails on the gutters) is usually available for kids at this 28-lane facility. *461 37th St., Sunset Park, 718/499–3848. Subway: 36th St.*

manhattan

`9` a-8

AMF CHELSEA PIERS BOWL

If it wasn't big (40 lanes) and new (Manhattan's first new lanes in decades) and state-of-the-art, it wouldn't be at Chelsea Piers. *Chelsea Piers (23rd St. and 12th Ave.), between Piers 59 and 60, 212/835–2695. Subway: C, E to 23rd St.*

`10` e-1

BOWLMOR LANES

This lively, old-time bowling center has 42 lanes on two floors. It stays busy with a downtown crowd until the wee hours. *110 University Pl. (between 12th and 13th Sts.), Greenwich Village, 212/255-8188. Subway: 14th St./Union Square.*

`9` c-5

LEISURE TIME BOWLING AND RECREATION

Bowling in the Port Authority? It makes sense when you think about it, given the central location and vaguely festive surroundings. Complete with a bar and billiards, this modern center has 30 lanes. *Port Authority Bus Terminal, 2nd level, Theater District, 212/268–6909. Subway: 42nd St./Port Authority.*

queens

`3` h-3

HOLLYWOOD LANES

This underground, 30-lane facility is the finest in Queens. *99–23 Queens Blvd. (at 67th Ave.), Rego Park, 718/896–2121. Subway: 67th Ave.*

`2` h-8

WHITESTONE LANES

Can't sleep? These 48 lanes are open 24 hours a day, 7 days a week. *30–05 Whitestone Expwy (at Linden Pl.), Flushing, 718/353–6300. Subway: Main St./Flushing.*

BOXING

Major boxing events are held monthly at **Madison Square Garden** (see Sports Stadiums, *below*). Many health clubs offer "Boxercise," a noncontact exercise involving boxing drills, gloves, and punching bags. The gyms listed here have bona fide rings.

brooklyn

`12` b-1

GLEASON'S GYM

Gleason's *is* boxing in New York. Since 1937 it's trained more than 100 world champions, including Muhammad Ali. You can spar (partners supplied, lessons available) or just watch, and women are welcome and encouraged. *75 Front St. (at Main St.), Brooklyn Heights, 718/797–2872. Subway: York St.; High St./Brooklyn Bridge.*

manhattan

`9` a-8

CHELSEA PIERS

In going after the best of everything, Chelsea Piers has joined up with Gleason's (see above) to offer a boxing program that includes first-time training and an equipment circuit. Nonmembers have to pay the steep day-pass fee to access the ring, which is in the Sports Center. *Sports Center, Chelsea Piers (23rd St. and 12th Ave.), Pier 60, 212/336–6000. Subway: C, E to 23rd St.*

`10` 6-e

HEAVY HANDS CHURCH STREET BOXING GYM

Its lack of glitz allows it to focus on quality personalized training. *25 Park Pl., Lower Manhattan, 212/571–1333. Closed Sun. Subway: Park Pl.*

`10` e-7

WALL STREET BOXING

. . . where stressed-out investment-banker types save themselves from heart attacks. Training sessions and sparring are open to all. *76 Beaver St. (at Wall St.), Lower Manhattan, 212/742–0038. Subway: Wall St.*

CRICKET

Pitching wickets is especially popular among West Indian immigrants. The **World Cricket League** (212/582–8556) has information on events.

bronx

2 *b-2*

VAN CORTLANDT PARK

There are 10 pitches at the Parade Ground, at approximately 243rd Street. Columbia University's cricket club plays home games here. *Park: W. 242nd Street to city line, between Broadway and Jerome Ave., 718/430–1890. Subway: 242nd St./Van Cortlandt Park.*

brooklyn

1 *f-7*

MARINE PARK

There are 4 cricket pitches at 33rd and Stuart streets. *Inlet between Gerritsen and Flatbush Aves., inland to Fillmore Ave., between Burnet and E. 32nd Sts.*

queens

1 *f-5*

FOREST PARK

There are three pitches at 80–30 Park Lane, Kew Gardens. *Park: Union Ave. and Union Tpke. to Park Lane S, between Park Lane and Cypress Hill Cemetery, 718/520–5900. Subway: J, Z to Woodhaven Blvd.; Union Tpke./Kew Gardens.*

staten island

1 *b-1*

WALKER PARK

This park has one cricket pitch. *Delafield Pl. and Bard Ave., Livingston.*

CROQUET

You need a permit to play on the croquet grounds in Central Park; call 212/360–8133 for information. You can also show up at 6 PM on Tuesday in the summer for a free clinic for perspective

members, hosted by **New York Croquet Club** (212/369–7949).

manhattan

9 *d-1*

CENTRAL PARK

Just north of Sheep Meadow is the city's lovely croquet ground, where players in bright white and flat shoes wield mallets. The season runs from April to early November. *Enter park at Central Park West and 72nd St. General information 212/360–3444. Subway: B, C to 72nd St.*

CROSS-COUNTRY SKIING

After a heavy snow, cross-country skiers emerge from their apartments and take to the streets in that brief period before the fluff becomes trampled and brown. Bridle paths and fields tend to remain fresh longer. The **Scandinavian Ski Shop** (40 W. 57th St., Manhattan, 212/757–8524) rents equipment. For park locations, *see Parks, above.*

bronx

VAN CORTLANDT PARK

The vast terrain, when it's smooth, makes for lovely skiing. *W. 242nd Street to city line, between Broadway and Jerome Ave., 718/430–1890. Subway: 242nd St./Van Cortlandt Park.*

brooklyn

4 *c-4*

OWL'S HEAD PARK

The views of the harbor just after a snowfall are otherworldly. The skiing is good here if you're comfortable on rolling hills. *Colonial Rd. at 68th St., Bay Ridge. Subway: Bay Ridge Ave.*

1 *h-6*

PROSPECT PARK

Long Meadow and Nethermead are good for beginners, though most will enjoy them. *Park bordered by Flatbush Ave., Ocean Ave., Parkside Ave., Prospect Park Southwest, and Prospect Park West, 718/965–8999. Subway: Grand Army Plaza; D, Q to Prospect Park; F to 15th St./Prospect Park.*

manhattan

9 c-9

CENTRAL PARK

Sheep Meadow, the Great Lawn, and North Meadow are big and relatively flat, but you'll need to get there early for best conditions. The bridle paths and pedestrian walkways are also lovely trails. *Enter park at Central Park West and 72nd St. or 85th St. General information 212/360–3444. Subway: B, C to 72nd St. or 81st St.*

queens

1 g-3

ALLEY POND PARK

The old Vanderbilt Highway provides good, gladed skiing for miles. The wetlands trail is another option.

3 h-2

FLUSHING MEADOWS–CORONA PARK

The bike paths and walkways throughout the park provide plenty of routes. *Union Tpke. from 111th St. and Grand Central Pkwy. to the Van Wyck Extension, Flushing, 718/699–4209. Subway: 7 to 111th St. or Willets Point/Shea Stadium; Union Tpke./Kew Gardens.*

staten island

1 b-2

HIGH ROCK PARK

The small hills and quick turns on the nature trails are best for experienced skiers.

1 b-3

LA TOURETTE PARK

Bucks Hollow is popular.

FENCING

Fencing can be recreational, competitive, or theatrical. Aficionados claim it's addictive.

manhattan

9 c-8

BLADE FENCING

Private lessons are by appointment. *212 W. 15th St., Chelsea, 212/620-0114. Subway: A, C, E to 14th St.*

9 b-1

FENCERS CLUB, INC.

Founded in 1883, this nonprofit organization is America's oldest fencing club. It teaches men and women of all levels and all ages, sometimes for free. The pickup area is open nightly. *154 W. 71st St., Upper West Side, 212/874–9800 or 212/501–0474. Subway: 72nd St.*

9 d-8

METROPOLIS FENCING CENTER

Group lessons provide a supportive atmosphere for novices. *45 W. 21st St., Chelsea, 212/463–8044. Subway: F to 23rd St.*

FISHING

You need a New York State freshwater-fishing license (ages 16–70) to freshwater-fish in the city; get an application from tackle stores or the **Department of Environmental Conservation** (718/482–4999). Saltwater fishing requires only a line and reel, though if you drive to a spot in the Gateway National Recreation Area, you'll need a parking permit (Breezy Point, Queens, 718/318–4300; Jamaica Bay, Brooklyn, 718/338–3799; Staten Island, 718/351–6970).

Fishers line the many waterways of New York City, from the East River Esplanade on Manhattan's Upper East Side to the Marine Parkway Bridge between Brooklyn and Queens. For some, fishing is a social event—secure your pole, kick back, and turn up the music. For others, it's a solitary, man-vs.-nature affair.

New York City Trout Unlimited (212/439–4741), dedicated to preserving cold-water fisheries, publishes a bimonthly newsletter, "The Urban Fisherman" (available through membership or at tackle stores), and sponsors events such as fly-casting in parks.

bronx

2 h-3

CITY ISLAND

Rent a skiff and head out into the sound for flounder and blackfish. Try Jack's Bait and Tackle (551 City Island Ave., 718/885–2042), Rosenberger's Boat Livery (663 City Island Ave., 718/885–1843), or any other outfitter that looks suitably salty. Fishing boats, including the *Riptide III*

(718/885–0236) and *New Daybreak II* (718/409–9765), generally set out for day trips. *Subway: 6 to Pelham Bay Park, then BX29 bus to City Island Ave.*

2 g-2
PELHAM BAY PARK
Cast for black bass, flounder, catfish, bullheads, and fluke from Orchard Beach and Hunter's and Twins islands. *Park: Bruckner Blvd. and Middletown Rd., 718/430–1890. Environmental Center (near Orchard Beach), 718/885–3466. Subway: Pelham Bay Park.*

2 b-2
VAN CORTLANDT PARK
The catfish and bullheads are biting in the Bronx's largest freshwater lake. *W. 242 St. east of Broadway, 718/430–1890. Subway: 242nd St./Van Cortlandt Park.*

brooklyn

1 h-6
PROSPECT LAKE
Fish in designated areas—you might catch catfish and carp. *Prospect Park, bordered by Flatbush Ave., Ocean Ave., Parkside Ave., Prospect Park Southwest, and Prospect Park West, 718/965–8999. Subway: D, Q to Prospect Park; F to 15th St./Prospect Park.*

1 f-8
SHEEPSHEAD BAY
Fishing boats line the piers along Emmons Avenue, crying out for you to join them in search of fluke, bluefish, striped bass, seabass, and blackfish, among others. Many boats head to Mudhole, a prime fishing ground, between 6 AM and 8 AM for all-day trips or at 8 AM and 1 PM for half-day outings. Options include the *Ranger* (Pier 3, 718/368–9902), *Dorothy B. VIII* (Pier 6, 718/646–4057), and *Blue Sea* (Pier 8, 718/332–9148). Check with Mike's Bait and Tackle (2201 Emmons Ave., 212/646–9261) for more information. *Subway: Sheepshead Bay.*

manhattan

7 d-4
CENTRAL PARK
The lake has carp, catfish, and bullheads. You can also use free bamboo poles and bait from the **Dana Discovery Center** to angle (catch and release) in the Harlem Meer, which is stocked with bluegills, bass, shiners, and catfish. No permit is required. This site is popular with families. *Dana Discovery Center, Harlem Meer (near 110th St. and 5th Ave.), 212/860–1370. Program runs July–Aug.; closed Mon.*

HUDSON RIVER PARK
Organizers supply bait and tackle for kids to catch and release in the Hudson. *Various piers, probably including 25 (N. Moore St.), 62 (W. 23rd St.), and 84 (W. 44th St.). 212/533–7275 for more information and locations.*

queens

1 h-6
ROCKAWAY
Catch bass, flounder, and porgies in the nontoxic saltwater at Breezy Point. There's freshwater fishing at Beach Channel Drive and Beach 32 Street. *Subway: Beach 36 St./Edgemere.*

staten island

1 b-4
WOLFE'S POND
There's freshwater fishing year-round and saltwater fishing October–May. *Wolfe's Pond Park: Holton to Cornelia Ave. on Raritan Bay, Prince's Bay, 718/984–8266.*

FLYING

You'll need a single or multi-engine license to fly a plane in the New York City area.

queens

3 e-4
ACADEMICS OF FLIGHT
A ground school and flying lessons (at Republic Airport, Farmingdale, Long Island) will get your feet off the ground. *43-49 45th St., Sunnyside, Queens, 718/937–5716. Subway: 46th St./Bliss St.*

FOOTBALL

The pro-football season extends from early September through December. All local games take place at New Jersey's **Giants Stadium** (see Sports Stadiums, below). Tickets are extremely difficult, if not impossible, to come by, though you might luck out at the stadium just before a game if the visiting team hasn't used up its share. Arena football, a chaotic game resembling a cross between indoor soccer and football, is played April–July.

teams to watch

NEW JERSEY RED DOGS

New Jersey's arena football team was new in 1997, but after winning the Eastern Conference of the Arena Football League, it saw postseason play. *Continental Airlines Arena (see Sports Stadiums, below), 201/507–8900.*

9 *c-6*

NEW YORK CITY HAWKS

The Hawks' 1997 inaugural season was, well, not so good, and some worried that this arena-football team might not make it to another. If the team survives, look for discounted tickets and family nights. *Madison Square Garden (see Sports Stadiums, below), 212/465–6741.*

NEW YORK GIANTS

The Giants played at the New York Polo Grounds, Yankee Stadium, and Shea Stadium before settling into their New Jersey home in 1976. Their 1995 and 1996 seasons were a disappointment, but that didn't make tickets any easier to come by: all are sold through season subscriptions. *Meadowlands Sports Complex, East Rutherford, NJ, 201/935–8222.*

NEW YORK JETS

Originally called the New York Titans, they now play in New Jersey, at Giants Stadium—how's that for an identity crisis? Though the Jets' record isn't the best (and that's an understatement), the waiting list for season tickets is 10,000 names long. *Giants Stadium, Meadowlands Sports Complex, East Rutherford, NJ, 516/560–8200.*

where to play

There are about two dozen municipal football/soccer fields in New York City; call the Parks Department (*see Parks Information, above*) for a permit and a field near you.

GOLF

Manhattanites may find this hard to picture, but there are 13 public golf courses in the other boroughs, and most are in good condition. Call the individual course to reserve your tee time. Fees are usually just under $20 for city residents (depending on tee time), slightly higher on weekends, and reservations and cart rentals cost about $2 extra. Golf season runs from mid-March through October or November.

bronx

2 *b-2*

MOSHOLU GOLF COURSE

The nine holes on this 3,119-yard course include many challenging shots. *Van Cortlandt Park, Jerome Ave. and 213rd St., 718/655–9164. Subway: 242nd St./Van Cortlandt Park.*

2 *g-2*

PELHAM GOLF COURSE

There are two scenic 18-hole courses here—the 6,281-yard **Split Rock,** one of the city's most challenging (USGA rating 70.6), and the 6,405-yard **Pelham** course. The former is hilly, with many trees (once convenient for disposing of Mafia kill), while the latter is flatter and open. *Pelham Bay Park, 870 Shore Rd., 718/885–1258. Subway: Pelham Bay Park.*

2 *b-2*

VAN CORTLANDT GOLF COURSE

Opened in 1895, this is the oldest public golf course in the country. Its 18 holes include two longer than 600 yards, for 6,102 yards total. *Van Cortlandt Park, Bailey Ave., 718/543–4595. Subway: 242nd St./Van Cortlandt Park.*

brooklyn

4 *d-6*

DYKER BEACH PARK

The wide fairways on this long (6,548 yards), busy course are tough but forgiving. *7th Ave. and 86th St., Bay Ridge, 718/836–9722. Subway: 86th St.*

1 *f-7*

MARINE PARK

Its 6,866 yards make this Robert Trent Jones–designed course the longest in the city, and its seaside location means it's flat and breezy. *2880 Flatbush Ave.*

(between Ave. U and Belt Pkwy.), Flat-lands, 718/338–7113.

queens

1 g-3

CLEARVIEW

One of the most heavily trafficked courses in the country, if not the world, Clearview is straight, flat, and good for beginners. The championship course is 6,473 yards. *202–12 Willets Point Blvd., Bayside, 718/229–2570.*

DOUGLASTON PARK

The 6,500-yard layout is rolling, with small greens and narrow fairways. *6320 Marathon Pkwy. and Commonwealth Blvd., Douglaston, 718/224–6566. Long Island Rail Road: Port Washington line to Douglaston.*

1 f-5

FOREST PARK

This newly renovated course is 6,300 challenging yards in aptly named Wood-haven. *1 Forest Park Dr. S, Woodhaven, 718/296–0999. Subway: J, Z to Wood-haven Blvd.*

1 f-3

KISSENA PARK

The fairways are well-used and close together at this relatively short, hilly course. *164–15 Booth Memorial Ave., 718/939-4594. Subway: Main St./Flushing.*

staten island

1 b-2

LA TOURETTE GOLF COURSE

The fairways are long and varied at this scenic and challenging (par 72) course. *1001 Richmond Hill Rd., 718/351–1889.*

4 a-7

SILVER LAKE

At this pretty, 6,050-yard course, hills and tight fairways challenge golfers, of whom there are usually many. *915 Victory Blvd. (near Forest Ave.), 718/447–5686.*

1 a-3

SOUTH SHORE

Formerly part of a country club, this 6,366-yard course is still very well maintained, with lots of trees. *Huguenot Ave. and Rally St., 718/984–0101.*

HANDBALL

Handball is usually played on a four-walled court. There are over 2,000 such municipal facilities throughout the boroughs, many of them at playgrounds. Call your local Parks office (*see Parks Information, above*) for one near you.

HOCKEY

The professional hockey season runs from October through April.

where to watch

NEW JERSEY DEVILS

New Jersey's tough and generally losing team surprised everyone by winning the Stanley Cup in 1995. *Continental Airlines Arena (see Sports Stadiums, below), 201/935–3900.*

9:

NEW YORK RANGERS

The beloved Mark Messier left after the 1996–97 season, but even this probably won't subdue the team's fanatical fans. *Madison Square Garden (see Sports Stadiums, below), 212/465–6741, hot line 212/465–6500.*

NEW YORK ISLANDERS

Of our three local teams, you'll have the easiest time getting tickets for this one—unless they ever play half as well as they did in the 1980s. *Nassau Veterans Memorial Coliseum, 1255 Hempstead Tpke., Uniondale, NY, 516/794–4100.*

where to play

7 d-4

LASKER RINK

You can drop in on games on weekends during the skating season; bring your own equipment. *Central Park at 106th St., 212/534–7639. Subway: B, C to 103rd St.*

HORSEBACK RIDING

It's always startling to see jodhpur-wearing riders trotting their way through city parks or down the street, but they have plenty of trails at their disposal. Manhattan's Central Park has 4½ mi of horse trails, including one around the reservoir (one level down from the jogging path). Though stables are usually busy, especially on weekends, the limited number of horses available means that your route won't be too congested.

bronx

2 *g-2*

PELHAM BIT STABLE

You can rent horses and Western saddles to ride on trails in Pelham Bay Park, or you can take lessons in an outdoor ring. Small children might enjoy the pony rides. *Pelham Bay Park, 9 Shore Road, 718/885–9723. Subway: Pelham Bay Park.*

2 *a-3*

RIVERDALE EQUESTRIAN CENTRE

This "centre" for learning and competing was created by two former Olympians, who renovated, expanded, and generally improved the Van Cortlandt Riding Academy. Facilities include an Olympic-sized indoor arena (100 by 200 ft) and outdoor rings, and the trails in Van Cortlandt Park. There are pony rides for kids daily. *Broadway and W. 254th St., 718/548–4848. Subway: 242nd St./Van Cortlandt Park.*

brooklyn

4 *e-2*

KENSINGTON STABLES

These horses are convenient to easy rides through Prospect Park. *51 Caton Pl. (between E. State St. and Coney Island Ave.), Park Slope, 718/972–4588. Subway: Fort Hamilton Pkwy.*

1 *f-6*

JAMAICA BAY RIDING ACADEMY

Choose from deserted wooded trails and sandy beaches as you explore the 300 acres open to you, or take a lesson on the indoor ring. *7000 Shore Pkwy, 718/531–8949. Subway: Rockaway Pkwy.*

manhattan

7 *b-6*

CLAREMONT RIDING ACADEMY

A National Historic Site, this academy has been in its Upper West Side location since it opened in 1892. Claremont has an indoor ring and prides itself on its teaching, but this is also the place to rent a horse for a ride through Cen-

tral Park. *175 W. 89th St., Upper West Side, 212/724–5100. Subway: 1, 9 to 86th St.*

queens

1 *f-4*

LYNNE'S RIDING ACADEMY

This low-key place has an indoor ring, guided trail riding through Forest Park, and lessons. *88-03 70th Rd., Forest Hills, 718/261–7679. Subway: 71st–Continental Aves./Forest Hills.*

staten island

1 *a-4*

EQUUS STABLES

Children's lessons are the specialty, but adults are welcome, too. Everything is done in rings; there are no trail horses. *2498 Veterans Rd. W, 718/948–9515.*

HORSE RACING

A day at the races can be exciting and very lucrative. Just don't bet more than you can afford to lose.

1 *g-5*

AQUEDUCT

Thoroughbreds have been racing at Aqueduct, the only racetrack in the city, since 1894. Its season runs from October to early May, Wednesday to Sunday. *Rockaway Blvd. and 110th St., Ozone Park, Queens, 718/641–4700. Subway: Aqueduct/North Conduit Ave.*

1 *g-3*

BELMONT PARK

Thoroughbred races move here from Aqueduct in mid-May, continue through June, and then pick up again from early September through October (Wed.–Sun.). Belmont Stakes, held in June, is the third event in horse racing's Triple Crown. The so-called Breakfast at Belmont—trackside breakfast and then a tram tour—can be fun (weekends and holidays 7–9:30 AM). *Hempstead Tpke. and Plainfield Ave., Elmont, NY, 516/488–6000 or 718/641–4700. Long Island Rail Road: Hempstead Line to Belmont.*

MEADOWLANDS RACETRACK

Trotters and pacers race January through mid-August; the flat-track season is Labor Day through December.

Meadowlands Sports Complex, East Rutherford, NJ, 201/935–8500.

YONKERS RACEWAY

There's harness racing every evening except Wednesday and Sunday year-round. Yonkers Ave., Yonkers, NY, 718/ 562–9500 or 914/968–4200. For bus information, call Westchester Bee Lines at 914/ 682–2020.

HORSESHOES

New York has hundreds of horseshoe pitches throughout the boroughs; all you need are horseshoes. Call the Parks Department (see Parks Information, above) for the pitch nearest you.

ICE SKATING

Skating is allowed on park lakes and ponds in all boroughs when we have a "hard freeze," but you shouldn't count on this happening even once in any given year. The Department of Parks and Recreation operates a number of rinks that get very crowded at predictable times; the season is November to April. Private rinks also fill up, but some have longer or year-round seasons. All rinks rent skates.

where to skate

All of these rinks rent skates—leaving you with no excuse not to give them a whirl.

brooklyn

4 f-2

KATE WOLLMAN MEMORIAL RINK

This popular outdoor rink is surrounded by Prospect Park's trees and offers both open skating and closed figure-skating practice sessions. It's open daily in season, and you can rent skates. East Dr. (near Lincoln Rd. and Parkside Ave.), Prospect Park, 718/287–6431. Subway: Prospect Park.

manhattan

7 e-8

ICE STUDIO

Just 35 ft by 55 ft, this tiny indoor rink (open year-round) is fun for children. 1034 Lexington Ave. (at 74th St.), 2nd fl.,

Upper East Side, 212/535–0304. Closed Aug. Subway: 77th St.

7 d-4

LASKER RINK

These large outdoor rinks are cheaper and less crowded than Wollman. Instead of skyscrapers, they have woodsy views. Central Park at 106th St., 212/534–7639. Subway: B, C to 103rd St.

6 c-6

RIVERBANK STATE PARK

This covered outdoor rink is popular with families. Riverside Dr. at 145th St., Harlem, 212/694–3642. Subway: 1, 9 to 145th St.

9 d-4

ROCKEFELLER CENTER

This small, very busy, private outdoor rink is the classic place to skate in New York. Just watching from above is very entertaining—seasoned locals and giddy tourists scuttle around together. With late-night skating under the famous Christmas tree in December, it's festive and romantic. Rockefeller Plaza (5th Ave. at 50th St.), Midtown, 212/332– 7654. Open Oct.–Apr. Subway: 47th–50th Sts./Rockefeller Center; E, F to 5th Ave.

9 a-8

SKY RINK

The entire Chelsea Piers Complex got started because its developer needed a place for his daughter to skate. Several years later, we have two private, Olympic-sized indoor rinks—one for events and the other for general skating—with lessons, hockey leagues, and special events galore. The views from the top of the pier are amazing but sometimes disorienting—when the sun is beating down and sails are flapping on the Hudson, for example. Chelsea Piers (23rd St. and 12th Ave.), Pier 61, 212/ 336–6100. Rink open 24 hrs year-round; call for open skating hours. Subway: C, E to 23rd St.

9 d-2

WOLLMAN RINK

Nestled within trees nestled within skyscrapers, Wollman has a picture-perfect urban setting. Even when its crowded, and it usually is, people are having the time of their lives. There's late-night skating to popular music on weekend evenings. Central Park, East Dr. near 63rd

St., 212/396–1010. Subway: N, R to 5th Ave.

queens

1 *f-3*

WORLD'S FAIR ICE RINK

This indoor rink gets crowded; the critical mass can be intimidating. *Flushing Meadows–Crotona Park, New York City Building, Long Island Expressway and Grand Central Pkwy., 718/271–1996. Closed Mon., Tues., Thurs. Subway: Willets Point/Shea Stadium.*

staten island

4 *a-7*

STATEN ISLAND WAR MEMORIAL RINK

These two enclosed outdoor rinks are the best places to skate on Staten Island. *Clove Lakes Park, Victory Blvd. at Clove Rd., 718/720–1010.*

IN-LINE SKATING

In just a decade, in-line skating has gone from barely existing to hooking nearly 2 million New Yorkers. Such phenomenal popularity attests to how well-suited this sport/transportation/way of life is to city streets—and city dwellers. Convenience, speed, and simplicity are among the draws: all you need are skates and padding (a helmet and wrist guards are highly recommended, and the former is required for children 14 and under), which can fit even in the tiniest apartment, and the most important skill to master is stopping. Need we mention that it's also a great workout and an excuse to wear skin-tight clothing?

For suggested routes beyond those listed here, *see* Bicycling, *above.* For lessons, *see* Roller Skating, *below.*

While skaters are allowed on sidewalks and on streets, neither is a good place for beginners, and sidewalks are really best left to pedestrians. When using your skates to get somewhere, remember to bring shoes—most buildings don't allow you to wear wheels inside. If you're new to blades, practice stopping on a deserted strip of pavement until you're good enough to be around other people. The **Central Park Skate Patrol**

(212/439–1234) holds free stopping clinics in Central Park (at both 72nd Street entrances, from April through October, 12:30–5:30 weekends) and in-depth classes.

Central Park—specifically the block-long stretch of Loop Road south of the West 67th Street entrance—is the heart of city skating. Hang out here to watch people navigate the cone slalom course (weekends) on one leg and backwards faster than most ever dream of moving. The less-traveled Cherry Hill, the Mall, and the "dead road" parallel to the Mall are good for practicing. The lower portion of the Loop Road is skate central, but only slightly more so than the rest of the park. Wollman Rink (*see* Rollerskating, *below*) is good for tinier laps. Other popular skating grounds in Manhattan are the north section of **Union Square Park** (when it's not a Greenmarket), the waterfront esplanade from **Battery Park** to **Hudson River Park,** and **Riverside Park.** Aggressive skaters do tricks at what's known at the **Brooklyn Banks,** the sloped asphalt directly under the Manhattan side of the Brooklyn Bridge. Vert ramps, half pipes, quarter pipes, rails, and other amenities specifically for skating are at the skate parks at **Chelsea Piers** (23rd St. and 12th Ave., 212/336–6200) and **Riverside Park** (Riverside Dr. and 108th St., 212/408–0264). Both charge admission.

Two skating institutions are the **Tuesday Night Skate** and Wednesday's **Blade Night Out,** both decidedly nebulous in organization. Wednesday's adventure, which meets at Union Square around 8 PM (times vary; 212/794–8513), covers a leisurely but exhilarating (and not always incident-free) few miles in Manhattan, drawing up to 200 people. The Tuesday Night Skate, which alternates between on- and off-island (Manhattan) trips, requires more endurance. It leaves at 8 from Blades Board and Skate (120 W. 72nd St.; route hot line 212/929–0003, ext. 5). **Time's Up** (*see* Bicycling, *above*) events also accommodate skaters.

EMPIRE SKATE CLUB

Founded in 1997 because New York skating needed at least some semblance of organization, Empire Skate runs recreational skating trips and skate-centric social events. *212/592–3674.*

JUGGLING

If you don't think keeping several objects in motion at once is a sport, just try it. Jugglers perform often outside South Street Seaport.

where to play

11 *b-3*

CARMINE STREET IRREGULARS

The time to stop by is Thursday from 7:30 PM to 10 PM, when well-practiced jugglers, entertainers, and beginners go at it. Drop in with a few things to juggle and someone will help you get started. *Carmine Street Gym, Clarkson St. and 7th Ave. S., West Village, 212/242–5228. Subway: Houston St.*

LAWN BOWLING

Brought to us by the Dutch, lawn bowling was probably the first sport played in New York City dating back to 1626—at Bowling Green. You'll need a seasonal permit to bowl on a municipal green; inquire with the Parks Department (*see* Parks Information, *above*).

where to play

9 *d-1*

NEW YORK LAWN BOWLING CLUB

You must be a member to use the bowling green in Central Park, north of the Sheep Meadow (67th St. near West Dr.). Lawn bowlers and croquet players share the greens and clubhouse. *212/650–9218. Subway: B, C to 72nd St.*

MARTIAL ARTS

The martial arts are an Eastern mix of physical training and philosophy for self-defense and mental discipline. Varieties include jiu-jitsu, judo, karate, iaido, and tai chi chu'an. Consult the Yellow Pages for an exhaustive listing of outlets.

brooklyn

4 *d-1*

brooklyn women's martial arts

This all-women center has many loyal students and volunteers. Beginners'

courses in self-defense, karate, and tai chi start at least once every three months. *421 5th Ave. (between 7th and 8th Sts.), 2nd floor, Park Slope, 718/788–1775. Subway: 4th Ave./9th St.*

manhattan

9 *d-5*

TAI CHI CH'UAN CENTER OF NEW YORK

Participants and observers are welcome at this small studio for tai chi and nei kung. *125 W. 43rd St. Theater District, 212/221–6110. Subway: 42nd St./Times Square.*

9 *d-7*

WORLD SEIDO KARATE ORGANIZATION

A traditional karate school, World Seido was founded by 9th-degree black belt Kaicho Tadashi Nakamura. Men, women, and children are welcome to observe or participate in classes, which run all day long and are excellent. The karate training can provide conditioning and teach skills useful for self-defense. *61 W. 23rd St., Chelsea, 212/924–0511. Subway: F to 23rd St.*

MINIATURE GOLF

brooklyn

1 *f-7*

GATEWAY SPORTS CENTER

Right on Rockaway Inlet, this 18-hole, rough-terrain course and 100-tee driving range offer peaceful putting. *3200 Flatbush Ave. (opposite Floyd Bennett Field), Flatlands, 718/253–6816.*

manhattan

9 *d-8*

HACKERS, HITTERS AND HOOPS

Kids love this fun complex. It's got a 9-hole course full of obstacles, a driving range, Ping-Pong, baseball, basketball, and other diversions, and is open late for the young-at-heart. *123 W. 18th St., Chelsea, 212/929–7482. 1, 2, 3, 9, F to 14th St.*

11 *a-8*

PIER 25

This outdoor course is open seasonally. The 18 holes are your typical miniature course, but the river breeze and views make it special. *Pier 25 (near Reade St.), Tribeca, 212/732–7467. Subway: Chambers St.*

7 *h-2*

RANDALL'S ISLAND GOLF AND FAMILY ENTERTAINMENT CENTER
There are two 18-hole minigolf courses and a driving range at this off-the-beaten-track site. *Randall's Island Golf Center, 212/427–5689. Shuttle bus leaves from 3rd Ave. and 86th St., Upper East Side.*

queens

1 *g-3*

ALLEY POND GOLF CENTER
These two indoor 18-hole courses are opposite the salt marshes of the Alley Pond Environmental Center. They have your basic greens, holes, and bumps, though the masters course is more challenging. *Alley Pond Park, Douglaston, 718/225–9187.*

staten island

1 *b-2*

ISLAND GOLF AND BASEBALL SPORTS PARK
With several watery obstacles, this 18-hole course is challenging, and you can move on to the batting cage or skate park when you're done. *215 Schmidts La., 718/370–7888.*

PADDLEBALL

Paddleball requires one wall and very little expense, which is one reason for its popularity, especially among agile young men. There are over 400 paddleball courts in the city—including **Coney Island,** Brooklyn; **Orchard Beach,** Bronx; and **Central Park,** Manhattan. Call the parks hot line in your borough for the nearest court. The National Paddleball Association organizes tournaments and instruction.

RACQUETBALL

Easier than tennis or squash to learn, racquetball sport requires more skill than force. Most clubs charge a guest fee in addition to an hourly court fee for nonmembers; many don't allow them at all.

brooklyn

12 *b-2*

EASTERN ATHLETIC CLUBS
The five courts host lessons and leagues in addition to regular games. Nonmembers pay a guest fee, but there's no court fee during off-peak periods. *43 Clark St., Brooklyn Heights, 718/625–0500. Subway: Clark St.*

manhattan

9 *d-8*

CHELSEA RACQUET AND FITNESS CLUB
This members-only club has four racquetball courts and standard fitness equipment. *45 W. 18th St., Chelsea, 212/807–8899. Subway: F to 14th St.*

9 *d-3*

CLUB LA RAQUETTE
Nonmembers pay a guest fee ($15 weekdays) on top of the court fee; there are two racquetball courts. *Hotel Le Parker Meridien, 119 W. 56th St., Midtown, 212/245–1144. Subway: 57th St.*

9 *b-5*

MANHATTAN PLAZA RACQUET CLUB
There's one racquetball court, open to nonmembers by appointment. Fees vary, so call ahead. *482 W. 43rd St., Hell's Kitchen, 212/594–0554. Subway: 42nd St./Port Authority.*

11 *b-3*

PRINTING HOUSE FITNESS AND RACQUET
The racquetball court at this full-service fitness club is for members only. *421 Hudson St. (at Leroy St.), West Village, 212/243–7600. Subway: Franklin St.*

queens

3 *e-3*

BQE RACQUETBALL CLUB
Guests pay a guest fee on top of the court fee to play here, but it's a very nice facility. There are seven courts. *26-50 Brooklyn-Queens Expressway W, Woodside, 718/726–4343. Subway: Northern Blvd.*

staten island

1 *a-3*

GOLD'S GYM

Gold's has six racquetball courts, all
open to nonmembers; call for prices.
300 W. Service Rd., 718/698–4500.

ROCK CLIMBING

The idea of you against the rock (or the
wall) is catching on in the city, mainly
because of the combination of strength,
flexibility, coordination, and endurance
that it develops. Several new walls have
opened recently, all requiring that you
take a lesson or pass a belay test (in
which you hold the rope while your part-
ner climbs) before you can climb or
spot, and they'll rent you equipment if
you don't have your own. Routes are
changed regularly (by moving the holds
around) to keep the climbing interesting.

manhattan

9 *a-7*

CHELSEA PIERS

There are two walls here, one 30 ft high
(primarily for children and nonmembers; in the field house) and the other
46 ft high (in the Sports Center). With
10,000 square ft total, the latter has
endless challenging routes. There's a
bouldering wall, too, for ropeless climbing. *Field House (between Piers 61 and
62), Chelsea Piers (23rd St. and 12th Ave.),
212/336–6500. Sports Center, Pier 60,
Chelsea Piers, 212/336–6000. Subway: C,
E to 23rd St.*

9 *c-2*

EXTRAVERTICAL CLIMBING CENTER

New in 1997, this wall ranges from 30 to
50 ft high, and since it's in the public,
open-air Harmony Atrium, it's is a fun
place to watch. There's also a climbing
store, where you can rent or buy equipment. ExtraVertical offers membership
packages, but its prices for day passes
(New York Sports Club members get discounts one day a week) are reasonable.
*61 W. 62nd St., Upper West Side, 212/586–
5718. Subway: 59th St./Columbus Circle.*

9 *b-2*

WEST 59TH STREET RECREATION CENTER

The first indoor wall in Manhattan, this
one has a fiercely loyal clientele despite

the opening of several more sophisticated climbing centers. Bring your own
equipment. Climbing membership is
separate from general rec-center membership, but the year-round and day-use
fees are reasonable. *533 W. 59th St., Midtown, 212/974–2250. Open weekdays 5
PM–10 PM, Sat. noon–5. Subway: 59th
St./Columbus Circle.*

MANHATTAN PLAZA HEALTH CLUB

Another pioneer on the Manhattan
climbing scene, the 20-ft indoor wall is
run by instructors with extensive outdoor experience. Use of the wall is
included in club membership, but nonmembers are welcome for a fee. *482 W.
43rd St., Hell's Kitchen, 212/563–7001.
Subway: 42nd St./Port Authority.*

ROLLER SKATING

Watch the feet of all the skaters
whizzing by on park roads and you'll see
a small number of traditional roller
skates, but since the advent of in-line
skating, the more traditional wheels are
most popular for dancing. As with in-
line skating, the five boroughs offer endless outdoor opportunities for skaters
confident enough to hit the streets.
Parks and rinks are preferred by many,
though, for obvious reasons. For more
tips, *see In-Line Skating, above.*

manhattan

LEZLY SKATE SCHOOL

A few skating lessons with Lezly's skating specialists (indoor and outdoor, traditional and in-line) will stop your ankles
from wobbling in no time. They also
teach roller dancing. This is also the
home of the **Central Park Dance Skaters
Association,** who you'll find disco dancing in a giant loop on the defunct park
road south of 72nd Street on weekend
afternoons. *212/777–3232.*

9 *b-8*

ROXY

Manhattan's only public indoor rink is
sometimes a dance hall, but on Tuesday
(predominantly gay) and Wednesday
(more mixed), it's a roller disco. *515 W.
18th St., Chelsea, 212/645–5156. Subway:
A, C, E to 14th St.*

9 *d-2*

WOLLMAN RINK

When the ice thaws, this wonderfully situated rink is turned over to the wheeled crowd. *Central Park, East Dr. near 63rd St., 212/396–1010. Subway: N, R to 5th Ave.*

RUGBY

The **New York Rugby Club** fields both men's and women's sides. In addition to training and games during the league seasons (spring and fall), the club schedules drinking practiced around televised rugby events—or for no reason. New members are always welcome; call 212/988–9201 for more information.

3 *C-1*

RANDALLS ISLAND

Playing fields are to the right of the ramp off the Triborough Bridge; there are games most Saturday mornings in spring and fall.

RUNNING AND JOGGING

The **Jacqueline Kennedy Onassis Reservoir** in Central Park is a beautiful, 1.6-mi gravel path that most Manhattan runners have circled more times than they'd care to count. Waterfront paths and trails through the larger parks in all five boroughs are all well traveled by runners. **Prospect Park** and **Central Park** both have popular running lanes around their loop roads. Manhattan's **East River Esplanade**, about 4 mi round-trip from Carl Schurz Park to 125th Street, is prettiest at sunrise, though you should probably run with someone at that hour. Watch the sunset from **Riverside Park** while running between 72nd Street and 116th, also about 4 mi round-trip. There are cross-country courses in the Bronx's **Van Cortlandt Park** (6 miles), Brooklyn's **Marine Park** (0.8 miles) and **Alley Pond Park** (1.5 miles), Queens's **Forest Park** (2.5 miles), and Staten Island's **Clove Lakes Park** (3.3 miles). The general rule for figuring mileage in Manhattan is twenty short blocks to a mile. Call the Parks office in your borough for the municipal running track nearest you, and for other distance-running ideas *see* Bicycling *and* In-line Skating, *above*.

NEW YORK HASH HOUSE HARRIERS

They call themselves drinkers with a running problem, but they actually organize fun scavenger *runs* throughout New York. If you successfully follow the trail, you end up in a bar with a cold drink. *212/427–4692.*

NEW YORK ROAD RUNNERS CLUB

Best known for the New York City Marathon (early Nov.) and the New Year's Eve fun run, this is the largest runner's club in the world. It offers a full range of classes, clinics, group runs, races, and even merchandise for everyone from beginning runners to elite champions. Members get substantial discounts and a subscription to *Running News*. The **Achilles Track Club** (212/354–0300) has programs for physically challenged runners. *9 E. 89th St., 212/860–4455.*

SAILING

New York City was the national center for sailing in the 19th century, and the New York Yacht Club is still very influential nationwide. The city's nautical heritage is most pronounced on City Island, whose shingled waterfront shacks, briny air, and salty characters seem more New England than Bronx; some people here still build sails or boats for a living. Experienced sailors should be able to help crew a boat off the island during the summer-long Wednesday-night race series (City Island Yacht Club, 718/885–2487). In a recent epiphany, Manhattanites realized what they were missing, and there are now several sailing options in New York Harbor as well.

manhattan

9 *a-8*

CHELSEA SAILING SCHOOL

Basic sailing, navigation, and seamanship are taught from Chelsea Piers' Hudson River marina. Alumni may join the Chelsea Sailing Club. *Chelsea Piers (23rd St. and 12th Ave.), Pier 59, 212/627–SAIL. Subway: C, E to 23rd St.*

10 *d-7*

MANHATTAN SAILING SCHOOL

The Manhattan Sailing School teaches sailing at all skill levels on J-24 boats in

New York Harbor; you can also rent or charter boats. The school was founded in 1991 by the Manhattan Yacht Club, which had just reintroduced recreational sailing to Manhattan in 1987 after the sport's absence for more than half a century. You can join the Yacht Club once you complete Basic Sailing. *World Financial Center, 393 South End Ave., Lower Manhattan, 212/786–0400. Subway: Cortlandt St./World Trade Center.*

10 *d-7*
NORTH COVE SAILING SCHOOL

An affiliate of the American Sailing Association and a neighbor of the larger Manhattan Sailing School, North Cove also teaches you to sail on J-24s. Experienced sailors can skipper or crew on boats from the fleet. *World Financial Center, 393 South End Ave., Lower Manhattan, 800/532–5552. Subway: Cortlandt St./World Trade Center.*

SCUBA DIVING

You never know what you might find off the coast—reefs, wrecks, subs, or garbage. Most scuba certification is either through **NAUI** (National Association of Underwater Instructors, 800/553–6284) or **PADI** (Professional Association of Diving Instructors, 800/729–7234), and both organizations can direct you to nearby programs. Classes include pool instruction and an open dive, which some people choose to complete while on vacation (your teacher should help you arrange this). Fees can vary from about $170 up to $400, and class sessions can last anywhere from one intensive week to a few months.

brooklyn

1 *f-8*
PROFESSIONAL DIVING SERVICES

Master Instructor and Captain Bill Reddan takes certified divers out on evenings and weekends on the *Jeanne II* to explore wrecks such as the *Algol* (80–120 ft) and the *Arundo* (125 ft). Call for a schedule and to make reservations. *Pier 5, Sheepshead Bay, 718/332–9574. Subway: Sheepshead Bay.*

manhattan

9 *e-1*
AQUA-LUNG SCHOOL OF NEW YORK

Using the pool at Hunter College, Fran Gaar, the first female master instructor in the country, and her instructors will prepare you for PADI or NAUI certification. Each student's record is kept individually, meaning you can show up for sessions whenever it's convenient. All equipment is provided. *Hunter College: Lexington Ave. at 68th St., Upper East Side. 212/582–2800. Subway: 68th St./Hunter College.*

9 *b-5*
PAN AQUA DIVING

Pan Aqua teaches certification courses at four Manhattan locations (92nd St. YM-YWHA, West Side YMCA, Vanderbilt YMCA, and Manhattan Plaza Health Club). Based at Manhattan Plaza, Pan Aqua also offers free scuba trials, rentals, and repairs. *460 W. 43rd St., Hell's Kitchen, 212/736–DIVE. Subway: 42nd St./Port Authority.*

queens

3 *h-3*
SEA HORSE DIVERS

This center has everything—instruction, sales, rentals, and occasional weekend trips along the Eastern seaboard. In addition to a 10-day PADI certification program, you can take an evening-long refresher course. *95-58 Queens Blvd. (near 63rd Dr.), Rego Park, 718/897–2885. Subway: 63rd Dr./Rego Park.*

SOCCER

Professional soccer was extremely popular in New York when Pelé played for the Cosmos in the 1970s, but the league died in the 1980s and many people forgot about it—until the U.S. hosted the World Cup in 1994. Will "football" ever catch on in this country?

where to watch

METROSTARS

Our local Major League Soccer team, born in 1996, hasn't realized its potential yet. The season is late March–September. *Giants Stadium, Meadowlands Sports Complex, East Rutherford, NJ, 201/935–3900.*

where to play

You need a permit to reserve any of the park soccer fields; call the appropriate Parks office for information and locations. At many fields you'll have to bring your own net.

SOFTBALL

New York has more than 600 baseball diamonds, heavily used by softball players. Many companies form softball teams and compete in leagues. If you're not part of a league, you'll need a permit; call your borough's parks office for fields near you.

SPORTING EVENTS

New Yorkers of all stripes come out for these sports and outdoor annuals.

ADVIL MINI MARATHON

Thousands of women race, jog, and walk the 10K course through Central Park, forming the world's largest race for women only. Runners start at the park's West Drive, near 66th Street, and finish at Tavern on the Green. *New York Road Runners Club, 212/860–4455. Early June.*

BELMONT STAKES

This prestigious track hosts the final race in the Triple Crown. *Belmont Park, Hempstead Tpke. and Plainfield Ave., Belmont, NY, 516/488–6000 or 718/641–4700. Long Island Rail Road: Hempstead Line to Belmont. June.*

BIKE NEW YORK

Bike New York is to cyclists what the New York Marathon is to runners. At last count, about 30,000 people have been turning out for this five-borough, 42-mi tour. It's all car-free, from the starting line in Battery Park to the long stretch on the Belt Parkway to the finish over the Verazzano Narrows Bridge (which doesn't otherwise allow bikes). A free ferry brings cyclists back to Manhattan. *212/932–BIKE. Early May.*

CHERRY BLOSSOM FESTIVAL

The Brooklyn Botanical Garden celebrates its cherry trees during Sakura Matsuri, a Japanese-themed festival that usually includes music and dance, Japanese-crafts demonstrations, special tours, and a tea ceremony in honor of the lush blooms. The trees form one of Mother Nature's most spectacular limited engagements. *718/622–4433. Early May.*

COREL W.T.A. CHASE CHAMPIONSHIPS

Closing an 11-month schedule of tennis tournaments, this is the biggest women's sports event in the world. *Madison Square Garden (see Sports Stadiums, below, 212/465–6000. November.*

EARTH DAY

Celebrations usually include numerous outdoor events. Check with the Parks Department and with Transportation Alternatives (*see Biking*), which traditionally sponsors a pollution-free ride. *Apr. 22.*

MANHATTAN ISLAND MARATHON SWIM AND WATER FESTIVAL

Individuals and relay team members, covered in Vaseline and shot through with immunizations, swim 28½ mi counterclockwise around Manhattan. In celebration of the race, Battery Park hosts a daylong Water Festival. *212/873–8311. July.*

MAYOR'S CUP

Schooners and classic yachts compete in New York Harbor in this race, organized by the South Street Seaport Museum. *212/748–8786. Late Sept.*

MILLROSE GAMES

These track-and-field championships are Madison Square Garden's oldest continuous sports event, and the longest-running invitational meet in the country. The prestigious Wanamaker Mile race is a highlight. *Madison Square Garden (see Sports Stadiums, below), 212/465–6000. February.*

NEW YORK MARATHON

Nearly 30,000 runners (about one-third of them New Yorkers) gulp Gatorade and wave at the cheering crowds on this five-borough foot race. Elite champions lead the pack; most of the runners are just looking to have a good time and to make it to the finish line in Central Park. *New York Road Runners Club, 212/860–4455. Early November.*

RUNNER'S WORLD/ ASICS MIDNIGHT RUN

Thousands of costumed runners ring in the New Year with fireworks and a 5K midnight run through Central Park. *New*

York Road Runners Club, 212/860–4455. New Year's Eve.

U.S. OPEN TENNIS TOURNAMENT

Celebrities always appear in the stands, and the boxes in the new Arthur Ashe Stadium are to die for, but the real excitement is the Grand Slam tennis. With a stadium ticket you can also catch matches in outlying courts and in the grandstand, where bleacher seating is first-come, first served. *U.S.T.A. National Tennis Center, Flushing Meadows–Corona Park, 800/524–8440. Late August–early September. Subway: Willets Point/Shea Stadium.*

SPORTS STADIUMS

CONTINENTAL AIRLINES ARENA

Formerly the Brendon Byrne Arena, this 20,000-seater has its hands full with the ferocious fans of the New Jersey Nets (basketball), New Jersey Devils (hockey), and, more recently, Mad Dogs (arena football). *Meadowlands Sports Complex, East Rutherford, NJ, 201/935–3900.*

7 *h-2*

DOWNING STADIUM

Pelé played for the New York Cosmos soccer team here in the 1970s, but now it's as likely to host a concert as a sporting event. *Randalls Island, 212/860–1828. Subway: 4, 5, 6 to 125th St.*

GIANTS STADIUM

It's rumored that Jimmy Hoffa rests in peace under the Astroturf trod by New York's two football teams (the Jets and the Giants), the MetroStars (soccer), and legions of concertgoers. The stadium seats almost 78,000. *Meadowlands Sports Complex, East Rutherford, NJ, 201/935–3900.*

9 *c-6*

MADISON SQUARE GARDEN

There's never a dull moment in Midtown's loud, 20,000-seat showcase. The New York Knicks and the New York Liberty shoot hoops, the New York Rangers slam pucks, and the New York City Hawks bounce off the wall in arena football. Many up-and-coming college athletes, track stars, boxers, wrestlers, and figure skaters find themselves here at some point. *7th Ave. between 31st and*

33rd Sts., Midtown, Manhattan, 212/465–6000. Tours daily.

NASSAU VETERANS MEMORIAL COLISEUM

Built in 1972, the New York Islanders' 16,000-seat home is showing its age, but hey, we haven't heard any rumors yet about the team moving to Manhattan. *1255 Hempstead Tpke., Uniondale, NY, 516/794–9300.*

3 *h-1*

SHEA STADIUM

New York Mets ballgames are always fun at this 55,777-seat stadium—the fans drown out the noise from nearby La Guardia Airport. *126th St. and Roosevelt Ave., Flushing, Queens, 718/507–8499.*

3 *h-1*

U.S.T.A. NATIONAL TENNIS CENTER

The venerable host of the U.S. Open lets the rest of us play most of the year (see Tennis, *below). Flushing Meadows–Corona Park, Flushing, Queens, 718/760–6200.*

6 *f-5*

YANKEE STADIUM

The 57,545-seat 1923 "House That Ruth Built" has watched its boys win 23 World Championships. Steinbrenner's not moving them anywhere. *161st St. and River Ave., Bronx, 718/293–6000. Subway: 161st St./Yankee Stadium.*

SQUASH

Squash is available at many private gyms. Court fees vary with supply and demand.

brooklyn

12 *b-2*

EASTERN ATHLETIC CLUBS

The Brooklyn Heights branch has two squash courts. Nonmembers pay a guest fee. *43 Clark St., Brooklyn Heights, 718/625–0500. Subway: Clark St.*

manhattan

9 *e-6*

ATHLETIC COMPLEX

Before this became a complete fitness center it was strictly racquet sports; now there's just one squash court left. Non-members are permitted for a fee. *3 Park Ave. (entrance on 34th St.), Murray Hill, 212/686–1085. Subway: 33rd St.*

9 *d-3*

CLUB LA RAQUETTE
There is one squash court. Nonmembers pay a guest fee on top of the court fee. *Hotel Le Parker Meridien, 119 W. 56th St., Midtown, 212/245–1144. Subway: 57th St.*

10 *e-8*

NEW YORK HEALTH & RACQUET CLUB
This racquet-sports specialist club has courts at two locations. Nonmembers pay an extremely steep visitor's fee. *39 Whitehall St., Lower Manhattan, 212/269–9800. Subway: Whitehall St./South Ferry.*

9 *e-4*

20 E. 50th St., Midtown, 212/593–1500. Subway: E, F to 5th Ave.

9 *c-2*

NEW YORK SPORTS CLUB
Take your pick of locations. *61 W. 62nd St., Upper West Side, 212/265–0995. Subway: 59th St./Columbus Circle.*

9 *d-6*

404 5th Ave. (between 36th and 37th Sts.), Midtown, 212/594–3120. Subway: 34th St./Herald Square.

7 *e-7*

151 E. 86th St., Upper East Side, 212/860–8630. Subway: 4, 5, 6 to 86th St.

12 *c-4*

110 Boerum Pl., Cobble Hill, Brooklyn, 718/643–4400. Subway: F, G to Bergen St.

11 *b-3*

PRINTING HOUSE FITNESS AND RACQUET
This full-service, members-only fitness club has six squash courts. *421 Hudson St. (at Leroy St.), West Village, 212/243–7600. Subway: Houston St.*

9 *c-2*

WEST SIDE YMCA
The two courts here are for members only. *5 W. 63rd St., Upper West Side, 212/787–4400. Subway: 59th St./Columbus Circle.*

SWIMMING

More than 30 city-run outdoor pools are open from the 4th of July weekend through Labor Day, and they're free—just bring a bathing suit, towel, and lock. Hours are usually 11–7, with an hour's break in midafternoon. The Aquatics Division of the Department of Parks and Recreation (718/699–4219) has information about pools, lessons, and lap swimming. Despite a few highly publicized incidents regarding sexual harassment at public pools, they're generally a safe (if crowded) diversion. Use common sense—city pools probably aren't the best place for your new thong, for example, and even with lifeguards on duty, you shouldn't swim alone. (*See* Beaches, *above*, for more outdoor swimming.) Indoor pools are open year-round, with the exception of those at public-recreation centers that also have outdoor pools. For more municipal pools, check the government listings pages of the phone book under Parks and Recreation—Swimming Pools.

bronx

5 *f-3*

APEX
The beautiful 50-meter, 8-lane indoor pool at Lehman College's new athletic center allows anyone to be a member for a reasonable yearly fee. *Lehman College, 250 Bedford Park Blvd. West, Jerome Park, 718/960–1117. Closed Sun. Subway: Bedford Park Blvd./Lehman College.*

5 *h-8*

CROTONA POOL
This outdoor pool is very large, but it still gets crowded. *E. 175th St. and Fulton Ave., Morrisania, 718/822–4440. Subway: C, D to 174th–175th Sts.*

2 *c-8*

ST. MARY'S RECREATION CENTER
The rec center has an indoor pool. *St. Ann's Ave. and E. 145th St.,, 718/402–5155. Subway: E. 143rd St./St. Mary's St.*

2 *b-3*

VAN CORTLANDT POOL
Van Cortlandt's outdoor pool is bigger than most. *W. 244th St. east of Broadway, 718/548–2415. Subway: 242nd St./Van Cortlandt Park.*

brooklyn

1 f-5
BROWNSVILLE PLAYGROUND RECREATION CENTER
For $10/year you can swim as a member in this 75-ft indoor pool. *1555 Linden Blvd. (at Christopher Ave.), 718/345–2706. Subway: L to New Lots Ave.*

1 d-6
RED HOOK POOL
This outdoor pool is Brooklyn's largest. *Bay and Henry Sts., 718/722–3211. Subway: Smith–9th Sts.*

1 e-6
ST. JOHN'S RECREATION CENTER
There's a 75-ft indoor pool at this public rec center. *1251 Prospect Pl. (between Troy and Schenectady Aves.), Crown Heights, 718/771–2787. Subway: 3, 4 to Utica Ave.*

4 d-3
SUNSET PARK POOL
This outdoor neighborhood pool is large and popular. *7th Ave. and 43rd St., 718/965–6578. Subway: 45th St.*

manhattan

7 g-6
ASPHALT GREEN AQUACENTER
This indoor sea—oops, pool—is state-of-the-art, with a movable bottom and bulkheads that can divide it into manageable subsections. It's Olympic-size—50 meters long—and nonmembers can swim at certain hours for a fee. *1750 York Ave. (at 91st St.), Upper East Side, 212/369–8890. Subway: 4, 5, 6 to 86th St.*

9 g-8
ASSER LEVY RECREATION CENTER
This public rec center used to be a bath-house, and its indoor pool is small but beautiful—natural light, high ceiling. There's a larger outdoor pool, too; the indoor one closes when the other is open. *E. 23rd St. and Asser Levy Pl. (between 1st Ave. and FDR Dr.), Gramercy, 212/447–2020. Subway: 23rd St.*

11 b-3
CARMINE RECREATION CENTER
The indoor pool closes when the out-door one opens. Both are no-frills but in good condition. *7th Ave. South at Clarkson St., West Village, 212/242–5228. Subway: Houston St.; W. 4th St.*

9 f-3
EAST 54TH ST. RECREATION CENTER
There's a small indoor pool here. *348 E. 54th St., Midtown, 212/397–3154. Subway: 6 to 51st St. or E, F to 53rd/Lexington Ave.*

7 g-8
JOHN JAY PARK POOL
Parks Commissioner Stern does his morning laps here. The park has a nice view from its perch above the East River. *E. 77th St. and Cherokee Pl. (near York Ave.), Upper East Side, 212/794–6566. Subway: 77th St.*

7 c-4
LASKER POOL
This is Manhattan's largest outdoor pool. *Central Park at 106th St., Morningside Heights, 212/534–7639.*

9 b-5
MANHATTAN PLAZA HEALTH CLUB
The 75-ft lap pool at this private club is a big draw, especially on bright summer days when the atrium roof opens. Non-members are welcome, for a fee. *482 W. 43rd St., Hell's Kitchen, 212/563–7001. Subway: 42nd St./Port Authority.*

6 c-6
RIVERBANK STATE PARK
This indoor lap pool is one of the cheapest nonmunicipal options ($3); there's also an outdoor pool in summer. *Riverside Dr. at 145th St., Harlem, 212/694–3600. Subway: 145th St.*

9 f-4
VANDERBILT YMCA
There are two pools here: a 75-ft shallow lap pool and a smaller pool with a deep end for lessons and classes. Nonmembers are welcome for a guest fee. *224 E. 47th St., Midtown, 212/756–9600. Subway: 51st St.*

9 *b-2*

WEST 59TH STREET RECREATION CENTER

This 60-ft indoor lap pool is underutilized. *533 W. 59th St., Midtown, 212/974–2250. Subway: 59th St./Columbus Circle.*

9 *c-2*

WEST SIDE YMCA

As at the Vanderbilt YMCA, there are two pools here. The one meant for laps has a beautiful tiled ceiling. *5 W. 63rd St., Upper West Side, 212/787–4400. Subway: 59th St./Columbus Circle.*

queens

8 *b-5*

ASTORIA PARK POOL

The 1936 Olympic trials were held in this large outdoor pool near the East River. *19th St. and 23rd Dr., Astoria, 718/626–8620. Subway: Ditmars Blvd./Astoria.*

1 *g-4*

ROY WILKINS RECREATION CENTER

There's an indoor pool at this St. Albans rec center. *177th St. and Baisley Blvd., 718/276–8686.*

staten island

1 *a-1*

FABER PARK POOL

This outdoor pool is good-sized. *2175 Richmond Terrace at Faber St., Port Richmond, 718/816–5558.*

4 *b-5*

LYONS POOL

Though the outdoor pool is fairly large and in good condition, it's not in the best neighborhood. *Victory Blvd. east of Bay St., Tompkinsville, 718/816–9571.*

1 *a-4*

TOTTENVILLE POOL

This standard-size outdoor pool is on the country club–inspired south shore. *Hylan Blvd. and Joline Ave., Tottenville, 718/356–8242*

1 *b-1*

WEST BRIGHTON POOL

This is a standard-size outdoor pool. *Broadway and Henderson Ave., West Brighton, 718/816–5019.*

TENNIS

Staten Islander Mary Outerbridge introduced Americans to tennis in the 19th century, and New Yorkers have expressed their (ahem) love for the sport ever since. To play on a municipal court (Apr.–Nov.), you'll need a permit. In Manhattan they're available at the Parks Department's headquarters at the Arsenal (830 5th Ave., at 64th St.) and from Paragon Sporting Goods (867 Broadway, at 18th St., 212/255–8026). Permits are $50 for the year; single-play passes are also available. Reservations, which are useful at some courts, cost extra, and many facilities have lockers for a charge as well. For complete information about permits, and for numbers to call in other boroughs, listen to the long recording at 212/360–8133.

where to watch

See **U.S. Open Tennis Tournament** and **Corel W.T.A. Chase Championships** in Sports Events, *above.*

where to play

All of these courts are city-owned unless otherwise noted. For an exhaustive list, call your borough's Parks office.

bronx

2 *d-3*

AGNES HAYWOOD PARK

There are 30 courts at this city park. *E. 215th St. and Barnes Ave., Williamsbridge. Subway: 219th St.*

2 *d-4*

BRONX PARK

Four new courts are expected here in 1998. *Bronx Park East and Brady Ave., Bronxdale.*

2 *c-6*

CROTONA PARK

These 20 hard courts are the among best in the Bronx. *E. 173rd St. and Crotona Ave., Morrisania. Subway: C, D to 174th–175th Sts.*

6 *f-4*

MULLALY PARK

There are 16 good courts here. *164th St. and Jerome Ave., Highbridge. Subway: 164th St.*

2 *g-2*

PELHAM BAY PARK

This park has 10 courts. *Bruckner Blvd. and Middletown Rd., Pelham Bay. Subway: Pelham Bay Park.*

2 *b-2*

VAN CORTLANDT PARK

There are six new hard courts and four older ones. *W. 241st St. and Broadway, Riverdale. Subway: 242nd St./Van Cortlandt Park.*

5 *g-1*

WILLIAMSBRIDGE OVAL

This area has eight hard courts. *E. 208th St. and Bainbridge Ave., Norwood. Subway: 205th St.*

brooklyn

4 *g-6*

BROOKLYN RACQUET CLUB

There are seven clay courts under a bubble and four more outside. This private facility opens early and doesn't close until the wee hours; courts are available for an hourly fee. *2781 Shell Rd. (near Avenue Z and McDonald Ave.), Brighton Beach, 718/769–5167. Subway: Avenue Z.*

4 *e-6*

DYKER BEACH PARK

There are nine hard courts here. *Bay 8th St. and Cropsey Ave.*

12 *e-2*

FORT GREENE PARK

This park has six hard courts. *DeKalb and South Portland Aves. Subway: Atlantic Ave.*

4 *g-7*

KAISER PLAYGROUND

There are 12 hard courts here. *Neptune Ave. and W. 25th St., Coney Island. Subway: Stillwell Ave./Coney Island.*

4 *d-4*

LEIF ERICSON PARK

There are nine hard courts here. *8th Ave. and 66th St., Bay Ridge. Subway: 8th Ave.*

1 *f-7*

MARINE PARK

There are 12 hard courts here. *Inlet between Gerritsen and Flatbush Aves., inland to Fillmore Ave., between Burnet and E. 32nd Sts.*

1 *f-8*

MANHATTAN BEACH

This small beach has 6 hard courts that aren't too busy. *Oriental Blvd. and Mackenzie St. Subway: Brighton Beach.*

4 *f-2*

PROSPECT PARK PARADE GROUND

There are 10 clay courts here. *Coney Island Ave. and Parkside Ave., Prospect Park South. Subway: Fort Hamilton Pkwy.*

manhattan

7 *d-5*

CENTRAL PARK TENNIS CENTER

Reservations are a good idea at these busy city courts. In addition to four hard courts and 26 newly reconditioned Har-Tru courts, the center offers professional instruction, tournaments, and locker rooms. *Park bordered by Central Park West, 110th St., 5th Ave., and 59th St. Courts midpark (enter at W. 96th St.), 212/280–0205. Subway: B, C to 96th St.*

9 *d-6*

CROSSTOWN TENNIS

Take note: on hot summer days, these four indoor courts are air-conditioned. They're available for hourly fees. *14 W. 31st St., Garment District, 212/947–5780. Subway: 34th St./Herald Square.*

10 *h-2*

EAST RIVER PARK

These 12 courts are in good shape but are not busy—perhaps because they're a little too close to the cacophonous East River Drive. *East River Dr. between 14th and Delancey Sts., East Village/Lower East Side. Subway: Delancey St.*

6 *e-6*

FRED JOHNSON MEMORIAL PARK

They turn the lights on at night for these 8 hard courts. *Adam Clayton Powell, Jr., Blvd. At 151st St., Harlem. Subway: 148th St./Lenox Terminal.*

5 *b-5*

INWOOD HILL PARK

These 9 courts aren't too busy except on weekends. *W. 207th St. at Seaman Ave. Subway: 207th St./Inwood.*

9 *b-5*

MANHATTAN PLAZA RACQUET CLUB

The five rooftop courts are covered by a bubble in the winter, open air (with great views) in the summer, and light after dark. They're open to nonmembers by appointment; fees vary, so call ahead. *482 W. 43rd St., Hell's Kitchen, 212/594–0554. Subway: 42nd St./Port Authority.*

9 *c-7*

MIDTOWN TENNIS CLUB

The eight Har-Tru courts—all under a bubble in winter and half bubbled (and air-conditioned) in summer—charge an hourly fee for nonmembers. *341 8th Ave. (at 27th St.), Garment District, 212/989–8572. Subway: C, E to 23rd St.*

1 *d-3*

RANDALL'S ISLAND

Four of these city courts are bubble-topped; the other five are outdoors. *Randall's Island.*

7 *a-5*

RIVERSIDE PARK

There are 10 clay courts at 96th Street and 10 hard courts at 119th Street. *Enter park at Riverside Dr. and 96th St. or 115th St., Upper West Side. Subway: 1, 2, 3, 9 to 96th St.; 116th St./Columbia University.*

9 *g-2*

SUTTON EAST TENNIS CLUB

From October to April there's a bubble under the Queensboro Bridge, with eight private clay courts inside. *488 E. 60th St., Upper East Side, 212/751–3452. Subway: 59th St.*

9 *e-5*

TENNIS CLUB AT GRAND CENTRAL

This club has the city's oldest and most uniquely located indoor courts, but the hourly fees top a whopping $100. *15 Vanderbilt Ave., 3rd floor, Midtown, 212/687–3841. Subway: 42nd St./Grand Central.*

queens

1 *g-3*

ALLEY POND PARK

In winter these 16 municipal courts are covered by a bubble to become the private **Alley Pond Tennis Club** (718/468–1239). *Grand Central Pkwy. and Winchester Blvd., Bayside.*

3 *d-2*

ASTORIA PARK

There are 14 courts here under the Triborough Bridge. *21st St. and Hoyt Ave., Astoria. Subway: Astoria Blvd./Hoyt Ave.*

1 *g-3*

CUNNINGHAM PARK

This park has 20 hard courts. *Union Tpke. and 193rd St., Holliswood.*

3 *c-4*

FILA SPORTS CLUB

You can take a shuttle bus from Manhattan to this large private tennis club. The 20 courts are outdoors in the summer, indoors in the winter. *44-02 Vernon Blvd. (at 44th Ave.), Long Island City, 718/784–0600. Shuttle from Sutton Theatre, 3rd Ave. and 57th St., Midtown. Subway: 21st St./Queensbridge.*

3 *h-1*

FLUSHING FIELDS

In the shadow of the U.S.T.A. Center, these eight courts are kept in excellent shape and are accordingly busy. *Flushing Meadows–Corona Park, Flushing. Subway: Willets Point/Shea Stadium.*

1 *f-5*

FOREST PARK

This park has 14 courts—seven hard and seven clay. *Park La. S and 89th St., Woodhaven. Subway: 85th St./Forest Pkwy.*

1 *f-3*

KISSENA PARK

This quiet section of the park has eight clay courts and four hard courts. *Rose Ave. and Parsons Blvd., Kissena. Subway: Main St./Flushing.*

1 *g-5*

ROCHDALE PARK

There are six hard courts here. *Guy R. Brewer Blvd. and 134th Ave., no phone.*

3 *h-2*

U.S.T.A. NATIONAL TENNIS CENTER

Considering the great playing that takes place on these courts, the hourly fees are pretty reasonable, generally topping out at $40. There are 29 courts, some of them indoors and lighted. *Flushing Meadows–Corona Park, 718/760–6200. Subway: Willets Point/Shea Stadium.*

staten island

1 *b-1*

SILVER LAKE PARK
These four courts have an idyllic locale, but they've seen better days. *Hart Blvd. and Revere St., Brighton Heights.*

1 *b-1*

WALKER PARK
There are six hard courts here. *Bard Ave. and Delafield Pl., Livingston.*

VOLLEYBALL

There are more than 330 volleyball courts in New York City; young 9-to-5ers spike hard after work. Call your borough's Parks office (*see* Parks Information, *above*) for the one nearest you.

manhattan

BIG CITY VOLLEYBALL LEAGUE
Show up for the four-hour Friday Night Club ($12) to spike and socialize. Call for locations, which depend on your level of play. *212/288–4240.*

NEW YORK URBAN PROFESSIONALS
It sounds like a yuppie group, and it is, but they have games open to all ($10) on Friday nights. Locations vary depending on level. *212/877–3614.*

11 *b-7*

PIER 25
There's an outdoor sand volleyball court right on the Hudson, on so-called Manhattan Beach Inc. A group can rent the entire court for an hourly fee; individuals can play for a daily rate. *N. Moore St. and 12th Ave., Tribeca, 212/571–2323. Subway: Chambers St.*

WRESTLING

Madison Square Garden (*see* Sports Stadiums, *above*) has championship, professional, and exhibition wrestling matches one weekend a month. For information, call 212/465–6741.

YOGA

A system of exercises for mental and physical well-being, yoga techniques teach breathing, postures, movement, and meditation. Most gyms around town offer some kind of yoga program, but you usually have to be a member to take the classes.

brooklyn

12 *g-7*

PARK SLOPE YOGA CENTER
The inner body is the focus at this center, which teaches kundalini yoga. Classes are $10 each, with quantity discounts. *473 13th St. (between 8th Ave. and Prospect Park W), 718/832–1559. Subway: 15th St./Prospect Park.*

manhattan

10 *c-1*

INTEGRAL YOGA INSTITUTE
This is New York's best-known yoga institute, with classes at all levels but not all prices—each costs under $10. *227 W. 13th St., West Village, 212/929–0586. Subway: A, C, E to 14th St.*

9 *b-1*

200 W. 72nd St., Upper West Side, 212/721–4000. Subway: 1, 2, 3, 9 to 72nd St.

9 *d-7*

IYENGAR YOGA INSTITUTE
The Iyengar method focuses heavily on postures and alignments; this institute offers a free introductory class and others at different levels for under $20 per class. *27 W. 24th St., Suite 800, Chelsea, 212/691–9642. Subway: F to 23rd St.*

11 *f-2*

KUNDALINI YOGA CENTER
Like Park Slope Yoga Center (*see above*), they use the kundalini method, focusing on internal organs. Call for schedule and class location. *419 Lafayette St., 5th floor, Greenwich Village, 212/475–0212. Subway: Astor Pl.*

9 *c-7*

SIVANANDA YOGA VEDANTA CENTER
One of the oldest and busiest yoga centers in Manhattan, Sivananda has classes for all ages and all levels. Both 1- and 1½-hour classes are under $10, with

member discounts. *243 W. 24th St., Chelsea, 212/255–4560. Subway: C, E to 23rd St.*

9 e-8

URBAN YOGA WORKOUT CENTER

Stress reduction and fitness are pursued through yoga, but without following a strict technique. Classes are $15, and memberships and quantity discounts are available. *900 Broadway (between 19th and 20th Sts.), Flatiron, 212/505–0902. Subway: N, R to 23rd St.*

9 e-3

YOGA ZONE

The teaching method is called ISHTAR (Integral Science of Hatha and Tantra Arts), and the studios are elegant. Classes are $15. *160 E. 56th St., Midtown, 212/935–9642. Subway: 59th St.*

9 e-8

38 5th Ave. (between 18th and 19th Sts.), Flatiron, 212/647–9642. Subway: N, R to 23rd St.

fitness centers & health clubs

With striking views, plush locker rooms, state-of-the-art equipment, and spa services at so many private gyms, you'd think people just showed up to relax. But no matter how much time they spend flexing in the mirror, adjusting their Spandex, and trying to meet others, people do go to the gym to work out. And only a city with such a fitness-obsessed populace could support such a variety of options. Don't take the decision of which gym to join lightly—you're choosing an identity. You're also probably forking over an arm and a leg initiation fee plus a chunk of your salary in monthly dues. Look for corporate discounts, join-with-a-friend specials, and sales, and ask if any fees can be waived or reduced.

Many of the more exclusive clubs are so intent on keeping the riffraff out that only members of people seriously considering joining are allowed past the front desk. These institutions are designated "Members Only" below. Those that allow members to bring guests are designated "Member Guests Only."

Others charge visitors fees for classes or one-day use of all facilities; often these fees are discounted or waived if a member brings you. All clubs have people to show you around personally if you profess an interest in membership.

PUBLIC HEALTH CLUBS

City-operated rec centers centers are unbelievable bargains. For just $10–$25 per year you have everything you'd expect from a health club—pools, basketball, weights, training equipment, machines, and even classes. The schedules aren't as packed as those at private clubs, but neither are the locker rooms. Manhattan locations include the magnificent, former public-bath building **Asser Levy** (see Swimming, *above*), **Carmine Street** (see Swimming, *above*), **East 54th Street** (1st Ave. and 54th St., 212/397–3154), and **West 59th Street** (10th Ave. and 59th St., 212/397–3159). All told, there are more than 30 centers throughout the five boroughs. For more information call the Parks Department (see Parks, *above*).

PRIVATE HEALTH CLUBS

9 c-8

AMERICAN FITNESS CENTER

This relatively new club is heavy on the strength straining, cardio equipment, and personal training, but it has a full schedule of aerobic and conditioning classes. *128 8th Ave. (at 16th St.), Chelsea, 212/627–0065. Subway: A, C, E to 14th St.*

7 g-6

ASPHALT GREEN

A unique public-private partnership turned an old asphalt plant into this fitness and arts complex. The 50-meter pool blows everything else in the city out of the water, but don't underestimate the rest of the place—weights and weight training overlooking the East River, aerobic and conditioning classes like Guts and Butts, an eye-catching AstroTurf field, and numerous community programs and programs for people with disabilities. *555 E. 90th St., Upper East Side, 212/369–8890. Subway: 4, 5, 6 to 86th St.*

9 *e-3*

BALLY TOTAL FITNESS

Inexpensive and convenient locations (in the city and across the country) are the pluses; waits for machines and limited class offerings and amenities are the minuses. For a full list of locations, call 800/846–0256. *45 E. 55th St., Midtown, 212/688–663. Subway: E, F to 5th Ave.; for other locations, 800/695–8111.*

7 *e-7*

144–146 E. 86th St., Upper East Side, 212/722–7371. Subway: 4, 5, 6 to 86th St.

10 *e-6*

233 Broadway (at Park Pl.), Lower Manhattan, 212/227–5977. Subway: Park Pl.

9 *f-2*

BALLY'S VERTICAL CLUB

A thousand-plus dollars per year buy you access to lots of machines, a good variety of classes, fun instructors . . . and the feeling that you're hanging out at a glitzy has-been. *330 E. 61st St., Upper East Side, 212/355–5100. Member guests only. Subway: 59th St.*

9 *a-7*

BASKETBALL CITY

With six full-size hardwood courts, electronic scoreboards, and computer-arranged pickup games, there's no denying the focus here. But Basketball City also has volleyball courts, a complete fitness center, and good locker rooms. *Chelsea Piers, Pier 63 (W. 23rd St. and 12th Ave.), Chelsea, 212/924–4040. Member guests only. Subway: C, E to 23rd St.*

9 *a-7*

CHELSEA PIERS SPORTS CENTER

Imagine passing endless rows of top-of-the-line weight machines, cardio equipment, and free weights; fitness studios with every imaginable class; a boxing ring; basketball/volleyball courts; and then a 46-ft climbing wall, and then seeing it all again on your way back to a 6-lane, 25-yard pool, and you're probably out of breath already. Now imagine seeing all that as you run around an *indoor* ¼-mi track, and you have some idea of what the Sports Center is like. The pool is at the end of the pier above the Hudson and has deck-to-ceiling glass windows on three sides, just in case you didn't notice the view. Add a sundeck and appropriately luxurious locker rooms and you don't feel so bad about

the $1,500 a year (or $31/day) it takes to be here. *Chelsea Piers (23rd St. and 12th Ave.), Pier 60, 212/336–6000. Subway: C, E to 23rd St.*

9 *f-3*

CRUNCH

A failed actor put his creative talents to good use in building this empire of fitness clubs and associated paraphernalia. The classes are loud, in-your-face, and sometimes unexpected—African Dancing, Thighs and Gossip, Fat Blaster. The machines are abundant, but locker-room amenities are not. The Second Avenue location has a small climbing wall. *1109 2nd Ave. (at 59th St.), Upper East Side, 212/758–3434; for other locations, 212/620–7867. Subway: 59th St.*

11 *f-1*

404 Lafayette St (at Astor Pl.), East Village, 212/614–0120. Subway: Astor Pl.

7 *e-7*

DAVID BARTON

Individual training, cardio equipment, and cushy couches, rather than extensive classes, are what draw people to this eponymous, bodybuilder-owned gym. *30 E. 85th St., Upper East Side, 212/517–7577. Subway: 4, 5, 6 to 86th St.*

11 *e-3*

623 Broadway (between Houston and Bleecker Sts.), Greenwich Village, 212/420–0507. Subway: Bleecker St., Broadway–Lafayette St.

10 *d-1*

522 6th Ave. (at 15th St.), Chelsea, 212/727–0004. Subway: F to 14th St.

12 *b-2*

EASTERN ATHLETIC CLUBS

These spacious Brooklyn centers have full programs of classes and numerous sports offerings, including swimming, martial arts, racquet sports, and dance. *43 Clark St., Brooklyn Heights, 718/625–0500. Subway: Clark St.*

12 *g-5*

17 Eastern Pkwy. (between Plaza and Underhill Sts.), Park Slope, 718/789–4600. Subway: Grand Army Plaza.

7 *b-8*

EQUINOX

All three of your selves—physical, mental, and spiritual—will be challenged here, with East-meets-West and martial arts–based classes taught by instructors who have become local celebrities. As you'd expect for the premium you pay to belong, equipment is up-to-date, plentiful, and in good working order. 344 Amsterdam Ave. (at 76th St.), Upper West Side, 212/721–4200, subway: 79th St.; other locations. Members only.

9 *b-5*

MANHATTAN PLAZA HEALTH CLUB

One of the few independent clubs in town, this Hell's Kitchen standout stays one step ahead of its bigger competitors without being outrageously expensive or intimidating. It has everything you expect in a complete health club—25-yard lap pool, quality equipment, and a full schedule of classes including the latest trends (Spinning, PowerBoards). Then there are the extras—the pool's retractable roof; the outdoor sundeck; the climbing wall that opened years before people had heard of such a thing; the tennis club's rooftop courts. 482 W. 43rd St., Hell's Kitchen, 212/563–7001. Subway: 42nd St./Port Authority.

10 *e-8*

NEW YORK HEALTH AND RACQUET CLUB

As the name suggests, this club is best for tennis and racquetball, but for people into those games it's a way of life—you get access to the club's party yacht, Westchester beach club, and social calendar. Its many locations offer plenty of courts, machines, and classes. Though visitors are allowed, the fee is unwelcoming. 39 Whitehall St., Lower Manhattan, 212/269–9800; call for other locations. Subway: Whitehall St./South Ferry.

9 *c-2*

NEW YORK SPORTS CLUB

The omnipresence award goes to NYSC—chances are you're within a few blocks of one now. They also win the high-strung–yuppie award: nine-to-fivers pack the clubs after work for reservation-only classes, willing to wait anxiously to burn their calories on equipment that's gathering dust the rest of the day. That said, it's worth mentioning that the equipment is kept up-to-date, the classes incorporate the latest trends, and thousands of people swear by this gym. 61 W. 62nd St., Upper West Side, 212/265–0995; for other locations call 800/796–6972. Subway: 59th St./Columbus Circle.

10 *e-7*

30 Wall St., Lower Manhattan, 212/482–4800, subway: Wall St.

NATURE TRAILS

You don't have to leave the city to bushwhack, wade through marshes, or get lost on wooded paths. Here are some favorite hikes.

Greenbelt
28 mi of trails incl. a 13-mi circular trail and the 7-mi La Tourette Trail.

Inwood Hill Park
Short nature trails pass tree identifications and an Indian cave.

Jamaica Bay Wildlife Refuge
Nearly 3,000 acres are reserved for nature walks and bird-watching.

Pelham Bay Park
The Sinawoy Trail.

Van Cortlandt Park
Old Putnam Railroad Track, Aqueduct Trail, and Cass Gallagher Nature Trail.

Wave Hill Ctr for Environmental Studies
A 1½-mi marked trail.

ON-LINE INFORMATION

Many of the organizations and parks listed here tell their stories on the Web. Here are some URLs for rainy-day exploration.

Central Park
www.centralpark.org

Friends of Van Cortlandt Park
www.isp.net.FVCP

New York Botanical Garden
www.nybg.org

New York Sports On Line
www.nynow.com/nysol/first.html

Parks Events
www.tricky.com/ nycparkspecialevents

Prospect Park Alliance
www.prospectpark.org

Wildlife Conservation Society
www.wcs.org

9 *d-6*
50 W. 34th St., Garment District, 212/868-0820. Subway: 34th St./Herald Square.

11 *b-3*
PRINTING HOUSE FITNESS AND RACQUET CLUB
With great West Side views, plenty of space, and diverse offerings, this is another down-to-earth independent option, and it draws some West Village celebs. Racquetball and squash courts are available, as is a classes-only membership. *421 Hudson St. (at Leroy St.), West Village, 212/243-7600. Members only. Subway: Houston St.*

9 *b-1*
REEBOK SPORTS CLUB NEW YORK
In true 1990s style, the line between theme park and what this purports to be is a thin one. The facilities are awesome—25-yard lap pool, ⅙-mile track, full-size basketball courts with stands, 45-ft climbing wall, every kind of machine you can think of. The classes, in 2,500-ft studios, also run the full range. The initiation fee is more than $1,000, after which the monthly rate is still no bargain. *150 Columbus Ave. (at 67th St.), Upper West Side, 212/362-6800. Members only. Subway: 66th St./Lincoln Center.*

11 *e-3*
WORLD GYM
For pumping iron and an outrageous number of classes 24-hours a day, this is your place. *232 Mercer St. (between Bleecker and W. 3rd Sts.), Greenwich Village, 212/780-7407. Subway: W. 4th St./Washington Square.*

9 *b-2*
1926 Broadway (between 64th and 65th Sts.), Upper West Side, 212/874-0942. Subway: 66th St./Lincoln Center.

9 *f-4*
YMCA
If you feel out-glitzed, out-priced, and old-fashioned at the city's other fitness emporiums, do yourself a favor and visit the Y. Built as veritable community centers, city Ys do a fine job of keeping you fit and making you feel good about the world. Make no assumptions about the offerings—equipment is in good shape, classes are challenging, locker rooms are clean, and pools are excellent. You might not end up ahead of this week's fitness trend, but you'll stay in shape. *Vanderbilt Y, 224 E. 47th St., Midtown, 212/756-9600; call for other locations. Subway: 51st St./Lexington-3rd Aves.*

7 *e-6*
92ND STREET YM-YWHA
Best known for its cultural programming, the 92nd Street Y deserves recognition for its fitness facilities, too. Classes here cover everything from yoga to spinning to line dancing, for all age groups; facilities include a 25-yard pool, racquetball courts, and a 5,000-square-ft, fully stocked "cardio court," fully stocked with machines that keep your heart in motion. *1395 Lexington Ave. (at 92nd St.), Upper East Side, 212/415-5729. Subway: 6 to 96th St.*

9 *e-3*
YWCA
This predominantly female center is another down-to-earth deal. It has a pool, a good array of machines, and an unusually large selection of self-improvement classes. *610 Lexington Ave. (at 53rd St.), Midtown, 212/735-9753. Subway: 51st St./Lexington-3rd Aves.*

chapter 7

HOTELS

...ecked the prices
...ty hotels lately,
...rude awakening—it is
tru... ...nd decent rooms for
less than $1... ...nd most cost twice
that. In addition, New York has more
than its share of deluxe hotels, where
one night costs about the same as a
month's rent for a studio apartment.

On a more reassuring note, you rarely
have to pay the full "rack rate," or standard room cost that hotels print in their
brochures and quote over the phone.
Hotels almost always offer corporate
rates, seasonal specials, and weekend
deals that typically include such extras
as complimentary meals, drinks, or tickets to events. Ask about specials when
booking; ask your travel agent for
brochures; and look for advertisements
in travel magazines or the Sunday
travel sections of major newspapers,
such as the New York Times, the
Washington Post, or the Los Angeles
Times. Of course, booking any all-inclu-
sive package, for a weekend or longer,
will also reduce the hotel rate.

In general, Manhattan hotels make up
for their small rooms and lack of parking with amenities befitting a cosmopolitan crowd: sophisticated
restaurants, top-flight service, fine fitness facilities, and in-room extras such
as phones with voice mail and modem
lines. Unless otherwise noted, hotels in
this book have air-conditioning and designated no-smoking rooms and/or
floors.

The majority of Manhattan's hotels are
in Midtown and the Theater District—
both convenient locations for those who
want to be in the heart of it all. The
more residential Upper East Side is
home to many of the city's small,
deluxe boutique hotels, such as the Carlyle and the Mark. Gramercy, Murray
Hill, and Chelsea are other choice
neighborhoods with plenty of hotel
options in most price ranges. Farther
downtown, the choices are more limited, especially in SoHo and the East

and West Villages. No matter where
you stay, though, Manhattan's small
size and excellent public transportation
make it easy to reach your destination
once you've freshened up.

price categories

CATEGORY	COST*
Very Expensive Lodgings	over $325
Expensive Lodgings	$265–$325
Moderately Priced Lodgings	$135–$265
Budget Lodgings	under $135

*All prices are for a standard double room,
excluding 13¼% city and state taxes plus an
occupancy charge of $2 per room, per night.

VERY EXPENSIVE LODGINGS

7 e-8

THE CARLYLE

It's tough to decide where to spend your
time in this Madison Avenue landmark:
Should you stay in your Mark Hamp-
ton–designed guest room, admiring the
fine antique furniture and artfully
framed Audubons and botanicals? Or
should you venture downstairs to the
cozy little Bemelmans Bar, with murals
by Ludwig Bemelmans, illustrator of the
beloved Madeline books? Either way,
you're sure to enjoy the swanky yet
refined ambience of this Manhattan
classic. 35 E. 76th St., 10021, Upper East
Side, 212/744–1600 or 800/227–5737, fax
212/717–4682. 145 rooms, 45 suites.
Restaurant, bar, café, in-room faxes, in-
room modem lines, kitchenettes, minibars,
room service, spa, laundry service and dry
cleaning, concierge, business services,
meeting rooms, parking (fee). AE, DC,
MC, V. Subway: 77th St.

9 e-3

THE DRAKE

Part of the Swissôtel chain, the Drake
reeks of Swiss-style efficiency; witness
the extensive business center, where
guests have access to three worksta-
tions, each with its own private desk,
telephone, and computer. The spanking-
new rooms have an Art Deco look, and
all have oversized desks and overstuffed
chairs and sofas. The Drake Bar is a
convivial meeting place, with Swiss spe-

cialties and some good Swiss wines. *440 Park Ave. (between 56th and 57th Sts.), 10022, Midtown, 212/421–0900 or 800/ 372–5369, fax 212/371–4190. 385 rooms, 110 suites. Restaurant, bar, in-room faxes, in-room modem lines, in-room safes, refrigerators, room service, spa, baby-sitting, laundry service and dry cleaning, concierge, business services, meeting rooms, parking (fee). AE, D, DC, MC, V. Subway: 59th St.*

9 d-3
ESSEX HOUSE
The lobby here is an Art Deco masterpiece fit for Fred and Ginger—and the restaurant, Les Célebrités, is one of New York's finest (see French in Chapter 3). Guest rooms and suites, some with Louis XIV–style furnishings and others with English Chippendale, are comfortable and classic enough to make you want to move in. Many have dazzling views of Central Park, which is right across the street. Service is excellent. *160 Central Park South, 10019, Midtown, 212/247–0300 or 800/645–5687, fax 212/ 315–1839. 520 rooms, 77 suites. 2 restaurants, bar, in-room faxes, in-room modem lines, in-room safes, minibars, room service, in-room VCRs, spa, baby-sitting, laundry service and dry cleaning, concierge, business services, meeting rooms, parking (fee). AE, D, DC, MC, V. Subway: N, R, B, Q to 57th St.*

9 e-3
FOUR SEASONS
Everything about this I.M. Pei–designed hotel is epic: the spired, limestone-clad structure itself; the giant guest rooms (average size is 600 square ft, and all have 10-ft-high ceilings); and, of course, the prices. Even if you can't stay here, step inside just to see the marvelous Grand Foyer, with French-limestone pillars, marble, onyx, and acre upon acre of blond wood. Guest rooms are soundproofed (a rarity in New York), and all have walk-in closets paneled with English sycamore. *57 E. 57th St., 10022, Midtown, 212/758–5700 or 800/332–3442, fax 212/758–5711. 310 rooms, 60 suites. Restaurant, bar, in-room modem lines, in-room safes, minibars, room service, spa, piano, baby-sitting, laundry service and dry cleaning, concierge, business services, meeting rooms, car rental, parking (fee). AE, DC, MC, V. Subway: 59th St.*

9 e-4
HOTEL INTER-CONTINENTAL
Though it doesn't achieve the same level of style as some of New York's other deluxe hotels, this member of the Inter-Continental chain does have the advantage of occupying a 1930s building whose grand, marble lobby still has its original ornate skylight and gilded crown moldings. Rooms are predictably traditional, with framed neoclassical prints and glass-top coffee tables; the only surprise is the brass-eagle doorbells mounted on the outside of each door—they're remnants of the building's former life as the Barclay Hotel. Bathrooms are tiny—even in the suites. *111 E. 48th St., 10017, Midtown, 212/755–5900 or 800/327–0200, fax 212/644–0079. 601 rooms, 82 suites. Bar, restaurant, in-room modem lines, minibars, massage, sauna, health club, baby-sitting, laundry service and dry cleaning, concierge, business services, meeting rooms, parking (fee). AE, D, DC, MC, V. Subway: 51st St./Lexington–3rd Aves; 42nd St./Grand Central.*

9 d-3
I.T.T. LUXURY COLLECTION HOTEL—NEW YORK
The hotel formerly known as the Ritz-Carlton is still the ultimate in luxury, with its prime Central Park South address, polished service, and tasteful decor. Fine art fills the public rooms, and guest rooms are little masterpieces, with rich brocades, polished woods, and marble bathrooms. Some rooms have breathtaking views of the park. *112 Central Park South, 10019, Midtown, 212/ 757–1900 or 800/241–3333, fax 212/757–9620. 192 rooms, 16 suites. Restaurant, bar, in-room modem lines, in-room safes, room service, massage, health club, laundry service and dry cleaning, baby-sitting, concierge, business services, meeting rooms, parking (fee). AE, D, DC, MC, V. Subway: N, R, B, Q to 57th St.*

9 e-2
THE LOWELL
You could pass right by this elegant, pied-à-terre–style boutique hotel on a neighborhood side street between Madison and Park avenues. Understated elegance pervades it, beginning with the tiny, Old World lobby. More than half the guest rooms are suites, and all are eminently inviting, with kitchenettes or minibars, stocked book-

shelves, and—in some rooms—working fireplaces and private terraces where you can dine al fresco. *28 E. 63rd St., 10021, Upper East Side, 212/838–1400 or 800/221–4444, fax 212/319–4230. 21 rooms, 44 suites. Restaurant, breakfast room, in-room faxes, in-room modem lines, kitchenettes, minibars, room service, in-room VCRs, massage, health club, baby-sitting, laundry service and dry cleaning, concierge, parking (fee). No pets. AE, D, DC, MC, V. Subway: 59th St.*

7 *e-8*

THE MARK

Along with its neighbor, the Carlyle, the Mark is widely considered the classiest small hotel in New York. On a tree-lined street just steps from Central Park, it's a bastion of serenity; the cool, Biedermeier-furnished, marble lobby is truly one of the New York's most charming small spaces. Guest rooms are luxurious and soothing, with cream-color walls, museum-quality prints, plump armchairs, fresh flowers, and Frette bed linens. *25 E. 77th St., 10021, Upper East Side, 212/744–4300 or 800/843–6275, fax 212/744–2749. 120 rooms, 60 suites. Restaurant, bar, in-room faxes, in-room modem lines, in-room safes, kitchenettes, minibars, room service, in-room VCRs, massage, health club, baby-sitting, laundry service and dry cleaning, concierge, business services, meeting rooms, parking (fee). No pets. AE, D, DC, MC, V. Subway: 77th St.*

9 *c-4*

MARRIOTT MARQUIS

This theater-district behemoth has nearly 2,000 rooms, plus a slew of restaurants (including a revolving restaurant and lounge on the 46th floor), shops, meeting rooms, ballrooms, and even a Broadway theater. It's a favorite with tour groups and conventioneers. Guest rooms are generic but clean and functional; some have nice city views. *1535 Broadway (at 45th St.), 10036, Theater District, 212/398–1900 or 800/843–4898, fax 212/704–8966. 1,911 rooms, 95 suites. 3 restaurants, 3 bars, café, coffee shop, in-room modem lines, in-room safes, room service, beauty salon, massage, health club, theater, baby-sitting, laundry service and dry cleaning, concierge, business services, meeting rooms, parking (fee). AE, D, DC, MC, V. Subway: 42nd St./Times Sq.*

9 *d-4*

THE MICHELANGELO

A touch of Italian luxury in midtown Manhattan, the Michelangelo welcomes you with multihued marble and quasi-Veronese oil paintings. Some guest rooms branch out to Art Deco and French-country styles, and all have marble bathrooms with bidets and 55-gallon bathtubs. Continental breakfast is served in the lobby lounge each morning. *152 W. 51st St., 10019, Midtown, 212/765–1900 or 800/237–0990, fax 212/581–7618. 123 rooms, 55 suites. Restaurant, bar, in-room faxes, in-room modem lines, minibars, room service, exercise room, baby-sitting, laundry service and dry cleaning, concierge, business services, meeting rooms, parking (fee). No pets. AE, DC, MC, V. Subway: 7th Ave.; 50th St.; 47th–50th Sts./Rockefeller Ctr.*

10 *d-6*

NEW YORK MARRIOTT WORLD TRADE CENTER

The World Trade Center bombing in 1993 virtually destroyed the former New York Vista, so this enormous hotel has a polished, new look. The skylit lobby has a grand curved staircase and a fountain, and there's an atrium restaurant off to the side. Guest rooms are modern and well-kept. The 22nd-floor health club has phenomenal views of Lower Manhattan. *3 World Trade Center, (between Liberty and Vesey Sts.), 10048, Lower Manhattan, 212/938–9100 or 800/550–2344, fax 212/321–2107. 795 rooms, 23 suites. Restaurant, bar, in-room modem lines, minibars, room service, indoor pool, health club, laundry service and dry cleaning, concierge, business services, meeting rooms, travel services, car rental, parking (fee). AE, D, DC, MC, V. No pets. Subway: World Trade Ctr.*

9 *e-4*

NEW YORK PALACE

After an 18-month renovation that ended in spring 1997, the former Helmsley Palace has reinvented itself from the ground up and is now one of Manhattan's most exciting deluxe hotels. Behind the hotel, the landmark 1882 Villard House, known for its Tiffany glasswork and frescoed murals, now houses the ultrachic, five-star restaurant Le Cirque 2000, an outrageous, futuristic riot of color (*see* French *in* Chapter 3). For more modest meals, there's a lobby-lounge restaurant with an olive bar and an afternoon "tapas" tea service with a Mediterranean twist. The newly redone guest rooms have retained their Empire flavor, with bold colors and dark woods, though some of the more luxurious rooms and suites in the Tower (Floors 41–55) have a brand-new, Art Deco look, with oversized furniture and polished blond-wood headboards. The health club has top-of-the-line equipment and an awesome view of St. Patrick's Cathedral. *455 Madison Ave. (between 50th and 51st Sts.), 10022, Midtown, 212/888–7000 or 800/697–2522, fax 212/303–6000. 800 rooms, 100 suites. 2 restaurants, 2 bars, in-room faxes, in-room modem lines, in-room safes, minibars, room service, spa, health club, baby-sitting, laundry service and dry cleaning, concierge, concierge floors, business services, meeting rooms, parking (fee). No pets. AE, D, DC, MC, V. Subway: 51st St./Lexington–3rd Aves.*

9 *e-3*

OMNI BERKSHIRE PLACE

Watch Siamese fighter fish swim in little bowls as you relax in front of the fireplace in the two-story atrium lounge— or just retire to one of the 375-square-ft guest rooms, where bedside comfort controls and fax machines are nice additions to the contemporary, Asian-influenced decor. This is Omni Berkshire's flagship hotel, and it easily lives up to that honor. *21 E. 52nd St., 10022, Midtown, 212/753–5800 or 800/843–6664, fax 212/754–5020. 396 rooms, 44 suites. Restaurant, bar, in-room faxes, in-room modem lines, in-room safes, minibars, room service, massage, health club, laundry service and dry cleaning, concierge, business services, meeting rooms, parking (fee). No pets. AE, D, DC, MC, V. Subway: E, F to 5th Ave.*

9 *d-3*

LE PARKER MERIDIEN

The atrium of this French-owned and -operated hotel strikes an exotic, eclectic note, with two-story arched mirrors, a mosaic ceiling, palm trees, and Doric columns. Equally dramatic are the glass-enclosed rooftop swimming pool (where it's fashionable to dine poolside), the rooftop outdoor track, and the enormous Club Raquette health club, with racquetball and squash courts. Rooms have an elegant neoclassical motif in soothing tans and browns. *118 W. 57th St., 10019, Midtown, 212/245–5000 or 800/543–4300, fax 212/708–7477. 449*

rooms, 249 suites. Restaurant, bar, in-room faxes, in-room modem lines, in-room safes, minibars, room service, indoor pool, spa, health club, racquetball, squash, nightclub, baby-sitting, laundry service and dry cleaning, concierge, business services, meeting rooms, parking (fee). AE, D, DC, MC, V. Subway: 57th St.

9 *e-3*

THE PENINSULA

The marble, Art Nouveau lobby of this opulent landmark recalls a grander era, when bell captains wore sailor suits and afternoon tea was on everyone's schedule. Guest rooms are vintage 1940s, with rose-color velour, mahogany furnishings, and framed Art Nouveau prints; many rooms have sweeping views down 5th Avenue. Don't miss the glass-enclosed, trilevel health club and spa, with an indoor, rooftop swimming pool where you can gaze down at midtown between laps. At press time a major renovation was slated to begin in early 1998; call to verify that the hotel is open. *700 5th Ave. (at 55th St.), 10019, Midtown, 212/247–2200 or 800/262–9467, fax 212/903–3943. 200 rooms, 41 suites. 2 restaurants, 2 bars, in-room faxes, in-room modem lines, in-room safes, minibars, room service, indoor pool, beauty salon, spa, health club, baby-sitting, laundry service and dry cleaning, concierge, business services, meeting rooms, parking (fee). AE, D, DC, MC, V. Subway: E, F to 5th Ave.*

9 *e-2*

THE PIERRE

Since the 1930s, the Pierre has occupied its 5th Avenue post with all the grandeur of a French château. The public areas drip with chandeliers, handmade carpets, and Corinthian columns. The king-sized guest rooms are resplendent with traditional chintz fabrics and dark-wood furniture; bathrooms have Art Nouveau fixtures. Service is predictably first-rate—the Pierre is a Four Seasons hotel. *2 E. 61st St., 10021, Upper East Side, 212/838–8000 or 800/332–3442, fax 212/758–1615. 149 rooms, 54 suites. Restaurant, bar, in-room faxes, in-room modem lines, in-room safes, room service, beauty salon, massage, health club, baby-sitting, laundry service and dry cleaning, concierge, business services, meeting rooms, parking (fee). AE, D, DC, MC, V. Subway: N, R to 5th Ave.*

(2 bath)
Rm 820, 822
$385

THE PLAZA

Ernest Hemingway is said to have advised F. Scott Fitzgerald to bequeath his liver to Princeton but his heart to the Plaza. Hemingway probably would have been shocked when Donald Trump bought the hotel, in 1988. This is also where the fictional Eloise ran riot—but you don't have to admire Donald Trump or Eloise to enjoy brunch at the fin-de-siècle Palm Court or a drink at the clubby Oak Bar, where horse-drawn carriages clip-clop past the windows. Though the guest rooms are small for such a luxury hotel, their high ceilings and lavish decor (including crystal chandeliers) give you a taste of real New York glamour. *5th Ave. at 59th St., 10019, Midtown, 212/759–3000 or 800/759–3000, 212/546–5324. 670 rooms, 135 suites. 4 restaurants, 2 bars, in-room faxes, in-room modem lines, in-room safes, minibars, room service, massage, exercise room, baby-sitting, laundry service and dry cleaning, concierge, business services, meeting rooms, parking (fee). AE, D, DC, MC, V. Subway: N, R to 5th Ave.*

PLAZA ATHÉNÉE

Step into this 16-story bastion of Louis XIV elegance on a quiet Upper East Side street and you may think you've landed in Paris. Rooms are extremely elegant, with French Directoire–style mahogany furniture and hand-painted silk drapery and bedspreads. The European-trained staff delivers polished service to a cosmopolitan clientele. *37 E. 64th St., 10021, Upper East Side, 212/734–9100 or 800/447–8800, fax 212/772–0958. 117 rooms, 36 suites. Restaurant, bar, in-room modem lines, in-room safes, minibars, room service, massage, exercise room, baby-sitting, laundry service and dry cleaning, concierge, business services, meeting rooms, parking (fee). AE, D, DC, MC, V. Subway: 68th St./Hunter College.*

REGAL U.N. PLAZA HOTEL

Beginning on the 28th floor of each of two sleek skyscraper towers, this dazzling 13-story hotel attracts an international, diplomatic set thanks to its location just a well-aimed stone's throw from the United Nations. Guest rooms are simple but tasteful, with breathtaking river views. There's a pool on the 27th floor, also with superb views, and a health club with indoor tennis courts. *1 United Nations Plaza (44th St. between 1st and 2nd Aves.), 10017, Midtown, 212/758–1234 or 800/223–1234, fax 212/702–5051. 393 rooms, 33 suites. Restaurant, bar, in-room faxes, in-room modem lines, in-room safes, minibars, room service, pool, massage, tennis court, health club, baby-sitting, laundry service and dry cleaning, concierge, business services, meeting rooms, parking (fee). No pets. AE, D, DC, MC, V. Subway: 42nd St./Grand Central.*

THE REGENCY

The Regency is a truly regal hotel, from the elegant lobby with its gilded antiques and massive chandelier to the posh Park Avenue location. The restaurant, 540 Park, has long been known as *the* place for power breakfasts, where top execs meet to discuss the market over omelets and orange juice; but more inviting is the Library, a cozy, wood-paneled lounge full of bookcases and comfortable seating arrangements—here drinks and light meals are served all day long. The traditional guest rooms have celadon carpets and salmon-color silk bedspreads. *540 Park Ave. (at 61st St.), 10021, Upper East Side, 212/759–4100 or 800/235–6397. 288 rooms, 74 suites. Restaurants, bar, lobby lounge, in-room faxes, in-room modem lines, in-room safes, minibars, room service, beauty salon, massage, exercise room, baby-sitting, laundry service and dry cleaning, concierge, business services, meeting rooms, parking (fee). AE, D, DC, MC, V. Subway: 59th St.*

RENAISSANCE

In the heart of Times Square, the Renaissance is one of the Theater District's classier hotels. Formerly the Ramada Renaissance, it was recently redone to suit business travelers. The third-floor lobby has an elegant, Art Deco look, and guest rooms are warm and inviting, with dark cherry wood and a black-and-tan color scheme. *2 Times Sq. (7th Ave. between 47th and 48th Sts.), 10036, Theater District, 212/765–7676 or 800/628–5222, fax 212/765–1962. 283 rooms, 22 suites. Restaurant, bar, in-room modem lines, in-room safes, minibars, in-room VCRs, massage, exercise room, baby-sitting, laundry service and dry cleaning, room service, business services, meeting rooms, parking (fee). AE, D, DC, MC, V. Subway: 49th St.; 50th St.*

9 *d-5*

THE ROYALTON

The most celebrated of Ian Schrager's and Philippe Starck's hotels is chic and minimalist. The cooler-than-cool lobby sees itself as the gathering place of the '90s, with chess- and checkerboard-covered tables where models and media folk gather to drink martinis. The showpiece of each spartan guest room is a low-lying, custom-made bed with a down comforter and Italian sheets; there are also window banquettes and fireplaces. *44 W. 44th St., Theater District, 10036, 212/869–4400 or 800/635–9013, fax 212/575–0012. 140 rooms, 28 suites. Restaurant, bar, in-room modem lines, minibars, room service, massage, exercise room, baby-sitting, laundry service and dry cleaning, business services, meeting rooms, parking (fee). AE, DC, MC, V. Subway: B, D, F, Q to 42nd St.*

9 *d-3*

RIHGA ROYAL

The Japanese-owned Rihga Royal has no plain old guest rooms, but rather 50 floors of contemporary suites, all with bay windows and French doors. The location suits many business travelers, as do the fax machines in every room. The Pinnacle Suites (on the top floors) have CD players, cellular phones, and "miniature business center" machines that print and copy. *151 W. 54th St., 10019, Midtown, 212/307–5000 or 800/937–5454, fax 212/765–6530. 500 suites. Restaurant, bar, in-room faxes, in-room modem lines, in-room safes, minibars, room service, in-room VCRs, massage, exercise room, baby-sitting, laundry service and dry cleaning, concierge, business services, meeting rooms, parking (fee). No pets. AE, D, DC, MC, V. Subway: 7th Ave; 57th St..*

9 *e-3*

ST. REGIS

Built in 1904 by John Jacob Astor for those who could afford and appreciate "the best of everything," this 5th Avenue landmark was bought by Sheraton in the early 1990s and restored to its original splendor. Highlights are the Astor Court tea lounge, with its trompe-l'oeil cloud ceiling; the King Cole Bar, with its famous Maxfield Parrish mural; and—for those who can afford it—the celebrated restaurant, Lespinasse (*see French in* Chapter 3). The opulent guest rooms have butler service, crystal chandeliers, silk wall coverings, and Louis XV–style furnishings. *2 E. 55th St., 10022, Midtown, 212/753–4500 or 800/759–7550, fax 212/787–3447. 221 rooms, 92 suites. Restaurant, bar, in-room faxes, in-room modem lines, in-room safes, minibars, room service, beauty salon, massage, sauna, health club, massage, baby-sitting, laundry service and dry cleaning, concierge, meeting rooms, business services, parking (fee). No pets. AE, D, DC, MC, V. Subway: E, F to 5th Ave.*

9 *e-2*

SHERRY-NETHERLAND

This Fifth Avenue grande dame is actually a cooperative-apartment complex, with a 3-to-1 ratio of permanent residents to guests. As a result, in-room amenities are somewhat hit-or-miss, depending on the whims of the individual owners; but all of the suites are utterly luxurious, with separate living and dining areas, pantries, decorative fireplaces, fine antiques, and marble baths. The dastardly expensive Harry Cipriani (*see Italian in* Chapter 3) provides room service; a liter of water costs about $20, no joke. *781 5th Ave. (at 59th St.), 10022, Midtown, 212/355–2800, fax 212/319–4306. 40 rooms, 35 suites. Restaurant, bar, in-room faxes, in-room VCRs, refrigerators, room service, barbershop, beauty salon, exercise room, laundry service and dry cleaning, concierge, business services, meeting rooms, parking (fee). AE, D, DC, MC, V. Subway: N, R to 5th Ave.*

9 *c-2*

TRUMP INTERNATIONAL HOTEL AND TOWERS

New on New York's luxury scene, the Donald's latest venture caters to business travelers with money to burn. The rooms and suites are more like contemporary apartments than hotel rooms; all have Sony sound systems, a selection of coffee-table books for guests to browse through, and minitelescopes for discreet spying on the action in Central Park. The restaurant, Jean Georges, is the latest project of acclaimed chef Jean-Jacques Vongerichten (*see French in* Chapter 3). *1 Central Park West (at 59th St.), 10023, Midtown, 212/299–1000, fax 212/299–1150. 86 rooms, 82 suites. Restaurant, bar, café, in-room faxes, in-room modem lines, in-room safes, kitchenettes, minibars, in-room VCRs, indoor pool, spa, baby-sitting, laundry service and dry cleaning, concierge, business services, parking (fee). No pets. AE, D, DC, MC, V. Subway: 59th St./Columbus Circle.*

9 e-4

WALDORF-ASTORIA

A New York institution, the Waldorf has attracted every president since Hoover and a handful of luminous longtime residents, including Frank Sinatra. Step inside the magnificent Art Deco lobby, with its original murals and mosaics, and you'll understand why. The individually decorated guest rooms are spread out on three different floors (the most deluxe and most expensive are at the top), but all are traditional and elegant. *301 Park Ave. (at 50th St.), 10022, Midtown, 212/355–3000 or 800/925–3673, fax 212/872–7272. 1,176 rooms, 276 suites. 4 restaurants, 2 bars, in-room modem lines, minibars, room service, massage, health club, baby-sitting, laundry service and dry cleaning, concierge, concierge floors, business services, meeting rooms, parking (fee). AE, D, DC, MC, V. Subway: 51st St./Lexington–3rd Aves.*

9 e-1

THE WESTBURY

British formality meets congeniality at the Forte Hotel chain's New York outpost. Leather banquettes look out on Madison Avenue at the clubby Polo Bar and Restaurant. Rooms and suites have a lived-in, English-country look, with floral chintz, Oriental rugs, and mahogany furnishings. *15 E. 69th St., 10021, Upper East Side, 212/535–2000 or 800/321–1569, fax 212/535–5058. 143 rooms, 85 suites. Restaurant, bar, in-room faxes, in-room modem lines, in-room safes, room service, massage, exercise room, baby-sitting, laundry service and dry cleaning, concierge, business services, meeting rooms, parking (fee). AE, D, DC, MC, V. Subway: 68th St./Hunter College.*

EXPENSIVE LODGINGS

9 d-5

THE ALGONQUIN

Once the meeting place of the famed Round Table of wits and critics, the Algonquin has attracted literary and theatrical types since it opened in 1902. In the clubby, oak-paneled lobby, overstuffed sofas and easy chairs encourage lolling over cocktails and conversation or afternoon tea. Victorian fixtures and furnishings give the comfortable guest rooms a traditional look; some are specialty suites dedicated to Dorothy Parker

and her contemporaries. *59 W. 44th St., 10036, Midtown, 212/840–6800 or 800/548–0345, fax 212/944–1618. 142 rooms, 23 suites. 2 restaurants, bar, in-room modem lines, in-room safes, room service, cabaret, library, laundry service and dry cleaning, concierge, business services, meeting rooms, parking (fee). No pets. AE, D, DC, MC, V. Subway: B, D, F, Q to 42nd St.*

9 e-5

DORAL COURT

On the low end of this price category, the Doral Court is a homey hotel in the peaceful residential neighborhood of Murray Hill. Its oak-paneled lobby is low-key and comfortable, as are its English country–style guest rooms. Guests can charge meals at the Adirondack Lounge, in the Doral Tuscany next door, to their rooms, and they also receive free passes to the nearby Doral Fitness Center. *130 E. 39th St., 10016, Murray Hill, 212/685–1100 or 800/223–6725, fax 212/779–0148. 248 rooms, 50 suites. Breakfast room, in-room safes, minibars, refrigerators, room service, massage, baby-sitting, laundry service and dry cleaning, business services, meeting rooms, parking (fee). AE, DC, MC, V. Subway: 42nd St./Grand Central.*

9 e-5

DORAL PARK AVENUE

An amusingly eclectic look sets the Doral Park Avenue apart from the other nearby Doral hotels (it's under separate management). The lobby showcases a giant painting of an ancient Greek city, but its seriousness is offset by palm trees and Art Deco details. Guest rooms are newly redecorated in a similarly playful style: beds might have neoclassical headboards with faux-leopard windowseat coverings. For $10, guests can work out at the nearby Doral Fitness Center. *70 Park Ave. (at 38th St.), 10016, Murray Hill, 212/687–7050 or 800/223–6725, fax 212/973–2497. 188 rooms, 6 suites. Restaurant, bar, in-room modem lines, minibars, room service, massage, baby-sitting, laundry service and dry-cleaning, concierge, business services, meeting rooms, parking (fee). AE, D, DC, MC, V. Subway: 42nd St./Grand Central.*

9 e-5

DORAL TUSCANY

The Doral Tuscany is similar in style to its sister hotel, the Doral Court, but it's slightly more luxurious. Rooms have Italian marble baths and vanities with sinks; suites also have walk-in closets and three phones. Like the Court, the Tuscany offers guests free access to the nearby Doral Fitness Center. *120 E. 39th St., 10016, Murray Hill, 212/686–1600 or 800/223–6725, fax 212/779–0148. 122 rooms, 24 suites. Restaurant, bar, in-room safes, minibars, refrigerators, room service, massage, baby-sitting, laundry service and dry cleaning, business services, meeting rooms, parking (fee). AE, DC, MC, V. Subway: 42nd St./Grand Central.*

9 *e-3*
HOTEL ELYSÉE

European refinement takes a friendly tone in this little midtown gem. There are only 99 guest rooms, which means the staff has time for personalized service and attention. What's more, all guests have access to the Club Room, where big, comfortable chairs and couches invite them to linger over coffee anytime, plus free wine and hors d'oeuvres on weeknights and complimentary breakfast in the morning. Other perks include free passes to the nearby New York Sports Club and easy access to the famed Monkey Bar, a trendy place for drinks and dinner. A few of the beautifully decorated guest rooms have terraces at no extra charge; request one far in advance. *60 E. 54th St., 10022, Midtown, 212/753–1066 or 800/535–9733, fax 212/980–9278. 87 rooms, 12 suites. Bar, restaurant, in-room modem lines, in-room VCRs, refrigerators, room service, massage, laundry service and dry cleaning, concierge, business services, meeting rooms, parking (fee). No pets. AE, DC, MC, V. Subway: E, F to 5th Ave.*

9 *e-3*
THE FITZPATRICK

Just south of Bloomingdale's, the Irish-owned Fitzpatrick is one of the friendliest hotels around. The mostly Irish staff loves to chat with the guests—especially when Gregory Peck, Liam Neeson, and Sinead O'Connor drop by. Rooms are spacious and cheerful, with emerald-green carpets and traditional furnishings. Guests have free access to the Excelsior Athletic Club, next door. *687 Lexington Ave. (at 57th St.), 10022, Midtown, 212/355–0100 or 800/367–7701, fax 212/355–1371. 42 rooms, 50 suites. Restaurant, bar, in-room modem lines, minibars, massage, laundry service and dry*

cleaning, room service, business services, meeting room, parking (fee). AE, D, DC, MC, V. Subway: 59th St.

9 *d-5*
MILLENIUM BROADWAY

The lobby is sleek and dramatic, with black marble floors; rich African-mahogany walls; enormous, outrageously stylized paintings of fleshy, classical figures; and striking flower arrangements. Rooms, too, have a sleek, modern look: leather and suede are the materials of choice; appliances are high-tech chrome; and everything is black, brown, and gray. The white-tile bathrooms, in contrast, are nothing special. *145 W. 44th St., 10036, Theater District, 212/768–4400 or 800/622–5569, fax 212/768–0847. 617 rooms, 10 rooms. Restaurant, bar, in-room modem lines, in-room safes, minibars, room service, massage, exercise room, baby-sitting, laundry service and dry cleaning, auditorium, concierge, concierge floors, business services, meeting rooms, parking (fee). AE, D, DC, MC, V. Subway: 42nd St./Times Sq.*

9 *e-6*
MILLENIUM HILTON

In keeping with its name, this large, sleek downtown hotel has a forward-looking style. The 500-plus rooms have contoured built-in furniture and are decorated in beige-and-wood color schemes. Almost all look out on landmark buildings and both the Hudson and the East rivers; you can even see St. Paul's Church from the glass-enclosed swimming pool. *55 Church St., 10007, Lower Manhattan, 212/693–2001 or 800/752–0014, fax 212/571–2317. 458 rooms, 103 suites. 2 restaurants, bar, in-room modem lines, in-room safes, minibars, room service, indoor pool, massage, health club, baby-sitting, laundry service and dry cleaning, concierge, business services, meeting rooms, parking (fee). No pets. AE, D, DC, MC, V. Subway: Cortlandt St./World Trade Ctr.; Chambers St.*

9 *e-6*
MORGANS

This was the first project of famed hotel designers Ian Schrager and Philippe Starck, preceding both the Royalton and the Paramount. It's a seriously high-style place; the minimalist, high-tech rooms are decked out with low-lying, futonlike beds and 27-inch Sony TVs on wheels. Bathrooms are modern masterpieces, with crystal shower doors, steel surgical sinks, and poured-granite floors. The room rate includes continental breakfast, and guests work out free at the New York Sports Club, a block away. *237 Madison Ave. (between 37th and 38th Sts.), 10016, Murray Hill, 212/686–0300 or 800/334–3408, fax 212/779–8352. 113 rooms, 26 suites. Restaurant, 2 bars, breakfast room, in-room modem lines, minibars, room service, laundry service and dry cleaning, baby-sitting, concierge, business services, meeting rooms, parking (fee). AE, D, DC, MC, V. Subway: 42nd St./Grand Central.*

9 *e-4*

PLAZA FIFTY

One of the nicest of the Manhattan East Suite hotels, this property has regular guest rooms as well as suites, but they may as well all be suites; the standard rooms are large and self-contained, each with a microwave, refrigerator, and coffeemaker. All quarters have a clean, modern look that makes them very livable—an excellent home away from home. *155 E. 50th St., 10022, Midtown, 212/751–5710 or 800/637–8483, fax 212/753–1468. 74 rooms, 138 suites. In-room modem lines, in-room safes, refrigerators, room service, excercise room, coin laundry, parking (fee). AE, D, DC, MC, V. No pets. Subway: 51st St./Lexington–3rd Aves.*

9 *e-4*

ROOSEVELT HOTEL

Though it's huge and somewhat impersonal, the Roosevelt is a sensible choice for those who like to be in the heart of the action—it's in a shopping arcade near Grand Central Station. There's a constant buzz in the grand, Corinthian-columned, marble lobby, which, alas, makes a much better impression than the slightly sterile guest rooms. All of the latter have the same decor: dark-wood reproduction furniture, loud floral bedspreads, and framed botanical prints. *45 E. 45th St., 10017, Midtown, 212/661–9600 or 800/223–1870, fax 212/687–5064. 1,040 rooms, 50 suites. Restaurant, bar, breakfast room, in-room modem lines, room service, massage, baby-sitting, laundry service and dry cleaning, concierge, parking (fee). AE, D, DC, MC, V. Subway: 42nd St./Grand Central.*

9 *d-3*

THE SHOREHAM

Almost everything here is metal or metal-colored—even the headboards are made of perforated steel and lit from behind. Cedar-lined closets and in-room VCRs and CD players add to the high-tech amenities. There are plenty of freebies here, including continental breakfast, a nightly dessert buffet, and 24-hour cappuccino and espresso (in case you need a jolt for that 4 AM flight out) that's good enough for coffee snobs. *33 W. 55th St., 10019, Midtown, 212/247–6700, fax 212/765–9741. 47 rooms, 37 suites. Breakfast room, in-room modem lines, in-room safes, in-room VCRs, massage, baby-sitting, laundry service and dry cleaning, business services, parking (fee). No pets. AE, DC, MC, V. Subway: E, F to 5th Ave.*

10 *d-4*

SOHO GRAND

Opened in August 1996, SoHo's first and only hotel is a remarkable amalgam of 19th-century SoHo–style architecture. A translucent, bottle-glass staircase with cast-iron embellishments leads to the second-floor lobby, where oversized furniture and neutral colors create cool comfort. Rooms have an industrial look: custom-designed drafting tables serve as desks, and the nightstands mimic sculptors' desks. The Canal House restaurant serves remarkably creative renditions of American comfort food—macaroni-and-cheese is a trademark dish. The hotel is owned by Hartz Mountain, the pet-food company, so dogs get extra-special treatment here. *310 W. Broadway, (between Grand and Canal Sts.), 10013, SoHo, 212/965–3000 or 800/965–3000, fax 212/965–3244. 363 rooms, 4 suites. Restaurant, bar, in-room modem lines, in-room safes, minibars, room service, massage, exercise room, baby-sitting, laundry service and dry cleaning, concierge, business services, meeting rooms, parking (fee). AE, D, DC, MC, V. Subway: A, C, E, N, R to Canal St.*

9 *d-3*

THE WARWICK

The Warwick has a loyal following, thanks to its prime midtown location and its sophisticated, but not stuffy, ambience. The Beatles stayed here when they first came to the U.S., to appear on the Ed Sullivan Show. Step into the elegant, marble-floor lobby—flanked by the convivial Warwick Bar on one side and Ciao Europa Italian restaurant on the other—and you'll want to stay awhile. Rooms are tastefully decorated, with soft pastel color schemes, mahogany armoires, and nice marble bathrooms. William Randolph Hearst, who built the place in 1927, would be proud. *65 W. 54th St., 10019, Midtown, 212/247–2700 or 800/223–4099, fax 212/957–8915. 341 rooms, 75 suites. Restaurant, bar, minibars, room service, laundry service and dry cleaning, business services, meeting rooms, parking (fee). No pets. AE, DC, MC, V. Subway: E, F to 5th Ave.; B, Q to 57th St.*

MODERATELY PRICED LODGINGS

9 c-3

AMERITANIA

This Broadway hotel draws a young crowd. The modern guest rooms are very much of the moment, with bright emerald-green, rose, and blue color schemes, and small, black marble bathrooms. Impersonate your favorite TV character at one of the restaurant's nightly karaoke sessions. *1701 Broadway (at 54th St.), 10019, Theater District, 212/247–5000 or 800/922–0330, fax 212/247–3316. 209 rooms. Restaurant, bar, exercise room. No pets. AE, D, DC, MC, V. Subway: 7th Ave.*

9 e-2

BARBIZON HOTEL

A women's residence club from 1927 to 1981, the Barbizon was home at various times to Grace Kelly, Joan Crawford, and Liza Minelli. A major renovation, completed in 1997, has brought the hotel back into the limelight. The chic lobby has a beautiful, marble-and-limestone floor and luxurious, gold-leaf chairs with mohair upholstery. The shell-pink or celadon rooms are more modest but thoroughly pleasant, with eclectic accents such as zig-zag wrought-iron floor lamps. The on-site health club has an Olympic-size pool. *140 E. 63rd St., 10021, Upper East Side, 212/838–5700 or 800/223–1020, fax 212/888–4271. 310 rooms, 13 suites. Breakfast room, in-room modem lines, in-room safes, minibars, room service, indoor pool, spa, health club, baby-sitting, laundry service and dry cleaning, business services, parking (fee). No pets. AE, D, DC, MC, V. Subway: 59th St.*

7 b-8

HOTEL BEACON

A true home away from home, each Beacon suite has a kitchenette with coffeemaker, full-size refrigerator, and stove—all for only $40 more than a standard room. What's more, the hotel is near Central Park, Lincoln Center, and scores of gourmet food stores such as Zabar's, so you can make good use of all those appliances. *2130 Broadway (at 75th St.), 10023, Upper West Side, 212/787–1100 or 800/572–4969, fax 212/724–0839. 110 rooms, 96 suites. Kitchenettes, refrigerators, business services, meeting room, parking (fee). No pets. AE, D, DC, MC, V. Subway: 1, 2, 3, 9 to 72nd St.*

9 d-6

BEST WESTERN MANHATTAN

Rooms come in three different styles—"Fifth Avenue" (ritzy), "Central Park" (lots of florals), and "SoHo" (bold colors)—and all have coffeemakers. Guests have access to a tiny exercise room. Just south of the Empire State Building, this heavily Korean neighborhood is lively, with lots of cheap shops and restaurants. *17 W. 32nd St., 10001, Garment District, 212/736–1600 or 800/567–7720, fax 212/695–1813. 136 rooms, 40 suites. Restaurant, bar, exercise room, business services, meeting room, parking (fee). No pets. Subway: 34th St./Herald Sq.*

10 f-6

BEST WESTERN SEAPORT INN

A cross between a colonial sea captain's house and a chain hotel, this place is thoroughly inviting, with a cozy, library-like lobby and a friendly staff. Though rooms are standard chain-motel fare, a few have whirlpool tubs and outdoor terraces with views of the Brooklyn Bridge. If you want to be near the Seaport and the Financial Center, this is a great choice. *33 Peck Slip (at Front St.), 10038, Lower Manhattan, 212/766–6600 or 800/468–3569, fax 212/766–6615. 72 rooms. In-room safes, refrigerators, in-room VCRs. AE, D, DC, MC, V. No pets. Subway: 2, 3 to Fulton St.*

9 e-4

THE BEVERLY

The Beverly's stylish, '40s-inspired lobby has fruitwood-paneled walls, gorgeous, art nouveau stained-glass windows, and an original terrazzo floor that dates from the hotel's birth in 1927. The newly renovated guest rooms and suites are every bit as classy, with carved wooden beds and high-quality fabrics. Continental breakfast is complimentary, and there's a good steak house on the premises. *125 E. 50th St., 10022, Midtown, 212/753–2700 or 800/223–0945, fax 212/759–7300. 30 rooms, 150 suites. Restaurant, bar, coffee shop, in-room modem lines, in-room safes, kitchenettes, room service, beauty salon, concierge, parking (fee). No pets. AE, DC, MC, V. Subway: 51st St./Lexington–3rd Aves.*

9 *c-7*

CHELSEA HOTEL

You may well be inspired by your muse at the landmark Chelsea Hotel, home at various times to Sarah Bernhardt, Arthur Miller, Thomas Wolfe, Dylan Thomas, Robert Mapplethorpe, Christo, and Willem de Kooning. You may not get away with leaving art as payment for your room, though, as some of these residents have—there's a gallery of their work in the lobby. Rooms are a mixed bag: some are high-style, while others look straight out of the '70s. *222 W. 23rd St., 10011, Chelsea, phone and fax 212/243–3700. 330 rooms, 310 with bath. Kitchenettes. No pets. AE, MC, V. Subway: C, E to 23rd St.*

9 *d-6*

COMFORT INN MURRAY HILL

Comfort is what you get here: all of the spacious rooms are equipped with big, comfy sofabeds for extra guests, and some have refrigerators and microwaves. On top of that, you get complimentary continental breakfast and a quiet but convenient location. The lobby is surprisingly elegant, with atmospheric lighting, fresh flowers, and a classical motif set off by Corinthian columns and tall, Greek-style vases in mirrored recesses. *42 W. 35th St., 10001, Garment District, 212/947–0200, fax 212/594–3047. 131 rooms. In-room safes. No pets. AE, D, DC, MC, V. Subway: 34th St./Herald Sq.*

7 *b-7*

THE EXCELSIOR

Directly across from the American Museum of Natural History, on a block full of fine old, doorman buildings, the Excelsior is an old-time hotel with an old-time feel. The lobby's inlaid-gold ceiling recalls earlier, grander days, and the down-home coffee shop serves breakfast all day. An extensive refurbishing has given the rooms a much-needed pick-me-up; they now have warm, earth-tone color schemes and traditional furnishings. *45 W. 81st St., 10024, Upper West Side, 212/362–9200 or 800/368–4575, fax 212/721–2994. 200 rooms, 66 suites. Coffee shop. AE, MC, V. Subway: 81st St.*

7 *e-7*

THE FRANKLIN

The Upper East Side's hippest, funkiest hotel has a pint-size lobby furnished with black granite, brushed steel, and cherry wood. The tiny rooms have custom-built steel furniture, gauzy white canopies over the beds, and cedar closets; bathrooms have steel-bowl sinks. Guests are invited to borrow CDs and videotapes for free (all rooms have CD players and VCRs). To add to the excellent value, there's a generous complimentary breakfast (including homemade granola) and a nightly dessert buffet, and—hold onto your seat—parking is free! *164 E. 87th St., 10128, Upper East Side, 212/369–1000 or 800/428–5252, fax 212/369–8000. 47 rooms. Breakfast room, in-room safes, in-room VCRs, library, free parking. No pets. AE, MC, V. Subway: 4, 5, 6 to 86th St.*

9 *e-8*

GRAMERCY PARK HOTEL

One of Manhattan's greenest, quietest, most delightful parks is locked to anyone who doesn't live right on its periphery—but you do, for as long as you're a guest at this aged, Queen Anne–style hotel. Guest rooms are a little the worse for wear, with worn furniture and old-fashioned bathrooms; but the cheerful location makes up for these flaws. *2 Lexington Ave. (at 21st St.), 10010, Gramercy, 212/475–4320 or 800/221–4083, fax 212/505–0535. 543 rooms, 157 suites. Restaurant, bar, beauty salon, meeting rooms. AE, D, DC, MC, V. Subway: 6 to 23rd St.*

9 *d-3*

HELMSLEY WINDSOR

Your first encounter with the cozy, wood-paneled, red-carpeted lobby tells you that the Helmsley Windsor delivers comfort as well as value. Rooms are spacious and pleasant enough; most have framed photos of old New York. Continental breakfast is complimentary. *100 W. 58th St., 10019, Midtown, 212/ 265–2100 or 800/221–4982, fax 212/315– 0371. 229 rooms, 15 suites. Breakfast room, meeting room, parking (fee). No pets. AE, D, DC, MC, V. Subway: B, Q to 57th St.*

10 *e-4*

HOLIDAY INN DOWNTOWN

The excellent dim sum at Pacifica restaurant is reason enough to stay at this downtown hotel, a favorite with Chinese business travelers. Rooms and suites are sleek and modern, with pastel walls and carpets, black-frame furniture, and framed watercolors with an Asian motif. This is a great location for anyone who wants to be near Chinatown and Little Italy as well as SoHo and the Financial District. *138 Lafayette St. (between Canal and Howard Sts.), 10013, Chinatown, 212/966–8898 or 800/465–4329, fax 212/966–3933. 188 rooms, 12 suites. Restaurant, bar, room service, parking (fee). AE, D, DC, MC, V. No pets. Subway: 6, N, R, J, M, Z to Canal St.*

9 *c-6*

HOWARD JOHNSON ON 34TH STREET

Once the dumpy Penn Plaza Hotel, this Midtown HoJo is now a decent business hotel. Though the tiny rooms are depressingly sterile, with jade-green and brown color schemes and tired-looking bathrooms (some have peeling plaster), it's a great location. Avoid the rooms facing 7th Avenue unless you don't mind street noise. *215 W. 34th St., 10001, Garment District, 212/947–5050 or 800/446–4656, fax 212/268–4829. 111 rooms. No pets. Subway: 34th St./Penn Station.*

9 *e-5*

JOLLY MADISON TOWERS

Part of the Italian Jolly Hotel chain, this is a great little bargain in Murray Hill. Rooms are cheerful and well-kept, and bathrooms have separate glass shower stalls. The colorful restaurant, Cinque Terre, serves good northern Italian cuisine. *22 E. 38th St., 10016, Murray Hill, 212/802–0600 or 800/225–4340, fax 212/ 447–0747. 212 rooms, 4 suites. Restaurant, bar, massage, sauna. AE, DC, MC, V. Subway: 33th St.*

9 *e-4*

HOTEL LEXINGTON

The Lexington attracts many tour groups because of its central location and on-site attractions, such as the Denim & Diamonds western dance club, Raffles coffee shop, and Sung Dynasty Chinese restaurant. There's usually lots of activity in the two-level lobby, which is elegantly appointed with a marble floor and rosewood pillars. Rooms are somewhat small, but all have nice marble bathrooms. *511 Lexington Ave. (at 48th St.), 10017, Midtown, 212/ 755–4400 or 800/448–4471, fax 212/751– 4091. 688 rooms, 12 suites. 2 restaurants, 2 bars, coffee shop, in-room modem lines, refrigerators, room service, exercise room, nightclub, laundry service and dry cleaning, concierge, business services, meeting room. No pets. AE, D, DC, MC, V. Subway: 42nd St./Grand Central.*

9 *e-4*

LOEWS NEW YORK HOTEL

This is a large, lively, reasonably priced hotel with an always-bustling lobby-lounge restaurant, a shopping arcade, and on-site parking. Prices drop substantially during low-occupancy periods; even suites are under $250. *569 Lexington Ave. (at 51st St.), 10022, Midtown, 212/752–7000 or 800/836–6471, fax 212/ 752–3817. 722 rooms, 40 suites. Restaurant, in-room modem lines, in-room safes, refrigerators, room service, barbershop, beauty salon, health club, business services, meeting rooms, parking (fee). AE, D, DC, MC, V. Subway: 51st St./Lexington–3rd Aves.*

9 *d-5*

THE MANSFIELD

Occupying a 1904 Stanford White building near the Royalton and the Algonquin, the Mansfield has a clubby, turn-of-the-century mood. Guest rooms have stylish, black-marble bathrooms, ebony-stained floors and doors, dark-wood venetian blinds, and sleigh beds. There are nightly piano and harp recitals in the intimate concert salon, where complimentary breakfast and after-theater dessert are served. *12 W. 44th St., 10036, Midtown, 212/944–6050 or 800/255–5167, fax 212/764–4477. 123 rooms, 25 suites. In-room VCRs, room service, library, meeting room, business services, free parking. No pets. AE, MC, V. Subway: 42nd St./Times Sq.*

9 *c-2*

THE MAYFLOWER

You'll feel at home the moment you enter the wood-paneled lobby of this friendly hotel on Central Park West, where a basket of apples and complimentary coffee and cookies are offered all day long. Rooms are large and comfortable, with thick carpeting, fruit-and-flower drapes, dark- wood colonial-style furniture, and walk-in closets. Some have park views, and most have walk-in pantries with refrigerators and sinks. *15 Central Park West (between 61st and 62nd Sts.), 10023, Upper West Side, 212/265–0060 or 800/223–4164, fax 212/265–2026. 365 rooms, 200 suites. Restaurant, bar, in-room modem lines, refrigerators, room service, exercise room, meeting rooms, parking (fee). AE, DC, MC, V. Subway: 59th St./Columbus Circle.*

9 *d-3*

NEW YORK HILTON AND TOWERS

This army-sized 46-story hotel is big with conventioneers, thanks to its many on-site business facilities, eating establishments, and shops. The Hilton spends vast amounts of money to keep the hotel trim, and it shows: There's a distinctive, landscaped driveway and a sprawling, brassy lobby; a lively sports bar; and, as a hypermodern flourish, TVs in the elevators. Considering the size of this property, guest rooms are surprisingly well-maintained, and all have coffeemakers, hair dryers, and ironing boards. Those in the towers have dazzling views—and access to the Towers lounge, where goodies are served all day long. *1335 6th Ave. (at 54th St.), 10019, Midtown, 212/586–7000 or 800/445–8667, fax 212/261–5902. 2,041 rooms, 20 suites. 2 restaurants, café, sports bar, in-room modem lines, in-room safes, minibars, room service, barbershop, beauty salon, hot tub, massage, health club, baby-sitting, laundry service and dry cleaning, concierge, concierge floors, business services, meeting rooms, parking (fee). No pets. AE, D, DC, MC, V. Subway: 47th–50th Sts./Rockefeller Ctr.*

10 *f-3*

OFF SOHO SUITES HOTEL

Though the Bowery is not the poshest of neighborhoods, it's not a bad place to stay if you want easy access to Chinatown, Little Italy, SoHo, and the Financial District. The two- and four-person suites here have fully equipped kitchens and are clean and functional, if totally generic. *11 Rivington St. (between Chrystie St. and Bowery), 10002, Lower East Side, 212/979–9808 or 800/633–7646, fax 212/979–9801. 40 suites, 28 with bath. Kitchenettes. No pets. AE, MC, V. Subway: 2nd Ave.*

9 *c-4*

THE PARAMOUNT

The dramatic, multilevel lobby is a creation of Ian Schrager and Philippe Starck, also responsible for Morgans and the Royalton. The young and the hip come here in droves; it's fashionable and fun. The tiny rooms have modern, angular furniture and beds with framed headboards, several of them bearing a print of Vermeer's *The Lacemaker*; bathrooms have bizarre conical sinks. *235 W. 46th St., 10036, Theater District, 212/764–5500 or 800/225–7474, fax 212/575–4892. 610 rooms, 12 suites. 2 restaurants, bar, café, in-room modem lines, room service, in-room VCRs, exercise room, nursery, laundry service and dry cleaning, concierge, business services, meeting rooms. No pets. AE, D, DC, MC, V. Subway: 42nd St./Times Sq.*

9 *c-2*

RADISSON EMPIRE HOTEL

This is one of the few hotel bargains near Lincoln Center, and it's thoroughly pleasant to boot. The lobby is modified English-country–style, complete with warm wood furniture and a hanging tapestry. Rooms are small but perfectly adequate, with textured teal carpets and dark-wood furnishings. *44 W. 63rd St., 10023, Upper West Side, 212/265–7400 or 800/333–3333, fax 212/244–3382. 355 rooms, 20 suites. Restaurant, bar, in-room modem lines, minibars, in-room VCRs, meeting rooms, parking (fee). AE, D, DC, MC, V. Subway: 59th St./Columbus Circle.*

9 *d-4*

HOTEL REMINGTON

The ornate awning outside hints at what you'll find in the lobby: faux-marble walls with mirror paneling, a ceiling painted gold to look like gilding, and glass chandeliers. Rooms are endearingly retro, with pink-shag carpeting and white-wood furniture—though at press time a complete renovation was in the works. Bathrooms are spacious, but many have only a shower stall (no tub). *129 W. 46th St., 10036, Theater District,*

212/221–2600 or 800/755–3194, fax 212/764–7481. 85 rooms. Airport shuttle. No pets. AE, DC, MC, V. Subway: 47th–50th Sts./Rockefeller Center.

9 e-4
THE ROGER SMITH

Here's a boutique hotel for art lovers, or for anyone who appreciates bold color schemes and unconventional combinations. Take the lobby, which might well be a very civilized nightclub—crimson carpet, splashy paintings, bronze busts here and there. All bedrooms are individually decorated, some with slightly outlandish touches such as ivy-trellis wallpaper. This is a very friendly place; you may even meet Roger Smith himself, as he owns the art gallery next door. 501 Lexington Ave. (between 47th and 48th Sts.), 10017, Midtown, 212/755–1400 or 800/445–0277, fax 212/758–4061. 134 rooms. Restaurant, bar, refrigerators, room service, laundry service, meeting rooms, parking (fee). AE, D, DC, MC, V. Subway: 51st St./Lexington–3rd Aves.; 42nd St./Grand Central.

9 e-6
THE ROGER WILLIAMS

The Gotham Hospitality Group has done wonders for this circa-1920s building, whose location suspends it ideally between midtown and downtown. The minimalist rooms are extremely stylish, with custom-made blond-birch furnishings and dramatic downlighting, and each comes with a 27-inch Sony TV, VCR, and CD player (guests have access to complimentary VCR and CD libraries). The bathrooms are artworks unto themselves, with chrome surgical sinks and recessed showers with cedar-grill floors. Don't miss the complimentary continental breakfast and nightly dessert buffets in the mezzanine—the coffee is divine. 131 Madison Ave. (at 31st St.), 10016, Murray Hill, 212/448–7000, fax 212/448–7007. 183 rooms, 2 suites. Breakfast room, in-room modem lines, in-room VCRs, free parking. Subway: 6 to 33rd St.

9 d-4
QUALITY HOTEL AND SUITES MIDTOWN

Because this hotel was independently owned until recently (as the Wentworth), its prewar building has more unique touches than the usual Quality franchise. Witness the slightly bizarre lobby, with its long, narrow corridor and loud, photorealist paintings. Rooms, on the other hand, have the sanitized look of a chain hotel, with teal carpeting, blond-wood furniture, and spacious, serviceable bathrooms. You're near theaters, Rockefeller Center, and a cluster of Brazilian restaurants. 59 W. 46th St., 10036, Midtown, 212/719–2300 or 800/228–5151, fax 212/768–3477. 193 rooms, 21 suites. In-room modem lines, in-room safes, barbershop, beauty salon, business services. No pets. AE, D, DC, MC, V. Subway: 47th–50th Sts./Rockefeller Center.

9 e-7
QUALITY HOTEL EAST SIDE

Patriotic types will appreciate the American-eagle wallpaper at this Murray Hill newcomer, originally called the Americana. Rooms are reasonably priced and come with such extras as hair dryers and ironing boards with irons; shared-bath rooms also have sinks. Checkered curtains and prints of American quilts add to the Yankee theme. 161 Lexington Ave. (at 30th St.), 10016, Murray Hill, 212/532–2255, fax 212/481–7270. 110 rooms, 85 with bath. In-room modem lines, exercise room, business services. Subway: 6 to 28th St.

9 e-4
SAN CARLOS

There's nothing remarkable about this small, conveniently located hotel—just friendly service and clean, modern accommodations. Every room has a kitchenette, walk-in closet, and two phones. Continental breakfast is complimentary. 150 E. 50th St., 10022, Midtown, 212/755–1800 or 800/722–2012, fax 212/688–9778. 75 rooms, 71 suites. Breakfast room, kitchenettes. AE, DC, MC, V. Subway: 51st St./Lexington–3rd Aves.

9 e-6
HOTEL WALES

The modestly priced Wales is a true find in the tony Carnegie Hill area. Built in 1901, it still has a turn-of-the-century mood; there's even a "Pied Piper" parlor decorated with vintage children's illustrations (this is where the generous complimentary breakfast and nightly dessert buffets are served). Guest rooms are small and show signs of wear and tear, but they do have fine oak woodwork, and all are equipped with CD players. Most of the suites face Madison Avenue. 1295 Madison Ave. (between 92nd *and 93rd Sts.), 10128, Upper East Side, 212/876–6000 or 800/528–5252, fax 212/860–7000. 87 rooms, 30 suites. Breakfast room, refrigerators, in-room VCRs, parking (fee). AE, MC, V. Subway: 6 to 96th St.*

9 *d-3*

THE WELLINGTON

The Wellington's traditionally decorated rooms are surprisingly tasteful for such a well-priced hotel, with dark-wood furniture, high-quality fabrics in soft color schemes, and nicely framed prints. The lobby is constantly crammed with tourists and feels hectic, but that's part of this old-timer's charm. Carnegie Hall is a stone's throw away. *871 7th Ave. (at 55th St.), 10019, Theater District, 212/247–3900 or 800/652–1212, fax 212/581–1719. 550 rooms, 150 suites. Restaurant, bar, coffee shop, beauty salon, parking (fee). No pets. AE, DC, MC, V. Subway: N, R to 57th St.*

9 *d-3*

THE WYNDHAM

Anyone who appreciates fine art and whimsical colors will love the Wyndham, whose lobby is a cross between a museum gallery and the comfortable salon of an art collector. The spacious, individually decorated guest rooms all have the feel of a summer house with a breezy rococo motif: light powder-blue, peach, or yellow fabric wall-coverings, flowers everywhere, and, of course, fine art. Closets are enormous. It's hard to find a better deal anywhere in Manhattan, let alone in such a prime location, right across from Central Park. *42 W. 58th St., 10019, Midtown, 212/753–3500 or 800/257–1111, fax 212/754–5638. 142 rooms, 70 suites. Restaurant, bar. No pets. AE, DC, MC, V. Subway: 59th St./Columbus Circle.*

BUDGET LODGINGS

9 *e-3*

ALLERTON HOUSE

Beware the rules at this women-only hotel in Midtown: A sign at the registration desk warns that men found above the third floor will be promptly arrested. For women, though, it's an excellent deal—it's secure and clean, and there's even a roof deck with views of the heart of Midtown. *130 E. 57th St., 10022, Midtown, 212/753–8841. 350 rooms, 30 with*

bath. Restaurant, bar, laundry. No pets. AE, MC, V. Subway: 59th St.

9 *d-7*

ARLINGTON HOTEL

Signs are in both English and Chinese at this Chelsea hotel, a favorite of Chinese businesspeople on their way to Chelsea's warehouses. Rooms are spacious, with generic decor. *18 W. 25th St., 10010, Chelsea, 212/645–3990, fax 212/633–8952. 96 rooms. No pets. AE, D, MC, V. Subway: F to 23rd St.*

7 *b-8*

BROADWAY AMERICAN HOTEL

In the heart of the Upper West Side, this place has a loyal following among budget travelers. The gray-tone rooms are simple but handsome, and guests have access to a communal kitchen and laundry facilities. *2178 Broadway, (at 77th St.), 10024, Upper West Side, 212/362–1100, fax 212/787–9521. 350 rooms, 84 with bath. Kitchen, laundry. No pets. AE, D, DC, MC, V. Subway: 79th St.*

9 *c-4*

BROADWAY BED & BREAKFAST INN

Though it isn't the kind of bed-and-breakfast where you linger over pancake breakfasts in the garden, the Broadway Bed & Breakfast is every bit as friendly and comfortable. Theater hounds can see their fill of Broadway shows, then fall into bed. In the morning, Continental breakfast is served in the brick-walled lobby, where stocked bookshelves and photos of Old New York create a homey mood. *264 W. 46th St., 10036, Theater District, 212/997–9200 or 800/826–6300, fax 212/768–2807. 40 rooms. Breakfast room. No pets. AE, D, DC, MC, V. Subway: 42nd St./Times Sq.*

9 *e-7*

CARLTON ARMS

Though the rooms here are phoneless, TV-less, almost free of furniture, and sometimes bathless, they score a perfect 10 when it comes to character. Over the years the free-spirited managers have commissioned artists to cover every wall, ceiling, and other surface with murals, some of them with outrageous themes. The Cow Spot Room, for example, has a Holstein motif of cow-spotted rugs, bedspreads, and walls; while the Versailles Room is a symphony of trompe l'oeil trellises and classical urns. Only in New York. *160 E. 25th St., 10010, Gramercy, 212/684–8337. 54 rooms. Fans. No pets. MC, V. Subway: N, R to 28th St.*

9 *d-8*

CHELSEA INN

Perhaps the best budget find in downtown Manhattan, this quaint old brownstone is just a few blocks from the Union Square farmer's market in a lively corridor of restaurants and boutiques. Rooms, most with shared bath, are inviting and economical, with dark-wood furniture, country-style quilts, big TVs, sinks, refrigerators, and hot plates. *46 W. 17th St., 10011, Chelsea, 212/645–8989, fax 212/645–1903. 24 rooms, 3 with bath. Refrigerators. No pets. AE, D, MC, V. Subway: 14th St./Union Sq.; F to 14th St.*

9 *c-4*

HOTEL EDISON

Fans of Al Pacino may recall Sophia's, the Edison's restaurant, from the loan-shark murder scene in *The Godfather.* The hotel is a hit with tour groups, with its reasonable prices and on-site facilities. The pink-plaster coffee shop is a great place to spy on show-biz types. *228 W. 47th St., 10036, Theater District, 212/840–5000 or 800/637–7070, fax 212/596–6850. 1,000 rooms. Restaurant, bar, coffee shop, beauty salon, airport shuttle. No pets. AE, D, DC, MC, V. Subway: 50th St.*

9 *d-7*

GERSHWIN HOTEL

There's always a lot going on at this young, arty mecca for foreign budget travelers—summer rooftop barbecues, gallery openings, and socializing in the giant, art-filled lobby. Rooms are as basic as they come, but they're painted in cheerful colors. Dormitories have four or eight beds and a remarkable rate of $22 a person. The hotel occupies a 13-story Greek Revival building, which adds to its funky character. *7 E. 27th St., 10016, Murray Hill, 212/545–8000, fax 212/684–5546. 160 rooms. Restaurant, bar. No pets. MC, V. Subway: 6, N, R to 28th St.*

9 *d-6*

HERALD SQUARE HOTEL

Housed in the former *Life* building, the Herald Square pays homage to its predecessor with framed vintage magazine covers in the hallways. The well-priced rooms are basic, with TVs, phones with voice mail, and in-room safes; what really stands out here is the service, which is remarkably attentive for such a cheap hotel. *19 W. 31st St., 10001, Garment District, 212/279–4017 or 800/727–1888, fax 212/643–9208. 127 rooms. In-room safes. AE, D, MC, V. Subway: 34th St./Herald Sq.*

10 *d-1*

LARCHMONT HOTEL

For many years, the quaint, residential West Village had no hotels at all. The Larchmont has solved that problem, though from the outside it still looks more like a charming brownstone home than a hotel. Rooms have a safari theme, with rattan furniture, ceiling fans, and framed animal or botanical prints. Bathrooms are shared, but they're clean, and every bedroom has a private sink. The staff is extra-friendly, and the reasonable rates include continental breakfast. *27 W. 11th St., 10011, West Village, 212/989–9333, fax 212/989–9496. 77 rooms. Breakfast room, kitchen. No pets. AE, D, DC, MC, V. Subway: W. 4th St./Washington Sq.*

9 *e-7*

MARTHA WASHINGTON

This women-only hotel has tight security policies that attract many long-term residents in their fifties and sixties. It's a good choice for short-term budget travelers as well, with kitchenettes (for weeklong stays only) and laundry facilities. *30 E. 30th St., 10016, Murray Hill, 212/689–1900, fax 212/689–0023. 450 rooms, 225 with bath. Coin laundry. No pets. Subway: N, R to 28th St.*

7 *b-8*

THE MILBURN

You may think you've entered King Ludwig's pied-à-terre when you step inside the lobby, which is full of heraldic doodads and gilt. The spacious rooms are more low-key, albeit slightly chaotic (witness the clashing color schemes in some)—but all have kitchenettes, which is key in this neighborhood of gourmet food stores. *242 W. 76th St., 10023, Upper West Side, 212/362–1006 or 800/833–9622, fax 212/721–5476. 102 rooms. In-room safes, kitchenettes, coin laundry. No pets. AE, DC, MC, V. Subway: 1, 2, 3, 9 to 72nd St.*

9 c-1

OLCOTT HOTEL

This semiresidential hotel occupies one of those fine old prewar buildings that line the main streets of the Upper West Side, with easy access to Central Park and the Museum of Natural History. There are daily and weekly rates for both comfortable studios (each with cooking pantry) and suites (with kitchenette). The lobby is large and inviting, with ornate gilded elevators and Corinthian columns that hint at the building's age. *27 W. 72nd St., 10023, Upper West Side, 212/877–4200, fax 212/580–0511. 150 rooms, 100 suites. Restaurant, bar, kitchenettes, parking (fee). No pets. MC, V. Subway: B, C to 72nd St.*

9 d-3

PARK SAVOY

Save money on a room here, and you'll have it to spend on a concert at Carnegie Hall or brunch at the Plaza—both just a few blocks away. Rooms may have rock-hard beds and no direct-dial phones or cable TVs, but they're colorful and sunny. The staff is friendly, and there's lots of repeat business. *158 W. 58th St., 10019, Midtown, 212/245–5755, fax 212/765–0668. 96 rooms. Restaurant, bar. AE, MC, V. No pets. Subway: 57th St.*

9 f-4

PICKWICK ARMS

A convenient location, a rooftop garden, and views of the Manhattan skyline (from some rooms) are among the advantages at this bargain favorite. What's more, the café spreads out an irresistible Middle Eastern buffet at lunchtime on weekdays—$6 for all you can eat. Drawbacks: the rooms are tiny, and the furniture is nothing special. *230 E. 51st St., 10022, Midtown, 212/355–0300 or 800/742–5945, fax 212/755–5029. 370 rooms, 320 with bath. Café, airport shuttle. No pets. AE, DC, MC, V. Subway: 51st St./Lexington–3rd Aves.*

9 d-4

PORTLAND SQUARE HOTEL

Built in 1904 as the Rio Hotel, this friendly little place was once the home of James Cagney and a few of his Radio City Rockette acquaintances. Prices are as cheap as they come—and you get phones with voice mail, in-room safes, a laundry room, and even a small exercise room. Rooms in the east wing have bigger bathrooms. *132 W. 47th St., 10036, Theater District, 212/382–0600 or 800/388–8988, fax 212/382–0684. 142 rooms, 112 with bath. In-room safes, exercise room, coin laundry. AE, MC, V. Subway: 49th St.*

7 a-8

RIVERSIDE TOWER

Rooms above the sixth floor have sweeping views of Riverside Park, the mighty Hudson River, and the New Jersey skyline. They're small, dark, and occasionally smoke-singed, but the location is good, and the price is right. European backpackers come here in droves. *80 Riverside Dr. (at 80th St.), 10024, Upper West Side, 212/877–5200 or 800/724–3136, fax 212/873–1400. 120 rooms, 116 with bath. Refrigerators, coin laundry. No pets. AE, D, DC, MC, V. Subway: 79th St.*

9 f-8

HOTEL 17

Madonna and David Bowie are among those who have frequented this trendy, dirt-cheap, Euro-style hotel. Most rooms are small and share a bath, but you come here for image, not luxury. *225 E. 17th St., 10003, Gramercy, 212/475–2845, fax 212/677–8178. 200 rooms, 12 with bath. Coin laundry. No pets. No credit cards. Subway: 14th St./Union Sq.*

9 d-6

STANFORD HOTEL

Near Macy's and the Manhattan Mall, the Stanford attracts a Latin American and Japanese clientele. Rooms are tidy, and all are equipped with TV and refrigerators. There's karaoke in the cocktail bar. *43 W. 32nd St., 10001, Garment District, 212/563–1500, fax 212/629–0043. 130 rooms. Bar, refrigerators. No pets. Subway: 34th St./Herald Sq.*

9 b-5

TRAVEL INN

Though it's way out in a desolate neighborhood near the Port Authority Bus Terminal, the Travel Inn is worthwhile for its generous amenities and low price. The spanking-new rooms—all with reproduction furniture, green carpets, and blue-tile bathrooms— occupy four wings that center around a lovely outdoor swimming pool surrounded by greenery and colorful plants. You also get free parking and a helpful travel-services desk. *515 W. 42nd St., 10036, Hell's Kitchen, 212/695–7171 or 800/869–4630, fax 212/967–5025. 160 rooms. Deli, room service, pool, meeting room, travel services, free parking. No pets. AE, D, DC, MC, V. Subway: 42nd St./Port Authority.*

9 *c-4*

WASHINGTON JEFFERSON HOTEL

The crammed rooms here have pink walls and are a far cry from luxurious, but each comes with cable TV, and some have mini-refrigerators. Though the hotel is on a somewhat lonely side street, away from the Broadway action, it's still convenient to the shows. Prices are rock-bottom. *318 W. 51st St., 10019, Midtown, 212/246–7550, fax 212/246–7622. 260 rooms, 130 with bath. Refrigerators. No pets. AE, MC, V. Subway: 50th St.*

10 *d-2*

WASHINGTON SQUARE HOTEL

This is *the* place to stay in the Village: It's quaint and historic (built in 1902), with a European-style lobby full of wrought iron and gleaming brass; it's convenient, especially for night owls (the Blue Note jazz club is just around the corner); and, more to the point, it's one of the only hotels in the area. There's a happening little restaurant, C3, on the premises, where complimentary breakfast is served; and there's even a tiny exercise room. Request a room with a window; the others are slightly dreary. *103 Waverly Pl. (at MacDougal St.), 10011, West Village, 212/777–9515 or 800/222–0418, fax 212/979–8373. 150 rooms. Restaurant, bar, exercise room. No pets. AE, MC, V. Subway: W. 4th St./Washington Sq.*

9 *b-3*

WESTPARK HOTEL

If you don't mind retro decor—pink or emerald-green shag carpeting, velour-covered seats, and mustard-yellow bathroom tiles—opt for this small hotel right off Columbus Circle, across from a major subway station that makes exploring the city a breeze. The management is friendly, and the price is right. *308 W. 58th St., 10019, Midtown, 212/246–6440 or 800/228–1122, fax 212/246-3131. 90 rooms, 9 suites. No pets. AE, D, DC, MC, V. Subway: 59th St./Columbus Circle.*

9 *d-6*

THE WOLCOTT

Beyond the gilded lobby lie unremarkable but functional guest rooms. All have phones with voice mail and color TV, and some have mini-refrigerators. You're just three blocks south of the Empire State Building, and have easy access to Macy's and the colorful shopping area surrounding 34th Street and Herald Square. *4 W. 31st St., 10001, Garment District, 212/268–2900, fax 212/563–0096. 200 rooms, 190 with bath. Coin laundry. No pets. AE, MC, V. Subway: 34th St./Herald Sq.*

HOSTELS & YMCAS

Independent hostels and those affiliated with Hostelling International (HI) are similar in price and style: they almost always have private rooms as well as dorms that sleep four to 12 people. The three private hostels in Harlem charge $14–$16 per dorm bed, while Midtown properties generally cost $20 or more. Very few hostels have air conditioning. Many hostels have an unadvertised policy of accepting foreigners only; those listed below accept Americans but require identification for check-in. Hostelers would be wise to carry a passport.

Another budget option is to stay in one of Manhattan's handful of YMCAs, where double rooms generally range from about $60 to $90. Though most YMCAs have bare-bones rooms and few facilities, they compensate by offering guests free use of their extensive gym facilities.

9 *d-4*

BIG APPLE HOSTEL

In the heart of Times Square, the Big Apple has brisk service, bathrooms that sparkle, and a big outdoor patio where you can sip free coffee with an international crowd. There are four-person dorms and a handful of private doubles. *119 W. 45th St., 10036, Midtown, 212/302–2603, fax 212/302–2605. 106 beds. Kitchen, coin laundry. MC, V. Subway: 42nd St./Times Sq.*

6 *d-6*

BLUE RABBIT INTERNATIONAL HOUSE

Don't let the location scare you off; this particular Harlem neighborhood, called

Sugar Hill, is relatively affluent and safe, and the hostel is just two blocks from St. Nick's Pub, one of Manhattan's best jazz clubs. Coed and women-only dorm-style rooms sleep four to eight, and there are also a few giant doubles. You can survey the street scene from a rooftop terrace. *730 St. Nicholas Ave. (between 145th and 146th Sts.), 10031, Harlem, 212/491–3892 or 800/610–2030, fax 212/283–0108. 25 beds. Fans, kitchen. No credit cards. Subway: A, B, C, D to 145th St.*

9 *c-8*

CHELSEA INTERNATIONAL HOSTEL

The free pizza-and-beer parties every Wednesday night draw a boisterous young crowd. The four-person dorm rooms are somewhat cramped, and only some have air conditioning, but they're half the price of the private doubles. An

---

OF BATHTUBS AND BIDETS

If you live in New York, chances are your bathroom is about the size of your closet. This is where luxury hotels come in.

Four Seasons (Very Expensive)
The enormous tubs fill in 60 seconds.

The Mansfield (Moderately Priced)
High-style, black-marble bathrooms.

The Michelangelo (Very Expensive)
Bidets and 55-gallon tubs.

Morgans (Expensive)
Crystal shower doors and poured-granite floors.

Omni Berkshire Place (Very Expensive)
Loos in the suites have TVs and CD players.

The Paramount (Moderately Priced)
Conical steel sinks designed by Philippe Starck.

The Pierre (Very Expensive)
Gleaming white marble with red and black trim; luxurious lighted mirrors.

Roger Williams (Moderately Priced)
Doorless, recessed showers with cedar-grill floors.

Trump International Hotel and Towers (Very Expensive)
Bath salts and loofahs are on the house.

---

international passport is technically required for check-in, but they (grudgingly) accept Americans when there's space. *251 W. 20th St., 10011, Chelsea, 212/647–0010, fax 212/727–7289. 200 beds. Kitchen. AE, MC, V. Subway: 1, 9, C, E to 23rd St.*

7 *e-6*

DE HIRSCH RESIDENCE AT THE 92ND STREET YM-YWHA

Right off Museum Mile in posh Carnegie Hill, the De Hirsch Residence is an excellent bargain: Every floor has its own kitchen, laundry, and shared bath, and you're steps away from the excellent fitness facilities as well as the Y's many cultural and social events. There's a three-night minimum stay, and you must reserve three weeks in advance. *1395 Lexington Ave. (at 92nd St)., 10128, Upper East Side, 212/415–5650 or 800/858–4692, fax 212/415–5578. 350 beds. Health club, pool, coin laundry. Subway: 4, 5, 6 to 86th St.*

7 *b-4*

HOSTELLING INTERNATIONAL–NEW YORK

Nineteenth-century architect Richard Morris Hunt designed this building, now home to the largest youth hostel in North America. Besides its sheer size, the main draws here are a garden and outdoor terrace and an excellent neighborhood location. There are about 100 four- to 12-person dorms, as well as some private rooms (with bath) that accommodate up to 4 people; these cost $75. Those with a Hostelling International card get a $3 discount. *891 Amsterdam Ave. (at 103rd St.), 10025, Upper West Side, 212/932–2300, fax 212/932–2574. 540 beds. Kitchen, coin laundry. MC, V. Subway: 1, 9 to 103rd St.*

6 *c-6*

SUGAR HILL INTERNATIONAL HOUSE

Like the Blue Rabbit International House (it has the same owners), this Harlem hostel is clean, comfortable, and friendly, with easy subway access and a sunny back garden. There are three four- to eight-bed dorms (some coed, some women-only) and one private double. Reserve in advance, check in before 9 PM, and remember your passport—it's required for check-in. *722 St. Nicholas Ave. (at 146th St.), 10031,*

*Harlem, 212/926–7030, fax 212/283–0108.
20 beds. Fans, kitchen. No credit cards.
Subway: A, B, C, D to 145th St.*

7 *d-2*

UPTOWN HOSTEL

This beautiful Harlem brownstone is a
real find thanks to Giselle, the hard-
working Canadian owner who loves to
debunk visitors' preconceptions about
Harlem. (It's the friendliest neighborhood she's ever lived in, she says.)
There are 30 coed dorms (four to six
beds) and two private doubles. *239
Lenox Ave./Malcolm X Blvd. (at 122nd
St.), 10027, Harlem, 212/666–0559. 30
beds. Fans, kitchen. No credit cards. Subway: 2, 3 to 125th St.*

9 *c-7*

YMCA–MCBURNEY

Despite the uninviting entrance—with a
security guard and a glassed-in reception
window—the McBurney is a good deal.
Rooms are small but decent, and guests
have free use of the gym. Beware,
though: there are only two large bathrooms for all 270 rooms. A $40 deposit
is required to secure your reservation,
unless you arrive before 6 PM. *206 W.
24th St., 10011, Chelsea, 212/741–9226, fax
212/741–8724. 270 rooms, none with bath.
Health club. Subway: 1, 9, C, E to 23rd St.*

9 *f-4*

YMCA–VANDERBILT

Tiny rooms with linoleum floors and
shared bathrooms are a small price to
pay for such a prime location and great
fitness perks: guests have free use of the
pools, cardiovascular equipment, and
Nautilus machines. *224 E. 47th St.,
10017, Midtown, 212/756–9600, fax 212/
752–0210. 377 rooms, none with bath. MC,
V. 2 pools, health club, airport shuttle.
Subway: 51st St./Lexington–3rd Aves.*

9 *c-2*

YMCA–WEST SIDE

A few blocks from Lincoln Center, this Y
has exceptionally extensive fitness facilities, including a pool, indoor track, and
squash courts. You must be at least 18
years old to stay here; reservations
(credit card required) are best made two
weeks in advance. *5 W. 63rd St., 10023,
Upper West Side, 212/787–4400, fax 212/
875–1334. 550 rooms, 100 with bath. Cafe-
teria, pool, sauna, health club, squash,
coin laundry, airport shuttle. AE, MC, V.
Subway: 59th St./Columbus Circle.*

HOTELS NEAR THE AIRPORTS

3 *f-1*

LA GUARDIA MARRIOTT AIRPORT HOTEL

A quarter of a mile from the airport
and—barring traffic—about 20 minutes
from Manhattan, this hotel is out of the
direct line of most flights. The airport
shuttle is free. *102–05 Ditmars Blvd., East
Elmhurst, Queens, 11369, 718/565–8900
or 800/882–1043, fax 718/899–0764. 432
rooms, 4 suites. Restaurant, sports bar, in-
room modem lines, room service, indoor
pool, health club, business services, meeting rooms, airport shuttle, parking (fee).
AE, D, DC, MC, V. Moderately priced.*

1 *b-7*

NEWARK AIRPORT MARRIOTT

The Marriott is right on airport premises
and provides free 24-hour shuttle service to all terminals, as well as free parking. It's only 30 minutes, in light traffic,
from Manhattan. *Newark International
Airport, Newark, NJ 07114, 201/623–0006
or 800/228–9290, fax 201/623–7618. 584
rooms, 6 suites. 2 restaurants, bar, room
service, indoor-outdoor pool, health club,
business services, meeting rooms, airport
shuttle, free parking. AE, D, DC, MC, V.
Moderately priced.*

B&B RESERVATION SERVICES

If you're looking for a more personal
(and significantly cheaper) overnight
experience in a more residential neighborhood than most hotels can offer, try
one of the hundreds of bed-and-break-
fasts throughout the city, especially in
Brooklyn. Beware, however, that
although you often pay less than $100,
the accommodations, amenities, service, and privacy may fall short of what
you get in hotels; and, despite the B&B
name, you often don't get breakfast. Ask
your B&B reservation agency for the
details on your property before checking
in.

B&Bs booked through a service may be
either hosted (you're the guest in someone's quarters) or unhosted (you have
full use of someone's vacated apartment, including kitchen privileges).
Needless to say, the latter option is the
more expensive. Most B&B services rep-

resent both kinds. Make reservations as far in advance as possible; refunds (minus a $25 service charge) are possible up to 10 days before arrival.

Abode Bed-and-Breakfast (Box 20022, New York, NY 10021, 212/472–2000 or 800/835–8880).

All Around the Town (150 5th Ave., Suite 711, New York, NY 10011, 212/675–5600, fax 212/675–6366).

Bed-and-Breakfast in Manhattan (Box 533, New York, NY 10150, 212/472–2528, fax 212/988–9818).

Bed-and-Breakfast Network of New York (134 W. 32nd St., Suite 602, New York, NY 10001, 212/645–8134 or 800/900–8134).

City Lights Bed-and-Breakfast (Box 20355, Cherokee Station, New York, NY 10021, 212/737–7049, fax 212/535–2755).

Urban Ventures (38 W. 32nd St., Suite 1412, New York, NY 10001, 212/594–5650, fax 212/947–9320).

chapter 8

HELP!

resources for residents

I t's easy to feel bogged down in a city like New York—but then, there is no city like New York. Many locals just don't have the time to take advantage of those hidden amenities that make it possible not just to survive but to thrive here. Yet nothing wipes away an especially grueling day like a reminder of why you live in (and love) New York. Take advantage of the city's best: Learn to tango. Take harmonica lessons—finally. Bone up on your Italian. Or get to know the folks who cater specifically to time-strapped New Yorkers in search of a good dog trainer, a trustworthy nanny, gay and lesbian social services, or advice on getting the landlord to fix the plumbing. Sit back, play your harmonica, and let New York help you unwind.

EDUCATIONAL RESOURCES

acting schools

9 b-4

Actors Connection Audition seminars attended by agents and casting directors. A popular vehicle for audition experience. *630 9th Ave. (between 44th and 45th Sts.), 212/977–6666.*

9 b-5

The Actors Studio Inc. One of the most exclusive workshops for professional actors. 50 years old in 1997. *432 W. 44th St., 212/757–0870.*

9 e-6

American Academy of Dramatic Arts Acting, speech, voice, movement, mime. *120 Madison Ave. (between 30th and 31st Sts.), 212/686–9244.*

9 b-8

Atlantic Theater Company Acting School Teaches the practical aesthetic technique developed by David Mamet and William H. Macy, founding members who drop by to teach periodically. Full-time two-year conservatory program; part-time programs for beginners and pros. Intensive summer program in Vermont. *453 W. 16th St., 212/691–5919.*

9 d-7

Creative Acting Company Beginner through pro. Scene study, monologue, commercials, sitcoms, more; some classes taught by casting directors. New sketch-comedy and improv group. Thursday is agent night: all the biggies, from ICM to William Morris. *122 W. 26th St., 212/352–2103.*

10 c-2

Herbert Berghof Studio All subjects, all levels. Founded by Uta Hagen and Herbert Berghof. *120 Bank St. (between Greenwich and Washington Sts.), 212/675–2370.*

10 e-1

Lee Strasberg Theater Institute, Inc. Pacino and DeNiro studied here. Founded by creative genius Lee Strasberg. *115 E. 15th St., 212/533–5500.*

adult education programs

10 e-2

New York University NYU's School of Continuing Education offers more than 2,000 credit and non-credit courses around the city, for both business and pleasure. *212/998–7080.*

10 d-1

The New School for Social Research Guitar Study, Foreign Languages, Business and Career, Music, Writing, Theater, Dance, and Culinary Arts in a cool, sociable atmosphere or via distance learning ("attend" classes on your computer). Year-round. *66 W. 12th St., 212/229–5620.*

7 e-6

92nd St. Y Language, literature, dance, music, arts, crafts, cooking, Jewish education. *1395 Lexington Ave. (at 92nd St.), 212/996–1100.*

art schools

9 c-3

Art Students' League Founded in 1875. Drawing, painting, sculpture. *215 W. 57th St., 212/247–4510.*

11 b-2

Greenwich House Pottery Wheel-throwing, hand-building, glaze, and more, including children's classes. *16 Jones St. (between Bleecker and W. 4th Sts.), 212/242–4106.*

11 *b-5*

Manhattan Graphics Center Not-for-profit printmaking workshop run by artists. Inexpensive courses in etching, lithography, silkscreen, and more. Fully equipped darkroom. $35 membership fee. *481 Washington St. (between Canal and Spring Sts.), 212/219–8783.*

10 *d-2*

New York Studio School Full-time studio programs and weekly figure-drawing classes. *8 W. 8th St., 212/673–6466.*

10 *d-1*

Parsons School of Design Painting, drawing, etching, color theory, life drawing, and more, at all levels. *2 W. 13th St., 212/229–8900.*

9 *f-7*

School of Visual Arts Drawing, painting, graphic design, illustration. *209 E. 23rd St., 212/592–2000.*

cooking schools

9 *d-7*

Peter Kumps New York Cooking School The city's most popular culinary-arts program. Hundreds of courses, including a well-attended knife-skills workshop and various ethnic cuisines. All levels. *50 W. 23rd St., 800/522–4610.*

7 *f-6*

307 E. 92nd St., 800/522–4610.

dance instruction

9 *c-3*

Broadway Dance Center This high-energy, five-floor dance hub offers jazz, ballet, tap, modern, hip-hop, African, flamenco, aerobics, and more. All levels, including children's classes. *221 W. 57th St., 212/582–9304.*

11 *e-3*

Dance Space, Inc. Most dancers come here for the Lynn Simonson jazz-technique and modern classes, but you can also study ballet, African dance, Middle Eastern dance, hip-hop, hula, yoga, and more, at all levels. The mood is serene and studious. *622 Broadway (between Houston and Bleecker Sts.), 4th floor, 212/777–8067.*

9 *c-2*

Paul Pellicoro's DanceSport All levels of mambo, salsa, tango, swing, waltz, hustle, quickstep, and other Latin and ballroom classes in a bustling and sociable atmosphere. *1845 Broadway (between 60th and 61st Sts.), 212/307–1111.*

11 *c-3*

S.O.B.'s You say you want to tango? Try this festive Brazilian club, with tango lessons one night a month. Dinner 6–midnight, lessons 7:30–9 followed by live music. Dance tickets $15. *(See Dance Clubs in Chapter 5.) 204 Varick St. (at Houston St.), 212/243–4940.*

language schools

9 *e-2*

Alliance Française/French Institute French at all levels. *22 E. 60th St., 212/355–6100.*

9 *d-4*

Berlitz Language Center Immersion courses for individuals and groups—in *all* spoken languages! *40 W. 51st St., 212/765–1000.*

10 *e-7*

61 Broadway (near Exchange Pl.), 212/425–3866.

11 *d-1*

The German House, NYU All levels plus business, conversation, and reading. "Meet the Authors" program: read 'em, meet 'em, discuss their work. Wunderbar. *42 Washington Mews (between 5th Ave. and University Pl.), 212/998–8660.*

9 *e-5*

Instituto Cervantes Spanish at all levels. *122 E. 42nd St., 212/628–0420.*

10 *d-1*

The New School for Social Research 16 languages, all levels. Accredited classes, such as "Italian for Italian speakers." Business-language courses in Chinese, Spanish, French, and, eventually, Russian. *66 W. 12th St., 212/229–5620.*

9 *e-2*

Parliamo Italiano Language School Italian at all levels, in a lovely town house. *132 E. 65th St., 212/744–4793.*

9 *d-6*

Russian Institute for Language and Culture Russian at all levels. *134 W. 32nd St., 212/244–5700.*

music schools

11 *b-2*

Greenwich House Music School Instrumental and vocal classes and workshops; preschool program in music and art. Free concerts and recitals of students' work. *46 Barrow St. (near 7th Ave. S), 212/242–4770.*

9 *b-2*

Juilliard School Evening Division regular faculty teach music, dance, and drama. The most popular course seems to be piano lessons, but offerings extend to a music criticism, studies of individual composers, and a wonderful class on overcoming performance anxiety. *60 Lincoln Center Plaza (Broadway at 65th St.), Upper West Side, 212/799–5040.*

New York Singing Teachers Association Evaluation (all levels), referral, master classes. *212/579–2461.*

10 *f-1*

Third Street Music School Settlement Founded 1894. Private and group instruction for all ages. *233 E. 11th St., 212/777–3240.*

RESOURCES

general

Emergency: Ambulance, Fire, Police Dial 911 or 0. For the hearing-impaired: TTY 311/800 342–4357.

9 *g-2*

Animal Emergency: Animal Medical Center 24 hrs. *Bobst Hospital, 510 E. 62nd St. (between York Ave. and FDR Dr.), 212/838–8100.*

AMBULANCE

In an emergency, dial 911 and a city ambulance will arrive free of charge. The patient will be taken to one of the city's 13 municipal hospitals, based on location and hospital specialty.

If the patient prefers a specific, nonpublic hospital, Keefe and Keefe provides 24-hour ambulance service to all five boroughs, for a fee. *212/988–8800.*

HOSPITAL EMERGENCY ROOMS

10 *e-6*

Beekman Downtown Hospital Mobile intensive care, two paramedic units (weekdays, 9–5), Basic EMT unit (24 hours, 7 days), coronary intensive care. *170 William St. (between Beekman and Spruce Sts.), 212/312–5070.*

9 *f-7*

Bellevue Hospital Center Intensive-care units: coronary, surgical trauma, pediatric, psychiatric, neurosurgical, and alcohol detoxification. *462 1st Ave. (at 27th St.), 212/562–4347, pediatrics 212/562–3025.*

9 *f-8*

Beth Israel Medical Center Coronary care, neonatal intensive care, alcohol and drug detoxification. *1st Ave. at 16th St., 212/420–2840.*

9 *f-8*

Cabrini Medical Center Coronary care, trauma intensive care, alcohol detoxification and drug-overdose units, psychiatric facility. *227 E. 19th St., 212/995–6000.*

6 *b-3*

Columbia Presbyterian Medical Center Intensive-care units: metabolic, neurosurgical, pediatric. *622 W. 168th St. (at Ft. Washington Ave.). Main: 212/305–2500. Emergency, adult: 212/305–2255. Emergency, pediatric: 212/305–6628.*

6 *e-8*

Harlem Hospital Coronary care; neonatal and respiratory critical care; alcohol and drug detoxification. Crisis intervention center for rape victims and battered wives and children. *506 Lenox Ave. (at 135th St.), 212/939–1000.*

7 *e-8*

Lenox Hill Hospital Coronary and neonatal intensive care. *100 E. 77th St., 212/434–3030.*

9 *f-2*

Manhattan Eye, Ear and Throat Hospital Ear, eye, nose, and throat emergencies. *210 E. 64th St., 212/838–9200.*

7 *e-5*

Mount Sinai Hospital Coronary, trauma, and medical intensive care; dental emergencies; emergency pharmacy until midnight. *5th Ave. at 101st St., 212/241–7171.*

10 *f-1*

New York Eye and Ear Infirmary 24-hour emergency service for eye, ear, nose, or throat problems. *310 E. 14th St., 212/979–4000.*

9 *g-1*

New York Hospital–Cornell Medical Center 24-hour paramedic unit; burn, coronary, neurological, and neonatal intensive care; high-risk infant-transport unit and treatment. *525 E. 68th St., 212/746–5454.*

9 *f-6*

New York University Medical Center Coronary care. *550 1st Ave. (at 33rd St.), 212/263–5550.*

9 *b-3*

St. Clare's Hospital and Health Center Coronary, medical, and surgical intensive care. *426 W. 52nd St., 212/586–1500.*

7 *b-3*

St. Luke's Hospital Center Coronary, trauma, and neonatal intensive care; alcohol detoxification; rape-intervention team; 24-hour psychiatric emergency room. *1111 Amsterdam Ave. (at 114th St.), 212/523–3335.*

9 *b-2*

St. Luke's–Roosevelt Hospital Coronary, surgical, and neonatal intensive-care units; alcohol detoxification. *1000 10th Ave. (at 59th St.), 212/523–6800.*

10 *d-1*

St. Vincent's Hospital and Medical Center of New York Coronary, spinal-cord trauma, and psychiatric intensive care; alcohol detoxification. *153 W. 11th St., 212/604–7998.*

POLICE STATIONS
Emergency Dial 911.

Police services are available 24 hours daily. For general information or the location of the precinct nearest you (in all five boroughs), call 212/374–5000.

COUNSELING AND REFERRAL
Citizens Advice Bureau Information, referral, and problem-solving center for housing, welfare, Medicaid, and Immigration, and Social Services. *178 Bennett Ave. (at Broadway), 212/923–2599; 2070 Grand Concourse (near Burnside Ave.), Bronx, 718/731–3117. Weekdays 9–3:30.*

Domestic Violence Hotline *800/942–6906.*

Mayor's Action Center Handles complaints about city agencies. *61 Chambers St., 212/788–9600. Weekdays 9–5; 24 hrs.*

Poison Hot Line *212/340–4494 or 212/764–7667 (dial POISONS).*

Public Assistance/NYC Emergency Shelter *212/513–8849.*

Salvation Army of Greater New York Information and referral for family problems, foster homes, senior-citizen residence problems, adoption, and alcohol and drug rehabilitation,. Two social workers on duty weekdays 8:30–4. Thirty-three centers throughout the city; summer camps; and a general hospital in Flushing, Queens. *212/337–7200.*

United Neighborhood Houses Information and referral for family and individual counseling; day care; nurseries; and senior-citizen programs. *212/967–0322. Weekdays 8–5.*

10 *d-5*

NEW YORK CITY HUMAN RESOURCES ADMINISTRATION
Provides public assistance in many areas; call for a referral to the appropriate division. *250 Church St., 212/274–5400 or 718/291–1900, weekdays 9–5.*

Child Services Foster care, adoption, day care, Head Start.

Crisis Intervention Unit Emergency housing, food, and clothing.

Family and Adult Services Home care, foster care for adults, protective services.

General Social Services Referral, interceding unit, outreach center.

Medicaid/Medicare Medical-insurance benefits.

Office of Income Support Child support from absent parents.

aids

AIDS Hot Line New York City Department of Health. *212/447–8200; national 800/342–2437.*

Advanced Counseling and Testing Service Board-certified counselors; FDA-approved test; results in 15 minutes. *212/246–0800.*

alcoholism

Alcoholics Anonymous Support system for alcoholics who want to stop drinking. Frequent meetings throughout the city. 212/870–3400.

National Council on Alcoholism Information and referral. 212/979–1010.

babysitting
The Babysitters Guild Licensed and bonded; in business over 50 years. Recommmended to visitors by major hotels. The staff, all 25 or older, speaks a total of 16 languages. Live-in sitters available; good roster of old-timers. Office open daily 9–9; sitters available 24 hours. 212/682–0227.

carriage rental
Chateau Stables America's largest working collection of horse-drawn vehicles. Rent any of 200 different carriages, including a stagecoach; hayride wagon; pony cart; hearse; and vintage ice, bread, and milk wagons. Return customers include Woody Allen. For an extra-special wedding, the glass-enclosed carriage is $1000 for 3 hours; and the half-carriages at Central Park (outside the Plaza Hotel, 5th Ave. and 59th St.) are on par with a very leisurely cab ride. 608 W. 48th St., 212/246–0520.

catering
Glorious Food Plan on perfection from this veteran city caterer. Classic French and international cuisines. 212/628–2320.

Simple Fare American regional cuisine. Prepares what the name suggests, with flair: breakfast pantry, salads, sandwiches, pasta, hors d'oeuvres, and desserts. 212/691–4570.

Taste From corporate events to private parties. Versatile: American regional, Mediterranean, Asian-influenced menus. Children's parties, too. 212/255–8571.

child crisis
24-hour Child Abuse and Maltreatment Register 800/342–3720.

coast guard
General information 212/668–7000

Emergency search and rescue 212/668–7936.

consumer protection
Attorney General's Consumer Help Line 800/771–7755.

Better Business Bureau 212/533–6200.

Department of Consumer Affairs Hotline 212/487–4444.

crime victims
10 e-5

Crime Victims Board of New York State Financial aid and reimbursement of out-of-pocket medical expenses for crime victims. 270 Broadway (at Church St.), 212/417–5160. Weekdays 9–5.

Crime Victims Hot Line 24-hour bilingual counseling and referral. 212/577–7777.

doctors on call
Private service for house calls by doctors in all boroughs except the Bronx. In Manhattan, daytime only. 718/238–2100 8 AM–midnight.

doctor and dentist referrals
Physician Referral Service of Beth Israel Medical Center 212/420–2000.

Dental Referral Service National service based in Southern California—where everyone has a fabulous smile. 800/511–8663.

drug abuse
9 d-5

Daytop Village Rehabilitation facilities to help addicts with drug and drug-related problems. 54 W. 40th St., 212/354–6000. Weekdays 9–5. 24-hr hot line: 800/232–9867.

New York State Division of Substance Abuse Services 24-hour referral to treatment programs, clinics, and hospitals. 800/522–5353.

11 g-1

Odyssey House Respected drug-abuse centers offer residential rehabilitation, vocational training, and reeducation, with a focus on reintegration into society. 309–11 E. 6th St., 212/477–9630; Ward's Island, Building 3, 212/860–6460. Open 24 hrs.

7 *b-8*

Phoenix House Foundation The city's largest drug-free residential rehabilitation program, with five facilities. Encourages responsibility, self-reliance, and trust. *164 W. 74th St., 212/787–3000. Open 24 hrs.*

family planning
Family Planning Information Service *212/677–3040.*

Planned Parenthood *212/541–7800. Daily 8:30–5. 24-hr clinic locator 800/230–7526.*

gay and lesbian concerns
Gay and Lesbian Anti-Violence Project 24-hour hot line arranges counseling, domestic-violence support groups, court and police accompaniment and monitoring, assistance in obtaining court-ordered protection, and legal services, all free. *212/807–0197.*

Gay Roommate Information Network *212/627–4242.*

10 *C-1*

Lesbian and Gay Community Services Center Counseling, therapy, education, library and museum, and resources for couples considering children. *208 W. 13th St., 212/620–7310. Daily 9 AM–11 PM.*

homework help
Dial-A-Teacher The United Federation of Teachers staffs this service to help children answer difficult homework questions. *212/777–3380. Mon.–Thurs. 4 –7 during academic year.*

housecleaning help
Best Domestic In addition to general house cleaning, this citywide agency provides maid service, butlers, nannies, housekeepers, husband-and-wife teams, chefs and cooks, chauffeurs, major domos, personal assistants, baby nurses, and office cleaners. Licensed, bonded, and insured, the company claims to reject about 85 percent of its candidates for employment (tougher than some of the Ivy League). 24 hours' notice is preferred, but they may be able to accommodate as little as 4 hours'. *212/685–0351.*

Green Clean General housecleaning in Manhattan, Brooklyn, and parts of Queens using nontoxic and environ-

mentally friendly products. Call a week in advance; 10 days in advance for large jobs. *212/255–7755.*

Pet Cleaning Services No, these Brooklyn pet cleaners won't clean the little darlings, but they will clean up *after* them. Specialty: shedding. *718/856–5657.*

landlord/tenant
10 *e-6*

Metropolitan Council on Housing This advocacy group advises tenants in rent-controlled and rent-stabilized apartments on their rights and helps organize tenants. *212/693–0550 Mon., Wed., Fri. 1:30–5. Walk-in location: 102 Fulton St. (at William St.), Room 302. Open Wed. 4–7.*

10 *e-7*

Division of Housing and Community Renewal Rent Administration City offices for tenants and owners of rent-controlled and rent-stablized apartments. *Information, 9–5 weekdays: 718/739–6400. Walk-in offices: 25 Beaver St. (at Broad St.), Lower Manhattan, 212/480–6227.*

7 *d-1*

163 W. 125th St., 5th floor, Harlem, 212/ 961–8930.

12 *e-3*

55 Hanson Pl., Downtown Brooklyn, 718/ 722–4778.

1 *g-3*

92–31 Union Hall St., Jamaica, Queens.

5 *g-4*

1 Fordham Plaza, Bronx, 718/563–5678. Walk-in hours: 9–4:45.

legal services
Legal Aid Society *General information 212/577–3300.*

Legal Referral Services Association of the Bar *In English, 212/626–7373; in Spanish, 212/626–7374.*

lost & found
TRANSPORTATION
JFK International Airport Found property will be held by the airline on which you traveled. If loss occurred on airport grounds or at the International Arrivals Building, call 718/244–4225.

La Guardia Airport (Port Authority Police) *718/533–3988.* Also call the airline on which you traveled.

New York City Buses Brooklyn, Queens, Staten Island *718/625–6200;* Bronx, Manhattan *212/690–9638.*

New York City Subways *718/625–6200.*

Newark International Airport *201/961–6230.* Also call the airline on which you traveled.

Port Authority Bus Terminal *212/435–7000.*

Railroads Pennsylvania (Penn) Station *718/990–8384;* Grand Central Terminal *212/340–2555.*

Taxicabs Items left in taxis should be turned in to the police station closest to your destination. To report a loss, call the Taxi and Limousine Commission at *212/302–8294.*

LOST ANIMALS

If your pet goes astray, post notices in the area of the pet's home and most recent whereabouts. Include a description and/or photo of your pet with your phone number only. Call all local veterinarians to check if your pet has been brought in, and inquire about posting notices at their offices. Report the missing animal to the ASPCA (424 E. 92nd St., 212/876–7700).

LOST CREDIT CARDS

American Express/Optima *800/528–4800.*

Chase *800/632–3300.*

Citibank *800/843–0777.*

Diners Club/Carte Blanche *800/234–6377.*

Discover *800/347–2683.*

mental health information & referral

Mental Health Counseling Hot Line State-certified therapists available for information and referral. Don't be put off by the answering machine—someone always calls back. *212/734–5876.*

on-line services

New York Convention and Visitors Bureau Visit www.nycvisit.com for an invaluable directory of Web addresses for new york organizations of every stripe.

The New York Times On America Online, enter keyword *times* for news or events listings; on the Web, read the *Times* at www.nytimes.com.

pets

ADOPTIONS

`7` *f-6*

ASPCA The national HQ of "America's first humane society" no longer kills unwanted animals. For an adoption fee of about $50, your new companion will be spayed or neutered and given the proper shots. *424 E. 92nd St., 212/876–7700.*

`9` *f-5*

Bide-a-Wee Very sweet mutts for dog lovers; domestic shorthairs for the feline-inclined. Adoption fee: $30–$50. *410 E. 38th St., 212/532–4455.*

North Shore Animal League Recommended by animal lovers regionwide. No adoption fee. *25 Davis Ave., Port Washington, NY, 516/883–7575. Long Island Rail Road: Port Washington.*

GROOMING

`9` *e-6*

Furry Paws professional grooming with natural products—no sedatives. Evening hours for the busy pooch. *120 E. 34th St., 212/725–1970.*

`9` *f-3*

Finishing Touches by Stephanie Dental care and therapeutic baths, in addition to basic grooming. *414 E. 58th St., 212/753–8234.*

Private Grooming by Terrie Vitolo A veteran groomer who makes house calls. *718/388–1442.*

TRAINING

American Dog Trainers Network resource and referral hot line. *212/727–7257.*

ASPCA Group training classes, two months long, range from Puppy Kindergarten to Therapy Training. *212/876–7700.*

Center for Applied Animal Behavior and Canine Training, Inc. Consulting and treatment of behavior, mainly for dogs. By appointment. *212/544–8797.*

Dr. Ellen Lindell Specializes in kittens and cats with behavioral problems, but

will work with Fido, too. Phone consultations and housecalls. *914/473–7406.*

VETERINARIAN REFERRALS
Veterinary Medical Association of NYC
212/246–0057.

pharmacies open 24 hours
Duane Reade *224 W. 57th St. (at Broadway), 212/541–9708; 2465 Broadway (at
91st St.), 212/799–3172; 1279 3rd Ave. (at
74th St.), 212/744–2668; 378 6th Ave. (at
Waverly Pl.), 212/674–5357.*

Genovese *Free delivery. 1229 2nd Ave. (at
68th St.), 212/772–0104.*

phone information
Long Distance Access Codes *AT&T
10288; MCI 10222; Sprint 10333.*

Bell Atlantic Dial the number within
your area code. Local service, billing
212/890–1550 or 718/890–1550; repairs
212/890–6611 or 718/890–6611.

AT&T *800/225–5288.*

MCI *800/950–5555.*

Sprint *800/538–0944.*

postal services
9 *c-6*
J. A. Farley General Post Office It's 3 AM
and you can't find your best friend's zip
code? 24-hour postal information is
here. *8th Ave. at 33rd St. 24-hour information 800/725–2161.*

rape crisis
**New York Police Department Rape Hot
Line** Female detectives provide counseling 24 hours a day and assist in filing a
police report. *212/267–7273.*

**Sexual Abuse Training and Treatment
Institute** *212/366–1490.*

senior citizens
New York City Department for the Aging
Extensive resources, including referral.
212/442–1000.

Legal Service for the Elderly Poor Part of
the citywide agency Legal Services for
New York City, LSEP provides free support for those elderly living below the
poverty line. *212/391–0120; for referral in
all boroughs, 212/431–7200.*

Legal Aid Society *212/577–3300.*

Senior Action Line A part of the mayor's
office, this information, referral, and
advocacy program for senior citizens is
staffed by volunteers. *212/788–7504.*

suicide prevention
Help Line *212/532–2400.*

Suicide Prevention Hot Line 24-hour hot
line *800/ 543–3638; 7:30 PM–midnight
718/389–9608.*

The Samaritans 24-hour hot line *212/
673–3000.*

television–cable companies
Call yours for service, repairs, and general information.

Manhattan South Time Warner of New
York. *212/674–9100.*

Manhattan North Time Warner of New
York. *212/567–3833.*

Bronx, Brooklyn Cablevision. *718/617–
3500.*

Brooklyn Time Warner of New York. *718/
358–0900.*

Queens Time Warner of New York. *718/
358–0900.*

Staten Island Staten Island Cable. *718/
816–8686.*

traveler's aid
1 *h-5*
Traveler's Aid Society of New York
Nationwide service helps crime victims,
stranded travelers, and wayward children and works closely with the police.
*International Arrivals Building, JFK Air-
port. Recorded information 718/656–4870.
Weekdays 10–10, Sat. 1–10.*

Crime Victims' Hot Line 24-hour bilingual counseling and referral. *212/577–
7777.*

utilities
GAS
Brooklyn Union Serves Queens (up to
Jackson Heights), Staten Island, and
Brooklyn. *718/643–4050.*

GAS & ELECTRIC
ConEdison Gas and electricity throughout city, except Brooklyn, Staten Island,

and part of Queens (where Brooklyn Union provides gas service). *212/338–3000. Gas leaks or emergencies 212/683–8830. Electric and steam emergencies 212/683–0862.*

zoning and planning

Department of City Planning Bookstore sells maps and publications; office dispenses zoning information and schedules of upcoming meetings. *22 Reade St. (between Broadway and Centre St.), 212/720–3300; Brooklyn 718/643–7550; Queens 718/392–0656; Staten Island 718/727–8453.*

Historic Landmarks Preservation Center *310 Madison Ave. (at 42nd St.), 212/983–1197.*

TRAVEL AND VACATION INFORMATION

airlines

The Central Airlines Ticket Office handles ticketing for all major airlines. *100 E. 42nd St., 212/986–0888.*

AeroMexico *212/754–2140 or 800/237–6639.*

Air Canada *212/869–8840 or 800/776–3000.*

Air Europa *800/238–7672.*

Air France *800/237–2747.*

Air India *212/751–6200.*

Air Jamaica *800/523–5585.*

Alitalia Air Lines *212/903–3300.*

America West Airlines *800/235–9292.*

American Airlines *800/433–7300.*

Austrian Airlines *800/843–0002.*

Avianca Airlines *212/284–2622.*

British Airways *800/247–9297.*

British West Indian Airlines *800/538–2942.*

China Airlines *800/227–5118.*

Continental Airlines *800/319–9494; international flights 800/231–0856.*

Czech Airlines *212/765–6022.*

Delta Airlines *800/221–1212; international flights 800/241–4141.*

Egyptair *212/586–2678.*

El Al Airlines *800/223–6700.*

Finnair *800/950–5000.*

Iberia Airlines *800/772–4642.*

IcelandAir *800/223–5500.*

Aer Lingus (Irish International Airlines) *212/557–1110.*

Japan Airlines *800/525–3663.*

KLM Royal Dutch Airlines *800/374–7747.*

LanChile Airlines *800/488–0070.*

Lufthansa Airlines *800/645–3880.*

Mexicana Airlines *800/531–7921.*

Midway Airlines *800/446–4392.*

Northwest Airlines *800/225–2525; international flights 800/447–4747.*

Pan American World Airways *800/359–7262.*

Qantas Airlines *800/227–4500.*

Royal Air Maroc *212/750–5115.*

Sabena Belgian World Airlines *800/955–2000.*

Scandinavian Airlines *800/221–2350.*

Singapore Airlines *800/742–3333.*

South African Airways *212/826–0995.*

Swissair *800/221–4750.*

TAP Air Portugal *800/221–7370.*

Trans World Airlines (TWA) *800/221–2000.*

United Airlines *800/825–9035.*

USAir *800/428–4322.*

Varig Brazilian Airlines *800/468–2744.*

Virgin Atlantic *800/862–8621.*

airports

1 *h-5*

John F. Kennedy (JFK) International Airport *Howard Beach, Queens, 718/244–4444.*

1 *e-3*

La Guardia Airport *Jackson Heights, Queens* 718/533–3400.

1 *b-7*

Newark International Airport *Newark, New Jersey* 201/961–6000.

car rental

SELF-DRIVE

Avis *Reservations: 800/831–2847; JFK 718/244–5400; La Guardia 718/507–3600; Newark Airport 201/961–4300.*

Budget *Reservations: 212/807–8700; JFK 718/565–6010; La Guardia 718/639–6400. From out of town, 800/527-0700*

Enterprise *Reservations: 800/736–8222; JFK 718/659–1200; La Guardia 718/457–2900.*

Hertz *Reservations: 800/654–3131.*

CHAUFFEUR-DRIVEN

Carey Lincolns, Cadillacs, stretch limos, and chauffeurs available 24 hours. Hourly rates. *212/599–1122; worldwide 800/336–4646.*

Fugazy Limousine Ltd. Limousines and sedans with courteous, uniformed chauffeurs serving all five boroughs, Westchester, and parts of Pennsylvania 24 hours daily. *212/661–0100. 24 hrs.*

Smith Limousine Located in Manhattan, Smith has Cadillacs and Lincoln limos, stretches, and sedans, plus vintage cars for special occasions. Big date? Ask for the 1948 Cadillac Limousine in dark blue. Cars available 24 hours daily. *212/247–0711. 24 hrs.*

embassies and consulates

British Consulate General *845 3rd Ave., 212/745–0200.*

Chinese Consulate of the People's Republic of China *520 12th Ave., 212/330–7400.*

Dominican Republic's Consulate General *1 Times Sq. Plaza 212/768–2480.*

French Embassy *972 5th Ave.,212/ 439–1400.*

German Consulate General *460 Park Ave., 212/308–8700.*

Irish Consulate General *345 Park Ave. at 51st St., 212/319–2555.*

Italian Consulate General *54 E. 69th St., 212/737–9100.*

Japanese Consulate General *299 Park Ave., 212/371–8222.*

Mexican Consulate General *8 E. 41st St., 212/689–0456.*

Portuguese Consulate General *630 5th Ave., 212/765–2980.*

Spanish Consulate General *150 E. 58th St., 212/355–4090.*

inoculations and vaccinations

Center for Disease Control's International Travel Line Knows which countries require which vaccines. *404/332–4565.*

9 *g-1*

International Health Care Service Staffed by specialists in infectious disease, the IHCS is devoted exclusively to the medical needs of international travelers, providing worldwide health information, immunizations, and post-travel tests and treatment. The fee varies, but it's always a worthwhile investment if you're traveling to a developing nation. Make an appointment four to five weeks before departure. *New York Hospital–Cornell Medical Center, 440 E. 69th St., 212/746–1601. Mon.–Thurs. 4–8 PM by appointment.*

1 *h-5*

Kennedy International Medical Office Building Vaccinations and inoculations for a fee. *198 S. Cargo Road and 150th St., Howard Beach, Queens, 718/656–5344. Daily 8 AM–10 PM; 24 hrs for emergencies. No personal checks.*

passport photos

Passports require two identical recent photos, each 2 inches square. These can be taken by any photographer; see the application for exact specifications.

passports

You can apply for a passport at any of New York's Passport Acceptance Agencies: designated post offices, county clerks' offices, and, in a pinch, the New York Passport Agency. Call the Ansonia Station post office (212/362–7486) for the passport-accepting post office nearest you. During peak travel periods— spring and summer—apply for a first-time passport three months before your trip. All passport information, including printable applications and a locator of the passport agency nearest you, is handily available on the State Department's Consular Affairs Web site: http://travel.state.gov.

Passport *renewal* is handled most easily through the mail. Renewal forms are available at many post offices (or on the State Department's Web site; *see above*) and can be submitted by mail or at any passport acceptance agency.

If you're short on time and/or don't have Web access, you can obtain passport information and forms by phone, for a fee. Call the National Passport Information Center at 900/225–5674 (35¢ per min.) or, with a major credit card, 888/362–8668 ($4.95). In a grave emergency after hours (such as the death of a relative abroad), call the passport duty officer at the U.S. State Department in Washington (202/647–4000).

A new U.S. passport costs $65 ($40 for those under 18); a renewal costs $55. If you need an emergency passport for travel within ten days, you'll pay an additional $30 fee for "expedited processing"; bring your plane ticket with you t the office.

10 *e-5*

County Clerk's Office The secret is out: there are no lines here. Come on down, for passports at least three weeks before departure. *New York County Courthouse, 60 Centre St. (at Pearl St.), lower level, 212/374–8361. Weekdays 9–2 except holidays. Bronx County Courthouse, 718/590–3643 (6/g-5). Brooklyn Supreme Court, 718/643–5897 (12/c-3). Queens County Courthouse, 718/520–3700 (1/g-3). Richmond (Staten Island) County Court, 718/390–5386 (1/c-8).*

11 *b-4*

New York Passport Agency This office issues emergency passports for travel within two weeks. You must have an appointment, but you're still bound to spend most of the day waiting on line. First-timers must bring proof of U.S. citizenship, photo I.D. (or I.D. with description), and passport photos *(see above). 376 Hudson St. (between W. Houston and King Sts.), 212/206–3500. Weekdays 7:30–3 except holidays.*

9 *e-4*

Passport Plus This private document service is for travelers with more money than time. It can get you a passport in as little as one day and arrange visas to all countries, as well as snap your pictures on-site. *20 E. 49th St., 212/759–5540.*

tourist offices

Considering a trip abroad? Tourist offices can send you colorful brochures and answer travel questions.

Antigua Department of Tourism and Trade *610 5th Ave. (at 49th St.), 212/541–4117.*

Argentine National Tourist Office *215 Lexington Ave. (at 32nd St.), 212/765–8833.*

Austrian National Tourist Office *500 5th Ave., 212/944–6880.*

Belgian National Tourist Office *780 3rd Ave. (between 48th and 49th Sts.), 212/758–8130.*

Bermuda Department of Tourism *310 Madison Ave. (at 42nd St.), 212/818–9800.*

Brazilian Tourism Bureau *16 W. 46th St., 212/730–1010.*

British Tourist Authority *551 5th Ave. (at 45th St.), 212/986–2200.*

Caribbean Tourism Association *80 Broad St., 212/682–0435.*

Cayman Islands Department of Tourism *420 Lexington Ave. (43rd St.), 212/682–5582.*

Colombian Government Tourist Office *140 E. 57th St., 212/308–6876.*

Cyprus Tourism Organization *13 E. 40th St., 212/683–5280.*

Czechoslovakia Travel Bureau *321 E. 75th St., 212/988–8080.*

Dominican Republic Tourist Information Center *1501 Broadway (between 43rd and 44th Sts.), 212/575–4966.*

Egyptian Government Tourist Office *630 5th Ave. (at 50th St.), 212/332–2570.*

French Government Tourist Office/French West Indies Tourist Board *444 Madison Ave. (between 49th and 50th Sts.), 212/838–7800.*

German National Tourist Office *122 E. 42nd St., 212/661–7200.*

Ghana Mission *19 E. 47th St., 212/832–1300.*

Greek National Tourist Organization *645 5th Ave. (at 51st St.), 212/421–5777.*

Grenada Tourist Information Office *820 2nd Ave. (between 43rd and 44th Sts.), 212/687–9554.*

Haiti Network Travel Service *211 E. 43rd St., 212/286–9692.*

Hong Kong Tourist Association *590 5th Ave. (between 47th and 48th Sts.), 212/869–5008.*

India Government Tourist Office *30 Rockefeller Plaza, 212/586–4901.*

Irish Tourist Board *345 Park Ave. (between 50th and 51st Sts.), 212/418–0800.*

Israel Government Tourist Office *800 2nd Ave. (at 42nd St.), 212/499–5660.*

Italian Government Tourist Office *630 5th Ave. (between 50th and 51st Sts.), 212/245–4822.*

Jamaica Tourist Board *801 2nd Ave. (between 42nd and 43rd Sts.), 212/856–9727.*

Japan National Tourist Organization *1 Rockefeller Plaza, 212/757–5640.*

Kenya Tourist Office *424 Madison Ave. (between 48th and 49th Sts.), 212/486–1300.*

Korean Tourist Office *460 Park Ave. (at 58th St.), 212/752–1700.*

Luxembourg Mission *17 Beekman Pl. (at 50th St.), 212/935–3589.*

Mexican Government Tourism Office *405 Park Ave. (at 45th St.), 212/755–7261.*

Monaco Government Tourist Office *565 5th Ave. (at 46th St.), 212/286–3330.*

Moroccan National Tourist Office *20 E. 46th St., 212/557–2520.*

Netherlands Board of Tourism *355 Lexington Ave. (between 40th and 41st Sts.), 888/465–5263.*

Philippine Department of Tourism *556 5th Ave. (at 45th St.), 212/575–7915.*

Portuguese National Tourist Office *590 5th Ave. (between 47th and 48th Sts.), 212/354–4403.*

Puerto Rico Tourism Company *575 5th Ave. (at 47th St.), 212/599–6262.*

Quebec Government House *1 Rockefeller Center, 800/363–7777.*

Romanian National Tourist Office *14 E. 38th St., 212/545–8484.*

Scandinavian Tourist Board *655 3rd Ave. (at 42nd St.), 212/949–2333.*

Tourist Office of Spain *666 5th Ave. (between 52nd and 53rd Sts.), 212/265–8822.*

Swiss National Tourism Office *608 5th Ave. (at 49th St.), 212/757–5944.*

Taiwan Visitors Association *1 World Trade Center, 212/466–0691.*

Turkish Tourism Information Office *821 United Nations Plaza (1st Ave. and 46th St.), 212/687–2194.*

U.S. Virgin Islands Government Tourist Office *1270 6th Ave. (between 50th and 51st Sts.), 212/332–2222.*

visa information & travel advisories

Call the embassy, consulate, or tourist office (*see above*) of the country you plan to visit for up-to-date information on visa requirements, travel advisories, and service strikes. For travel advisories on specific countries, call the U.S. State Department at (202) 647–5225.

Ask Immigration (800/375–5283) answers questions on immigration—citizenship, visas, relatives abroad, and more.

U.S. Customs Service (800/697–3662) refers you to the appropriate authority on importation of goods.

DIRECTORIES

alphabetical listing of resources & topics

restaurants by neighborhood

shops by neighborhood

resources & topics

restaurants by neighborhood

WEST VILLAGE

shops by neighborhood

ASTORIA, QUEENS

BAY RIDGE, BROOKLYN

BRONX

BROOKLYN HEIGHTS

CHELSEA

CITY NOTES

CITY NOTES

CITY NOTES

CITY NOTES

Escape
from the city

Great weekend getaways for people who enjoy country walks and off-the-beaten-path excursions with romantic inns, scenic spots, and historic sites.

At bookstores everywhere.
www.fodors.com/

Fodor's Travel Publications has guidebooks to fit the needs of all kinds of travelers from families to adventure seekers, from nature enthusiasts to urban weekenders. With the range of coverage and the quality of information, it is easy to understand why smart travelers go with **Fodor's**.

At bookstores everywhere.
http://fodors.previewtravel.com/